Project Management Communications Bible

William Dow, PMP, and Bruce Taylor

WILEY

Wiley Publishing, Inc.

Project Management Communications Bible

Published by
Wiley Publishing, Inc.
10475 Crosspoint Boulevard
Indianapolis, IN 46256
www.wiley.com

Copyright © 2008 by Wiley Publishing, Inc., Indianapolis, Indiana

Published simultaneously in Canada

ISBN: 978-0-470-13740-6

Manufactured in the United States of America

10 9 8 7 6 5 4 3 2 1

For general information on our other products and services or to obtain technical support, please contact our Customer Care Department within the U.S. at (800) 762-2974, outside the U.S. at (317) 572-3993 or fax (317) 572-4002.

Library of Congress Control Number: 2008927909

About the Authors

Bill Dow, PMP, is a published author, PMP Certified Project Management Professional, with more than 18 years in Information Technology, specializing in software development and project management. Bill has a strong passion for project management, project management offices, and software development lifecycle methodologies. Bill has a strong methodology background and has been very successful in every company he has worked for in ensuring the projects methodologies matches the project while still guaranteeing the highest of quality for the customer. Bill has worked all across North America, starting his career in the late 1980s as a computer-programming analyst, worked in the consulting field for many years, led a large project management office at AT&T Wireless/Cingular and is now working in IT at the Microsoft Corporation in Redmond, Washington. Bill has also taught IT courses in several Canadian colleges.

Contact Bill Dow at billd@projectcommunication.org.

Bruce Taylor is an expert in the field of project management. He regularly provides professional assistance to top management and has accumulated impressive experience in developing project scheduling and cost control systems continuously since the mid 1960s. He has worked worldwide on some of the largest projects, including some huge offshore platforms in the North Sea and the Northwest shelf of Australia.

Mr. Taylor is a pioneer in project management software tools. He and a partner founded a small project management consulting and software development company, which quickly grew internationally. Using his experience, the company developed, and marketed an automated project scheduling, and cost control system. Included in this development was the first automated network logic diagram chart using the critical path method of scheduling. He built a client base of over 150 major companies worldwide. This included branch offices in France and Australia.

Over the past 40+ years, he has conducted many project management classes and seminars throughout the United States, Canada, Europe, Japan, Australia, South America, and the Near and Far East.

Contact Bruce Taylor at brucet@projectcommunication.org.

To Our Wives & Families

We want to thank Kath and Nancy for their constant dedication and never-ending support while we wrote this book. The development of this book became a major project for all of us and we spent many hours apart. We both thank you for being so understanding and giving us that time. We also want to thank you for all the time you put into reviewing, adding suggestions, and making this a wonderful book. It was truly a team effort.

Credits

Acquisitions Editor
Kim Spilker

Project Editor
Beth Taylor

Technical Editor
Jim Lefevere

Copy Editor
Beth Taylor

Editorial Manager
Robyn Siesky

Business Manager
Amy Knies

Sr. Marketing Manager
Sandy Smith

Vice President and Executive Group Publisher
Richard Swadley

Vice President and Executive Publisher
Bob Ipsen

Vice President and Publisher
Barry Pruett

Project Coordinator
Erin Smith

Graphics and Production Specialists
Claudia Bell
Carl Byers
Jennifer Mayberry

Quality Control Technicians
David Faust
Jessica Kramer

Media Development Project Manager I
Laura Moss

Media Development Coordinator
Jenny Swisher

Associate Producer
Shawn Patrick

Proofreading and Indexing
Aptara, David Faust

Contents

Contents

Part II: Project Knowledge Areas   73

Contents

Contents

Contents

Contents

Contents

Foreword

No human social process is as pervasive nor as important as communications. It affects all human relationships and endeavors; be it a marriage, a football game, the classroom, or a project. Somehow, we all seem to be able to recognize poor communications or the lack of any communication, but we cannot seem to see it coming. That makes it difficult to intercept the problem because it is generally too late by the time we identify the problem. One solution might be proper planning. You have likely heard the old adage that "Those who fail to plan, plan to fail!" Yet even planning requires some forethought, help, and tools to be done right.

Project teams and stakeholders require information as rapidly as possible. Receiving a monthly progress report four weeks after the status date is like reading a several-months- old magazine in your doctor's office. Team members require accurate and comprehensive details on the scope of their work. Stakeholders want to know the status and the performance of the project execution. Contractors need to have clarifications on any ambiguous issues in the specifications and drawings. Funding agencies want to know that their funds are being used as planned. Participants want to know what to expect at upcoming meetings so they can prepare or be prepared. International teams face the added challenge of different time zones and cultural issues such as perceptions and practices.

The technology for communications has evolved and allowed for much greater speed in communicating. Similarly, the newer technology for executing the project activities has allowed for more rapid production and execution of the work. Along with this speed increase, we face problems and issues arising more rapidly and in increasing volume. This, in turn, requires more rapid capabilities to respond and tools for dealing with the vast array of data and information. Nothing has revolutionized human communication capability as much as the Internet since Gutenberg invented the printing press. Radio and television come close, but even they are limited in scope by the presentation format, the geographic boundaries of broadcasts and the regulatory limitations of governments.

Communication is the key to keeping team members, managers, and stakeholders informed and on track to pursue the project objectives. Communication is also the key to identifying issues, risks, misunderstandings, and other challenges to project completion.

The task of dealing with all of these challenges and demands can be daunting. However, there is abundant help available. The literature is full of books on communication skills and methodologies. The challenge is to find a single, comprehensive publication that covers the subject from head to toe for project management in particular.

I am delighted to congratulate you on holding in your hand a volume that has met that challenge. Bruce Taylor and Bill Dow, PMP have concluded a superb effort to bring the subject into focus while covering all aspects of the issues. Using the Project Management Institute's Project Management Body of Knowledge Guide as a framework, they have organized the material in a logical fashion that will aid the practitioner in homing in on a particular subject. The reader will also find the material broken down into two major parts: the tools and the processes. In addition, they have compiled a significant set of tools and references on the CD that accompanies this book.

Whether you are looking for tips on planning your communications process on your project, or want to gain insight on specific tools and techniques that can help you, you will find the answer here. The material is also up to date in light of the ever-changing technology that we humans make use of in communicating with others. Just as the technology of communications tools has evolved, so has the type of information and the formats used to present information. Performance reports, earned value techniques, information distribution systems, document control systems, contract management systems, configuration control processes, and risk handling are just a few of the many project communication tools used all around the globe. Many of these have evolved over time. This volume covers it all.

So please, keep this book at your elbow, mark the pages, use paperclips or Post-it notes as bookmarks. It will be your friend for life. Enjoy! And may your future communication problems all appear before they are problems.

Tammo T. Wilkens, P.E., PMP

Preface

One of the project manager's top priorities is to ensure he or she has a handle on all project communications. It is critical that he or she controls every "major" message flowing in and out of the project. There is an old but wise saying, "A project that communicates poorly is going to perform poorly." That is such a true statement, and one that should guide project mangers on every project where they are involved.

The book leverages the Project Management Institute's Project Management Body of Knowledge®, better known as the PMBOK. The communication tools in the book tie directly with PMBOK's knowledge areas and lifecycle processes. There is a direct one-to-one mapping of communication tools and knowledge areas. There is also a one-to-one mapping of communication tools to project lifecycles. This mapping allows instant understanding of what tools to use in both the knowledge area and lifecycle process of the project.

This book is a guide for all project managers, team members, and customers or clients regardless of the project's size, industry, or complexity. The book acts as a single source of project communication tools for immediate utilization on your projects. The attached CD provides a working template for the tools explained in the book, and the data used to build the tools. In some cases, the CD has a couple examples of the communication tool to allow you to determine which example closely matches your project. The CD can be a helpful asset to managing and communicating effectively on your project.

The CD also includes a spreadsheet that provides Tools at a Glance for your instant reference of the communication tools located in the book. The spreadsheet's main purpose is to provide a reference between the communication tool and the project lifecycle or PMI$^{(r)}$ Knowledge area. It will offer guidance as to what tool to use in what lifecycle phase or what knowledge area you are trying to communicate. This spreadsheet has sorting capabilities that will allow you to slice and dice the communication tools by a number of different methods. This includes; by lifecycle, knowledge area, size of project, type of tool, part of book (chapter number), recommended usage (best practice), and industry type. This spreadsheet is a complete reference to the communication tools located in the book. The spreadsheet guides your project communications throughout your project. You may find this spreadsheet to be priceless in managing your project's communications!

As a customer or a client of the project, having the knowledge as to which communication tool the project manager should utilize and which tools are available is invaluable. There will be an expectation you will have from the project manager and project team members as to how they will communicate this throughout the project. It is important that you are obtaining the information you need to make project decisions and guide the project to completion. Using the tools in this book, you can suggest to the project manager or team members the tool you would like utilized on your project. The project manager will have examples readily available from the CD to utilize on your project. This book will become valuable to you in ensuring you are continually receiving the project status information you need.

To communicate more effectively, the book offers a series of communication tools to anyone involved in the project. There may be times when a team member or the project manager is unfamiliar with how to communicate a certain aspect of the project, and, therefore, can reference any one of the tools in the book to help communicate this type of message. Since there are a number of tools in this book, there is a high probability that one of the tools will be applicable for their particular projects situation. It is important to note the tools in the book are applicable for most projects, across most industries, and only a couple tools are deemed software specific.

Acknowledgments

We want to thank everyone who was involved on this project for his or her help and support in the writing of this book. It is impossible to write a book of this magnitude without having a large number of people to thank. It has taken us over four years to develop, research, and write this book. We still have many new tools and concepts for future editions of this book. We would like to thank everyone for the great effort provided in the support and development of the book.

The Project Management Institute (PMI) has been a great source of inspiration, resources, and friendships. We strongly recommend this nonprofit organization to anyone pursuing the field of Project Management. You can obtain information about local PMI chapters at www.pmi.org.

A special "thank you" to the following people for helping us along the way:

Bill Dow (my son, who has gone out of his way many times throughout the book, and helped us in ways you will never know! Thanks Bill! We have learned a lot from you throughout this journey, and we appreciate it!)

We would like to thank the following people in their support for this book:

Beth Taylor, Barry Pruett, Al Callan, PMP, Carl Chatfield, PMP, Tammo Wilkins, Greg Hutchins, Mike Fisher, PMP, Andrew Friedrich PMP, Luc Brisard, Len Lewis, Murray Rosenthal, Heather Clark, Dean Rosenthal, Irene Holt, and Carl Adams, and Janice Y. Preston.

Special thanks to Scott Button and Tony Rizzo for writing the critical chain sections in the book; we could not have done either of those tools without you!

Special thanks to our friend Len Lewis for his extensive knowledge in project management and the editing and support that he supplied. Also, a special thanks to Mike Fisher for his EPM section in the book. Thank you Luc Brisard for your international knowledge and support.

How to Get the Most out of this Book

Here are some things to know so you can get the most out of this book:

- For general knowledge of project communication in a working environment, review, and analyze Part I of the book.
- Review the planning questions and answers thoroughly for each communication tool in Part II.
- In the third part of the book, use as reference for creating and using the tool. If you already know the tool, there are tips on how to utilize the tool that you may not have realized.
- Utilize the Project Management Master Tools spreadsheet as a reference to ensure you are using as many tools as you can for your project.

Icons: What Do They Mean?

Although the icons are pretty standard and self-explanatory (they have their names written on them!), here's a brief explanation of what they are and what they mean.

TIP — Tips offer you extra information that further explains a given topic or technique, often suggesting alternatives or workarounds to a listed procedure.

NOTE — Notes provide supplementary information to the text, shedding light on background processes or miscellaneous options that aren't crucial to the basic understanding of the material.

CROSS-REF — If you want to find related information to a given topic in another chapter, look for the Cross-Reference icons.

ON the CD-ROM — This icon indicates that the CD-ROM contains a related file and points you to the folder location.

TOOL VALUE — This is the value of the tool for the project manager and in some cases, customer, team members, and other stakeholders.

How This Book Is Organized

The book is broken down and organized in three main parts. In the first section, we discuss general project management communication. The second section of the book covers communication tools that support the nine project knowledge areas. The third part includes the same communications tools, however, it demonstrates the creation and use of the tools in the planning, executing, and close-out processes of a project. And the fourth part provides extra information you may find helpful.

Part I: An Introduction to Project Communications

Project communication planning is the task of identifying the information needs and requirements of the project customers. Customers require information about the project such as risk events, budget data, and schedule information. You are the project manager, so you must be proactive and plan for your customer needs.

When working in a project environment, one of the most challenging aspects of being a project manager is project communications management. As projects become complex and more challenging, project managers need to step up and become effective communicators. The challenges that project managers are facing today are greater than in the past. These challenges include virtual project teams, shorter product time to market, advancement of technology or technology changes in middle of project, and diversity of product availability (new products coming out daily). The communication planning activity includes documenting the where, how, and to whom project information is communicated. This communication planning effort will guide the project manager and the team members through the lifecycle from a communication perspective.

Part II: Project Communication Tools by Knowledge Areas

The second part of this book, which includes Chapters 4 through 13, describes and highlights the communication tools applicable to the nine knowledge areas. Communication tools can have primary knowledge areas and secondary knowledge areas. For example, a communication tool can be a primary tool in the cost knowledge area and can be a secondary tool in quality knowledge area. Using best-practice techniques and historical reference determines where each tool fits within each knowledge area.

In these chapters, we describe each tool in detail. Each tool has a series of 10 planning questions that assist project managers in their planning discussions with their customers on how they will utilize this particular communication tool. These questions each have our suggested answers or ideas as to how you could use this tool on your project. These answers are simply ideas and are not complete as they are only a starting point to get you thinking about how the tool could be utilized on your project.

Part III: Project Communication Tools by Process Groups

This part describes and highlights the communication tools applicable to the five lifecycle processes. In this section of the book, the goal is for you the reader to master the creation and use of these tools on your projects. This process is the same one utilized for mapping communications tools to knowledge areas. In this mapping process, the communications tools can map across one or many of the project processes in the same manner as the communication tools that mapped across multiple knowledge areas. Therefore, no hard rules exist as to where project managers can utilize communication tools. Actually, the more processes the better, which often enhances project communications. Using the best practices techniques and historical reference determines where each communication tool fits within the project lifecycle process.

In chapters 14 through 22, each tool has the following major areas associated to them:

- Project scenario
- How to create the tools (if applicable)
- How to use the tools on your project (if applicable)

Tools at a Glance

We have included on the CD-ROM a spreadsheet that provides an easy to understand mapping of the communication tools to both knowledge areas and to the processes. We based our mapping of tools to knowledge areas and processes, based on best practices, historical references, and years of practical project management experience.

The spreadsheet called Master Project Management Communications Tools list.xls is included on the CD-ROM for your immediate use. This table provides not only an easy mapping communication tools to knowledge areas and processes, it also provides a listing of other important factors related to the tool. These factors include:

- Tools to recommended usage (high, medium, low) on projects
- Tools that are critical to all projects
- Tools to knowledge area

- Tools to process groups
- Tools to industry type
- Tools to size of project
- Tools that are managing or reporting
- Tools that are reports or forms

This table and the associated mapping of communication tools is an incredible resource to any project manager because it provides you the ability to determine what tool you use in your particular project situation. For example, you just kick off the planning phase; what communication tools should you be using in this phase?

It is highly recommended that every reader take the time to discover the power of this table, print it, and hang it on your wall for ongoing use.

Projects fail due to one main reason only, and that is poor project communications. A lack of clear and concise communications prevents projects from succeeding. It is that simple! Regardless of what you read or what experts on the Web say, when a project manager or his or her team members do not communicate effectively, they will have a hard time implementing a successful project. This is also true for clients or customers of the project. They also own the responsibility for communicating effectively on their projects. Project communications is a two-way effort and both parties are responsible for ensuring that their messages are clear and concise. Without that, project failure is inevitable!

The following list represents the results from a project management survey conducted by a leading U.S.-based training company © ESI International, Inc. This list indicates the results as to why projects fail. In reviewing this list, you will see that that the survey results have deemed 50 percent of the reasons are due to Poor Requirements Definition. The other 50 percent represents various other reasons. In closer analysis, you will see Communication Problems is only 14% of the reasons. We strongly believe that number is too low, and think that Communication Problems are actually 90 percent if not higher, as to why projects fail. Let us take you through our reasoning below. This data was presented in the 2007 Project World November 13–16, 2007 Conference Guide. Here is the list of reasons in order:

1. Poor Requirements definition = 50%
2. Inadequate risk management = 17%
3. Poor Scope control = 15%
4. Communication problems = 14%
5. Lack of qualified resources = 3%
6. Other = 1%

© ESI International, Inc. Reprinted with permission.

The following list represents the reasons and percentages as to why we feel that projects fail. When looking at the various reasons for failures, it comes down to one or two main reasons. In most cases, that reason is poor communications by the project manager, team members, or customers of the project. Someone is not communicating effectively on the project such as deadlines missed, budgets overrun, team members not talking, and customers not receiving the information they need nor communicating their requirements clearly. In this table, you will clearly see that Communications Problems represents 90% of the reasons why projects fail, and the remaining areas represent only 10%. It is common knowledge that it is easy to resolve technical problems. Here are the reasons why projects fail:

- Poor Requirements definition = 2%
- Inadequate risk management = 1%
- Poor Scope control = 1%
- Communication problems = 90%
- Lack of qualified resources = 1%
- Other = 2%

Can you see the clear differences between the two lists? If not, let us break this down and explain.

A common saying in the Project Management profession is, "Project communication is the most important aspect of managing a project." If you happen to be a poor communicator, this can make it difficult to be successful. If you are a great communicator, and proactive in managing your communications, then your life as a project manager will generally be much easier.

The most important aspect of project communications is the way you approach it. Most project managers just let communications happen and they do not plan for it. It is common for project managers to send out project status reports, issues lists, and risk registers in support of their regular project communications. However, do you think they are stopping to realize if these reports are valuable or provide the information the customers need? They may be, but without the pre-planning and understanding of all of the customer's requirements, these typical project periodic reports may or may not be getting the job done.

In order for a project manager to be successful, it is important for them to look at the tools they are currently using today and ask themselves if they feel they are communicating effectively. Then ask your customers and see how they respond. The project managers should ask themselves if they are delivering project information effectively to their customers. If not, then they should take the time to plan which communication tools will be most effective on their projects. The project manager should work directly with the customers or clients to ensure they are receiving the information they require. This upfront planning, and working with the clients or customers to understand exactly their needs will help to ensure effective communications between the two parties. This "Project Communication Planning" concept is relatively new to the profession and is quickly becoming a standard with all project managers.

Planning communications is a fundamental change for most project managers and it is important to understand this culture shift immediately. Changing the way you think about project communications will allow you to be more successful. You must understand what information you need to manage your project successfully. Typically, most project managers ask for project information, but do not explain how or why they want it. When project managers do not explain how they want project information, they are not properly communicating. Successful communicators change the way they think about communicating by planning ahead and communicating their project information and other communication needs. When your team members send you the basic project information, they are not thinking how to communicate that information properly. In most cases, they do not even consider whether the information they send is even usable. Often, team members send the information and hope you go away. If you worked closely with them and explained why and how you want the information from them, it opens the dialog between both parties and improves communications tremendously.

Without making this fundamental paradigm shift, you can get by, and most likely, your project will complete, but you are not communicating as effectively as you could be without that upfront planning. However, what a difference you could have made if you had just given some thought as to how you were going to communicate the information and then send it throughout the life of the project.

Your customers can benefit greatly from this effective and proactive communication style. When project managers are proactive and plan their communications with their customers, it provides them the confidence that they will get the information they need for effective project decision making throughout the life of the project. Project managers who take this proactive approach become more effective and in more control of their projects than the project managers who tend to be more reactive and always in a mode where they are reacting and fighting problems on the project. You are in greater control of your project when you are a proactive communicator then when you are a reactive communicator.

Part I
Introducing Project Communication Concepts

Chapter 1

Introducing Project Communication

Many project managers take good communication for granted. They start working on a project without even thinking about how to communicate with others. The lack of a communication plan is possibly the biggest mistake the project manager and the team members make. Project communication is composed of three components:

- Communicating project information in a timely manner
- Generating the right level of information for the customers
- Collecting, distributing, and storing project information

TIP The combination of these areas results in proper project communication. Take the time to see the bigger picture and fully understand the project communication aspects of your project.

Each team member communicates with other team members on a variety of subjects, issues, and processes daily. One common difficulty with project communication is that the project manager and team members assume they have communicated properly with each another, when most often they have not. In this chapter, we cover why you, the project manager, should plan project communication, work with personal communication, understand knowledge areas, and discover lifecycle processes.

Going over a Project Scenario

Here is a typical communication scenario of a day in the life of a project:

1. A stakeholder requests an unexpected report.

2. A team member who is familiar with the data or has the skills to run a particular tool generates the report.

3. If the person who requested the report wants to receive it every week, the team member who created it will update it weekly and continue to send it indefinitely.

This scenario happens every day on thousands of projects. The customer requests a report, and it gets created, printed, and then sent off as soon as possible. The process is routine and requires no thinking or planning, just getting the information to the customers as soon as possible.

However, what just happened here? Or rather, what did not happen? Absolutely no planning occurred. The project manager should ask questions of the requestor as follows:

- What information does the report provide?
- What are you trying to achieve with this information?
- Who needs this report and how will they use it?
- How often is the information needed?
- How quickly do you need the report developed?
- Do you have the budget to develop this report?
- Is there an existing report that includes similar information?

Using this technique of question and answers actually develops the customer requirements for this report. This technique saves time and money by clarifying the needs of the customer before developing anything. Using this technique, the project team members gather information to develop the report and assemble enough detail to determine how to use the report with multiple stakeholders. It becomes a win-win for everyone.

When a project team member does not use this technique and simply develops the report on the fly from the initial request, it is setting a bad example and is filling a short-term request and not considering the long-term use of the information.

NOTE Certainly, some reports should be turned around quickly, but without having a planning discipline in mind, short-term reports can quickly become long-term reports that never go away. Planning how you will communicate your project information is the responsibility of both the project team member and the customer.

Plan to Communicate, Communicate the Plan

We recommended that, as project managers begin new projects, they step back and look at how they will communicate effectively. This technique of upfront planning of your project communication is a brand new technique for the Project Management industry. Using a series of predefined planning questions forces the project manager and customers to think in a completely different way about how to deliver or receive project information. Each communication tool, such as a status report, is going to present and carry different project information. Therefore, project managers should plan how they will communicate this information to their customers, and customers should plan how they will utilize the information after they receive it. The days when project customers received and accepted generic status reports from project managers are over! For example, customers who plan the information they need for project level decision-making purposes, will no longer accept a status report that does not provide the information they need. If customers are not seeing the information they require, then the project manager has failed to communicate properly.

CROSS-REF In Chapter 2, we cover the different ways customers want to receive project information.

CAUTION Project managers must use their communication tools correctly. These tools enable them to deliver a variety of project statuses and, therefore, they should utilize as many tools as often as possible.

Normally, the project manager *provides* the project status to the customer, but rarely do both parties spend time together actually planning the information that is going back and forth between them. Generally, the project manager or team member sends the information to the customer without asking if the information is valuable or helpful to them, and that is the fundamental problem with project communications today. If the project manager sits down with the customers and asks them what kinds of information they need from the project, there will be a much better understanding of the information that should flow between them, and the project manager can then plan accordingly.

Upfront planning of projects is not new; project managers have been doing that for years. However, upfront planning specific to project *communication* is new but is rarely done by project managers today. We advise all project managers to plan not only their projects but also how they will communicate their project's information. We suggest learning all the communication tools in this book and then selecting the right tools based on the size of the project. Upfront planning goes a long way in effectively communicating with your customers, and some of the tools located in this book are going to help you become a great communicator.

After the upfront planning is complete and the project manager and customers agree on what communication tools will work, the project manager should send out a communication plan to all customers, clients, and upper management containing the agreed-upon information and the tools to be used on the project.

In this book, we also cover two brand-new communication tools to the project management indus-try. The first tool, the project communication requirements matrix, documents project roles, reports timing and frequency, and includes the names of the staff members receiving project infor-mation. The second tool is the people report matrix that provides a table displaying the project roles and the different reports those roles will receive. This allows anyone to be able to determine at a glance who is receiving what report, and this is helpful to the project manager when the cus-tomer is asking for project information. The project manager can refer to a report that the customer is already receiving that contains the same information. Finally, we highlight and discuss in detail the impact and benefits of using a project communication plan. As we all know, project communi-cation plans are one of the most important tools a project manager can use on their project and is the tool that establishes the rhythm of project communications. Without it, the project manager, team members, or customers have no idea who is managing, controlling, or reporting project information.

CROSS-REF   See Chapter 2 for more information on the project communication requirements matrix and the people report matrix.

One method you can use to plan project communication is to gather the project team members and stakeholders into a communication planning meeting. This meeting allows the group to jointly plan on who will be involved in communicating project information. During the meeting, the com-munication requirements matrix and the people report matrix are developed and included as part of the communication plan. The group then selects the communication tools for utilization on the project, so that everyone is aware from the start of the project what tools are used and who is responsible for creating them. After the planning meeting occurs, the project manager completes the communication plan and everyone agrees to it. The project manager sends the plan to all cus-tomers, clients, upper management, and team members to document what was agreed upon, allowing them to use the plan throughout the project. That communication plan becomes the offi-cial plan for the project.

The project management office (PMO) is important in the role of project communication. A project management office is a formal organizational structure that supports all projects and project methodologies for the organization. Normally, a Project or Program Director heads the project management office along with project managers and administrative support. The size of the project management office will vary depending on the company size and the number of projects being exe-cuted. Large corporations have had project management offices for many years. Often, project management offices set the standards for project communication tools, such as status reports, issues lists, risks, communication plans, project schedules, and so on. As a project manager, you must be aware of the governances that the project management offices have established and adhere to those rules while managing your projects. It is important that after reviewing the communica-tion tools in this book and the different aspects covered about project communications that each project manager looks at the current policies and procedures of their own PMO to determine if there are any differences. If there are large differences, it may be because the PMOs are not follow-ing the same rigor and processes outlined in this book. This is okay because it simply represents a lack of immaturity in the PMOs at this time. As the PMO grows and establishes itself, it will learn to put great value on how important it is to communicate project information effectively and will start to enforce the new policies and procedures that enhance project communications. A project manager who discovers large discrepancies may find value in discussing the inconsistency with the leaders of the PMO. Not everything covered in this book will be applicable to every project, or across every industry, but the foundation is solid and is an incredible starting point for any project manager in enhancing their project communications.

Understanding Project Management Knowledge Areas

The project manager and team members are involved in all aspects of the project; therefore, one of the most important things a project manager and team members can do is understand the project's knowledge areas. Knowledge areas are the nine components of any project, which are common to all projects, regardless of their size or industry. There are nine knowledge areas defined by the Project Management Institute (PMI). To be a successful project manager you should know and understand each of the areas. We cover them in the following sections.

NOTE The Project Management Institute's Body of Knowledge (PMBOK) has called these areas Knowledge areas. The Project Management Institute (PMI) was founded in 1969 to promote the project management profession. The membership is now over a half million and growing fast. The PMI organization has developed a standard for the profession of project management and has documented those standards in the Guide to the Project Management Body of Knowledge (PMBOK).

The Project Management Institute's Project Management Body of Knowledge has included the following areas as their knowledge areas: Project Integration, Scope, Time, Cost, Quality, Human Resources, Communication, Risk, and Procurement.

Project integration management

The *project integration management* concept area includes all concept areas and activities that require coordination throughout the life of the project. The Integration knowledge area is the work required to integrate all areas of project management: Integration, Scope, Time, Cost, Quality, Human Resources, Communication, Risk, and Procurement. Most projects are undergoing continuous change that requires constant integration. A typical day for a project manager can have her shifting attention from communication issues to cost and budget concerns, and then to addressing quality issues, and so on. Project managers spend their day spread thinly between each of the nine knowledge areas, so they must have a solid understanding of each knowledge area to be able to address the project situation properly. Project managers who are unsure of a particular knowledge area will struggle until they learn that area well enough to work effectively in it. It is important that project managers understand the knowledge areas well to help them be successful in their jobs.

Project scope management

The *project scope management* identifies how to manage all the work that is required to complete the project. In many cases, creating a work breakdown structure consisting of project activities, costs associated with activities, project resource names, and the project schedule acts as a central repository for the entire project's scope. Therefore, using the work breakdown structure for project scope management is a valuable tool. The other important communication tool within the scope management area is the project communication plan. The communication plan documents and describes how the project manager or team members will communicate project information throughout the life of the project. Project scope control is a critical task that project managers undertake while managing their projects. Project managers should ensure that their project has well-defined scope and ensure that customers and management approve that scope before getting too far along in the project. Without that approval, the project's scope can easily get away from you, and your project may be negatively impacted. To prevent scope getting out of hand, project managers must ensure that at the beginning of the project they have a change control process defined and in place. A *change control process* is an important method of scope control. A common term within scope management is *scope creep*. Scope creep is adding additional work items to the original scope without going through a change control process.

NOTE   Scope creep is a common risk to projects today. Scope creep can consist of a small change like adding two or three new reports to a software development project to complex change where designers add 1000 square feet to the building.

The project scope approval process is normally project specific and is important to every project manager to understand and drive continually. There are two major groups that handle scope approval. The first group is the customers requesting the additional work, and the second group is the project manager or the team members who perform the work. In most cases, the customers or owners have the final say as to whether the additional scope is added to the project, but that often comes with a price; it is either the price of extending the project schedule or adding more costs or resources to the project.

Time management

Time management includes all aspects of managing the time components of the project. Activity estimating is a difficult component of a project to manage because, in many cases, these estimates are pessimistic *best guesses*. Your project team members normally give these to the project manager. The team members give a best guess as to how long they feel it will take to complete their assigned area of the project. Unless your project is using machines, such as in manufacturing, where scheduling the time it takes to perform a task is exact, activities estimating and working with your project team members' best guesses can be challenging. As a project manager, you are basing the success of your project on the best guess estimates given by your team members. If there are any miscalculations from anyone, your project time lines can suffer.

Time management consists of many different aspects on your project. It can range from project activities start and end dates to resource allocation, such as equipment used on a construction project. Time management also includes schedule development and resource schedule management. Each of these activities is a component of time management.

Cost management

Cost management includes all aspects of managing the costs of your project. It is another key component of your project and is one of the core areas managed tightly by most project managers. Because cost management can be challenging, every project manager should watch it closely and regularly throughout the life of the project.

Successful cost management will require cost estimating and tracking tools. Without tools in place, cost management can be difficult, and in some cases impossible to manage. It is important that all companies provide the appropriate cost estimating tools for their project managers. If the project is cost driven, you must perform cost management activities on the projects.

Quality management

All the aspects of managing quality of your project are included in *quality management*. Quality can be a subjective measurement on a project, but by putting metrics in place, it can help quantify these measurements. In software development projects, a common measurement of quality is the count of the bugs in a program based on their severity level, for example, 10 severity 1 bug, 23 severity 2 bugs. A software project manager measures quality by measuring the number of bugs in the Severity 1 level. If a project has 5 severity 1 bugs, and the measurement of quality is 3, then the project would have failed its quality measurement.

All areas of the project should measure quality, and project documentation is no exception. All projects will have numerous documents as part of the lifecycle of the project, and those documents should be of the highest quality. The project team members review each document for content as well as acceptable levels of quality before giving their final approval.

On the majority of projects, quality management is one of the concept areas that is often overlooked. A project manager's main responsibility is to ensure the highest acceptable level of quality on a project. Quality should equal but never exceed what is in the scope of the project. For example, the manager should never approve the building of a more expensive project than what the scope requires. Quality can also refer to documentation, validation, final approval. Quality management plays an important role on all projects.

Human resource management

Human resource management includes all aspects of managing the team members who are working on a project. On most projects, managing project team members can be challenging because often, the project manager is not the team member's direct supervisor. Therefore, the project manager is working under a weak matrix structure and must continually work closely with the functional manager for their resource's time. This can be a difficult situation for project managers, but unfortunately, it is the norm in most companies.

> **NOTE** A weak matrix structure is a structure where the project manager does not have any formal reporting responsibilities or authority, but acts more as a coordinator when leading the project. A weak matrix structure organization is not a project-driven type of organization, but more of a functional-driven organization.

An important aspect of human resource management is consultant management. Project managers often have consultants working on their projects as regular members of the team. Consultants assigned to projects need to be managed in a different way than a team member who is an employee of the company. Project managers must be aware of these differences and look to their own human resource rules and policies to determine their management responsibilities. For example, consultants do not normally receive end-of-the-year formal performance reviews. These are usually associated with employees only.

Project human resource management is not the equivalent of the standard human resource manager in every company. A human resource manager in a company is concerned with the rules of hiring, firing, categorizing positions, and other human resource administrative aspects of people management. A project's human resource manager is responsible for the allocation of the right team members to the right activities at the right time.

Communication management

Communication management includes all aspects of managing the communication of your project. Communication management consists of the following areas: communication planning, distribution of project information, and the management of the recipient's information.

Communication management is the most important concept area on your project. Project managers who fail to communicate effectively negatively affect their projects; and in some cases this can lead to failure. All projects require constant communication to their stakeholders.

The reason that communication management is so important is that it covers every aspect of the project. For example, from the initial approval of the project to the final closeout, a project manager will consistently be communicating various aspects of the project to the team members, upper management, and their customers. If a project manager is unable to communicate effectively, in most cases they are going to struggle in this type of role. Constant communication with team members and customers will increase the chance of a project succeeding. This ongoing communication will give customers the information they need to make project level decisions.

Communication management consists of

- **Communication planning:** Plans the project information and communication of the team members and other stakeholders
- **Project information distribution:** Defines the distribution of the needed information and makes it available to the team members and other stakeholders in a timely manner

- **Performance reporting:** Identifies and reports all progress status, measurements, forecasting, and analysis on the project
- **Managing communication of internal and external stakeholders:** Managing all communication to satisfy the requirements of the project stakeholders while addressing all communication issues occurring during project execution

 Communication management is providing the right information to the right people at the right time.

The acquisition and distribution of project information is the most important aspect of communication management. For example, a project manager may create a weekly project status report generated by end of day Friday, and then send it to the stakeholders for review and comments. Project managers are fully responsible for deciding what project information is created and distributed to their stakeholders.

You can communicate three ways:

- **Verbal:** Speaking to one another
- **Written:** Writing documentation or memos
- **Visual:** Presentations, body language, and video

As the project progresses, project managers need to establish a rhythm for the project and ensure that their stakeholders receive the project information in a timely manner and on a consistent basis. For example, a project manager can create a weekly performance report depicting the rate of progress on cost and schedule. Doing this allows the project manager to calculate the remaining work on the project.

Risk management

Risk management includes all aspects of managing project risks. Project managers must be observing and monitoring risks on a regular basis to ensure they do not affect the project negatively.

Risk management consists of the following areas:

- **Risk planning:** Plan for risk events and process
- **Risk identification:** Identifying possible sources of risks and risk events
- **Risk analysis:** Analyzing and qualifying risk
- **Risk response planning:** Planning the response of risk events
- **Risk monitor and control:** Monitoring, controlling, and mitigating the impacts of risk events
- **Risk closeout:** Documentation of risk events and lessons learned

Project managers must be very diligent in the tracking and managing of their project risks. Often project managers use a risk assessment form for tracking project risks; the use of this form allows for easy sharing with anyone interested in the project. Project managers need to ensure that they are tracking risks on an ongoing basis and at a minimum discussing the risks with the team members weekly. If project managers spend the time going over and reviewing project risks with their team members at weekly status meetings, it will provide the project manager with assurance that team members are still actively tracking and working the project risks. Without a weekly review, project risks can go undetected and could end up negatively affecting the project.

In the project risk management knowledge area, there are many tools available to assist project managers in planning, analyzing, and controlling project risks. These tools, such as the risk matrix, decision trees, and expected monetary value, are all available to assist the project manager in risk tracking.

CROSS-REF   See Chapter 12 for more information on these tools.

Risk classification is simple: risks are normally classified as low, medium, or high, and the type of project determines the classification. For example, in the construction industry, a tilt-up building (warehouse) is a relatively low-risk project because warehouses are relatively easy to build from a construction perspective. A hospital or research lab is a high-risk project due to the number of complexities and customizations that go into these types of buildings. In construction, a medium-risk project would be somewhere in between a warehouse and a hospital; for example, a residential complex could be a medium-risk project. The project manager determines the risk level at the beginning of the project and decides the meaning of low, medium, and high. To classify a risk correctly, the project team, customers, and upper management should agree on the definitions and rating factors of these three classifications. When the classification is determined and understood, the team will work jointly to assign risk classifications to every risk event.

Procurement management

Procurement management includes all aspects of managing the procurement concept area on your project. As an example, procurement activities can include everything from when to hire team members from outside your company, to ordering weekly lunches throughout the project. On construction projects, procurement management is an important aspect of project management, with much more rigor than would be applied on a software type project. With the large number of contractors (electrical, plumbing, laborers) all working on a single project, the project manager is heavily involved in the procurement management process. Tasks such as hiring, firing, scheduling work tasks, and negotiating contracts and payouts are just a few of the activities a project manager performs in the procurement management area.

Project procurement can be a difficult area of your project to manage, especially when working with vendors or outside contractor companies. Change requests can impact the contract or budget, and every time a change is approved it can engage the project manager in the procurement area to process the change accordingly. Change requests often put strain on the relationship between the two companies, especially when money is involved and someone is expecting payment. If one company continues to drive change requests throughout the process and expects payment for every additional work item, the relationship between the two parties may be at odds. Often an understanding exists between the two parties that not every work item is chargeable to the project; even in a fixed-bid project there is often work that is completed free of charge. When there is an expectation on both sides that not everything will be a change request, it offers goodwill between the two companies and improves the chance of future projects between them. Change requests come up most often on fixed-price (fixed-cost) contracts where additional work items are requested for the project and contractors are expecting payment, but the owner or stakeholders who requested the work expect it to be part of the original project. When such a situation occurs, it is scope creep and handled through the change request process. If the change request extends beyond the original agreement of the requirements and additional work is required, the contractor is going to expect additional payment for this work.

One important aspect of procurement management is the contract management. Contract management includes negotiating and creating contracts. Contracts can include the following:

- Labor
- Equipment
- Materials
- Agreement between two parties

 A contract is a great communication tool and is legally binding.

One aspect of the procurement concept area is administrative closeout. Administrative closeout is different from the technical aspects of closeout because administrative closeout pertains to the closing down of the activities on the project. Closing out a project includes tasks such as budget auditing, inspection and final approval, sign-off on a subcontractor's contract, archiving documents for long-term storage, and project turnover. Project managers must ensure that there is legal closeout of their project before its final turnover.

Contract administration includes the activities to start the engagement process between two parties and manage it throughout the project until closure. After the project is completed, contract administration includes the activities to formally accept and close the contract.

CAUTION Ignoring one concept area, or leaving it for someone else to take care of, may hurt your project's chances of success.

TIP Knowledge areas are not all created equal. As a project manager, you may not spend equal time on all areas. Therefore, your time needs adjusting accordingly when working in each knowledge area.

Explaining the Project Lifecycle Process

Project managers can use many different methodologies to manage projects, and each industry has a unique methodology for managing projects. For example, a software development project has an industry-specific methodology, and each methodology has a unique project lifecycle process. Regardless of the particular lifecycle process, common processes exist among them. These processes may have different names across the industry or methodology, but the core phases remain the same. The descriptions and details are below.

There are five process groups within the PMBOK. The groups are Initiating, Planning, Executing, Monitoring and Controlling, and Closing. Every project has these process groups.

Figure 1.1 shows a graphical presentation of the *project lifecycle* process. As you can see, the five processes in this chart all relate in one way or another. The Initiating process starts a project and then moves to the Planning process, and the Executing process starts at the actual creation of the product. A back-and-forth process occurs between the Executing process and the Planning process throughout the project, and finally, the Closing process completes the project. During the lifecycle, the Controlling process oversees the activities occurring in each process area and provides rigor and structure to how the team accomplishes each task.

FIGURE 1.1

This is an example of a typical project lifecycle process chart and all the interactions between the processes.

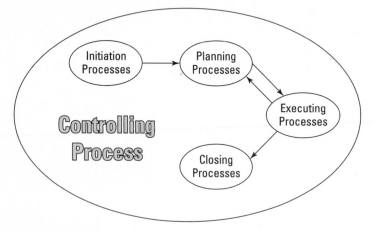

TIP   It is critical for a project manager to understand the project lifecycles process, and it will certainly increase your chances of success.

Initiating progress group

The project initiation activities are the startup tasks required on every project to get it under way. A wide range of activities is included in project initiation tasks for every project. These activities include initial project setup documents, creating budget forecasts, hiring consultants, and project schedule creation. In most cases, it takes time to start up a project correctly, so do not rush through creating the work deliverables; it will only hurt your project. If you forget something important early on in the project, it may be difficult to go back and make corrections. The schedule baseline is a good example of something that, if missed initially, cannot be re-created easily. Schedule baselines are taken before any process is recorded on the project. When the project moves to the executing phase, it is next to impossible to go back and take a baseline snapshot. Ensure every deliverable you complete is the highest level of quality the project can sustain. To ensure a high level of quality, the project manager will describe the quality standard for the team for each deliverable. For example, when completing a requirements document, all sections of the document must be either completed or noted as not applicable to the project. When doing so, this improves the quality of the document because it does not look like sections are missing; they just may not be needed for this type of project.

Depending on the methodology selected for your project, these activities can take weeks or months to complete. On larger construction projects, the start-up activities can sometimes take years before the project actually starts. In software projects, the small to medium size projects can often take a couple of weeks to a month to begin. Most methodologies define in detail the start activities required to move to the next phase. In many cases, the start-up activities for project managers are consistent across the same industry and project type. The different methodologies have different start-up activities, and that information is available to anyone interested in the methodologies documentation or training materials.

Planning progress group

Project planning activities include the expansion of the project charter and the gathering of the necessary information to plan and design the product of the project. The project manager and the team members plan the project execution. During the planning phase, the project manager performs the following:

- Plans and defines project scope
- Develops work breakdown structure
- Creates the project schedule and assigns resources
- Creates a project budget
- Generates a risk plan and analysis
- Develops a quality plan
- Creates a communication plan
- Develops a procurement and contract administration plan

NOTE Each of the preceding activities is applicable to the planning area. The project manager decides what order to perform these activities, but each needs completing before finishing the planning phase.

Executing progress group

Project execution is the process of performing the activities assigned to all stakeholders of the project. These stakeholders include the project manager, project team member, and other individuals who are assigned work tasks for the project. Only the work activities executed and documented in the project management plan should be included in the project. The executing phase of the project is one of the project manager's top responsibilities.

One of the tasks of the project manager at the beginning of the executing process is the creation of the project team. Throughout the executing phase, the project manager mentors the project team members. It is the project manager's role to ensure that team members execute their work activities in a timely manner while maintaining a high level of quality. The execution phase is also the most difficult and time consuming for a project manager; as the team members execute their work activities, and as problems and issues arise, the project manager needs to be on top of the problems and drive them to successful completion.

Quality assurance monitoring is also an important aspect of the executing phase of the project. All project team members who have work assignments complete quality assurance activities. The project manager has the ultimate responsibility to see that the quality meets the project requirements.

Controlling progress group

Project monitoring and control includes the process of performing the activity of oversight and control of all the work necessary to complete a successful project. The monitoring and controlling of work on the project spans all lifecycle activities. Portions of work from the initiating process to the closeout process require constant monitoring to ensure a successful completion. This aspect of the project lifecycle is the most time consuming for any project manager because of the need to understand every component of the project and to know whether the individual project activities are under control. If not, the project manager would step in and take control of the process until it has recovered and is back under control.

 **TIP** The controlling process spans across the entire lifecycle of the project.

Monitoring and controlling the process requires the active engagement of the project manager at all times. All projects will have the monitoring and controlling process integrated within them to ensure there is oversight by the project management team. The monitoring and controlling of a project is where project managers either do a great job or fall down and perform miserably. The constant monitoring and controlling of your project is an area where a project manager who is on top of their project can enhance the chances of success.

Closing process group

The project closeout process includes the finalization of all activities across all of the knowledge areas of the project. These activities include everything from finalizing contracts, reassigning staff, archiving documents for long-term storage, final documentation audits, and other shutdown activities.

There are two types of closeouts on a project:

- Technical closeout is the activities performed to complete the delivery of the product. The product delivered must meet the agreed-upon technical specifications. Therefore, to confirm this requirement, the project team must refer to the technical documentation and the final product to ensure it meets the required specification. During this phase, the project manager and team members must continually verify the quality of the project.

- Administrative closeout is the signing and archiving of all final documents and contracts and turning over of the product to the owner. An important aspect of administrative closeout is capturing the final approval and acceptance on all contract conditions by the project owner and team members. It also includes the reassigning of project staff and any final budget transfer or closeout processes. Many times during the administrative closeout process, an audit of the work's activities is required.

One of the important aspects of project closeout, specifically administrative closeout, is the capturing of the lessons learned information. Normally captured at the end of the project, lessons learned information is invaluable for the future projects that are of a similar nature. The information compiled and reported to the project team and stakeholders is historical knowledge of the project's events. It is important to store the lessons learned information as part of an overall knowledge base repository for other project teams to review.

CROSS-REF See Chapter 2 for more information on the lessons learned document.

Finally, project managers should remember how important the warranty period is on a project. The warranty period starts after delivery of the product to the owner. Project managers should be alert and have the project's maintenance team ready to respond to any issues or problems with the delivered product after the warranty period begins. The warranty period is going to differ for each project based on the industry, priority, and the impacts to the customers. A lower-priority project may not have a long warranty period, where a high-priority, high-criticality project would. Another example would be a construction project's warranty; in most cases this would be longer than a warranty period for a software development project. Warranty periods are not applicable to every project.

Summary

This chapter covered the importance of project communication. Successful project managers utilize both knowledge areas and lifecycle processes to communicate effectively their project information. Understanding and using the knowledge areas and lifecycle processes are fundamental to your success as a project manager. It is important that project managers and team members understand their roles and are comfortable with their responsibilities of communicating project information.

The most important aspect this chapter covers is the planning of communication tools used on your project. In most cases, this is a paradigm shift for the project management industry and to project managers in general. Project managers should spend the time at the beginning of the project to select the communication tools that they plan to utilize. The tools selected can affect the overall outcome of the project. This selection process includes both the project manager and the customer selecting the tools they feel are necessary for communicating effectively. A lack of communication planning can have the team scrambling and producing information that may or may not be valuable and potentially become a time waster.

Chapter 2

Planning Project Communication

Project communication planning is the task of identifying the information needs and requirements of the project customers. Customers require information about the project such as risk events, budget data, and schedule information. You are the project manager, so you must be proactive and plan for your customer needs.

In large companies, quite often, there are project management offices or project management groups that set standard requirements for company-approved projects. The standard includes areas such as the timing requirements on how often to send project information, types of project information captured, the types of reports utilized, and many other areas. An example of the standard is the timing of the data collection for status reports. Typically, the data collection is due by the end of the workday on Thursday, so the actual status report can be complied and sent on Friday.

One of the components of communication planning is the understanding of who generates project information and how. At times, both the project manager and the team members are required to generate joint project information and report to the customers. In some cases, a project team lead must generate project information specifically for a particular customer. For example, in a software project, a list of all bugs in the development phase requires a developer to create a report. Capturing the specifics of who is responsible for creating project information is a valuable part of the communication planning process and establishes at the beginning of the project who is responsible for what type of reporting.

Project communication planning is a relatively new concept in the project management field, but one that, if you embrace it, will change the way you manage projects forever. The project's success can depend on how well you embrace this change and how willing you are to take a chance on doing things a bit differently then you have in the past.

Struggling with Proper Project Communication Planning

Project managers often struggle to communicate their project information effectively. They are either sending too many reports or generating status information that makes no sense or provides little value, or they are sending too few reports and not providing a complete and satisfactory picture of the project. Communication planning can be difficult. Understanding the customers or clients is challenging when trying to determine exactly what information they want to see. It takes years to become a good communicator and a lot of practice working with customers and trying to understand their communication needs.

Project managers either ignore or struggle to perform project communication planning properly. The following list explores some of the common reasons.

- Bringing together the various parties involved in the project is challenging. These parties range from the project manager, team members, customers, clients, owner, and any other stakeholders involved in the project. Bringing together this large group of people is difficult in its own right mainly because everyone is so busy working on so many different activities and in some cases are offsite and not readily available. However, in order to have a fully documented project communication plan, the project manager must have all these participants involved as much as possible.

- Project managers and team members have been communicating all their lives and, therefore, wrongly assume that they can communicate project information just as easily. For this reason, many project managers tend to avoid or completely ignore any communication planning techniques. If project managers do not establish project communication as one of their higher priorities, they will miss being an effective communicator.

- Project managers fail to plan project communication requirements. They do not allocate the proper time to this task to effectively understand and document the communication needs of their customers. Often, the project manager must initiate the project or has higher priorities such as determining a budget, finding team members, understanding requirements, or creating a schedule. The actual task of identifying the communication requirements becomes overlooked or not addressed at all. Because of this pressure on the project, it is easy to skip the planning effort and start right into the details of the project. This is a bad practice and you should avoid it.

- Not every project manager has the understanding or knowledge to be able to create a communication plan. This is often due to he/she not having the proper training or experience on this subject, and he or/she therefore struggles to understand even how to proceed. Using the techniques in this section will help you and your project team members with this learning curve and will provide you the basic understanding of how to create a project communication plan, present project information, and be an effective communicator.

Project managers who miss planning their project communication may find themselves in a difficult situation when trying to communicate project status. Without upfront planning, they or their team members will be lacking a full understanding of their customer's requirements. The project manager may have one concept on how the project team will communicate, and the customers could have a completely different concept altogether. This leads to a communication breakdown, which, in the end could lead to a project failure.

Preventing Common Communication Problems

Communication problems occur throughout a project's lifecycle. These problems can be anything and have a large impact on the project.

The following list explains some common communication techniques that successful project managers have utilized. Project managers should be aware of these techniques and if applicable utilize them on their projects.

- Hold weekly in-person status meetings with key project customers. This establishes a rhythm for project communications with these customers. Regular project communication creates confidence in the customers that you are in charge of their project and watching it closely. Some project managers never spend any amount of time with their customers and when issues and concerns arise, they have no relationships to fall back to in the difficult situations. Project managers should take that time to work closely with their customers and form a good working relationship with them. Those relationships can last forever.

- Project managers should establish a cadence for delivering their project's status reports on the same day, at the same time. In doing so, the project manager builds yet another level of confidence and trust with their customers that they can deliver the information on time and on a regular basis. Customers will come to expect that reporting cadence from the project manager and will appreciate them sending that information on a consistent basis. They will feel like they can rely on the project manager, which is a great place for anyone to be in with their customers.

- Project managers disperse the status report and the meeting agenda prior to the day of the meeting. It should be enough time to allow the project stakeholders to absorb the information before the actual meeting. By doing this, you are actually allowing your customers to prepare for the meeting. If they are required to bring additional information or talk about a particular subject, you take the surprise out of the conversation and allow them to prepare ahead of time because they have the information already. In almost every case, managers do not like surprises; therefore sending out this information early prevents any surprises from arising at the meeting. This technique usually speeds up the meeting because the meeting attendees have the opportunity to review the material early and for the lesser important items, they can be discussed briefly and moved past. Using this advance notice technique may resolve some issues before the meeting.

- Project managers should follow up with attendees after a status meeting by asking questions, sending meeting minutes, and being available. If questions do come up be sure to respond in a timely manner. Doing so goes a long way in great project communication, and your customers will appreciate it!

- Creating a project control room for the project and assigned project team members for the duration of the project is often helpful. The control room includes performing all the tips stated early (status reports, in-person status meetings) as well as having a central communication room for displaying and discussing project information. Very large scale projects tend to have these project control rooms as standard operating procedures. The larger projects will have the time, money, and complexity to establish these rooms as an important part of their project communication.

- Project managers can use the two-question technique (small stakeholder groups only). Project customers or stakeholders are to bring two questions to the meeting after reading the status report. This is a fun way to get the stakeholders engaged in the project and ensures they read the status report.

Understanding Communication Links

In this section, we discuss communication links between people. Do you remember the game everyone called telephone? You know; someone says a sentence, tells a friend, that friend repeats it, but adds something to it and tells someone else. At the end of the chain, the original sentence is completely different from the start of the chain. In some cases, what comes out in the end is the complete opposite of the original sentence.

The more people involved in the communication chain, the harder it is to communicate accurately. Adding people almost guarantees that someone will jumble the information between the parties.

The following formula represents the calculations for communication links. This formula is widely used by project managers around the world. Note the number of links created when you are communicating and working with so many different people. In Figures 2.1 and 2.2 it displays how quickly the communication links grow as you add people. For example, if you are communicating with ten people, your links are not ten. No, your links would equal 45. Let us look at the following formula to get the real picture of how many people are in your communication path.

Number of Links = $n(n-1)/2$ where n = number of people communicating

Actual Example for 10 People: $10 (10 - 1)/2 = (10 \times 9)/2 = 45$ Links

Therefore, if you plan to send your communication to ten people, expect the message to be repeated at least 45 times. The repeating of this information could have a huge negative impact on your project, especially if the message was not clear and to the point when originally sent. The result could be total miscommunication on your project.

Figure 2.1 describes how quickly the communication links grow as you add more people to the conversations.

FIGURE 2.1

This figure represents the number of communication links.

2 = 1

7 = 21

20 = 190

50 = 1,225

NOTE The formula is simple to understand after you start working with it. Initially, it takes some time to see just how large the impact is on people when sending your messages, and it provides project managers a number to focus on when creating their message. No longer should a project manager just think he is sending a message to ten people. The message must be addressed to a larger group initially.

Figure 2.2 shows that as the number of people involved in your project communication increases, the number of communication channels increases geometrically. The changes in this figure actually hit the 300 mark for 25 people.

ON the CD-ROM The communication links spreadsheet on the CD allows you to create your own calculations and determine communication links for as many people as you want on your project.

FIGURE 2.2

This figure represents the number of communication links for 1 to 25 people.

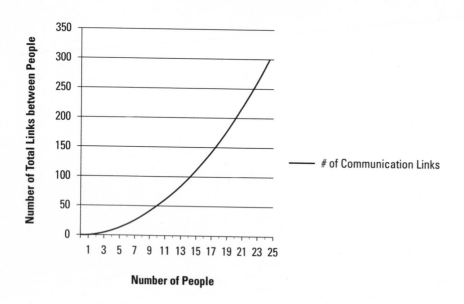

Sending and receiving models

There are two components of communication—sending and receiving. This sounds simple, one sends, and one receives. It occurs every day in regular conversations. However, understanding and implementing the process of sending and receiving is not quite that simple. The challenge is in the interference or the noise introduced when communicating between multiple parties.

Figure 2.3 shows several steps that occur in a simple conversation between two people. Both people are transmitting and receiving messages as the conversation occurs. Because of interference, these messages are sometimes altered as they go through filters. Interference could be a personal filter. Interference is just about anything that can alter or interfere with the message sent. Each of us has a *personal filter* that can alter the understanding of the message communicated to us. Personal filters develop over time as our personalities are developed and we experience life's daily challenges. These personality traits create and develop a person's communication filter. Therefore, one person can hear a message one way and experience that message based on their background and experiences. A different person could interpret that same message a different way. These differences can really become evident when two people are communicating from different countries. Each may have a different understanding of the message sent. This can be especially true when dealing with two different cultures, such as Eastern and Western cultures.

FIGURE 2.3

This example represents a typical conversation between two people.

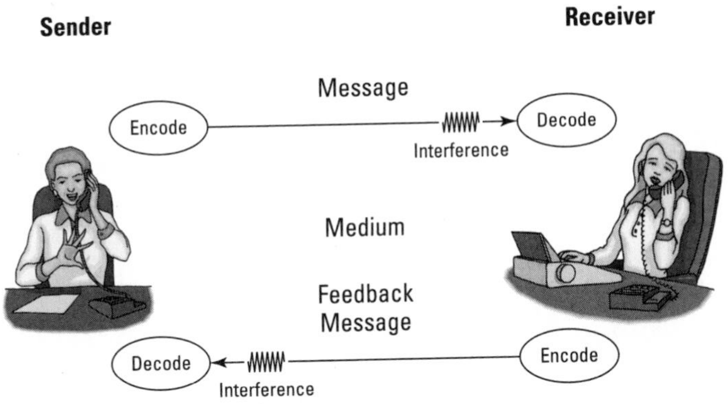

Figure 2.3 displays two women having a typical conversation. Both women are engaged in encoding and decoding the conversation. As you can see, interference is added to the conversation occurring before the decoding happens and after the encoding process. This interference could change the sent message. A simple conversation can become complex. The encoding, decoding, and interference, all occurring throughout the conversation, can really make communication difficult between the two people.

Knowing the following terms can be helpful:

- **Sender:** Person sending message
- **Receiver:** Person receiving message
- **Encode:** Sending thoughts that are understood by others
- **Decode:** Translation of message into thought process
- **Message:** The results of the encoding process
- **Medium:** Any form of conveying the message
- **Feedback message:** The results of the encode process sent by receiver

Sending model

Sending information, regardless of the type, can be tricky and needs careful handling. When sending a message, you need to put yourself in the place of the receiver and understand the information sent to try to avoid any miscommunication. Sometimes, sending the same message a couple of times in a slightly different format is beneficial. Other times, people may not clearly understand the message if it is only delivered in one format. As the project manager, ensure that you cater to more than one style of learning when sending your project messages. For example, if possible add both text and graphics to your messages to enhance not only the message but also the chances of your readers being able to comprehend the information. Project managers should be aware of the cultural differences and personal bias people may possess. Having that knowledge beforehand will allow you to tailor the message to that individual, and the chances of understanding the information is higher.

Receiving model

From the line graph in Figure 2.2, you can see that even when you think you are communicating with a small number of people, behind the scenes you are actually dealing with a much larger group. Trying to communicate a specific message, when it has to go through that many people, means it is going to go through a number of different filters. Everyone will be filtering it differently to some existent. It is amazing that any verbal communication accurately transmits at all when going through so many people!

Preparing and Delivering Presentations

Project managers are responsible for presenting project information throughout the life of the project. In most cases, these presentations require the project manager to plan and deliver the material about the project. In this section, we discuss how to plan and deliver a great project presentation. We also cover some tools and techniques to use to ensure every presentation delivered achieves its desired goals.

 Presentations are the opportunity for a project manager to shine and show off his or her presentation skills. Be prepared and give them your best presentation every time!

 If your presentation skills are lacking, we recommend joining Toastmasters International to improve your skills. Find them at www.toastmaster.org

Preparing for a presentation

Preparing for a project presentation is like preparing for anything important. If you go in unprepared, you may have some disastrous results while standing in front of your team members and customers. Here are some tips that you can use when you are planning and preparing for a presentation.

Some of these tips are just common sense, but all are helpful reminders that can help you become a better communicator.

- **Know your audience.** Although knowing your audience is important, knowing how knowledgeable your audience is on the subject you are presenting is even better. You can create a more detailed presentation when your audience is familiar with the material. This also determines the amount of time you need to spend on each section. If you feel your audience is going to be fully conversant in one area, you may want to focus more of your presentation in that area and leave the areas that everyone is less familiar with alone.

Catering to the needs and wants of your audience will help you deliver a successful presentation.

- **Establish the correct tone.** You need to decide what will work best for your presentation. Should it be serious or informal? Will humor work? How much is too much?

- **Dress for success.** Always dress professionally when presenting your materials. Even if every other day you dress informally, the day of the presentation you need to look professional and look respectable to your audience.

- **Know the room and facilities.** Familiarize yourself in advance with your presentation room and any equipment that you plan to use. This upfront planning should help with any technical issues that may arise.

- **Present your credentials to establish creditability.** Present your credentials at the beginning of the presentations so your audience knows your background and you can build a level of trust and respect from them right from the start.

- **Schedule informal meetings with stakeholders in advance.** Presenting information to some of the key stakeholders ahead of the actual formal meeting should eliminate any major surprises during the actual presentation. Project managers should schedule preview meetings ahead of the final presentation, to allow both management and stakeholders the chance to see the raw materials before the final meeting. Doing this can also help the presentation by incorporating management and stakeholders' ideas into the presentation.

- **Practice, practice, and practice.** Practicing your presentation is the key to presenting it well.

Presenting your project materials

After all the preparation is complete, it is time for you, as the project manager, to present your project material. As you continue to hold project presentations, you will learn from your mistakes and improve your presentation skills. In the meantime, here are some helpful tips and ideas to prepare you now for your presentations.

- **Introduce your topic well.** Your introduction will vary in length and detail, depending on the length of your talk, your topic, and the level of sophistication of your audience. Determine what you are trying to impart. Give the necessary information but be careful not to include large amounts of extraneous material. Visual aids are particularly important here to grab your audience's attention. If you have a snappy photo, an interesting thought, or a catchy phrase, use it here. The point of the introduction is to capture your audience's attention, let them know what you will be talking about, get them excited about the topic, and let them know why your topic is so interesting.

- **Limit your use of animation.** Too much animation can be distracting and reduce the impact of your presentation. This problem is encountered in presentations today, especially because the animation software has become easier to use. On the flip side, having just the right amount animation or graphics in your presentations can positively impact your presentation. Remember, the presentation is your time to shine, and you want to provide some fun and excitement with your presentations. Regardless of how serious the message, it may be easier to sell with some levity.

■ **Don't overwhelm your audience with information.** Limit the total amount of data you present and limit the amount of information you show on any single slide. Busy slides and complex graphs are not helpful at all and can end up confusing your audience. A confused audience is not a happy one. Keep slides brief and to the point and never have more than five bullets per slide.

■ **Begin with a title slide and show a brief outline of the topics.** Use text slides to designate the beginnings of individual sections of your talk or to introduce a major topic. Usually a prominent title in bold letters is adequate. Text slides can be important and helpful to you and your audience. They demonstrate your organizational skills, help audience members to follow your talk more easily, and let them know where you are heading with your presentation.

Avoiding common mistakes

When making project presentations, it is common to make simple mistakes that can detract from the overall presentation itself. These are frequently made mistakes, but easily avoidable. Here is a list of tips that will help you avoid these common mistakes.

■ **Paraphrase your text slides, don't read each major point.** The audience will be reading the slides. You can read a point or two, but then go into the details you want your audience to understand.

■ **Clearly label all axes on figures (if applicable) and give each figure a brief, informative title.** Doing so is good practice and makes your slides clear and easy to follow.

■ **Choose your graphs carefully.** Graphs should follow a logical progression, and you should be able to explain each graph fully. Use the best graphics available but be careful not to distract your audience by making the artwork more interesting than the information. Watch for colors, patterns, and the various combinations of each. Make sure you focus on content and clarity.

■ **Cite all sources of information, especially if you did not generate the data yourself.** It is important to give credit where credit is due when using material you did not create.

■ **Always give a synthesis or conclusion.** Display a brief summary of your conclusions on a slide while you discuss the significance of the material you have presented. Your conclusions should match your talk objectives and should complete your story.

You must include a segment of time for questions and answers following a project presentation. Adding a question and answer period is the key to a successful presentation and allows everyone to walk away with more knowledge about the subject. When project managers fail to provide a question and answer period, the audience may feel rushed and less informed. The question and answer period is the time that you are able to show your audience that you really know your subject, so whenever possible, plan and prepare for that time in meetings. Try to think about all the questions that could come up and be ready to answer them if possible. You should be ready and prepared to answer questions that come up about the materials or the project in general.

TIP Always remain relaxed and calm throughout the question period, even though, you may be stuck on a question, or put on the spot. Do not worry about this, as even the best presenters are stuck sometimes, but the more experienced ones can normally get themselves out of it. In most cases, this is as easy as saying "I don't know the answer" or "I will get back to you this afternoon." This provides the presenter the opportunity to get off the spot and gives them a follow-up action item to track down after the presentation.

When answering questions during the presentation or even in the question and answer period, take the time to gain composure, make sure you understand the question clearly, and think about it before you answer. If the question is unclear or does not make sense, ask politely for clarification. Experienced project presenters encourage questions and answers during the presentation. They can control the time remaining for the presentation and move the presentation along appropriately.

Understanding Stakeholder Risk Tolerance Level

Risk tolerance level (or often, *risk level*) describes the willingness of the customer to take various risks. In most cases, the customers' risk tolerance level and the project manager's risk tolerance level is different. Therefore, those differences can cause communication problems. Personality conflicts arise when one person is more risk-adverse than is the other person. Understanding and knowing the differences in risk tolerance levels between the two interested parties early in the project allows the project manager to make better decisions. Without this information, any project decisions made by the project manager could be the opposite of what the customer would have expected or wanted the project manager to make for them.

The following list describes the three levels of risk tolerance.

- **High:** Willing to take more project risks and make decisions based on that risks level.
- **Medium:** Willing to take on some risks but careful in those risk decisions.
- **Low:** Very fearful of project risks and unwilling to make a decision that would increase the risk to the project.

We describe the three different risk tolerance levels in detail in the following sections.

High risk tolerance level

A person who has a *high* risk tolerance level is an individual who has a tendency to take and allow more risks on a project. A *Risk Seeker* is a person in project management who is willing to take on additional risks on a project. For example, a project customer accepts a budget forecast that has been overrunning for several months. Because it is only a forecast, he is willing to take the chance that the forecast will go down and the project will end on budget. The high risk tolerance person generally takes more chances on their projects and in their personal lives. These people tend to be the bungee jumpers of the world. Therefore, when assigned to a project, and depending on the role the Risk Seeker is playing, they could end up jeopardizing the project because of the risks they are willing to take. Over the years, we have found that a person who has a high risk tolerance tends to be an optimistic person and is usually positive.

A person who has a high risk tolerance level will not tend to require as many status updates or various project information reports throughout the project. Generally, these people are not micro-managers and tend to let the team members do their job and manage the project with little to no interference.

Medium risk tolerance level

A person who has a *medium* risk tolerance level is an individual who has a tendency to take and prevent risks on their projects. A *Risk Neutral* is a person in project management that is willing to take on some risks, but not high risks. Using the same budget overrun example, a person with a medium risk tolerance level would be someone who would accept the risk of the project going over budget, but would be looking into the possibilities of preventing that from occurring as soon as they heard about the situation.

A person who has a medium risk tolerance level requires some level of project reporting but doesn't request needless or extra reports. Generally, most customers have a medium risk tolerance level and do not tend to require excess reporting or hand-holding throughout the project, but are usually willing to accept the regular cadence of project information to which they agreed to at the start of the project.

Low risk tolerance level

A person who has a low risk tolerance level is an individual who will not accept many risks. A *Risk Avoider* is a person in project management who is not willing to take any kind of risk on a project. This person often worries unnecessarily about all aspects of the project. This type of individual will be someone that focuses on what could go wrong and puts measures in place to prevent those events from occurring. Using the same budget overrun example, a person with a low risk tolerance would be worried about the forecasted overage and be adamant in trying to resolve these issues as soon as possible, potentially causing extra work for the project. Over the years, we have found that this type of a person is pessimistic and tends to require extra attention.

A person that has a low risk tolerance level requires constant project reporting, updates, and reassurance that a project is continuing on track toward completion. This person will be one who will often require a number of on-demand reports and a high demand for ongoing project information.

Table 2.1 shows an example of the three risk tolerance levels and the amount of requested reporting for each level. In this chart, when reviewing the first example (High – Risk Seeker) you can see that this person requires high-level project information at a lesser frequency (Monthly/Quarterly). Review the other two risk tolerances to get an understanding of their requirements. This chart does not require you to add your specific project details too. We present it as a guide to help you understand and plan how to communicate effectively at these levels of risk tolerance.

TABLE 2.1

Sample Risk Tolerance versus Reporting Frequency Matrix

Customer's Risk Tolerance Level	Level of Reporting to Provide to Customer	Frequency
High (Risk Seeker)	High level of project information: i.e., Project End Date: September 2009, Budget: $1,000,000	Monthly / Quarterly
Medium (Risk Neutral)	Medium. Combination of high level and detailed level of project information i.e. Project End Date: September 12-15, 2009, Budget: $1,123,200	At least weekly
Low (Risk Avoider)	Low. Very detailed project information, covering all aspects of the project, i.e., Project End Date: September 15, 2009 @ 5:00pm PST, Budget: $1,123,202.22 + -5% accuracy	Daily/hourly and on-demand reporting volumes of reports

This chart is a smart communication tool, because it directs and guides you as the project manager in understanding how much communication you will be required to send to your particular customer based on their risk tolerance level.

Determining customer tolerance levels

Successful project managers assess their customer's risk tolerance level on the first meeting. They may simply ask them how they deal with project risks or have a general conversation with them about risks on a project. After that conversation, a project manager should notice how much risk that customer is willing to take. With this knowledge, the project manager should be able to understand how to communicate more effectively with that customer.

NOTE When discussing risk tolerance levels some customers may have different risk tolerances for different areas of the project. For example, in a cost-driven project, a customer may have a lower risk tolerance for the cost aspects of the project, but tend to have a higher risk tolerance for the schedule or scope aspects. On a completely different project, that same customer could change his or her risk tolerance levels based on the conditions or type of project. On a schedule-driven project, a low-risk person is going to take fewer risks on the schedule component, but may be freer with the budget and scope components.

By missing this important aspect of your customer's personality and their particular tolerance on handling risks, you may not be communicating as effectively as possible with them.

Defining a Project Communication Plan

A project communication plan is the document that defines the process and procedures involved with communicating project information. The plan is the link between the process of managing the project information and distributing the information to the appropriate stakeholders in a timely manner. It does not communicate the actual project information itself; it only generates the procedures the project manager or team members will follow to gather and create the project information. The content of the project communication plan includes areas such as timeframes to receive the data, recipients of the communication plan, distribution and storing methods, and the information collection process. One of the factors of the communication plan that needs watching closely is the timely delivery of project information. If you distribute project information one or two weeks late, it makes the information useless for your customers. They will not be happy or put up with the delay for long. You should ensure the information you send is the latest possible. This is important, specifically, when it comes to budget data and the frequency of reporting that type of data. Financial information can swing from week to week;, therefore timely reporting of this data is critical to keeping the project budget on track.

> **NOTE**   Part of creating a project communication plan is the understanding of the appropriate generation of project information. This ensures that the right people receive the right information at the right time.

Creating a project communication plan

A project manager should ensure that one of the earliest tasks in initiating and kicking off a project is the development and creation of the project communication plan. Follow these steps to create a project communication plan.

1. **Plan and document the communication components of your project.** For example, the project manager documents the information he believes is needed to communicate effectively as well as what the customers or team members required to communicate successfully, covering areas such as

   - Why do the customers need project information?
   - Who is working on the project?
   - What information do they need?
   - When do they need it?
   - How will they want it generated (such as format)?
   - How will the communication materials be stored and retrieved?

   Other areas to be aware of are virtual communication requirements of the project and specific requirements of the project stakeholders, such as sensitive or confidential information or the documents generated from the methodology used on the project.

NOTE The project manager should understand what everyone on the project would like to see for project communication deliverables to ensure they are communicating effectively.

2. **Consolidate and plan using the results of the Step 1 planning activities.** For example, the project manager gathers the specific project requirements captured in Step 1 and plans how to generate these communication requirements. For example, the customers have asked for a monthly newsletter. The project manager must track down the process of generating a newsletter in this project environment. The project manager works with the customer to ensure that the information in the newsletter is what they expect to see. The newsletter, in this case, represents the vehicle to deliver project information. The project manager continues working with the customer until he has completely reviewed and understood what the communication requirements are from the customer (documented in Step 1).

NOTE Take the time, summarize the requirements in Step 1, and determine if they are even possible to create in your project environment. A project Web site may not be possible to create for your type of project or your project environment but could be a legitimate wish of the customer.

3. **Document the customer communication requirements within the project communication plan.** For example, the customer has asked for a project Web site, a monthly newsletter, and quarterly press conferences in Step 1. The project manager would document those requirements within the communication plan. After the project manager obtains the customer's approval on the plan, its creation is complete and the project manager attempts to create the communication requirements from the customer.

ON the CD-ROM See the project communication plan template in the Communication_Managing folder as you begin Step 3.

4. **Record your findings into your own communication management plan.** Table 2.2 is a sample table of contents for a communication management plan.

Every company that practices formal project management should have some form of project communication plan for their project managers to utilize. Project managers need to review the communication plan and make sure that it works for their projects. Not every section will be applicable to the project, and some sections may need adding because of the uniqueness of the project. The main structure of the document should be sufficient to provide the project information to the stakeholders or owners of the project, and the results of the document once completed are a comprehensive communication plan.

Table 2.2 represents a table of contents for a communication plan. You can use this generic plan immediately if a template is not already available for you to utilize.

TABLE 2.2

Communication Plan Table of Contents Example

Section #	Description
Section 1	Project Communication Plan
Section 2	Project Organization Chart
Section 3	Project Communication Requirements Matrix
Section 4	People Report Matrix
Section 5	Timeframe
Section 6	Lessons Learned

The following tips can increase your chances of success and can be used as a check list in creating a communication plan.

■ Follow established project management office procedures within your company or organization for capturing communication requirements. The project office also sets up the cadence and rhythm of how often project reporting is required, so you need to understand that cadence and use this information in gathering customers' communication requirements. (For example, the PMO establishes a monthly newsletter, and the customer wants a weekly newsletter.)

■ Hold brainstorming sessions with project team members and project customers or stakeholders to capture their communication requirements for the project. In these sessions, the project manager or an administrative assistant will document the customer's communication requirements. This includes what reports, forms, Web sites, communication tools, and specifically the documents or spreadsheets the customer requires for their project. The goal of every communication plan identified in these sessions is to provide the customer with the information they need to make project level decisions and gain status of the project.

■ When the project customers require media or press conferences as part of their communication requirements, you should find out the steps or processes involved for delivering messages to the media.

■ One important aspect of understanding the actual communication plan is determining the expectation the customers have on the reporting timeframe for this information. For example, the project customer requests a project status report, and the project manager must determine exactly how often the customer wants the status report. The project manager will work directly with the customer for this information and jointly agree on an acceptable timeframe.

Kingdome roof replacement project

A project that received a great deal of media attention was the Kingdome roof replacement project in Seattle, Washington, back in 1994. The Kingdom was Seattle's multipurpose stadium used for professional baseball, football, concerts, and many other events. The problem arose when the roof tiles on the inside of the Kingdome started falling randomly on the baseball field and were endangering the players during a regularly schedule practice. When this occurred, the team members were immediately removed from the field, and the safety manager of the Kingdome closed the stadium for safety reasons. This drew instant media attention to the Kingdome. This created an investigation, which concluded the tiles in the Kingdome needed to be replaced before they could continue with any concerts or athletic events. The media agencies were actively tracking this high-profile project and demanded up-to-date information throughout the life of the project. The project office decided the best way to handle the constant pressure of replying to the media was to create a project management office, take over a conference room, and put all relevant project information up on the walls for review by team members, media, and the public. This information was constantly kept current because of the demand. The media had the latest information on the project at any time. The room was open 24 hours a day, seven days a week. The project team was working around the clock to meet a tight deadline, and therefore the latest update information was available to the media at any time without having to bother the project manager or owners.

- Understand exactly who the audience is for each communication deliverable. Ensure that you do not misjudge the recipients of the project when sending out project information. Take time to ensure that the right people have the latest project information at all times.

- Use the company's standard template if possible; do not recreate your own version of the communication plan if there is already one available. Companies will often have a generic communication plan, missing the key steps and processes outlined above but an excellent starting point for your project.

NOTE You must understand how important it is to learn the reporting frequency of your company. The earlier you learn this, the better off you will be making the deadlines that you are expected to make for project reporting.

Defining the Project Communication Requirements Matrix

A *project communication matrix* is a chart that shows how communication flows on a project. It states who communicates to whom and what level of communication is used. It also shows who develops the information and who receives it. The direction and flow of information shows readers how the information transfers to different parties. The communication matrix is effortless to understand and appears easy to build; however, a lot of information needs to be obtained before you can even start to create this powerful tool. It does not usually take a great deal of time to build the matrix after you have the information, but acquiring the information can be difficult. It is the gathering of that information when building the communication requirements matrix which helps the project manager or team member understand the real communication needs of everyone involved in the project.

Table 2.3 shows a communication requirements matrix. This matrix represents who receives what information on the project and lists project stakeholders across the top and down the side. Also noted are any applications specific to the company that requires project status. The actual reporting or information generated is in each cell of the matrix.

Understanding how to read the matrix chart

In the first row in the matrix, noted as the Project Manager, you see that the project manager sends the Stakeholders (Internal / Core team) weekly status reports and attends monthly stakeholder meetings. This intersection cell documents the specific communication requirements the project manager has with that particular role, in this case the Stakeholder (Internal/Core Team). As you are reading the matrix, look closely at the intersection cells as they tell you the information passed between the two parties. This continues for every role on the project. As you read across the row for the project manager specifically, you should also notice that he or she is responsible for entering status into the company's financial and reporting systems. This data includes color status (green, yellow, red), project dates, budget information, risks, issues, action items, and so on. The project manager enters it into the system directly. Continue to review each row for every role on the project and review the intersection cells for each role. This process continues until the project manager documents all the different roles on the project.

The benefit of using the communication requirements matrix is that the project manager can see, on a single page, the passing of information between the various roles on the project. Early in the project, it is the responsibility of the project manager to obtain sign-off of the project communication requirements matrix. The customers will appreciate approving this matrix at the beginning of the project so expectations on their communication needs are set and fully understood. They know exactly what information they will receive during the life of the project.

Creating a communication requirements matrix

The following steps provide the project manager with support in the creation of a communication requirements matrix.

1. **Plan and document the roles required for the project.** As an example, the project manager will document all roles that are involved on this project. Once identified, add these roles to the template across the top and down the side cells. This establishes specific project roles that will obtain or distribute project information throughout the life of the project.

2. **Document the individual communication requirements for every project role.** The project manager will work directly with each role and gather their information needs for

TABLE 2.3

Communication Requirements Matrix

Team Member Tool	Project Manager	Stakeholder (Internal/Core)	Stake-holder (External) Team)	Owner	Estimator/ Estimating Team)	Company Financial and Reporting System(s), Estimator System(s)	Medium
Project Manager		Communicates status weekly and participates in monthly stake-holder meeting		Communicates status weekly and participates in monthly stakeholder meeting		Puts project in red status Add dates Add budget information	Electronic
Stakeholder (Internal)	Feedback, Issues/ Concerns						Verbal
Stakeholder (External)	Issues/ Concerns	Feedback, issues, concerns					Document and verbal
Owner	Issues/ Concerns						Document
Estimator/ Estimating Team						Cost of project, size of project, duration of project	Document
Company Financial and Reporting System(s), Estimator System(s)				Budget information Project status Issues/ risks			Electronic

the project. A great example of this would be the customer and the project manager roles. Both parties would sit down together and discuss the communication needs between them. The information captured during these sessions fits directly into the intersection cells on the communication requirements matrix between the project manager and the customers. The interview process continues as the project manager meets with each role and documents what they require for project information. At the end of every session, the project manager would enter those requirements directly into the intersection cells between the two roles. The communication requirements matrix is complete after the project manager finishes interviewing all the team members working in the project roles and the cells where applicable are completed. In some cases, there will be specific systems where the project managers have to enter project data. These systems should go on the matrix as well. It is up to the project manager to understand what his or her requirements are for entering this data.

3. **When the communication requirements matrix is complete, store it as part of the project documents and send it to customers for approval and future reference.** As an example, the project manager finalizes the communication requirements matrix, stores it in the document control system, and then sends it to the customer for approval. If the project has a control room, hang the matrix on the wall for anyone to observe and update when applicable.

Understanding the role report matrix

A *role report* matrix identifies the reports that a project manager will create for the various roles on the project. The role report matrix is different from the communication requirements matrix. The main difference is the communication requirements matrix contains the information sent between the two roles (either people or applications), while the role report matrix is documenting only the reports between the parties. The communication requirements matrix has areas where the project manager can enter data into a financial reporting system, whereas this data would never go on the Role Report matrix. The Role Report matrix is going to be valuable in describing and documenting the various types of reports the stakeholders of the project are receiving.

Table 2.4 shows a role report matrix. This table represents project reports sent to the different roles and people involved with the project. The matrix lists the different types of reports across the top and the actual roles and people's name down the side. Like the earlier communication requirements matrix, the intersection cells represent the main information passed between the two people on the project.

In this example, the first row of data represents the CEO/CFO for the project. In reviewing that particular row, the CFO (John Smith) can request a status report or a cost report at any time and has another requirement that is a monthly variance report on the budget. As you progress through the table, you will observe the roles and their associated project reports.

TABLE 2.4

Role Report Matrix

People (receive the report)	Name	On-Demand Report	Daily Report	Weekly Report	Monthly Report	Quarterly Report
CEO/CFO	John Smith	Status/ Cost Report			Variance Report	
Owner	Peter Adams	Status/ Cost Report			Schedule, Cost Report, Issues/Risks Report	
Stakeholder	Mark Taylor	Stakeholder Report		Schedule, Cost Report, Issues/Risks Report		
Project Manager	Bruce Jones		Daily Status Report	Weekly Status Report, Cost Report, Issues/ Risk Report		
Risk Manager	Sally Smith	Risk Report	Issues/Risks Report	Risk Report		
Media	Tim Robbins	Media Report				
Cost Manager	Evan Campbell			Cost Report, Performance Report, Variance Report.		
Functional/ Resource Managers	Mary Keele	Resource Utilization Reports			Resource Utilization Reports	
Quality Control Manager/Team	David James				Quality Report, Issues/Risk Report, Status Report	
Project Engineer	Peter Parker			Status Report, Cost Report		
Foreman	Tom Jones			Look Ahead or Activity Report		

The benefits of using the Role Report matrix include the following:

- It documents who receives what reports and how often the reports are distributed.

- It documents the available reports. The matrix displays who is receiving what report. If stakeholders see a report they are not receiving, they can simply ask for that report. It may not be possible without this type of matrix.

- A project manager can control the project information distribution to their stakeholders and team members and determine quickly who is receiving what project information.

- It can be used in an ongoing review process to determine if reports are still a requirement for each project stakeholders.

Creating a role report matrix

The following steps provide the project manager with support in the creation of a role report matrix.

1. **Plan and document the roles and report types available for the project.** For example, the project manager will document the different types of roles on the project and place them down the left-hand side of the matrix. Across the top, the project manager will add the various standard project reports. These reports will include at a minimum, Daily, Weekly, Monthly, or Quarterly reports.

2. **Document the individual project reports required for every project role.** The project manager works directly with each role and gathers what type of status reports they want to receive from the project. A great example is the Owner Role, in which the owner has asked for a Status and Cost report on demand, a Monthly Status report(s), and a Quarterly Status report. The project manager then works with all the other project roles and determines which reports they want to receive. The project manager, as he or she interviews each role, is continually updating the Role Report matrix and adding the information obtained directly into the intersection cells. At the end of the interview process, the role report matrix is complete and ready for use on the project.

TIP When creating the role report matrix, try to complete this at the same time you are completing the communication requirements matrix. Both tools are required documents within the communication plan and have the project manager interviewing the stakeholders only once.

3. **After the role report matrix is complete, store it as part of the project documents and send it to customers for approval and future reference.** For example, the project manager finalizes the role report matrix and then stores it in the document control system and sends it for the customer's approval. Similar to the communication requirements matrix, if the project has a control room, hang the role report matrix on the wall for anyone to observe and update when applicable.

The following list represents the various types of communication reports used in a role report matrix and would be listed as an option across the top of the table.

- **Weekly status reports:** Provides a status of the project mainly from a scheduling and cost perspective.

- **Project schedule:** Provides the time lines for the work activities on the project.

- **Daily report:** Provides a daily snapshot of the project activities, addressing any risks, issues, or concerns occurring on the project.

- **Monthly report:** Provides a monthly snapshot of the project activities, addressing any risks, issues, or concerns occurring on the project.

- **Quality report:** Provides a quarterly snapshot of the project activities, addressing any risks, issues, or concerns occurring on the project. This is normally a summary level report.

- **Cost report:** Provides a snapshot of the project costs at time of running report. This includes planned and actuals.

- **Variance report:** Provides a snapshot of the variance across cost and time from an established baseline.

- **Issues report:** Provides a list of all project issues.

- **Risk report:** Provides a list of all project risks and risk issues.

- **Performance report:** Provides a snapshot of the current project performance metrics and trends.

- **Resource utilization report:** Provides a snapshot of the resource utilization across all project team members.

- **Resource leveling report:** Provides a snapshot of the project's resource leveling project.

- **Quality report:** Provides a current snapshot of quality status and issues for the project.

- **Media report:** Provides a media release.

- **Lesson learned report:** Provides ongoing lessons learned for the project.

- **Look ahead report:** Provides a look ahead for short-term activities.

- **Stoplight report:** Provides a high-level graphic summary report on the cost and schedule status of the project.

 Determining who will be receiving what report is critical in the development of this role report matrix

Developing Lessons Learned Information

One of the techniques and best practices that senior and experienced project managers utilize is the developing and creating of *lessons learned* information throughout the life of the project. Most of the time, if project managers do collect lessons learned information, it is developed as a last-minute thought in the final days or at the end of the project. This is during the closeout process, where the project manager scrambles for bits and pieces of project history to develop and compile it into a lessons learned document. In most cases, because the project is in its closing phase, the project manager has only a few team members remaining, and compiling and obtaining project information from them to consolidate in the lessons learned information can be difficult. This scenario is common for a project manager who waits until the end of the project before collecting and developing the project's lessons learned information.

A best-practice technique that is starting to gain popularity is the collection of the lessons learned information during the life of the project. We recommend that you plan and develop your lessons learned that way on your projects. From the kick-off meeting, capture and store the lessons learned information into a central repository for everyone to review. As the project progresses, one technique that you might utilize is the capturing of lessons learned information during the project's status meetings. This is the best time to collect this information because you and your project team members are present and able to provide the week's lessons learned information at the same time. Everyone can hear and discuss what is happening or what has happened during the week. When developing your weekly status meeting agenda, add a lessons learned agenda item. As the meeting progresses to the point where you are about to collect lessons learned information, ask each team member about their positive and negative experiences for the week. You may not even mention the word lessons learned to them, just capture what went right and what went wrong from every team member. They will provide the data and not even realize they are giving you the lessons learned information. You can lead the discussion around the lessons learned information from past projects or even weeks on the current project to ensure that the team is not repeating the same mistakes. Each week, continue this process, capturing exactly what went right, what went wrong from each team member. At the end of the project, compile the information into a final presentation.

Communicating lessons learned information

When communicating project information, project managers should have as much knowledge about the project as possible to ensure that the message they are communicating is as accurate as possible. One method of obtaining the knowledge is utilizing the lessons learned information from past projects.

When you are reviewing lessons learned information from past projects, you are personally gaining a wealth of knowledge from the last project manager and their team members on the events of a previous project that would not normally be available. We recommend that if there is lessons learned information from past projects or if the project manager who ran those projects is still around, that you review the material and interview or discuss the project with that project manager. You will be able to learn more details about what happened on the project. In some cases, the project manager can determine what information to share and what information not to share. Sometimes sharing too much information can cause unnecessary bias that could negatively impact the project. For example, there may be information captured in the lessons learned information about an individual or a particular group that was valuable to capture for the past project but does not offer any benefit for this particular project.

When planning your project communication, as the project manager, it is to your advantage to utilize lessons learned information. When you have the knowledge of what went right and what went wrong on projects similar to yours, you can communicate that knowledge to your team members and customers on your current project.

Benefiting from lessons learned

One of the advantages of sharing lessons learned information is the positive impact that information can have on your project. Sharing these past experiences and the specific knowledge that team members gained allows the next project to benefit greatly. One example is when design teams create cost-saving techniques on the earlier project and then utilize those same techniques on the existing project. These design and cost techniques can save time and money on the current project.

Another important benefit of sharing lessons learned information is the advantage that the team members, customers, and other stakeholders obtain from understanding the mistakes and benefits of previous projects. Understanding these mistakes and benefits at the start of the project can help reduce the chance of the current project team making the same mistakes as previous teams. When managing a second iteration of a project, you should be clear on how the other efforts occurred and at the minimum be aware of the major issues or concerns within those other projects. A project manager, when utilizing and reviewing information from past projects, looks for the following information to share with his or her team and customers to help benefit a new and upcoming project.

- **Project budget information.** You want to understand how the other project managers managed their budgets and what tricks and techniques they used to be successful or not.

- **Project schedule information.** You want to understand the duration of the new project to be able to compare the project schedules of the previous projects to the current project's schedule. This comparison is important because you can find out if your project can or should be utilizing the same timeframes as the previous projects. This information may show you if your project will make its final delivery date.

- **Project resources.** Find out the various utilization of each worker, the process of finding the resources, and whether those resources were allocated properly across the lifecycle of the project. The more information you can determine and extract from the lessons learned information allows you to plan more appropriately for your new project.

- **Risks and issues.** Understand the previous project's risks and issues and try to eliminate the chances of those reoccurring on your project. Try to learn from what went right and wrong on the previous projects. Understand the method the previous projects used to create, track, and reduce risks.

- **Communicate with the previous project manager.** One of the techniques that senior project managers often utilize when reviewing lessons learned is talking directly to the project managers of the previous projects. Those conversations can often provide additional ideas from the details not documented but that are valuable nonetheless. Some of the stories and best practices that the previous project managers can offer you are undocumented. Without these conversations, the new project manager would miss some valuable management points.

While collecting the lessons learned information, the project manager must enter the data into a central location such as a database or document format. When companies take the time and effort to produce lessons learned information on a project, they are building a tremendous wealth of information that can benefit future projects for years to come.

 Collecting lessons learned information on a project could be difficult. Do not let lessons learned sessions turn into complaining sessions!

Distributing Project Information

Project managers must decide what methods, manner, and style to choose in delivering project information. You can deliver information in three different ways: verbal, written, and visual. Each of these offers benefits and risks when delivering project information. The challenge is to determine what method to utilize when distributing specific project information.

We recommend that you ask the customers what kind of communication style they prefer at the start of a project. Often customers or stakeholders will unknowingly offer it. For example, if a customer is one who uses a lot of diagrams and pictures when describing something, she is often graphic oriented and will be quick to mention or say, "Draw me a picture, I learn better that way." On the other hand, some customers learn quickly using a text document of a spreadsheet with rows of data. In both cases, you have discovered the learning preferences of your customers and therefore can structure all your messages going forward to that learning style.

Communicating verbally

Verbal communication is simply having a conversation. It is basic, common, and something every project manager should be good at doing with his or her customers, team members, or upper management staff. Project managers who do not communicate well should focus on improving those skills to advance their chances of being successful in their career. There are many courses and training materials available for project managers to utilize.

One of the challenges of verbal communication is the challenge of conversations occurring over the telephone or functioning in a long-distance environment. Because many project managers often take verbal communication for granted and everyone feels they are good at it, they often don't remember that there is a layer of complexity added when communicating verbally over the telephone. You must be aware of your tone on the phone compared to how you come across in person. Your communication styles may have to differ based on the situation and the method (phone or face to face) you are using. Something said in person may be inappropriate over the phone (a joke, for example). Some of your customers or stakeholders may prefer to learn and understand the message using a verbal type of communication. They may be the type of people that can learn more effectively by having project information explained to them directly in verbal conversation and conference calls compared with getting the same information through an e-mail, a report, or a document. To help a customer who learns better using a verbal method, try the following:

- Develop status reports, issues, or risks formally on paper or e-mail and send them to the stakeholders prior to the first face-to-face meeting.

- Go through the report with the customer either on the phone or in person. The preferred method, if possible, is in person. That way, you have a formal record on paper, but you also have explained the report and addressed any questions or concerns the customer may have.

The following list details the verbal communication options available to project managers.

- **Face-to-face conversation**
  - **Formal:** Formal communication includes presentations, status meetings, budget reviews, milestone reviews, providing information to media (interviews), meeting with customer or stakeholders
  - **Informal:** Talking around the watercooler, conversations in halls, gossip, and talking over social functions with your customers or project team members
- **Telephone conversation**
  - **One on one:** Typical one-on-one conversations are usually informal. Talking on the phone and dealing with project issues, in most cases, is an informal conversation. Unless both parties agree that it is a formal conversation, most people consider it informal. If either party records a call for future playback, it is vital to obtain permission from the other party, but in those cases, those conversations are formal. Recording a phone call is a good way to capture conversations in case there is a need to go back for future reference or the subject is so complex that a person would need to go over the call a number of times to understand the information completely.
  - **Conference call:** Conference calls are communication among a number of people and in most cases are formal. Often costs are associated with these calls and are scheduled formally with multiple project team members and customers or stakeholders. Conference calls usually have multiple participants and can have participants from multiple locations around the world. For example, a person working on a technical problem can contact his peers working in India and Ireland, and all three parties can actively participate on the call at the same time. These conference calls can solve problems more quickly than a one-on-one call.
  - **Computer calls (LiveMeeting, Skype, and Icall):** Computer calls are similar to standard conference calls in which you can have a one-on-one call or have multiple people on the line. Using communication software is becoming a popular way to communicate rather than using the standard phone line to make your calls. Many different products are available on the Internet to perform these types of calls, and depending on the Internet connection, most of them are free of charge. In situations where project team members are located around the world, this technology narrows many communication gaps between the team members and allows everyone to always feel that they are connected. Not only can you communicate verbally, but also you can be explaining what is on the computer screen at the same time. These tools are wonderful for virtual teams!

Communicating in writing

Written communication seems to be the most popular method of communicating project information. In project e-mails, memos, or official documents, communicating in writing is by far the most popular choice for project managers. For example, when someone writes a policy and distributes that policy to the staff in an organization, because it is in a written documented format, people consider that policy as accepted and the new rules of the organization. Sending that same information verbally, such as in a large company meeting or through a presentation, does not have the same impact as a document with the same information.

There are three main written communication formats that most project managers utilize while communicating project information. These formats include:

- **E-mail:** E-mail has become the most common form of communication in the 21st century. Project team members utilize e-mail more than ever before and often more than using the telephone. E-mail has become so popular that even staff members working in the same department tend to communicate via e-mail instead of talking face-to-face. The recipient can answer the message when he chooses; thereby eliminating the need to provide the information immediately as they would in a face-to-face conversation or on a phone call. The downside of e-mail is that you can phrase things in a tone that you may not use in a face-to-face conversation or phone conversation. It provides distance between the two parties that sometimes can be quite negative. Framing your e-mail message and spending the time to understand how your audience will receive the tone of your e-mail will go a long way in bettering your project communication skills on e-mail.

- **Paper:** Paper has been around for thousands of years and is the standard when it comes to project information reporting. Even in the age of electronics, some stakeholders and management want to see paper reports. Project managers need to understand the reporting format requirements for their project, and in many cases, they continue to report on paper.

  - **Formal:** Project managers utilize formal reporting for deliverables such as project status reports, presentations, and cost reports. They file and save these documents for long-term storage and future reference.

  - **Informal:** A project memo would be informal when there is no signature attached and it is used for temporary communication. Normally, people discard them when no longer needed.

- **Electronic:** You can get your messages sent instantly using tools such as Instant Messenger on your computer and text messaging on your mobile phone. These tools are great communication tools, but are not a method of formal communication. They are the wrong type of tool for any formal communication. Instant messaging tools are great for quick status, high-level actions, and general communication touch points. Project managers should never communicate formal project information using an instant messaging tool without immediately backing it up with an e-mail, document, or telephone call. Another aspect of instant messaging you must consider is the lack of security. Most of the popular instant messaging tools today do not have strict security standards in place because of the nature of how and why the tool was originally developed. These tools do not have strong security standards built in. Project managers and team members must be careful how much and what type of information they send with these tools. Be careful when using these types of tools and watch closely what you write. You must be careful and expect that millions of people can see anything you type. As the tools improve over time, watch for security features to be added and formal statuses will start flowing out on these tools; but in the meantime, informal communication is the rule.

Communicating visually

Project managers have the luxury of presenting their data in graphs, charts, and tables. This format is easy to read and understand. Never has there been a truer statement than a picture is worth a thousand words. Most often, project customers or stakeholders have an easier time reading and understanding project information visually. Project managers should utilize visual communication whenever possible. Generally, stakeholders or team members can visualize project information almost instantly compared to reading pages of text with the same data. With this in mind, you need to understand how important these presentations can be and use them appropriately throughout your project. When doing so, ensure that everyone provides feedback and comments on your presentations so that the material you present is sending the right message.

NOTE When you obtain feedback on the presentation material, this acts as a mini lessons learned session.

A good presentation strategy is to approach them as if you are telling a story. Guide the audience through that story as you go through the material. Even though you are presenting a serious subject, have fun with it. Do not be afraid to add some animations, graphics, and color to your material. It will often lighten the mood, raising their learning level and adding some fun to the material.

One benefit of visual communication is that customers or stakeholders generally prefer graphics and drawings to be able to grasp the information quickly. On the flip side, if your customer does not favor graphics or charts, then you could produce a text version of the same slides to cater to their preferred learning style. A great example of this is the marketing of junk mail. It often contains a large, glossy foldout page of marketing material, but it also contains in the envelope the same material in a plain text format. Marketing companies have figured out that to market to everyone effectively, they have to cater to the learning styles of everyone in the material they send. As noted earlier in this chapter, this is another area or opportunity to understand and cater your material to the learning styles of your customer.

Project managers after deciding to present their project information in a visual format have a number of different options to use. With the advancements of technology, and the Internet specifically, project managers should not be short of any option when deciding what method to choose for their presentations. Often their imagination is the only criteria they will face. Here are a couple of the many visual methods:

- **Presentations:** One of the most popular and widely used tools for developing presentations is Microsoft PowerPoint. If you are unfamiliar with PowerPoint or any of the other presentation-type tools on the market, you should gain familiarity with them as soon as possible and if required take some training. Using them enhances your ability to deliver powerful and effective project presentations.

- **Documentary of the project (video/DVD):** One method of delivering a powerful impact about your project is to create a video documentary. These videos can contain a lot of valuable information displayed in a short time period. These videos usually have a high cost to them. However, if your project is one of high visibility, this kind of video is a great way to get your project information communicated in a concise and professional manner. Larger construction projects tend to use these videos as a standard tool for communication. A new trend has larger software development companies producing videos to capture and simulate their software to potential customers. Companies are offering short videos of what the software can do and show simulations of their products in action. You can see many examples of these videos on company Web sites all over the Internet. Microsoft has many of these videos on their Web sites for Office products and their game suites. Some of the products that create videos for project presentations include Camtasia, Articulate, Snag-it, WebEx, and Live Meeting. One major advantages of using this type of format is the ability to repeat and reuse the same information as a learning aid. If you run the video in a loop, the information is repeating continually for the customers to review and understand. These videos are often shown in conferences, auto shows, boat shows, and home shows, and they are even appearing in local stores now (showing you how to use their product to paint your house). The other advantage of this type of media format is the ability to start, stop, reverse, and fast-forward the information, allowing you to review specific areas of the material a number of times.

The greatest advantage of this type of media is capturing time motion–type photography that captures step-by-step development of the project throughout its various phases. The construction, manufacturing, and security industries all use this photographic technique successfully for a variety of reasons. In construction, for example, time motion photography is used to display a time-lapsed review at the various stages of development.

Summary

We explored the essence of planning your project's communication.. We discovered and discussed some communication challenges, showed you how to solve or work with those challenges, and covered the details on communication links. We also described the importance of understanding your customer's risk tolerances and learning styles. We stressed how that knowledge will help you communicate more effectively.

At the end of the chapter, we discussed two of the most important aspects of planning your project's communication. This included the creation of a communication plan and the capturing of lessons learned information throughout the life of the project. Those two items alone, if you understand and utilize both of them, will increase your chances of managing a successful project.

Chapter 3

Working with Project Communications

When working in a project environment, one of the most challenging aspects of being a project manager is project communications management. As projects become complex and more challenging, project managers need to step up and become effective communicators. The challenges that project managers are facing today are greater than in the past. These challenges include virtual project teams, shorter product time to market, advancement of technology or technology changes in the middle of the project, and diversity of product availability (new products coming out daily). These complexities make managing projects a challenging task in today's market. Project managers, throughout the life of their projects, should focus their attention on working with these new challenges in communicating project information. The communication planning activity includes documenting where, how, and to whom project information is communicated. This communication planning effort will guide the project manager and the team members through the lifecycle from a communication perspective.

In this chapter, we explore the various aspects of working with project communications. Some of the areas covered include information overload, the importance of communicating face-to-face, challenges of virtual teams, and dealing with personality conflicts on large, diverse teams.

Overloading on Project Information

Project team members, customers, and stakeholders are receiving an overwhelming amount of project information on a regular basis. Almost every team member complains about the amount of information he or she has to produce or sift through to determine an actual status, a particular update, or an assigned action item. E-mail is quickly becoming the source of information overload. Managing e-mail is time consuming; people are struggling to keep up and effectively manage their time.

When communicating and distributing project information, project managers must be clear about what they are asking for and when they need it. If project managers are looking for answers, decisions, or a quick turnaround, this may require a new level of follow-up and tracking with the customers to ensure they receive the information they need.

> **NOTE** Effective project communication avoids overloading a team member or customer with too much information. It is actually the exact opposite. Effective communication is actually providing only the information people need in an appropriate format to access and process the information as quickly as possible.

It appears that project managers or team members can do little to resolve this issue, but having the general awareness and consideration when communicating project information can go a long way in mitigating this problem. The following activities occur on projects today causing this information overload:

- **Too many e-mails.** There is little to discuss here. Just make sure that project team members and customers are more conscious of what they are sending in their e-mails. A lot of the problem is not project oriented; it originates from outside the project. If the information you are receiving is not pertinent to your job request remove it from a project e-mail list.

- **Too many detailed status reports.** For project customers who are overseeing multiple projects, project managers should consider that those customers might be receiving at least one status report from every project every week. To a project manager, this may mean your customers are not reading your project information as thoroughly as you would like because of the large number of reports they are receiving. Alternatively, customers may not read your project status reports because they have too much information; and, therefore, they are having difficulty finding the information they need.

- **Too many status meetings.** Customers, project managers, and team members are required to attend and provide project status at a number of status meetings each week. Because project managers, in particular, are often required to provide status to both the customer and a number of different internal status report meetings, they often end up repeating the same project information many times.

- **Too much micromanagement.** Often project managers face the reality of dealing with and communicating with a number of higher-level managers who are actively engaged on their projects. This engagement can lead to communicating the same project information to each of the managers and fielding a series of questions from each manager on a continual basis. The ongoing support and communications with these senior managers often lead to project managers being micromanaged and not in control of their projects. Micromanagement is the over-managing of detail at a level lower than what the project manager should be actively involved in. For example, a project manager is unlikely to review computer code on a software development project. In this case, the project manager would be overextending his or her boundaries and interfering with their team member's work.

- **Not enough time to process information.** So much project information passes among the project team and their customers, and often there is little or no time to actually process and understand the information. When an e-mail message sent on one particular subject is reviewed and returned multiple times, the original intent of the message may be lost.

- **Working on multiple projects and competing priorities.** Project managers, project team members, and customers normally have multiple projects assigned to them. In doing so, they have competing priorities. Splitting the team member's commitments and work efforts is leaving most team members with information overload and with the possibility of not being effective on any single project. Having too many competing priorities may cause team members to burn out.

Burnout has become a major concern, and without a solution or a method to handle information overload, experienced team members and employees are continually leaving their companies. It is advisable that project managers try to understand the importance of communication overload and plan their project communications appropriately. Project managers can be diligent in the information they are sending. We recommend that the project manager and team members control the project information instead of the project information controlling them.

The following activities are potential solutions to handling and processing information overload. (These are only two solutions outlined out of the possible hundreds.) The two noted will be the most familiar and the most applicable to project managers and team members.

- **E-mail processing:** Most of the popular e-mail applications have rules within them that will automatically move e-mails, based on selected criteria, to various folders. When an individual creates special rules, the individual is no longer looking at a massive amount of unread e-mail when trying to determine where to start. Automatically moving these e-mail messages to the various folders reduces the overloaded feeling an individual has when looking at all their unread and unanswered e-mails. They can process the messages in the different folders on an "as needed" or "priority" basis.

- **Multiple projects and priorities:** Utilizing Eliyahu M. Goldratt's *Theory of Constraints methods*, one of the first processes that a project manager can suggest when assisting in the overloading problem is the reducing of project team members multitasking and assignments to multiple projects. Reducing a person to one project and having each person complete their work on the one project before starting a new project help reduce the overloaded feeling.

CROSS-REF For further information, on the Theory of Constraints, see Chapter 9.

Interacting Face-to-Face

Spending some time with each team member, even if it is limited, may resolve concerns where and when applicable. We call this method face-to-face communications. Face-to-face conversation is at least two people discussing something. A group session of at least three people communicating and interacting is also face-to-face communication. Project managers should try to establish face-to-face communications with each project team member on a regular basis. These individual sessions will help enhance the overall group session that is held when the project manager leads the regular scheduled status meetings.

Although having face-to-face conversations by no means prevents all project problems from escalating, these face-to-face meetings do provide rapport and relationship connections between the team members that can often reduce many escalations.

> **TIP**   Regardless of the role each team member plays, or their specific organization structure, project managers should establish that rapport as early as possible. You should allot some time and try to meet with your team members, customers, or stakeholders, and anyone else involved in the project, each week throughout the life of the project.

The following list represents some of the various benefits and values of performing face-to-face communications both professionally and personally:

- **Build and establish rapport.** Face-to-face meetings establish a rapport and a working relationship between various parties.

- **Build and establish credibility.** You can establish credibility and respect by utilizing face-to-face communication techniques. Like trust, earning credibility and respect occurs between the parties over time, and as people continue to meet commitments and expectations of the parties this respect comes more quickly. Credibility is something that can quickly be lost as well if someone feels you are not telling the truth, or have betrayed him or her in some way. It takes a lot of work to maintain credibility.

- **Build and establish friendships.** Using the one-on-one communications over a time period, personal and professional friendships are often established. By building and establishing a rapport and credibility, this often turns into a friendship between the two parties.

> **TIP**   Project managers should encourage face-to-face meetings among the different skills sets of the project. Often face-to-face communication occurs between the project manager and the particular team members, but a best practice is to encourage the team members to meet on a regular basis, building their own rapport and often working issues out amongst themselves.

Making face-to-face communications work

In the following sections, we discuss solutions that project managers can implement to enhance their face-to-face communications with the project team members, customers, or stakeholders.

In-person meetings

When meeting in person with your project team, you must remember that your body language and facial expressions are going to be harder to conceal than when communicating by phone or e-mail. Avoid making any expressions, comments, and remarks that could express your true feelings and reveal information unintentionally. Doing so is essential when visiting team members in foreign countries. (See Appendix H on the CD-ROM for further information on foreign communications.) The wrong actions or communication can easily offend team members, customers, or stakeholders and be perceived as inappropriate or even offensive.

When preparing to meet your project team or project stakeholders for the first time in person, remember the following actions and techniques:

- **Body language:** As a project manager, you need to be careful about how you approach people on the first meeting. You need to be professional and ensure that your body language is not giving a different message than what you are saying. Project managers should avoid crossing their arms constantly when communicating to their team members. People may consider this to mean that you are concealing information or not totally opening up.

- **Emotions:** Control your emotions when communicating your project information to both the project team members and customers. Project managers are seen as leaders; therefore, a project manager who cannot keep his or her emotions in check will be viewed as someone who is either not a leader or not strong enough for the job. A best practice and recommendation is for you to show you have some emotions — that you are not emotionless — but control your emotions when required.

- **Facial expressions:** Facial expressions tell it all. So many things can be "said" with facial expressions either on purpose or by accident that you must really be careful. You must project a strong, confident image; therefore, ensure that your expressions do not reflect something that you do not want to reflect. Think positively and keep a smile on your face at all times when delivering positive project information. When delivering negative information, your facial expressions are also important and should reflect the seriousness of the problem.

- **Dress:** Dress professionally so that you project an image of authority when delivering project information. Project managers gain a level of confidence when they dress professionally. This does not necessary mean that you have to wear a suit and tie all the time. Just dress appropriately, especially when delivering your project information.

Informal conversations with team members and customers or stakeholders can enhance the communication aspects of your project tremendously. These conversations can take place just about anywhere, and serve to establish a rapport with team members or stakeholders that is unlikely to happen in a formal setting. Informal conversations also build trust between people and increase the bond between the two parties. Often long-lasting friendships develop when establishing informal conversations with team members or customers. The project manager should try to encourage informal discussions whenever possible to help the team members and customers build stronger relationships.

Social events

Often project managers have the opportunity to improve their communications with their team members by creating social events. Social settings often lower the working anxiety between team members and create a relaxed and friendly atmosphere for everyone. Another positive aspect of hosting or attending a social event is the opportunity to resolve communication issues with team members or customers.

Business lunch

A business lunch is one of the most valuable venues for one-on-one communication. The low cost of having the occasional business lunch pays off tremendously in the rapport established and relations built between the two people. However, if the two people tend to go to lunch too often, such as daily, for example, the value of the rapport building and increased communications diminishes because it becomes too informal, and even unprofessional in some cases.

Understanding the value of face-to-face communications

You cannot assign a dollar value to the benefits of using face-to-face communications. Building trust is building credibility among team members on the project. When project managers work with team members who are credible, they know they can assign them work and it will be completed and with good quality. Building trust with team members early in the project can reduce a lot of wasted time that could negatively affect the project. If people do not trust each other, they will spend extra time following up and checking up on each other. This hurts the project and the people continuing to do the checking because it makes for unnecessary work. An ongoing meeting between the two parties can reduce the possibilities of miscommunications.

Exploring Virtual Communications

The project management profession is clearly changing, moving away from boardroom meetings and group gatherings, and favoring virtual project teams at various sites around the world. Companies are allowing full- and part-time employees to work from home (home office employees) or a remote office (corporate or remote office) in another town or state, 100 percent of the time. Along with the onset of companies moving development and testing teams to offshore countries, one of the professions left at home most of the time is the project manager. The project managers, when left to managing 95 percent virtual project team members, often have no virtual team skills or any particular communication tools to help them. The project managers are literally required to figure out how to manage virtual project teams on their own. In some cases, training is available, but that is often rare and the project managers have to figure out how to manage these teams with little training. If project managers have never had the experience of managing virtual teams before, they could be in for a big surprise and serious trouble while managing their first virtual project. Virtual team management is often quite difficult and something that takes time and energy to master. The communication aspect of virtual teams is difficult and something project managers should not take lightly and should prepare for when first starting into their virtual project.

A real-world project communication lesson

A software development company wanted to find out if it was practical to develop a software system by working around the clock across three different countries, each in a different time zone. It appeared there were only two options: Work three teams, first shift, second shift, and third shift, 24 hours a day in one location; or work three teams located strategically around the world, each working first shift only.

The objective of the project was to develop a software system in less than half the normal time it would take to develop the software with a single onshore project team. Senior management decided to experiment with this global project and attempted to create three virtual teams to fulfill that objective.

Here is how the virtual teams worked together. The team in the United States developed their portion of the program during their eight-hour shift. Near the end of the shift, they documented what they had accomplished that day and transmitted all the files and documentation to the team in Japan. The two teams would communicate and establish what the Japanese team would do on their shift. At the end of the shift in Japan, those team members repeated the process of documenting the day's work and then submitted the work to the European team. At the end of the shift in Europe, that team communicated back to the U.S. team on the progress. The U.S. staff then took over, working on the remaining tasks. This process would continue throughout the life of the project. It turned out to be a successful project, and the three teams produced a project in half the time of a single U.S.-based team. The team actually used the different time zones around the world to their advantage and to the project's advantage. Using teams in three different countries, the project ended completing a total of 24 hours a day worth of work, compared to the standard 8 hours worked within the United States and most other countries. The passing of the information from one team to another keeps the project progressing on a daily basis.

It became immediately apparent when the teams first started the process that it was critical that communications were concise and accurate for two main reasons. The workers needed to communicate the technical information between teams in a way that everyone could understand and in a way that would allow the process to continue when that team handed over the work. In addition, the communications had to be in different languages because English was not their first language in Japan. This complication made for a difficult situation when translating the work back from Japanese to English for continuation and completion of the project's work.

Another benefit not often called out is that companies are limiting their overtime payouts because as the project teams get close to the end of their day, they wrap up their work and pass it over to the next team, located in a different country, to continue working while they are off.

Communicating with a virtual project team

Working with project teams can be challenging, but working with virtual teams is even more challenging. The challenging aspects of virtual teams come in all areas of the project. These challenges include communication challenges, such as time zones, and language barriers, resource challenges, obtaining the right skill sets, cost challenges (exchange rates changing), adding additional team members to bridge the gap between the two countries, and scheduling and quality challenges where team members are not able to fulfill the needs of the project. Different religious holidays in different countries can become an issue. These issues are generally the same as those the project manager faces on a regular project. However, these issues magnify tremendously with virtual teams. The communications with virtual teams is one of the areas of the project in which the project manager could end up suffering greatly if he or she is not careful. The language barrier, to start with, often has a huge impact on the project team; and it often takes months to resolve, or outside parties to act as an intermediary between the two projects in the different countries. After the communications barriers and difficulties are resolved and properly handled, the project communications should become easier.

There are many different methods to communicate effectively with virtual project teams. These methods include the following:

- Telephone
- Weekly telephone conference calls
- Site visits
- Video conferencing
- E-mail and written communications such as faxes or letters
- Shared company Web sites such as SharePoint
- Shared applications where project status information is stored and updated; i.e., project server
- Instant messaging
- Online Communication tools such as Live Meeting or Skype
- Online Collaboration tools
- File transfer software such as FolderShare
- Document Control systems

As you continue to gain work experience with virtual project teams, you acquire different communication methods to enhance your knowledge of communicating in this difficult environment. The more time they have working with virtual teams the better they become, and you end up discovering your own methods for working with virtual teams.

Managing virtual project teams

Like working with project teams, managing project teams is often challenging. Managing project teams with a virtual component is usually much more challenging. There are many challenges with virtual teams including struggles with communications (language barriers or time zone differences), resource management, technical problems (English versus Metric systems), and so on. These challenges are often less influencing for onsite project teams where the project manager is readily available and can resolve the issues as they arise. For virtual teams these issues could go for days before being resolved. This could affect the project if it goes on too long.

Here are some tips and techniques you can use to manage virtual project teams:

- **Conduct a kick-off meeting.** At the beginning of a virtual project, the project must hold a project kick-off meeting. This meeting may be the first time that some members have a chance to meet each other and converse. The project manager must define the scope, goals, and objectives of the project and motivate the team to approval before the meeting concludes. A strong project manager (meeting leader) can accomplish this goal with all team members. This may be the last time some team members will ever see each other.

> **TIP** If the project manager does not have great meeting skills, hiring a motivational speaker to bring the project team members together will facilitate ownership in the project.

- **Build a rapport and establish trust.** Another aspect of managing people is to build rapport and trust with each team member. This is twice as hard with a virtual team. Project managers need to establish this early in the lifecycle and ensure that they spend time with each team member and establish a relationship with them. A project manager needs to put in face time and bond with the team members to form relationships. Sometimes the only way to accomplish this is by site visits periodically. Rapport and trust is a two-way street. People must earn trust and be given trust by others. Project managers need to go out of their way and trust that their team members will deliver on their respective tasks at the times they have said they will deliver.

- **Create good team dynamics.** In virtual environments, establishing a buddy system is a good idea. When the team is located in multiple locations, each individual team member needs the psychology, morale, and technical support from at least one other person. Establishing a buddy system enables virtual team members to have someone to reach out to who can provide help when needed. This partnership between two or more team members creates a buy-in and ownership for the tasks assigned on the project. Having a buddy system eliminates that issue by providing someone for each of the members to be able to contact, and with whom they can collaborate. Buddy systems are also valuable to onsite teams, but in a virtual environment they become a necessity.

- **Meet in person.** When working in a virtual environment, the team spreads out and does not meet face-to-face often, if at all. Therefore, as a project manager, you need to determine how to meet and continue to build the rapport between the team members. As the bonding between you and the different team members increases, the dedication increases. Project managers become even more committed to each team member and therefore to the project. It is a win-win for everyone. Project managers need to ensure that they force these face-to-face meetings with the team members by trying to establish dollars in the budget and time in the schedule to allow these meetings to occur. We recommend ensuring that virtual team members are in person at the larger and more important project meetings; team members gain a connection to the project and feel that they are important to the team and should attend the critical meetings.

> **TIP** Project managers should ensure there are dollars set aside in the budget for virtual team members' travel and expenses; and, if applicable, they can come to the main office for these types of meetings.

- **Keep tasks short for early success.** If project managers create tasks that are short, they allow easy tracking and performance reporting from the beginning of the project. The advantage to the team member who is in a remote location is they know exactly what to do, how short it will take, when it is due, and what to deliver. Working and reporting on five short tasks is easier than having to do so for one or two long tasks. The short task technique should keep the team member motivated and wanting to complete the tasks with more enthusiasm.

- **Ensure the project team member has work.** In a virtual environment, project managers can feel like they are unclear on what tasks the team members are working on because they are not physically present. This sometimes can create some worry and concern for project managers since they do not know if they are getting the maximum productivity out of their team members. To ensure motivation and ownership for the team members, project managers must continually ensure that the project team members have enough work to do, and if not, the project manager should point out that offering their assistance to other team members can benefit the project. Project managers need to continue to stay on top of the work assignments of their team members (regardless of location) to ensure productivity and to ensure motivation of each individual team member.

- **Give team members more responsibility.** Gauging the amount of work each virtual team member can accomplish can be tough if the project manager is not working closely with these individuals on a day-to-day basis. We suggest visiting the team member's virtual location as often as possible. Nothing is more productive than face-to-face communication to maintain a team member's motivation on the project. When visiting the team member onsite, the project manager should ensure they are not under a lot of stress due to their workload or not enough stress due to lack of workload. During the visits, the project manager should have continual conversations with the team member about taking on more work and responsibilities for the project.

Motivating virtual project teams

Motivating project teams, either virtual or local, can be challenging but can also be a lot of fun and rewarding. Project managers must treat both the onsite team and the virtual team members equally.

Here are some of the fun events and activities you can do to celebrate and show your appreciation toward your team:

- **Hold morale events.** Project managers should work to create a project environment where they have morale-boosting events, as often as possible. Morale events are great pick-me-up events where the team members get together, can relax, chat about nonbusiness-related topics, and get to know one another in a relaxed environment. Typical morale events include team lunches, or after-work drinks. Other events include outings such as mini-putt golf, baseball games (sporting events), or other fun outings. These events are successful when many team members join and share their experiences and personalities outside of the office. These types of events are critical to larger teams on longer-term projects. When team members work together for long periods and never get to spend quality non-work time together more personality conflicts arise on the project. Holding the occasional morale event, regardless of the cost, can do wonders for the success of the project.

A virtual project team member conflict scenario

Avirtual project team member felt that his project manager was nagging him too much about project status information. He decided to stop communicating with the project manager. He stopped answering e-mails stopped attending status meetings, and no longer filled out status reports. He believed that if he stopped communicating, he could spend more time on his work and get his tasks done without interruptions. In the meantime, the project manager continued to work with him and tried to communicate that this was unacceptable behavior and that he was affecting the progress of the project. The team member allowed the project manager to call him at specific times during the workday, he would only come into the office when he wanted to, and he would only respond to e-mails during a limited window during the day. These demands helped him feel like he would be able to accomplish his tasks quicker and not have to spend time responding to the project manager, let alone anyone else asking him questions. This scenario went on for about a month, and the project manager then asked management if the team member could be removed from the project. After ongoing communications with the team member and stressing that his behavior was unacceptable, the project manager raised this issue to upper management. Upper management advised the project manager to remove him from the project.

- **Recognize and reward people.** If your company has a reward and recognition program, the project manager should use it. If the company does not have a formal program, the project manager needs to take the time and effort to create/write up these rewards for their project team members. It is amazing how far a well-received fun certificate, hand toy, or marketing gadget given to a hard-working team member goes toward building morale and a great working relationship. A low-cost reward system pays off in the end for the project manager and the project.

- **Create fun.** It is the responsibility of the project manager to create fun on the project. They need to instill having a fun environment, but also keep the project team focused to deliver a successful project. There are many ways to have fun on a project, from giving gifts at status meetings, morale events, and generally keeping the environment light and motivating.

- **Monetary rewards and pay raises.** The last tip that a project manager can do is to offer money or pay raises to a team member, either at the beginning or during the project to help motivate him. Some team members are highly motivated by monetary rewards.

Communicating consistently

Sending regular and timely project communications is a necessity for every project manager. The need is greater for project team members working in a virtual environment. Virtual team members may often feel as though they require additional communications in order to stay better connected to the project. Project managers utilize as many tools or processes as necessary to ensure that the virtual team members are receiving as much information as they need to make project decisions.

One of the main areas project managers should look for is any inconsistency when sending out project information to their virtual team members such as the project status report. For example, when the individual team leaders send in their Team Lead's report it is commonly distributed weekly; however, if the team leader is inconsistent in sending their information on a weekly basis, it is difficult for the project manager to stay active in that area of the project. Therefore, be able to report updated project information in the weekly project status report. Hence, the virtual team member, along with everyone else, is not getting the latest project status information.

Establishing communication guidelines

We suggest that project managers develop guidelines for virtual project team members. If guidelines were in place before the project began, the scenario in the previous sidebar would not have happened. Project managers should look to their project management offices or to specific company policies, if applicable, to determine if there are any virtual project team member guidelines or procedures in place and use those policies whenever possible. If there are no policies in place, we recommend the following as a starting point for your project:

- **Establish work hours.** The work hours of a virtual team member will be the standard operating hours of the company. These hours normally include an eight-hour day with the weekends off. If both parties agree, they can change these hours. Being offsite does not guarantee them any additional "away" time from the regular office responsibilities.

- **Create home office infrastructure.** A virtual team member should have a company-standard computer that is loaded with the company image of software products. The home office should be a separate location, away from any distractions for the team member to be able to work effectively. A virtual team member cannot have a standard dialup connection as their only source of connecting to the Internet.

- **Require progress and status reporting.** A team member working onsite or virtually will follow the same requirements as onsite team members and must report, at a minimum, project progress and status once a week. This could include completing status reports, one on one communications, newsletters, or completing online status information, such as updating the project's schedule.

> **NOTE** Establish, document, approve, and adopt firm guidelines to set the virtual team member's expectations for communication, infrastructure, work hours, and progress reporting. These expectations are set as policies, not guidelines, and ensure that virtual team members follow them when working offsite. The project manager requires the virtual team member to sign and approve these polices before they start in this virtual work position. If they do not sign the agreement, they should not be eligible to work remotely.

Exploring virtual team member qualifications

The qualifications and skill sets of the team member that will work virtually are quite often different from someone assigned to a local office. There are six basic skills and qualities a person should have before they can work in a virtual environment. If one of these qualities is missing, the project could suffer because that individual may not be pulling his or her own weight and is therefore slowing down the progress of the project.

A virtual team member should have the following qualities:

- **Be an excellent communicator.** The number one quality of a person in a virtual role is that she must be a good communicator. If a virtual team member is a poor communicator, he or she is putting projects at risk.

- **Have experience in existing project or similar position.** A team member who has worked on a project before, or worked virtually in the past, can be a great asset to the project team. If a team member is new and has little experience, then starting them in a virtual role could be risky.

- **Be a self-starter.** A virtual team member must be a self-starter and proactive. A self-starter is a person that can immediately jump into their workload and be dedicated enough to perform their work without ongoing supervision. A proactive person is one that will see problem areas and will jump to address these areas without any direction or asking from the project manager. That type of person will "just do it" and take on the extra workload.

- **Have self-discipline.** A virtual team member needs to have a high degree of self-discipline. This person is not easily distracted and can focus on the work projects during their established working hours.

- **Have a high level of dedication.** A virtual team member must be highly dedicated to the project. One of the areas of understanding a person's dedication level before actually hiring them is to test them in the interview process. These tests can include psychological tests and in-depth questioning on previous dedication on projects. The use of references in the interview cycle will also help with this process.

- **Be able to prioritize.** A virtual team member must have the attitude that the project is a high priority to them and focus their attention on delivering their work products. If the team member does not feel this project is of a high priority or feels like he can only work at a half capacity, this is not the right fit for a virtual team member.

Figure 3.1 displays a Spider Chart that evaluates the qualifications of potential virtual team members for working on your virtual project. In this case, you can see that Sally B has the highest level for each factor to make her the best fit for the project.

ON the CD-ROM We have included a sample of this Spider Chart and associated data in the Chapter 3 folder. Use it as a guide to help you create your own personal version of a team evaluation Spider Chart.

FIGURE 3.1

This is an example of a Team Member Evaluation Spider Chart.

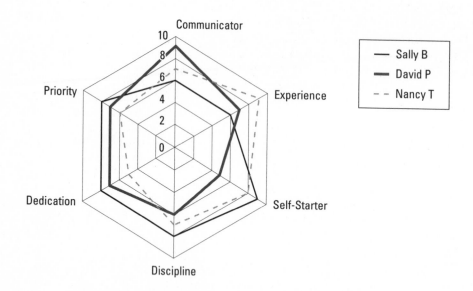

Team Member Evaluation

Dealing with Conflict in the Project Environment

In project management, all projects have conflicts — some big, some small but they are going to occur. People inherently deal with conflict in two ways; they use *flight* or *fight*. Flight is simple; it involves removing yourself from the conflict and avoiding it completely. Fight is much more difficult because it involves you standing up, protecting yourself, and "fighting" for what you believe. In most cases, flight is the easiest and what people tend to do most often. Your first impression may be to take the flight action, but be aware that it is usually the worst choice. The flight characteristic is not a good choice because the conflict does not usually go away, and the longer you avoid it the worse it gets.

 Tackle conflicts directly. Avoidance can make the situation worse.

Project managers need to address a conflict directly. They need to be professional about how they deal with the conflict, but they also cannot back away from it.

Projects consist of many people, each with their own ideas, styles, and personalities. These differences will create conflict situations on your project every time. Some conflicts are minor, such as a difference of opinion on how to tackle or approach a problem, and some are large such as when two team members just cannot get along. In both cases, if not managed correctly, either conflict can hurt the chances of a successful project. Team members need to treat each other with respect at all times. With that respect, there should be a level of common understanding and the ability to work with each other on a project, even though you may or may not like each other. As a project manager, you will encounter conflicts on your projects, and how you deal with them will be critical to the success of the project—and to your career as a manager. One large conflict can sideline the whole project. If you ignore one small conflict and it goes out of control, it can derail a project and your success as a project manager. A real-life example and good example of a small conflict becoming major is a project risk such as losing available funding for contracting staff as the project transfers over the fiscal year boundaries. At the early stages of the project, the risk is low because the end of the fiscal year is six months away, and the project is big enough and important enough to the company that the dollars will always be available. As the project progresses and transfers over the fiscal year, if for one reason or another it loses the contracting dollars and the contractors working on the project leave, the project could be at a dead stop. The project could be derailed and may not recover.

Project managers can use five approaches to resolve conflicts on their projects. These styles are common resolution techniques across all industry.

- **Cooperative problem solving:** Cooperative problem solving is working together to solve issues and problems in a workable environment. It is two or more people sitting down, discussing the issue/problem, and coming up with a workable solution for both parties. This method is usually the best method to handle problems because the result is a win/win for all parties. Generally, it also ends in a better working relationship by both parties and therefore this makes the project environment that much stronger. In every situation, especially the first time a conflict arises, project managers should use the cooperative problem solving method" to work the problem. If the specific conflict comes up repeatedly then this method is not working. It is time to try a different method.

- **Competing:** The competing style is about the gaining of power and control over the person you are in a conflict with. Competing is learned behavior from early childhood and is reinforced by the thousands of conflicts you encounter every day. This style is difficult to use all the time. Competing is gaining power, and a person cannot use it every time. Nobody is strong enough mentally to compete in every situation, every day, against every person. However, using the competing style when judgment and skill are used can be a powerful, effective, and appropriate technique for solving some of the conflicts on your projects.

- **Compromising:** When at least one person wants to compromise with the other person they are in a conflict with, the compromising resolution style is used. Some people feel that it is better to get something, rather than nothing, and those people tend to use the compromising method every time a conflict arises. The project manager cannot use the compromising style all the time without it reflecting poorly on him. If you are always "rolling over" and not standing up for what you believe in, then you become an ineffective leader and in turn a poor project manager. Compromising is more like cooperative problem solving in some cases.

- **Accommodating:** When one person in the conflict surrenders and puts his interests behind the other persons the accommodating style is used. That person (who surrenders) feels that it is more important to keep a close relationship and harmony with the person they have a conflict. When using that style too often, a project manager will appear to be a poor leader and will quickly lose the respect of their project teams.

- **Avoiding:** A person who does not want to be involved in any conflict and feels it is easier to avoid them is using the avoiding style. Generally, this is not a good approach for any project manager because the conflict tends to fester and in most cases gets worse if not addressed. If that does occur, project managers can have serious issues on the project. Using this style solves few conflict issues. Most project managers tend to be leaders and do not tend to follow this conflict resolution style. There are some cases where the conflicts are intense, where the project managers can choose to avoid it temporarily, let the situation cool down, and address it later. That way, the conflict is still on the radar of the project manager, but time is going by and the tension should ease up. That will allow the project manager and the conflicting parties to readdress the conflict in a more calm and reasonable manner.

Table 3.1 displays typical areas of communication problems occurring on projects today across the five basic conflict resolution styles. This chart is a suggested guide — no style can cover every project communication issue. Project managers and team members can use it when conflicts arise and they are unfamiliar with how to approach them. When conflicts do arise, quite often project managers just use a gut reaction and do not think of the best possible resolution style. However, if project managers had a chart such as the one below and believed in it, then when conflicts arose they could bring it out and use it to help them approach the conflict.

TABLE 3.1

Conflict Resolution Chart (During the Project)

Problem Statement/Style	Cooperate Problem Solving	Competing	Compromising	Avoiding
Establish budget for the project		No	Yes	No
Engineering design problems	Yes	No		
Communication problems	Yes			
Contract negotiations		Yes	No	
Project schedule conflicts	Yes			No
Resource conflicts		No		Yes

ON the CD-ROM We include a sample of this table in the Chapter 3 folder. Use this as a guide to create your own version of this Conflict Resolution table.

You can use this chart as a scoreboard for how you personally handle conflicts. Whenever your team has a conflict, identify the problem area where it arose, and put a simple Y (Yes) or an N (No) and keep score to see where the majority of Yeses falls on the chart. After a period of time, reanalyze your conflict resolution score and determine where the majority of Yes(es) and No(s) are placed on the chart. After you have this chart completed, identify where you had the most successes and use that conflict style for future situations in that category. If you are working a problem for a category that is not in the chart already, simply add it to the chart. There are so many possible project problems so putting them all on a single chart is impossible. However, this chart is a good starting point and can point you in the right direction on how to handle your conflicts. Over a period, you will have maxed out your categories, but the historical trends of how you handled the different conflicts will be an essential tool to enhance your communication skills.

At the end of the project, use this conflict chart as your own personal lessons learned. If you maintain a chart such as this one throughout the life of the project, you can learn something about yourself. On the next project, you can use the same chart as a template, but fill in the style to the conflict matrix where you were the most successful with a dot or a shaded background to distinguish that style as the most successful for the project situation. Having the most successful styles per conflict situation identified gives you a head start on your next project. You will most likely have the same or similar situations occur and you will know exactly what resolution style worked well the last time.

NOTE If you are looking for some fun, create your own conflict chart identifying project conflict situations that occur and then gray out or identify in some way the conflict style you would use for each situation. At the end of the project, you can see how accurate you were. This would be a good test of how well you judge your own character and how you feel you would handle a situation.

Communicating with Enterprise Portfolio Management

How does your organization create an environment where project management communications flourish? Intentional conversations from the executive suite and project issues needing senior level resolutions connect throughout the culture by an Enterprise Portfolio Management (EPM) process. In the project management vernacular a *portfolio* is a collection of projects and other work grouped together to support the management of those projects to meet the strategic business goals and objectives of the enterprise. Portfolio management is the strategic management of one or more portfolios. EPM incorporates a projectized process of management that delivers the visibility and communications essential to align strategies with available resources and budgeting across the enterprise orchestrating top-down strategic planning with bottom-up execution. The leader of an

EPM is the craftsman of the foundation that will sustain project management communications focused on achieving the strategic objectives. The foundation building blocks cover the entire spectrum of project, program, and portfolio management, not the least of which are:

- Governance alignment
- Portfolio risk management
- Resource management
- Dispute resolution

When your organization commits to reaching the goals defined by the executive's strategic objectives, communications must exist that make it clear to the project manager that they are in sync with the direction the organization is heading. However, how does this happen in your organization?

Because project managers normally do not hang out with executives and conjure up strategies that guide the enterprise, perhaps they are receiving the message in the form of metrics and incentives, such as a headline in the weekly internal newsletter or a chance conversation at a weekly bagel break.

Unfortunately, without the communication conduit of the EPM providing feedback to the executives about receipt of the message, leaders will find themselves reacting to unfavorable trends reported by the accounting department.

The EPM organization exists to bring focus and clarity to the people, processes, systems, and technology that enable project managers' and their teams' delivery of projects that achieve the strategic objectives of the enterprise.

Figure 3.2 displays an EPM applying to both client and internal projects. Each project type requires an EPM in order to achieve strategic goals.

The communications environmental influences by the EPM organization result in their successful execution of culture change. Using the successful formula of making small changes quickly after listening actively to what the culture needs, particularly attention in collecting feedback from entry-level technical and administrative staff and announcing the successes publicly, the EPM should look to improve the project and portfolio management capability by driving clarity and accountability to

- Project management processes and tools
- Project management training
- Workload leveling and forecasting
- Work exporting and virtual teaming
- Communication and collaboration
- Project portfolio stage gates

FIGURE 3.2

The Enterprise Portfolio Management (EPM) Communication Model.

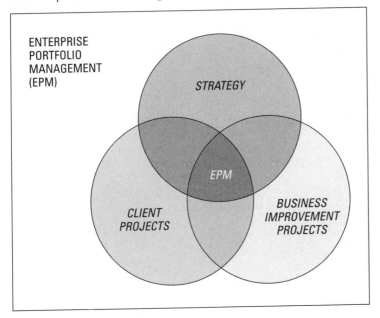

For the EPM organization to fulfill its role in creating a sustainable project management communications environment, the leader of the organization must have access to and support from the executive team while being accepted by the project manager environment as the leader of all aspects of processes that affect their project delivery and quality of their work life. Ideally, these individuals will be in a Chief Project Officer (CPO) role with a seat at the table in the executive suite. Other roles such as Director of Project Management or Project Management Office Director will work. The key is executive access and support. Being a peer executive is the ideal role for the leader of the EPM organization.

Aligning governance

Observation of public and private organizations clearly reveals that governances exist in different forms for each organization hierarchy. The executive suite is responsible for defining the enterprise governances that flow into the culture. Typically, the governances provide a framework for responsibilities and practices that:

- Provide strategic directions
- Ensure achievable objectives
- Identify and manage risks
- Focus resource assignments strategically

As the levels of culture embrace the enterprise governances, each level develops its "governance" or defines roles and responsibilities within its hierarchy to achieve the higher-level governances. You may know these as work approaches, best practices, QA/QC process, or desktop procedures. Whatever the name, they represent actions people execute and are accountable for the results of their actions.

The CPO and his or her EPM organization are responsible for review, validation, and leading changes to the hierarchical governances until they align and enable achievement of strategic goals. Achieving the alignment of the strategic goals will require the EPM organization to communicate up and down the cultural structure to reach successful alignment. The CPO needs to influence the executives to modify governance to accommodate the tough questions and resistance from the project management culture. At the same time, the CPO must influence the project managers to accept compromises to their objections.

Successful change management through influence is the job of the CPO and the EPM organization. Achievement of these established changes requires the power and relationships with the EPM team through the leadership skills of the CPO. It is critical to the project management communications environment that the CPO and his EPM organization are able to operate freely within the culture to achieve alignment of governances. The people working with the CPO in the EPM organization will need exceptional interpersonal skills, political astuteness, and most important must know how to communicate with each member of the culture such that they feel that they have been heard. This will take special people with special efforts. This is what is required to create a sustainable project management communication environment.

Managing portfolio risk

Project teams that desire to meet client and enterprise management expectations by minimizing threats to cost and schedule objectives and maximize opportunities use some sort of risk management practice. Project managers need not act alone to mitigate risks when an EPM organization is in place. The CPO will assist project managers by allocating project portfolio resources to mitigate project risks that threaten or enhance the achievement of strategic goals. This collaboration between the CPO and project managers creates a shared responsibility to manage risks throughout the project portfolio that meets both enterprise executive management and client expectations.

When the CPO communicates regularly with the executives and project managers, then it would be easy to leverage project portfolio management resources to mitigate risk events. The conversation with the executives focuses on how asset deployment will help mitigate project risks and the impact to enterprise goals, and how the PM culture will benefit from timely EPM intervention in the risk management process. The CPO's conversation with the project manager will point out the importance of identifying risks early and reporting impacts and responses quickly to enable the CPO to plan effectively risks responses that meet the client's expectations while minimizing the impact to strategic goals. It is vital for the CPO to circulate freely in both the executive and project management communication circles to respond to project risks using project portfolio resources in a way that increases the likelihood of achieving strategic goals.

Managing resources

Resource planning and deployment are the highest-value service the EPM organization can provide the enterprise. Executives need to understand current and future delivery capacity from which to base strategic goals. Project managers need to plan and deploy resources to deliver current projects and be ready to delivery future opportunities.

The CPO will lead his or her EPM team to collect and analyze the basic data needed to meet the needs of the enterprise. Initially, staff availability data is collected. Preferably, the project manager collects the centric data generated such as:

- Staff planning data from the set up of new projects and budget revisions following client approved change orders
- Staff forecast utilization data developed for estimates at complete (EAC) and routine staff labor revenue forecasts

While the project managers submit this data, other resources collect data for non-project work as well as project pursuits that may result in future work.

Successful resource management is measured by the project manager's usage of resource availability data to make project delivery decisions and present options that affect clients' goals as well as achievement of enterprise strategic goals. The CPO will collaborate with the project managers and those responsible for staffing to determine their needs for this data. This would include:

- Quickly planning for resource utilization for changes, risk responses, and presenting options to the client
- Developing "what if" delivery scenarios that help the client respond timely to their management team
- Working with the EPM to deploy resources to their project to meet deadlines
- Updating recruiting needs

When project managers are distracted from project delivery to provide workload forecast data that they feel exists in project setups, estimate at complications, and revenue forecasts, the process becomes inefficient for the enterprise. When project manager and staff morale is impacted, data arrives only after follow up to the original request, and quality is inconsistent. The CPO will need to convince the executives to invest in the resource capacity system integration, but will also need to show project managers how they can provide additional client service using the workload forecasting data. The CPO will likely meet resistance to this process from senior PMs who rely on personal relationships to manage the resource availability for their projects. It will test the CPOs leadership skills, but resource planning and capacity are better suited to satisfy the needs of the portfolio in order to achieve strategic goals.

Achieving the desired results and acceptance of resource capacity planning and deployment will depend largely on the creation of a sustainable project management communication environment. The culture in the environment will accept and pursue the greater good of portfolio and enterprise performance through peer alignment. The EPM organization's highest responsibility is to create the environment where communications and relationships support the notion that each individual benefits by the performance of the portfolio to meet or exceed the strategic goals.

Resolving issues and disputes

Expedited project issues resolutions are an effective way to avoid risk events that threaten cost and schedule performance. The EPM organization will design a process that creates communications needed to resolve the issue identifying the impacts to strategic goals. The characteristics of an effective issues resolution process include:

1. Use and issue log to track resolution.
2. Evaluate and identify the levels of unresolved issues beginning with project staff and ending with the executives.
3. Staff define the issue, analyze issue impacts, discuss the issue and impact mitigation to resolve the issue.
4. If issue is unresolved, document Step 3 and discuss proposals to unresolved issue.
5. If you are unable to achieve resolution, elevate to the project manager the unresolved issues documentation from Step 4.
6. Continue this process by updating documentation and issues log until issue is resolved.
7. If the executive committee cannot resolve the issue, then submit documented issue and feedback to the Dispute Resolution Board comprised of enterprise employees.
8. Issue documented dispute resolution agreement.

Although numerous variations exist for resolving issues and disputes, the key to the process steps is to collaborate and communicate in a safe environment design to resolve project level issues while minimizing the impact to strategic goals.

Walk through your hallways, read your corporate blogs and staff e-mail. Chances are that technical mentoring and coaching is going on without a second thought. Why? Because the environment created by the technical staff to collaborate while solving a technical problem for their clients allows for open and honest communications.

The CPO and his EPM organization need to create a similar environment to allow project management communications to occur as routinely as technical problem solving. The path to making this happen is involvement of project managers in the creation of the environment such that the time spent in this space feels like it benefits them and their clients. The chapters in this book describe components of the project management communication environment, and while the EPM organization achieves success by assisting in the delivery of the project portfolio that meets strategic goals.

Summary

Project managers are continually working with the various aspects of project communications on their projects. They can be both the victims and the causes of project information overload and need to ensure they are aware of this overload when working with the team members and customers. Another area where project managers will require solid project communication skills is working with the team members and customers in building a rapport and relationship. It is important that every project manager builds great relationships and that they can rely on their team members when the project is in difficult times. One of the best methods for building relationships is having face-to-face meetings and building both a bond and relationship with each team member.

Another challenge the project manager will deal with in managing project teams is the virtual team member. Managing resources that work offsite can be challenging from a resource perspective and a project activities perspective. When virtual team members have conflicts, the complexity of handling them becomes much harder. Project managers need to be trained and ready to deal with virtual team member conflicts and their offsite working arrangements. Virtual project management is becoming more and more a standard accepted practice in many companies today.

Finally, conflict management in the projects is an extremely difficult challenge for any project manager. Using the appropriate conflict resolutions techniques discovered in this chapter will help project managers and team members tackle these challenges and prevent any negative impact to the project.

In this chapter, we explored the various aspects of project communications in a project team environment. Some of the areas and ideas covered in the chapter will enhance project managers' and team members' overall communications while working on their projects and in their day-to-day lives.

Part II

Project Knowledge Areas

Chapter 4

Defining Communication Tools to Manage Project Integration

In this chapter, we explore the project communication tools that support project integration management. This is one of the nine knowledge areas recognized by the Project Management Institute.

Project integration management involves all of the other eight knowledge areas and activities that require coordination and integration throughout the life of the project. (See Chapter 1 for more information on each of the knowledge areas.) All projects undergo continuous updating and change throughout the life of the project that require constant integration. Project managers are constantly shifting from knowledge area to knowledge area while managing their projects. Project Integration is the coordination and the working of the activities across the knowledge areas on a project.

The management of project integration is mandatory throughout the project. This becomes apparent when you observe any aspect of a project. Any time the individual knowledge areas interact with each other, you have integration.

Introducing Project Integration

The main purpose of the management of project integration is to smoothly integrate the eight other knowledge areas to complete a successful project. The eight knowledge areas are scope, time, cost, quality, human resources, communications, risk, and procurement.

Project integration management involves several steps as you work your way through a project. These management steps are essential on all projects. The most important process steps are:

- Creating a project charter, which formally authorizes the project and assigns a project manager.

- Producing a project management plan. This supports the definitions and integration of all subordinate plans, including the scope on the project.

- Developing a scope document that integrates all the management processes.

- Managing, monitoring, and controlling the execution of the project work as described in the project management plan.

- Establishing a change control system to track and approve change requests.

- Integrating all closeout activities of the project by incorporating them in the project management process.

The tools in this chapter support the process steps to integrate the work needed to initiate, plan, execute, control, monitor, and close out the project from conception through production and turnover. The tools listed in this chapter specifically support project integration management and each has its own purpose and use for this knowledge area.

Introducing the Project Charter

The purpose of the *project charter* tool is to authorize the project and to assign a project manager and officially kick-off the project. The project manager in this process will decide to utilize the company's resources or hire externally for this effort. The project charter establishes the budget and the duration for the project. It describes and communicates the project's high-level components, such as scope, goals, and objectives to upper management, customers, or any interested parties. The project charter is a document that anyone can use to understand what the project is all about without needing to understand the details or its technical aspects of the effort. It also authorizes the utilization of material and equipment. You can think about the project charter as the major components of the project that you would normally put in a formal presentation to management. The project charter communicates the overall concept of the project to anyone involved or interested in learning about the project.

NOTE The Project Management Institute's knowledge area for this tool is the Integration area. The secondary area that this tool could be associated with is Scope.

ON the CD-ROM We have included a sample of this Project Charter tool in the Integration folder. Use this as a guide to create your own version of this tool.

TOOL VALUE Project charter authorizes the project and sets it in motion. It also assigns the project manager, as well as the budget, the start date, and duration.

The project charter, because it sets the project in motion, is the first official document on the project. It describes the project at a high level. It is not the scope document, but one of its functions is to act as a high-level guide to create the scope document. It describes what to do, not how to do it. Without the project charter the project team has literally no direction or idea what they should be accomplishing.

A project charter document is generic enough across the industries that it is adaptable to most projects, and each industry will have specific requirements covered in those documents unique to them. The common sections of the project charter document describe the project's purpose, scope, budget, resource requirements, schedule, and critical success factors along with assumptions and constraints. The project sponsor or owner who has the responsibility of developing the details behind the document will often require assistance from you, the project manager, and some of your project team members in completing the document's specifications. It is also their responsibility to communicate the project charter document to the project manager and team members to ensure they understand what they are required to develop and complete.

A well thought-out project charter communicates and guides the project to a successful completion. It will allow the team to understand what they must accomplish to complete the project successfully. Most of the important aspects of a project are contained within the project charter document. It usually is at a summary level at this point in the project because there has been little if any planning to date. The document is more for kicking off the project and does not contain details. From a communication perspective, each of the components in the project charter document can stand alone in communicating valuable project information. For example, in the major deliverables section of the document, the project manager can use that section and communicate to their stakeholders or owners of the project what the deliverables will be. The deliverables could become the milestone list.

Table 4.1 represents a sample project charter document. In this sample, the major aspects of the project are all covered and documented. The project charter becomes the driving document behind the project's planning; therefore, it is vital that the information is contained in this one document for easy retrieval and reference.

TABLE 4.1

Project Charter Table of Contents

Section	Description
1	Introduction
2	Overview of Project
3	Purpose of Project
4	Objective of Project
5	Project Scope
6	Project Budget
7	Project Start and Finish Dates
8	Major Deliverables
9	Resources
10	Business Need or Opportunity

continued

TABLE 4.1	(continued)
Section	**Description**
11	Financial Benefits of the Project
12	Critical Success Factors of Project
13	Expected Benefits
14	Assumptions and Constraints
15	Sign-offs

Defining the roles

Many people are involved in the development and communication of a project charter. The following roles and descriptions can help you understand who is involved in this process:

- **Project manager:** Provides support to the project sponsors on development of the project charter and carries out the implementation of the project after senior management approval. She communicates any activities occurring throughout the project charter development. In some organizations, only senior management creates the project charter document, and assigns the project manager only after the document is complete.

- **Team members:** Carries out activities of project once the project kicks off. The team members may be involved in communicating various aspects of the project charter. For example, they could be responsible for describing the project's planning tasks as it relates to the details described in the project charter.

- **Project sponsors:** Develop the idea of the project, communicate the idea by presenting a project proposal, and support the development of the project's charter document.

- **Project owner/client:** Holds financial responsibility, is responsible for overall acceptance, and communicates their approval of project.

Planning to use a project charter

When planning to use a project charter, the project manager must first work with the sponsor and owner and review the document and acquire an understanding of the proposed project. Doing this, allows the project manager to review and accept the responsibility for the project as described in the project charter document. After the project manager is familiar with what the project is about, he or she has enough information to build their project team and start the project planning process. As the project kicks off, the project manager along with the sponsor or owner will sit down with the project team members and go over the project charter. This will give them time to ask questions and get a great understanding of the project. After performing these steps, the project manager has adequately prepared for the use of a project charter on their project.

Before you can create the project charter, you must formulate a plan. In the following "Planning Questions" section, we provide some initial thoughts to help you start thinking about how to implement the tool on your project.

Planning Questions

1 *When would development of the project charter occur?*

During the initiation process (phase) of the project

2 *Who is going to use this tool, both from an input and output status?*

Upper management, owners, executives, project manager, team member, subcontractors, media

3 *Why are you going to use this tool?*

To communicate the scope, goals, and objectives of the project

4 *How are you going to use this tool?*

Upper management will use document to decide whether to proceed with project, determine cost estimates, determine schedule estimates, determine proposed solutions, and determine resourcing needs, Project Manager will use it as an authorization to acquire the team members and utilize the budget allocated to the project

5 *How will you distribute the information?*

Document format such as Microsoft Word, document control system, e-mail, in-person presentation

6 *When will you distribute the information?*

When selling the project to upper management or customers who need to approve the project, project kick-off meeting, on-demand

7 *What decisions can or should you make from this tool?*

Upper management or customers make go/no go decision on the project, schedule decisions, cost decisions, resource and scope decisions; making all these from the tool

8 *What information does this tool provide for your project?*

Describes the project, provides an idea how long it may take, how much it may cost, identify technical challenges, comparisons of similar projects, if applicable

9 *What historical and legal information do you need to store?*

Decision on why project was approved or rejected and lessons learned information

10 *What will be the staffing requirements (Role Type) to run and maintain these tools?*

Customer or sponsor, senior management, possibly the project manager

Reporting using a project charter

The project owner or customer creates the project charter document. The document communicates and guides the project manager and the team members in the areas of scheduling, budgeting, and the quality aspects of the project.

There are two distinct reporting levels for distribution of the project charter.

■ The first level is the project owner(s) who utilizes this document for presentations to their peers and financial areas for the support and approval of the document before and after final approval of the project.

■ The second level of distribution is the project manager and project team members chosen to work on the project.

During the conceptual and startup phase (project initiation process), the project management team constantly refers to the project charter document. The project charter is developed and distributed in a document format for ease of distribution and presentation. Quite often, the project manager extracts some of the information in the project charter for project presentations during the initiation of the project.

This is a one of a kind document and is distributed once and then on demand. The project manager does not report from the project charter each week because this tool does not have project status information. It is stored as part of the document control system for long-term archiving and is accessible by any interested stakeholder on the project.

CROSS-REF See Chapter 14 for additional discussions on how to create and use a project charter.

Introducing the Project Kick-Off Meeting

The purpose of the *project kick-off meeting* tool is to formalize the start of the project and to initiate the project activities. The project kick-off meeting tool engages the project team members and enables them to become a cohesive team. The project kick-off meeting helps establishes the atmosphere of the project. Some of the benefits that holding a project kick-off meeting provides are that it creates the ability to bring the team together, helps form relationships among the team members, and improves the communication aspects of presenting the same information at the same time to everyone involved in the project.

NOTE The Project Management Institute's knowledge area for this tool is the Integration area. There is no secondary area for this tool.

Holding a project kick-off meeting gives the project manager and team members the chance to establish a bond. The team members should feel that they can work together to resolve any project issues and by meeting and getting to know each other a bond establishes in most cases. Without a project kick-off meeting, the team members may never have that bonding experience and therefore the project manager could have challenges with the team working together and dealing with project issues as they arise.

ON the CD-ROM We have included a sample of the project kick-off meeting tool in the Integration folder on the CD-ROM. We believe that this sample is a great starting point for the creation of this tool for your project. Your company or project may have specific requirements that will enhance this communication tool further.

TOOL VALUE Project kick-off meeting sets the direction, tone, focus, and goal of the project and all team members and stakeholders.

Normally, the project kick-off meeting generates a great deal of positive energy for your team members and customers attending the meeting. This is the time to establish initial opinions and first impressions of each other. These opinions may last throughout the project. For team members that are working in a virtual environment, the project kick-off meeting may offer the only opportunity to meet the other team members for the first time.

Table 4.2 represents a common project kick-off meeting agenda for use on most projects. The agenda items covered are typical for any type of project discussion. The agenda is generic enough for any project, and enhancement could include areas particular or specific to your type of project.

ON the CD-ROM Included on the CD-ROM is a template Project Kick-off Meeting Agenda presentation for your reference and use on your project.

TABLE 4.2

Example of a Project Kick-off Meeting Agenda

Agenda Item	Description
1	Project Scope, Goals, Objectives
2	Project Out of Scope
3	Project Risks
4	Project Issues
5	Budget Estimate
6	Project Schedule
7	Methodology Deliverables
8	Requirements Deep Dive
9	Design Deep Dive
10	Development Deep Dive
11	Test Deep Dive
12	User Acceptance Criteria Deep Dive

Creating a great first impression with your team members at the project kick-off meeting can help you gain a high level of respect. Most team members quickly determine if they want to work for you. You must make a good impression to the team members as well as customers when you are ready and prepared for the meeting.

The project kick-off meeting is the official start of the project. The content of the meeting explains the scope, goals, and objectives to all stakeholders and interested parties. It ensures that everyone has the same information about the project at the same time and everyone can focus on what the team has to deliver. The kick-off meeting provides the first chance for the owner to present what they expect from the project and the team as well and explain what they are hoping to achieve. The owner presentation provides the opportunity for the team to hear them and to ask necessary questions. This connection is also important in building relationships between the owner and the team members. The project kick-off meeting is often the first and the only chance these two parties will have to meet.

Some owners may refuse to participate in the project kick-off meeting. They may feel they have turned the project over to you and do not want to interfere. Other owners want to run the meeting. The best practice is for you and the owner to present the project kick-off meeting together, so the owner is not feeling that they own the meeting, but are a valuable participant.

If the project manager decides that having a project kick-off meeting is not important, then the project team members are normally much slower to engage in the project. The individual team member most likely will feel lost and unsure of the project's goals or their particular roles. This can have a devastating impact on communicating with your project team members. Bad morale is not something a project manager wants to face any time during the project, and especially when it is just starting.

Planning to use a project kick-off meeting

The project kick-off meeting in many ways is an example of project planning. The pre-work (planning) for any project kick-off meeting is required to ensure that the meeting meets the goals and objectives of the owner and project manager. The importance of this pre-work is to ensure that you have all the information on hand to kick off the project and that you are communicating effectively with everyone involved.

Using these tips can help make your project kick-off meeting a success:

- **Complete the investigation of the project.** You can do preliminary work to help you understand what the objectives of the project are and to do research based on those objectives.

- **Meet customer and outline their expectations.** Sit down with the customers, and understand and document their expectations of the project. Good communications skills will be necessary at these customer meetings when discussing their expectations. Make sure you meet with every person that signed the project charter.

- **Gather appropriate documentation and information.** Research the project whenever possible and get a high-level understanding of it.

- **Gather lessons learned and any relevant information.** Work with any previous project managers. Read similar projects lessons learned documents and understand the project's challenges it previously dealt with and implement appropriate ones on your project.

- **List the team member's expectations of the project.** Meet with each team member, explain the project, and gather his or her expectations and feelings about the project.

- **Include company specific tasks.** If the company has any specific tasks within the project kick-off meetings, utilize these tasks when applicable.

Before you can create the project kick-off meeting, you must formulate a plan. In the following "Planning Questions" section, we provide some initial thoughts to help you start thinking about how you would utilize this tool on your project.

Planning Questions

1 *When would you create, develop, and write the Project Kick-off Meeting tool?*
During the initiation phase of the project and prior to starting the planning or developing of the project's scope

2 *Who is going to use this tool, both from an input and output status?*
Upper management, owners, executives, project manager, team member, subcontractors

3 *Why are you going to use this tool?*
To bring everyone together, meet and focus on the goals and objectives of the project, start the buy-in of the team members on the project, allow everyone to be in-sync with the project from the start

4 *How are you going to use this tool?*
To kick off the project and communicate project information

5 *How will you distribute the information?*
Presentation format such as PowerPoint, document format such as a Microsoft Word, document control system, e-mail, in-person, and meeting environment

6 *When will you distribute the information?*
Once during the kick-off meeting and then it would be available in the document control system for historical reference

7 *What decisions can or should you make from this tool?*
Project Decisions based on the kick-off meeting time lines, feedback, scope, and resources are all possible from using this tool.

continued

continued

8 *What information does this tool provide for your project?*

Describes the project, provides an idea on how long it may take, how much it may cost, identifies technical challenges and any other information relevant to getting the project started.

9 *What historical and legal information do you need to store?*

Any relevant documents or presentations used in the meeting, minutes of the meeting, and any lessons learned information

10 *What will be the staffing requirements (role type) to run and maintain these tools?*

Project manager, project analyst, possible project team members, possible upper management, or customers providing their insight and approval of the project

Reporting using a project kick-off meeting

Usually at least two groups are involved in creating the presentation materials for the project kick-off meeting: project managers and their customers. Each of them will have specific areas to cover during the meeting. Therefore, each party should have ownership as to what they will cover in the materials. In some cases where the project is technical, there may be an opportunity to invite a subject matter expert that would be responsible for that specific area of the project. This subject matter expert would also have material they would present as well. They could also join the meeting to provide encouragement or technical backup for the team members.

The project kick-off meeting is a one-time event. Therefore, there is only this one document used to report just once at the beginning of the project. The presentations and the project kick-off meeting materials created are all stored as part of the document control system for long-term archiving and are accessible by any interested stakeholder on the project.

CROSS-REF   See Chapter 14 learn more about how to create and use a project kick-off meeting.

Introducing the Project Management Plan

The purpose of the project management plan is to compile a series of management plans to guide you, your project team members, and your customers through the management and controlling of the project. This series of management plans includes time management, quality management, risk management, and cost management that covers all project knowledge areas and communication aspects. It is a collection of those management plans into a single package (volume). One of the valuable aspects of the project management plan is the inclusion of the project strategies. These strategies are items such as the project's scope, goals, and objectives and are included in the project management plan.

You can use two main methods to create or utilize a project management plan on a project.

- You can create a single blank shell electronic document and title it the project management plan and then use hyperlinks to link or point to the major areas of the project (scope, risk, cost, and schedule). For example, a project management plan using this method would have a page dedicated to risk management, but that page would only include a hyperlink to the actual risk management document for the project.

- The second method is to create a fully documented and detailed project management plan by copying and pasting the contents from various management plans (risk, issue, schedule, quality, and so on) into a master project management plan document. Hyperlinks are not used in this plan, and it requires someone, normally the project manager, to copy the details from one management plan to the master project management plan. For example, in risk management, the major contents of the risk management plan are copied word for word into the master Project Management plan as well. The disadvantage to this method is keeping the information current in multiple documents and ensuring that the customers or team members are using the most current information. It would be harmful to change a process within the master project management plan and not have those same changes or updates implemented within the individual management plan themselves or vice versa.

NOTE The Project Management Institute's knowledge area for this tool is the Integration area. The secondary knowledge area for this tool is Scope.

ON the CD-ROM You can find a sample of a project management plan in the Integration folder. This is a guide to the first step in creating your own personal version of this tool.

TOOL VALUE The project management plan provides a direction and a process for the project manager to follow during the life of the project. It is the executing and controlling roadmap for the project.

Table 4.3 represents an example of a project management plan table of contents. The sections described in the table are suitable for most projects regardless of the industry. If you work for a company that does not have a project management plan in place, use this project management plan as a starting point. This document should cover all areas of the project in as much detail as possible to avoid any miscommunications or confusions. When a project situation occurs, you or your team members would have a consolidated place to go to find the process and procedures for handling it.

NOTE Sections 1 through 19 in Table 4.3 should be included in every project management plan regardless of what method you have chosen to create the plan. Whether you select the shell document or the all-inclusive document, the first 19 sections should be the same.

TABLE 4.3

Example of a Project Management Plan Table of Contents

Section	Description
1	Introduction
2	Project Descriptions
3	Application
4	Scope
5	Constraints and Assumptions
6	Risks
7	Issues
8	Relationship to Other Project
9	Mission Statement
10	Project Objectives
11	Project Team Members
12	Project Roles and Responsibilities
13	Project Plan Management
14	Project Approach
15	Conflict Management
16	Project Tasks, Deliverables, and Milestones
17	Planning Approaches/Methodologies
18	Key Deliverables
19	Major Milestones Dates / List
20	Scope Management
21	Issues Management
22	Risk Management / Including Risk Register
23	Problems Management
24	Financial / Cost Management
25	Communication Management
26	Quality Management Plan
27	Staffing Management Plan
28	Procurement Management Plan
29	Schedule Management Plan
30	Summary

A project management plan is vital for any project, no matter the size, type, or industry. The plan is a communication and support tool that documents and assists team members and customers in the managing and control of the project. When a management situation arises, the project management plan or one of the various documents within the plan describes in detail the process to handle the situation. The project management plan covers the management plans for each of the project knowledge areas at a high level. For example, the risk management plan documents the process and procedures for opening and closing project risks in detail. The risk management plan is part of the overall project management plan and therefore team members can go to either document for the risk management information. Project managers should be careful to understand that they are not duplicating documentation in two sets of documents. The best approach is for the project management plan to be a consolidated document to bring all the plans together in one location. Doing this avoids the necessity of people having to go from plan to plan or looking for some disparate information

NOTE Some companies refer to the project management plan as a project governance guide. These documents represent essentially the same components of the project management plan but with company specific information or requirements. Ensure that you capture this additional information for your project, if applicable, especially if the company has deemed it as important.

A common misconception about project management plans is that they are the same as a project schedule. They are not, and it is important to keep these two separate. Project schedules are a list of tasks with intended start and finish dates normally created by the Project scheduling tool. The project schedule does not provide the detail, process, and procedures that the project management plan covers. Its purpose is to capture the lists of tasks and timeframes for the project. Project managers should be aware of the differences between the two and ensure that they are clear when discussing each of them with their customers, stakeholders, or team members. For example, if a project manager is communicating his project schedule information, she could say, "I just created my project schedule by using the latest version of my scheduling package and discovered it had some new features in the software to allow for specific cost reporting." When going into this kind of detail, it will clearly state to anyone what you are talking about, which in the end avoids any confusion. Anytime you are talking about features or cost reports, people are going to be aware that you are not talking about the project management plan and that you are talking about in most cases the project scheduling tool.

The project manager is responsible for creating and maintaining the project management plan during the life of the project. Project managers also become one of the main users of the document, and they rely on it quite heavily to help them manage their project. The project customer or team members will also use the project management plan as well, mainly though, as a guide to how a particular process should work. For example, a customer would look closely at the change control plan and refer to the change request process within that plan. That way, when the customers do have change requests, they have a documented process to follow.

Project managers are responsible for ensuring that the project team members have bought into the project management plan before the start of the project. Obtaining agreement from the team members also can prevent miscommunication and chaos. The management documents within the project management plan should have the information the team members require to control most situations as they occur.

Planning to use a project management plan

In preparing to create and use a project management plan, the project manager must first decide what method he or she will implement for a project management plan document itself. The decision is to use either a blank shell document that links to the different management plans or an all-inclusive document that actually describes each knowledge area in enough detail to cover adequately the plan. The project manager needs to make this decision as early as possible in the project. He or she then must work to ensure that the knowledge area management plans (Risk, Scope, Quality...etc.) are complete, approved, and stored in the document control system for easy access. That way, the project manager can just link to the plans or go in and copy the text from each and store in the master project management plan. The project manager then needs to understand and prepare for some of the technical details around the project management plan. This includes where the documents are to be stored, who receives security access, and long-term archiving. Finally, in planning to use the project management plan, the project manager determines the proper owner of each of the management plan(s) and starts to work with that owner until the documents are complete and ready. After performing these tasks, the project manager has adequately prepared for using the project management plan on their projects.

Before you can create the project management plan, you must formulate a plan. In the following "Planning Questions" section, we provide some initial thoughts to help you start thinking about how to utilize this tool on your project.

Planning Questions

1 *When would you create, develop, and write the project management plan?*

During the planning phase, after the management plans are complete and can be compiled into an overall master plan.

2 *Who is going to use this tool, both from an input and output status?*

Project manager, team members, subcontractors, customers, stakeholders, anyone who needs guidance and direction on handling various project situations

3 *Why are you going to use this tool?*

To establish the framework that allows team members and stakeholders to understand when and how to manage and control communications and various aspects of the project; for example risk management, quality management, and so on.

4 *How are you going to use this tool?*

Guide the execution of the project and refer to the various plans for different project situations

5 *How will you distribute the information?*

Document format such as Microsoft Word, document control system, e-mail

6 *When will you distribute the information?*
Once, when all management plans are complete and the project management plan is complete and ready for use on the project, on-demand

7 *What decisions can or should you make from this tool?*
Decisions on the management and execution of the project throughout the various knowledge areas

8 *What information does this tool provide for your project?*
How to execute the processes and procedures in each of the knowledge areas, such as risk management, issue management, and cost management.

9 *What historical and legal information do you need to store?*
Document itself and any modifications, lessons learned dealing with any process or procedures that have not worked well during the project

10 *What will the staffing requirements (role type) be to run and maintain these tools?*
Project manager, project team members, document control manager

Reporting using a project management plan

The project manager normally compiles the project management plan information at the beginning of the project, and as the subdocuments are complete, the project manager continues to update, monitor, and ensure that the information in the project management plan is accurate through the life of the project. Because the project management plan consists of a series of documents compiled into a single document (or a shell document that has links to the actual management plans), if policy or process changes occur on the project, the project management plan will need to be updated to reflect those changes. (If you chose to implement the shell document, you would have to reflect the changes as well in the individual documents.) Regardless of what method you choose to build the plan, the project manager communicates the updates and changes to the stakeholders, team members, and upper management involved in the project on an ongoing basis.

The following list represents the management plans included in a standard project management plan. These plans represent the major areas of most projects. Each of these categories represents a document for creation and inclusion into the project management plan.

The following plans are included as part of a standard project management plan:

- Project scope management plan
- Schedule management plan
- Cost management plan
- Quality management plan

- Staffing management plan
- Communication management plan
- Risk management plan
- Procurement management plan
- Milestone list
- Schedule baseline
- Cost baseline
- Quality baseline
- Risk register

The manager will not have to report from the project management plan each week because it does not include project status information. The project management plan is more of a reference and guidance document used throughout the life of the project. It is stored as part of the document control system for long-term archiving and is accessible by any interested stakeholder on the project.

CROSS-REF   See Chapter 14 to learn more about how to create and use this project management plan.

Introducing Project Meeting Minutes

You can use *project meeting minutes* to capture the activities and action items that occurred during a project meeting and to communicate that information to anyone interested. Project meeting minutes enable anyone interested in the project to learn what occurred and what was committed to during the meeting. Meeting minutes are helpful for those team members who could not attend the meeting. Project managers should take meeting minutes or have someone capture those meeting minutes for them. (We recommend that project managers ask someone else to take the minutes — it's difficult to run the meeting at the same time.) The minutes' taker should capture as much relevant information as possible and leave all the extra discussions or noise out of the meeting minutes.

NOTE   The Project Management Institute's knowledge area for this tool is the Integration area. This tool works in every other knowledge area as well.

 We have included a sample of the Project Meeting Minutes tool in the Integration folder on the CD-ROM.

TOOL VALUE   Project meeting minutes are a document of what occurred during the meeting, which provides everyone with knowledge and identifies accountability for what was said and agreed upon at the meeting.

Project meeting minutes are the notes taken that capture the action items and main points that rose during a meeting. You should always review the captured and summarized meeting minutes after each meeting to ensure that they are accurate. Then distribute them to your team members and customers for their review of the issues and action items. You should follow through on the action items. Doing this is an important step in your ongoing project communication management because the continuous flow of project information to your stakeholders and team members is invaluable.

> **TIP** You might want to capture a certain part of a meeting such as a subject matter expert's material to make sure the communication is accurate. If this were necessary, you would record only that part of the meeting for future playback. You can use a number of recording tools such as the Dictaphone, computer camera, tape recorder, movie, camcorder, and so on.

Figure 4.1 represents common meeting minutes for a typical project. (Look on this book's CD for a copy.)

An excellent tip for taking meeting minutes is to capture the action items from the last meeting and bring them forward to the current meeting to ensure that nothing is lost from week to week. Often project managers miss this and assume that their team members will perform the action items captured in the last meeting. Most team members require that extra push to ensure they remember the action items assigned to them, and bringing them forward on a week-to-week basis reduces the chances of them forgetting.

Meeting minutes are great communication tools because they communicate the action items and outcomes from a meeting event. One of the best practices is for the project managers to communicate meeting minutes at the end of every meeting by sending out those minutes and relevant action items to all stakeholders, and project team members. The project manager should also post those minutes within the document control system for easy access and review. By doing so, you are continuing the ongoing project communications with your interested stakeholders, thus keeping project information flowing. Project managers should also follow up on each issue or action item during the week to ensure that the team is making progress on the items. As action items complete, the project manager should communicate this to everyone on the team.

As the project progresses and you or your team members capture the meeting minutes on a week-to-week basis, these minutes become invaluable. This repository is a wealth of project information that is valuable to the project team, customers, and other stakeholders. When it is necessary to look back at past decisions or discussion points, the first place to review is the historical repository of meeting minutes. This information becomes easy to use and to find the information you are searching for. The meeting minutes become a source for to-do lists (action items) or formal project tasks. The action items in the weekly minutes carry through each week until they are completed or noted, then dropped.

Capturing the lessons learned information during the course of the meeting is a best practice technique. In Figure 4.1, you noticed that there is an agenda item called "This Week's Lessons Learned." During that time on the agenda, the project manager opens the subject to the meeting attendees and notes the lessons learned (What went right? And what went wrong?) for the week. The compiling of this information each week will eliminate the lessons learned meeting(s) at the end of the project. Then at the end of the project, the project manager just summarizes the lessons learned log to complete the lessons learned document and presentation. The project manager then presents it to the project team, customers, and upper management at the formal lessons learned meeting.

FIGURE 4.1

This figure represents a typical set of meeting minutes from a project.

Meeting Minutes for PROJECT XXX

Project Name	:	
Meeting Title	:	
Date	:	
Time	:	
Place	:	
Phone Information	:	
Chair Person	:	
Invitee List	:	
In Attendance	:	

AGENDA	
1.	Last Week's Minutes Review
2.	Project Schedule Review
3.	Major Area Updates
4.	Project Issues Review
5.	Project Risk List Review
6.	This Week's Lessons Learned
7.	Walk-on's

Action Items:

#	Action Item	Owner	Status	Due Date	Comments
1.					
2.					

Carry-Over Items for Next Meeting

#	Description
1.	
1.	

Next Meeting Details:	:	
Date	:	
Time	:	
Place	:	

All members of the project team should use the project meeting minutes to review and recap what occurred. Individuals will have different purposes for how and why they will utilize the meeting minutes but generally each will be looking for specific action items assigned to them. The project manager and team members should ensure that they make the meeting minutes available to the project's stakeholders, so there is full disclosure, and anyone wanting to see what occurred during the meeting can access the project information if needed.

NOTE The accuracy of meeting minutes is crucial. In some cases, these documents are valuable in litigation, so project managers ensure that they keep them current and as accurate as possible.

Planning to use project meeting minutes

In *preparing* to create and use project meeting minutes, the project manager must first develop or utilize an existing project meeting minute's template from the company or a past project. In doing so, the project manager establishes how and what he or she will communicate during the meeting. Next, the project manager needs to determine where the meeting minutes will be stored. Then determine how to set up security access, and any technology (document control system) or non-technology solutions for these minutes. Then the project manager creates a meeting agenda to match or feed the meeting minutes' template. This can take some time to ensure the agenda and the minutes are aligned and the project manager gets the information he /she needs to help manage the project. Finally, the project manager should work with the scribe, go over the template, and ensure that she knows what to capture. A project manager should never select someone randomly at the start of the meeting because that person may not fill in the template correctly and valuable information could be lost. The project manager should the think about how often the meeting should occur. Should it be weekly? Could it be biweekly and not lose the communication that needs distributing? (Refer to the project management plan to help you make this decision.) After preparing and performing these planning steps, the project manager has adequately prepared for using meeting minutes on their project.

Before you can create project meeting minutes, you must formulate a plan. The "Planning Questions" section provides you with some guidance to help you start thinking about how to utilize the tool on your project.

Planning Questions

1 *When would you create, develop, and write project meeting minutes?*
You want to create a meeting minute's template at the beginning of project and then use it throughout the project during every project meeting

2 *Who is going to use this tool, both from an input and output status?*
Project manager, team members, clients, customers, upper management, the minute's taker

continued

---

continued

3   *Why are you going to use this tool?*

To document the information and discussions that occurred during the meeting and assign action items and to-do lists to project team members and stakeholders

4   *How are you going to use this tool?*

Capture the information discussed, report to project team members, report to customers or clients if applicable, develop status report data from meeting minutes information, create and distribute action item list for team members

5   *How will you distribute the information?*

E-mail, document format such as Microsoft Word, document control system

6   *When will you distribute the information?*

As soon as possible after the meeting, within 48 hours

7   *What decisions can or should you make from this tool?*

Depending on type of meeting, decisions could be made on status, project direction, resources, time-frames, budget, issues, risks, and dependencies.

8   *What information does this tool provide for your project?*

Depending on the type of meeting held, the information will vary greatly but areas could include scope, cost, time, resources, risks, issues, and other project-related details

9   *What historical and legal information do you need to store?*

All versions of meeting minutes, lessons learned information

10   *What will be the staffing requirements (role type) to run and maintain these tools?*

Any one of the typical project managers would maintain and develop meeting minutes, scribe, project manager, cost manager, quality manager, and resource manager

Reporting using project meeting minutes

In most cases, you as the project manager are responsible for creating the meeting minutes on your projects. In the larger projects where there are a number of project managers or there is support staff assigned, they would be responsible for capturing, compiling, and reporting the project meeting minutes. We suggest hiring a stenographer to capture the information and create the minutes for the meeting. Another scenario, if your project is small, is to have the team members rotate each week and capture the meeting minutes for the project. After the meeting, the meeting attendees should receive the minutes no later than 48 hours later.

The project manager has to report from the project meeting minutes each week or whatever the cycle (bi-weekly or monthly, for example.). The project meeting minutes are full of valuable project information, status, current events, and a valuable wealth of project data. The meeting minutes are stored as part of the document control system for long-term archiving and are accessible by any interested stakeholder on the project.

CROSS-REF See Chapter 20 to learn more about how to create and use the project meeting minutes.

Introducing the Project Organization Chart

The purpose of the *project organization chart* is to display the project's organizational structure. The goal of having this chart in place is to allow team members (especially new ones), customers, or upper management to see who is working on the project and to understand their various roles and positions. The project organization chart helps team members determine who to communicate with on the project. When reviewing the assignments of each team member, you can cater your communications to the people in those various roles. For example, you would not send a plumber a work request for something electrical, or vice versa. The project organization chart also offers an at-a-glance view of what roles are missing (if applicable) and where the team could use extra staff. In many cases, the project may have a full team but may not have enough of a particular resource skill. In those cases, the project organization chart may not specifically show holes in the staffing, but when you understand the amount of project work required, it can indirectly show that there are not enough resources at the existing level. Additionally, having a project organization chart on a large project allows the team members to see across roles and determine contacts, team leads, and assist in the communications between all team members. On smaller projects, the team dynamics are easier to manage, but a project organization chart still offers the same benefits as it would on a larger project, just at a smaller scale. In either case, just by looking at the project organization chart, anyone has the ability to see how big or how small of a project they are involved in.

NOTE The Project Management Institute's knowledge area for this tool is the Integration area. There are no other knowledge areas for this tool.

ON the CD-ROM We have included a sample of a project organization chart in the Integration folder. This is a guide to the first step in creating your own personal version of this tool. Your company or project may have specific requirements that will enhance this communication tool further; however, we believe this is a great starting point for the creation of this tool for your project.

TOOL VALUE A project organization chart communicates a diagrammatic representation displaying the functions of the project and the relationships to one another along lines of authority. It shows the position of all team members and it is easy to read and understand.

The project organization chart provides a lot of information at a single glance. This format allows anyone to identify quickly a person's role and level on the project. It also allows for identification of the individual team members' reporting structure, which is usually required during the course of a project.

A project organization chart can also help project managers understand the communication links associated with the project. In Chapter 2, we discuss the various advantages and challenges of project links, and when reviewing the project organization chart, you can determine how challenging your project will be from a communication link perspective as well. Totaling the number of the people on the organization chart will provide you a number to add to the link calculations as described in the formula in Chapter 2.

CROSS-REF   **See Chapter 2 for more information on communication links**

Figure 4.2 represents a basic example of a project organization chart from a construction project. This project organization chart represents two levels of organization structure. The first level is the project manager, and the second level represents the major areas on the project. These team leaders are not necessarily the individual workers on the project, but more of the functional leaders of the groups and have team members under them performing the work activities. On this construction project, the project manager may not know the names of each team member but will work directly with the lead person in a particular area. That lead would coordinate the work for their team. In this example, the project manager would work closely with Bill Johnson, the Foundation lead, but may not ever work with a single team member in Bill's group.

FIGURE 4.2

This figure represents a basic example of a project organization chart.

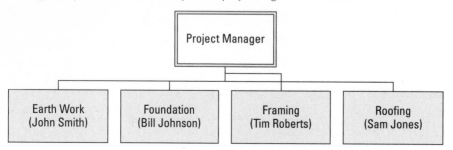

An organization chart is a chart that represents the structure of the project, generally in terms of the rank of each team member for that project. The project organization chart is different from a *company's* organization chart; the project chart is only valid for the length of the project. In defining this structure, you will notice that the communication channels form indirectly for you. Referring to Figure 4.2 as an example, if there is a lead for a particular area of the project (Foundation for example), the project manager would communicate with that lead (Bill) first to request approval to talk to Bill's team members, and only then approach any of the team members in the Foundation group. This approach is a respectful way of approaching project communications as well as acting as a guide as to how you should structure your communications on the project (for example, send the report directly to Bill and let Bill decide to send to his team members).

In most cases, you as the project manager are responsible for creating the project organization chart for the projects you manage. When creating this chart, do so at the beginning of the project when there are few team members because it is easier to create with a smaller number and then add onto the chart as more team members arrive. As new members join the project, add them to the project organization chart as soon as they sign onto the project. If you wait until it is late in the project, or when all assigned team members are on board before starting to create the organizational chart, it may never get finished. Normally, this is because it does not have the priority of the other project items and therefore could get lost in the project's work activities. In larger projects where there are a number of project managers or there is administrative support staff assigned, they are normally responsible for capturing, compiling, and reporting the project organization chart.

Project organization charts are graphical in nature and therefore are a wonderful communications tool. The project organization charts may have color to communicate the different work streams. The chart is used in a variety of ways to communicate, such as in project offices displayed on a wall or in a central location, and it is used in presentations as a representative of the team structure. Project managers should as a best practice create the project organization chart as early as possible and update it as team members come and go on the project.

> **TIP** Another best practice, if possible, is to take pictures of each of the team members and add these pictures directly onto the organization chart. When new team members are looking for a person or want to put a name to a face, these pictures are invaluable.

The project organization chart shows the managers and team members who staff the project. The chart shows the different relationships between various staff members, consisting of:

- **Line:** Shows direct relationship between superior and subordinate.
- **Lateral:** Shows relationship between different departments on the same hierarchical level.
- **Team Member:** Shows relationship between the project manager, the leads, and the team members. Most likely, project managers have no authority over a team member as normally the team member reports to a function manager.
- **Functional:** Supplies resources to the project and is not shown on the chart.

> **TIP** Project managers should take a copy of their project's organization chart and display it during the weekly status report for easy reference.

Planning to use the project organization chart

In preparing (planning) to create and use a project organization chart, the project manager must first determine who are the team members on their project and what roles are they filling. The project manager needs to know how to structure the project and determine who will assume leadership roles on the team. Different projects have different leadership roles; the project manager sets up the structure based on the roles. The project manager communicates the project structure to the various project leads to ensure those leads are accountable and responsible for their work areas. When working with the leads, the project manager determines who the assigned team members are, and what team members are still missing. He can complete the organization chart accordingly.

Before you can create the project organization chart, you must formulate a plan. In the "Planning Questions" section, we provide some initial thoughts to help you start thinking about how you can utilize this tool on your project.

Planning Questions

1 *When would you create or develop the project organization chart?*

During the Planning process of every project, when a new member of the team rolls on and off the project

2 *Who is going to use this tool, both from an input and output status?*

Upper management, owners, customers, project manager, team members, subcontractors, and media (TV, radio, newspapers) and everyone involved in the project

3 *Why are you going to use this tool?*

To determine who is working on the project and where to communicate or receive specific information

4 *How are you going to use this tool?*

Determine who is on the project, and who is responsible and leading what areas, determine team size and any open positions, possibly display complexity to the project based on team size, reporting relationships, leadership roles

5 *How will you distribute the information?*

Document format such as PowerPoint, Microsoft Visio, and hard copies posted on project walls, document control system, e-mail, other software packages for creation and distribution of organization charts

6 *When will you distribute the information?*

Once when created, and when the team members roll on and off the project, keeping it current

7 *What decisions can or should you make from this tool?*

Who's who on the project, staffing decisions based on holes in resource areas, costing and estimating based on team sizes, who to see for particular information, size of team and work location or offices for team members

8 *What information does this tool provide for your project?*

Project Team structure, hieratical reporting, point of contact, responsible areas of project, any missing resource skills sets, possibly any over-allocation of resources

9 *What historical and legal information do you need to store?*

Lessons learned information on development of the project organization chart, org charts versions themselves, potentially any reasons why staff rolled on and off the project

10 *What will be the staffing requirements (role type) to run and maintain these tools?*

Project manager, project analyst, possible project team members, functional managers, HR representatives, graphics department

Reporting using a project organization chart

The reporting process of the project organization chart is straightforward. When the first rough draft is complete, report it to the project team members, customers, and upper management. Then whenever a new team member joins or if someone leaves, update the project organization chart. At the start of the project, it is dynamic because of the staff build up. An update of once a week is appropriate during this time. Update the chart only when necessary, because most of the time, it is stable and people do not come and go that often. At the end of the project when team members leave the project a simple "X" through their box may be enough to keep the chart current if there is no time to update formally the chart. Otherwise, update it when there is time and put a new copy on the project wall to keep everyone informed on the project.

Figure 4.3 represents a more advance project organization chart because it has more than one level shown in the chart. This figure represents not only the team leaders, but also their assigned project staff. This would be a great example of a project organization chart where you are discussing staffing options and trying to determine if there is enough staff in place for the workload of your project.

Other than the first time, only when updating the project organization chart will the project manager produce a new chart. Project managers use a presentation format such as PowerPoint to create this chart. It is stored as part of the document control system for long-term archiving and is accessible by any interested stakeholder on the project.

CROSS-REF   See Chapter 14 to learn more about how to create and use this project organization chart.

FIGURE 4.3

An advanced organization chart for a project team.

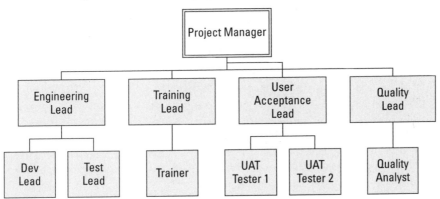

Introducing the Project Proposal

The purpose of the *project proposal* is to capture the requirements of a project in a usable format for bidding on a project. When companies do not have the in-house expertise or use contractors for their project work, they turn to outside companies to help fulfill that need. The project proposal should contain all the details on how to assemble the project. The contracting company bids on the work based on that information. The communication aspects of this project proposal are important because if anything is missing, the companies that are bidding on the work are doing so without all the information. When project managers create the project proposal, they must look at this bid document from a communication perspective and ensure that everything is included. If any portion is missing, the bidding companies may end up turning in a low bid, not realizing that the project proposal is incomplete. In that case, the project manager or their company was not communicating effectively with the bidding companies and it will cause future problems on the project. A perfect project proposal document equals a perfect bid process.

> **NOTE** The Project Management Institute's knowledge area for this tool is the Integration area. There are no other knowledge areas for this tool.

> **ON the CD-ROM** We have included a sample of the project proposal tool in the Integration folder. Use this as a guide to create your own version of this tool.

> **TOOL VALUE** Project proposals present ideas and project suggestions to create a project of which senior management will accept or reject.

The proposal document is beneficial from a communication perspective because it communicates the understanding of the proposed project to anyone involved in the project. When developing a project proposal that is complete and thorough, the estimates received from the contracting companies should closely match the expectations of the project. If it does not, you could run into some project issues involving schedule, costs, scope, and quality, to name a few. Some companies that produce many proposals a year have a template, sometimes called a boilerplate, to follow, which comprises a large portion of the proposal document before adding specific project information. Therefore, the individual project managers or team members assigned to develop the document only have to add the specifics to the project to the document and it is complete.

A well-written project proposal communicates the information needed to create the future project in such detail that there will be little need for additional information. To develop a proposal of such high quality requires dedication and effort that will save time and cost on the project itself. A well-written proposal makes it easier for the bidders to define how they are going to do their work and their estimate on costs and schedule. With a poorly written project proposal (meaning poor communication occurs to the bidders), the estimates will vary and have wide ranges. If the bidding companies are not clear when they start the project, this will cause many issues during the bidding process and throughout the life of the project.

Table 4.4 represents a typical project proposal table of contents. The documents can vary slightly from industry to industry and require much of the same information regardless of the project type. The bidding process is relatively the same across the different industries.

TABLE 4.4

Example of a Project Proposal Table of Contents

Section	Description
1	Introduction
2	Proposal Submission Deadlines
3	Terms and Conditions
4	Pricing
5	Warranty Coverage
6	Mandatory Conditions
7	Mandatory Evaluations Criteria
8	Background and Current Practices
9	Project Description
10	Project Overview
11	Requirements Section
12	Project Structure
13	Technical Requirements
14	Critical Success Factors
15	Project Management Plan
16	Deliverables
17	Work Packages
18	Project Cost Control
19	Integration with Other Projects

The project proposal should represent the total scope of the project. Knowing the total scope of the project allows the bidding companies to estimate correctly their costs of completing the project because there is nothing else in the project that they do not know about.

One technique that helps both the bidding company's personnel and the proposal company's team members is for the proposal project manager to hold a bid review meeting and communicate the information in the project proposal document to the different companies involved in the bidding. The project manager can address any question or concern the bidding companies may have with the project proposal document at the meeting. This meeting allows full disclosure and communication of the details of the project. The project proposal may not have had this information clearly described; and, therefore, bidding companies will have questions they want addressed before they start the bidding process. The proposal team members should also join these bid review sessions to ensure they are comfortable, and understand their roles and the bidding company's roles on the project. The project manager will have other opportunities to communicate the project proposal to the team members, but if they do join the bid review meetings it allows them to hear the various questions and concerns the bidding companies have before the project ever starts. Many times, the company puts a small number of its resources on the project when bidding the project work; therefore, communication among the team members who work at the proposing company and the team members at the bidding company can be challenging.

The project proposal can have many names in the project management field, such as statement of work, bid document, request for quotation, and request for proposal, to name a few. Different industries can have other names, but the core function of this document is the requesting of outside services to perform the work activities of the project.

Planning to use a project proposal

Long before the consideration of a project proposal document the company that has the skills to do the project may not have enough of the resources to work on the project. A software development company may have a need for a new utility system. They have the skills, but they may not be able to afford to take them off the development project they are currently creating. They would go through a "Make/Buy" process to analyze whether it would be better to make the new utility system in-house (Make) or contract the work (Buy) to an outside company. If the decision was to contract the work outside of the company, the project manager must write a project proposal. In preparing to create the proposal, the project manager should start this process by communicating with the procurement group to initiate the development of the project proposal template. In working with this group, the project manager will understand and learn about the legal aspects of contract management, determine what companies he or she can use, and the process involving procurement. Then, the project manager would start to gather a limited number of team members to assist him or her with the creation of the document. After performing these steps, the project manager has adequately prepared for using a project proposal on their project.

Before you can use a project proposal tool, you must formulate a plan. In the "Planning Questions" section, we provide some initial thoughts and ideas to help you start thinking about how to use this tool on your project.

Planning Questions

1 *When would you write the project proposal tool?*
At the start of the initiation phase of the project

2 *Who is going to use this tool, both from an input and output status?*
Upper management, owners, customers, executives, project manager, team members, subcontractor, outside contracting companies who are bidding on work, media, procurement group, legal team, contract teams

3 *Why are you going to use this tool?*

To communicate the work of the project to an outside company or group for bidding purposes, To frame the work of the project and use it as a guide throughout the life of the project, to monitor and test against, from a contract management perspective, with the outside companies

4 *How are you going to use this tool?*

Represents scope of project and therefore will use it to allow companies to bid on work, assists in documentation of contract terms and conditions for project, to respond to all bidding and contracting companies' questions and concerns through the bidding process, checklist to ensure everything is included for the scope of the project

5 *How will you distribute the information?*

Document format such as Microsoft Word document control system, e-mail, in-person presentations, bid meeting, regular mail, or courier

6 *When will you distribute the information?*

Once, for the official bidding of the project and only a limited time after that based on the procurement process. The distribution of this document is highly secure and formal. Legal actions may ensue if the project manager or team members do not follow the procurement rules and regulations.

7 *What decisions can or should you make from this tool?*

Scope decisions, cost decisions, schedule decisions, quality, resource, infrastructure, purchasing, leasing, environmental, engineering, design, and construction

8 *What information does this tool provide for your project?*

All project related decisions, such as the big three: scope, cost, and schedule

9 *What historical and legal information do you need to store?*

All interactions with all companies, Proof of correspondence between one company and evidence that it was sent to all companies, Lessons learned information, contract negotiations, all other legal aspects of the proposal/bid process

10 *What will be the staffing requirements (Role Type) to run and maintain these tools?*

Owner, project manager, designers, procurement staff, contract staff, and legal staff.

Reporting using a project proposal

When project proposals are required, it is often the business group or individual staff members within those business groups that actually create the physical document. Project managers are rarely involved in the development of the project proposal, but can be in some cases.

Normally it is too early in the life of the project to have assigned a project manager. These proposals may never actually become a project, so assigning a project manager too early often is expensive and a waste of time. Every company is going to have their individual processes for creating a project proposal document, and standard documentation to use depending on the type of project and the industry.

Depending on the company, the project proposal process could be quite different. In most companies, this is a formal process and the legal team and various members of upper management watch it closely.

The project manager will not have to report from the project proposal each week because it does not have project status information and as noted may not even be involved in the project until after the creator of the proposal completes it and it is ready for bidding. The project proposal is a one-time document used for generating the bids for the project and supports the contract and procurement management process as the bids are accepted. It is stored as part of the document control system for long-term archiving and is accessible by any interested stakeholder on the project.

CROSS-REF See Chapter 14 to learn more about how to create and use the project proposal tool

Introducing the Project Status Meeting

The purpose of *project status meeting* is to obtain and communicate status for the project. There are two types of status meetings on a typical project.

One type of status meeting is for the project team specifically, where each team member communicates the status on their deliverables and discusses any issues, concerns, or risks that they may have. These status meetings are normally weekly and are more like working "status" sessions than just pure status meetings. These meetings are one of the only meetings where the project team gets together each week and communicates about the project in person. These meetings are critical to the success of the project, and they must occur throughout the life of the project.

The second type of status meeting is a "customer" status meeting where you meet directly with the customers and communicate the overall status of the project. This second meeting should stay at a high level when possible, and you should limit the details.

For some projects, as the project manager, you may choose to have one large project status meeting where the team members work through the project deliverables, issues, and concerns in front of the customer. The project team can ask the customers questions pertaining to their specific areas of the project without having to go through formal communication channels. This meeting would be more effective on a monthly basis, where the issues are less and the customers are not hearing the day-to-day problems of the project. The negative side of having one large project status meeting is the fact of having no time for the team to work together without the customer present. The team may have issues, problems, and other concerns, and if they have no opportunity to work on these concerns outside of this one meeting the customers are going hear all the problems. We recommend keeping the two meetings separate to allow the project team members to work out their issues and allow you as project manager to incorporate all the issues into a status report you would like to present to the customers.

On the higher-profile projects that have media attention, project managers need to schedule *media-based status meetings*, where you and your team members are available to answer questions from the media.

NOTE   The Project Management Institute's knowledge area for this tool is the Integration area. The project status meetings are applicable to all knowledge areas.

ON the CD-ROM   We have included a sample of this project status meeting in the Integration folder on the CD-Rom. This is a guide to the first step in creating your own personal version of this tool. Your company or project may have specific requirements that will enhance this communication tool further; however, we believe this is a great starting point for the creation of this tool for your project.

TOOL VALUE   The project status meeting maintains the ongoing communication of the project between the team members. It keeps the owner up to date and keeps the communication between the owner and the project manager open.

The project status meeting is a decisive communication tools. The ability to pull all team members together once a week, twice a week, daily, hourly, or whenever the project requires them provides you, as the project manager, and your team members with the latest and most up-to-date information about the project. There is no other opportunity for you and your team members to get this much information about the project at one time other than in a written status report. And even in a written report, there may be areas not covered in the status report that would come out in a meeting. The communication aspect of getting everyone in a room is tremendous and allows for a lot of project information to flow between multiple people. Best practices require project status meetings on all projects, regardless of the industry or type of project.

Table 4.5 provides a typical project status meeting agenda. It contains the most relevant agenda items for most projects. The agenda of the meeting sets the tone and the format as to how the meeting will run. Using a formal agenda for a project meeting makes it easy to create meeting minutes from that agenda.

TABLE 4.5

Example of a Project Status Meeting Agenda

Agenda Item	Description	Owner / Responsible
1	Review Last week's Minutes	Project Manager
2	Review Current Action items	All Team
3	Review Project Schedule	All Team
4	Major Area Updates	All Team Leads

continued

TABLE 4.5 *(continued)*

Agenda Item	Description	Owner / Responsible
5	Review Current Budget information	Project Manager
6	Project Risks	All Team
7	Project Issues	All Team
8	Lessons Learned Information	All Team
9	Walk-ons	All Team

Project status meetings are extremely helpful for you, your team members, and your stakeholders. They provide the opportunity for the team to present status and work together on project-related issues. Project status meetings can be fun and have a playful atmosphere to them that will enhance morale and team relationships. Project managers are responsible for the mood and atmosphere of those meetings so they should take every opportunity to obtain as much information as possible but also make the meetings fun and enjoyable. Many times team members are interested in the overall direction and health of the project, and project status meetings are the team members' opportunity to acquire that information from you. During the week, project managers, for the most part, leave the project team members alone; so getting them all together to discuss accomplishments or next steps is important for both parties.

Getting the team members together on a regular basis to check status, discuss issues, risks, and next steps is critical to the success of the project. Without project status meetings, you can easily lose control of the project, and you could have project team members sitting around and not knowing how to proceed. Quite often, on software projects, you call status meetings weekly, but in some higher profile projects, it is common to see daily checkpoints. If projects are in situations that need immediate attention or management oversight, then daily meetings are required. A daily status meeting would be an exception to the rule and would occur only for a short duration while critical issues need attention. Projects would go back to regular status reporting (weekly) when the critical issues have resolution.

On most projects, weekly project status meetings are required. If project managers do not get together or tend to push off status meetings to more of a bi-weekly basis, they can lose sight of what is really happening. On the average project, two weeks is a long time-period to wait between status meetings and too long before getting updated project information.

There are many different examples of the various types of status meetings that project managers call on a regular basis. The communication aspects of these meetings can also vary. Project Managers should look at each of these meetings from a communication perspective and determine what status they want to communicate in each meeting. The following is a list of some common status meetings:

- **Daily checkpoint.** A daily meeting with most or all team members to discuss what is occurring on the project. This provides the project daily coverage, normally when there are pressing issues or concerns. The communication aspect of this type of meeting is tremendous because the customers hear how the project is progressing each day. If they have any issues or concerns, they have the opportunity to affect those issues.

- **Weekly project status.** The regular project status meeting occurs on a weekly basis. At this meeting, you will typically describe and record the project issues, risks, schedules, and budgets. The communication aspect of this meeting is beneficial because it provides a weekly look at the project, and the customers can track and maintain these components easily at the weekly level. Presenting all this information daily may be overwhelming to them, and be more of a negative communication experience than a positive one.

- **Weekly financial/budget review.** This is a weekly financial status and budget review. This meeting presents the opportunity for you and your customers to go over the finances of the project in detail and determine if the project is running over or under budget. Often this meeting can be bi-weekly or monthly, depending on the financial cycle of the project. If the project is over-running the budget, additional meetings may occur. The communication aspect of this meeting is also beneficial because the customers will know and understand each week how the project is progressing from a financial perspective. Normally, project dollars calculate on a monthly basis, but doing a weekly sync will allow the project customers to have a tighter control or handle on the forecasts for the project. Even though the money does not change on a weekly basis, keeping a grasp on how the team is forecasting it is important.

- **Monthly media status.** This is a monthly checkpoint with the media, where the project manager, the communications manager, and possibly the owner's representative discuss the updates and status of the project. The media outlets from around the city, town, or country can attend this meeting. This meeting provides the media with the latest status of the project and gives them ongoing and regular communications. When working with the media, it is important to be as open as possible when providing them the project information they want. Preparation for this meeting is an absolute necessity.

- **Monthly management checkpoints.** This is normally a high-level status meeting where the project team, led by the project manager, discusses the status of the project. This meeting includes schedule, budget, issues, risks, key requests, or challenges. The communication aspect of this meeting is beneficial because these meetings are more of a monthly status, high-level checkpoint to provide executives with a project status that they normally would not receive on a week-to-week basis. The benefit of this kind of meeting, from a communication perspective, is that you are providing senior-level decision makers the information about your project that can change its course. Whether it be additional resources, additional dollars — whatever the case — these monthly meetings are helpful in communicating this type of information.

Project status meetings are critical to the success of the project because of their communication value. The ability to present project information from the team members working the actual deliverables of the project is invaluable. Customers can hear firsthand the issues of the project and can work together with the team to resolve them.

Planning a project status meeting

In preparing to create and use a project status meeting, the project manager must first determine the type of project meeting he or she will call. Once they determine the type of meeting, they must create a good project agenda. Every project manager should determine the structure and format for the meeting and determine if they will have any co-leaders or presenters at the meeting. Other planning aspects of the project status meeting include booking the actual meeting room, determining the duration of the meeting, securing any audio or video equipment or special equipment, determining the attendees, preparing for any food or beverages. and starting to prepare the meeting materials.

Before you can create the project status meeting, you must formulate a plan. In the "Planning Questions" section, we provide some thoughts and ideas to start you thinking about how to utilize the tool on your project.

Planning Questions

1   *When would you create, develop, or have the project status meeting?*
Every reporting cycle throughout the project there will be at least one project status meeting (normally weekly), On-demand and as needed meetings will occur.

2   *Who is going to use this tool, both from an input and output status?*
Project manager, team members, clients or customers, executives, upper management, superintendent (construction)

3   *Why are you going to use this tool?*
To obtain and deliver project status information on a regular basis, to get the team members together to collaborate on project information, deliver project status information to customers or clients. analyze project performance, evaluate risks and issues, financial aspect review

4   *How are you going to use project status meeting tool?*
Capture project information from team members, Delivery project information to customers or stakeholders, update project metrics indicators, such as cost, schedule, issues, risks, and resource information

5   *How will you distribute the information?*
Document format such as Microsoft Word, e-mail, document control system, project presentation, in-person meetings, video conferencing meetings

6   *When will you distribute the information?*
Depending on the needs of project for frequency and after the actual project status meeting occurs

7 *What decisions can or should you make from this tool?*
Project schedule decisions, cost decisions, issues and risk decisions, quality decisions, resource decisions, scope decisions, and overall direction of project

8 *What information does this tool provide for your project?*
Update status information for the project in each of the major areas

9 *What historical and legal information do you need to store?*
All versions of status meeting minutes, agendas, and any possible recordings of presentation materials presented, lessons learned

10 *What will be the staffing requirements (role type) to run and maintain these tools?*
Project manager, team member, clerk, or scribe

Reporting from a project status meeting

On most projects, the project manager creates the agenda and format for the project status meeting. They own the agenda, the meeting minutes, the preparing for, and providing the contents of the meeting. It is expected of team members to show up, report status, and provide project-related information. On the larger projects where there are a number of project managers or there is support staff assigned, these staff members would be responsible for providing administrative support to the project manager, such as capturing and compiling the project meeting minutes.

Project status meetings normally occur weekly. On most projects, this rhythm meets the requirements of the customer. After the project status meeting is complete, you, or whoever is responsible for creating the meeting minutes, have 48 hours to produce them. If you wait any longer than that, the team members will have moved on in their work activities and may forget their new assignments or action items. It is important that you distribute the minutes as soon as possible after the meeting so this does not happen.

The project manager reports from the project status meeting using the meeting minutes each week. The project status meeting has a wealth of project information about the progress that occurred over the last week. The project manager creates the project status meeting agendas by using a document format. The status meeting agenda is stored as part of the document control system for long-term archiving and is accessible by any interested stakeholder on the project.

CROSS-REF See Chapter 19 to learn more about how to create and use project status meetings.

Introducing the Project Status Report

The purpose of the *project status report* is to communicate project information in a formalized method to the customers, upper management, and the team members. The project status report is one of the most common communication tools used on projects today. There are thousands of examples on the Web to choose from for your project. Most companies have standard project status reports. The project status report is a living, breathing document utilized throughout the life of the project. However, it is important that the report represent the latest status of the project at a given time. You should establish expectations with your customers that you will distribute the project status report to them on the same day each week. Once you set that standard, they will come to expect this regular project communication. The most common day each week is Friday, by end of business day (EOD). Friday's EOD is a common timeframe across most companies, and it provides management that "stake in the ground" date when everyone knows when they can obtain the latest project information. It is a great idea to establish that cadence of when to deliver the project status report at the beginning of the project and stick to that reporting cycle throughout. This will provide ongoing communications with your customers and stakeholders of the project.

NOTE The Project Management Institute's knowledge area for this tool is the Integration area. The project status reports are applicable to all knowledge areas.

ON the CD-ROM We have included a sample of the project status report in the Integration folder. Use this as a guide to create your own version of this tool.

TOOL VALUE Project status reports document the communications of the current project information among project stakeholders on an ongoing basis.

The project status report is the official plan of record for the project. This report contains all relevant project information with the latest status of each of the areas of the project. It is beneficial because it provides the information for you to discuss what is happening on the project with your team members or customers. You can set the expectation with your team members that they will discuss the contents of the project status report each week and report those same contents to upper management and customers. This allows the verbal report and the written status report to match and keep consistent the information about the project.

Figure 4.4 is an example of a summary level status report for use by any project. The data contained in the report stays at a high level with no detail at all. This is a common format for status reports in the project management profession today. There are thousands of different types of status reports. Your company, in most cases, will have a template for you to follow. Each status report will cater to the specific type of project and industry of the company managing the effort.

TIP Every project must produce a status report on a regular basis. Customers expect this regular communication from the project.

The project status report provides status of the project. Depending on the audience for the status report, the information can be quite detail oriented, or provided at a high level. The details within the report depend upon the person asking for the report and their requirements for project information.

FIGURE 4.4

A sample project schedule.

Example of Project Status Report (High Level)

Reporting Period: 4/14/2009 – 4/18/2009

Project manager: Bob Smith, PMP

Accomplishments this Period:

- Tech specs completed
- Design Started
- 5 Developer Resources hired and started on-boarding process

Scheduled Items Not Completed:

- Approvals obtained from customers
- Final Budget approved

Activities Next Period:

- Design to Continue
- Developers to continue on-boarding

Issues:

- None at this time.

Schedule Changes:

- None at this time.

Budget Changes:

- Project is running $5,000 under budget at this time.

Staffing Changes:

- None at this time.

Notes:

One of the best practices project managers can perform when working with project status reports is working with their customers and ensuring these reports meet their reporting and communication needs. This consists of a project manager sitting down with the customers, going over the report together, and modifying it to match the requirements of the customer. The customers may not be happy with the generic status report selected by the project manager or the project management office, and may have specific requirements in what they need to see about the project. Project managers cannot assume that a generic report will provide enough information for their customers. That assumption could cause some communication problems.

If you create your project status report with too much detail, then the senior-level management who are looking for summary level status will be lost in those details. They will not want to weed through all the detail information to find the particular status they are looking for. On the other hand, if your status report only summarizes the status information, you may have problems communicating this information to your team members or customers who are looking for the details. Your goal is to mix both detail and high-level information into a single project status report and communicate that information for your project appropriately.

Many times, when producing status reports the primary audience is upper management or customers and not someone looking for the granular details of the project. If those kinds of details are required, the individuals should be talking directly to you or the project team members working on the effort, and not looking for a report to obtain this information.

The information on a project status report has two main purposes: Action or Informing. When stakeholders receive the project status and realize that there are decisions or project-related items that they need to address (take action), they do so by reacting from the data provided on the report. Without a project status report, project issues could sit and, in some cases, negatively affect the project if not attended to. The other purpose of the project status report is informing customers and upper management of the latest status and project information. In this case, the project status report is to inform only and is not to make decisions or take action.

Two main audiences have a need for the project status report: one is the project team and the other is the customers or stakeholders. Each group has a different purpose for the report. The project team uses the project status report to report the latest project information and provide particular status updates on their specific areas of the project. The customers or stakeholders of the project use the information in the project status report to make project-level decisions.

 Let your customers determine how often you should deliver the project status report. In most cases, this is on a weekly basis.

Planning to use a project status report

In preparing to create and use a project status report, the project manager should first determine the reporting template he or she will use on the project. Most companies will have templates which they use but may require the project manager to tweak a little. The project manager should be sure to match the project status report with the weekly project status meeting agenda to ensure they are obtaining the information they need on a week-to-week basis. Project managers should ensure they review the minutes from the last meeting when preparing the next project status report, to ensure if there are any outstanding items from the last report they are either addressed or closed. The project manager would then have to set up and prepare for long-term storage of the reports or the inclusion of the report data into any company-level status report tool. There may be occasions in which the project manager produces a single project status report and then has to transcribe that report into a company-wide reporting tool for consolidation. Project managers must plan and prepare for this process if it is applicable in their company. Finally, the project manager must prepare how he or she will obtain the project status information, where they will acquire the data, and what sources can they utilize for finding the information. For example, each team lead's report will be an excellent source of project status information that that project manager will draw from on a regular basis.

Before you can create a project status report, you must formulate a plan. In the "Planning Questions" section, we provide some initial ideas answers to help you get started.

Planning Questions

1 When would you create, develop, and write the project status report?
From the first time status is collected and then throughout the life of project

2 Who is going to use this tool, both from an input and output status?
Everyone involved in the project will utilize this project status report to obtain the latest information about the project

3 Why are you going to use this tool?
To provide the latest status information about the project on a periodic basis, guide the execution of the project deliverables, to identify, monitor, and control project issues and risks, keep the project on schedule and within budget

4 How are you going to use this tool?
Gather the updated project status information from team members and other stakeholders, develop and distribute the actual status report to all interested parties

5 How will you distribute the information?
Document format such as Microsoft Word, e-mail, document control system, presentations, in-person discussions

6 When will you distribute the information?
On a periodic basis, where projects often report on a weekly cadence for reporting status, a larger project can go bi-weekly or in some cases monthly. The distribution needs will vary from project to project and customer to customer

continued

continued

7 *What decisions can or should you make from this tool?*

Project-level decisions such as project schedule decisions, resource decisions, cost decisions, and issue and risk decisions can be made from this tool.

8 *What information does Project Status tool provide for your project?*

The latest project status of all major aspects of the project such as scope, schedule, costs, issues, and risks

9 *What historical and legal information do you need to store?*

Previous versions of status reports, lessons learned information, and final status report

10 *What will be the staffing requirements (role type) to run and maintain these tools?*

Everyone involved in executing and controlling the project is involved in developing or adding information to the project status report on a periodic basis

Reporting using a project status report

You may not actually develop the physical report (although in most cases you probably will), but the responsibility for creating and delivering the project status information is yours. On large projects, you can have an administrative assistant, a junior project manager, or a team member assisting you in creating and compiling this report. It is important for the project manager to communicate constantly with the team to acquire data to include in the status report.

Figure 4.5 shows a detailed project status report. Your project stakeholders who feel they need to understand all the details of the project will request this type of status report from you. This format is common for status reports in the project management industry because additional information or details are required.

NOTE   Many times, there is little or no activity on a project over the weekend, so in most cases status reporting is not required during that period. If deadlines are in jeopardy and work occurs over the weekend, in many cases the project manager must report project status updates on those days as well. This occurs rarely and for short periods until the project is back on track.

FIGURE 4.5

This figure represents a sample project status report used in the industry today.

Example of Project Status Report (Detailed):

Date:

Project name: _____   **Prepared by:** _____

Week ending: _____

Planned Tasks for Reporting Period:

Task Name:	**Start Date:**	**End Date:**	**% Complete**
Start foundation	1/22/08	3/12/08	22%

Status	**Resources Assigned**
On Track	Bob, Sam, Frank

Conflicts:

- The project is running into a conflict with the Jones project and resources from each project are running into conflicts on which project they should be working on. Joe Smith is spending 100% of his time on the Jones project but has to develop the detail designs for the walls on the east side of the building next week. We have to determine what we can do about this conflict, or the project could have an impact hit to the schedule.

Action Plans:

- Jon Hellenbeck needs to spend time securing the extra budget for the second structure. The change request approved, but the funding taken longer than expected. Jon will spend next week on this funding delta and report back to the stakeholders.

Next Week's Planned Activities:

- Complete foundation work, on the Jones and Smith structures.
- Johnson Stones Company is delivering 20 ton of bedrock for the main structure. That is due next Tuesday between 4–5pm. Larry Smith will be on site receiving the rocks and will sign all relevant paperwork.

Other Notes:

Introducing the Team Charter

The purpose of the *team charter* is to provide the project manager the ability to communicate to his or her team members a high-level of project information regarding their assignments, timeframes, budgets, and assumptions and constraints they will have on the project. This document also acts as a staffing plan and allows the project manager and upper management to determine when team member's allocations and assignments are required for the project and allows them to staff the project accordingly. The team charter describes any special training or skills the team members will need in order to accomplish the scope of work on the project. As the resource managers makes the resource assignments on the project, the project manager works closely with them to ensure that the team members have the skills required, or are able to take the appropriate training to gain the skills required, to complete the work activities of the project.

NOTE The Project Management Institute's knowledge area for this tool is the Integration area. There are no other applicable knowledge areas for the team charter.

ON the CD-ROM We have included a sample of this team charter in the Integration folder on the CD-ROM. Use this as a guide to create your own version of this tool.

TOOL VALUE Team charter communicates the various staffing plans for the project and provides the information to the team members to plan their assignments across multiple projects.

The team charter documents the human resource requirements for the project. There are no requirements for equipment or material covered in this document. The resource plan tool covers the requirements for equipment and materials. The team charter document communicates to the team members the scope, goals, and objectives of the project as well as all other relevant assignment information. The team members are able to review the team charter and determine exactly their roles and responsibilities as well as timeframes that are associated with the project.

CROSS-REF See Chapter 9 for more information on the resource plan.

Companies will have different names for this document, but each will represent the same purpose, that is the allocation of the team members across the project. Without a team charter, a project team could have challenges and have a hard time coming together and understanding what their roles and responsibilities are on the project. The team charter document is a valuable tool for every project regardless of the size of complexity in bringing the team together to a common understanding of the project.

Table 4.6 represents a typical team charter table of contents. This document is common across projects and provides an excellent reference for communicating the purpose, goals, resource schedule, roles, budget, and project staffing information. The sections of this document cover all areas of staffing and are updatable.

TABLE 4.6

Example of a Team Charter Table of Contents

Section	Description
1	Project Name
2	Team Charter Description
3	Purpose / Goals of Project
4	Resource Time Period (Start and Finish)
5	Project Resource Roles
6	Project & Resource Budget
7	Team Members List
8	Project and Team Interfaces
9	Assumptions and Constraints
10	Resource Skills and Training Requirements
11	Approvals

NOTE Another name for the team charter is the staffing plan.

The team charter is valuable as a communication tool for every project manager because it captures and communicates the following information:

- For resource requirements, you can use the team charter document to communicate the project's resource requirements with consulting companies where you are looking to hire resources. An example would be a software project, where a project manager is trying to fill a resource gap of ten testers from outside the company. The project manager has documented this requirement in the team charter; and, therefore, when using that document to discuss the needs of the testers it contains all the information you need. Having the information in one place makes it easier to communicate the needs to all parties involved in providing the resources for the project.

- The team charter represents a commitment to set aside the resources for the project by both upper management and the sponsor. Each of the parties sign off on the document before the project begins, so the project manager understands that from the beginning they have the resources they need to be successful. Failure to sign off on this document can spell trouble for the project because it could mean the required resources are not available or may not ever be available for your project.

Project managers must understand how they are to use the staff assigned to them and therefore must communicate those needs into a team charter document. Very few functional managers will allocate staff members to projects without the full understanding of their utilization on the project. Functional managers in most companies have management authority and are the direct hiring or

HR manager of the team members. Functional managers are sometimes called "Line manager." Knowing this information allows functional managers to determine future projects and other opportunities for their staff members. When every project manager in an organization utilizes a team charter, the combination provides a complete staffing plan for that organization. Functional managers can look holistically across all projects and all resources and plan accordingly.

Another advantage of the team charter document is the cost information it captures. After compiling the resource information into a single document, it becomes easy to review and communicate the project's cost information when required. Budget and staffing decisions can be determined from this document. Any future projects that are close or of a similar size to this effort, they can utilize the information in the team charter document to plan accordingly for their staffing needs on the project.

The team charter document becomes valuable not only to you and to the functional managers, but also to the team members themselves. The team members can plan their work activities and estimate how long their assignment will last based on the information within the document. Team member assignments can be across different projects; the team charter document provides every team member their view on the workload for this particular project. In order for the project team member to benefit from this document, the team charter must contain enough detail that there are no questions on their assignments. The team charter needs to communicate clearly and concisely, and it must be easy to retrieve the staffing assignment information. Each team member should understand his or her role and timeframes as to when their assignments occur on the project and can get the information directly from the team charter document. It provides them an excellent planning tool to understand when they will be working on this project and available for others.

Another area where the team charter document provides value is the gathering and compiling of the training and specific skills required for the project. In the team charter document, the project manager would describe their training requirements for each team member or the specific skills to perform the roles. For example, on a software project, the project manager can require data warehousing experience, and the team members that are filling the roles may not have this experience. In this case, the project manager would document the training he or she would expect the team members to take to satisfy this requirement.

Planning to use a team charter

In preparing to create and use a team charter, the project manager must first determine what roles, skills sets, budget, and timeframes are needed on the project. After understanding this information, the project manager documents this information into the team charter to communicate with the organization's functional managers the staffing requirements for the project. The project manager then works with those managers to fill the roles required for the project. This process normally has the project manager working with a number of different functional managers that are responsible for specific roles in the company. Therefore, a project manager would go to a developer manager, tester manager, and design manager to fill the project's staffing needs. As part of the project's budget planning process, the project manager uses the team charter to understand the expected costs for the resources and can plan his or her budget on staffing accordingly. After performing these planning steps, the project manager has adequately prepared for using a team charter on their project.

Before you can create the project team charter, you must formulate a plan. In the following "Planning Questions" section, we provide some initial thoughts and ideas as to how we would respond to each of the questions. Each of these responses provides you with guidance so that you can start thinking about how you want to utilize the tool on your project.

Planning Questions

1 When would you create, develop, and write the team charter tool?

During project initiation process, and in the planning process when determining the team members for the project

2 Who is going to use this tool, both from an input and output status?

Project manager, team members, subcontractors, upper management, client, or customers, functional or resource managers

3 Why are you going to use this tool?

To provide the project team members their specific roles, responsibilities, and assignment durations on the project, provide a staffing plan to senior management and resource managers as to what the specific resource needs will be on the project

4 How are you going to use this tool?

Document the requirements of the project's staffing needs, work with resource managers to fulfill those needs; drive the resource cost and estimating for the project, report the team charter document to all relevant stakeholders

5 How will you distribute the information?

Document format; such as Microsoft Word, e-mail, presentations, document control system, in-person discussions

6 When will you distribute the information?

Beginning of project, on-demand as resources roll on and off the project

7 What decisions can or should you make from the team charter tool?

What resources are required, types of resources, costs decisions based on billing rates, schedule resources, dependencies decisions, training and skill set decisions

8 What information does this tool provide for your project?

All the information pertaining to the human resources allocated to the project

continued

continued

9 *What historical and legal information do you need to store?*
The document itself and lessons learned information

10 *What will be the staffing requirements (role type) to run and maintain these tools?*
Project manager, resource, or functional manager, team members, clients or owners of project

Reporting using the team charter

The project manager creates the team charter document. Even though you are not the sole contributor to the document, you do hold accountability for its accuracy and ongoing upkeep. Project team members rely on this document to understand their commitments to the project. Functional and resource managers rely on the document to understand when they have committed their resources to your project. Therefore, the communications aspects of this tool range from the project team member to upper management and customers, to functional or resource managers all involved in your project one way or another. The project manager reports updates to the document throughout the project when adding or removing resources from the project.

There is no formal reporting of the team charter from a standard project reporting perspective. This is not a document reported on weekly, or even on a monthly basis; it is more of an on-demand type document and heavily utilized in the managing of the project. The team charter document is stored as part of the document control system for long-term archiving and is accessible by any interested stakeholder on the project.

 The team charter is almost identical to the project charter, except that it focuses only on the team members and their skills.

 See Chapter 21 to learn more about how to create and use the team charter tool.

Introducing the Team Lead's Report

The purpose of the team lead's report is to communicate to the project manager the status from each team leader's area of the project. The team lead's report often carries the same information as the regular project status report, but the main difference is that it only contains information from a single area of the project, not the complete project. Each team leader communicates the issues, risks, and concerns from their portion of the project through a team lead's report. On a typical software development project, the team lead's report would come from each of the four team leaders, leading the development, training, user acceptance testing, and the release areas of the project. After you have this information from each of your team leaders, you can consolidate it into a single project status report for the project. The team lead's report also provides you with the ability to review specific details of each area and offer your assistance where applicable. If you are reading the report and discover an issue or risk in a particular area, you can work directly with the team leader to determine how to resolve it. The teams lead's report is beneficial in that it enables you to focus specifically on one particular area of the project at a time, while not overwhelming you with all information at once. Customers, when needing more detail, will often look for the project manager or one of the team leaders to communicate the specific team lead's report for a specific project area.

NOTE The Project Management Institute's knowledge area for this tool is in the Integration area. This tool is applicable to the other knowledge areas as well: Scope, time, cost, quality, human resources, communications, and risk.

ON the CD-ROM We have included a sample of a team lead's report in the Integration folder. Use this sample as a guide to the first step in creating your own personal version of this tool. Your company or project may have specific requirements that can enhance this communication tool further; however, we believe this is a great starting point for the creation of this tool for your project.

TOOL VALUE Team lead's report communicates the detailed status of an individual area on the project.

The team lead's report is an excellent communication tool because it contains the updated project status of only one area of the project, not the whole project. Whether it is labor, electrical, plumbing, or quality, the team lead's report describes in detail what is occurring in his or her particular area only. There is often mention in the report of the dependencies with other areas of the project, which is beneficial to the project manager to ensure that he or she keeps the communication active between everyone involved, but the real value to this type of report is that it is only one area of the project.

The team lead's report encourages discussions between the team leader and you as the project manager. The formal communications between these two roles should occur at a minimum weekly to ensure that there is proper communications and so nothing falls through the cracks. The team lead's report allows you to feel that you are connected and have the information you need from that particular area without being constantly involved. That is extremely important on a large project where you do not have all the details on each area but must have an understanding of how a project is progressing as a whole.

Figure 4.6 represents a typical team lead's report. This report is an example from a construction project that represents the activities from the week ending 2/22/2008 time period. This example has enough detail to determine exactly what is happening in that area but does not provide full project status — which is the true benefit of this report!

As each of the areas on the project submit their team lead's report, you as project manager are responsible for consolidating the information and determining the overall status of the project. The team leaders could each report their portion of the project in one particular color, based on how their area is progressing, but as project manager, you make the final call as to the overall status of the project. You also make the decisions on what information from each of the reports you will place on the master or overall project status report.

FIGURE 4.6

A sample team lead's report from a construction project.

Date: 2/18/08
Project Name: Jones Apartment building Construction
Weekending: 2/22/08

Prepared by: B. Smith
Project Status Report Submit Date: 2/20/08

Planned Tasks for Reporting Period:

Task Name	Start	End Date	% Date	Status	Resource Assigned
Start Foundation on North Wall	2/20/08	3/12/08	75%	On Track	Bob, Sam, Frank
Budget secured for additional floors	2/18/08	2/18/08	100%	Complete	Bill
Complete Forms on South Wall	2/22/08	2/22/08	100%	Complete	Bob, Sam, Frank

Conflicts:

- Structure rebar was not delivered on time for foundation build, but expected next Tuesday, on site. This is on track and not expected to be delayed.

Current Action Plans:

- Plan to reschedule foundation construction due to delay in delivery of rebar.
- Final hiring of plumbing Crew scheduled for end of next week for underground utilities.

Next Week's Activities:

- Order site crane for delivery on 3/12/08
- Remove forms from North wall

The timeframes for the team lead's report are the same as the overall project status report, normally weekly. The team lead's report requires that each leader send their status information two days before the project status report is due for final reporting. That buffer gives you time to compile all the information into the final weekly status report and ask questions if there are any miscommunication or misunderstandings.

The project team members value a team lead's report because the information stored about a particular area of the project allows them to understand exactly what is happening in that area. If the project manager does not have a great deal of insight in a particular area of the project, the team lead's report provides an excellent update on the status of that area. If there is a situation where a team member from one area has to provide information to another area, the team lead's report is an excellent tool for these purposes. For example, if a software developer misses a deadline to provide data to a software tester, the test lead would add that issue to their team lead's report. If the software developer who missed the deadline read the test lead's report, he or she would know that their missed deadline is being escalated to the project manager. In this case, that developer would be able to react to the missed deadline and possibly resolve the issue in a timely manner. Without the team report, there could be many project's issues going unnoticed and potentially causing negative impacts without the project manager or teams members really understanding why.

CROSS-REF See Chapter 2 for further details around communicating with virtual teams.

Planning to use a team lead's report

In preparing to create and use a team lead's report, the project manager must first develop or utilize a status report template for the team lead's report. The project manager would then go over the team lead's report with each team leader to ensure that they are comfortable with it, and understand what information they need to provide to them. The project manager in those discussions would also work with the team leaders and set the timeframes as to when they will send them the team lead's report for overall consolidation into the master project status report. After performing these steps, the project manager has adequately prepared for using the team lead's report on their project.

Before you can create the team lead's report tool, you must formulate a plan. In the following "Planning Questions" section, we provide some initial thoughts and ideas as to how we would respond to each of the questions. Each of these responses provides you guidance to start you thinking about how you would utilize the tool on your project.

Planning Questions

1 *When would you create, develop, and write the Team Lead's Report tool?*
It is normally during the initiation process then throughout the life of project when updates are required

2 *Who is going to use this tool, both from an input and output status?*
Everyone involved in the project will utilize the team lead's report to gather and obtain information about a specific area of the project. Project managers will use the report for consolidation into the master project schedule.

continued

---

continued

3 *Why are you going to use this tool?*

To provide the latest status information about a single area of the project on a periodic basis, to guide the execution of the project deliverables within a specific area, to identify, monitor, and control project issues and risks in a specific area, monitor and ensure that area of the project is running on schedule and within budget

4 *How are you going to use this tool?*

Gather the updated project status information from team leads and incorporate this information into the overall status report, determine the issues or concerns in that particular area of the project

5 *How will you distribute the information?*

Document format such as Microsoft Word, e-mail, document control system, presentations, in-person discussions

6 *When will you distribute the information?*

On a periodic basis, where the project is often weekly as a cadence for reporting

7 *What decisions can or should you make from the Team Lead's Report tool?*

Project area specific decisions such as area schedule decisions, resource decisions, cost decisions, issue and risk decisions...etc.

8 *What information does this tool provide for your project?*

Latest project status of a single area of the project such as scope, schedule, costs, issues, and risks

9 *What historical and legal information do you need to store?*

Previous versions of team lead's status reports, lessons learned information (these reports can be effective in litigation)

10 *What will be the staffing requirements (role type) to run and maintain these tools?*

Project manager, team leader for each specific area of project, project team members

Reporting using a team lead's report

The individual team leaders of the different project sub-areas (construction for example: there are electrical, mechanical, plumbing and survey crew) are responsible for creating their individual team lead's report. As the leaders of these specific areas, they are closer to the details and therefore responsible for compiling their information and reporting to the project manager on a periodic basis. Usually once a week, but it could be daily. The project manager has the overall responsibility of compiling this information into an overall project status report for reporting on the project.

 Each week, project managers can obtain the lessons learned information from a team lead's report.

 See Chapter 21 to learn more about how to create and use a team lead's report.

Summary

We explored project communication tools that support the Integration knowledge area. The tools in this chapter help you improve your project communications across the nine knowledge areas. Tools such as the project kick-off meeting, project management plan, and the project status report should all be utilized to ensure you are communicating as effectively as possible. The project status report will be the most common tool to project managers across every industry. Ensure you talk to your customers about how effective the current project status report is in providing them the information they need to make project decisions.

All the tools in this chapter are beneficial across the nine knowledge areas, and project managers should utilize as many as possible on their projects.

Chapter 5

Defining Communication Tools to Manage Project Scope

I n this chapter, we explore project communication tools in the Scope Management knowledge area. Scope management consists of the processes and procedures that you use to ensure that the project consists of all the work required and only that work required creating and completing the project. The Scope Management knowledge area encompasses scope planning, scope definition, scope verification, and scope control. It would also include creating and maintaining the work breakdown structure. Project managers monitor the scope management processes throughout the life of the project. It is important to understand that without solid project scope, you cannot have a good solid project.

Projects that are scope driven do not focus on the time or cost aspects of a project, but are focused on quality and scope, and delivering the exact customer requirements. Scope driven projects try to match the customer's requirements 100 percent. An example of a scope driven project would be an airplane engine. In aerospace, the engine cannot fail and therefore regardless of the time or cost it takes to complete this project, it will continue until it passes all quality checks.

In this chapter, we present the tools used to control project scope and assist project managers with managing that scope. These tools are helpful in communicating effectively on your project. Each tool has its own purpose and use in the Scope knowledge area.

Introducing Customer Requirements

The purpose of using a *customer requirements* tool is to capture, document, and communicate the customer's wants and needs for the project. Projects should not start or become even projects without some form of requirements document from the customer. The customer requirements document acts as the main repository for storing their requirement information. There are many different formats of customer requirement documents and each differs from industry to industry and from company to company. The Internet has many different samples of customer requirements documents for anyone to choose from and then to implement on their projects. When using the documents, it is beneficial to understand the type of project you will be managing and the specific customer requirements template to utilize for that type of project. Even in the software world, an application development project and a data warehouse project for example are two completely different types of projects, and therefore the methods in which you capture customer requirements for them would be different.

No project can be successful without some form of documented customer requirements. The communicating and the capturing of these requirements between a project analyst and the customer are important in this process. The customer requirements document is the end result of those communication sessions. Relative to the total duration of a project, capturing the customer requirements only takes a short amount of time, and not usually the longer portion of the project. These sessions occur during the planning phase of the project, when the project team is getting its directions on what it is all about and what the customers are looking for on the project.

NOTE   The Project Management Institute's knowledge area for the customer requirements tool is the Scope Management area. This tool can be associated with the following knowledge areas: Integration, Time, and Cost.

ON the CD-ROM   We have included a sample of this customer requirements tool in the Scope folder. Use this as a guide to create your own version of this tool.

TOOL VALUE   Use the customer requirements to communicate and document the customer's wants and needs to the project team members.

The project requirements analyst captures and documents customer requirements and then provides them to the project team members to help them to understand the project. This customer requirements document provides detailed descriptions of the business needs including the scope, goals, and objectives for the project. One important concept to understand is the customer requirements do not capture the technical aspects of the project; those are in the various technical documents. The customer requirements document contains only the business needs from the customer. In gathering this information, there are often a series of back and forth discussions and communications occurring between the requirements analyst and the customer all the while capturing and understanding this information. This dialog continues until all requirements are complete and all parties approve the document.

Table 5.1 shows an example of a table of contents for a customer requirements document. The document contains all the sections required to capture and communicate the business needs of the project. This example is generic and can work for most industries across most projects.

TABLE 5.1	

Customer Requirements Table of Contents

Section	Description
1	Scope
2	Customer Needs (Goals and Objectives)
3	Policies and Procedures Definitions
4	Business Use Cases and Scenarios
5	Business Unit Interactions (if applicable)
6	Deployment Requirements
7	Output Reporting Requirements
8	Operational Requirements
9	Testing Requirements
10	User Documentation and Training Requirements
11	Requirements Priority Matrix
12	Assumptions, Risks, and Constraints
13	Participating Markets

The project requirements analyst gathers and stores the customer requirements in a series of one or more documents. Customer requirements do not often span more than one document usually, especially in software projects, but can, depending on the size and complexity of the project. In these cases when the customer requirements span multiple documents, the project requirements analyst is responsible for ensuring the information is stored together and the information is available when required.

The capturing of customer requirements is a special skill set and is difficult to do effectively or efficiently. Most project managers do not enjoy or feel comfortable capturing these requirements to the level the project team will need to create the product. Some do, but often in software projects specifically, they leave the gathering and capturing of the project requirements to the experts and requirements analysts on the team who specialize in this type of work. The requirements analyst communicates directly with the customers and is responsible for capturing and creating the customer requirements document.

A customer requirements document is a communication tool used throughout the life of the project. In the beginning, the document is used to collect and communicate the customer's requirements. As the project progresses, it is a tool that project team members refer to and compare what is being created to what the original requests were of the project.

Capturing and collecting customer requirements are often challenging tasks. In the following example, the first item in the list demonstrates how to capture customer requirements information.

Good requirement from customer: Customer would like a ten-story apartment building constructed in downtown Seattle on XXX Main Street. **Assessment:** When the construction crew starts their work, they know exactly where to go, and how big the building is going to be. When the team completes work on the fifth floor of the building, they know they have completed approximately half of the project.

Bad requirement from customer: Customer would like the team to build an apartment building, in downtown Seattle. **Assessment:** The problem with this requirement is the team would have no idea how high to build it, or where even to start the building project.

If the customer does not state clearly what he or she wants, a project team will struggle to deliver what the customer wants. Project managers play a vital role in this process, because they have to be diligent in what requirements they accept and must constantly communicate the requirements of the project back to the customer to ensure everyone is in full agreement. If the project manager accepts incomplete requirements, this could have a huge affect on the project's schedule and budget. Especially, in the construction phase when the customer finds out what the team is building is incomplete or, worse, completely wrong. The project team could end up building one thing whereas the customer has something completely different in mind.

One of the skills that a project manager must acquire is the ability to recognize when the customer requirements are complete or not complete, and if not, what is still missing? Doing this enables the project manager to go into these projects with their eyes wide open and situations such as the example noted above will occur less often or not at all. When a project manager fully understand the requirements of the project there is far less of a chance that he or she will run into requirements problems.

Planning to use customer requirements

During the planning process when preparing to use a customer requirements tool, the project manager must first ensure that they have the correct requirements analyst staff on the team to capture the requirements. Next, the project manager works with the project requirements analyst(s) and goes over the customer requirements template to make sure that it is in an acceptable format and applicable for this type of project. The project manager then works with a customer to ensure that they will dedicate themselves to the project while responsible for delivering the requirements to the project requirements analysts. The project manager then sets up various requirement-gathering sessions between the requirements analysts and the customer to ensure that everyone is engaged in requirements gathering. After accomplishing these tasks, the project manager has adequately planned for using the customer requirements tool.

Before you can create the customer requirements tool, you must formulate a plan. In the following "Planning Questions" section, we provide some initial thoughts and ideas as to how we would respond to each of the questions. Each of these responses provides you guidance to start you thinking about how you would utilize the tool on your project.

Planning Questions

1 When would you develop and write the customers requirements document?

During the initiation process of the project into the planning process

2 Who is going to use this tool, both from an input and output status?

Customers, owners, executives (summary only), project manager, team members, subcontractors

3 Why are you going to use this tool?

To communicate to the project team the work involved to develop the product

4 How are you going to use it?

Understand and document user requirements. Calculate potential cost and schedule estimating, resource team sizing, resource requirements (non-human), risk analysis, quality analysis, procurement activities from the requirements gathered

5 How will you distribute the information?

Document format such as Word, document control system, and e-mail

6 When will you distribute the information?

After the requirements phase completes, as needed after that especially when modifications occur to the document, or major scope changes occur on the project.

7 What decisions can or should you make from this tool?

Determine what is in and out of scope, possible schedule, and cost decisions, types of quality assurance requirements, resource and staffing requirements, purchasing decisions, facilities decisions, risk decisions, and business decisions

8 What information does this tool provide for your project?

Customer requirements and expectations, detailed descriptions of product from customer's perspective

9 What historical and legal information do you need to store?

All requirements and changes to requirements (approved, non-approved) for legal reasons, lessons learned (what was captured, what went right about the requirements, what went wrong?)

10 What are the staffing requirements (role type) to run and maintain these tools?

Project manager and team members

Capturing customer requirements is critical to the success of the project.

Reporting customer requirements

On most projects, a project requirements analyst creates the customer requirements document. After created, the project analyst communicates the project requirements to the other team members, including the project manager, so everyone is completely aware of their roles on the project. The project requirements analyst works throughout the project as the customer liaison and communicates between the team and the customer until the project completes. The requirements analyst who captured the customer requirements initially has the knowledge that the project team members will heavily rely on to build the project and will not have to continually go back to the customers for more information.

There is no regular reporting of the customer requirements document on the project because the document does not contain project status information. However, the project manager does report on the progress of the work defined in the requirements document using a different form, like a project status report. For example, the project manager reports that various stages of the document are complete, and reports the approval and sign-off of the document to the point that no future changes can occur without the change control process.

The project team members utilize the customer requirements document throughout the project as a reference guide and support for further technical documentation. The project requirements analyst creates the customer requirements document using a document format, and it is stored as part of the document control system for long-term archiving and is accessible by any interested stakeholder on the project.

 See Chapter14 to learn more about how to create and use the customer requirements tool.

Introducing the Feasibility Study

The purpose of the *feasibility study* tool is to identify whether the concept of a project is viable. Senior management or the owners must decide whether the concept advances into a project. Most industries use feasibility studies to communicate the concept and idea to senior management and owners of the proposed projects. A feasibility study determines if the proposed project is feasible, cost beneficial, and aligned with the company strategic goals. Feasibility studies can range from small to complex, and depend on the industry and type of project requested. All projects should have a feasibility study that documents the concepts, ideas, and suggestions proposed for the project. An example of a feasibility study is a new cancer-fighting drug. The feasibility study would include the components that create the drug, any negative side effects, cost analysis, risk analysis, and research that support the combination of the components into a new single drug.

 The Project Management Institute's knowledge area for this tool is the Scope Management area. There is one other associated knowledge area for this tool: Integration.

ON the CD-ROM We have included a sample of a feasibility study in the Scope folder. Use this as a guide to create your own personal version of this tool.

TOOL VALUE A feasibility study lowers the risk of companies spending unnecessary time and costs on a project that has minimal or no long-term benefits.

A feasibility study is a great communication tool for any project because it provides the details for the decision makers as to whether the project is worth continuing. This study can save a company time and money on an initiative that may not benefit the organization. Project managers are rarely involved in the creation of a feasibility study, but do tend to use the document in assessing the study or as reference in executing and controlling phases of the project. For example, during a project execution, if the feasibility study has indicated some initial test results were positive, the project manager during the project's testing phase would want to ensure that they create the same test scenarios so that the results match. This feasibility study is a reference point in this case, to prove that the project and the study are testing the same parameters and are in alignment with each other. A project manager can also use the feasibility study to learn and understand the decisions made that lead to the approval of the project. The feasibility study lets the project manager and team members understand what the owner was thinking when approving the project that is helpful when working on the project. This allows the project manager to manage the project more efficiently while also being aligned with the customer or owner's thinking.

Table 5.2 shows a table of contents for a feasibility study document. As you can see this is a document that expects enough detail in the various sections that the feasibility review board will have enough information to allow them to make a go or no/go decision.

TABLE 5.2

Example of a Feasibility Study Table of Contents

Section	Description
1	Executive Summary
2	Background Information
3	Description of Current Situation/Problem
4	Description of Proposed Idea
5	Project Timelines
6	Feasibility Review Board
7	Go/No-Go Decision

The communication process of this feasibility study is twofold. The first is that the requestor takes the initial idea and request through the feasibility process and obtains approval from the feasibility review board. In completing the feasibility study document (refer to Table 5.2), the project requestor follows the company-defined process and completes the template. Once complete, the second communication aspect of this tool is the project manager and the project requester's review of the proposed project idea and associated feasibility study.

Feasibility studies come in all shapes and sizes and span across all industries. Some of the actual examples of feasibility studies include the following:

- **Upgrading a software/hardware system.** A company in this case would initiate a new feasibility study to develop a new system that would closely align with the organization. This could be a new payroll systems, HR system, financial system, or CAD system to name a few.

- **Designing a new aircraft.** An aerospace company can initiate a new feasibility study that documents a new airplane design that includes costs, lifespan, manufacturing time, market need, and safety considerations.

- **Planning to purchase new software.** A company in this case can initiate a new feasibility study that documents a new software package for the company. This documents the benefits to the software, the return on investment (ROI), the costs, and the impacted users. It could also include a make or buy decision.

- **Constructing a new building.** A development company in this case can initiate a new feasibility study that proposes a new design for a building, including costs, construction considerations, environmental concerns, and construction timeframes.

Many types of feasibility studies are implemented across a variety of industries. These types are often broken into different categories such as business, government, technical, and so on. Here are some types of the feasibility studies used today:

- **Schedule feasibility study:** Analyze how long it will take a project or process to complete and what the go-no/go decision point will be.

- **Organizational feasibility study:** Analyze what the impacts would be on cost and resources if the company decides to reorganize their current resource base.

- **Legal feasibility study:** Analyze whether it is worth pursuing a particular litigation.

- **Technical feasibility study:** Analyze if a technical concept will work within the current environment.

- **Cultural feasibility study:** Analyze whether offshore teams and onshore teams can communicate and effectively execute a project.

- **Construction feasibility study:** Analyze if it is cost effective to construct a building, based on the height and location.

- **Environmental feasibility study:** Analyze whether the environmental conditions at a particular location are suitable.

NOTE Projects require justification before approval. Feasibility studies provide the detail and information that decision makers need to approve or reject a project.

Planning to use a feasibility study

In planning and preparing to use the feasibility study tool, the project manager must first read and understand the document, which may include going over the document with the requester or originator. In these discussions, the project manager may want to have a team lead or two with him or her, so they are each getting the background and history of why the requestor is proposing the document. A technical resource may also be required in case the requestor has technical questions. After obtaining this information, the project manager then creates a project charter document to obtain official approval to proceed with the project. After performing these steps, the project manager has adequately prepared for using a feasibility study on their project.

Before you can create the feasibility study tool, you must formulate a plan. In the following "Planning Questions" section, we provide some initial thoughts and ideas to start you thinking about how you would utilize the tool on your project.

Planning Questions

1 *When would you create or write this tool?*
Initiation stage of project, before planning begins

2 *Who is going to use this tool, both from an input and output status?*
Project manager, team members, developer, customers or client, senior management, feasibility review board, financial manager, risk manager

3 *Why are you going to use this tool?*
Justify the proposed concept or idea of a possible new project

4 *How are you going to use the feasibility study tool?*
To obtain knowledge on approval factors and criteria, cross reference and validity check while managing and executing the project

5 *How will you distribute the information?*
Document format, e-mail, possible presentation(s), document control system, presentation

6 *When will you distribute the information?*
As soon as it is complete, and after that on demand

7 *What decisions can or should you make from this tool?*
Type of project charter to create, decisions on assumptions and constraints applied to project, possible decisions on success criteria, and the go-no/go decision on the concept

continued

continued

8 *What information does this tool provide for your project?*

Factors on approval decisions, guide on the direction of the project, reference, authority on going ahead with project

9 *What historical and legal information do you need to store?*

Lessons learned, feasibility study document itself, justifications behind the approval decisions, possible backup, and research material on studies to support document

10 *What will be the staffing requirements (role type) to run and maintain these tools?*

Project planner or initiator (requestor of proposed project), possible support from project manager

Reporting using a feasibility study

The project customers or owners are responsible for creating and communicating the initial reporting of the feasibility study. The analyst working in the business or for a particular owner leads the creation of the document. The reporting of this feasibility study occurs officially once during the formal feasibility study review meeting. In this meeting, the customers, upper management, and the staff gather to review the document, ask questions, communicate, and collect the additional facts they need to make a go-no/go decision. The upper management resources comprise the feasibility study review board.

The project manager does not have to report from the feasibility study each week because it does not contain any status type of information. The feasibility study uses a document format and is stored as part of the document control system for long-term archiving and is accessible by any interested stakeholder on the project.

CROSS-REF See Chapter 14 to learn more about how to create and use the feasibility study tool.

Introducing the Scope Definition Document

The purpose of the *scope definition document* is to create a project document that communicates in detail the project's scope. The scope definition document drives the project's work activities. Both the customers and the project team members utilize the scope definition document throughout the project as the mechanism to confirm the approved scope of the project. The project manager compares the project change requests to the contents of this scope definition document and determines if the work has already been included in the project. If it is not in the scope definition document, it is a new request to the project and is processed accordingly.

The project manager should communicate the scope definition document throughout the life of the project to team members and customers. From evaluating change requests to working the deliverables of the project, constant communication is occurring between the project manager, customers, or clients, on the contents of this document. Project managers should communicate the project's scope on a regular basis, often during a weekly status meeting or working meetings and ensure that at all times everyone agrees and understands the project's scope. Because of all the details within the scope definition document, it also becomes valuable to the project manager in controlling the execution and the delivery of the project. The project manager can refer to this document when needing to understand the scope of the project or discussing the scope with customers and team members.

NOTE The Project Management Institute's knowledge area for this tool is the Scope Management area. There is one other associated knowledge areas for this tool: Integration.

ON the CD-ROM We have included a sample of a scope definition document in the Scope folder. Use this as a guide to create your own version of this tool.

TOOL VALUE The scope definition document defines all the work on the project that drives the team members to project completion. The project team should avoid work that is not contained in this document.

The scope definition document describes all the actual work deliverables for the project. Any customer, client, or upper management staff, if they require, can read this document and understand the project's scope. The project manager and team members communicate the details of the project using the scope definition document throughout the life of the project. This communication discussion would include the deliverables, scope issues, quality, risks, and the work breakdown structure.

TIP The more time spent developing the scope document, the less time spent executing the project.

Because the scope definition document is the driving force behind the project, all other documents are reliant on this document. Therefore, understanding this document and communicating it efficiently to everyone involved in the project is in the project manager's best interest. This is no small task and something project managers will need to spend considerable time and effort doing. Best practices for the project manager is to be proactive with this document, communicate regularly with it, and ensure everyone is onboard by obtaining sign-off and approval on the document.

CROSS-REF See change requests in Chapter 4 for more information on this tool.

Table 5.3 shows an example of a scope definition table of contents. There are many important sections of this document, each applicable to most types of projects, across any various industries. As you can see from the document, there are many categories covered. The most important section is Section 18 in the document, the scope section. Notice that there are actually two scope sections to identify what is in and out of scope. Most projects have both *in scope* and *out of scope* items, and it is important to explicitly identify both to the customer. The customer needs to be clear on what the project will and will not deliver. The other sections of this document are also important, such as risk events, quality procedures, communication plans, budget, and schedule, but from a scope perspective, the two scope sections are critical.

TABLE 5.3

Example of a Scope Definition Table of Contents

Section	Description
1	Overview
2	Vision of the Solution
3	Vision Statement
4	Business Environment and Justification
5	Business Opportunity
6	Business Risks
7	Customer or Market Needs
8	Scope Statement and Purpose
9	Success Criteria
10	Project Background and Objectives
11	Project Description
12	Major Features
13	Scope and Limitations
14	Scope of Initial Release
15	Scope of Subsequent Releases
16	Limitations and Exclusions (Out of Scope)
17	Work Breakdown Structure
18	Scope Items Defined
18.a	Scope Items
18.b	Out of Scope Items
19	Risk Event Items
20	Quality Procedures
21	Communication Plan
22	Resource Assignment
23	Project Budget
24	Timetable/Schedule
25	Stakeholder Profiles
26	Project Priorities
27	Operation Environments
28	Assumptions, Constraints, Dependencies

The scope definition document is a large, complex document that covers many aspects of the project. Items covered include background, customer needs, business risks, vision statement, major features, and scope, out of scope, project priorities, and the operating environment. Without this document, your project team members would struggle in understanding the project's work items, and what specifically they need to work on. You as the project manager would struggle to determine what you have to deliver as well. You would have questions: What are the parameters and assumptions do you have to deliver the project? How do you actually execute and control major areas of the project? Without a scope definition document, your team members could be literally sitting around waiting for their next assignments and they would have no idea how to move forward after completing what you gave them. A scope definition document provides team members with the next deliverable and keeps them constantly engaged on the project.

It is critical that the customer or owners approve the preliminary scope definition document before the project initiates. This approval officially defines the scope of the project and an agreement between the customer and the project team as to what the deliverables will be for the project. If any additional changes occur after the approval, they are candidates for change requests and need to follow that process accordingly.

The scope definition document plays a major role in managing and controlling project change requests. The project manager uses this document throughout the project to control the changes requested by comparing the new requests to the current scope and then evaluating the differences. If the request is new, then it follows the change request process already established for the project. If the requested change is existing and in the approved scope of work, the project manager notifies the requestor that the item is already in scope and confirms on the schedule when the work is scheduled to be complete.

Contract-based projects that utilize outside contracting companies for staffing purposes will use the scope definition document to help create the project's contract. It is normally an addendum to the actual contract itself. The scope definition document is then part of the project's legal contract and managed accordingly. In doing this, the contract stays free of scope, and the scope items are in the scope definition document where they belong.

Planning to use a scope definition document

In planning and preparing to use the scope definition document, the project manager must ensure that the customer has approved and signed the customer requirements document first, before starting the process of creating a scope definition document. That customer requirements document is the basis for developing the scope definition document and requires approval and completing before any other work starts. After the customer requirements document is complete, the project manager must then prepare his or her project team to develop the scope definition document. This requires hiring the right-skilled person(s) to be able to transform the customer requirements into the actual scope of the project. After selecting and obtaining the skilled team members, the project manager works with them and determines the applicable template for creating the scope definition document. Once the project manager creates the template, the project manager then schedules the series of meetings with the customers and team members and jointly completes the template and defines the scope of the project.

Before you can create a scope definition document, you must formulate a plan. In the following "Planning Questions" section, we provide some initial thoughts and ideas to start you thinking about how to use the tool on your project.

Planning Questions

1 *When would you create and write the Scope Definition Document tool?*

After the customer requirements document is complete, during the planning process, before work starts on the project

2 *Who is going to use this tool, both from an input and output status?*

Everyone on the project will use at least a part of this document, as it is the driving force of the project

3 *Why are you going to use this tool?*

It defines all the work on the project and helps the project manager control that work; It is the guide for the entire project.

4 *How are you going to use is tool?*

Documenting the scope items and work deliverables into a central repository acts as the single source of product scope and planning tool for project teams, determines resource assignments, estimates project costs, and schedule, determines potential risks, determines potential quality issues, determines materials required, supports project communications

5 *How will you distribute the information?*

Document format such as Microsoft Word, e-mail, document control system, presentation format

6 *When will you distribute the information?*

After initial creation, as approving the changes to the scope and the document requires updating, and throughout the project as requested, most often the document is moved to a document control system for access by anyone requiring it

7 *What decisions can or should you make from this tool?*

Any decisions relating to the scope management and control of the project

8 *What information does the tool provide for your project?*

This document is comprehensive and covers most areas of the project including time and budget

9 *What historical and legal information do you need to store?*

Lessons learned information, scope definition document itself, change requests applied to the document and to the project (could be different), Issues resolved, risks reduced, Resource assignments made.

10 *What will be the staffing requirements (role type) to run and maintain these tools?*
Project manager, team members, risk manager, cost manager, quality manager, resource manager, procurement manager, communication manager, and legal team when applicable

 Understanding your scope from the start of the project will provide you the justification you need to prevent additional scope from creeping into your project.

Reporting using a scope definition document

There is no regular weekly reporting of the scope definition document because it does not contain project status or progress information. The reporting of the scope definition document occurs once when the project team members and customers gather and approve the document for the project. When changes occur or the document needs re-approving for some reason, the project manager will redistribute it to the original approvers for re-approval. The project manager often uses the scope definition document in project reports or formal presentations, but that is usually as a one-off reporting and not part of any weekly or monthly reporting cycle. The document is stored as part of the document control system for long-term archiving and is accessible by any interested stakeholder on the project.

 See Chapter 17 to learn more about how to create and use the scope definition document.

Introducing the Scope Management Plan

The purpose of the *scope management plan* is to ensure that there are processes and procedures in place to create, maintain, and control project scope. As described earlier in the scope definition document, managing and controlling the project's scope is one of the project manager's most important tasks and therefore having a tool such as a scope management plan can help guide and benefit the project manager tremendously.

The scope management plan includes scope planning, scope definition, the work breakdown structure (WBS), scope verification, and scope control. One of the more important areas is scope control. Scope control is the process and procedures that the customers or project team follow to add or remove value (scope) on the project. The scope management plan also documents how the project utilizes the acceptance and verification processes as well as being important in identifying the processes to develop the project's work breakdown structure. The work breakdown structure splits the larger elements of the project into smaller easier to work with subelements. By using a work breakdown structure, you can increase the chance of project success.

The important aspect of working with the scope management plan is to ensure the project manager communicates the process and procedures within the plan as soon as the document is complete.

The project manager must communicate the various processes and procedures within the document with the customers and team members to ensure they are comfortable and understand how the project manager will manage the scope on the project. The change request process especially requires the project manager to go over that section with the customers and make them aware of how to process changes. When the project manager takes this proactive approach and communicates the plan, doing this prevents any surprises or concerns that a customer may have in following the processes when requesting a change. If the project manager waits to communicate the change request process at the time the first change request occurs, this will cause issues and concerns to the customers. They do not want to be learning a new process when they are trying to get a change in on the project.

NOTE   The Project Management Institute's knowledge area for this tool is the Scope Management area. The associated knowledge area for this tool is Integration.

ON the CD-ROM   We have included a sample of this scope management plan in the Scope folder. This is a guide to the first step in creating your own personal version of this tool. Your company or project may have specific requirements that will enhance this communication tool further; however, we believe this is a great starting point for the creation of this tool for your project.

TOOL VALUE   Use the scope management plan to establish processes and procedures to control project scope.

There are five major aspects of a scope management plan, and each assists the project manager with managing the project's scope. Project managers should take the time to ensure that their projects have a scope management plan in place at the beginning, so that there are no issues or concerns throughout the project managing the project's scope.

Table 5.4 shows the table of contents for a scope management plan. This table of contents covers each of the major areas of scope management. The planning, definition, verification, and control areas are all essential components in managing and handling the project's scope. Project managers should be proactive in each scope management area and should cover all areas with as many details as possible when developing the document. After obtaining approval on the document, the importance of it becomes obvious the first time the customer wants to make a change to the project. When that change request occurs, the project manager and project team have a documented process to follow and handle the change preventing any negative impacts to the project.

TABLE 5.4

Example of a Scope Management Plan Table of Contents

Section	Description
1	Project Overview
2	Scope Planning
3	Scope Definition

Section	Description
4	Work Breakdown Structure (WBS)
5	Scope Verification
6	Scope Control

The scope management plan benefits both the project manager and the team members by describing in detail the processes and procedures they will follow in managing and controlling the project's scope. Both the customers and project manager need a process to guide them when working with their customers in the planning and defining of the project's scope. Within the scope management plan, it should have enough detail that the project team and their customers will know exactly what is required of them to complete this process. For example, when customers or upper management ask for a scope change (add or remove value on the project), the project manager will follow the process defined in the document to process the change. When customers or the project teams try to manage scope without a process it could have the customers going directly to team members asking for changes that may or may not be possible. This takes time away from team members to perform the work on the project and in most cases is disrupting to them. Another area of the scope management plan is the scope verification process. This process describes how the customer has the opportunity to verify the scope they requested for the product. It also documents the processes and procedures they have to undertake to approve or reject the scope. There is a communication aspect of the scope verification process that project managers must handle carefully. Project scope is a sensitive area for most customers, especially during the later stages of the project when it comes to accepting and rejecting scope items. During this process, the customers feel like they have most of the control and it is the project team's responsibility to meet their needs and requests for the project, based on the project scope. This is acceptable in most cases. Some customers are quite good about this and work closely with the project team to achieve the goals of the project. Other customers take a much harder line and become quite difficult with the project team members when finalizing and approving scope items. During the scope verification process, the customers can be demanding and hard to please, other times the approval process can go easily. Project managers in both cases must communicate with the customers and ensure that they are scheduling meetings, distributing status, and communicating regularly with everyone involved during this critical time. Otherwise, this delicate situation in some cases can turn out to be difficult for the customer and the project team members if the project manager does not manage it correctly.

The scope management plan also documents the change management process. The change management process can actually prevent the customers, designers, or owners from submitting too many unnecessary change requests by establishing the change control process and procedures that they must follow to submit any changes. When documenting and developing the scope control section (Section 6 in Table 5.4), project managers should make the process difficult enough that customers or owners will not ask for random changes as often as they would without a process, however easy enough, that the customers feel they can process change requests without a lot of red tape.

The five processes of scope management interact with each other throughout the life of the project. During the planning phase, there will be identification of new scope items and the determination of how they fit into the project. The five components are:

- **Scope planning:** Creating a document that includes definitions, verification, and controlling of scope items on project.

- **Scope definition:** A scope statement is the basis for all project decisions.

- **Scope verification:** Acceptance and approval of scope items by stakeholder, customer, and owner.

- **Scope control:** The scope change control process is established and monitored throughout the life of the project.

- **Work Breakdown Structure (WBS):** Breakdown of work items into smaller and more manageable deliverables.

 Scope management is critical to a project's success.

Planning to use a scope management plan

When planning to use the scope management plan, the project manager must first work with the team members to determine how they jointly will control the project's scope. Because the scope management process is all-inclusive, it is going to require the team's full efforts to work together and monitor closely or the project will never be successful. For example, if a team member takes on additional scope work from the customer without telling the project manager, it leaves the project manager unaware of the change and in less control of the project. Additional scope can add cost as well as time to the project. With few exceptions, there should be no work effort without some additional compensation in either cost or time or both allowed to the project. In the planning process, the project manager must establish the direction with the team members that all scope additions will go through the change control process. After determining from a team's perspective how they will handle scope changes, the project manager will then approach the customers to ensure that they understand the scope management process completely. This includes how and when to introduce scope changes, how scope is verified, and any other steps in the scope management process. Part of that same discussion with the customer will include their reporting requirements, including special reports they want to review, timeframes on when to send them, and any special reporting requirements. For example, one customer wanted a count of all scope change requests every week, so the project manager agreed to generate that report for the customer. In this example, when the project manager captured the reporting requirements early in the planning process, it allowed the project manager the time to produce the reports the customer desired. After performing these planning and preparation steps, the project manager is adequately prepared to use the scope management plan on their project.

Before you can create the scope management plan tool, you must formulate a plan. In the following "Planning Questions" section, we provide some initial thoughts and ideas to help you start thinking about how to utilize the tool on your project.

Planning Questions

1 *When would development of the scope management plan occur?*

During the initiation process (phase) of the project, the scope management plan is created as to how the project will handle scope changes and modifications.

2 *Who is going to use this tool, both from an input and output status?*

Upper management, owners, executives, project manager, team member, subcontractors, media (TV, radio, newspapers)

3 *Why are you going to use this tool?*

To communicate the scope, goals, and objectives of the project

4 *How are you going to use this tool?*

Upper management will use documents to decide whether to proceed with the project, determine cost estimates, determine schedule estimates, determine proposed solutions, and determine resourcing needs. Project manager will use it as an authorization to acquire the team members and utilize the budget allocated to the project.

5 *How will you distribute the information?*

Document format such as Microsoft Word, document control system, e-mail, in-person presentation

6 *When will you distribute the information?*

When selling the project to upper management or customers who need to approve the project, project kick-off meeting, and on-demand

7 *What decisions can or should you make from this tool?*

Upper management or customers make go/no go decision on the project, schedule decisions, cost decisions, resource and scope decisions

8 *What information does this tool provide for your project?*

Describes the project, provides an idea how long it may take, how much it may cost, identifies technical challenges, provides comparisons of similar projects, if applicable

9 *What historical and legal information do you need to store?*

The scope management document itself. Lessons learned information.

10 *What will be the staffing requirements (role type) to run and maintain these tools?*

Customer or sponsor, senior management, possibly the project manager

Reporting using a scope management plan

In most cases, the project manager and the team jointly create the scope management plan for the project. When the project is small, the project managers themselves can create the scope management plan for the project. If the company has an existing template, then the project manager can use that template, making adjustments where necessary to suit the needs of the project.

There is no formal reporting of the scope management plan each week because it does not have project status information. At the beginning of the project, there would be a one-time walkthrough of the scope management plan with the customers and team members who are seeking approval and acceptance of the plan. Other than that, the scope management plan is more of a reference guide, used by the owner, project manager, and team members, and therefore does not require the formal weekly reporting. The scope management plan uses a document format for its creation and is stored as part of the document control system for long-term archiving and is accessible by any interested stakeholder on the project.

 See Chapter 14 to learn more about how to create and use this tool.

Introducing the System Requirements Document

The *system requirements document* captures the technical requirements for a project. This type of document tends to be software focused if the project has a heavy technical component to it. The document needs to describe what the customer is requesting in technical terms.

NOTE Some companies call this document "system requirements," some call it the "technical requirements," and other companies have different names. The most important thing to remember, regardless of the name, is the type of information within the document and the type of project where it is used.

The system requirements document often matches closely with the business requirements document. On most projects, there is a one-to-one mapping table between technical requirements and business requirements. For example, when a customer states a business requirement that he would like to see a weekly report that indicates the budget forecast, the technique requirement is the creation of a weekly budget forecast report. This mapping table ensures that every business requirement has a corresponding technical response. One of the most important goals of the document is the mapping between the two different requirements and ensuring that the specific requests of the customers have a technical solution.

The communication of a system requirements document is two-fold: one for the customers to make sure the requirements meet their requests and the other for the team members to understand what they are to create for the project. The one document meets two different needs. Therefore, it requires the project manager to communicate the same information to both customers and the project team members to ensure everyone is on the same page. When presenting the systems requirements document to the customers and senior management it would be at a summary level, not detailed at all, because the document itself can get quite complex, and they would rarely want that kind of detail explained to them. The details of the system requirements document would be generally for the team members only, who need it to create the product of the project.

NOTE The Project Management Institute's knowledge area for this tool is the Scope Management area. The other knowledge area associated with this tool is Integration.

ON the CD-ROM We have included a sample of this system requirements tool in the Scope folder. Use this as a guide to the first step in creating your own personal version of this tool.

TOOL VALUE Value of a system requirements document is to document and describe in detail the technical components of the project's solution for the designers, developers, and testing team members.

During the design and development phases, the project team members will use the system requirements document to understand the technical aspects of the project and what it is that they have to build. Project managers should ensure that all team members who need to utilize the system requirements document have access to it. In some cases, this may mean calling meetings and bringing multiple team members together to review the document, e-mailing or adding the document to the document control system, and doing whatever they need to ensure the people who need it do actually have access to it.

Table 5.5 shows an example of a table of contents for the systems requirements document. The template covers many aspects of the technical aspects of the project and when completed becomes a very comprehensive document for the project team members to work from.

TABLE 5.5

Example of a System Requirements Table of Contents

Section	Description
1	Document References
2	Sign-off Section
3	Document Conventions
4	Business Procedure Mapping
4.1	Business Requirements Identification
4.2	Business Process Analysis
4.3	Initial System Requirements Summary
5	System Description
5.1	System Overview
5.2	System Objectives

continued

TABLE 5.5	*(continued)*
Section	**Description**
5.3	System Process Specifications
5.4	System Constraints
5.5	System Risk/Impacts/Assumptions
5.6	System Interfaces
6	User Interface Designs
7	Source System Model
8	Functional Processes
9	Functional Process Model
10	System Operational Requirements
11	System Deployment Requirements
12	Context Diagram
13	Conversion/Migration Needs
14	Data Communication Requirements
15	Inter-Project Dependencies
16	Testing Requirements
17	Report Requirements

The system requirement document requires sign-off and approval from the project team and in some cases, the customer, before it becomes final. Because the documentation and details contained in this document become the final solution, the project manager must obtain approval and sign-off from everyone required before releasing it to the design and technical teams for creation of the product. The project should not move forward until the project manager obtains all approvals and those approvals are stored in a safe location, in most cases, the document control system.

Most of the time, the technical aspects of software projects do not require customer's approval, unless they specifically ask for it, or have a technical background to be able to understand the contents of the document.

When covering the mapping between business requirements and system requirements, the project manager and team members should understand the importance and the close ties these two documents have to one another. A missed business requirement can mean a missed system requirement and therefore more than likely a missing functionality in the final product. When creating a mapping between these two types of requirements (business and system), it provides and communicates to the customer the exact understanding of how the business requirements map to the system requirements. In doing this mapping, the project team members and customers will have a better understanding of how the requirements end up being in the final product.

Listed below is an example of a business requirement and its mapping to a systems requirement:

- **Business requirement:** Capture customer contact information within a software application.

- **System requirement:** Develop Visual Basic Screen that allows user input of personal contact information. The form should be web enabled and have all relevant security features contained within it. The screen should be red and have the ability to add, delete, and edit any entries.

The project team members while developing the system requirements document will need to understand if the customers are looking for minimum requirements or recommended requirements for their product. This is important because if the project team members spend a lot of time and effort capturing information that is not needed or never utilized (such as capturing recommended requirements when the project can only afford minimum requirements) then the project team members have wasted that time and effort. The team could have been working on the next step in the project after the system requirements were complete.

Listed below are definitions of minimum requirements and recommended requirements on a typical software or systems project:

- **Minimum requirements:** Documents the lowest requirements needed to make the software usable at all. The system requirements document should state that if users are running the software under the minimum requirements, they will not be getting the best experience out of the software and therefore may have unexpected problems that a more robust system would not experience. These minimum requirements are just guidelines and not rules and are put in place to give the users the best possible experience with the minimum application.

- **Recommended requirements:** Includes the details involving what are the "recommended" requirements for a system, and when a user has the hardware to match those requirements the software should run in an ideal state. When users have the recommended hardware to run the application it should provide the best possible performance to the user.

Planning to use a system requirements document

In planning and preparing to use a system requirements document, the project manager should first ensure the project has the correct resources in place to map the business requirements to a technical solution. (This skill set is not easy to obtain, and doing so requires a person that knows the subject and can communicate well with the customers.) The project manager then works with the analyst who will create the system requirements document and go over the template to ensure it is applicable to the type of project. The requirements analyst will adjust the template accordingly. The next step is for the project manager to ensure that the customer's business requirements are complete, to be able to use and start the development of the project's system requirements. If the document is not complete, the system requirements document cannot finish. It can be started but not finished until the business requirements are complete and approved. Doing so could cause major rework on the project. After performing these steps, the project manager would have adequately prepared for using the system requirements document on their project.

Before you can create a system requirements document, you must formulate a plan. In the following "Planning Questions" section, we provide some initial thoughts and ideas to help you start thinking about how you would utilize the tool on your project.

Planning Questions

1 When would you create, develop, or write this tool?
During planning and requirements phase, before design or technical details required for development, also when requirements change

2 Who is going to use this tool, both from an input and output status?
Project manager, client or customer, team members (specifically system analysts), subcontractors or specific skill areas

3 Why are you going to use this tool?
Capture, document, and understand technical information about the project to apply to the design of the product, determine cost, and schedule impacts for the project

4 How are you going to use this tool?
Create design and development deliverables for project

5 How will you distribute the information?
Document format, such as Microsoft Word, document control system, and e-mail

6 How often will you distribute the information?
Once, as needed if any major changes occur in requirements

7 What decisions can you make from this tool?
Technical decisions, constraints and assumptions, preliminary staffing requirements or skills sets required, cost decisions, schedule decisions

8 What information does this tool provide for your project?
All technical requirements of project

9 What historical and legal information do you need to store?
Lessons learned information, technical decisions, technical assumptions, or constraints, requirements document

> **10** *What will be the staffing requirements (Role Type) to run and maintain these tools?*
> System analysts, designer, project manager, owner, developers, testers, subcontractors

> **NOTE** System requirements are critical to capture and bring a team to a common understanding of the technical aspects of the project.

Reporting using a system requirements document

The system analyst(s) assigned to the project develops the system requirements document. The analyst(s) works with the developers and designers when creating the document so they have an understanding of the project and are not surprised by the document when they receive it. The system requirements document stores technical information about the project, not status information, so it is not reported on. There is a one-time approval and sign-off meeting when first creating the systems requirements document so the project team approves it officially. The approval and sign-off meeting enables the project team members to individually approve the document allowing the project to move to the next phase.

At the beginning of the project, the system requirements document is reported and approved, and then stored as part of the project regular documentation. The system requirements document contains more reference and technical information about the project than any other document. The system requirements document is stored in the document control system for long-term storage and assessable by any interested stakeholders.

> **CROSS-REF** See Chapter 15 to learn more about how to create and use a system requirements document.

Introducing the Work Breakdown Structure

The purpose of the *work breakdown structure* is to ensure that the project includes and identifies all the work items needed to complete the project successfully without the addition of any unnecessary work elements. The work breakdown structure breaks down the work into manageable work packages. The project manager uses it to define the total scope of the project. It can include the description, cost, time, risks, quality, resources, and scope of each activity (work package). Within each work package, the work breakdown structure assists the customers and team members in identifying the deliverables of the project.

> **NOTE** The Project Management Institute's knowledge area for the work breakdown structure is the Scope Management area. The Scope area is where the project team creates the work breakdown structure; however, everyone uses it throughout the entire project.

> **ON the CD-ROM** We have included a sample of a work breakdown structure in the Scope folder on the CD-Rom. This is a guide to the first step in creating your own personal version of this tool. Your company or project may have specific requirements that will enhance this communication

tool further; however, we believe this is a great starting point for the creation of this tool for your project.

TOOL VALUE The main value of the work breakdown structure is it identifies and defines all the work on the project. It also displays the work in a graphical presentation, which is easy to read and understand.

The work breakdown structure communicates all the work on the project. A single repository displays all the information for every deliverable on the project. Having a single source saves time and effort from searching for project information, and potentially saves cost. The top level of the work breakdown structure displays the organization of work elements and how they fall into large categories. For every element in the work breakdown structure, the parent and child of that element are easily identifiable.

Figure 5.1 shows the top level (the project) and the major level (the phases). This is the first stage in the development and reporting of a work breakdown structure. A "Project Management" element should always appear to the left of the major elements (Phase 1 in this example).

FIGURE 5.1

The project level and the top level of a WBS.

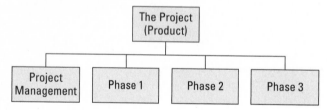

The work breakdown structure is helpful to all members of the project team. It can graphically display all the work items for the project on a single chart, making it easy to understand the deliverables of the project. Every project team member and stakeholder can utilize the work breakdown structure as a tool to understand what the project expects to deliver. If is also valuable to team members for them to understand what are their work items for the project.

The work breakdown structure provides detail on each activity, possibly not documented anywhere else in the project standard documentation. By developing a work breakdown structure dictionary, the project manager and team members can identify any work activities belonging to any part (category) of the project. This dictionary contains all the information about a work package (task). The project manager communicates the work breakdown structure to both the stakeholders and project team members throughout the life of the project and works to ensure that the project activities complete on time and on budget. When change requests occur on the project, the work items (tasks) become additions to the work breakdown structure.

The work breakdown structure should be a large part of defining, executing, and managing the changes to the project. The work breakdown structure is the skeleton and the foundation for every project regardless of the size and acts as the project's major support mechanism.

This list identifies some of the benefits of using a work breakdown structure on your project. The work breakdown structure does the following:

- Identifies all work on the project
- Includes a breakdown of the project into specific work packages
- Includes a mechanism to roll-up items to a parent level
- Accounts for all work on the project
- Helps identify all project deliverables
- Supports activity estimates, both in time and cost

When developing a work breakdown structure, consider the following points:

- It is a systematic breakdown of the project objective(s) in a hierarchical format
- The project level is the project objective and deliverable assigned to it
- The next level defines the major segments of the planned objective and deliverables
- Upper and mid-levels define a decomposition of the major segments into components
- Lower levels define the integration work to create each lower-level product
- By definition, the lowest level is the work package
- Each WBS element should represent a single tangible deliverable
- Each element should represent an aggregation of all subordinate WBS elements listed immediately below it
- Each subordinate WBS element must belong to only one single parent WBS element
- The deliverables should be logically decomposed to the level that represents how they will be produced
- Deliverables must be unique and distinct from their peers, and decompose it to the level of detail needed to plan and manage the work to obtain or create them
- Define deliverables clearly to eliminate duplication of effort within WBS elements, across organizations, or between individuals responsible for completing the work
- Deliverables should be limited in size and definition for effective control — but not so small as to make cost of control excessive and not so large as to make the item unmanageable or the risk unacceptable

The work package

A *work package* represents a work activity (task). The combination of all the work packages defines all the work on the project. Only defined work falls in a work package. The work package description should always have a verb and a noun (create the drawing, erect the steel, design module 6, and so on). Each work package communicates a deliverable to the project. A work package is the bottom level of the work breakdown structure.

CROSS-REF For a detailed description of the work package tool, see Chapter 10.

WBS dictionary

A work breakdown structure dictionary is the document that defines and describes all the work performed in each work breakdown structure element. The following list describes characteristics of a work breakdown structure dictionary:

- WBS should sufficiently describe the work of the project but does not need to be lengthy
- WBS forms or templates are helpful to all project stakeholders
- WBS can have different formats at different WBS levels
- Each WBS element contains enough description that they could be used alone to generate a comprehensive statement of work
- WBS addresses all work scheduled to be performed
- The WBS clearly and comprehensively defines the entire project's scope

The majority of the time the project team members only work on a single project. They may work on more than one project at different times. Each single project has the project defined at the top level of the WBS. The next level down (major level) identifies the type of breakout the project will have. This major level starts the main categories of a project. Below this level, the subcategories start and then are broken down into more detail. As an example, the major level could be broken down by location, resources, phase, system, subcontractor, or by module. The bottom level is the work package.

The functional levels of a work breakdown structure

When you develop a work breakdown structure, there will be many levels of summary and detail elements. Below the top level, you can have many varying levels under each one of the elements. You could have four levels under one element and seven levels under another element. There are four *distinct* levels of a work breakdown structure. The top level is the project level. The next level is the major level, and it defines all the major components of the project such as project management, phase, and module. All levels below the major level, except the work package level, are considered mid-level and are parents of the level below them. The bottom level is the work package level where it lists the project deliverables. The definitions of levels are as follows:

- **Project level:** Charter and project scope
- **Major level:** Project management, components, assemblies, subprojects, or phases
- **Mid-level:** Subassemblies
- **Bottom level:** Work package (such as a task or activity)

WBS in a project management office environment

When you work in a Project Management Office (PMO) environment, you work with multiple projects. A PMO generally oversees the management of the company or organizations' projects. The PMO group is responsible for the coordination, support, and policies of the company's projects. In most PMOs, the reporting is the summary of the integration of the projects and called the program level. Most work breakdown structures in a PMO environment roll up to the summary level for reporting to senior management.

Figure 5.2 shows a sample of a Project Management Office's WBS with the program at the project/program level and projects at the top level. Below the top (project) level in this example are various phases.

FIGURE 5.2

A program WBS with three projects at the top level.

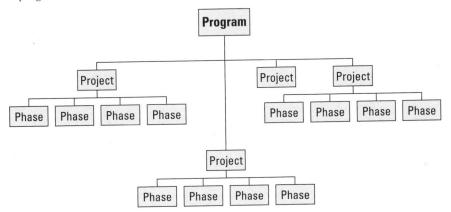

In the early stage of a project, it may be feasible to develop only a two- or three-level work breakdown structure since the details of the project may not be available. As the project planning process advances into the project definition phase, the work details become more apparent. The subdivisions of the work breakdown structure elements are developed at lower levels. These final subelements, the lowest level of work packages, are the detail descriptions of the work performed on the project. The product of this decomposition process is the completed work breakdown structure.

Figure 5.3 shows a sample where the work breakdown structure integrates into the planning process of the scope. Note the development of the scope definition and the WBS occur at the same time. As you learn more about the scope, you can apply that information to the WBS. The WBS will then help in developing the scope. They work as a team with each other.

FIGURE 5.3

How the work breakdown structure integrates with the planning process

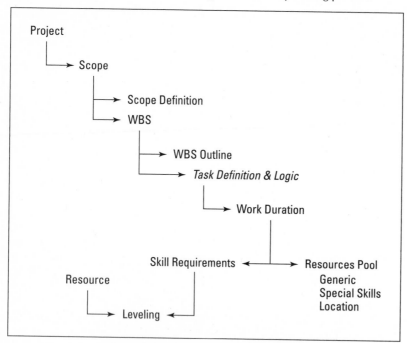

The Planning Process and the WBS

Figure 5.4 represents a sample of a WBS and the *work packages* creating the activities for a logic network diagram tool. Note the logic network diagram uses only the *work packages,* the bottom level of the WBS. The project schedule uses only the work packages to determine the start and finish dates for each activity that creates the project schedule. As an example: *Work Package* "Design B1" in the WBS becomes *activity* "Design B1" in the logic network diagram.

As you work on the creation of the scope of your project, more detail is developed. This detail becomes available to the WBS, which will be broken down to lower levels. In turn, the WBS can support the development of the scope detail. If a team member starts creating or identifying work that is not in the scope, it is important to remove those activities from the project. There should be no work included in a project that is not in the scope of work. If you do that extra work, you are adding value to the project that was not called for and you are doing it free of charge. The owner will love it and the project manager will not be as happy as it is taking unplanned time and money away from the project.

FIGURE 5.4

The transition of the work packages into the activities of the logic network diagram.

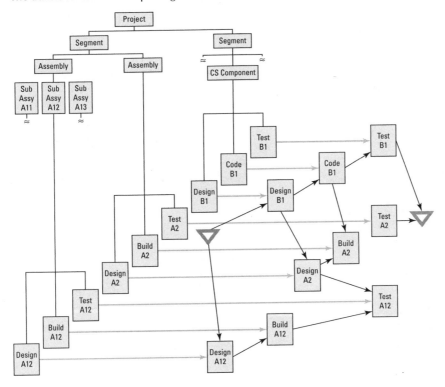

Planning to use a work breakdown structure

Since the WBS is all encompassing in identifying and defining all the work on the project, when you plan to use one make sure the project team members and the other stakeholders participate. If possible, include the functional managers in the planning sessions. Plan a short training class for the people who have never used a WBS.

Establish some rules on the maximum time (duration) or maximum cost a work package will be, such as the work package duration being no more than one reporting cycle or cost no more than a fixed amount and has a maximum amount of labor hours assigned to it. Make sure one of the branches on the second level is a project management branch. This branch will define all the work the project will need to plan, execute, control, and close.

Before you can create the Work Breakdown Structure tool, you must formulate a plan. In the following "Planning Questions section, we provide some initial ideas to help get you started thinking about how to utilize this tool on your project.

Planning Questions

1 When would you create, develop, or write this tool?

Planning process, update as required based on approved change orders

2 Who is going to use this tool, both from an input and output status?

Upper management, owners, project manager and team members, subcontractors or specific skill areas, the media

3 Why are you going to use this tool?

Defines all work for the project, hierarchal order to determine parent and child of any element of work breakdown structure, to extract any information from any element of work breakdown structure, graphic display is easy to read and understand

4 How are you going to use this tool?

Put on wall in graphic or picture form, WBS Dictionary Document

5 How will you distribute the information?

Dashboard format (small sections), electronic, tabular, plotter, project server, document control system

6 When will you distribute the information?

After initial creation and on-demand and after changes or updates

7 What decisions can or should you make from this tool?

Almost any project-related decisions are possible from this tool

8 What information does this tool provide for your project?

All project work activities such as schedule, costs, risk, quality, resources, communications, constraints, and assumptions

9 What historical and legal information do you need to store?

Work breakdown structure, WBS dictionary, any identifiable changes to the WBS, lessons learned

10 What will be the staffing requirements (Role Type) to run and maintain these tools?

Project manager, schedulers, cost control manager, risk manager, procurement manager, and quality manager

Reporting using a work breakdown structure

The work breakdown structure is such an important communication tool because at one time or another every person working on the project needs the information from the work breakdown structure — it describes all the work on the project. Therefore, the work breakdown structure must be in a general area where everyone can get to it. Work breakdown structure charts can become quite large, especially horizontally. Because of this, the project manager often dedicates an entire wall displaying the information of the work breakdown structure.

Another way to report the work breakdown structure is through the work breakdown structure dictionary. It is usually kept somewhere near the work breakdown structure chart or is accessible within the document control system. Generally, the dictionary has more detail to supplement the work breakdown structure. These two tools go hand-in-hand.

 A work breakdown structure is one of the most important tools, if not the *most* important tool, on the project.

Figure 5.5 represents a four-level WBS chart. This is a typical work breakdown structure where the top levels represent team leaders and the mid-levels represent senior staff representatives. The bottom level in this case is the actual workers in each subarea of the project. Remember the mid-levels can be many levels deep. The WBS identifies the level and the position that will require reporting. As an example, the team leaders will report from their top-level position. In this case, there will be three reports. If a detail report is required, the team members at the mid-level or possibly the bottom level will produce the report. The project manager will report (weekly status reports, budget report, performance report, etc.) from the project levels.

FIGURE 5.5

The four major levels in a WBS. The bottom level is always the work package.

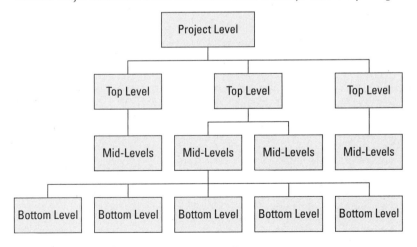

Because the work breakdown structure is on a wall displayed in the project office, it is update only when the work changes on the project. This will become less frequent as the project matures. Change orders most likely will change the WBS because they are adding work, which adds work packages. Project managers update the work breakdown structure on demand only if it is not part of a regular periodic reporting cycle.

 See Chapter15 to learn more about how to create and use the work breakdown structure tool.

Summary

The tools described in this Scope Management knowledge area support project managers and team members in controlling the Scope areas of their projects. As we all know, managing project scope is critically important and something that is not taken lightly. Therefore, project managers and team members need to monitor and control scope management closely throughout the life of the project as it is the quickest area to get away from you if not watched closely.

The chapter includes tools such as feasibility studies, scope definition document, system requirements document, and the work breakdown structure. Each tool focuses on controlling the scope aspects of the project. With these tools, project managers or team members will be able to control the activities on the project better and drive the project team toward a successful completion of the project.

Chapter 6

Defining Communication Tools to Manage Project Time

The Time Management knowledge area encompasses activities project managers perform to effectively manage the time aspects of their projects. Time management is one of the top three areas that project managers must be skilled in when communicating project status. Project customers do not want to hear that their project is going to be late or that the team has missed a key milestone date and therefore if a project manager must present this information, they need to do so very carefully.

Some projects are time driven because they have an absolute end date that cannot slide. An example of this is the Y2K projects managed before the turn of the millennium. Because Y2K projects were time driven, project managers focused their efforts on managing the schedule of the project and did not need to focus as much on the cost or scope aspects of the project because those factors were not the driving force of the projects. In other words, during Y2K projects, customers rarely cared about the cost of the project; the focus of the team was ensuring the project team hit the date. Hence, the communication aspects of the project manager focused mainly on date specifics, ensuring the project team was driving toward the December 31 deadline.

In this chapter, we explore project communications tools in the time management area where we present the tools project managers should utilize in managing the activities specific to time on the project. The tools noted are to help the project manager communicate effectively in the time and schedule aspects of their projects. The tools included in this chapter will help you become a better communicator and work much more effectively with your customer.

Introducing the Baseline Schedule

The purpose of the *baseline schedule* tool is to establish a depiction of the initial (original) schedule before any work begins on the project. The baseline schedule is the original project schedule before the project manager makes any progress or updates to the plan. The customer usually approves the project's baseline schedule. The value of having a baseline schedule is to track how well the project team is progressing and to compare and communicate any variances between the original schedule and the current schedule as the project moves through its lifecycle. The project manager is responsible for communicating those variances to the customers and upper management staff. The baseline schedule allows comparisons of the project's original schedule, costs, and resource assignments to the progress the team is making on the project at any time. The different comparisons project managers can make are project costs, start and finish dates of specific project activities, and resource assignments, to name a few. The benefit of using the baseline schedule is how clearly it communicates the project timelines and how well it communicates if the team is tracking to the original schedule or not. The ability to see the differences from the baseline schedule to the current day progress is easy. The current schedule shows the slips and delays on the schedule alongside the original baseline dates for each project task. When reviewing the project schedule it is clear which dates have changed at the task level. Project managers should have an easy time communicating the slippage to their customers because of the ease of use and clarity of the baseline schedule.

Without a baseline schedule, the project manager or customer would have a considerably harder time understanding or seeing where there is a project slip and what project areas are still causing the delay. Using a baseline schedule is the only method to track and record the current schedule slips.

> **NOTE**   The Project Management Institute's knowledge area for this baseline schedule is the Time Management area. The secondary concept area for this tool is Scope.

> **ON the CD-ROM**   We have included a sample of the baseline schedule tool in the Time Folder. Use this as a guide for creating your own personal version of this tool.

> **TOOL VALUE**   A baseline schedule tool allows you to compare the original project information with current information, and provides the ability to show trend analysis and variance analysis with your project data.

The baseline schedule allows for a simple comparison between two project schedules (the original and the current) to determine whether the project is still on track or needs attention. You as project manager, or your team members, can use the baseline schedule throughout the project to communicate project schedule status and compare the two schedules regularly to prevent any possible slips or delays in the project. The baseline schedule also uses cost data to track over and under runs. This baseline schedule can communicate positive information if the project is on track and hitting the schedule dates (no slips), and negative information if the plan is off track and not tracking to the original plan (slips). In both cases, the baseline schedule is a valuable tool because it keeps the project customers and project team members constantly communicating project schedule information and working together to ensure that the project stays on track and on budget. If the project manager decides he or she will not use a baseline schedule, they are missing the chance to use a valuable communication tool that could help them manage their projects more effectively. Without the tool, it is harder to see where the delays actually occurred and where overruns are at the task level. Without the tool, it actually takes away the ability of the project manager to communicate with their customers about the schedule delays and cost variances in the project schedule. It is much more difficult to show the customer the delays without seeing a graphical representation.

Figure 6.1 displays an original project schedule and a baseline schedule shown from a project-scheduling tool. In this example, you can see that the project's original start date was December 26, 2007; however, it actually started one week late, on January 2, 2008. The original duration was three days for Task 1 but the actual duration took five days. When reviewing Task 5, the last task of the project, you will also notice this project on track now to finish eight days late.

FIGURE 6.1

A typical project schedule, including the baseline schedule.

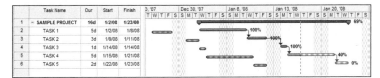

	Task Name	Dur	Start	Finish
1	– SAMPLE PROJECT	16d	1/2/08	1/23/08
2	TASK 1	5d	1/2/08	1/8/08
3	TASK 2	3d	1/9/08	1/11/08
4	TASK 3	1d	1/14/08	1/14/08
5	TASK 4	5d	1/15/08	1/21/08
6	TASK 5	2d	1/22/08	1/23/08

TIP   A baseline schedule is necessary to calculate any performance measurements on your project.

If you record any work on the tasks and create the baseline schedule with that work included, and then perform a schedule comparison between your baseline schedule and your current schedule, the results would be incorrect because you have reported actuals (start and finish dates) that are different from the original plan. For example, if you start the project one week late and create a baseline, all the dates on your plan will represent that one-week slide.

To capture the progress of your project at different times during the project, you may want to create more than one version of the baseline schedule. For example, at the start of the project you create a baseline schedule and then as the project progresses, you create a new version of the baseline schedule at the beginning of each major phase. As you progress, you can compare the new baseline schedule to the current schedule and determine quickly how well the project has moved forward. Using the baseline schedules at the beginning of each phase, you can compare the progress of one phase to the progress of another phase. Many project managers take advantage of this comparison and often have multiple copies of the baseline schedule on their project.

With the baseline schedule, you have the comparison data you need to analyze the performance of the project using the earned value technique. This can provide the typical performance s-curve report, schedule performance index, and cost performance index. By using this information, you can analyze the rate at which the work is progressing and make decisions based on the rate of progress.

 See Chapter 7 to learn more about the earned value technique, s-curve, and the schedule and cost performance indexes.

TIP Always create a schedule baseline, although you may not think you are going to need it! You will in the future!

Planning to use a baseline schedule

In planning to use a baseline schedule, the project manager must first have a completed and approved project schedule with no progress on any of the activities. The project manager should then work with his or her customers to determine the different times they want baseline snapshots taken during the project; doing this will establish your customers' reporting requirements. The project manager will then identify whether the customer wants only one baseline (the original schedule with no progress reported) or a baseline recorded at the beginning of each month or at the beginning of each phase. This is important to know, because a project manager must perform these baselines and needs to know ahead of time the expectation. Remember, there is usually no going back. After determining that, the project manager has adequately planned to use the baseline schedule on their project.

Before you can create a baseline schedule, you must formulate a plan. In the following "Planning Questions" section, we provide some suggestions of how we would respond to help get you thinking about how you would utilize the tool on your project.

Planning Questions

1 *When would you create, develop, or write this tool?*
Executing process just before work activities begin, different stages of the project

2 *Who is going to use this tool, both from an input and output status?*
Upper management, owners, executives, project manager, team members, subcontractors, or specific skill areas, the media (TV, radio, newspapers), anyone involved in working or dealing with the impacts of late delivery on a project

3 *Why are you going to use this tool?*
To display the original plan and baseline schedule and compare how the project is progressing and performing

4 *How are you going to use this tool?*
Keep the current project schedule and baseline schedule up-to-date to allow for comparisons between the two, upper level management reporting, and show both time and cost variances on the project.

---

5 *How will you distribute the information?*

Project-scheduling tool, plotter, newsletter, document control system, e-mail, in-person meetings

6 *When will you distribute the information?*

At the start of the project, then at major milestones throughout the life of project, and also once a month

7 *What decisions can or should you make from this tool?*

Schedule and cost decisions, investigate potential project problems, risk decisions, resources decisions, performance decisions

8 *What information does the tool provide for your project?*

Schedule information, cost information, resources information, and performance information

9 *What historical and legal information do you need to store?*

Lessons learned information, actual costs, actual start and finish dates, resource assignments, variances between different project components

10 *What will be the staffing requirements (role type) to run and maintain these tools?*

Project manager, team members, scheduler, resource manager, cost manager

Reporting using a baseline schedule

The project manager is responsible for creating and reporting the baseline schedule throughout the project. This normally occurs at various times during the project, such as major project events, delivery dates slip or any other major milestone on the project.

The project manager may use the baseline schedule on a weekly basis to compare the work accomplished during the week with the baseline, to see if the team is performing as planned. Using a weekly reporting cadence provides customers and upper management with a constant checkpoint of how well the project is progressing. The project manager creates the baseline schedule within a project-scheduling tool. In most cases, the project manager stores the project files outside the project-scheduling tool and in the document control system for long-term archiving.

CROSS-REF   See Chapter 17 to learn more about how to create and use this baseline schedule tool.

Introducing the Change Control Plan

The purpose of the *change control plan* is to document the processes and procedures for controlling project changes. When someone requests a change, a project manager needs to have a process in place to follow in order to adopt or reject that change. The change control plan helps a project stay in line with its goals, and requires that most change requests go through this process. The change control plan is *critical* to the success of a project. Project managers should create and distribute the change control plan before any work activity begins; otherwise, they most likely will have a difficult time controlling the scope of the project. When value is added to or removed from a project, the scope change process includes following the processes within the change control plan. Most change requests add value to the project because they are correcting errors found or improving other features. Other types of changes remove value. Removing features follows the same rigor as adding a feature to a product. This type of removal request would also follow the processes outlined in the change control plan.

For example, when a deadline for delivery of the software is approaching, the client may decide to remove some functionality that was originally in the scope in order to meet the delivery date. If a customer presents a request and it is within the scope of the project, then it is not a change request. Project managers must be aware that the new request could already be included in the project's scope, so they should always compare the new request to the original project scope before calling it additional work. It may already be in there, just named something different.

> **TIP** Be reasonably flexible and do not make everything requested a formal change. In doing so, you create goodwill and a positive relationships between you and your customers.

Project managers may find that the customer's change request is so small that it takes less time to perform the task than it would to process it through the formal change request process. On occasion, it is beneficial for the project manager to consider doing the work requested in order to build a stronger relationship with the customers.

> **NOTE** The Project Management Institute's knowledge area for this tool is the Integration area. The secondary areas that this tool could be associated with are Scope and Risk.

> **ON the CD-ROM** We have included a sample of a Change Control Plan tool in the Integration folder. Consider this as a guide to create your own version of this tool.

> **TOOL VALUE** The change control plan allows project managers to control project scope and costs by using an established process. It allows the project manager to identify scope creep by comparing the existing scope to the change requests.

The change control plan helps facilitate conversations between the project customers and the project team, on how the project manager will manage and control all change requests. When you are using a standard change control plan for your project, your customers may already be familiar with that process and therefore will accept it and use it readily. One of the responsibilities of a project manager is to ensure customers sign off on the change control plan at the beginning of the project. This sign-off provides accountability to the project customer that they will follow the process every time they have a change. It also limits any communication problems the two groups may have on the document or the change request process itself. After introducing the change control plan, the customers may have questions or concerns that the project manager needs to respond to and ensure that everyone understands the document completely. Usually, the customers just accept the change control process and procedures and abide by them throughout the project, but some customers challenge the rules and therefore their sign-off and approval is important.

It is important that your customer understands how to document change requests and that they are comfortable with the process as early as possible in the project. If they are just learning the process, and at the same time are trying to implement a change request, it is going to be disrupting and a bad experience for both the project manager and the customer. Project managers want the change request process to run as smoothly as possible whenever used because it is something that will be utilized throughout the life of the project.

 Hold a short training session for your customers explaining how to complete a change request, and how the change control process works.

Table 6.1 is an example of a change control plan's table of contents. This document is set up to have the customers document their responses to a series of questions regarding the impact that their change request will have on the project. The answers and details relating to those questions will be decision points for the change control board to approve or reject the change.

TABLE 6.1

Example of a Change Control Plan Table of Contents

Section	Description
1	Change Control Board, Roles, and Responsibilities
2	Change Board Iimpact/Considerations Review
3	What Process Does Requestor Have to Follow to Initiate a Change? What Is the Flow?
4	Change Board Timeframes and Response Expectations
5	Change Request Documentation and Expectations
6	Any Additional Information on the Change Control Plan or Process
7	Mandatory Change Process Explained Here
8	Approvals and Responses from Change Control Board
9	Mandatory Change Process
10	Final Recommendation and Approval

Project stakeholders play a large role in the change control plan and procedures document, and can make or break a project by the number of changes that they request of the project team. If there are too many changes, the project team has little time to work on the actual scope of the project; instead they are working on change requests and the customers may not achieve what they had expected of the project. Not every project change request is acceptable; in some cases, the change is too great and the impact to the schedule too large, or the cost too high. The project manager may totally reject a large change or delay it until a later date in the project live cycle. On a software project, a large change request may wait until the next version. As project manager, you are responsible for ensuring that you work closely with your stakeholders by using the change request process to ensure that changes suggested are necessary.

Project managers should communicate to the customer how the team will react to being overwhelmed with change request work added onto their already overloaded schedule as overloading and overworking the team members will have a negative impact to the project. A change control plan communicates the processes and procedures, but not necessarily the impact to morale. That communication is the responsibility of the project manager.

Here is an example of the steps you would take in processing a change request in the construction industry. The steps would be similar in both software or research projects.

1. Initiate the change request and log it into a change request system.
2. Analyze the specific change request and distribute a request for information.
3. Create and submit a change request form for analysis and cost estimating.
4. Submit the change request form and cost and schedule impacts to the change control board (or appropriate persons) for review.
5. Once reviewed, make a decision on the request (approved/denied).
6. Plan a time to do the work if approved.

Some change requests, if small enough or mandated by government, do not require approval. The change control board automatically accepts these changes as required and incorporates them into the project's work activities. After the change control board notifies the project manager of the approval decision, they ask the project manager to communicate that decision to the project team and customers.

Understanding change control roles

Every change control plan has both the roles and responsibilities of each team member outlined so that everyone understands exactly what is required of them on the project. The change control plan documents and describes the following roles:

- **Change initiator:** Person who communicates the request and who ultimately will confirm its completion.

- **Project sponsor/owner/customer:** Communicates the approval of funds for the change request. The change owner assigns specific tasks to the task owners and communicates the progress on those tasks through completion.

- **Change administrator:** Carries out initial categorization and assessment, monitors progress of the change requests, and communicates progress throughout the process.

- **Impact assessors:** Assesses the impact of the change by communicating impacts and risks of the change request.

- **Change owner:** Typically the person who communicates the change required and manages it through the process.

- **Task owners:** The person responsible for doing the work to complete and deliver the change request.

- **Change manager:** Manages the overall change process, acts as a point of escalation for change requests, communicates change request information, exercises judgment in assessing requests, and escalates the change requests to a change board if appropriate.

- **Change board:** An appropriate management board that reviews the change process and specific change requests where required. This board typically is comprised of the service delivery manager, customer representative, and change manager who makes the final acceptance or denial of the change request, and communicates that information to the project team and the change initiator.

A limited number of projects have a solid scope, there is always something that happens that complicates the scope discussion. In most cases, the project manager must issue change requests because of poorly written requirements, and therefore missed scope items. The more information that is included in the project requirements document, the less number of changes are required. If the project team members communicate the requirements to the customers and gain approval on those requirements, they are less likely to continue to seek changes to the project as it progresses through the lifecycle; without that approval, the project is almost guaranteed a large number of change requests.

When you utilize the change control plan, you are also responsible for reporting and communicating status from the change request process. This status could be during a weekly status meeting or a status report, or anything that communicates with your customers on the tracking and handling of change requests. This ongoing status is a great method to communicate techniques that provide full visibility to your customers on the status of their proposed changes.

Planning to use a change control plan

In the planning to use a change control plan, the project manager must identify a standard change control process for their project. This includes items such as change control forms, change control board members, weekly change control meetings, and establishing a change control repository or central Web site for tracking and storing changes. The project manager must also plan the team member's allocation of time for handling and reviewing changes outside project activities listed on the project schedule. In most cases, the work of reviewing and evaluating change requests by team members is part of their regular project activities, and not outside of their normal day-to-day project work, although some team members think it is. That is for the project manager to work out with each team member at the start of the project. Each team member should allow time to work on change requests as well as their scheduled work. Project managers should plan to allocate time to evaluate change requests to their team members, and communicate that expectation at the beginning of the project. After performing these steps, the project manager has adequately prepared for using the change control plan on their project.

> **NOTE** Remember the work effort that it actually takes to complete an approved change request should be included in the master schedule and the baseline schedule.

In the following "Planning Questions" section, we have provided some suggestions to help you start thinking about how you can utilize the tool on your project.

Planning Questions

1 When would you create, develop, or write this tool?

During the planning process, then modified and update as needed. Also prior to the first change request by the customers or team members.

2 Who is going to use this tool, both from an input and output perspective?

Upper management, owners, customers, executives, project manager, team members, subcontractors, or specific skill areas will all use this change control plan

3 Why are you going to use this tool?

Describe to project team, including clients and customers, how the change process works, document the process steps to control changes to allow anyone to request change without negatively impacting project or its team members

4 How are you going to use this tool?

Present process and procedures to clients, customers, and team members ensuring everyone follows process to submit change requests on project. Use as a training document to ensure everyone can follow the process of submitting changes.

5 How will you distribute the information?

Distribute via document format such as Microsoft Word, document control system, and e-mail

6 When will you distribute the information?

When someone has requested a change, or as they occur, the project manager sends the document as a friendly reminder to follow the process

7 What decisions can or should you make from this tool?

Decisions on controlling and managing the change request process, what and who will be communicating the change request information to end user or team members

8 What information does this tool provide for your project?

Process steps and procedures for controlling project changes, communication audiences, roles and responsibilities, review considerations, mandatory changes, and approval or denial process

9 What historical and legal information do you need to store?

Lessons learned, actual process steps in process that worked or didn't work for future reference and corrections or updates for the plan

10 What will be the staffing requirements (Role Type) to run and maintain these tools?

Project manager, scheduler, purchase manager, designer, owner or client, subcontractors

Change control reporting types

You should ensure that you have a change control reporting process established at the beginning of your project. That way, when the project starts, the reporting method is in place and ready and you can utilize it to ensure everyone is up-to-date on all the change requests and their statuses. Many different types of reports are available to use during the change control process of which you and your team members, or customers, should be aware. Some of the common reports include:

- Outcome of the change control board (approve/reject)
- Communicating how to complete the change request form
- Overall change control process (project manager and team members report this data)
- Total number of change requests per month form

Although your most important task is to run the project, reporting and staying ahead of changes is a critical aspect of your work activities as well. Reporting a change request's approval or rejection can be tricky. It is much easier to let your customers know of an approval for their change request, however, if the impact to that approval puts the project over budget or behind schedule, then the message needs proper attention before delivery. For you and your team members to be great communicators, you need to control the flow of project information at all times. A rejected change request could mean an unhappy customer, and you want to make sure that you communicate this rejection with sensitivity.

Reporting can also include the reporting on, and communication of, the contents of the change request form. You and your team members may not develop the contents of the change form, but are responsible to drive the change through to completion. In most cases, you report the change request form to different levels of management, other stakeholders, and a variety of staff that are required to either accept or deny the change. The change request form becomes a valuable communication tool because it describes in detail the changes requested.

The timeline for reporting from the change request process and procedures depends on the number of changes requested for the particular project. If the team members did not capture the scope correctly, or the project has active and demanding customers, then change requests can flow into the project daily. If this is the case, you may want to consider weekly reporting of this change request process to the key project stakeholders. The reporting of this information will be formal via e-mail and documented for reference and legal purposes in most cases.

CROSS-REF See Chapter 16 to learn more about how to use or create this Change Control Plan and Procedures tool.

Introducing the Change Request Form

The purpose of the *change request form* is to monitor and control the changes requested on the project. The customer or team member completes a change request form to document and communicate the changes to the project that they want to occur. The project manager should review each change request form with the customer and train them on how to complete the form in a manner that is acceptable to you and your project. There must be enough information on the form that a project team can review it and determine how they would incorporate the change once approved. The form must also communicate enough information that the change control board can approve or deny the change request as well, therefore, one or two lines of detail on a change request form will not be enough information.

The change request log's purpose is to analyze change requests on a project. The log stores the changes for historical purposes and assists in identifying lessons learned information. It does not matter if requests are accepted or denied; they are all stored within the change request log. The change request log is a central repository for all change requests.

Both the change request form and the change request log communicate the change request details that are proposed by the customer or team member. The change request log does not contain the same level of detail that a change request form carries, but does carry enough detail that anyone reviewing the document can understand the request at a summary or high level. We have included both of these tools in this section because of their high dependence on each other and the align-ment they have from a communication aspect. For example, there would be no value to having a change request log unless there was at least a single change request filed for the project. A change request does not require a change request log for reporting, although a best practice technique is to ensure that, once reporting on a particular change request, the project manager enters it into the change request log to keep both tools in sync. Change request forms store all information about the actual requested changes, but the change request log stores only the high-level summary infor-mation, although it does provide a picture of all the changes that were either accepted or rejected on the project. If the project is running late or over budget, the change request log communicates that information clearly by displaying all the changes within it.

 The Project Management Institute's knowledge area for this tool is the Integration area. The secondary areas that this tool could be associated with are Scope, Quality, and Risk.

 We have included a sample of a change request form and a change request log in the Integration folder. Use these as guides to help you create your own version of this tool.

 The change request form identifies all changes to the project. It provides a common look and form for capturing change request information.

Change request forms provide formal documentation on the proposed or suggested changes to the project. The change request form is easy to use by any project manager, team member, or cus-tomer. The change control plan discussed earlier in this chapter sets the standards and guidelines to process these change request forms. Some projects will use many change request forms as the project progresses. Submitting change requests does not derail a project, it just forces a project team to review and determine how to incorporate the change within the project, if applicable. This process occurs repeatedly throughout the project and requires the project manager to supervise this review process closely and communicate the information to everyone involved in the proposed changes.

Project managers need to communicate to their customers when, in the project's lifecycle project, it is possible to make the changes documented in the change request form. It is the project manager's responsibility to communicate with their customers that if change requests come in by them, they could have a negative impact on the project, and may be rejected. There should be strict guidelines around the timing of change requests for every project, but there must be a point in the project's lifecycle when a change request is no longer accepted.

Change request form

Many companies have their own version of a change request form, and based on the industry and project type, these forms capture the information required to understand the proposed changes to the project. A construction company will have a different change request form than a software company, because the industries are so different. Some of the core information captured in the document is standard, including scope changes, schedule changes, cost impacts, and quality change. Therefore, when someone requests a change, some of the same areas, regardless of project type, are impacted.

Figure 6.2 displays an example of a standard change request form. This form is common among all industries and usable on any project. Without a doubt, forms are going to vary from company to company and industry to industry.

The change request form is a great communication tool used to document changes requested on your project. Project managers use these forms as the communication vehicle to talk with stakeholders and obtain approval to proceed with additional work requested. The project manager must ensure that no one is working on an unapproved change request. All change request forms need reviewing and approving before any work occurs on the requested activities. Time and effort spent on an unapproved request take time away from the project's current activities, jeopardizing the time and budget of the project. The change request form tracks a wealth of project data for easy communication to everyone involved in the project.

You can use a change request form in the following situations:

- To communicate and request scope additions or removal of changes, including owners who request new functionality within a project that is different from original scope of work.

- To communicate to the customers or management, a request to increase the project's budget.

- To communicate to upper management and request additional project staff.

- To communicate and request changes found causing design errors; this includes reporting the discovery of problems found that will change the direction of the project.

- A customer requests new functionality within a project that is different from original scope of work.

FIGURE 6.2

The change request form is a standard document across all industries, with variations to allow industry differences.

Name of Project:	Project manager:
Change Request #	Change Request Date:
Change Requested By Name:	Current Project Phase:

Description of Change:
Scope Impact:
Schedule Impact:
Cost Impact:
Quality Impact:
Possible Risks:

Reviewed By: Position: Date:

Recommended Action: Approve Or Reject:

Change request log

Project managers use a change request log to keep a historical reference of the project's change requests. Project managers quickly discover the importance of change request logs and utilize them to communicate the change requests at a summary level for the project. A project manager should create a change request log at the beginning of a project and add change request information (high level) to the log as changes occur. Most projects require one change request log. Filters can select the closed and active change requests.

Project managers will find great value in the change request log from a lessons-learned perspective. When storing the project change information, the log provides a record of what the project accepted and rejected as changes. Therefore, if the project goes over budget or behind schedule, has quality issues or staffing problems, the reasons may be determined by reviewing the change request log and the information contained in that log. As projects progress, project managers should continue to store project change requests within the change request log, and then utilize this tool for obtaining lessons learned information. A change request log can communicate a running tally of the costs and the number of accepted and rejected change requests. This is valuable information if the project is cost or schedule driven.

Table 6.2 shows an example of a change request log. This is a basic example, but one that contains valuable change request information. If someone requires further detailed information on a specific change request, have him look at the change request form because this is where all details of the requested change are contained. This change request log stores only high-level information about the change requests; it does not contain detailed information. The log enables the viewer to see at a high level, all the changes proposed for the project, and determine quickly which were accepted or rejected. The log is also valuable for storing changes on a long-term or historical basis.

TABLE 6.2

Example of a Change Request Log

CR#	Description	Date Req	Decision	Date Authorized	Approved by	Requested by	Implementation Date
A6-55	Modify main wall	02/03/2008	Y	04/14/08	JSmith	MJones	05/14/08
BJ-07	Add new baseboard	07/01/2008	N	N/A	Rejected	BThomas	N/A

The project manager is responsible for reporting the information contained in the change request log to upper management and the project's stakeholders, usually on a monthly basis. The number of times to report this information depends on the specific project's needs.

Planning to use a change request form

In preparing to use a change request form and a change request log, the project manager must first determine if the company has these two tools. If they do, the project manager should begin to use these tools immediately on their project. Otherwise, if there are no tools available, the project manager can use the templates of both these tools supplied on the CD-ROM in this book. Both tools should be modified to meet the project's specific requirements. However, before starting to use these tools, a project manager should consult with the customer to determine if there are any special requirements or requests associated with the change request process that need to be considered. If the customer does have special requirements, then the project manager should consider these requests, incorporating them into the change request form and change request log where applicable. After performing these tasks, the project manager will have adequately prepared for using the change request form on their project.

Before you create the change request form, you must formulate a plan. In the "Planning Questions" section, we have provided some initial thoughts to help start you thinking about how to utilize this tool on your project.

Planning Questions

1   *When would you create, develop, or write this tool?*
During the planning phase of the project for both tools

2   *Who is going to use this tool, both from an input and output status?*
Project manager, team members, client or customers, designers, architects, and engineers, or anyone involved in the project

3   *Why are you going to use this tool?*
The change request form documents the specific requirements of the change, and the change request log tracks and stores the changes for long-term reference.

4   *How are you going to use this tool?*
Change Request Forms capture change request information and provide the information to make an assessment on the impacts to the project. The Change Request Log displays all changes on the project and communicates that information to the stakeholders and provides input to lessons learned information, and will provide a one-stop shop for high-level project change information.

5   *How will you distribute the information?*
Document format, e-mail, document control system, presentation format such as PowerPoint

6   *When will you distribute the information?*
As change requests forms are completed and requested, as well as when the final determination of approval or rejection occurs. Continually reported throughout the project.

7   *What decisions can or should you make from this tool?*
Decide on what information is required to complete the request, establish impacts to project based or core components (scope, cost, schedule), and decide if the request has merit to implement based on information captured in the form. Decisions on a change request log are limited as this is an informal tool capturing high-level summary changes only.

8   *What information does this tool provide for your project?*
All requested changes, approval and rejection decisions, and assessment results

9   *What historical and legal information do you need to store?*
All change request forms, the change request log itself, and any lessons learned information

10   *What will be the staffing requirements (role type) to run and maintain these tools?*
Project manager, team members, cost manager, risk manager, resource manager, and quality manager

Reporting using a change request

The project manager is responsible for reporting the number of change requests associated with the project. The project manager uses a documented format for the change request form to communicate the requested change information. Usually, the form is e-mailed to all project team members for assessment of impacts, and then to the change control board for final determination on its approval or rejection.

The project manager displays the change request log in a presentation format as part of a larger overall presentation that presents it to the customers or upper management. To use this tool, you must have additional project information, for example, the project is over budget by 50 percent, and there are 20 approved change requests; those two pieces of information support each other. That many change requests on a project require additional dollars that the project manager may not have allocated in the budget, hence the over-budget situation; one piece of data would not be relevant without the other. If the project is projecting over budget by 50 percent, and the customers or management have not seen the change request log with 20 change requests in it, they would have no explanation as to why the project is over budget.

TIP Ensure that project managers properly document and log all changes for the project. Changes that come in on the back of a scrap piece of paper are not acceptable and project managers must reject them.

CROSS-REF See Chapter 19 to learn more about how to use a change request.

Introducing the Gantt Chart

The purpose of a *Gantt chart* tool is to communicate the project's activities to the customers, stakeholders, and team members. It is one of the most widely used tools in a project manager's toolbox and is invaluable in communicating a wealth of project information. At a single glance, a Gantt chart helps you determine, and communicate the status of the project to any interested parties. The project manager uses the Gantt chart throughout the life of the project to display project activities, start and finish dates, task and project costs, resource assignments, and dependencies.

One of the most valuable aspects of the Gantt chart is the "what if" scenarios you can perform when moving activity dates, adjusting project costs, or adjusting resource reassignments on your current project. When adjusting any one of these items, each of them can change the project dramatically; and, therefore, you can see what the changes will look like without affecting the actual project. A Gantt chart allows you to change, and change back, any data values with little or no effort. There are few tools that can react "on the fly" to adjusted project data, and display the impacts of the changes immediately for evaluation. Just imagine what your project will look like when a design task originally planned for 5 days took 30 days! A Gantt chart communicates both graphical and tabular information on a single page in an easy to understand format.

NOTE The Project Management Institute's knowledge area for a Gantt chart is the Time Management area. The secondary areas that this tool could be associated with are Scope, Cost, Human Resources, Communication, and Risk.

ON the CD-ROM We have included a sample of a Gantt chart in the Time Folder. Use this as a guide to create your own version of this tool.

TOOL VALUE A Gantt chart allows you to display project information on an easy-to-read and understand, graphical and tabular format. Your customers, team members, or upper management staff will find this tool helpful when delivering and presenting project information.

A Gantt chart is simple to create and provides a complete view of the project's information. It displays a large amount of information about a project at a single glance. It is also one of the best methods to communicate different types of data on the project. For example, when using a Gantt chart view, project managers can display costs fields, resource fields, or any other type of field available within the tool. The choices are almost unlimited, sometimes leaving the project manager with the challenge of which fields to exclude.

The Gantt chart, shown in Figure 6.3, is easy to customize. You can add and delete, move and size project columns however you chose. Regardless of the method that the project manager chooses to effectively communicate project information, if she is adding columns of fields that are not relevant or do not provide value, there is no sense even reporting on it.

FIGURE 6.3

A sample Gantt Chart Report displaying five activities with their duration, start, and finish dates, based on the relationships between the activities.

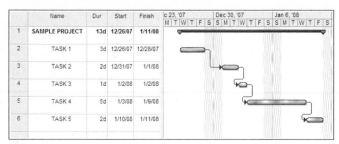

When reviewing the chart, it is easy to see the sequence (order) of the activities by reviewing the black arrows shown in the graph area, and the directions and connecting points of those arrows. In this example, Task 1 connects to Task 2, which connects to Task 3 and so on. This is a simple example, but one that effectively displays and communicates the task relationships. When creating a project schedule, the project managers will often miss these logical relationships between the tasks because the schedule is created on the tabular side of the project schedule and is not usually a graphical setting. This is also true when the project manager is trying to troubleshoot issues with dates aligning correctly, or getting the computer generated end date to hit on the desired end date. It is far more difficult to find the problems when viewing a list of activities on the tabular information side compared to looking at them in a graphical view. The project manager should ensure the logical relationships between tasks are correct if they are having problems with project schedule dates. Using the graphical area of the Gantt chart displays valuable project information and the various relationships between the tasks, and provides the project manager with the ability to work in a graphical environment and move dates around on the project.

Project managers often use the Gantt chart tool to communicate with the customer or the team on a regular basis. Most often customers call for this information on a weekly basis, however, this information is available at any time when stored in a document control system or in a project-scheduling tool. Project managers should expect to report formally only once a week. Your stakeholders or customers will come to expect this chart (report) weekly once you initiate that cadence with them, and they will look forward to reviewing what has changed and what has progressed from the last time they saw it and will better understand the challenges you are facing on the project.

Using a Gantt chart provides many advantages to the project manager, one being the ability to report on cost and schedule data concurrently on the same chart; the tabular information is on the left side of the chart and the graphical bar chart on the right. There are only a few other tools that exist — such as a tabular report and a spreadsheet report — that have similar abilities for reporting both cost and schedules together. Another advantage of the Gantt chart is the ability to communicate the schedule in a graphical format showing the bars for each project task over a time scale. Using the graphical aspects of the tool, you can sit with your customers and easily review the project details and timelines.

A Gantt chart can also be a cost report, a schedule report, or a combination of both. The data contained on these charts includes work activities, cost data, resource assignments, time lines, and percent complete, to name only a few. The choice of what columns of project information to communicate is unlimited. In most cases, it is up to the project manager to decide what is applicable on their projects and what they will or will not communicate.

The most popular project management scheduling packages on the market offer Gantt charts as part of their normal functionality. The Gantt chart is a specific view within the tool that project managers actually select as they would any other view. Many software packages, such as Microsoft Project, Primavera, Workbench, and Scheduler, include Gantt charts. For more advanced project management, the Gantt chart can present earned value information within the tool and actually become a complete earned value communication system.

CROSS-REF For more earned value information, see Chapter 7.

Planning to use a Gantt chart

In planning to use a Gantt chart tool, the project manager must first understand what fields and columns of data they will utilize on the chart. In preparing for that, the project manager meets with the customers and determines what they require on the chart and how often they want it reported. Many times, companies set standards as to what columns and fields they will make available, and sometimes project managers have limited options as to what they can choose. If companies are using an enterprise project server, project server administrators may lock down project Gantt charts fields and only make a standard set available for reporting purposes. In most situations, project managers and customers can choose the fields they want to review based on what makes the most sense for the project. Other activities project managers perform in preparing to use a Gantt chart require determining who will maintain and own the project schedule, what resources are working on the project, resource labor rates, project time lines, and project methodology. In all cases, when these steps are completed, the project manager should be ready to utilize the Gantt chart immediately on their projects.

Before you can create a Gantt chart, you must formulate a plan. In the "Planning Questions" section below, we have provided some initial thoughts and ideas to help you start thinking about how to utilize this tool on your project.

Planning Questions

1 *When would you create, develop, or write this tool?*
Initiation phase, during initial planning, and during the planning phase when developing the project schedule for the project

2 *Who is going to use this tool, both from an input and output status?*
Project manager, team members, project scheduler, resource manager, cost manager, and customers

3 *Why are you going to use this tool?*
To display project-scheduling information graphically, to display and communicate information via a tabular format project managers will use this tool to guide execution of project

4 *How are you going to use this tool?*
Report project information, display and update activity, and report and display progress on tool

5 *How will you distribute the information?*
Project-scheduling tool, e-mail, document control system, presentations, and hang charts on the wall

6 *When will you distribute the information?*
After creating initial schedule, as part of a periodic reporting cycle, on-demand as requested

7 *What decisions can or should you make from this tool?*
Scheduling decisions, cost decisions, resource decisions, performance decisions, dependencies decisions

8 *What information does this tool provide for your project?*
Scheduling, cost, resource, dependencies, and control information

9 *What historical and legal information do you need to store?*
Lessons learned information, original plan, and final version of project schedule

10 *What will be the staffing requirements (role type) to run and maintain these tools?*
Project manager, team member, project scheduler, cost manager, resource manager, and anyone involved in managing or updating the project schedule

Reporting from a Gantt chart

In most cases, you as the project manager are responsible for creating and reporting the project's Gantt chart. The project information on the report will most likely vary from project to project depending on the different needs of your customers.

Here is a list of possible Gantt chart reports available for your project. These charts are popular on most projects:

- **Cost chart:** This report displays budget and actuals.
- **Earned value chart:** The report displays cost and schedule performance indexes and variances.
- **Time chart:** This report displays activities based on their schedule dates.
- **Labor hours chart:** This report displays planned and actual labor hours over time.

It is relatively easy to create any of these charts, but it does require some background information before the Gantt chart becomes valuable. For example, entering the relevant costs, time, and resource information into the project-scheduling tool makes creating these types of reports very easy. Without that information, the reports would be difficult to produce in the tool.

Figure 6.4 shows a more enhanced project Gantt chart. This chart has additional information than the Gantt chart in Figure 6.3, although both are from the same project. The purpose was to communicate how easy it is to add valuable project information in a short time. Figure 6.4 displays the project team members assigned to the project and the associated costs allocated for each team member. Figure 6.4 displays the first line (line 1) as the summary activity for the project. On this summary line, you can see the project information rolled up (summarized) from the five detailed tasks associated with it. These tasks are connected (network logic), and those connections provide the overall cost and time allocations for the project. In this example, the project duration is 13 days and costs $1,275 to complete.

Figure 6.5 represents a typical Gantt chart for a book-publishing project. In the Gantt chart, you can communicate a great deal of information such as the costs of the project, duration, start, and finish dates, and resource assignments. Your customers may be overwhelmed with all the information that the Gantt chart actually provides. Present it in a way that provides them with the information they need without getting lost in the details. For example, removing some of the columns can be a powerful way to communicate the necessary information without overloading your customer with all the data on the chart.

FIGURE 6.4

This Gantt chart is an example of a more robust chart built from the project schedule in Figure 6.3.

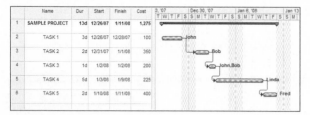

FIGURE 6.5

A sample Gantt chart for a book-publishing project.

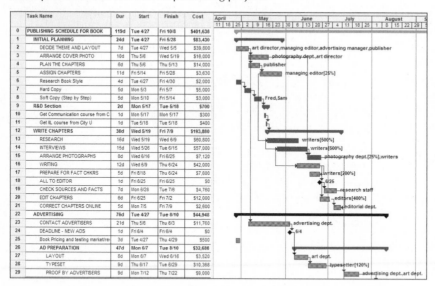

Most project managers use Gantt charts to manage and control projects on a daily basis, and they generally use a Gantt chart as a communication tool more often than any other tool because of all the data it contains and the ease of presentation. Team members, customers, senior management, or anyone else wanting detailed project information are going to look to a Gantt chart to provide them with the data they need on the project.

The project manager will report using the Gantt chart each week because of the valuable project information contained in the chart. There are different formats for reporting Gantt charts — electronic, paper, and presentations. The Gantt chart resides within the project-scheduling tool but is manually copied and stored each week in the document control system for long-term storage and archiving purposes.

CROSS-REF See Chapter 21 to learn more about how to create and use a Gantt chart.

Introducing the Logic Network Diagram

The purpose of a *logic network diagram* is to communicate project activities, their predecessors, their successors, and logical relationships. Project managers or project planners use a logic network diagram as a visual aid to communicate and ensure the relationships between the project tasks are correct before finalizing the project schedule. This tool is graphical and easy to use when determining the correct order of your project tasks. Medium to large projects use a logic network diagram because they often have a great amount of complexity in the task relationships; the project manager needs a graphical tool to select the tasks and logically order the tasks into the sequence that makes sense for the project. In some cases, it is too hard to explain how tasks relate without using a diagram, whether the project is complex, or people are unclear on how the relationships between different tasks are to occur, the project manager will use this tool to assist in the communications. The project manager also utilizes the logic network diagram when the project goes awry, or major logic changes occur that force the re-planning of the project; in this case project managers or project planners can start with the existing project tasks and arrange them in the correct order.

NOTE The Project Management Institute's knowledge area for a logic network diagram is the Time Management area. The secondary area that this tool is associated with is the Scope concept area.

ON the CD-ROM We have included a sample of a logic network diagram in the Time Folder. Use this as a guide to create your own version of this tool.

TOOL VALUE Logic network diagrams allow for easy understanding and viewing of the project tasks and their logic relationships to each other in a graphical format.

The logic network diagram communicates the logical relationships between project tasks and activities in a clear and concise manner. Using the tabular format of a project schedule does not allow for the same clear view of the project tasks and does not lay out the tasks in a format that is easy to read or understand. The logic network diagram also displays the project's critical path. Having critical path information mapped and diagramed early in the project will help the project manager and team members understand where they should focus their attention to ensure success of the project.

The logic network diagram is great in determining if there are any activities or relationships missing on the project schedule. When reviewing the project tasks and laying them out across a logic network diagram, project managers or project planners can determine if there are major portions that have not yet been added to the project schedule. Project customers will be able to tell if they have specific areas of the project assigned to them or if the project manager has listed all the tasks in their area. It is a great self-checking tool and only a handful of other tools can offer the same benefits, however none can offer it graphically like the logic network diagram tool can.

Figure 6.6 represents a typical logic network diagram. In this example, you can see the project has six main activities, two milestones, and start and finish boxes. The diagram communicates the logical relationship between these activities as well. They are Start to A, A to B, B to C, C to Finish on one path, and the second path includes Start to D, D to E, and so on. An important relationship to watch is the D to C relationships on the logic network diagram. That relationship shows that C cannot start until B and D are complete. From a project perspective, this is a finish to start relationship and something a project manager should watch closely.

FIGURE 6.6

A pure logic diagram of activities for a particular task on a project. In most cases, when logic diagrams show this level of detail, the activities represent the work tasks for a single activity, not a complete project.

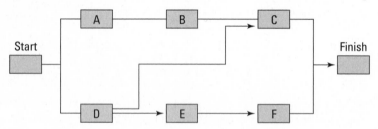

The interdependencies of activities can be challenging to understand on complex projects. In Figure 6.6, the relationships shown between A to B, B to C, and so on are easy to understand and therefore easy to communicate. Interdependencies are the relationships between two project tasks. The logical relationships show the order to accomplish the tasks on the project. This logical network diagram also shows the information that passes from activity to activity. As an example, in a pharmaceutical research company that is performing research on a new drug, the government requires several phases that the drug must pass through before the company can introduce it to the public. In a logic network diagram, you see the different phases of the research cycle and the relationship lines drawn between the phases required before the drug moves to the next phase. This example would be a single row in Figure 6.5 (Start to A, B, and C, to Finish) where the letters A, B, C, could represent the actual phases of the drug research process.

The logic network diagram comes in two basic formats. The first is a pure logic diagram showing activities as boxes and the relationships between those activities noted by arrows. The second format is the timescale diagram that displays the activities as bars, similar to a Gantt chart tool.

Pure logic diagram

The pure logic diagram (see Figure 6.6) highlights the order and relationships between project activities and is easy to read and follow because the activities are simple boxes and relationships on a diagram. The boxes represent work activities such as in a software project, Design, Dev, Test. The main benefit of a Pure Logic Diagram is to help debug project logic. If there are complexities in that logic, it is important that the diagram represent it; for example, the D to C relationship in Figure 6.6 portrays a small level of complexity in the logic. On a pure logic diagram, activities follow one right after the other.

Time scale diagram

The logic network diagram is a time scaled chart. In Figure 6.10, the drawing displays a time scaled logic diagram drawn with bars instead of boxes. These bars are of varying lengths based on the duration of each activity. On a time scale diagram, the length of the bar is proportional to the duration of the activity and scaled to the calendar. To understand how long a particular activity can be, scale it against the calendar. Time scale diagrams look similar to the graphic portion of a Gantt chart, but many activities can be on a single row.

Figure 6.7 represents a display of three activities and the logical relationships between the activities. The project planner determines how to create the links between the activities. The diagram below illustrates that in order to link the boxes, the project planner should indicate the relationships between Task A and Task B is ID 1 as the predecessor, and ID 2 as the successor for the logic linking Task A and Task B. This process is the same between Task B and Task C.

FIGURE 6.7

Represents a small but accurate logic network diagram.

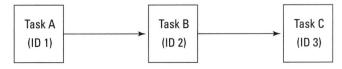

Now that you have seen that activities can link together, it is a good idea to understand the four ways of defining those relationships (links). The following explains the four types of relationships between activities:

- **Finish to start:** When one activity finishes before the next activity can start, this is the default relationship between activities.
- **Start to start:** When one activity starts, the succeeding activity can also start.
- **Finish to finish:** When one activity finishes, the succeeding activity can finish.
- **Start to finish:** When one activity starts, the succeeding activity should finish.

Figure 6.8 graphically displays the four types of task dependencies used on a logic network diagram. These are important to note when creating and communicating the diagram when there are questions about the relationships between the individual tasks. The fifth dependency noted in Figure 6.8 is "None" and not considered a task dependency, but is worth noting because "None" often appears on logic network diagrams and is valid.

FIGURE 6.8

Common project task dependencies.

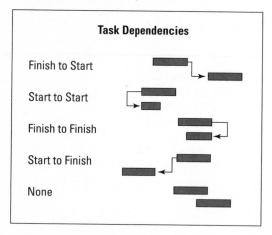

CROSS-REF See Chapter 17 for further details on creating these relationships for your project.

Planning to use a logic network diagram

In planning to use a logic network diagram, the project manager must first understand the tool of choice for this modeling process. In most cases, project managers use a typical project-scheduling tool that has a logic network view associated within it. In preparing to use this tool, project managers must add work tasks to the project schedule as a starting point. In some cases, it is good to start with the current activities of the project, then lay them out on a logic network diagram so they can be moved around and reorganized at will. After the tasks are loaded into the schedule, the project manager can start to utilize the tool.

There are other times when the project manager must draw the project activities, even at a high level, using a manual method (pen and paper), and this would be a good short-term solution, but long term the information needs entering into a formal tool in order to utilize all the benefits of the tool.

Before you can create the logic network, you must formulate a plan. In the following "Planning Questions" section, we provide some thoughts and ideas to help start you thinking about how you can use this tool on a project.

Planning Questions

1 *When would you create, develop, or write this tool?*
During the planning process when initially creating a project schedule and when updating is necessary

2 *Who is going to use this tool, both from an input and output status?*
Project manager, project planners, team members, subcontractors, or specific skill areas looking to determine the logical order of the project tasks

3 *Why are you going to use this tool?*
To determine the logic and relationships between the activities, graphically view the layout of the project tasks, and determine if any are missing or key areas of the project are missing

4 *How are you going to use this tool?*
Ensure the relationship between the activities (predecessors, successors) is correct. Determine if tasks are missing in the project task list; display a graphical layout of your project tasks.

5 *How will you distribute the information?*
Plotter, document control system, project schedule, e-mail, tabular form

6 *When will you distribute the information?*
During the planning process when creating the project tasks and after the final schedule completes

7 *What decisions can or should you make from this tool?*
Logical relationships decisions, order of activities correct, decisions about missing areas of the project

8 *What information does the tool provide for your project?*
Logical diagram of project tasks, schedule start and finish dates, durations of tasks

9 *What historical and legal information do you need to store?*
Baseline network, modifications to network itself, final version of logical network

10 *What will be the staffing requirements (role type) to run and maintain these tools?*
Project manager, team members, scheduler, cost manager, project planner

Reporting with a logic network diagram

The reporting of the logic network diagrams can occur throughout the project lifecycle. The two methods of reporting the logic network diagram include a hand-drawn method (rarely used) and software. Usually software products, for example Microsoft Project, will draw a pure logic network diagram for the project but not a time scale diagram. Using software ensures that the diagrams are easy to read and easy to edit. Project managers and team members commonly have logic network diagrams on white boards or on paper, and when they finish those discussions the project manager should immediately use software to clean up the diagrams and make them readable. When updating and moving the project activities, the project-scheduling tool automatically changes the project schedule. When using a manual method such as pen and paper, you lose the ability to move tasks around automatically, determine the impact of those moves, and communicate that impact to your customers. You should finalize the diagram first, go to a software tool, move the tasks around, and then determine the impacts of that move.

Figure 6.9 represents a time scaled logic network diagram. This diagram clearly shows the critical path in darker bars, A, D, G, M, N, and R along the bottom of the chart. You can observe that the bars are of different lengths, and these lengths represent the duration of the activity. Please note that activity "I" is a lighter color because it has more float then the other activities. A diagram in color usually displays the critical path in red.

CROSS-REF See Chapter 17 for more information on this tool and definitions around lead and lag.

FIGURE 6.9

A logic network diagram.

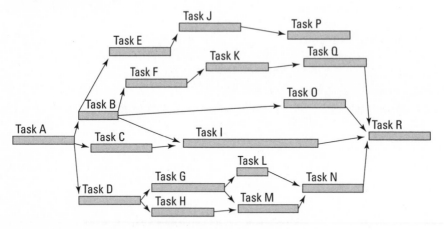

Figure 6.10 represents a time scaled logic diagram from a book-publishing project. It is a small portion of a total project and is a real-life example. The numbers at each end of the bar represent the start and finish dates relative to the calendar above it. The number beneath the bar in the center is the duration of the activity, the number in the bar is the activity's ID.

FIGURE 6.10

A logic network diagram from a book-publishing project.

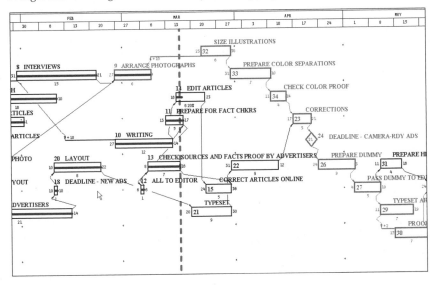

There is no need for formal reporting of the logic network diagram during the project lifecycle. The diagram is not part of the standard project reports because it does not contain project status.

Because the logic network diagram can be so large and difficult to draw on a standard piece of paper, the most appropriate format for printing is a plotter. Using the diagram on a computer screen, or over a series of screens, is also possible but may be challenging because the diagram can become large, complex, and hard to read on the screen.

CROSS-REF See Chapter 17 to learn more about how to use or create a network logic diagram.

Introducing the Project Milestone List

The purpose of the *project milestone list* is to communicate the project's milestone tasks and dates in a presentation format for upper management, customers, and project team members. The project's development or lifecycle methodology usually documents the major project phases. In some cases, the project milestone list and the major methodology phases are the same, making the creation of the project milestone list a lot easier. In some cases, companies have their own versions of the popular project methodologies, and sometimes they tweak it and organize it in a different way to match the needs of their industry or specific company.

There are many different methodologies available for projects, and each one is specialized to the industry that is executing the project. Rarely do project methodologies cross industries or merge in a single project. A construction project's methodology would differ greatly from a research project's methodology.

Project managers should establish a project's high-level milestones and publish them to the team for review at the beginning of the project. After the team or management approves the dates, they are set for the project and the dates are only changeable if there are scope changes, major change requests, or major impacts to the project that affect the project's time lines. The high-level milestone dates are on the baseline schedule and set the guiding periods for project team members to work on the project.

NOTE   The Project Management Institute's knowledge area for this project milestone list is the Time Management area. There are no other secondary areas for this tool.

ON the CD-ROM   We have included a sample of a project milestone list in the Time folder. Use this as a guide in creating your own version of this tool.

TOOL VALUE   A project milestone list provides the major components of a project and the delivery dates of those components in a simple and easy to read format.

The project milestone list represents the major phases of a project determined by the methodology chosen for the project. On software development projects, the project manager can choose from multiple methodologies to use on their projects. Two of the most popular include Waterfall and SCRUM. Each methodology has different dates and deliverables, even though they are in the same industry. In these examples, there are two different and distinct deliverables for the project milestone list. Table 6.3 represents a good example of the project milestone list for a software project (Waterfall).

Table 6.3 represents a typical software milestone list. The milestones displayed in the table are consistent with common software development methodologies used by the market today. When reviewing this list you can see that the milestone names are the major deliverables of the project, and the associated date is the expected delivery date for that milestone. You can also see that the asterisk (*) is an indicator of the phase the project is currently in and tracking to the delivery date.

TABLE 6.3

Example of Software Milestones (Waterfall only)

Milestone	Due Date
Project Initiation	01/17/2009
Requirements Complete (*)	03/03/2009
Design Complete	04/07/2009
Development Complete	06/09/2009
Testing Complete	10/11/2009
User Acceptance Testing Complete	11/09/2009
Production – Go Live	11/20/2009

One of the most important communication aspects of using a project milestone list is that the major delivery points represent a communication touch point with the customer. In almost every case, each one of the milestones on the project milestone list represents major communication points, normally in a presentation format, and a special meeting for the customers and upper management. You are responsible for this special meeting and deliver the latest status of the project (with the assistance of his or her team). This is a major communication event for the project and one that, if the team completes the milestone on time and within budget, project managers should recognize and celebrate with the team members and reward them for their efforts. The customers will appreciate the project presentations as they provide them with the latest project information. Often customers will monitor the project milestone list to ensure the project is tracking to the deliverable dates.

The project milestone is a high-level communication tool that is popular with the media. On large projects such as building airplanes, skyscrapers, or other large construction efforts, project managers send the project milestone list to the media for reporting in order to communicate project information to the public.

A project milestone list helps both you and your team members to communicate the critical dates of the project to your customers or upper management. The project milestone list, once established, communicates to all stakeholders what stage the project is in, and what the next stage of the project will be.

To understand a project milestone list and the different phases that are included on these lists, let us use a software example. Common milestone phases for software projects include requirements, design, development, testing, user acceptance, and production. In a construction example, common milestones consist of notice to proceed, start of project, start, and completion of various areas, testing and balance completion, certificate of occupation, and turnover to owner phases. As you can see from these two examples (software and construction), the project milestone lists can be different and it would be difficult for them to come together for a single project.

Figure 6.11 represents a typical project milestone list shown is a graphic format. This version is perfect for presentations, Web sites, newsletters, and so on and is an effective way to communicate project information to customers, upper management, or any interested stakeholder. Project managers should have this project milestone list available and handy to communicate to their customers at all times.

Each industry has its own way of dividing a project into major sections or parts; some use phases, such as the software industry; the construction industry uses location, and some use go/no-go decision points, such as the pharmaceutical industry. These major phases, or subdivisions, give executive management the ability to manage by milestone dates and have check-in points to ensure that the project is still on track. Management staff and stakeholders can identify if projects are ahead of schedule or behind schedule by reviewing milestones lists with associated dates and comparing them to the current progress of the project. It is common for management to use project milestones lists and manage by exception rather than looking at all the details of the project. This is quite common in organizations where there are a large number of projects and limited executive staff to oversee the portfolio of work.

FIGURE 6.11

A project milestone list in a graphical format.

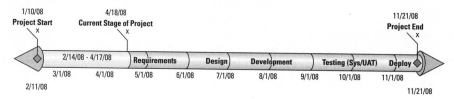

Project Milestone List

Planning to use a project milestone list

In the planning process when preparing to use a project milestone list, the project manager must first determine the methodology the project will utilize. After that is determined, the project manager should look for templates or existing versions of the project milestone list using that same methodology. This saves time and effort and prevents the project manager from reinventing something that already exists. After everyone agrees on the diagram, the project manager determines where and how to communicate information on the project — what Web site, newsletter, how often, and so on. After the project manager performs these planning steps, he or she has adequately prepared for the use of this tool.

Before you can create the project milestone list, you must formulate a plan. In the "Planning Questions" section, we provide some initial thoughts to help you start thinking about how to utilize the tool on a project.

Planning Questions

1 **When would you create, develop, or write this tool?**
In the planning process during methodology selection

2 **Who is going to use this tool, both from an input and output status?**
Upper management, owners, executives, project manager, team members, and subcontractors of specific skill areas, the media, marketing departments

3 **Why are you going to use this tool?**
To map the project major milestones to the project schedule and present a project roadmap to customers

4 *How are you going to use this tool?*

By reviewing the milestones and associated dates at each status meeting, deliver in presentation format to clients, drive project team to deliverables based on milestone dates

5 *How will you distribute the information?*

Plotter, newsletter, document control system, presentation, e-mail

6 *When will you distribute the information?*

Once, when created for a presentation, approval of project milestones phases or timeframes, status meeting, on-demand, major milestone check point meetings/presentations

7 *What decisions can or should you make from this tool?*

Schedule decisions, risk of schedule slide, methodology decisions, including which phases to add, or not to add to milestones

8 *What information does the tool provide for your project?*

Schedule information, major milestones dates, methodology selected, phase overlapping dates

9 *What historical and legal information do you need to store?*

How variance issues were resolved with the milestone dates, lessons learned Information, actual finish dates

10 *What will be the staffing requirements (role type) to run and maintain these tools?*

Project manager, team members, and scheduler

Reporting using a project milestone list

The project manager creates and updates the project milestone list continually throughout the life of the project. Project managers will report the project milestone at least weekly, and then again during major milestone events.

Table 6.4 represents a typical construction milestone list. The milestones represented in this list are consistent with the construction methodologies. One of the big differences in the methodologies and corresponding project milestone lists for construction projects deals with the various locations the project team is working on at the time of taking status. For example basement, first floor, second floor, and third floor are major elements on the project and therefore should be noted on the milestone list.

TABLE 6.4

Example of Construction Milestones

Milestone	Date
Notice to Proceed	01/01/2009
Start to Mobilization	01/09/2009
Foundation Complete	02/11/2009
Rough-In (Electrical Complete) (*)	03/07/2009
Finished Inspection Complete	07/08/2009
Certification of Occupation	11/13/2009
Turn Over to Owner	12/31/2009
Punch List Complete	01/17/2010

The project manager reports the project milestone list continually throughout the project. The project manager and team members, in most cases, report status against the milestone lists on a weekly basis until the project completes. Many times the project manager uses the project's ability of making a major milestone as to what color they will report for the week on the stop light report (red, yellow, or green). The status color of the project is often determined by the team's confidence level regarding whether or not they can hit the project's major milestones listed on the milestone list.

To ensure that customers are aware of the different milestones, the project manager should post the project's milestone list on the project Web site, project rooms, or advertise it via the media for reporting and awareness.

 See Chapter 17 to learn more about the project milestone list.

Introducing the Project Schedule

The purpose of a *project schedule* is to create, monitor, and control project activities. The project plan drives the project schedule. The project schedule acts as a central repository for all project task information and helps get the right information in the hands of those making company or project-level decisions. Project managers utilize their project schedules almost daily to determine what activities are currently in progress, what cost information has changed, what activities are critical, and who the resources on the project are. The project schedule is your one-stop shop to communicate this detailed project information. The goal of the project schedule is to identify what needs to be done (activities), when it needs to done (start and finish dates), and who is going to do it (resources). Without a project schedule, even the smallest of projects can turn into a disaster because the project manager will have limited ability to control the tasks and people on the projects. Even on small projects, project managers should remember to understand the order of the work, what are their dependencies, what are the costs associated to the project tasks, and in the end, who is responsible for each activity. This information, regardless of whether the project is large or small, is valuable information, and is required in order to run a successful project.

When you resource load your project schedule (add resources to the tasks on the plan) and then continue to add resource costs, you start to realize the functionality built into this tool. You can perform several types of analysis with this information loaded into your project schedule (information such as resource commitments, costs at a certain date on the project, resource allocations, and so on). A fully loaded resource schedule is important in managing a project.

NOTE The Project Management Institute's knowledge area for this project schedule is the Time Management area. The secondary concept area for this tool is Scope.

ON the CD-ROM We have included a sample of a project schedule tool in the Time folder. Use this as a guide to the first step in creating your own personal version of this tool. Your company or project may have specific requirements that can enhance this communication tool further; however, we believe this is a great starting point for the creation of this tool for your project.

TOOL VALUE A project schedule is the plan of record for the project. It displays where you have been, where you are, and where you are going on your project. Very few projects can be successful without this tool.

The project schedule is one of the most important tools a project manager has to communicate project information. The wealth of data within this tool can help resolve problems of complex questions on the project. Project schedules include project activities, start and end dates, resource assignments, costs per activity, activity dependencies, and earned value indexes, to name a few. The project manager builds the project schedule from the project plan because the project plan consists of activities, duration, and the logical relationships between the activities (the order of activities that are going to be processed) that are all key elements of the project schedule. Once defined, the project manager runs the information though an automated scheduling tool to create the project schedule. The project schedule includes the start and finish dates for each task, calculated by the scheduling tool. The automated scheduling system does not have the ability to plan; its only job is to crunch the numbers and input from the project manager or project scheduler. Therefore as the project manager, you must provide the tool with the following information before it will calculate the schedule. This includes activity description, duration, and logical relationships between activities at a minimum. After doing so, the tool completes the calculations for your project.

Project managers must make a diligent effort to constantly update and maintain the project schedule for their projects. Sometimes, on larger and more complex projects, the project manager hands the scheduling responsibilities to a project scheduler for ongoing maintenance of the project schedule. In this case, the project manager is still actively involved, but does not perform the actual updating or maintenance of the file; but the project manager is still responsible for the maintenance of the project schedule.

Project stakeholders expect a weekly communication of the project schedule from the project manager. In most cases, this is an acceptable timeframe because more frequently would provide too much information and less frequently could leave the customer's feeling lost or out of touch. When communicating this information, the project manager should start by going over the project milestone dates and then drill into the specific tasks that are occurring during the timeframe he or she is presenting on the schedule. When communicating the project schedule on a weekly basis, it provides an excellent opportunity to keep the customers in-sync with what is occurring on the project at all times.

The project schedule is so popular that before long, the stakeholders will demand nothing less from the project manager and will learn to appreciate and value the wealth of the project data it provides.

Figure 6.12 represents a typical project schedule using the Gantt chart view. This project schedule shows duration, start dates, finish dates, and predecessor ID number for each activity. The project manager can add many different columns of information to the project schedule, but depending on size, may struggle with paper size for printing or screen size for presenting the information. In most cases, it is up to the project manager to decide what columns and fields they want to display as part of their project schedule default view. The choices are almost endless.

FIGURE 6.12

A typical project schedule for a book-publishing project.

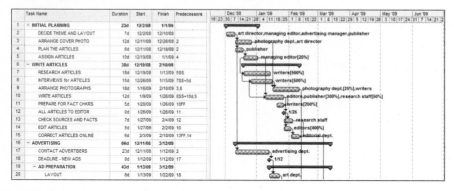

TIP   Make sure the durations of your activities are no longer than one reporting cycle. Anything longer, project managers have a much more difficult time estimating and reporting progress. When starting an activity in a reporting cycle, you want to make sure that activity finishes no later than the next reporting cycle.

The minimum information that exists on a project schedule includes a task description, duration (in hours/days/weeks/months), and the logical relationships. A project-scheduling tool cannot plan. You must describe every activity, you must estimate every duration, you must define what order (sequence) the activities will be worked. Without at least these elements, the project information cannot become a project schedule. You can add many other fields to the project schedule, but when creating the initial project schedule, you should have at least the aforementioned fields as a starting point. When communicating project schedule information you should be communicating at least the minimum number of fields to your customers, but plan to report many more fields to provide the complete picture of the project.

NOTE Rarely can a team complete the creation of a project schedule on the first attempt; it is a dynamic process ongoing throughout the project.

When communicating to your project team members using the project schedule, you should be looking at the lowest possible granularity on that schedule, because team leads and team members will want to discuss the individual tasks and any issues or concerns they are having at that task level, not necessarily at the overall project level. You also want to discuss with your team members specifics at the task level, so you have a true understanding of the status of your project. When you dive deep into the details to report project information, you are prepared to answer questions on those details that you would not be able to without that deeper level of knowledge. Identifying and discovering the details of your project is invaluable as you communicate your project information.

TIP Do not overload your project schedule with too many time constraints such as, start no earlier than, must finish on, finish no later than. Keep time constraints to an absolute minimum, and let the project-scheduling engine do the work.

The project schedule can display hundreds of fields (columns) of information related to a project. Some of these fields include, but are not limited to costs, resources, duration, percent complete, earned value, total float, and the activity's relationships. In most cases, it is best to keep the fields to a minimum so as not to overwhelm people with detail they do not need. Additional fields can cause confusion and may be unproductive to a project manager while offering little extra value to the schedule. We recommend creating two separate reports with different fields rather than trying to crowd the fields onto one report. One could be a schedule report, and the other could be a cost report. In most cases, they would go to two different people — one for schedule, and one for cost.

- Microsoft Project
- Primavera
- Project Scheduler
- Open Work Bench
- Deltek Open Plan

When reviewing and choosing a project-scheduling tool, you should be looking for features that you can utilize often on your projects. Some of the features these tools provide include:

- Great reporting features such as the ability to select, sort, summarize, and group your information
- User friendliness — easy to read and understand and the ability to create schedules with little to no training
- Resource capability assigning, leveling, and detail reporting
- Cost analysis, budgeting, and tracking
- Earned value analysis

 The actual reviewing and selecting of a project-scheduling tool for your company is beyond the scope of this book.

Planning to use a project schedule

In the planning process for preparing to use a project schedule tool, the project manager must first select the methodology she will use on the project and then choose the correct company's scheduling tool for their project's schedule, or if given the option, choose her favorite tool. If the project manager is not familiar with the project-scheduling tool, she must first receive training on the product before creating the schedule. Finally, before the creation of the schedule, the project manager should determine if she is responsible for creating the schedule, or if the project is hiring a project scheduler to perform this work. On larger efforts, most often, there is a project scheduler on the team and the project manager does not own the responsibility of creating the project schedule. The project manager works with her customers and stakeholders to understand their wants and needs on the project schedule (cost or resources, both or neither). The project manager will decide how often to communicate the information to them. When these planning steps are in place, the project manager or project scheduler can create the project schedule.

Before you can create a project schedule, you must formulate a plan. In the "Planning Questions" section, we have provided some initial thoughts to help you start thinking about how to use this tool on your project.

Planning Questions

1 *When would you create or develop the project schedule?*
Initiating process, throughout the planning process and the project, as changes occur

2 *Who is going to use this tool, both from an input and output status?*
Upper management, owners, executives, project manager, team members, subcontractors of specific skill areas, and the media

3 *Why are you going to use this tool?*
To be able to display the tasks on the project and create performance reports. To show resource assignments, dependencies between tasks, costs per task, time lines per task and variances in costs and schedules

4 *How are you going to use this tool?*
To keep the current and baseline schedule up to date, provide upper level management reporting, detailed reporting and manage by exception (stop light report). To show both time and cost variances, resource loading and performance analysis.

5 *How will you distribute the information?*

Tabular report, plotter, newsletter, document control system, e-mail, and presentation format

6 *When will you distribute the information?*

When created, status meetings, on-demand, weekly status reports

7 *What decisions can or should you make from this tool?*

Decisions about risk, cost, quality, resources, purchasing, and performance analysis

8 *What information does the tool provide for your project?*

Schedule information, cost information, resource assignment information, dependencies, activity list, network logic diagrams, Gantt chart, and time constraints

9 *What historical and legal information do you need to store?*

How variance issues were resolved (through notes), lessons learned Information, actual costs, actual start and finish dates, resource assignments, dependencies between tasks, cost and schedule variances

10 *What will be the staffing requirements (role type) to run and maintain these tools?*

Project manager, team members, project scheduler, resource manager, cost manager, risk manager, financial manager

Reporting with a project schedule

The project manager relies on their team members to help them create the project schedule. On larger projects, project schedulers create the project schedule because the project manager would not have the time to spend on it and still be able to manage the project. Many times your company has project schedule templates to use as a starting point, across the different types of projects. No template will work exactly for every project, so you are going to have to make changes and updates to the template regardless. This project schedule template creates the initial categories and tasks, but requires modifying to make it applicable to your unique project. These project schedule templates communicate the various project methodologies your company uses to implement projects. If your customers or stakeholders have specific project tasks or requirements, the project manager adds them to the project schedule to ensure the team completes these activities.

When reporting and communicating with the project schedule, the project manager rarely uses the project schedule alone because the supporting details contained in the project status report assist in telling the whole story of the project. The project schedule needs the status report and the supporting information.

Before you can do any project reporting you have to plan what types of reports you will communicate and how you are going to create those reports. To create the reports, you need to establish the detail information to be able to sort, select, summarize, and group your tasks. For example, you may want to group the project activities by phase or location. To accomplish this, you must plan how you are going to extract the activities that fit into the various groups. How you implement this depends solely on the software system you are using to manage your project schedule. Each of these software programs also has built-in reporting capabilities that you may want to utilize when communicating your project information to your customers and other stakeholders.

Different formats are available for reporting the project schedule. The first and most commonly used format is on paper (document format) where the project schedule is printed and analyzed with the customers or stakeholders in person at a review meeting. This commonly used method allows the customers to ask questions of you and your team members on the various components of the project schedule.

The other method of reporting is electronic publishing of the project schedule, via presentations, e-mails, and Web sites. This reporting technique is good because the information becomes instantly available to the customers, subcontractors, and vendors and allows them to drill into the details of the tasks at their convenience. Often companies create project dashboards that contain project schedule information for communicating this information. This type of communication is real time, and extremely valuable to customers and upper management.

CROSS-REF See Chapter 11 for more information on project dashboards.

Introducing the Schedule Management Plan

The purpose of the *schedule management plan* is to ensure that there is a process in place to create, monitor, and control the project schedule. Some companies call the schedule management plan a time management plan; they are actually the same document. Project managers should communicate the schedule management plan to everyone involved with the project so that they understand that formal processes and procedures are in place when they need to make any changes to the project schedule. The schedule management plan establishes that no project schedule changes occur without formal approval from different staff members on the project, such as the project manager or the project scheduler. Team members randomly changing the project schedule is not good and can really impact the project negatively.

Project managers should make sure that a schedule management plan is in place during the project initiation phase and before any project activities begin.

NOTE The Project Management Institute's knowledge area for this Project Milestone list is the Time Management area. The secondary concept area for this tool is Scope.

ON the CD-ROM We have included a sample of the schedule management plan in the Time folder. Use this as a guide to help you create your own personal version of this tool.

TOOL VALUE A schedule management plan establishes the process to create, execute, monitor, and close out the project schedule. The value of this tool is the structured process that a project manager, team member, or customer follows to make any schedule enhancements and changes. It also defines the process of updating the schedule to keep it current.

The schedule management plan describes the various elements of actually developing, maintaining, and closing out the project schedule. This includes any report generation, creating a baseline schedule, and any other aspects such as resource assignments or the inclusion of cost. The plan also includes who is responsible for making various updates to the schedule and the level of details needed to create the project schedule. The project manager must determine the level to which he or she will report progress as well. For example, a lower-level project schedule, used by the project manager to drive the day-to-day project activities, may not be the same level of detail used for project reporting to the customers or upper management. Often, project managers choose to report their project schedules at the highest level only to keep customers or senior management from unnecessary worry, or getting into the details of the plan.

Table 6.5 represents a typical schedule management plan table of contents. As you can see from the table of contents, the major sections of the plan include the baseline process, parameters, change control, reporting and so on. It is not a large or complex plan, but important when it comes to keeping a tight control on the project's schedule.

TABLE 6.5

Example of a Schedule Management Plan

Section	Description
1	Schedule Management Plan Overview
2	Schedule Management Responsibilities
3	Schedule Baseline
4	Schedule Parameters
5	Schedule Change Control
6	Schedule Reports

The schedule management plan documents in detail the process and procedures for the project schedule change control process. Note Section 5 of the table of contents: this section contains the processes and procedures for making any changes, named Schedule Change Control. This section includes how often you can make schedule changes (weekly), who can make the changes (the person responsible on project), and who provides the overall approval for these changes (project manager, customer). When anyone requests changes, they must follow this process before making any changes to the schedule. Normally schedule changes are limited to a few individuals on the project and are rarely open to all team members. Imagine the chaos and impacts to the project if there was no process in place, and team members were able to get into the schedule and change dates or move resource assignments randomly without approval.

On larger projects that have a scheduling staff performing as project planners and schedulers, a schedule management plan sets the processes and procedures for them to follow as part of their daily work. A project scheduler is responsible in a full-time role to create and maintain the project's schedule. On large construction projects, one, two, or even more full-time project schedulers manage the work tasks on the schedule. The project planner or scheduler is responsible for all changes and updates to the schedule under the project manager's direction. As the project progresses and changes occur to the schedule, you as the project manager will provide guidance to the project planner/schedulers to update the project schedule reflecting the latest status. For example, a key group requests an extension on the schedule of one week or they will miss a project deadline. You allow that request under the approval of the project customers and then instruct the project schedulers to make the changes to the schedule.

One of the main aspects of the schedule management plan is the process of creating a schedule baseline. As a project manager, make sure you create a schedule baseline for your project even if you do not think you will need one.

The schedule management plan is one of the most important tools in controlling and managing the time aspects of your project. The plan is broken into six major areas. The schedule management plan includes the following sections:

- **Overview:** This section includes the processes that incorporate report generation and include a baseline schedule for reporting project performance.

- **Responsibilities:** This section identifies who is responsible for developing the schedule, who will be accountable for creating the baseline and updating the current information, and who will generate the performance report for each reporting cycle. Also identified should be the person responsible for data entry and the scheduling tools.

- **Schedule baseline:** This section includes the details and processes for creating a project baseline, and the importance of it.

- **Schedule parameters:** This section includes any constraints, assumptions, and schedule limitations on the project. It identifies the duration of the reporting cycles (weekly, monthly, etc.), which should establish the maximum duration of the activities in the schedule.

- **Schedule change control:** This section covers how changes occur on the project schedule. This section also includes details on how, when, and why the modification of the schedule occurred, and the process to approve any change requests. It defines the process for updating the baseline when change requests are included.

- **Schedule reports:** This section includes any reports and the timing of those reports to the customers of the project. This may include the method to select, sort, group, and summarize the schedule. One of the breakouts could be the Work Breakdown Structure.

Planning to use a schedule management plan

In the planning process for preparing to use a schedule management plan, the project manager must first determine the number of scheduling resources required and their responsibilities for the creation, updating, and changes to the project schedule. The project manager must also determine if there are any parameters on the schedule (such as hard or external constraints), determine a schedule change control process, and finally meet with the customers and document their schedule reporting requirements. Performing these planning steps allows the project manager to complete the planning steps to adequately prepare to use the schedule management plan.

Before you can create the schedule management plan, you must first formulate a plan. In the "Planning Questions" section, we have provided some initial thoughts to help you start thinking about where you can use this tool.

Reporting using a schedule management plan

The schedule management plan is not part of the project's regular status reporting because it is a management and controlling document, not a status document. The document does not contain

---

Planning Questions

1 **When would you create and write the schedule management plans tool?**
In the planning process when documenting the other management plans for the project (such as scope, cost, quality)

2 **Who is going to use this tool, both from an input and output perspective?**
Project manager, team members, subcontractors, and project schedulers

3 **Why are you going to use this tool?**
To document the process and procedures for making schedule changes on the project, document responsible parties for those schedule changes, document any constraints or assumptions around schedule changes, document how to create and maintain the project schedule, and document the reporting requirements

4 **How are you going to use it?**
By guiding and directing team members and customers on the schedule management process, and working with project schedulers to ensure the process and procedures are followed and not deviated from, use as a guide in ensuring the reporting aspects of the project schedule are being adhered to

5 **How will you distribute the information?**
Document format such as Microsoft Word, document control system, e-mail, possible presentations

6 **When will you distribute the information?**
At document creation, on-demand, to new project scheduler resources, otherwise when required

continued

continued

7 *What decisions can or should you make from this tool?*

Decisions on schedule management and control processes, how often to report schedules, tool decisions for schedule creation, how often changes are made, updating and reporting cycle

8 *What information does this tool provide your project?*

The management and control process and procedures for schedule changes, identifies and clarifies the project team members who have responsibility for updating the schedule, captures the assumptions and constraints, processes for creating a baseline, resources and roles, and various reporting requirements

9 *What historical and legal information do you need to keep?*

Lessons learned information, schedule management plan itself and changes to the plan

10 *What will be the staffing requirements (role type) to run and maintain these tools?*

Project manager, team member, project scheduler

detail project information, just processes and procedures for controlling the schedule. One key aspect of this document is the reporting component and the description of when project schedule reporting will occur. For example, the schedule management plan can call for weekly Gantt charts, monthly cost reports, and on-demand resource leveling charts. In each case, the schedule management plan documents the reports and the specific reporting requirements of the customers.

The schedule management plan also documents when you will collect project status, allowing you to create the project reports with the latest information.

The schedule management plan describes in detail the generation of the reports, such as titles and their placements, various columns of information (fields), and how to sort, select, group, and summarize the reports. The plan also includes the communication aspects of who receives the reports, type of media (electronic/printer/plotter) used, and how often reports are to be distributed.

Some of the typical reports outlined in a schedule management plan that your customers may require include:

- Gantt chart
- Project calendar
- Stop light report
- Resource allocation report
- Various cost reports
- Network logic diagram reports
- Earned value report

The schedule management plan is also one of the management plans within the project management plan tool. The document once approved is stored in the document control system for long-term archiving and is accessible by anyone interested in obtaining this information.

CROSS-REF See Chapter 16 to learn more about how to create and use a schedule management plan.

Summary

The tools described in this Time Management knowledge area support project managers and team members in controlling the time aspects of their projects. Managing project schedules is an important task and something to take seriously throughout the project. Project managers need to monitor and control time management closely because it is something that can quickly get away from you.

This chapter includes tools such as schedule management plan, Gantt chart, logic network diagram, project schedule, project milestone list, and the baseline schedule. Each tool focuses on helping the project manager and their team members become more efficient in project communications in the Time Management knowledge area. With these tools, project managers and team members can control the activities on the project and drive the team toward a successful completion.

Chapter 7

Defining Communication Tools to Manage Project Costs

In this chapter, we explore project communications tools in the Cost Management Knowledge area. Cost management includes the process and procedures to manage and ensure that the project stays on budget. The tools listed in this chapter are vital to communicating the cost and budget components of your project. Project cost management is not business finance.

Much like time management, cost management is one of the areas that most customers watch closely, and the success of the project can hinge on this area being successful. On a cost-driven project, the project manager must be cost conscious and track the budget closely. Tasks such as running various budget reports, determining contractor costs, watching the forecasts closely, and closing out purchase orders are some of the critical aspects of budget control.

The tools presented in this chapter can help you and your project team members become better at communicating project cost information to customers, and upper management staff. Each of the tools in the chapter has their own unique purposes within the Cost Management knowledge area and each will benefit the project manager on their projects.

Introducing the Budget Spreadsheet

The purpose of a *budget spreadsheet* is to track, record, and communicate the project's budget and cost information. The budget spreadsheet is a critical tool in managing and controlling project costs, and without it, project managers can struggle to stay on top of their finances. Project forecast management is another area in cost managing and yet another example of why project managers should use a budget spreadsheet as often as possible to monitor and control their budgets.

The communication aspects of budget spreadsheets can be challenging. Project managers must ensure that they handle communicating budget information carefully. When communicating this information, the project manager must choose the appropriate form to communicate this information. It can be in person, by e-mail, or by other means, depending on the budget and the message to deliver. Sending an e-mail to your customers stating that your project is millions of dollars over budget without first communicating in person or over the phone is not a proper method to handle that situation.

NOTE The Project Management Institute's knowledge area for this tool is the Cost Management knowledge area. The secondary area that this tool could be associated with is Communications.

ON the CD-ROM We have included a sample of this Budget Spreadsheet tool in the Cost folder. Use this as a guide to help you create your own version of this tool.

TOOL VALUE Budget spreadsheet provides the project's financial picture from an executive level down to the details, and provides project managers with total control over the project's financial data and reporting.

Project managers, because of their responsibility of monitoring and controlling the project monies, have benefitted for years by using budget spreadsheets. Some companies have formal applications that enable them to manipulate project money; but in most cases, the common tool for project managers is the budget spreadsheet. Even if companies have tools, the tools often generate budget spreadsheets. The complexities and the formulas in the spreadsheet will differ from company to company and industry to industry. Some companies only track the basic information; others have complex formulas that allow a project manager to watch every dollar and how it is spent. Some projects require a strict level of budget tracking and some are looser and, therefore, do not require the project manager to track with the same rigor. In most cases, companies have standards for tracking dollars that the project manager must adhere to on their projects. Over time, project managers have found a best practice is to track the project's spending on a weekly basis. This allows you to feel like you have a constant handle on your project's budget. For example, projects' forecasts often change on a week-to-week basis, and knowing that information can lead to uncovering potential issues in the budget much earlier, giving impacted parties a chance to resolve before it ever actually occurs.

Table 7.1 represents a basic budget spreadsheet for a small project. This spreadsheet shows four separate groups having maximum dollar amounts allocated to each group, and the average dollars spent on similar type projects. In this example, the project has up to $38,000 to spend, but will most likely spend in the ballpark of $23,000. (Note: Group A and D have not completed their portions of the project, therefore this project is not yet complete.)

TABLE 7.1				
Example of a Budget Spreadsheet (Cost by Group)				
ITEM#	Avg. Cost	Max Cost	Forecast Costs	Final Cost
Group A	$5,600	$10,000	$8,000	
Group B	$2,300	$5,000	$3,500	$3,805
Group C	$4,750	$8,000	$7,650	$5,654
Group D	$10,000	$15,000	$13,200	
Totals	$22,650	$38,000	$32,350	

Every company should have a budget spreadsheet template for project managers to use on their projects. If one is not available, this example provides a starting point for a small effort. (This template is on the CD-ROM included in this book.)

Budget spreadsheets, as noted, differ from project to project but contain some common key elements to the budget management process; these key elements include average costs, maximum costs, forecasted costs, actual costs, and final costs. There is no perfect format or number of columns to use on a budget spreadsheet. As long as you are getting the information you need to manage and control your project's budget, use whatever will work for you. If another project manager is tracking different fields and different information, it does not mean your spreadsheet is wrong or not effective; it could simply mean that your projects are different and he is tracking more or less information. In the end, most customers are not going to care how you track the details or the methods you use, as long as you are tracking correctly and not overspending on the project's budget.

 **Control your activities by setting a maximum cost amount. For example, set a limit that no activities can cost more than $10,000.**

Upper management and customers hold project managers accountable for controlling the project costs. As the project comes closer to closing out, their scrutiny heightens on the project's spending. The budget spreadsheet can assist you with answering and responding to a higher level of scrutiny from upper management or from customers. For example, as the scrutiny becomes more intense, project managers can use the budget spreadsheet to understand how the project has used the budget, projecting future expenditures, and the overall costs of the project. These three areas are the major components of any budget spreadsheet, and you should be watching those as closely as possible. One of the most scrutinized areas of the budget is the forecast information that provides the project's current estimate at completion. This information is excellent in determining whether the project is projecting to complete over or under budget. The projects forecast is complex, and is an often-overused formula in the project budgeting process because many project team members will over forecast to ensure they have the dollars allocated to their portion of the project, without understanding or caring about the overall budget. Project managers must be watchful of the forecast data on a regular basis and have a clear understanding of the people and resources that make up those estimates. If they have this information, if heated discussions occur, they can stand up for their team members and justify why and how the money is projecting.

One of the key aspects of a successful and useful budget spreadsheet is the data and the process behind the numbers. Without all team members entering their estimates in a consistent manner, the numbers on the budget spreadsheet can be all over the map. For example, if they estimate resources differently, or do not control them in their data entry from a week-to-week basis or a day-to-day basis, the forecasts and estimates can swing all over the place. Most companies control this swing from within the Finance departments, but it also takes the diligence of the project manager to stay on top of this process and monitor it closely. Because the project manager is responsible for standing up and reporting on these dollars, you must be sure the process for entering the dollars is correct.

NOTE When working on a foreign project, an unexpected exchange rate change can raise havoc with the project's estimated cost. It is possible to lessen the impact of this change by establishing a contract agreement before the project start, and if the rate changes the impacts are accounted for in the budget.

Most budget spreadsheets display the dollars allocated to the project by specific functional areas. For example, in a software project the design, development, and testing teams each have a specific budget amount for their portions of the project. When the team leads for each of the different areas provide a budget estimate, the project manager's responsibility is to hold these team leaders accountable to their budgets; otherwise, budget overruns can occur in many different areas, causing a negative impact to the overall budget. The tracking of the budget amounts to a specific area of the project is important and beneficial because it increases the accountability of the team leaders responsible for those areas. If you are seeing that a group is forecasting over their maximum amount, you can work directly with that team's lead in that group and correct the situation immediately. You as project manager provide the maximum budget amount to each group and expect them to stay on budget throughout the project. This allows the team leaders in their own groups to look at their forecasted amounts, look at the maximum amounts, and determine if they have a delta (variance). If so, you should work closely with the team lead and resolve the delta. In the end, it will help bring that portion of the project's finances back in line, and in most cases correct the overall budget for the project.

NOTE A delta is the difference or the variance in two amounts. If one amount is expected to be $10 and it ends up being $15, the delta is $5 dollars. Delta is a common term in the project management industry when discussing variances between the two terms.

One advantage to using budget spreadsheets is the total control you have over the data. In some cases, project managers like to create budget scenarios in which they adjust the dollar or resource hour allocations and determine what the new project costs would be under that scenario. These are *what-if* scenarios, and they become powerful communication tools when managing your project's budget and answering those difficult questions from your customers or upper management. Ongoing communicating of this information to the customers is beneficial because if they have any specific requests, you can adjust and play with values in the budget to attempt to satisfy their requests. You can easily create what-if scenarios in your budget spreadsheet, and store them in a separate spreadsheet, leaving your original budget spreadsheet intact. Creating these scenarios can help you understand the impact if something occurs unexpectedly, and you have to make some "real-life" changes. Stockholders can make future planning and decision making using what-if scenarios. Here are three what-if scenarios for managing your project costs:

- How would changing employee rates affect the bottom line project budget?
- What happens to the project's budget if the resources incorrectly allocate their hours?
- What happens to the budget if overtime is required?

Planning to use a budget spreadsheet

In the planning for using a budget spreadsheet tool, the project manager must first understand the rules and processes defined for budget management within the company. The project manager needs to work with the Finance or PMO teams and understand templates, timeframes, and other expectations for managing and controlling a project's budget. After the project manager understands this information, he /she will have the ability to develop the project's budget spreadsheet. The next step is for the project manager to work with the customers and determine their reporting requirements for budget reporting. Knowing when the customer would like to see the financial data and making sure that those expectations match the processes established by the company is an important step for the project manager to take in this planning process. For example, customers who want to see actual cost on a weekly basis but the company processes actuals on a monthly basis are going to be out of luck. There would be little a project manager could do to get the actuals from the financial system more often than monthly. The project manager would have to set an expectation with the customer that in this case, it is not possible. Without having these conversations, the project manager would never know the customer's expectation on budget reporting and may cause future communication issues on the budget reporting side of the project. After completing these steps, the project manager has adequately prepared for using a budget spreadsheet on their projects.

Before you can create a budget spreadsheet, you must formulate a plan. In the "Planning Questions." ection below, we provided some suggestions to help you start thinking about how to utilize a budget spreadsheet in your project.

Planning Questions

_1_ _When would you create, develop, or write this tool?_
Planning process, when getting the budget aspects of the project started, and long before project execution begins.

_2_ _Who is going to use this tool, both from an input and output perspective?_
Upper management, owners, customers, executives, project manager, team members, subcontractors, cost manager, financial analyst

continued

continued

3 *Why are you going to use it?*

Estimating budget for the project, detail cost reporting on actuals, estimate project schedule, estimate, and track actuals of project

4 *How are you going to use this tool?*

Update and monitor cost of project and report results, determine staffing needs for project, determine schedule constraints

5 *How will you distribute the information?*

Document format such as Microsoft Word, spreadsheet format such as Microsoft Excel, document control system, e-mail, graphic charts

6 *When will you distribute the information?*

Weekly, most often regarded on projects as the timeframe for capturing and ensuring projects are on track, monthly reporting on actuals in most cases

7 *What decisions can or should you make from this tool?*

Cost and budget decisions, vendor versus in-house staffing model, project scope decisions based on costs, quality decisions, overtime allowance

8 *What information does this tool provide for your project?*

Cost information, resources information, contractor rates, employee and contractor actuals, budget forecasting, month-by-month spend chart/rate.

9 *What historical and legal information do you need to store?*

Lessons learned information, actual costs versus projected costs, actual hours versus projected hours, variance reports

10 *What will be the staffing requirements (role type) to run and maintain these tools?*

Project manager, financial analyst, cost control manager, clerk

Reporting using a budget spreadsheet

On most projects, the project manager is responsible for the creation of the project's budget spreadsheet. On larger projects when there is an administration team in place, reporting is normally a key activity for that type of group and they often become responsible for creating and maintaining budget spreadsheets for the project. The budget spreadsheet is a regular project standard report and distributed during the reporting cycle established by the company. This is often a weekly cadence and working with your customers, weekly is a common expectation they have for this type of report.

A best practice that project managers should utilize is the ongoing tracking of the project's budget. Regardless of the company's formal reporting cycle, project managers should track, capture, and store their budget data on a weekly basis during the life of the project. If there is a situation in which the finance department develops a budget restatement or has issues concerning the budget, project managers need to have the information stored in case they need to revisit it.

During the project status meeting, which in most cases is weekly, the project manager communicates the budget to the customers and addresses any concerns or issues they have on the budget at that time. Communicating this information in person adds a level of accountability for the project manager to ensure their team members are spending the budget wisely throughout the project. Without a weekly checkpoint, expenditures will rise, and money may not be recoverable.

Table 7.2 represents an advanced monthly tracking budget spreadsheet. In this example, you see that this budget spreadsheet tracks per month two separate variances, one on labor hours, and the other by project costs. This information ensures that the project manager and team members are estimating their hours accurately each month. After the month ends, the project manager enters the actual hours for calculating total project costs. If the project manager sees that a project team member's hours are not consistent with the original estimate, then the project manager pays special attention to that resource's hours and determines how they developed their estimates and what factors they used in their calculations. It may be that a particular resource just needs training to become a better estimator so that their future estimates are more accurate.

TABLE 7.2

Example of a Budget Spreadsheet (Hours/Project Costs)

Name	Emp Rate	Contactor Rate	Jan Act	Jan Est	Actual Total Costs per Month	Est. Total Costs per Month	Hour Var	Cost Var
Employee 1	$45		2	2	$90	$90	0	0
Contractor 1		$96	5	5	$480	$480	0	0
Employee 2	$35		2	3	$70	$105	-1	-35
Employee 3	$25		5	1	$125	$25	4	100
Employee 4	$44		6	6	$264	$264	0	0
Contractor 2		$100	10	6	$1,000	$600	4	400
Employee 5	$22		2	2	$44	$44	0	0
Employee 6	$45		10	15	$450	$675	-5	-225
Employee 7	$65		2	2	$130	$130	0	0
Employee 8	$45		15	5	$675	$225	10	450
Totals			59	47	$3,328	$2,638	12	690

This example is another one of the thousands of budget spreadsheets available to project managers to utilize on their projects. As noted earlier, there is no right or wrong format, and project managers must select one that works for their projects. Most often, project managers pick a format they like and have worked with before and use it from project to project.

CROSS-REF See Chapter 16 to learn more about how to use a budget spreadsheet.

Introducing the Cost Estimate Report

The purpose of the *cost estimate report* tool is to provide an initial cost estimate to the owners or customers of the proposed project. Before any work activities begin or the project is in its initiation process, an estimating team develops the estimates for all resources and materials the project team will need to execute the project. The cost estimate report also contains any assumptions and justifications for calculating those project costs. This allows anyone who needs that information full disclosure in order to help make the final decision on proceeding with the project. In the early stages of project funding, the cost estimate report is valuable because it provides the cost estimate to the project and a method of determining whether there are enough funds available to proceed. If the funds allocated do not meet the needs of the project, there is little reason for starting the project. In many cases, customers or executive staff cancels the project before they ever fund it — cost estimate report helps in that decision-making process. On the other hand, if funding does receive approval, the project manager's first responsibility is to ensure that the cost estimate and approved funding amounts are the same, and if they are not, determine the difference. The cost estimate report can generally have either a project customer or owner, or a project manager takes the responsibility for creating a cost estimate report. The method of choosing the responsible person for creating it depends on the company's internal process for creating them in the first place.

The communication aspects of the cost estimate report are critical. Communicating the costs of the project without solid justifications or reasons behind the costs can cancel the project before it even starts. Communicating an extremely high cost estimate without laying out the tradeoffs and benefits of that high cost does not provide the decision makers with enough information to decide whether to proceed with the project. Project managers must be fully aware of the importance, and the different methods to which they communicate this cost estimate information. The methods and manners to which they present this information can make or break a project.

NOTE The Project Management Institute's knowledge area for this tool is the Cost Management area. The secondary area that this tool could be associated with is Human Resources.

ON the CD-ROM We have included a sample of a cost estimate report in the Cost folder. Use this as a guide to create your own version of this tool.

TOOL VALUE Cost estimate reports communicates any interested stakeholder the knowledge of the estimate for the project. Using this information helps executives or upper management to make decisions on approving or rejecting the project. Past cost estimate reports of similar projects can be of great value.

The cost estimate report is especially beneficial on cost-driven projects; however, project managers should utilize them on every project. Even though the project manager uses the document normally at the beginning of the project to determine the project's initial estimates and the funding allocations, it is an important document to utilize throughout the project. In project situations where particular project areas (design, development, and test) actually go over budget or project to go over budget, the project manager can use both the cost estimate report and the budget spreadsheet report to compare the estimates and initial assumptions to determine why the project is off track. In those cases, if there is a valid reason, then often the senior management or customers will provide the extra dollars (especially if they are confident in how the project is progressing) and will understand that those dollars are required to complete the work. However, if there is a lack of confidence and the project manager handles the budget unwisely, the owners or customers are less likely to add additional dollars to the project and the project will be forced to find other ways. In either case, without a cost estimate report, the project manager will struggle to justify the project's funding and could have a difficult time obtaining the money.

TIP Continue tracking the project's budget to compare the accuracy of the initial estimates and the actuals on an ongoing basis. Cost estimates help keep the project dollars on track; and if tracked weekly, it keeps a project manager on top of the dollars for the project.

Figure 7.1 represents a cost estimate report for a software project. The multiple systems in this example have each provided an estimate on their impacts on this proposed project. Their estimates included size, scope, and complexity on how they understand the project will affect their areas. The project manager or owner of the project (depending on the company) compiles all the impacts from each system and any resources or hardware (in this case, it is a software project) and then calculates the cost estimates for the project.

FIGURE 7.1

A sample of a cost estimate report.

Impact Assessment - +/- 100% (range)							
Project Name: ABC Software Development Project	Size/Scope/Complexity					Earliest Possible Start Date	
	Very Low	Low	Medium	High	Very High		
System A	$ 40,000					5/14/2008	
System B			100,000			5/22/2008	
System C					60,000	10/14/2008	
System D			65,000			9/12/2008	
Project Team (Resources)				400,000			
Project Hardware and Ongoing Maintenance			200,820				
Bundling Systems	$ –	$ –	$ –	$ –	$ –		
Total Expected Costs of Project: $835,820						$ 835,820	

The cost estimating process is a relatively straightforward process where the project manager is responsible for consolidating the information from the affected parties and entering it into a spreadsheet or cost accounting system. This process normally begins with a business requirements document that indicates the scope of the project, and the project manager sending that document to the impacted systems for their initial review. After all the impacted systems have performed their assessments on the work based on those requirements, they can determine the costs it will take for them to update their systems if the customers approve the project. Their estimates are then complied and sent back by the impacted systems or groups to the project manager for consolidation into a single cost estimate report. The project manager then enters that information into the overall cost estimate report for the project. In Figure 7.1, four systems provided estimates to the project manager for consolidating into the cost estimate spreadsheet. After the project work begins, changes or tweaks to the project estimates occur in the budget spreadsheet only, not in the cost estimate report. The cost estimate report is for pre-project work only and you use it for decision-making purposes, not for the ongoing management and control of the project.

Almost every company has a unique method for estimating project costs and refining those costs throughout the project. This is a dynamic process for companies, and project managers need to continue to be involved and aware of that process to be successful. The first time through this process can be challenging for project managers, but once they get the hang of it, they will find it becomes second nature to them. When project managers take their projects through this process, many companies have stages where team members, upper management, and customers can review and adjust the project's costs accordingly. Some companies have three stages, some have two, and some have five or more. These stages coincide with the various stages of the project lifecycle methodology used to drive the project. The stages are often in this format:

- The first round of project funding is normally an initial rough order of magnitude. That is generally a confidence level from the team members of +100 percent and -50 percent. This + 100 percent indicates that the estimate provided could be 100 percent more than the estimate, and the -50 percent indicates the estimate can be 50 percent less than the estimate. As you discover more about the project, the funding is refined and the estimates become more accurate.

- The second stage of project funding reviews occurs during the initial requirements phase where the team has a confidence level of + or -20 percent. The third pass on project funding occurs at even a later stage in the project lifecycle and the project team has even further details of the project and a higher level of confidence.

- The third and often final stage of project's funding reviews, the project team has a very high level of confidence and therefore the project estimates get to a point where they are + or -5 percent accurate. Rarely do projects hit exactly, and holding them to a + or -5 percent estimate accurate is a very tall order for most projects today.

In some cases, companies decide to fund projects automatically and adjust accordingly if applicable. In those cases, the managing of the project's budget to the dollars allocated is much more difficult. When companies fund projects without a cost estimate, the project manager has no choice but to manage the budget with the dollars provided and request additional dollars down the line if applicable. The lack of a cost estimate report often sets project managers up to fail from a budget perspective. Without adequate opportunity to provide input to the funding of the project or little control to obtain additional funds, project managers have very little they can do to help the budget situation. In this case, even though the project does not use the cost estimate report initially, creating one can help in justifying any additional dollars requested and therefore would still be valuable for the project manager to have in their toolbox.

CROSS-REF See Chapter 5 for more information on the WBS tool and the various calculations and estimates within a work package.

On construction projects, they call the cost estimating process takeoff. *Takeoff* is the process of identifying specific materials and their associated costs from the design drawings. Using the information in the takeoffs — such as materials, equipment, labor hours, and administrative costs — provides the estimated total for the construction of the building. This estimate is what companies will use to bid on the construction of a building.

Planning to use a cost estimate report

In planning for using a cost estimate report, the project manager must first decide the internal process and procedures at the company to develop cost estimates. This could include working with the Finance departments or the Project Management Office (PMO) to understand their processes for obtaining project cost estimates for your project. The next step in this process is for the project manager to decide on what the cost estimate report will look like for their project, and adjust the fields and the spreadsheet accordingly. Once the project manager understands the process and has a template ready, the project manager would then work with the requirements analyst or the customer to obtain the initial requirements for the project. The project manager then decides from those requirements the impacted parties or systems for the project and sets up discussions with each group to go over the cost estimate report and process. After performing these steps, and the different impact groups have the template and know what to do, the project manager should be prepared to use the cost estimate report.

Before you can create the cost estimate report, you must formulate a plan. In the following "Planning Questions" section, we provide some suggestions to help you start thinking about how to utilize the tool on your project. Planning on how to use the tool and thinking about where to use it makes sense. This is an effective way to plan and utilize this valuable communication tool.

Planning Questions

1 When would you create, develop, or write this tool?
Initial project request phase, often during planning phase when estimating the cost of the project

2 Who is going to use this tool, both from an input and output status?
Upper management, owners, executives, project manager, team members, subcontractors, or specific skill areas, cost estimators, contacts from impacted systems who are providing costs based on their expected changes (software projects)

continued

---

continued

3 *Why are you going to use this tool?*

To estimate the costs of the project and provide those costs to owners or clients for setting the budget and approving the project, any revisions to project requiring estimating, capture the costs for changes to various systems (software projects)

4 *How are you going to use this tool?*

Determine cost estimates for project by capturing the different impacted areas and calculating those areas

5 *How will you distribute the information?*

Spreadsheet format such as Microsoft Excel, document control system, e-mail, presentations

6 *When will you distribute the information?*

As needed, this tool is to drive the creation of the project estimate for budget planning. Change request may require changes and redistribution of the cost estimate.

7 *What decisions can or should you make from this tool?*

Cost decisions, resources decisions, impacted system decisions (software projects)

8 *What information does the tool provide for your project?*

Cost information, impacted project information, possible duration information

9 *What historical and legal information do you need to store?*

Lessons learned information, actual costs, actual estimates, impacted system list (software projects), original budget

10 *What will be the staffing requirements (Role Type) to run and maintain these tools?*

Project manager, team members, resource manager, cost manager

Reporting using a cost estimate report

Many companies have different approaches as to how they handle the developing cost estimate reports. In some cases, the project manager plays a role in developing it, and in other cases, the project manager does not. In either case, the actual creator of the document is not as important as how the project manager communicates and utilizes the cost estimate report on their projects.

There are many different varieties of the cost estimate reports. Each differs from industry to industry and takes different shapes and sizes. Each report will have its own unique purposes and be valuable in compiling the overall costs of the project. The different types of cost estimate reports include:

- Materials estimate report
- Labor estimate report

- Equipment estimate report
- Administration report (overhead)

Project managers must be proactive with communicating the cost estimate report in the early stages of the project. From working with the customers and obtaining additional dollars to working with each group or impacted system and determining their costs, the project manager can be quite active in using a cost estimate report during the early phases and getting that information out to as many people as possible. Project managers should ensure that during this early project phases, they communicate the information on the report as often as possible and ensure that everyone involved can access the information if necessary.

The format to develop the cost estimate report is a spreadsheet. In some cases, the cost estimate report appears in a presentation format, such as PowerPoint, or a document format such as Microsoft Word or Microsoft Excel. Normally the cost estimate report is a spreadsheet. Some companies have systems that handle the budgeting process, but even in those cases, most systems can generate a cost estimate report spreadsheet for the project manager to work with on their projects. The cost estimate report is stored within the project document control system for long-term storage and historical reference.

CROSS-REF See Chapter 17 to learn more about how to use a cost estimate report.

Introducing the Earned Value Analysis

The main purpose of *earned value analysis* is to measure continuous project performance and predict the final cost and schedule results. The earned value analysis displays the performance trends on the project. It allows calculations to occur at the project level as well as the detail level and can display different categories of performance.

The earned value concept has been around for at least 40 years. Earned value is synonymous with performance measurement. The core of the earned value analysis method is the measurement of the actual effort being performed on the project and then comparing it to the original plan called the baseline. One of the major attributes of the earned value method is the fact that it integrates time and cost to display trends occurring on the project. Prediction of future rates of progress calculations are one of the main advantages to using the earned value analysis tool. Other advantages include tracking the schedule and monitoring costs. This tool is one of only a few tools that actually does integrate cost and schedule information. It also tracks variances in cost and scheduling to display how far the project is ahead or behind schedule as well as over or under budget. Earned value analysis is a tool that compares the current budget to the original budget, and the current schedule to the original schedule.

NOTE The Project Management Institute's knowledge area for this tool is Cost Management. The secondary areas that this tool could be associated with are Time, Human Resources, and Communications.

ON the CD-ROM We have included a sample of an earned value analysis tool in the Cost folder. Use this as a guide to create your own personal version of this tool. Your company or project may have specific requirements that can enhance this communication tool further; however, we believe this is a great starting point for the creation of this tool for your project.

TOOL VALUE Earned value analysis allows project managers to track performance continuously throughout the life of the project. It displays the rate of performance in both time and cost.

The earned value analysis tool can generate earned value S-curves, which are great for presenting the true performance of your project. After work starts on the project, the earned value charts can display trending information as to how the project is performing and how it expects to perform. The earned value analysis displays exactly how the project is trending and if there are any anomalies from a cost or time perspective, the project team can investigate them and determine where and how to resolve the problems.

Figure 7.2 shows a typical earned value trend chart. The chart shows the planned value (PV) of the project before it has started. You create the PV (baseline) by adding the cost of each activity to the chart during the period in which it will be complete. Then, totaling the cost of all the activities in each period provides the value for that period. Plotting these values creates a cumulative curve like the one in Figure 7.2. This curve is an S-curve report because it resembles the shape of the letter S. It represents the projected rate that the project should perform in the future. When the project is under way, applying the other two values, earned value (EV), the performance, and actual cost (AC) shows the performance trend of the project. The example below is communicating the project is not performing as planned (PV versus EV) and is over spending its EV by about two times (EV versus AC).

FIGURE 7.2

This figure represents a sampling of a planned budget from a software development project.

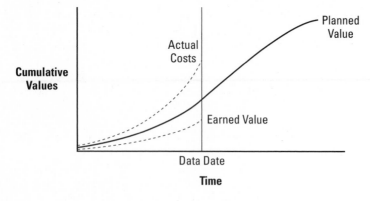

The project manager benefits from using the earned value analysis tool because he /she sees the rate of progress the project is making and compares it to the original plane (baseline) to determine the differences. Using the results of the tool gives him/her a better understanding of the project and determines the actual status and performance of the project team. Without a tool like this one, the project manager does not have the same ability to understand or have the same level of confidence. The earned value analysis has a tremendous wealth of project data that you, the project manager, can review in depth and determine where and how well your projects are performing.

Government project managers have been using the Earned Value Analysis tool for many years. The construction industry has mandated earned value for larger-size projects and the software industry has seen it become more popular. More recently, the trends in the private sector of project management are showing earned value becoming more prevalent and popular across the industry. As project managers start understanding the value in using earned value, it will become a standard report in their reporting process, especially when their customers are demanding performance analysis types of reports from their projects.

Project managers may find the best time to use the Earned Value Analysis tool is when working on medium to large projects because tracking performance is a fundamental request of customers. When project managers are not tracking costs or hours at the activity level, then earned value analysis tracking and performance reporting is not practical and rarely used. You can track costs or labor hours, or both when performing earned value analysis as long as you have set up the project schedule to collect this data on your project. Doing so opens a suite of earned value analysis types of reports.

Even though we noted previously that when projects do not have costs or hours recorded at the activity level, then earned value analysis is not practical; it does not prevent project managers from still utilizing this tool. In those situations, where the project has not implemented cost or labor hours, earned value analysis is still possible and of some value, just not the full value it would have implementing it completely. Project managers can create their own units to perform the earned value calculations. The reason for this is that earned value analysis does not require a particular type of unit to measure or calculate performance. If you want to calculate earned value analysis, you can literally develop any unit type you want, and you can track your project's performance using that unit. It is common for project managers to use the value of the "duration" to create the earned value analysis types of reports.

 See Chapter 16 to determine how to create an earned value analysis with your own units of measure.

Measuring a project's earned value

Before you are able to measure the earned value of a project, one of the first tasks to perform is to understand the terminology of these calculations. This terminology is standard across the industry and is important to understand. The following elements of earned value calculations include planned value (PV), actual costs (AC), and earned value (EV). These calculations compute the earned value parameters and reports.

Here is a definition and an example of each of these elements:

- **The planned value:** The portion of the work that is planned on a task between the task's start date and the finish date. For example, the total planned budget for a four-day task is $1000. The PV is $1000.

- **The actual cost:** The total actual cost incurred while performing work on a task during a given period. For example, if a four-day task actually incurs a total cost of $350 on each of the first two days, the AC for this period (two days) is $700 (but the PV and EV are equal to $500 each, which is 50 percent of the value of the task).

- **The earned value:** The value of the work accomplished, the portion of the work spent for a given percentage of work performed on a task. For example, if after two days, 50 percent of the work on a task is completed, you have earned $500 of the activity's $1000. In this case, you are performing right on schedule.

 Earned value analysis is a great project performance measurement. Project managers should utilize all concepts of earned value on their projects.

Calculating earned value analysis performance

When calculating earned value analysis, the industry uses a standard set of calculations. These calculations include:

- **Cost Variance (CV):** The difference between a task's earned value and its actual cost. CV = EV – AC

- **Schedule Variance (SV):** The difference between a tasks earned value and its planned value. SV = EV – PV

- **Cost Performance Index (CPI):** The ratio of earned value to actual costs. CPI = EV / AC.

- **Schedule Performance Index (SPI):** The ratio of earned value to planned value. SPI = EV / PV

Performing and interpreting earned value analysis

When performing earned value analysis on a project, the answers to some standard project questions become readily apparent. How much money is needed to complete the project? Is there enough time to complete the project on schedule? When having this type of information available, it provides a new level of detail for the project manager that they would not have without executing an earned value analysis.

Earned value variance indicators, such as cost, can be either positive or negative. A positive variance indicates that the project is ahead of schedule, and the cost is under budget. Positive variances might enable the reallocation of money and resources from tasks or projects to projects that are in trouble.

A negative schedule and cost variances indicate that the project is behind schedule and over-running its budget, and immediate action needs to be taken to ensure that the project gets back on track as soon as possible. If a task or project has a negative CV, the budget may need to be increased or the scope of the project revisited. If a project has a negative SV, then an option might be for the team members to work overtime to bring the project back on schedule.

 Controlling costs on your project is critical and is just as important as time and scope management — the big three!

The earned value performance indicators that are ratios, such as the CPI and the SPI, can be equal to 1.0, greater than 1.0, or less than 1.0. A value greater than 1.0 using CPI communicates an under-running budget and less than 1.0 indicates you are running over budget. For SPI, if the value is less than 1.0, you are ahead of schedule, and if it is greater than 1.0, you are behind schedule. For example, an SPI of 0.84 means that you are working at a rate 16 percent faster than you had planned. It has taken you only 84 percent of the planned time to complete that portion of a task in a given time period, and a CPI of 0.8 means you are running over budget by 20 percent.

The earned value (EV) of an activity is the percent complete of work on the activity multiplied by the budget (baseline) of the activity (EV = % complete X activity cost). When an activity is 100 percent complete, it has earned all of its value. When reporting progress on an activity you only need a few percentage points. There are several methods for reporting progress on an activity. One method to make reporting progress easier is to give an activity an agreed upon percent when it starts. As an example, a project scheduler would automatically assign 25 percent complete when an activity starts. When an activity has reached 26 percent complete, but less than 50 percent, the activity would automatically receive 50 percent complete. The next progress step of an activity would automatically receive a 75 percent complete when the activity's percent complete was between 50 percent and 75 percent complete. An activity would only receive 100 percent complete upon completing the activity.

 Some projects are set up where the project manager only receives the value of the activity when it is complete. That is, it is either 0 percent or 100 percent complete. This progress reporting method does two things for the progress of a project: it forces short activity durations and it all but eliminates arguments when reporting progress. Either the activity is finished or it is not!

These performance values are used to analyze the rate (speed) at which the project is being worked and to estimate future progress.

Planning to use an earned value analysis

During the planning for using an earned value analysis, the project manager should review the company's process and procedures that may be in place. If they are in place, learn them and follow them. If there are no procedures, you will have to make sure that a coding system is in the scheduling program to be able to select, group, and summarize the activities you want to use to do an earned value analysis. Before developing an earned value analysis, we recommended that you use the Work Breakdown Structure tool to make sure you have a fully defined scope of work for the project. The coding system should be set up in the work packages of the WBS, and then transferred to the scheduling program. The cost for each work package (activity) must be developed next. Before you can run an earned value analysis, you must create a cost loaded baseline schedule to do your variance reporting and create the plan value curve on the S-curve chart.

CROSS-REF See Chapter 6 for more information about the baseline schedule.

Before you can create the earned value analysis, you must formulate a plan. In the following "Planning Questions" section, we provide some suggestions to help you start thinking about how you can utilize an earned value analysis on your project. Ask yourself the following questions:

Planning Questions

1 When would you create, develop, or write this tool?

After creating a project baseline and immediately after the first update of the project for reporting progress

2 Who is going to use this tool, both from an input and output perspective?

Upper management, owners, clients, executives, project manager, team members, subcontractors, or specific skill areas

3 Why are you going to use this tool?

Performance measurement, schedule variance, cost variance, schedule performance index, cost performance index, estimate at complete, trending for S-curves, compare plan versus actuals

4 How are you going to use it?

For reporting to upper level management, detailed reports, manage by exception, shows both time and cost, cost and schedule decisions

5 How will you distribute the information?

Dashboard format, spreadsheet format such as Microsoft Excel, e-mail, tabular, plotter, newsletter, document control system

6 When will you distribute the information?

After the first set of activities have progress reported, and then throughout the life of project

7 What decisions can or should you make from this tool?

Schedule and cost decisions, Investigate potential project problems, quality, risk, resources, purchasing, and legal decisions

8 What information does this tool provide for your project?

Schedule information, cost information, resources, comparing current schedule to original plan (baseline)

Reporting using an earned value analysis

On most projects, the project manager is responsible for the creation of the projects earned value analysis reports. On larger projects where there is an administration team in place, reporting is often an aspect of that group's responsibilities. The group commonly called a PMO or a project management office that works on larger projects and provides both the processes and the structure for running various aspects of the project is responsible for creating the earned value analysis process. Reporting is normally included in those processes. The earned value analysis reports are part of regular project standard reports and distributed on a weekly or monthly basis to the stakeholders of the project. Some report types include the following:

- Cost variance report
- Cost performance index report
- Schedule variance report
- Schedule performance index report
- S-curve report
- Schedule and cost forecasting report

Table 7.3 shows a typical earned value table for a construction project. The table displays the three values of an earned value analysis including the planned value (PV), the earned value (EV), and the actual costs (AC). In this example, the project is about halfway through its completion. With a quick glance, it is easy to see that this project is performing close to the original plan by the values in the Cost CPI and the Schedule SPI fields. As an example of an activities performance, in reviewing the final plan activity, it is good to know how to read the data values in each column to determine how that particular activity is performing. In the PV, EV, and AC fields, it has the values of 250, 210, and 210. Using the formulas above, the cost variance calculates as CV = EV – AC (210 – 210) = 0, the schedule variance calculates as SV = EV – PV (210 – 250) = -40. To calculate the two indexes CPI and SPI, the formulas are CPI = EV/AC (210/210) = 1.0 and SPI = EV/PV (210/250) = 0.84. Reviewing the values that display the performance of the activity "Final Plan," you are working according to plan on the costs, and at a rate of 84 percent of the schedule. Overall this project is performing well.

TABLE 7.3

Example of an Earned Value Analysis Tool Report

Activity	Planned Value	Earned Value	Actual Cost	Cost Var.	Schedule Var.	Cost CPI	Schedule SPI
Preliminary Plan	100	95	110	-15	-5	0.86	0.95
Final Plan	250	210	210	0	-40	1.00	0.84
Move Out	300	280	265	15	-20	1.06	0.93
Remodel	1200	1200	1300	-100	0	0.92	1.00
Move In	250	250	240	10	0	1.04	1.00
Totals	2100	2035	2125	-90	-65	0.96	0.97

Figure 7.3 represents an earned value chart that displays the performance trends on a project. You can see from this example, the project is behind schedule (EV – PV) by approximately two quarters and running over budget (EV – AC) by about double (200%). To estimate how far behind schedule the project is from the point where the EV touches the status date line, go horizontally back (left) to the PV curve. This imaginary line would touch the PV curve at the end of the third quarter of 2008. The project is running roughly a little over a half year behind schedule. When reviewing the costing aspects, the project is spending about twice as much as it has earned (the difference between the point of AC on the status date line and the EV point on the status date line). If this trend continues, the project will deliver late (40% behind schedule) and be significantly (200%) over budget.

Each week, during the standard reporting cycle, the earned value reports become part of the regular project reporting cycle. The earned value reports are an important aspect of project reporting and should be stored as part of the standard project reporting. The format best used for reporting earned value analysis information is a spreadsheet, and quite often the information ends up in other formats, such as PowerPoint presentations or on internal Web sites. The earned value analysis reports are stored within the project document control system for long-term storage and historical reference.

CROSS-REF See Chapter 16 to learn more about how to use an earned value analysis.

FIGURE 7.3

This figure represents typical trending curves on earned value calculations for a project.

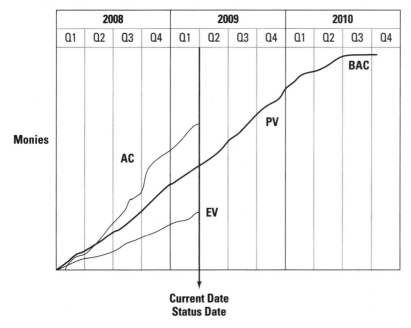

Introducing the Estimating Tool

The purpose of the *estimating* tool is to create high-quality and accurate estimates for the project based on future trends and possible unknown events. When team members add their estimated working hours on a software project, the estimating tool uses those hours to calculate the estimate at completion (EAC). After the project starts, the EAC calculation requires the actual as well as the forecast estimates to calculate properly. Using an estimating tool is beneficial to the project manager because it allows him /her to make decisions based on whether the project is running over or under budget. In the construction industry, professional estimators create the estimates for a project where software, for example, the impacted systems, would provide the estimates.

When working with forecasters and estimators, it is good to have a clear understanding of what each one of them provides to your project. A forecaster provides future labor rates, equipment costs, and material costs. The estimator calculates the estimates using these future costs and rates. When a forecaster is involved, the projects are generally longer in length and well into the future.

NOTE The Project Management Institute's knowledge area for this tool is the Cost Management area. The secondary areas that this tool could be associated with are Scope, Time, and Human Resources.

ON the CD-ROM We have included a sample of an estimating tool in the Cost folder. Use this as a guide to create your own version of this tool.

TOOL VALUE An estimating tool allows the project manager to have a forecast of the cost in advance of starting the project. Senior management can make a go/no-go decision before spending any monies on a project.

A project estimate is a great communication tool to communicate the future costs of the project. After the project's estimate is complete, the project manager shares that information with the project customers and stakeholders. In some cases, the estimate is higher than the allocated budget. When that occurs, you must work with your customers and determine if changes can occur to the project to bring the estimate within the budget or request additional money for the project to cover the expected overage. In some cases, estimates come in as expected and the project's funding requires no further actions.

A project customer on a software project, for example, can obtain great benefits from using an estimating spreadsheet on the project. Not only will the estimating spreadsheet provide a ballpark of the project's costs, it also provides the different team member's roles expected to be involved on the effort. Also included are the various components of a project (such as lifecycle process breakdown), and other direct costs expected for project (such as equipment). When customers have this information, it allows them to perform course corrections early in the life of the project, possibly preventing any budget reallocations or overruns. A number of project managers take advantage of the estimating process because of the value it brings to their projects and the look into the future it provides to their project's funding.

TIP Project forecasting is challenging because it is estimating based on many unknown factors. Bring in experts and accurate data for the best-quality forecasting results!

There are times when professional forecasters are involved with creating the project estimates. Usually when forecasters are involved in projects, the projects are often large and long in duration. Professional forecasters are costly and larger efforts warrant bringing them in to perform this service. The longer projects benefit the most from having forecasters because it can provide you insight into the labor rate and equipment costs, two, three, five — even ten years in the future.

The forecaster predicts labor rates, material rates, and equipment costs in the future and applies those costs to the project to determine a future cost estimate. These forecasts, which are broken down by time periods, allow for a granular level of project reporting for the project manager to utilize. The further out the forecasts, the less accurate they are for the project. Making accurate predictions far into the future is almost impossible because the number of unknowns is too great.

Calculating formulas for estimating

Every project needs an estimate in both time and cost. Regardless of the scale of the project (small /medium/large), forecasting and estimating are required to determine future costs. The project manager, the cost manager, and customer use several different calculations to estimate the cost at the completion (EAC) of a project; these are standard across all industries. The estimate at completion formula is included:

- Estimate at completion using remaining budget: Calculated by using the actual costs (AC) to date plus the budget at completion (BAC) minus the earned value (EV). The formula: EAC = AC + BAC – EV

- The project manager uses this estimate when the project management team assumes they can meet the budget of the remaining activities and ignores the past performance.

- Estimate at completion using cost performance index: This calculates by using the actual costs and the budget at completion minus the earned value divided by the Cost Performance Index. The formula: EAC = AC + ((BAC – EV)) / CPI

- The project manager uses this estimate when the project team assumes the performance rate of the work completed and that rate will continue throughout the rest of the project. In most cases, this is the most accurate forecasting technique for establishing the estimate at completion.

- Estimate at completion using cost performance index and schedule performance index: Calculated by using actual costs plus total budget, minus earned value divided by cost performance index times the schedule performance index. The formula: EAC = AC + (Budget – EV) / (CPI * SPI)

- Use this estimate when the project team assumes that this will be the most likely outcome for the forecast of the cost of the project. This formula takes into consideration both cost and schedule performance to date and uses it to estimate the future completion cost.

- Estimate at completion using forecast data: This calculation uses the actuals plus the forecast (remaining estimate of work) to calculate the estimate at completion. The formula: EAC = Actuals + Forecast

- Estimate used when the project team enters their forecast amounts toward the project and there are actuals already hitting the budget. The two values determine simply the estimate of monies required for completion.

  There are three components to a standard estimate at completion formula: the answer, the actual cost component, and the remaining portion of the formula. (This is a standard definition for all formulas.)

The following forecasting methods are the most popular today in Project Management:

- Time series methods: Uses historical data as the basis for estimating future outcomes
- Causal /econometric methods: Take economic conditions and come up with a forecasted estimate
- Judgmental methods: Expert knowledge
- Other methods include:
  - Simulation
  - Prediction market
  - Probabilistic forecasting

Planning to use an estimating tool

In the planning for using an Estimating tool, the project manager must first decide the internal process and procedures in place to develop their project estimate. This could include working with the Finance department or the Project Management Office (PMO) to understand their processes for obtaining the project cost estimates first. The project manager then decides from these processes the best way to obtain an estimate for their project. After the project manager understands the process, and decides on the best way, the next step is to work with the estimating team and the customers to obtain the initial requirements for the project.

Another method for estimating a project if the project manager and some of the team members do not have a lot of experience in estimating and they have to create the estimate themselves is to develop a full and complete WBS. Creating the WBS with small, detailed work packages helps to estimate the cost of each work package. When all work packages have an estimated cost, roll up the cost to the project level and you have an accurate estimate for the project. Then transfer this cost into the master schedule activities for use in doing the earned value analysis.

CROSS-REF See Chapters 5 and 15 to learn more about how to create and use a work breakdown structure.

Before you can create the estimating tool, you must formulate a plan. In the following "Planning Questions" section below, we provide you with some suggestions to help you start thinking about how to utilize the estimating tool on your project.

Planning Questions

1 *When would you create, develop, or write this tool?*
Initiating process, planning process, for obtaining the initial estimate on the project

2 *Who is going to use this tool, both from an input and output status?*
Upper management, clients, project manager and team members, subcontractors, or specific skill areas, project forecaster

3 *Why are you going to use this tool?*
Estimate and forecast the future costs of the project, budget planning, schedule planning, resource planning

4 *How are you going to use this tool?*
To determine material, equipment, schedule, costs for resources future use

5 *How will you distribute the information?*
Document format, e-mail, document control system, charts and graphics, drawings

---

6 *How often will you distribute the information?*

After initial estimate, and on as-need basis, or as management approves changes

7 *What decisions can you make from this tool?*

Go/no-go for project, schedule decisions, cost decisions, resource decisions, material decisions, and equipment decisions, purchasing decisions

8 *What information does this tool provide for your project?*

Schedule information, cost information, resource information, equipment information, and materials information, future labor rates, future costs

9 *What historical and legal information do you need to keep?*

Lessons learned from forecasting process, research data on forecasting trends, and documents created during process

10 *What will be the staffing requirements (role type) to run and maintain these tools?*

Forecaster, estimator, owner, or client, upper management, project manager

Reporting using an estimating tool

Project managers and their team members on smaller efforts create project estimates. On large projects, the owner often hires professional estimators to create the project's estimates. These estimates are valuable throughout the life of the project and project managers tend to utilize them the most at the beginning of the project when the initial cost estimates are required and the allocation of the budget is occurring and then don't use them that often during the project. The purpose to bring the estimator in is to predict the future costs at the beginning, and if there are any concerns or the project projects to be higher than what is expected, the project has the chance of being cancelled before it ever gets started.

NOTE Project teams try to estimate and forecast based on unknowns early in the project and can never hit the estimates exactly!

The estimating report is an important part of the budgeting process and something occurring at the beginning of the project. The estimating report is not part of the standard project reporting cycle and is reported normally once or twice at the beginning of the project only. The estimating report uses a spreadsheet format and often ends up in other formats, such as PowerPoint or on internal Web sites. The estimating reports are stored within the project Document Control System for long-term storage and historical reference.

CROSS-REF See Chapter 15 to learn more about how to use and create the estimating tool.

Summary

The tools described in this chapter help project managers and team members control the costs of their projects. As we all know, managing the project cost is one of the most important aspects of project management and should be an area the project manager watches closely throughout the project.

As you review this chapter, the one tool that will jump out and helps control project costs the most is the Earned Value Analysis tool. The different calculations and ability to understand the project performance at a most granular level are invaluable to you as you manage your project. This tool is still relativity new, especially in software, but is catching on as one of the most effective and important cost management tools available to you. Project managers using the earned value analysis techniques have a much better understanding of their project's performance and costs than the project managers who do not utilize the tool.

The chapter also includes tools such as budget spreadsheets, cost estimate report, and the Estimating tools. Each of them helps the project manager manage and control their project costs.

Chapter 8

Defining Communication Tools to Manage Project Quality

In this chapter, we explore project communications tools in the project Quality Management knowledge area. These communication tools are critical to controlling and managing the quality aspects of your project. Each tool can help you communicate the different areas of quality of your project to your customers, upper management, and project team members.

The Quality Management knowledge area on a project includes activities dealing with how the project team handles quality planning, quality control, and quality assurance. Quality is a subjective measurement where a level of quality that is acceptable to one manager may be unacceptable to another manager.

One of the tools noted in this chapter called quality metric can help the project manager control the management of quality on their project. Within this tool, there is an explanation of the term quality measurement. This describes the level of quality a customer is trying to achieve on their project. On software projects, a common measurement for quality is the number of errors or bugs in an application. A customer would want that number as low as possible. They could demand that it be zero.

The following tools cover the management and control of the project's quality along with how to communicate this important information to your customers and upper management staff. Not only is it important for a project manager to process the project's quality correctly, but it is also important to understand how to communicate this information.

Introducing the Comprehensive Test Plan

The purpose of the *comprehensive test plan* is to document and identify a standard approach to planning, executing, and communicating the activities in a project's testing phase. A comprehensive test plan contains the processes and procedures to eliminate as many failures as possible before releasing the project for user acceptance testing. The comprehensive test plan tends to focus more on the software industry, more than any other industry. The reason for this is the large number of variables a software system has and how many things could go wrong. The comprehensive test plan is making its way into construction, health, and drug industries. For example, the comprehensive test plan is popular in the health industry to ensure that the project teams eliminate safety and health hazards in their products before releasing them to their consumers. In the construction industry, a comprehensive test plan is part of the commissioning process.

The goal of every comprehensive test plan is to ensure the highest-quality standards on the project at the level the project can afford. Unfortunately, the budget of the project is often the driving factor as to the level of quality applied to the project. The project manager manages the budget and therefore plays a big role in determining how much quality to apply to the project. Therefore, the project manager is constantly working with the project's customer and working to ensure that the testing phase has the money it needs to be successful. The cost of applying rigor to the testing effort is very beneficial to the project. Not only does it take additional time, but also it could take additional monies from the budget. On the other hand, testing an application that is required for NASA to launch a spacecraft would be required and would warrant the time and money spent on the testing process.

Communicating the comprehensive test plan is simple and straightforward. Generally, it consists of the test analyst who created the document (normally a tester or test lead) bringing the project team together and reviewing the document to ensure everyone understands how testing will occur. This would occur a couple times through the document creation process to ensure everyone is onboard and agrees with the testing process and procedures being outlined. At the end of the document creation process, the project manager sends the final document for approval and sign-off to the relevant stakeholders.

NOTE   The Project Management Institute's knowledge area for this tool is the Quality Management area. The secondary area that this tool could be associated with is Risk.

ON the CD-ROM   We have included a sample of this comprehensive test plan tool in the Quality folder on the CD-Rom. This is a guide to the first step in creating your own personal version of this tool. Your company or project may have specific requirements that will enhance this communication tool further; however, we believe this is a great starting point for the creation of this tool for your project.

TOOL VALUE   The comprehensive test plan ensures quality control of the product. The value of the test plan document defines the process to achieve that quality through testing processes using set limits.

The comprehensive test plan is an important communication tool for communicating testing information internally amongst the project team members. The plan has a high amount of detail and contains many areas such as testing scope, success criteria, quality test deliverables, environmental needs, schedule, safety, and associated testing risks. The project manager communicates the comprehensive test plan to the project team leaders by e-mail and formal meetings to ensure everyone is on board and aware of the testing processes. Testing is a key component to any project, so it is important that everyone understands the testing components outlined in the document and they make sense for the project.

Table 8.1 represents an example of a table of contents for a comprehensive test plan. Different industries utilize this plan for their testing needs and change the contents of the document to reflect what they require for their specific project. When completing the testing information in each of the sections, it should cover the testing components in enough detail to fill the testing needs of most projects.

TABLE 8.1

Example of a Comprehensive Test Plan Table of Contents

Section	Description
1	Test Plan Identifier
2	References
3	Introduction of Testing
4	Test Items / Cases and Scripts
5	Risks and Issues
6	Features to Be Tested
7	Features Not to Be Tested
8	Approach
9	Item Pass / Fail Criteria
10	Entry and Exit Criteria
11	Suspension Criteria and Resumption Requirements
12	Test Deliverables
13	Remaining Test Tasks
14	Environment Needs
15	Staffing and Training Needs
16	Responsibilities
17	Schedule
18	Planning Risks and Contingencies
19	Approvals
20	Glossary

The comprehensive test plan benefits all members of the project team because it contains the process and procedures for every aspect of project testing. The project team members that are not directly on the test team can also use this plan to understand how testing occurs. If those team members are related or have to support testing in any way, they will have to understand the details of this plan and know how they can support this testing effort. For example, the development group and the testing group on a software project are tightly integrated. The development group looks closely at the comprehensive test plan document developed by the test team and determines where they pass testing deliverables back and forth, where they interact, and where they come together in the testing process. Without this comprehensive test plan, the two teams will have no idea where or how they interact with each other with the testing effort and as a result, this problem would have a negative impact on testing.

One of the areas the comprehensive test plan *does not* cover is the user acceptance testing. The comprehensive test plan does not describe in detail any of the customers' testing — that information is in the user acceptance document. The customer's acceptance testing involves the users testing the functionality of the product before releasing to them officially and ensuring what they documented in the customer's requirements document is what they actually received in the system or product their testing. When developers and test teams perform their testing, they end up testing the code behind the application and may not necessarily run the same test cases that the customers would run, so it may make sense to keep them in two separate documents.

 Make sure that stakeholders/owners sign off on the comprehensive test plan.

Planning to use a comprehensive test plan

In planning and preparing to use a comprehensive test plan, the project manager should first connect with his /her test team to ensure that they are onboard with creating this document for the project. They should be, but a project manager would need to check to ensure the test lead is onboard and realizes that they are responsible for the document. Normally, it requires a number of team members to generate this comprehensive test plan document, so the project manager should ensure he/she lines up all applicable team members required in this creation process and receives their approval and commitment to help create the document. When the project manager determines who is going to create the document, they can then works with the test lead who normally takes the lead role in development to ensure that the template for the comprehensive test plan matches the specific needs of the project. After completing that step, the project manager can focus his or her attention on the communications aspects of the test plan. This will include the project manager and the test team members working together to determine when does the test document need reporting, what other reports are required, what are the timeframes associated to reporting, and so on. In performing this step, it allows both the project manager and testing team to understand who is communicating the testing information before any testing begins and it avoids communication problems in the future. After performing these planning tasks, the project manager has adequately prepared for the use of the comprehensive test plan on their project.

Before you can create the comprehensive test plan, you must formulate a plan. In the following "Planning Questions" section, we have provided some suggestions to help you start thinking about how to utilize a comprehensive test plan on a project.

Planning Questions

1 When would you create or write the comprehensive test plan tool?

In the planning process before actual testing starts, during final design of the requirements

2 Who is going to use this tool, both from an input and output perspective?

Project manager, team members, subcontractors, test manager, individual testers

3 Why are you going to use this tool?

To ensure comprehensive and extensive testing occurs on the project, to ensure product quality

4 How are you going to use it?

Guide team members through all areas of the testing process, including determine staffing and training requirements, determine project schedule and timeframes for testing, determine risks and issues associated with testing, meet product quality standards

5 How will you distribute the information?

Document format such as Microsoft Word, document control system, e-mail, presentation

6 When will you distribute the information?

Once at creation to ensure development and testing resources sign-off on plan, then again at the beginning of the test phase to ensure testing team has direction and guidance to execute testing, and after any changes occur on plan

7 What decisions can or should you make from this tool?

Decide on particular testing process for project, decisions on test cases, testing assumptions and constraints, testing resources decisions. All other areas around testing, go/no-go conditions and decisions.

8 What information does this tool provide for your project?

Process and procedures for end-to-end testing, test cases and scenarios, testing resources, testing timeframes, testing risks, and issues

9 What historical and legal information do you need to store?

Test cases, test results, test timeframes, test costs, lessons learned Information

10 What will be the staffing requirements (role type) to run and maintain these tools?

Project manager, test manager, testing resources

Reporting using a comprehensive test plan

The testing team members assigned (normally the test lead) to the project are responsible for developing a comprehensive test plan. Normally a single tester or test lead owns the responsibility of creating the plan and ensuring that everyone on the project accepts and approves it. That single person also owns the communication of the comprehensive test plan throughout the life of the project, and they will ensure that anyone who needs the document can access it when they have too. The Document Control system is the usual storage tool for the document, which is open to all team members or customers.

The communication of the comprehensive test plan requires careful consideration. This plan is quite detailed. It more than likely will require long sessions with the project team discussing each section of the document and acquiring clarification before it reaches the point of approval. Project managers should ensure that the test lead is communicating the comprehensive test plan between all members of the project team that require it for testing. If not, the people needing it for their jobs will be at a disadvantage if they have not seen the document before or have lots of questions and concerns.

The comprehensive test plan is a one-time document that does not need weekly reporting because it does not contain project status. It requires the test team members sign off the document at the beginning of the test phase and approve that they will execute the test process as outlined in the document. The comprehensive test plan is stored in the document control system for long-term archiving and is accessible by any interested stakeholder on the project.

CROSS-REF   See Chapter 16 to learn more about the comprehensive test plan.

Introducing the Control Chart

The purpose of a *control chart* tool is to track data points relative to upper and lower limits of a particular controlled range. These ranges can vary dramatically and depend greatly on the type of project and the data generated in the project that is to be tested. Following are two examples of how project managers use control charts: tracking highway speeds and comparing the number of accidents occurring at specific speeds; and tracking the cloudiness level in a water sample, the clearer the water the less chemical content. Both cases are valid control chart tests and important in understanding the level of quality being performed in the tests.

A control chart provides a graphical view of test results, making those results easy to comprehend and communicate. Much easier to understand in a chart then they would be in a tabular column of data. At first, the chart may seem difficult to understand and may require some explanation on how to read it, but as you continue to use it, reading and analyzing the data becomes much easier. Control charts tend to be popular with senior management because they are graphical and require little time to process and comprehend the information on the chart. It is so much easier for a project manager to communicate the results of a single chart compared to forcing the executives to sift through pages and pages of test results. Project managers will often be required to sit down and review the control chart with executives on the project. Depending on the results of a control chart, the executives or upper management may observe that many of the data points are out of range and deem the project too risky to continue going forward. In this case, those same executives may step in and prevent some of those risks from occurring, but would never have had known they had to without seeing the results documented on a control chart.

The project manager must realize that, depending on the type of project and the data behind it, a control chart may not be applicable. However, if they utilize one, and the data is tracked in this fashion going forward, the project managers and team members will discover how impressive this tool is and how beneficial it will be to track and communicate the test results.

NOTE   The Project Management Institute's knowledge area for this tool is the Quality Management area. The secondary area that this tool could be associated with is Risk.

ON the CD-ROM   We have included a sample of a control chart in the Quality folder. Use this as a guide to create your own version of this tool.

TOOL VALUE   Control charts identify data that exceeds acceptable limits necessary for a quality product. It is easy to identify the data outside of the limits and then determine the action plan required to correct that data going forward.

A control chart is a great tool for assisting the project manager in managing and controlling the project's quality. Because a control chart is so easy to create, maintain, and update, project managers should use this tool whenever possible and work with their test team to ensure they use it on their projects for reporting test results.

Most team members can benefit from the project having a control chart. For example, when a team member reads a control chart, they can tell immediately if their role on the project has anything to do with the data represented on the chart. The team members can look at the data and determine if their work, regardless of what it is, actually influences the data on the chart. A chemist can review a water cloudiness control chart and will know that his role is influencing the data on the chart. A team member on the same team, who is a marketing representative, could look at the same chart and know that the work they do every day on the project will not affect the data on the chart. Why is this important, is it because both people have completely different roles on the project and have different abilities of influencing the control chart, but both people use the chart for different purposes? Therefore, as a project manager it is important for you to ensure that all team members have access to the control charts regardless of their roles and ensure you are communicating it to them on a regular basis.

Figure 8.1 represents a typical control chart for a project. This example of a Water Cloudiness control chart represents the cloudiness conditions of the water. A value of 0.0 represents no visibility and cloudy, and a 7.0 represents a very clear condition with complete visibility. In reviewing the chart, you can see that on March 5, 2006, the cloudiness condition hit a value of 6.0. Which meant it was almost clear and there was no or very little cloudiness to the water. On March 12, 2006, the cloudiness value hit a 1.6 and the condition of the water was very poor.

FIGURE 8.1

This figure represents a sample of a daily control chart testing the cloudiness conditions of the water.

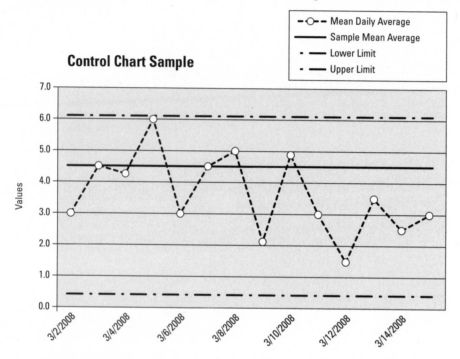

When creating or reviewing a control chart, there are four components to consider. These include the following:

- A central line (mean or average) of what you have set for the test or derived from the data
- An upper control limit, the maximum acceptable limit for the data collected
- A lower control limit, the minimum acceptable limit for the data collected
- Process values plotted on the chart (data points)

During the planning process, the test team will plan the various control charts they will produce during the testing process. The project test team will work directly with the project manager and customers to ensure that the different control charts they are creating capture the correct data points and help to communicate the project's overall quality. It is important during this session that the customers also agree on the charts that the test team is producing to ensure they are not wasting their effort in that process. During those design sessions, the customers and the test team will jointly develop the upper and lower level limits for the data conditions for the testing process. The project test team can develop their own criteria for the upper and lower limits but need the customers, project managers, and subject matter experts to approve these conditions for the control charts. Only the customers can state what they believe is an acceptable quality level for the project. If the project team members or the project manager makes assumptions on what the level is, it can possibly lead to disaster or at the least disappointment.

> **TIP** Always let the owner or the customer select the quality limits. They are the only ones that can. After all, they are paying for the project.

One aspect often missed when communicating and working with a control chart is the establishment of the upper and lower limits for the specific data points. These upper and lower limits are also known as thresholds. In discussing this with the customers, everyone must reach the same understanding of what is an acceptable level of quality and what level is unacceptable. Based on this communication, the data points for both limits (upper and lower) are set, and the project's test team has values they can use as a guide in the testing processes. For example, on a software project, a control chart could capture and display the number of bugs detected during the test phase of a project. The threshold limits for the number of bugs detected at the upper end is five and lower end is three. Therefore, if the project exceeds that threshold and the project has six or more bugs, the customer, project manager, and test team lead must decide what to do with that many bugs occurring on the project. If the project is receiving six to ten bugs per test pass and only five are allowed, as the upper limit, then the customers or stakeholders could decide to stop all testing and send the project back to the development team to correct the errors. Other possible solutions include acquiring additional staff for testing to understand why the bugs are occurring or changing the test criteria. The project team members would then react and adjust work activities based on the changes to ensure that the project gets back on track (acceptable quality) as soon as possible.

Some of the challenges in developing a control chart include the communicating of the chart and getting everyone to understand what the chart means from a quality perspective. Everyone needs to know how the results will impact the quality of the project. For example, if there are many data points over either an upper or a lower line, there could be real quality problems on the project. Other challenges include getting the testing team engaged and developing their own control charts, and determining what types are most applicable to that type of project. Almost every project has a level of quality associated with it and therefore almost every project can create control charts of some fashion to track specific quality limits. Project managers should work closely with the testing team to ensure there are some levels of quality tracked on the project and then communicate those control charts whenever possible.

Planning to use a control chart

In planning and preparing to use a control chart, the project manager must first work with the project's test team, determine and identify the appropriate charts that are applicable for the project. After they have decided on the various charts, the project manager works with the test team to determine how they will initiate and implement the various tests that will produce the data for the control charts. The next step in this planning process is for the test team to work directly with the project manager and the customer to consider how they will report the control charts results. This includes deciding on the method of delivery (in-person, e-mail) to deliver the control charts. After performing these planning steps, the project manager has adequately prepared for the use of control charts on their project.

Before you can create the control chart, you must formulate a plan. In the following "Planning Questions" section, we provide some suggestions to help you start thinking about how to utilize a control chart on your project.

Planning Questions

1 When would you create, or develop the control chart?
In the planning stage of the project when the test team is deciding what charts are applicable to the project, when determining quality checkpoints and discussing how the team is going to achieve maximum quality on the project

2 Who is going to use this tool, both from an input and output status?
Project manager, quality manager, team members, executives, owner or client, upper manager, quality staff if applicable

3 Why are you going to use this tool?
To document and communicate the data control limit results, and decide on actions based on the results

4 How are you going to use this tool?
Capture test results, analysis results, make decisions from results, and present and create change requests due to results

5 How will you distribute the information?
Chart format, e-mail, presentation, document control system

6 When will you distribute the information?
After the test results, or on-demand

7 What decisions can or should you make from this tool?
Decisions dealing with results of test, decisions on upper and lower limit levels, decisions on how to deal with results outside of those ranges

8 What information does this tool provide for your project?
Test results based on control limits

9 What historical and legal information do you need to store?
Previous test charts, previous charts, testing process assumptions and constraints, lessons learned information

10 What will be the staffing requirements (role type) to run and maintain these tools?
Project manager, tester, team member, quality manager

Reporting using a control chart

The project's test team creates the various control charts for the project. In some cases, the project manager is responsible for creating control charts but requires the test team to provide them the results to create the actual control charts. A control chart contains specific project level data and becomes part of the regular project reporting cycle on most projects. The project test team and project managers should reach an agreement ahead of time as to when it makes sense when reporting on the project's control charts.

There are many different types of control charts today. Any project that focuses on quality most likely will have control charts that are applicable for their projects. Some of these include:

- Balancing a building; temperature readings within various rooms in construction industry
- Determining an acceptable limit; for example, five out of ten thousand parts are unusable
- Detecting software code defects or bugs tracking
- Determining traffic flow volumes over a stretch of highway during different times each day
- Detecting particles per solution of runoff over time
- Analyzing the effect of a change on the design
- Counting the number of operating room delays per day
- Determining the number of days ahead of schedule, behind schedule, or on schedule

Each week, the project manager reports using the control chart as part of his or her regular project reporting. If the test is ongoing, the control chart report should be included as part of the standard project reporting and stored in the project's document control system.

CROSS-REF See Chapter 20 to learn more about how to use a control chart.

Introducing the Delphi Method

The main purpose of the Delphi method is to solve large, complex problems without a dominating bias. The Delphi method uses well-researched principles solidified and tested over time. Similar to the concept of brainstorming, this method uses a secret ballot. Whenever a group of experts gathers to solve a problem, one or two people always tend to dominate the group. Because of this, there is a slanting or bias in the solution because of those dominating people. The goal of the Delphi method is to eliminate that dominance and thereby produce the best solution. It is a way for a group of experts to reach a consensus.

This method also works for smaller projects as well, where one or two dominating people can impact the direction and solution of a smaller effort as they could on a larger effort. Usually, however, the Delphi method is more applicable to use on larger projects.

The communication aspects of the Delphi method are often challenging because you are dealing with large and complex problems that often go on for months and can be challenging in their own right.

NOTE The Project Management Institute's knowledge area for this tool is the Quality Management area. The secondary area that this tool could be associated with is Risk.

ON the CD-ROM We have included a sample of the Delphi method in the Quality folder. Use this as a guide to create your own version of this tool.

TOOL VALUE The Delphi method discourages and attempts to eliminate any bias in the solution of a problem.

The Delphi method may take months or even years to solve a problem because of the large size and complexity of the problems. Here are some challenges that face teams using the Delphi method process. As you can see, these are not simple or straightforward projects where a single project manager can try to tackle these problems alone. These problems are complex and may not be possible to resolve entirely. Here are some examples where the Delphi method is applicable:

- Putting a colony on the Moon or Mars
- Discovering an alternative fuel for the transportation industry
- Designing a new airplane or building a ship
- Solving world peace
- Solving world poverty
- Designing the new Panama Canal
- Designing a mechanism for controlling the weather

When facing a challenging problem, project managers often turn to industry experts for help. (Examples of large-scale problems include a complex structural problem, complex database design issue, and a complex drug formula.) The Delphi method is actually an easy process to execute. To eliminate the dominance of the one or two people in a group, the Delphi method uses a technique of having each expert describe a solution to a given problem without consulting any of the other experts. The method takes these multiple solutions and summarizes them into the best solution involving all experts. It provides each expert an equal say in the process. The project manager then communicates the results of the process back to the project experts for another round of comments. The group may reach consensus of the solution in a few iterations of this process or it may take years (put a man on the moon and bring him back safely, for example). The method continues until the experts' solutions no longer change, and then the process stops. The final round of this process is face-to-face meetings with all the experts. Using this method usually produces the best solution and is more feasible than if the group of the same experts met from the beginning and tried to resolve it together at the same time. This is where the dominant personalities come in and sway the results of the process.

The Delphi method is important to utilize when there is a bias in their team members and the project manager has no ability to control a dominant and controlling person on the team. Using this method, it provides the ability to control the results by isolating each team member's solution and going through several rounds of analysis to generate the best results.

The Delphi method is applicable to any type of projects, across every industry. One of the best examples of using the Delphi method is in a training class. When the instructor breaks the students into workgroups to solve a class problem, this is a form of using the Delphi method. Project managers and team members are engaged in the Delphi method on a regular basis and may not even realize it.

As the project manager, you and your team members benefit from using the Delphi method by obtaining unbiased solutions to your project problems. For example, if your project faces a large and complex issue and cannot continue forward, the project manager decides how to proceed. If the project manager decides to use the Delphi method, the results of the Delphi method process provide a possible solution on how to proceed. This solution takes the responsibility away from the project manager who is trying to solve the problem and moves it onto a group of trained experts.

Planning to use the Delphi method

In the planning process for using a Delphi method, the project manager must first identify if the problem is one that is solvable by using the method or could it be possible to obtain the solution by using another method or technique. If the project manager decides to use the Delphi method, the next step would be to identify and qualify the people that can possibly derive a solution. They could be team members or off-site experts. The project manager must assemble the solution team as a group (not physically together though) but making sure none of them communicates with each other about the problem. The next task would be to describe the problem in detail and document it for the solutions team. The project manager can either do it himself if he has the expertise or hire an expert. The project manager then develops a plan and a schedule to circulate the documentation to the experts. Next, the project manager develops a process to respond, summarize, and re-circulate the solutions until achieving a consensus. After performing these steps, the project manager has adequately prepared for using the Delphi method on their project.

Before you can create the Delphi method, you must formulate a plan. In the following "Planning Questions" section below, we provide some suggestions to help you start thinking about how to utilize the Delphi method on your project.

Planning Questions

1 **When would you create, develop or write this tool?**
When the planning process begins, or even before initializing the project because the answer to the problem may depend on whether the project will even start, or if it is not the project its self when various project issues need resolving

continued

continued

2 *Who is going to use this tool, both from an input and output status?*
Client, project manager, team members, subject matter experts, and owners or customers

3 *Why are you going to use this tool?*
To resolve large complex problems, with an unbiased solution

4 *How are you going to use it?*
Execute the Delphi method

5 *How will you distribute the information?*
Documented format, document control system, presentations, e-mail

6 *When will you distribute the information?*
Upon completion of the Delphi method process and a solution is obtained

7 *What decisions can or should you make from this tool?*
The main decision made from this tool is the solution derived from the method. To implement the solution or not, budget and schedule impacts based on solution

8 *What information does this tool provide for your project?*
Delphi method provides a solution to the problem addressed and can provide multiple solutions, assisting in providing an assumed best answer. Design of the solution, method to implement solution and possible technical aspects of solution

9 *What historical and legal information do you need to store?*
Project procedures, legal requirements from client, Insurance issues, decision making background and history, documentation generated within the solution process, lessons learned, possible patient information if applicable

10 *What will be the staffing requirements (role type) to run and maintain these tools?*
Facilitators, subject matter experts or users, project manager, team members, clients or owner

Reporting using the Delphi method

The reports generated from the Delphi method are not necessarily the sole responsibility of one person. At the beginning of the process, assigned team members can guide the reporting process. The Delphi method is a series of developing reports. Every time the team goes through an iteration of the Delphi method, additional information is created that brings the solution of the problem closer. When reaching consensus, the writing of the final report commences. The person responsible distributes it to the appropriate parties in a timely manner. The person responsible for the report could be the project manager, an assigned analyst, or anyone involved in the process that has the ability to document the results of the group's effort during this complex process. Without knowledge of the Delphi method process occurring, the summary or final recommendation (solution) report is difficult to develop. The Delphi method report is delivered only once at the time of solution of the problem. After that, it is on demand. The documentation and analysis is stored as part of the regular project archives.

CROSS-REF See Chapter 15 to find out how to create and use the Delphi method.

Introducing the Design Specification Document

The purpose of the *design specification document* is to describe the detailed technical specifications of the product. Every product in the world has a design specification of some kind, ranging from a scrap of paper to many elaborate computer-generated detailed documents; yours probably will be somewhere in-between. This document provides enough information, with enough detail that, if complete, the project team developing the product can actually create the product from the specifications. The design specification document covers various aspects of the project including but not limited to design maps, design considerations, assumptions, constraints, and design methodology. Project managers will drive the development and use of this document on every project when developing a final product. This will ensure that the design team and developers have a solid foundation to develop and the best possible solution for the customers.

The communication aspects of a design specification document are challenging because it is a technical document and because various people must be involved and issue approval before considering it final and ready for construction. The project manager must drive the communication and ensure those on the project are receiving the documents, making comments on it, and approving or rejecting it where applicable.

NOTE The Project Management Institute's knowledge area for this tool is the Quality Management area. The secondary area that this tool could be associated with is Risk.

ON the CD-ROM We have included a sample of the design specification document in the Quality folder. Use this as a guide to the first step in creating your own version of this tool.

TOOL VALUE The design specification document communicates the detailed requirements to construct the product.

Most industries use design specification documents. Software development projects have been using these documents for years to record the details involving design considerations on the project. For example, on software projects these documents describe components such as screen layouts, report specifications, and user interface design. Without a design specification document, the software developers would have to rely on their own opinions for screen and report designs. Doing so and giving the design team the complete responsibility of the screen or report layouts can be risky, because most likely it will not match what the customer is expecting. The design specification document bridges the gap between the customer and the project team. In the construction industry, the architects and engineers create the design specification document for their customers.

Figure 8.2 represents part of a design specification for the layout of a sailboat. As stated, many industries use this tool as a method of communicating actual specifications to the team constructing the product. In this example, the specification is a sailboat and provides excellent detail of the layout and the different areas and compartments. A boat builder will be able to use this document, along with other specification documents associated with this boat, to build the boat. This is just an example of a design on the market today across thousands of industries creating millions and millions of products.

The process for using a design specification document starts with the design engineer/architect or the analyst working with the customers capturing the details of the product designs. For example, in the boat specifications shown in Figure 8.2, a marine architect would have worked with the boat designers and customers to decide where to install the shelves, and where the linen lockers and navigation table go. Someone would also have provided input on the design for capturing it in the design specification document. That process continues until all aspects of the sailboat are complete. Depending on the product, this process can take months to complete, or a short time if utilizing an existing product's design specification document.

The development process consists of many rounds of interviews, capturing requirements, and eventually compiling those results to develop the design specification document. The process is often a long process and involves many customers, developers, and project team members, all providing their input to the overall design of the project. Throughout the process, the customers and analysts will become familiar with the design requirements and will have an understanding of what the final product will look like before ever creating the actual product.

Before starting the interview process, the engineer (or architect) or analyst will discover the correct design specification document for the type of project they are creating. The majority of design specifications documents have a standard template of one form or another to use as a starting point. A software design specification document and a construction design specification document will be completely different and will not look even remotely the same. However, each document has the same purpose — to provide a location to store the details, requirements, and specifications for the developers or the construction crew to utilize when constructing the product.

Using a design specification document presents challenges to the project manager. Because the document contains so many details around the design of the final product, sometimes customers have expectations that do not match what the analyst captured in the document, and other times the analyst captures it correctly. The biggest challenge is to capture what the customers want from a design perspective and put that into a format that is workable by the development team. Sometimes overcoming the different needs of the two parties is hard, and other times it is impossible. When this scenario occurs, and customers are asking for something the development team has no idea how to produce, it becomes an area where many projects go wrong. When this occurs, the project goes into a holding pattern until finding a resolution and the customers and team members come to an agreement on the design of the product. Fortunately, this does not happen very often.

FIGURE 8.2

A sample of a design specification document for a motor boat.

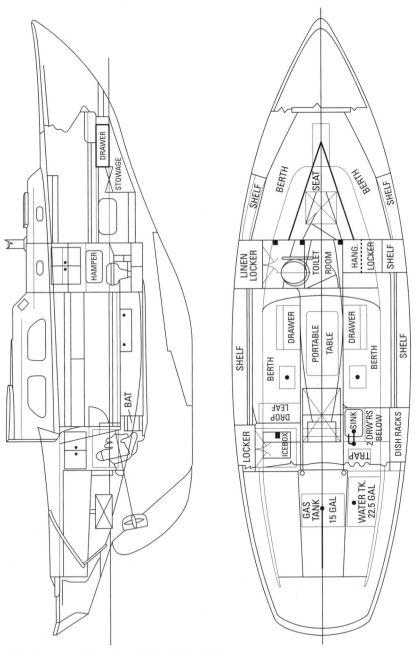

Printed with permissions from: Lackey Sailing, LLC

CROSS-REF See Chapter 5 for more information on the customer requirements document tool. The customer requirements document will contain the specific design requirements from the customer and will need updating or referring to when there are design issues on the project.

TIP Design specifications span all industries. Ensure focus and attention is on these specifications at all times. The success of your project depends on it!

Planning to use a design specification document

In planning and preparing to use a design specification document, the project manager must first work to ensure that an analyst or an architect/engineer is assigned to the project that will be capable of producing the document and working with the customers to gather their requirements. When it has been determined who will write the document, the project manager works with that person to review the design specification template and determine if it is applicable for the project. Rarely do the design specification documents ever match exactly the needs of the project so some adjustments to the template will be required. After determining the right format for the document, the design analyst is ready to start creating the document, and the project manager will work with the customer and the team members to support the creation of the document to ensure that they are willing and able to dedicate the amount of time necessary to assist the analyst during this effort. The analyst will also require assistance from team members and customers to complete the document. This will eliminate times the analyst would otherwise spend guessing or researching answers to questions that are readily available by their team members more familiar with their own areas of the project. Without that time commitment from the customers, the analyst will find it difficult to complete the document in a timely manner and may not end up capturing the information correctly the first time. After performing these planning steps, the project manager will have completed the necessary steps to prepare adequately for the use of this tool.

NOTE The design specification document works hand in hand with the requirements documentation. The requirements document feeds the design specification document.

Before you can create a design specification document, you must formulate a plan. In the "Planning Questions" section below, we provide some suggestions to help start you thinking about how to utilize this tool on your project.

Planning Questions

1 When would you create, develop, or write this tool?
During the planning process for the template itself, but during the design phase of software the project

2 Who is going to use this tool, both from an input and output status?
Clients, project manager, team members, subcontractors, architects, engineers, or specific skill areas will use this tool.

3 *Why are you going to use this tool?*

To understand the design of the product, cost estimating based on materials is required

4 *How are you going to use this tool?*

Document the details and design concepts for developing the final product.

5 *How will you distribute the information?*

CAD drawings, document control system, e-mail, presentations (portions), document format, such as Microsoft Word

6 *How often will you distribute the information?*

Initial document creation the design and developers teams will be looking for the document to be able to start their designing and development process.

7 *What decisions can you make from this tool?*

How to develop the final product, material decisions, cost decisions, schedule decisions, resource decisions, risk decisions

8 *What information does this tool provide for your project?*

The how-to in constructing the product, what material would be required, method of construction, possible equipment details

9 *What historical and legal information do you need to store?*

All historical drawings, all specification documents

10 *What will be the staffing requirements (role type) to run and maintain these tools?*

Architect, engineer, designer, subject matter experts, project manager, customer

Reporting using the design specification document

The engineer or design analyst assigned to the project has the responsibility of creating the design specification document. This is a technical document, which limits who can produce it. The analyst will leverage the work of the technical staff members to help them complete the document from a design perspective.

The analyst or architect/engineer assigned to creating the design specification document is responsible for communicating it to anyone involved in the project. The project manager can help with the process, but it is up to the creator of the document to share with whomever they see fit. The project manager is responsible for obtaining sign-off from the team members and the customer on the design specification document. That approval ensures that everyone is in agreement with the information in the document and allows the project to move into the development phase.

Table 8.2 represents the table of contents for a software development design specification document. The document covers a wide range of topics such as design considerations, architectural strategies, policies, and detailed system designs. Each area contains enough information to develop the final product, and the project manager and team members who work for a design company will use that company's design methodology to create all their design specifications.

TABLE 8.2

Example of a Software Design Specification Table of Contents

Section	Description
1	Introduction
1.1	Design Template Purpose
1.2	When to Use
1.3	Capturing the Design information
1.4	How to Use the Design Template
1.4.1	Packaging the Design
1.4.2	Trade-offs and Alternatives
2	System Overview
2.1	Design Map
2.2	Supporting Material
2.3	Definitions and Acronyms
2.4	Design Considerations
2.5	Assumptions
2.6	Constraints
2.7	System Environment
2.9	Design Methodology
3.0	Risks and Volatile Areas
3.1	Architecture
3.2	High Level Design
3.3	View/Model
3.4	Low Level Design
3.5	Module 1..n
3.6	User Interface Design
3.7	Application Control
3.8	Screen 1..n

This template is © Copyright Construx Software Builders, Inc. and is used with permission from Construx.

The project manager is not required to report from the design specification document every week because the document does not contain project status information. The only time it would require any type of reporting or approval would be during initial development, throughout the requirements sessions, and when obtaining final approval. The most popular format for the design specification document is to create them in a document format, but oftentimes, presentations use sections of the document. The design specification document is stored as part of the document control system for archival and long-term storage and is accessible by any interested stakeholder on the project.

CROSS-REF See Chapter 21 to learn more about how to use a design specification document.

Introducing the Flow Chart

The purpose of the *flow chart* is to display a graphical set of steps in a process or procedure. Almost everyone is familiar with flow charts because of the thousands of different applications and purposes we see them used for on a daily bases. The flow chart is something that project managers should take advantage of on their projects to improve communications. Communicating complex or difficult processes or procedures can often be hard to explain in a text format, but if you draw them using a flow chart format, they become much easier to explain and communicate to both the team members and customer.

The communication aspects of a flow chart are amazing and often overlooked because project managers rarely consider these tools as something to use on a regular basis. Flow charts are simple and easy to use and many project managers do utilize flow charts on their projects and find great value in them for a variety of reasons. For example, on a software development project, flow chart examples include step-by-step instructions to enter data, processes for completing a series of developing code, or training steps when starting to take a training course. The project manager has the responsibility of ensuring that project team members communicate their flow charts to all team members or project customers. For those team members needing to use a flow chart to follow a process or procedure, it is beneficial that the project manager spends time and goes over the flow chart with them so they have a better understanding of all the processes before executing any of the steps in the chart.

NOTE The Project Management Institute's knowledge area for this tool is the Quality Management area. The secondary area that this tool could be associated with is Risk.

ON the CD-ROM We have included a sample of a flow chart in the Quality folder. Use this as a guide to create your own version of this tool.

TOOL VALUE The flow chart tool communicates the information necessary to understand and use a representation of the flow of a process or procedure.

The benefit of using a flow chart on a project is its familiarity and ease of use. In some industries, flow charts are known as logic flows, process modeling, and control flow diagrams, to name a few. In general, because of how easy they are to understand and use, flow charts have a high acceptance rate by all team members. Upper management and customers will appreciate using a flow chart to explain procedures or a series of steps that relate to an issue on their projects. A common use of flow charts in software development projects is the flow of a particular software application, from screen to screen, or around the user interface. As the application is developed, software developers will use flow charts to describe the flow of an application or a section of the application. They will then use the Flow Charts to help them explain the different application paths to the customer. This makes it easier for the customer to understand the chart and to determine immediately if they like the flow or not and suggest changes if there are issues.

Figure 8.3 represents an example of a flow chart. This basic flow chart is displaying the graphical nature of the tool. This example demonstrates how a project manager would go through the process of hiring staff for the project. This flow chart has a series of steps and questions to walk through in this hiring process.

FIGURE 8.3

This figure represents a sample flow chart.

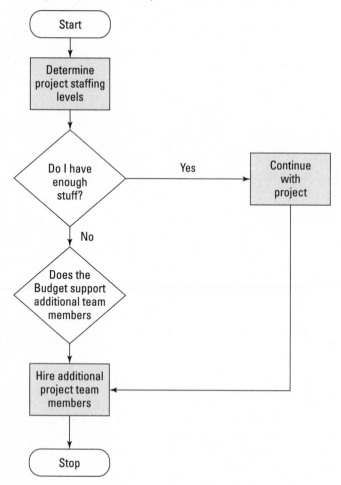

NOTE Flow charts are strong communication tools when trying to understand where information flows in, out, and through a process or procedure. Flow charts span all industries and are a common tool for project managers.

One of the beneficial aspects of using a flow chart is to determine flaws or missing areas in a process or procedure, especially, processes that are brand new or relatively new. Developing a flow chart is an excellent method to establish what the steps are and determine if anything is missing. The process for correcting this situation is relatively easy and initially requires the project team and the project manager working together to develop the initial flow chart based on the process or procedure, and then as a group to determine if anything is missing on the existing flow chart. A common mistake project managers make on projects when they create complex processes or procedures is never to develop the flow charts associated with the processes. Creating a flow chart acts as a learning tool to supplement the text describing the processes. Not only will it help the customers understand the processes quicker, it could potentially determine that a process was missing something not caught in the text.

Here are some possible flow charts that are applicable to projects today:

- **Complex system process flow chart:** Used in the software industry, it describes how systems will interact and transfer data between the two systems.

- **Structural design flow chart:** Used in engineering, it describes the steps necessary to accomplish a structural design.

- **Safety flow chart:** Describes the steps to explain a safety procedure on a job site, for example the safety steps in exiting a helicopter after a crash into water.

- **Shop flow chart:** Used in the manufacturing industry, it describes the flow of a product through a manufacturing process.

Planning to use a flow chart

In planning and preparing to use a flow chart, the project manager must first understand the various project areas where the flow chart will be beneficial and considered valuable for communicating project information. In some rare cases, there are projects that do not require flow charts, or creating them would not benefit the project. They are rare, but do occur. The flow chart is not challenging from a planning and communicating perspective because many people are familiar with the tool. The project manager must plan how and where he will use the tool and what processes should have a flow chart associated with them.

NOTE A flow chart is like a road map showing you how to get from point A to point B.

Before you can create a flow chart, you must formulate a plan. In the "Planning Questions" section, we provide some suggestions to help you start thinking about how to utilize the tool on your project. Planning on how to use the tool and thinking about where to use it makes sense. This is an effective way to plan and utilize this valuable communication tool.

Planning Questions

1 *When would you create, develop, or write this tool?*

Project managers create flow charts throughout the project in a variety of different areas and processes

2 *Who is going to use this tool, both from an input and output status?*

Everyone involved in the project will utilize the flow charts

3 *Why are you going to use this tool?*

To assist in demonstrating a process or a procedure that may be difficult to communicate, but much easier to communicate using a diagram or chart

4 *How are you going to use this tool?*

Training process and procedures, project presentations

5 *How will you distribute the information?*

Document format such as Microsoft Word, Microsoft Visio, plotter, document control system, e-mail, presentation

6 *When will you distribute the information?*

After creation to ensure everyone is in the loop of how the process or procedures run.

7 *What decisions can or should you make from this tool?*

The tool is about teaching and helping people understand a process or procedure. Possible decisions on flows in the procedures and any changes to those flows.

8 *What information does the tool provide for your project?*

Process and procedures to follow through a process

9 *What historical and legal information do you need to store?*

Lessons learned Information, flow chart revisions, and the document itself

10 *What will be the staffing requirements (role type) to run and maintain these tools?*

Project manager, team members, and subcontractors

Reporting using a flow chart

Any member of the project team member can create a flow chart; however, the type of flow chart depends on what the project manager or team member is trying to explain. Some projects may need multiple flow charts. This need depends on the complexity of the project and what the project manager or team members feel they want to communicate to their customers or senior management. Another example would be for explaining administrative items and complex developments for a project.

Project managers or team members will have an easy time communicating the project's flow chart because of the graphical nature of the tool and how familiar people already are in reading and understanding them. One of the best practices project managers should consider while communicating their flow charts is to bring everyone together either in person or on the phone and go over the flow chart to ensure that there is a common understanding on every step or process and it is clear on the outcomes and decision paths documented in the chart. Project managers should be aware that even though the charts are easy to read, some people might struggle to understand and comprehend them. In this situation, communicating to them in person, one-on-one, usually works well in helping them through their challenges.

In most cases, flow charts do not fall into the weekly status reporting cycle because they do not contain any project information. There may be some exceptions, and discussing the Flow Chart on a weekly basis makes sense, but that would be only on the rare occasion and for a limited time. For example, project managers can use a flow chart at a press conference to report the various stages of the project and each week report the next stage through the end of the project.

A flow chart documents a process or procedure. Project managers will report at the initial creation of the flow chart and then on-demand. Charting and presentation applications create the flow charts normally in a presentation-type format. A flow chart is stored as part of the document control system for long-term archiving and is accessible by any interested stakeholder on the project

 See Chapter 17 to learn more about how to use a flow chart.

Introducing the Quality Management Plan

The purpose of the *quality management plan* is to identify and document the project's quality processes. This plan is important to put in place early in the project before activities begin and before testing can occur on the deliverables or the product. The goal of the quality management plan is to ensure the highest level of quality possible for the project's budget and to provide team members with the processes for managing quality assurance and the quality control areas on the project. Projects that do not utilize a quality management plan are ignoring an important aspect of project management and doing a disservice to their customers. By ignoring quality, project managers are not providing the best possible project results to their customers.

Communicating the information contained in a quality management plan is the responsibility of the project manager on most projects. Some larger projects have quality control managers that lead the quality areas of the project and are responsible for the quality management plan. In this case, the quality managers are responsible for communicating the quality management plan, not the project manager. In either case, whoever is in charge of quality is responsible for ensuring that team members are delivering quality, as outlined in the plan, and work with the customers to ensure they are not demanding a level of quality they cannot afford, or have allocated in the budget. Unfortunately, this is something that happens regularly; customers ask for higher quality than what is in the budget, in some cases impacting other areas of the project. Project managers should make the customers aware that if they are demanding a higher level of quality then what is in the quality management plan, then additional budget will most likely be required to support that quality level. That budget could mean extra testers, longer test periods, and so on all in the efforts to increase the level of quality on the project.

NOTE   The Project Management Institute's knowledge area for this tool is the Quality Management area. The secondary area that this tool could be associated with is Risk.

ON the CD-ROM   We have included a sample of a Quality Management plan in the Quality folder. Use this as a guide to the first step in creating your own personal version of this tool.

TOOL VALUE   A quality management plan communicates the understanding of what process to follow to establish and maintain the standard of quality on a project.

The biggest benefit of utilizing a quality management plan is the focus and attention that it brings to the project team members and the customers on the quality aspects of the project. Without a quality management plan, quality becomes something of a second thought and something that may not even be considered or addressed. With an active quality management plan in place, the customers and team members have to consider quality as a priority in their work efforts. This will eventually reflect on an overall superior final product. The quality management plan helps in providing assurance that the final product will meet the expectations of the customers, because the project manager would have worked with those customers to ensure they have included a level of quality (satisfaction level) into the quality management plan as a guideline and a quality level for the project team to follow.

Table 8.3 shows a table of contents for a quality management plan. Every project requires a quality management plan to drive the team members and customers into ensuring that quality is the highest level possible and that quality techniques and processes continue throughout the project. This quality management plan is applicable across multiple project types and is not industry specific. Depending on the project, like all other templates, the quality management plan requires updating to fit the specific needs of the project, and rarely does one plan fit the needs of every project.

TABLE 8.3

Example of a Quality Management Plan Table of Contents

Section	Description
1	Quality Management Approach
2	Project Overview
3	Quality Standards and Metrics
4	Quality Tools
5	Quality Planning
6	Quality Assurance
7	Quality Assurance Procedures
8	Quality Assurance Roles and Responsibilities
9	Quality Control
10	Quality Control Procedures
11	Quality Control Roles and Responsibilities

The project manager is responsible for communicating the quality management plan to their team members and customers to ensure that everyone is in alignment with the level of quality they are providing and receiving on the project. The team members are providing quality in their work products and the customers are receiving a quality product. An example of the test team requiring their work to align with the quality management plan the project manager would document this in Section 9 (Quality Control). In a scenario where the testing on a project is scheduled for two three-day periods, but due to complexities and time restrictions, the test team only completes one of the three-day period test cycles, there will be a perception from the customer that they are not getting everything they agreed to in the Quality Control section. Even if there are no additional defects found in the first test cycle, the customers will want that extra cycle because not only did they pay for it and agree to it, they will feel like the project is forcing lesser quality into the project by not performing that extra test cycle. If the project ends and the test team does not complete any additional testing, they will potentially be forcing a lower level of quality on the product and onto the customers. They could be potentially missing errors or problems by not performing that extra test cycle. Completing a second round of testing would provide the level of quality that the customers agreed to, and completing a third round of testing would appear to be exceeding the level of quality. In this line of analysis, the customers are equating a level of quality with the number of test passes the test team will perform. On the other hand, if the logic is that every test pass will find additional errors, then technically the project team may never stop testing, or may never get to a point where there are zero errors. In this case, the project manager has to work with the customers and stand behind what they agreed to as the level of quality they were willing to accept and approved in the quality management plan.

The quality management plan does not provide a step-by-step process or act as a how-to-guide, but it does provide the guidelines and procedures for each quality area. When quality issues arise, the project manager utilizes a quality management plan for an understanding of how they will correct those issues. For example, if you have an issue in the quality control area, you can review both the quality control section and the quality control procedures section in the plan to determine how to resolve the issues. The plan acts as a reference guide to assist you in managing and controlling all quality aspects of your project.

There are only a few disadvantages of using a quality management plan. Some include, implementing the rigor on quality activities for a project that does not warrant it, or another would be adding time and money to quality tasks that would not be cost effective. Other than that, the quality management plan sets the framework to ensure quality exists, and there should be limited customers that do not want the highest-level quality possible on their projects. For individuals or customers who do not want quality to be the focus of the project, the project manger should question if they are a good fit for the team. In some cases, the project manager should arrange for a reassignment of that team member. If a customer feels that other areas are more important than quality, as long as they approve and document that expectation, the project team should respect those wishes and react accordingly.

The quality management plan covers many aspects of the quality components, including the following:

- **Quality planning:** Identifying and enforcing the level of quality expected on the project. Project managers need to discuss the level of quality with the stakeholders early in the project to ensure that everyone maintains that level of quality throughout the life of the project. If the quality level drops or is not maintained, then the project manager must implement the quality control and quality standards processes to regain the quality level. Quality planning includes the determination of how many test cases does the test team run for each test scenario.

- **Quality assurance:** Quality assurance activities focus on the processes for managing and delivering the solutions. The project manager, team members, and other stakeholders, perform various quality assurance processes throughout the project. Examples of a quality assurance activity would be user acceptance testing. By projects having UAT built into their project methodology, they are assuring that some level of quality testing will occur and the customers will be happy with their product in the end.

- **Quality control:** The project team performs quality control activities continually throughout the project to verify that project management and project deliverables are of high quality. Quality control activities include testing to ensure testing is passing at acceptable levels and customers are excepting the results of the testing.

- **Quality standards:** Quality standards certify processes and systems of an organization, not the product or service itself. In 1987, the International Organization for Standardization (ISO) created a series of quality standards named ISO 9000-1987. These standards are applicable in many different industries based on the following categories: design, production, and service delivery. Many companies try to achieve the ISO 9000 quality standard to improve their operations. This standard is a benchmark used in industries around the world.

■ **Quality tools:** The discipline of total quality control uses a number of quantitative methods and tools to identify problems and suggest avenues for continuous improvement in fields such as manufacturing. Over many years, total quality practitioners gradually realized that a large number of quality-related problems use the seven basic quantitative tools to resolve problems.

Planning to use a quality management plan

In planning and preparing to use a quality management plan, the project manager must first determine where in the project quality testing should occur and how the team can improve quality on the project. After determining where on the project quality testing should occur, the project manager would then work with a test team member or the quality manager to own the development of the quality management plan. Otherwise, the project manager would own the plan for the project. After finding an owner, the project manager and that owner would work with the customers and determine areas on the project where they want to focus on the quality testing. In those discussions, the project manager will gather the reporting and communication requirements from the customers as well as determine how often they want to have quality testing results reported to them. After adequately planning and working through these planning areas, the project manager will have prepared for the use of the quality management plan on his project.

Before you can create a quality management plan, you must formulate a plan. In the following "Planning Questions" section, we provide some suggestions to start you thinking about how you can utilize the tool on your project.

Planning Questions

1 *When would you create, develop, or write this tool?*
During the planning process when determining the areas of the project that have the largest impact on quality

2 *Who is going to use this tool?*
Project manager, team members, quality manager, subcontractors, customers, and upper management

3 *How are you going to use it?*
To define how quality management will occur on the project and act as a guideline of how the team members and customers control quality.

4 *How will you distribute the information?*
Document format such as Microsoft Word, document control system, e-mail

continued

---

continued

5 *What information would you distribute from this tool?*

The quality process and procedures, identification of quality tools, identification of quality roles and responsibilities, sets and establishes quality levels

6 *How often will you distribute the information?*

Once at the creation and approval of document and then throughout the project as required, or as quality becomes a major aspect of the project.

7 *What decisions can you make from this tool?*

High-level cost estimating based on quality, quality execution decisions and quality specifications decisions, how to allocate and control quality procedures or process, quality assurance process decisions

8 *What information does this tool provide for your project?*

Quality approach, quality tools, quality assurance procedures, roles and responsibilities for managing quality, quality matrix, quality checklists, quality improvement process, and quality baseline

9 *What historical and legal information do you need to keep?*

Lessons learned Information, document itself, modifications and updates, quality assurance measures taken on project, issues related to document

Reporting using a quality management plan

Any project team member can create a quality management plan for the project. In some cases, the project manager will take on the responsibility of creating this plan with the help and support of their team members and in other cases, when the project is large enough, the project hires a quality manager to ensure that a person is tracking and controlling the project's quality.

Many times, it is a best practice for the project manager to review other projects' quality management plans as a starting point for their project to leverage the good work already completed both in the plan and on the actual project. In most cases, these processes and procedures are already familiar to the organization and in all likelihood, tested to be successful on prior projects. Another technique a project manager should take advantage of is any lessons learned information from prior projects as it relates to quality testing or quality management. If there is information available to the project managers as to what was done special in the testing of the project, that information is beneficial to a project manager. Specifically, what went right and what went wrong on the testing aspects of the project.

The quality management plan does not fall into the weekly status reporting cycle because it does not contain any project status information. The project manager develops the quality management plan using a document format and stored in the document control system.

Understanding the Shewhart cycle

Walter Shewhart developed the Shewhart cycle in the 1920s. The concept behind the Shewhart cycle chart is to improve the quality of the organization or product. As project managers learn about quality and its importance on their projects, understanding the origin and the history is important. The Shewhart cycle is a concept well known in quality, and therefore project managers should learn about this process to enhance their own skills in this area.

The Shewhart cycle chart is defined by four main areas:

1. Plan: To improve results by designing or revising the process components.
2. Do: Implement the plan and measure its performance.
3. Check: Evaluate and report results to stakeholders.
4. Action: Make a decision on possible process changes for improvement.

Project managers apply the concepts documented in the Shewhart cycle chart to their projects where quality is a critical aspect of success to the project. Project managers should understand the importance of this chart and the cycle as it pertains to not only the process of controlling quality, but also how they will communicate quality at each step throughout the process. As the project progresses through the various steps, the project manager communicates the progress and results of those steps to their customers while still maintaining the level of quality that the customers approved in the Quality Management Plan. The quality process steps repeat throughout the life of the project and communications between the project manager and the customer occurs at the end of each step.

The following figure represents an example of the Shewhart cycle chart. The chart starts at Plan and runs continually until achieving quality on a project. This is a popular chart and has many different versions out on the Internet using the same format and same information. It has become the standard in a Quality Management area.

This figure represents a sample of the Shewhart cycle chart.

 See Chapter 16 to find out more about how to use a quality management plan.

Introducing the Quality Metrics Tool

The purpose of a *quality metrics* tool is to establish the level of satisfaction of the customer as it pertains to the quality of the product. A metric comprises one or more measures. It is a measurement of how satisfied the customer is with the results. Therefore, a quality metric is the measurement of the satisfaction level of the customer on the quality of the product or the deliverable.

Every project has some metric that can measure the satisfaction level of the customers with what they are receiving. For example, for every 1000 screws, a customer will accept 25 defective screws. This example represents the accepted satisfaction levels, or their levels of quality. Other examples could include the number of code defects in software, specific building codes in construction, and sample sizing in drug research. In all cases, regardless of the test, there will be a metric or an acceptable level for the customer that the project manager and team members will strive to achieve. If that is not possible, the customers may simply refuse the project and reject the product until they are satisfied. This could lead to lawsuits, civil cases, and the project could be a complete failure.

Project managers should be aware of the difficulties in obtaining quality metrics from their customers and working with them in establishing an acceptance level. This is difficult because some of the demands the customer has are to achieve the highest level of quality possible, irrespective of the project's budget. This may or may not be possible, and it requires the project manager to ensure that the customer's demands match the dollars allocated to the project. If there are not enough allocated funds for the customer to obtain the higher level of quality than what they originally paid, adding more funds to the budget will be necessary. These additional funds will need approving by the customer and upper management staff but in the end, the project is going to need the additional budget to support the request of higher quality on the project.

NOTE The Project Management Institute's knowledge area for this tool is the Quality Management area. The secondary areas that this tool could be associated with are Integration and Risk.

TOOL VALUE Quality metrics allows the controlling and tracking of the quality on a project. Customer satisfaction is rated by how well the project team meets or falls short on individual quality metrics.

Quality metrics are about satisfying the customer's expectations whenever possible. However, meeting the customer's satisfaction does not always mean that the quality has to be 100 percent; in some cases, they will accept a much lower percentage and still be satisfied. It is important that the project manager or quality manager ensure the customers approve a range of what they feel they would be comfortable with before the project's activities start, and if the project stays below the lower point in the range, the customer should be satisfied with the results. When you are dealing with millions of screws produced every day, a failure rate of 25 per 10,000 could be significant, but small in comparison to all the manufacturing that is occurring.

The following describes some quality metrics examples on projects today:

- **Software metric:** The number of bugs or software errors reported in an application. Severity level bugs are between one and three and each indicates the level of impact the bug would have on the operations of the system. One is the most severe level.

- **Database metric:** The database must return results within 5 to 10 seconds independent of the number of records stored or the number of users accessing the database.

- **Office metric:** Office cubical units must be a minimum 6 feet in height and V-shaped so that they fit in a corner and have overhead storage units. The units should have lighting under each overhead storage unit so that the desktop provides enough light. The desktop should be 2 feet by 6 feet for a total of 24 square feet of surface area. The units will have standard file drawers at each end of the V-shape and enough room for a file cabinet.

- **Cross border times metric:** When entering between Canada and the United States, the maximum wait time is 15 minutes. Any longer than those wait times will result in unhappy travelers.

- **Project cost and schedule metric:** It is best to establish metrics at the beginning of the project. The project should never be greater than one week behind schedule and never over budget by 2 percent.

> **NOTE** The project manager must manage his customer's expectations as they relate to quality on a project.

When dealing with the challenges of quality metrics, breakpoints is a common term for exceeding the level of satisfaction of the customer. *Breakpoints* or non-acceptable quality levels are the dissatisfaction events that occur when the project reaches or exceeds a certain metrics level; however, just prior to that point the quality level is still tolerable. In other words, breakpoints are levels that if crossed, fail to meet the customer's expectations.

When developing quality metrics, one of the important aspects of developing the metrics is determining the breakpoints for every metric. The customers should set the expectation of what their breakpoints are because that expectation is customer specific. The project manager's responsibilities are to determine what steps to take when the project hits those points, and how to direct the team in responding to those issues. For example, when the project is constantly hitting 100 bad screws out of 10,000, the project manager should stop the manufacturing line and walk through each process upstream using a fish bone chart to determine where the failure rates take place on the line. It is in the upstream analysis that the project manager and team determine where the failures are occurring, address the failures at the point of malfunction, and then move forward in the manufacturing cycle.

Planning to use a quality metrics tool

In planning and preparing to use quality metrics, the project manager must first determine the various areas on the project where quality is essential. Some projects may have multiple areas where quality plays a factor and other projects may have limited areas. When planning for this testing, project managers should determine where the customer wants the focus to be and ensure that the process and procedures are set up. After the project team members in each project area (testing, development, or design) determine what quality testing means in that area, the project manager will work with the customers to determine if they want to be involved in the testing cycle. In some areas of the project, there will be no customer involvement. Other areas, such as design, screen layout, or report testing, the customers are heavily involved. Sometimes, it can be challenging when customers are involved in this process and testing. The project manager has to keep a good handle on those challenges and manage the customer wisely. The project manager can achieve this by something as simple as producing daily or weekly reports for the customer and keeping them completely in the loop during the testing process. How the project manager handles customer engagement without derailing the progress of the project is an important step in the planning process.

Before you can create the quality metrics tool, you must formulate a plan. In the "Planning Questions" section below, we have provided some suggestions of how we would respond to each of the questions. Each of these responses will provide you guidance and start you thinking about how you would utilize the tool on your project. Planning on how to use the tool and thinking about where to use it make sense. This is an effective way to plan and utilize this valuable communication tool.

Planning Questions

1 When would you create, develop, or write this tool?
During the planning process, after locking customer requirements, and well before execution of any project deliverables occur so quality has not yet become something that is measurable

2 Who is going to use this tool, both from an input and output perspective?
Upper management, owners, customers, executives, project manager, team members, subcontractors, quality assurance team members, quality manager, risk manager

3 Why are you going to use this tool?
To document the customer's quality requirements and then use them for project team members as yardsticks to meet.

4 How are you going to use it?
Determine the acceptable quality level for project deliverables, rate satisfaction level of customers, determine breakpoints and non-acceptable levels (control chart)

5 How will you distribute the information?
Document format such as Microsoft Word, document control system, e-mail, presentation

6 When will you distribute the information?
During the test cycle, this is normally once a week and in some cases daily. At the minimum weekly, to ensure that the project continues to meet its quality metrics during the testing phases

7 *What decisions can or should you make from this tool?*

Decisions on what quality metrics to use, decide on the upper and lower limits for the test results, determine if metrics are being met or not

8 *What information does this tool provide for your project?*

Identify tolerance levels, decisions to add additional testing or not, go/no-Go decisions on phase release and final release based on quality metrics results

9 *What historical and legal information do you need to keep?*

Test results, assumptions for each test, lessons learned information

10 *What will be the staffing requirements (role type) to run and maintain these tools?*

Project manager, team member, quality analysts, quality manager, risk manager, testers

Reporting using quality metrics

The project manager communicates quality metrics during the testing phase using the results from the test team while comparing them to the expectations of the customers. If during the planning process the customer has created a number of different metrics, the project manager is responsible for communicating those metrics during the testing process to ensure the test team meets the needs of the customer. As the testing process continues, the project manager communicates the results of each metric. This communication continues throughout the testing cycle.

Quality metrics fall into the weekly or daily status reporting cycle. Because the metrics do not contain project status information but do contain the information to which the team judges quality, regular reporting of this information is essential. Information such as number of bugs achieved in software testing, wait timeframes, or defective product amounts are examples of the status reported during the weekly status meetings. The customers and project team members must ensure the ongoing quality of the project, and watch the quality metrics closely each week and react accordingly if the team does not meet those metrics. Quality metrics use a document format for creation and are stored within the document control system for long-term archiving and access by interested stakeholders on the project. They must be available in case of litigation procedures long after the project has closed.

CROSS-REF See Chapter 16 to learn more about how to use quality metrics.

Introducing the Scatter Chart

The purpose of a *scatter chart* or (scatter diagrams) is to plot data points based on two sets of independent variables. You can use them when a project team needs to show relationships between two independent data points on a project. Scatter charts usually display patterns in the data and can help project customers or team members determine what the patterns mean. You can then base any project-level decisions on those patterns. Scatter charts are used to test theories, ideas, or possible relationships that team members have on two variables that are related in some way and observe what happens to one of them when the other variable changes. Other uses include cause and effect relationships charts; where data changes are made to one or the other variables, the scatter chart shows those changes immediately. Generally, there is no proof that one variable causes the other one or visa-versa.

NOTE The Project Management Institute's knowledge area for this tool is the Quality Management area. The secondary areas that this tool could be associated with are Time, Cost, and Risk.

ON the CD-ROM We have included a sample of a scatter chart in the Quality folder. Use this as a guide to create your own version of this tool.

TOOL VALUE A scatter chart displays the relationship between two variables when you need to find out what happens to one variable when the other one changes. It communicates if there is a relationship between the two variables.

A scatter chart can display large amounts of data identifying groups of information in a trending format. As the project manager, you should monitor this type of chart closely because it provides you with information that can increase your chances of success on the project. You should watch these scatter charts throughout the project and make course corrections if the data is trending in the wrong direction (i.e., CPI versus SPI).

When a scatter chart contains both project schedule and cost information, it is easy to communicate this information to your customers by going over the contents of the chart. This information keeps them informed on two of the most important areas of the project by utilizing this communication tool.

The relationships on a scatter chart fall into various patterns or categories. Figure 8.4 shows no correlation between the X and the Y variables. Y is not dependent on X or the other way around. The data points of Figure 8.4 have no relational pattern and are scattered over the whole chart.

FIGURE 8.4

This figure represents a no correlation scatter chart.

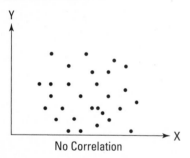

No Correlation

Figure 8.5 shows a positive correlation between the X and the Y variables. An increase in Y may depend on an increase in X or the other way around. The data points of Figure 8.5 have an upward slope. This indicates a control in X may bring about a control in Y.

FIGURE 8.5

This figure represents a positive correlation scatter chart.

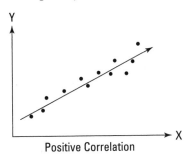

Positive Correlation

Figure 8.6 shows a negative correlation between the X and the Y variables. A decrease in Y may be dependent on an increase in X or the other way around. The data points of Figure 8.6 have a downward slope. This indicates a control in X may bring about a control in Y.

FIGURE 8.6

This figure represents a negative correlation scatter chart.

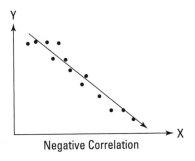

Negative Correlation

Figure 8.7 represents a typical scatter chart. The chart shows the difference between wait times between eruptions (mins) and the duration of the eruption itself (mins). The Y-axis on the chart is the wait time between eruptions ranging from 40 minutes to 100 minutes. The X-axis displays the duration of the eruption time itself ranging between 1.5 minutes and 5.5 minutes. Notice how the scatter chart forms a dumbbell pattern. Also, notice that if an eruption is short, the time between eruptions is also short. If eruptions are long, the times between the eruptions are also long.

FIGURE 8.7

This figure represents a sample scatter chart.

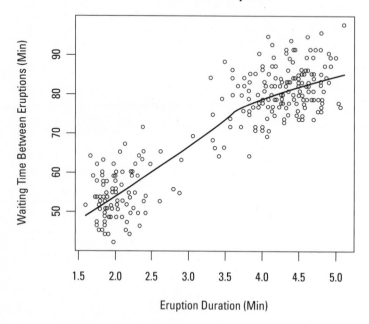

Old Faithful Eruptions

Depending on the type of chart, the project manager, team members, and customers (or stakeholders) can benefit from using scatter charts. Project stakeholders benefit because scatter charts can graph specific product level data that, once placed on a chart, makes it much easier to make a product-level decision based on that data. You, as project manager, can also benefit from scatter charts, especially when you are charting schedule and cost information. After that information is on the chart, it makes it much easier to make project-level decisions, such as pushing out deadlines or adding more dollars to the budget.

The scatter chart plots data points based on two independent variables on an X-Y grid. The relationship between the two variables plotted may form a pattern that could reveal information not acquired in any other way. Using these two-dimensional X-Y axes scatter chart you can display patterns or trends in the data by drawing an average curve through the data points. It is important to note that in scatter charts, the time dimension plays a major role in the data collection. For example, data can collect and chart at any time, but the power of the scatter chart is that it will continue to chart the data regardless of the time it was acquired (time is not a factor, unless it is one of the independent variables). Therefore, data can continually be charting and plotting on the graph. This also holds true for sequential data — it does not matter the order the data is in, it is just a point on the scatter chart. The scatter chart is much different from a line graph even though it uses a line on the chart. It is not like a line graph because it does not matter which order the data is in, it just becomes a point on the scatter chart. On a line graph, the order of the data collection and charting is important.

A scatter chart can have multiple types of data points. Each set of data points has a unique identifier. It can be a symbol, number, color, or size or any combination. If you desire, you can average the data points as a line graph and not display the data points. However, if you want to, you can also show the line and the data points to display possible trends.

Planning to use a scatter chart

In planning and preparing to use a scatter chart, the project manager must first plan and analyze the data to determine if it will match the scatter chart format. In most cases, the data matches the format. The project manager then works with the project team members to discuss their role in gathering data to support the creation of a scatter chart. Normally, this is usually one or two team members who throughout the project will be responsible for collecting and providing data. The project manager then works with the project customers, and determines what types of scatter chart reports would they like created for the project. One of the purposes of talking to the customers is so they understand the format and can read and understand the scatter chart when delivered to them. Some customers may not understand these charts initially and need the project manager to explain how to read the charts.

Before you can create as charts, you must formulate a plan. In the following "Planning Questions" section, we provide some suggestions to help you start thinking about how you can use the tool on your project.

Planning Questions

1 *When would you create, develop, or write this tool?*
On demand, and anywhere in the life of the project

2 *Who is going to use this tool, both from an input and output status?*
Thoughts and Ideas: Everyone on the project

3 *Why are you going to use this tool?*
Plot data points based on two sets of independent variables, report results of comparisons

4 *How are you going to use this tool?*
Set up criteria to create the data points from the two variables and plot against each other in X/Y chart

continued

---

continued

5 *How will you distribute the information?*

Plotter, newsletter(s), document control system, e-mail, presentation, document format such as Microsoft Word

6 *When will you distribute the information?*

Once created and throughout testing cycle, on-demand

7 *What decisions can or should you make from this tool?*

Decisions based on comparison results of independent variables, decide what independent variables to use

8 *What information does the tool provide for your project?*

Resulting data from two independent variable data points

9 *What historical and legal information do you need to store?*

Documentation and graphs, results, lessons learned

10 *What will be the staffing requirements (role type) to run and maintain these tools?*

All project team members can create a scatter chart

Reporting using a scatter chart

There is no one creator of scatter charts on a project. If the project is small, the project manager or analyst assigned to the project often creates the reports for the project. The scatter chart report falls into that category of predefined regular project reports. If the project is large enough, it often has a large administrative group responsible for creating various reports and then someone in that group is responsible for creating the scatter chart.

Here are the possible chart types for scatter charts:

- Cost performance index and schedule performance index charts
- Average overtime hours worked to mistake count
- Activate ingredients in a product to its shelf life
- Experience versus salary
- Concrete cure time versus chemicals
- Hours light bulb burns versus temperature of room
- Performance for each floor constructing a skyscraper

Figure 8.8 scatter chart shows budget and schedule information. This chart shows a project tracking ahead of schedule and under budget as the most dominate pattern on the chart. Each diamond (data point) on the chart represents a month's worth of progress based on the Schedule Performance Index (SPI) versus the Cost Performance Index (CPI) for the month. Considering the SPI, the axis is along the bottom and any diamond to the right of 1.0 is ahead of schedule. Diamonds to the left of 1.0 are behind schedule. The farther away from 1.0 the farther the schedule was either ahead or behind schedule.

The same holds true for the CPI. In this case, it would be the Y-axes or vertical axes. Any diamonds above the 1.0 represents a performance of under budget, and any diamond below the 1.0 mark is over budget.

CROSS-REF See Chapters 7 and 16 for more information on CPI and SPI calculations.

FIGURE 8.8

This figure represents a second different example of a scatter chart.

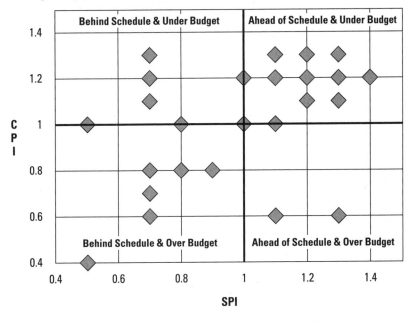

◆ CPI vs. SPI

Scatter charts fall into regular weekly status reporting cycle because they contain project status information that is relevant and applicable to the project. Scatter charts provide the best possible picture of the project to the project manager, project team, or customers. A scatter chart uses the spreadsheet or charting format and is stored as part of the document control system.

CROSS-REF   See Chapter 17 to learn more about how to use a scatter chart.

Summary

This chapter touches on many tools to help project managers, customers, and team members manage and control the project's quality areas. Project managers are required to drive quality into their team members and the deliverables they are producing. Team members also are responsible for quality and should ensure everything they produce is of the highest quality level.

The one tool that stands out in this quality chapter is the scatter chart. Project managers should take time and learn about the capabilities of the scatter chart. They will see quickly how effective it is and how they can utilize it on their projects immediately. When project managers create scatter charts, to assist them in managing their projects, the information they include on the chart is mainly schedule and cost information, but when combining earned value calculations, this tool becomes an invaluable asset to them.

Chapter 9

Defining Communication Tools to Manage Project Human Resources

On most projects, managing project team members can be quite challenging because most of them are not your direct employees. They are on loan to you from their functional manager(s). If they are contractors, they do not even work for your company. In most cases, you have no authority to hire or fire them. You are not even responsible for their paycheck. You are simply a project manager with the resources that were available when the project started. Therefore, it can be a struggle at times to motivate them to work late, perform extra tasks, or any other project task that may be over and above the actual duties. Another important aspect about managing resources is planning and ensuring that the resources assigned to your project are not overworked; as a project manager, you want to ensure that your team members have a balanced workload. You must prevent resource burnout in order to have a successful project. For example, a project team member has multiple project assignments, and your project is only one of their total workload. This multiple project situation causes a completely new level of complexity for you as the project manager because you are attempting to plan and balance your team member's workloads, and you may not have exposure to all the other projects they are working on. In this situation it would be wise for the multiple-project managers to get together to communicate and plan the work efforts of those shared resources.

One of the biggest responsibilities of the project manager is to acquire the project team. They need to obtain the right skills for the right roles on the project. Project managers must also ensure that their team members understand their roles and specific responsibilities on the project. At the same time the project is executing, the project manager should be continuously improving the skills, performance, and competency of each team member.

In this chapter, we explore project communications tools in the project Human Resources Management knowledge area. These tools are important in communicating effectively and managing the resources associated with your project. Each of the tools can improve your overall project communications.

Introducing the Critical Chain

The main purpose of the *critical chain* method is to enable a typical organization to complete projects at twice the rate of conventional methods. The critical chain tool can significantly reduce the amount of multitasking that happens in the organization by providing cross-project measurements and priorities so that each person on the project team knows, across all active projects, which task to work on at a full level of effort until they can make a handoff to the next team member.

The critical chain also installs project buffers and feeding buffers in each project. The *project buffers* protect the customers from delays in the project's critical chain and provide a measurement of the risk of missing each project's commitment date, and the feeding buffers protect the project's critical chain from delays in the feeding chains. There is an add-in tool for Microsoft Project as well as other stand-alone project management products that incorporate the critical chain features directly into the scheduling software tools.

NOTE The Project Management Institute's knowledge area for this tool is the Human Resources Management area. The secondary area that this tool could be associated with is Time.

ON the CD-ROM We have included a demo of a popular critical chain tool for your review in the Communication Tools Human Resources folder.

TOOL VALUE Critical chain reduces multitasking to a minimum and shortens the project schedule considerably in a multiproject environment.

Most projects use the standard critical path method (CPM), but there are alternatives to project scheduling and control, with the most popular being the critical chain. The *critical path* is the sequence of project network activities that add to the longest overall duration, and the critical chain is the sequence of project network activities after resource leveling that adds up to the longest overall duration. The critical chain tool adds a number of other features, discussed below.

In a multiproject environment with shared resources, the biggest problem is the constant pressure resources face to complete tasks in multiple projects. The result is frequent task switching by the resources, also known as multitasking. Multitasking jeopardizes any task that requires dedicated focus. Management often incorrectly presumes multitasking is good because you seem responsive to their changing priorities. However, recent studies support the conclusion that multitasking is very damaging to productivity. This frequent task switching drains productivity — especially in team knowledge work. By using the critical chain tool, the problem is manageable.

The project team members benefits the most from using a critical chain on any project because they can focus on single tasks and dedicate time and effort toward one task at a time. It increases their productivity and quality on the products they are developing.

The *buffer report* enhances the communication of the condition of the project to all stakeholders. Figure 9.1 shows an example of a buffer report. This report provides information that enables the stakeholders to judge the condition of the project and feeding buffers. *Feeding buffers* are buffers that protect the ability of the critical chain (the chain being the longest series of work activities or tasks for the project) to maintain its performance by buffering the variation of noncritical tasks and chains where they feed into or merge with critical chain tasks. Total float is normally a happenstance of the network. Using feeding buffers, the necessary amount of total float (protection) for a chain is deliberately installed.

As an example of the information in the buffer report, consider the last row, which starts with Task ID 57. The name of the buffer is given, and in this case the name starts with PB protecting, indicating that this is a project buffer. The buffer end date of 11/19/2003 is the commitment date for the project. The expected finish of a day earlier, 11/18/2003, is the unprotected expected finish. This varies as the project commences.

The buffer length of 14.3 days indicates how many days of protection the buffer contained at the project start. The buffer guide of -9.76 days shows that at this point in the project, 9.76 days should contribute back to the buffer to have the appropriate protection for the remaining work. Time can contribute back to the buffer by completing tasks in a shorter duration than the original estimates. The *protection ratio* provides similar information, but in different units. Protection ratio is the ratio between the protection remaining and the protection required for the remaining work. The protection remaining is shown in the Buffer Left column of 0.3 days, and the protection required can be computed from the Chain Left column of 51 days, indicating that the longest (critical) chain of work remaining is 51 days. The protection required of 10 days can be found by subtracting the buffer guide (-9.76 days) from the Buffer Left (0.3 days). And 0.3 days / 10 days yields the protection ratio of 0.03. Finally, the check task shows the task ID of the task that, if expedited, would have an immediate effect on the condition of this project buffer.

Planning to use a critical chain

When planning to use a critical chain tool, the project manager must first create or obtain a list of projects for the enterprise that is forced-rank ordered by priority. Publishing this sequence broadly is the first step to stopping the multitasking. The projects that are under way already require finishing first, with each resource focusing first on the highest project on the list that he or she can move forward. Next, the project manager identifies a cutover project. A cutover project is one that has sufficient remaining work to merit re-planning with the critical chain model, which includes project and feeding buffers. The project manager works with this project and all later projects according to the critical chain approach. After the first critical chain project is planned according to the critical chain model and put into work, then the project manager reports project status weekly by initiating a buffer management meeting in most cases. After completing these planning steps, the project manager is adequately prepared to use a critical chain on a project.

Before you can create the critical chain tool, you must formulate a plan. In the following "Planning Questions" section, we provide some initial thoughts and ideas to help you start thinking about how you can use a critical chain on your project.

FIGURE 9.1

A text-based buffer report.

Task ID	Buffer Name	Buffer End Date	Expected Finish	Buffer Length	Buffer Guide	Protection Ratio	Buffer Left	Chain Left	Chain Left
19	FB protecting Plumbing	8/28/2003	9/4/2003	3.61 days	−8 days	−1.67	0	3 days	18
21	FB protecting Drywall	9/17/2003	9/3/2003	2.83 days	8 days	5	2.83 days	2 days	20
31	FB protecting Interior Complete	10/1/2003	9/11/2003	4.12 days	10.39 days	3.88	4.12 days	7 days	18
33	FB protecting Interior Complete	10/1/2003	9/26/2003	2 days	1 day	1.5	2 days	2 days	10
40	FB protecting PAINT TOUCH-UP	10/13/2003	10/28/2003	2 days	−13 days	−5.5	0	4 days	10
42	FB protecting PAINT TOUCH-UP	10/13/2003	10/30/2003	2 days	−15 days	−6.5	0	2 days	10
46	FB protecting PAINT TOUCH-UP	10/13/2003	10/24/2003	2 days	−11 days	−4.5	0	2 days	10
48	FB protecting FINAL INSPECTION	10/21/2003	9/15/2003	1 day	25 days	26	1 day	1 day	10
51	FB protecting PAINT TOUCH-UP	10/13/2003	10/28/2003	2 days	−13 days	−5.5	0	4 days	10
57	FB protecting End of Project	11/19/2003	11/18/2003	14.3 days	−9.76 days	0.03	0.03 days	51 days	10

Planning Questions

1 When would you create, develop, or write this tool?

When planning the project, consider using the critical chain approach, and including project and feeding buffers. During execution, create a buffer report on a weekly basis, and use this during the buffer management meeting.

2 Who is going to use this tool, both from an input and output perspective?

Project management director, project managers, project team members, resource managers

3 Why are you going to use this tool?

Increase the throughput of applications in the company, reduce project team members multitasking on projects, control resources utilization, and reduce schedule duration from Critical Path Method schedule

4 How are you going to use it?

Create and analyze buffer reports and looking glass reports, identify project risks and what-if scenarios using the critical chain models of remaining work, identify project impacts and potential solutions.

5 How will you distribute the information?

Task lists, looking glass buffer and dashboard reports, document reports, posted on a bulletin board, e-mail, document control system, project server

6 When will you distribute the information?

Starting during the planning process and throughout the life of project

7 What decisions can you make from this tool?

Decisions about the near-term deployment of resources decide on moving resources from one project to another to prevent missing commitment date decisions on critical buffers; what tasks are scheduled for completion by each team member so they can be assigned to their next task

8 What information does this tool provide for your project?

Buffer provides information about the risk of meeting the project's commitment date; prioritized task lists for each resource and indicates which task is most urgent on a relative and absolute basis

9 What historical and legal information do you need to store?

The planned and completed project duration, difference between the planned and the completed project duration, completed project staff-days, lessons learned

10 What will be the staffing requirements (role type) to run and maintain these tools?

Project manager, team member, resource manager, project scheduler, cost manager

Critical Chain Methodology

The critical chain concept, developed at Israel Aircraft Industries in 1996 and later applied to many industries ranging from large-scale assembly and residential construction (largely physical processes), has now spanned into software development and product development industries. The improvement obtained when using the critical chain method on simple projects (few weeks long) to multi-year complex projects is dramatic.

The Theory of Constraints (critical chain) advocates five focusing steps in order to improve the throughput (amount of work over a given period) of a system. The five focusing steps may start after the system boundaries, the goal, and establishing the measures of the system.

1. Identify the constraint. Given the system boundaries and the goal of the system, what is keeping the system from moving toward its goal? For a multiproject system, it is the most highly loaded resource.

2. Decide how to exploit the constraint. This involves evaluating the constraint and finding opportunities to get the most output from the constraint.

3. Subordinate all other processes to the above decision. This means no factors should hold up correcting the constraint.

4. Elevate the constraint. The Exploit and Subordinate steps enable you to squeeze as much productive capacity out of the constraint, for little investment. Once finishing with this it may be time to invest in more capacity for the constraint.

5. If, because of these steps, the constraint has moved, return to Step 1. Do not let inertia become the constraint.

Critical chain project management uses buffer management instead of earned value management to assess the performance of a project. In one example, the project team implemented critical chain method on Boeing's F/A-22 Wing Assembly operations. When implementers discovered a conflict between the team members working tasks that earned value, compared to those working on urgent (according to the buffer management measurements) tasks, management decided to shift the team's focus to completing tasks that were urgent according to buffer management. The result was that the hours per unit were reduced 33–50 percent. This was a huge positive impact on getting each wing completed faster.

Reporting using a critical chain

On a weekly basis, the project management director creates or supervises the creation of some type of multiproject buffer report, using the critical chain software. The type of report depends on the critical chain software in use. PowerPoint or Web pages are popular methods of reporting this data to a wide audience, or a meeting that includes the project management director, the resource managers, project managers, and key technical personnel on the project. The use of a buffer report enables the project management director to assess the health of every project in the portfolio and take actions, such as resource reallocation, scope changes, or another type of intervention for projects that are in danger of missing their commitment dates.

There are at least three types of buffer reports in use today:

- **Text-based reports:** A tabular report that lists each buffer and provides various buffer measurements
- **Fever charts:** A time series report that charts the buffer consumption over the course of the project
- **Looking glass:** A Portfolio Report shows the current condition of each project in the portfolio, coupled with a time series report for each project that shows trends

Text-base report

Most critical-chain software tools produce a dispatch list for each resource. The purpose of a dispatch list is to let resources know what to do after they finish their current task. Figure 9.2 answers that question by displaying a dispatch list. The Task Prioritization Metric column sorts the report so that each resource can see the most urgent task from all their assigned projects. The Task Prioritization Metric is based on the type and condition of the buffer that is threatened by the listed task. The Task Prioritization Metric is computed as 10 X Buffer Protection Ratio/Buffer Weight. The Buffer Weight is 10 for project buffers and 1 for feeding buffers. This way, tasks that threaten project buffers will sort above tasks that threaten feeding buffers.

Fever chart

A fever chart is a type of chart that plots a variable over time. Named by the medical community to chart a patient's temperature over time, Figure 9.3 is an example of a fever chart used for buffer management; this chart provides a time history of the condition of the project buffer. The report plots the percentage of buffer consumed as black dots in the figure with each status date update. The vertical line near the right side indicates the commitment date for the end of the project. When the percentage of buffer consumed enters the light gray zone, the project manager should formulate a recovery plan. When the percentage of buffer consumed enters the dark gray zone, it becomes time to implement the recovery plan. These charts display electronically with green, yellow, and red zones rather than gray zones.

Looking glass

Looking glass reports create a graphical executive information system, a dashboard, which brings statistical process control (SPC) and buffer management to the world of project management. Figure 9.4 illustrates a portfolio view that presents a graphical multiproject view, which allows executives to assess at a glance the state of their multiproject system. The left-most light gray bars display the completed duration, and the dark gray bars indicate remaining duration. The black-outlined bars indicate the amount of buffer remaining, and the number to the right of the black-outlined bars is the value of the protection ratio. The numbers inside the bars are in business days, and the chart plots the bars along the calendar time line shown at the top of the figure.

FIGURE 9.2

The protection ratio of the buffers enables prioritized task lists for the resources.

Project Name	Resource Name	Task Prioritization Metric	Open Preds?	Expected Start	Remaining Duration (Days)	Task ID	Notes
MYouth Center2	Builder[2]	1.09	No	10/28/2003	2 days	24	
MYouth Center2	Builder[3]	1.09	No	11/11/2003	3 days	34	
MYouth Center1	Builder[2]	−0.14	Yes	11/4/2003	2 days	52	
MYouth Center4	Builder[4]	0.79	Yes	10/29/2003	2 days	5	
MYouth Center1	Builder[2]	−0.14	Yes	11/6/2003	3 days	53	
MYouth Center4	Builder[6]	0.79	Yes	10/31/2003	5 days	6	
MYouth Center1	Builder[2]	−0.14	Yes	11/12/2003	3 days	54	
MYouth Center4	Builder[6]	10	Yes	11/13/2003	4 day	14	

FIGURE 9.3

A sample fever chart showing the condition of the project buffer as a function of the status dates.

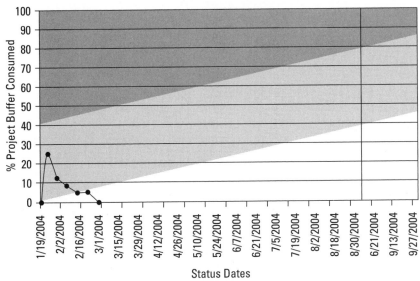

When needing a time history for a particular project, selecting the text to the left of the project bar produces a single-project time history; Figure 9.5 shows this single project time history. The light gray bars at the bottom of the chart display the completed duration, the dark gray bars indicate remaining duration. The black-outlined bars indicate the amount of buffer remaining, and the numbers inside the bars are business days. The software plots the bars at each status date along the horizontal axis, with a height in business days.

Critical chain reports are part of a standard reporting cycle. The data presented is so valuable in managing and controlling the project that team members and stakeholders must review the data on a regular basis. Many applications develop critical chain reports, and once developed, the project manager redistributes the data in many other formats for reporting purposes. The critical chain reports should be stored as part of the project's document control system.

CROSS-REF See Chapter 16 to learn more about how to plan, create, and use a critical chain.

FIGURE 9.4

In the portfolio view, the second project from the top is at the highest risk of missing its commitment date with a protection ratio of 14 percent.

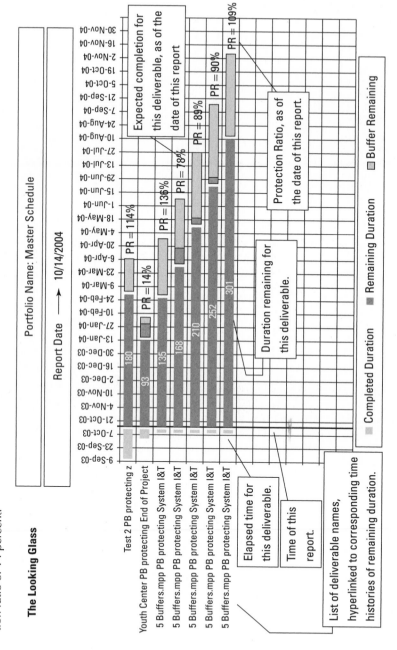

The Looking Glass

FIGURE 9.5

An example of a single-project time history.

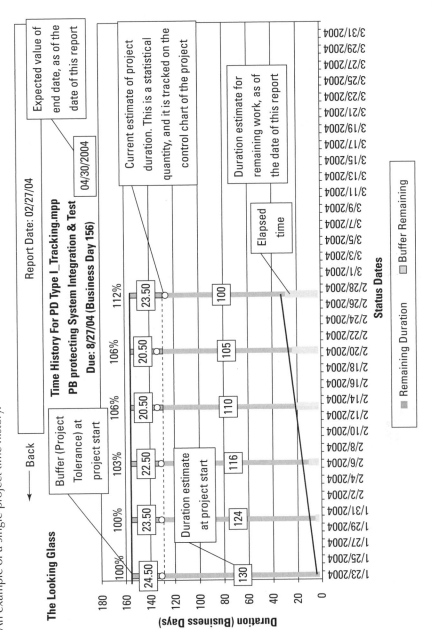

Introducing the Histogram Report

The purpose of the *histogram report* is to display project information using an easy-to-read graphical format. The histogram report consists of vertical bars across multiple categories along the horizontal axis. The report shows what proportion of data falls into each category and where the data can spread across those multiple categories. Project managers use histogram reports for a variety of reasons. Examples include cost and labor hours, percentage of time to a certain area, and number of staff sick and vacation days per quarter. It is unbelievable the number of different reports that are possible using the histogram format. It is really up to the imagination of the project manager to decide what he or she wants to create for their projects.

> **NOTE**   Stacked charts or skyline charts are other common names for histogram reports.

The project manager and team members will regularly communicate the histogram report on their project. This communication normally occurs at the start of the project and carries on throughout the lifecycle until the project ends. Some customers want multiple histogram reports created to keep a continual watch on the project, and others may only want a few reports to ensure that they stay on top of the project but not bogged down by report after report. In both cases, the project manager works with the customer to ensure that they are comfortable with the number of histogram reports they are receiving and if they end up needing more, the project manager can react accordingly.

> **NOTE**   The Project Management Institute's knowledge area for this tool is the Human Resources Management area. The secondary area that this tool could be associated with is Risk.

> **ON the CD-ROM**   We have included a sample of a histogram report in the Human Resources folder. This is a guide to the first step in creating your own personal version of this tool. Your company or project may have specific requirements that can enhance this communication tool further; however, we believe this is a great starting point for the creation of this tool for your project.

> **TOOL VALUE**   A histogram report provides an instantly recognizable chart to the customers that will show variances in data categories. The chart displays simple variances between the horizontal data and the vertical values on the graph.

When working with histogram reports it is quite common for those reports to be confused with bar charts (Gantt chart). Most people outside of the project management profession consider a histogram and a bar chart to be the same chart. Therefore, we thought it was important to let you know the differences immediately to avoid any further confusion.

Figure 9.6 shows the histogram report on the left and the bar chart on the right. You can easily see the difference in the two charts.

The process for creating histogram reports is project dependant and often falls on the project manager to determine how the process occurs on their project. In most cases, the project manager selects the different types of information he/she plans to create with the histogram report format. Depending on the type of report and the data captured, the project manager creates the report and then shares that information with all applicable stakeholders on the project.

FIGURE 9.6

This figure represents both a histogram and a bar chart (Gantt chart) to highlight the differences in the reports.

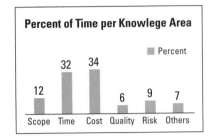

Percent of Time per Knowlege Area

Task Name	Dur	2009					
		Oct	Nov	Dec	Jan	Feb	Mar
Plan Project	20d						
Design	35d						
Model	20d						
Prototype	30d						
Test	15d						

CROSS-REF See Chapter 21 for more information on how to create and use a histogram report.

There are few challenges in creating a histogram report as long as the data is constantly available and refreshed for the reporting cycles. If there is a challenge, it is determining if the data is available, relevant, and updated in a timely manner. The actual creation of the report is relatively simple. Project managers cannot rely on establishing a regular reporting cycle of histogram reports for their customers if there are challenges or problems bringing in refreshed data on a constant basis.

There are many areas of a project where histogram reports are useful for reporting. The primary uses for histogram reports include:

- **Cost management:** The histogram report displays information such as actuals, budget over time (by week, month, quarter, etc.), and comparisons of vendors costs over a stated period. The histogram report is a great choice for reports ranging from costs of rental equipment, consultant hours, and other project costs, where it is important to have visibility on ranges such as time. The possibilities and number of histogram reports are almost unlimited.

- **Resource management:** The histogram report displays various resources availability over time. The chart displays the amount of budgeted and actual work hours per week by the individual resources. By analyzing Figure 9.7, it appears that Bill is working the most hours in the group, and by determining who is working the most hours, it is easy and quick to determine who is working the least amount of hours. Histogram reports are excellent in showing resources that have work on project activities over their current workload. When using histogram reports on a periodic basis (daily, weekly, monthly), the resources can see their project allocations for their work assignments. Based on the allocated hours per resource, the histogram report is an effective way for management to determine the workload of all resources.

There are many benefits of using histogram reports; one benefit is that it displays multiple levels of comparison data on a single chart. Multiple-level histogram reports or stacked histogram reports provide multiple data points on a single column of data. A second benefit is the drill down capability that histogram reports offer as part of its standard features. Customers, or any users of the report, can select data at the highest level (summary level) and then click into that data for further details. Histogram reports are developed by using spreadsheet applications and the built-in chart wizards; they are developed horizontally or vertically, with two or three dimensions, all within the spreadsheet application.

Because the histogram report is beneficial to so many different areas on a project, the data contained in the report determines who will benefit the most from the tool. For example, if the data in the histogram report consists of resources or resource allocations, then the functional managers of the individual resources will utilize the histogram report to determine their resource assignments and determine how they are allocating staff across various projects. If the finance department creates histogram reports based on the project cost data, it then becomes a key financial report and therefore beneficial in the financial area. This can continue from project area to project area, where each project lead creates their own version of the histogram report for their areas. The histogram report is a robust and key communication tool for many members of the project team to utilize.

Planning to use a histogram report

When planning to use the histogram report, the project manager must first determine what areas of the project are going to benefit the most from the use of this report. Areas such as resources, costs, and scheduling are potentially best suited for this type of report, but it could vary from project to project. Once the areas are determined, and the project manager feels he/she is comfortable in what areas of the project to use it on, then the next focus is to determine the customer's needs for the reports. Customer needs include the data the customer wants to see on the charts, and how often they expect them. Sometimes, customers have specific reporting requirements, and the histogram is one of the tools that can fill the needs of the customers in most cases. The next step in this process is for the project manager to focus on which project team member will create the actual reports during the project. The project manager must ensure they allocate enough time to the resources schedule to allow them to perform their work activities and create the reports for the project. After performing these planning steps, the project manager has adequately planned for using the histogram report on the project.

Before you can create a histogram report, you must formulate a plan. In the following "Planning Questions" section, we provide some initial thoughts and ideas to help you start thinking about how you can use a histogram report on your project.

Planning Questions

1 *When would you create, or develop the histogram report tool?*
Throughout the project, the project manager can help manage the project by using the histogram on a series of histogram reports.

2 *Who is going to use this tool, both from an input and output status?*
Anyone involved in the project can utilize this tool in some manner. Either the project manager is using it for cost and schedule management, or the functional managers are using it for resource management.

3 *Why are you going to use this tool?*

The ability to communicate project information in an easy to create format is beneficial to both the customers and the project manager.

4 *How are you going to use this tool?*

Resource management, cost management, schedule management (report depending)

5 *How will you distribute the information?*

Presentation format, e-mail, document control system, document format such as Microsoft Word, Plotter

6 *When will you distribute the information?*

Part of reporting cycle and as need arises

7 *What decisions can or should you make from this tool?*

Cost decisions and resource decisions are two areas for the project manager to utilize this tool in their decision-making process.

8 *What information does this tool provide for your project?*

Graphical representation of cost and resource and other information such as a Pareto chart

9 *What historical and legal information do you need to store?*

Lessons learned information, final version of chart

10 *What will be the staffing requirements (role type) to run and maintain these tools?*

Any stakeholder can create the histogram report for the project

Reporting using a histogram report

In most cases, the project manager is responsible for the creation of a histogram report on a project. However, on larger projects where there is an administrative team in place, the project manager would let that team own the responsibility of creating and communicating the histogram report for the project.

The histogram report is a great communication tool for messaging specific project information to project customers. Project managers will quickly enjoy how fast they can create the report and communicate it to their customers. Their customers will appreciate getting the information in a format that is easy to read and understand and providing them valuable project information.

Figure 9.7 is an example of a histogram report. This report displays the hours per week of four of the project's resources across a five-week period. The histogram report is helpful when tracking project problems. The data such as resource burnout, resource budgeting, or other project issues are all valuable to report with using this tool. For example, if Sam is falling behind in his work, you can see in the third week that he had a short week, and therefore you can tell he is still catching up from missing that time and his work products may be suffering.

FIGURE 9.7

A sample of a histogram report reporting on the number of hours worked per week by a support team.

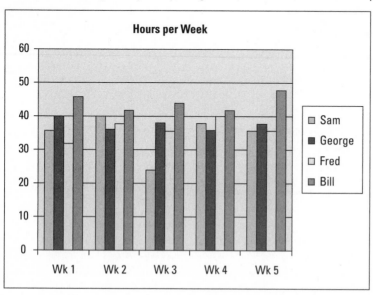

Figure 9.8 represents a second histogram report showing a stacked histogram report using a 3-D format. In this chart it is difficult to determine the hours per week for a particular resource but easy to see the cumulative hours per week for all resources. You can determine the number of hours worked across a chart like this better than with most other reports. For details concerning an anomaly on this chart, you can create a detailed chart showing what data is causing the anomaly.

The project manager generally adds histogram reports to his or her standard reporting cycle on a weekly, bi-weekly, or monthly basis. The actual histogram report depends on the reporting cycle used on the project and the specific data required for the report. The project manager generates a histogram report using the graphic functionality within a spreadsheet tool and often makes the report available in PowerPoint or on an internal Web site. The histogram report is stored as part of the document control system for long-term archiving and is accessible by any interested stakeholder on the project.

CROSS-REF See Chapter 21 how to plan, create, and use a histogram chart.

FIGURE 9.8

A sample of a histogram report, reporting on the number of hours worked per week for all resources on a support team.

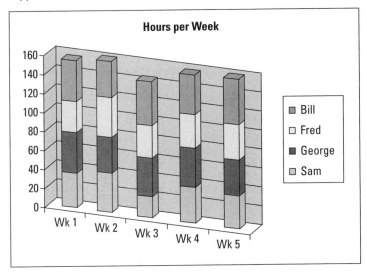

Introducing the Human Resource Plan

The purpose of a *human resource plan* is to capture and document the projects staffing requirements. The project manager captures all the resource names and the roles required for the upcoming project. The project manager works directly with the functional managers to ensure that team members needed to execute the project are available for the project at the appropriate times. The project manager should finish the human resource document as early as possible in the planning phase because it provides the functional or resource managers with as much time as possible to obtain the staff needed for the project. Otherwise, if you left it too late, you could be out of luck getting the staff you need to execute the project. There could be nobody available at the time you need them on your project and you may have to go outside and acquire resources from the consulting companies. This could add time and costs to the project not originally factored into the budget.

From the planning process to the execution and closeout, the project manger communicates the human resource plan to everyone involved in the project. Because of the wealth of information contained in the document, the team members will appreciate this information as well because it helps them understand when they are involved (timeframes) in the project and what their project roles will be. The project manager also keeps the functional managers involved with the human resource plan throughout the project, especially as team members roll on and off the project. The human resource plan will help the functional managers organize and plan their team's different project assignments to ensure there is no overload or burnout. In the cases where the functional managers have multiple human resource plans available and can see all of the different commitments for their team members across the different projects, they have a much easier time determining how to allocate their staff across the projects. With project managers completing the human resource plans in the same format, it makes it easy for the resource managers to review the same information in the different plans and then plan their staffing assignments accordingly.

NOTE   The Project Management Institute's knowledge area for this tool is the Human Resources Management area. There is no other secondary area for this tool.

ON the CD-ROM   We have included a sample of a human resource plan in the Human Resources folder. Use this as a guide to create your own version of this tool.

TOOL VALUE   The human resource plan provides the project manager with the ability to know in advance when they will need to utilize their resources and the associated costs of those resources on the project.

One benefit of using a human resource plan is the tracking and storing of the associated team member's costs. As team members roll on and off of a project, the costs to the project associated to those team members fluctuates accordingly; for example, during the design phase there is a large team of designers assigned and charging full time to the project. When the design phase finishes, that large team moves onto a different project and no longer charges to the current project. As you can imagine the costs associated to the project also change dramatically at this time because you no longer have a large group of designers charging 100 percent of their time to the project. Having this information documented in a human resource plan provides the project manager and customers with the information they need to adjust the budget accordingly, or allocate funds differently during different phases of the project that require the additional funds.

Another benefit of using a human resource plan is that the project manager can try different what-if scenarios with the budget and staffing models. This works well for project managers who are managing a cost-driven project and need the flexibility to add and remove team members based on the current spending of the project. The what-if scenarios are an excellent way of obtaining costing information by adjusting the costs, the number of team members, or start and finish dates, without actually changing resources or assignments on the actual project. With this flexibility, it allows the project manager much more control over the project's resources. When something does actually go wrong on the project and the project manager must make adjustments with staffing, the project manager can make the adjustments first in the staffing plan and determine the overall impact to the project. Without a plan like this in place, the project manager has less flexibility and less control of the project's resources.

NOTE   Human resource plans keep staffing assignments organized and under control. Without a plan in place, the project may have resources assigned with no justifications and reasons to apply the resources.

Table 9.1 shows a table of contents for a human resource plan. As you can see, the document contains many sections around the staffing requirements for the project. This includes training needs, skills required, timeframes, and resource qualifications. This is a comprehensive document and valuable to the project throughout the course of the project.

The human resource plan spans all industries and all project types. All projects require staffing, regardless of whether the project manager captures the requirements on a back of a napkin or in an advanced document such as the human resource plan, everyone, the customers, senior management, and the project manager need to understand the staff, materials, and any other resources needed to deliver the project. There are many factors for needing this resource information, such as cost estimating, schedule management, and budget setting and controlling. Therefore, documenting it correctly in a human resource plan provides everyone involved in the project the information needed to be successful in the resource area.

One important note that project managers should consider in developing the human resource plan is to consider both the staffing requirements and the other types of resource requirements required for the project. These other types of requirements include machines, hardware, and materials. Other examples include cranes for a construction project, personal computers for a software projects, or the amount of plastic material for a manufacturing project. The project manager frequently documents the staffing needs in one document and the materials or equipment needs in another document. The information ends up in two separate documents, which is not normally beneficial at all, because information can be forgotten or written in one document but not aligned to what it says in the other document. As noted, sometimes these other requirements fall into two separate documents. One best practice that project managers should follow is the combining of a project's human resource needs (staff) and the non-human resource needs (materials) into a single document. This saves time and expense, and reduces the overhead of containing project requirements in multiple documents.

As project manager, you must have a good handle on your project's resource requirements at all times. You must ensure that your project is covered, and every area has the proper resources required to complete that portion of the project.

As project manager, you should communicate the project staffing requirements with the functional managers to ensure the resources are assigned and ready when you need them. The human resource plan is excellent for having those conversations and supporting why you need particular staff or the costs associated to staffing on the project. Having these conversations as soon as the company officially announces the project, and then as you progress through the development of the human resource plan, keeps the functional manager planning and thinking about your staffing needs. That way there are no surprises, and as the start of the project nears, the functional managers are ready to assign the staff you need. Avoiding these conversations, or waiting until closer to the time the document is ready, will actually hurt your chances of getting the staff you need, and you may be scrambling for team members to start the project. The project manager will utilize the human resource plan as the legal agreement (contract) between the two companies. In this case, when hiring project resources from outside the company, the human resource plan could become the legal document.

One helpful tip that some project managers like to do is create a human resource plan based on the work breakdown structure or in some cases on the project's organization chart. Project managers should realize how important it is to develop an organization structure and then use that structure as the framework to develop the human resources plan. That way, you can clearly see what roles are missing on the organization chart.

Planning to use a human resource plan

When planning to use a human resource plan, the project manager must first determine the staffing and resource requirements on the project. Projects vary in complexity and size, but most projects in a particular industry have the same roles and deliverables, and therefore the project manager will have a past project's staffing models that they can use as templates and starting points to begin developing the human resources plan. After determining the initial staffing needs, the project manager should work with the functional managers and communicate the initial draft plan to them; this includes timeframes, number of resources, skills sets, and so on. The project manager will work with the customers and communicate the various timeframes on the project they will need to engage. The project manager should obtain a commitment from the customers on the timeframes of their engagement and after planning for staffing needs, equipment needs, and other materials needs the project manager should plan and work with the budget to ensure there are enough funds to staff the project accordingly. When doing this during the planning process, the project manager can identify if there are any problems or concerns with the budget before the project ever begins, and either adjust staff according to the funds, or request additional funds for the staffing and material needs of the project.

In the following "Planning Questions" section, we provide some initial thoughts to help you start thinking about how you can utilize a human resource plan on your project.

Planning Questions

1 When would you create or develop this tool?
During the planning process of the project, after official announcement of project

2 Who is going to use this tool, both from an input and output status?
Project manager, team members, functional managers, customers, upper management, and resource manager

3 Why are you going to use this tool?
To document the staffing, equipment, and material requirements for the project; run "What if" scenarios for staffing and costing, and determine initial staffing costs

4 How are you going to use this tool?
Planning resource for staffing requirements, throughout project as staff roll on and off; to document costs, and as a tool for management and control of project resources

5 How will you distribute the information?
Presentation format, e-mail, document control system, document format such as Microsoft Word

6 When will you distribute the information?
Throughout the project mainly as staff roll on and off, the human resource plan will provide the plan to which to move the resources, planning stage is also an important time in the project where the project manager distributes the document to various areas leaders of the project for resource assignment and allocations

7 What decisions can or should you make from this tool?
Resource increase and decrease decisions, resource reassignment decisions, material decisions, staffing decisions, cost and budget decisions

8 What information does this tool provide for your project?
Human resource requirements, estimates on costs for project budgeting, training needs and schedule, resource, and material requirements

continued

continued

9 *What historical and legal information do you need to store?*

Resources usage, lessons learned information on human resource planning process, comparisons between actual resources requested and used, cost comparisons, resource assignment comparisons

10 *What will be the staffing requirements (role type) to run and maintain these tools?*

Project manager, resource manager, financial analyst

Reporting using a human resource plan

On most projects, the project manager is responsible for creating the human resource plan. When developing the plan, the project manager will rely on the functional managers to understand the staffing requests and be able to provide the necessary staff needed to execute the project from their work groups. For example, the project manager can determine that the project needs five designers and works with the functional manager of the design team to obtain those resources. A team lead in the design area will document their staffing requirements for the project by having the project manager add the requirements of the five designers in the human resource plan. The functional managers are responsible for actually providing the staff to execute the project and therefore it is important they are active in the creation of the human resource plan.

Table 9.2 represents a human resource staff plan for a typical project. This plan is a major component of the human resource plan, but works well as a standalone tool. This staffing plan highlights the various staffing needs across the project. For example, there are three team members required for the project, and on this staffing plan, the functional managers who are responsible for filling these roles will see the expected hourly rates and expected finish dates for those resources. This staffing plan should contain enough information for the functional mangers to be able to fill the project roles requested.

TABLE 9.2

Example of a Human Resource Staffing Plan

Project Name	Group Name	Resource Type	Resource Count	Hourly Rate	Finish Date
ABC Project	Development	Developer	1	$80	7/1/2008
ABC Project	Analyst	Functional Analyst	2	$60	12/31/2008

One best practice found in using a staffing plan such as Table 9.2 is to expand its use across multiple projects, therefore having the company's project resource requests documented in a single table. This provides great exposure to the organization's staffing needs across all projects. When combining multiple projects, the executives can see the trends and the consistent need for staff; they may end up making hiring decisions for the company, not just the project. Executives can look over the entire list of staffing needs across the company and determine where they are missing or lacking in resources. They can then hire for those areas where necessary. For example, if the Project Management Office (PMO) staff consolidates all the staffing plans, this would be an easy way of seeing across all the projects and determining which projects need staff. Not only can you tell the type of staff need, in many cases, you can get an accurate count of the number of staff needed.

Project managers should report on the human resource plan weekly while the project is still missing resources or hiring to fill open positions. The human resource plan contains project status information and therefore requires weekly exposure and attention from customers, management, and team members. The project manager creates the human resource plan document using a document format, and in most cases the information is transferred to other types of presentations as well. The human resource plan is stored as part of the document control system for long-term archiving and is accessible by any interested stakeholder on the project.

 See Chapter 15 to learn more about how to plan, create, and use a human resources plan.

Introducing Resource Leveling

The purpose of the *resource leveling* tool is to balance (level) the resource workloads and assignments over the life of the project. Resource leveling is one of the more complex tasks that project managers must complete during the planning and executing processes. Project managers and resource managers must constantly reevaluate the workloads of their team members so they do not get overworked. The term *leveling* means to limit the maximum number of hours a project team member should work in a day. This leveling process usually extends the duration of an activity to accommodate the set limit of 8 hours per day. Some companies use 7 hours, some companies use 10 hours, and some use 12 hours. Companies establish their own hours per day factor, but in some cases, for example in projects such as the Olympics opening day or highway bridge openings, they alter the factor to cater to the specific project needs. In some cases, if the project gets in trouble or is running behind and needs to catch up on a deliverable, the project manager can change the factor to something higher than 8 hours. In any case, regardless of the hours per day factor, the resource leveling process is the same.

Project managers are actively involved in the resource leveling process and communicating the impact of the resource leveling results. It is in the best interest of the project manager to ensure they communicate any changes in the project's resource assignments to the team members to allow them to plan accordingly. During the leveling process, the project manager must be communicating the results to the team members and the functional managers to ensure everyone is involved in the leveling process. The functional managers may expect resources to be rolling off the project, and that may not be happening if the leveling process requires the resources to stay longer due to the amount of time estimated for the particular task. The resource leveling process often extends project timelines, breaks budgets, and assigns resources longer to the project than originally estimated. This is because the leveling process is correctly assigning the resources at the appropriate level

(8 hours a day) not overloading them with unrealistic hours and deadlines. In most cases, the leveling process results match closely with the actual results and time lines of the project. Because of these factors, project managers should be active in communicating results from the resource leveling process whenever possible and set the right level of expectations to the team members that the project is focused on making changes based on the results of this process.

> **NOTE**   The Project Management Institute's knowledge area for this tool is the Human Resources Management area. The secondary tools for this area are Time and Cost.

> **ON the CD-ROM**   We have included a sample of the Resource Leveling tool in the Human Resources folder. Use this as a guide to create your own version of this tool.

> **TOOL VALUE**   Resource leveling prevents over-allocation of the project team members, maintains a preset limit of labor hours per day per resource, and creates a more realistic schedule that usually causes the project to increase in duration.

Most projects use the critical path method for scheduling, and because of that, there is a high probability that the project manager over-allocates their resources on the project. The reason is the project manager or the project scheduler assigns individual resources to individual activities and the scheduling system, ignoring maximum resource allocations. The scheduling system in turn will schedule the activities as early as possible and therefore resources end up over-allocated. To eliminate this problem, most of the project-scheduling tools have an automated resource leveling feature that calculates the team member's maximum assignments on the project per day (hours per day factor). Project managers assign the resources to the tasks and then use the automated resource-leveling feature to assign and level the team. In most cases, after running this process, the project schedule and costs grow, but the resources have a more realistic allocation to the project. We have found the automated schedule systems are a first step in resource leveling. You should always do further manual leveling to acquire a better schedule. There are leveling situations and decisions the automated systems simply cannot handle correctly.

Figure 9.9 shows an example of an over-allocation chart for project resources. The example shows the average weekly hours across seven months of work. Notice that the project resources in every month but one (June) were working over 40 hours per week. In most cases, resources should stay within a 40-hour workweek, but in April, that allocation doubled to 80 hours. The project manager cannot increase and then decrease the resources on the project as depicted below, so they must resource level the work. Before the project manager resource levels the project, they should have a good idea as to how much more time is required to complete the project. By totaling the over-allocated hours (140), you can estimate this project will extend another 3.5 months.

Project managers should work with their team members to understand what other assignments and work commitments they have on all their projects. Having this bigger picture provides the project manager with the knowledge of whether the team members are able to complete both assignments and make the deadlines on their respective projects. Using these details, the project managers can resource level their individual project resources across multiple projects and communicate the new estimates and timeframes to all impacted project managers. Project managers obtaining this information can adjust their projects accordingly, and possibly look to reduce the individual task assignments of the over-allocated resources. Doing this will most likely increase their chances of success on the project. Working in a Project Management Office environment, those team members can help drive the resource leveling process across multiple projects. In doing so, it allows those staff members to understand their resource assignments across multiple projects and adjust their schedules accordingly to meet the needs of the project.

| FIGURE 9.9 |

A resource over-allocation chart.

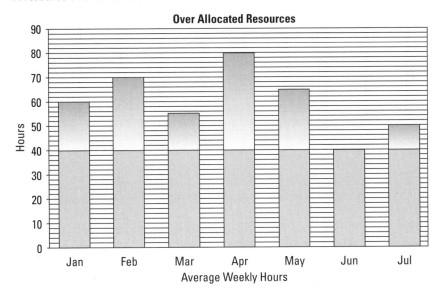

The tracking and monitoring of resource assignments is critical on every project and an ongoing task throughout the project for the project manager, team leaders, and resource managers. Any overloaded or overworked team member may be less motivated to give a 100 percent effort because of being stretched too thin. Any resource manager should be proactive in their planning and managing of resources and should be constantly monitoring their team member's project assignments to prevent any over-allocations or burnouts as well. The resource managers should also work directly with the project manager or if working in a PMO environment, multiple project managers, to move activity dates or look for additional resources when there are scheduling conflicts across a resource. The resource leveling process can help prevent any possible burnout of the team members and create a longer and happier commitment to the company.

TIP Every project is resource constrained so taking the time to level the resources may gain you some extra availability that you were not expecting.

When project managers or resource managers are completing the resource leveling process, they usually review and analyze leveling information on a resource usage chart or directly within the project-scheduling tool. During the review process, the project manager or resource manager determines how they have allocated the team members across the project and if those allocations are correct. If the allocations are not correct, the project manager should determine which team member needs reallocating. Sometimes there should be a reduction in a team member's workload. Because this is an automated process using software, the project manager should check to confirm that the process completed successfully.

As project managers engage in the resource leveling process, they quickly learn the software algorithms are not perfect. Usually there is some manual checking and/or tweaking that needs to take place after the resource leveling process to ensure accurate project assignments. While checking and tweaking their team's assignments, the project manager can determine immediately whether he or she requires additional resources to keep the project on track.

The resource leveling process also applies to materials and equipment used on a project. Like humans, the equipment and materials for a project require planning and monitoring throughout the project. When resource leveling the project's materials and equipment, you are applying the same processes and techniques you do with people. The only exception would be that materials or equipment is not limited to a standard eight-hour workday. Technically, because equipment, for example, can have multiple team members operating it, it can go non-stop as long as the operators stick to the standard working hours they have agreed to. Another example of resource leveling includes dump trucks on a construction project; you may have a situation where you are constrained to the number of dump trucks available to carry material. Your schedule may have the project expected to lay more asphalt (material) per day than is physically possible. Because, in this example, there are only 13 dump trucks available, you may need to resource level the material (asphalt), therefore limiting the cubic yards produced and limiting the number of trucks needed for the project. This is one of the hundreds of different examples where materials and equipment both are involved in the leveling process.

Planning to use resource leveling

When planning to level the project's resources, the project manager must first determine their project staff allocation and their current work assignments. This includes both assignments for the staff (people) and the machines. This planning process includes working with various team members and reviewing their individual work activities to determine if they are capable of making their various commitments on the projects. The project manager would then meet with the project team members' resource managers and determine if they can reduce any over-allocations. Once the project team members look like they have a chance of being successful, the project manager can then assign the resource onto his or her project accordingly. This planning and preliminary work should lower the chance of the project manager overloading the project team members by factoring in the time commitments they have on other projects. After ensuring the team members are available and ready for assignment, the project manager turns the attention to the equipment or machines (if applicable) and determines those assignments. The goal here is to ensure the equipment is on site when required and staff is available to operate it. The project manager may go to tremendous lengths to ensure the scheduling of the equipment and machines and forget to schedule the staff to operate it. This mistake could cost the project time and money to correct. After determining the staff requirements and properly allocating the equipment needs, the project manager should then work with the resource managers or upper management to determine the reporting and communication requirements. For example, the resource leveling process may be something that the project manager completes on a weekly basis, but actually makes staffing changes or reports on the information monthly. Resource managers may be interested in seeing the results of the resource leveling process more often than monthly because rarely will they have the time to pull resources or adjust assignments on a weekly basis. However, if at the beginning of the project, the project manager establishes a monthly look at the resource assignments, the resource managers can plan and prepare for that type of reporting and moving of the staff if required. After planning and preparing these steps, the project manager has done everything they can to use the resource leveling process on their projects.

> **NOTE** You will resource level! You can either plan it or do it on the fly, but you will resource level.

Before you can create the resource leveling, you must formulate a plan. In the following "Planning Questions" section, we provide some initial thoughts to help you start thinking about how to utilize the tool on your project.

Planning Questions

1 *When would you create and develop the resource leveling process?*
During the planning phase the project manager establishes contacts with resource managers and establishes the resource leveling process, during the life of the project resource leveling process is ongoing

2 *Who is going to use this tool, both from an input and output status?*
Project manager, team members, subcontractors, or specific skill areas, resource managers, superintendents, and foreman

3 *Why are you going to use this tool?*
To level resources that are currently over-allocated, determine staffing over-allocations on projects, to assist with the resource cost planning and project budgeting exercises, determine missing resources or resource gaps, reassign staff after leveling process occurs and potentially do not have any assignments left on project

4 *How are you going to use this tool?*
Moving resource assignments based on conflicting timeframes, reducing overlapping and multiple project deliverables, schedule resources at a constant level, determine project schedule changes, determine budget impacts based on longer schedule

5 *How will you distribute the information?*
Spreadsheet format such as Microsoft Excel, tabular report, document control system, plotter reports, e-mail

6 *How often will you distribute the information?*
As needed, weekly, potentially monthly which depends on the needs of the resource managers

continued

continued

7 *What decisions can you and should you make from this tool?*

Schedule and cost decisions, reassigning resource decisions, scheduling equipment and material decisions

8 *What information does this tool provide for your project?*

Resource schedule information, potential cost information, resources loading information, resource allocation information

9 *What historical and legal information do you need to store?*

Historical activities and resource assignments, lessons learned information, resource reports, decisions based on resource leveling, assumptions during scheduling processing

10 *What will be the staffing requirements (role type) to run and maintain these tools?*

Project manager, resource managers, scheduling team, team members

Reporting resource leveling

The project manager is responsible for creating and driving the resource leveling process. Regardless of how large the project is, the project manager drives this process to ensure that they are keeping their team members properly allocated and not overwhelmed on their project activities. The project manager must also bring in the resource managers during this leveling process to ensure that they are looking at their resource assignments across all the projects to eliminate over-allocations.

The resource leveling process consists of different reports used to keep over-allocations under control, including the following:

- **Resource usage chart:** Identifies resources and activities assigned to them. The chart also displays the project resource usage over time.

- **Task usage chart:** Identifies activities and the resources assigned to those activities. It is the reverse side of the resource usage chart.

- **Resource allocation chart:** Identifies the resources allocated to the project. It displays the amount of hours and materials allocated. It can be in a graphic or tabular format.

- **Histogram report:** A graphical representation of the amount of hours or units, both planned and actual, over a given time span.

- **Over-allocated report:** Displays the resource over-allocation amounts on the project.

Figure 9.10 represents the result of the resource leveling process applied to the chart in Figure 9.9. The project resources are all working as close to a 40-hour per week limit as possible. There are some cases, in which the resources are both over and under the 40-hour limit, but in general, each resource is as close as possible. An automated system never allocates resources exactly at the

40-hour limit – it is almost impossible. Also note, on the resource-leveled chart, the project has extended three additional months from the chart in Figure 9.9. This is common when you resource level because the over-allocations are corrected, and the schedule is extended to account for it. The resource leveling process often extends the project schedule and makes it even more accurate.

FIGURE 9.10

A sample resource level chart after the resource leveling process occurred.

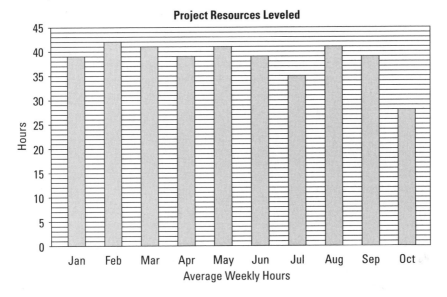

The project manager and resource managers report the results of the resource leveling process on a weekly basis to ensure that focus and attention occurs on the resource assignments. The project manager, or the resource manager, may not take any actions on a weekly basis except to review the resource over-allocations charts and determine if there are any project impacts. Depending on what the project manager and resource managers agree upon at the start of the project, resources may only reduce their over-allocations and assignments monthly.

The first pass of the actual process of resource leveling occurs in a project-scheduling tool and is rarely done manually. The resource leveling occurs in the project schedule itself and is often sent to graphic and charting tools, such as Figures 9.9 and 9.10, for presentation purposes. Therefore, the results of the resource leveling process are in a project schedule format and then transferred into charting tool format, such as Excel. The project schedule is stored in both the project scheduling application and in a document control system for long-term archiving, and is accessible by any interested stakeholder on the project.

CROSS-REF See Chapter 15 to learn more about how to plan, create, and use resource leveling.

Introducing the Responsibility Matrix

The purpose of the *responsibility matrix* (RACI) is to determine the responsibilities of each role on the project. The responsibility matrix defines the roles and responsibilities across the project by documenting role-by-role and activity-by-activity what each person or role will accomplish during the project. At the start of the project, the project team jointly completes the responsibility matrix by filling in the accountability levels of each role. For example, the project team would add a designer role to the responsibility matrix and then go through each activity on the project and determine where the designer is responsible for the activity. At the end of this process, a designer can have multiple activities associated to their role. This process continues for all roles on the project until the matrix is complete and at the end, the project team together signs and approves the responsibility matrix.

To understand the responsibility matrix (RACI) in more detail, and to be involved in the creation process, it is important to understand the accountability levels that are possible assignments within the RACI itself. Therefore, the RACI diagram splits the project tasks or deliverables into four main responsibility levels. The responsibility levels include the following:

- **Responsible:** Those who complete the work task or develop the deliverable to achieve the task. There can be multiple resources responsible.

- **Accountable:** The resource that is ultimately accountable for completion of the task, but may not complete the work themselves.

- **Consulted:** Those who the project managers sought to provide opinions or consulted with, but are not responsible or accountable to the work deliverable or task.

- **Informed:** Those who the project manager is responsible to keep informed about the project and up-to-date on progress, but are rarely involved in the actual project. This is normally a one-way communication only.

On a software development project, where there is a focus on developing databases, a responsibility matrix called the CRUD Matrix is used. CRUD stands for Create, Read, Update, and Delete, which are specific levels of access assigned to an individual for the application controlling data in the database table.

The following responsibility/security levels define the access level the various roles on a project can have when accessing the data within the software application. These security levels include:

- **Create:** Create ability on database tables. The user would have the ability to add database tables to the system, change column names, change column sizes, etc.

- **Read:** Read access on database tables. The user would have the ability to read data from the tables where they have this access.

- **Update:** Update access on database table. The user would have the ability to update data in the tables where they have this access.

- **Delete:** Delete access on database table. The user would have the ability to delete data in the tables where they have this access.

In the construction industry, the project manager uses responsibility matrixes on most projects. For each person on the responsibility matrix, there is a role for them. The communicating of the responsibility matrix can be challenging because of the volatile nature of this tool. Here is an example: A project manager is asking a team member if he/she has completed a particular activity on the project. Because the team member was not aware of this assignment, he/she never started working on it. The project manager then refers the team member to the responsibility matrix and points out they are assigned to the activity. During this communication, the project manager can handle this situation in two ways. First approach would be for the project manager to be very demanding and tell the team member he or she should have known all along this was their assignment and to only work on the tasks assigned to him/her in the responsibility matrix (RACI). That usually does not work out that well in the long run. The other approach the project manager could take is a more gentle approach and discuss the outstanding task with the team member and ask him/her to take on the work now that they know it is their responsibility to complete it. In both cases, the project manager must approach this matter carefully and determine how they want to approach each situation. The responsibility matrix is one of the more challenging communication tools for this reason and project managers should be aware of that fact for this particular tool.

NOTE The Project Management Institute's knowledge area for this tool is the Human Resources Management area. There are no other secondary areas for the responsibility matrix.

ON the CD-ROM We have included a sample of a responsibility matrix and the CRUD matrix in the Human Resources folder. Use this as a guide to the first step in creating your own personal version of both of these tools.

TOOL VALUE Responsibility matrix displays the task the team member is associated with on the project. Some matrixes further identify the level of authority assigned to the particular role.

Using a responsibility matrix has many benefits, the most important being establishing accountability and responsibility to individuals on the project. This benefit is by far the most valuable, and the one tested throughout the life of the project. For example, the project manager would refer to the RACI when assigning team members specific tasks on the project. On the other hand, when team members receive the assigned tasks they will check/test the RACI to confirm that this is something they are responsible for and should take on. It is common for the project manager to assign tasks to team members and team members should check the RACI to confirm the assignment is appropriate. The RACI may have something completely different than they would normally be assigned and he or she should approach the project manager with that and let him/her know it is not appropriate.

Figure 9.11 shows a responsibility matrix. In this example, you can clearly see the project roles across the top and the project activities down the side. Notice that the project's methodology, business requirements, system requirements, and design are breaking the RACI into logical sections. In the intersecting cells between the roles and the project activities, you see a series of letters, R, A, C, and I. These letters represent the accountability level of the project role to that project task. The legend for this chart is located in the top-left corner of the chart and describes the different accountability levels noted in the chart.

The creation of the responsibility matrix occurs at the beginning of the project, before work activities begin. After selecting the project's team members, the project manager gathers everyone together into a meeting and goes through every role and item in the RACI chart. The goal of these meetings is to select the appropriate accountability and responsibility for each project role. Many times, the project team members are unclear what their roles are, so reviewing the RACI as a team is one way of ensuring all team members understand their roles. Even on the smallest of projects, understanding who owns a task or deliverable at the beginning of the project is important.

In many cases, there are many project roles that have a combination of responsibilities and it is common to see a dual role of R/A for a single activity, meaning the project role (Customer) is both responsible to create the deliverable (requirements document) and also accountable to ensure it is completed and ready for use. An example of this would be a project manager who is responsible for developing a project schedule and accountable that it is developed and shared with the project team.

Software projects have a unique aspect to them when it comes to using the responsibility matrix. In some cases, these projects utilize both a responsibly matrix (RACI) and a CRUD matrix on a single project. When software projects are database or table driven, a large part of the project will be ensuring security, and a CRUD matrix is the mechanism to enforce security on the tables within the systems. Every software project that has tables will have some form of security and will require the project manager and the database administrator to work together to determine the roles on the project that require database access. Without a CRUD matrix, the project's database administrator will have no security set for the tables, and that would subject the tables to being completely open and available for anyone to utilize, or completely locked down allowing no one access. Both of these situations are avoidable if a CRUD matrix is in place and security is on all the project tables.

Table 9.3 represents a basic example of a CRUD matrix used on a project. The CRUD matrix defines the roles of the application to the tables and responsibility levels. It is easy to understand and easy to create the report. When reading this chart for example, it states that an Administrator has full access to all the tables in the system, where in the other extreme, the "Guest" role, has limited "Read only" access. As you review the chart and the various roles, it is easy to see each role assignment in this particular application. You can also see how easy this chart would be to communicate with everyone involved in the project to ensure it is correct and set correctly.

In the CRUD matrix example, there is a role to table assignment made for every table. The role assignments have a C, R, U, or D, entered in the intersecting cells to indicate the table security level. Software projects use this matrix on the specific roles in the application when they need the ability to access or update the database. The application could have roles such as Administrator, Power User, or Guest, and each role would have an assignment at the minimum of C, R, U, or D for the tables in the application. A common example of this role assignment would be an Administrator who would have an assignment of a CRUD, meaning that role could do anything they need to with all the tables within the application. A second example of this would be a Guest role within the application assigned an R role, meaning when they can "READ" any table in the application, but have no ability to create tables, update, or delete data in the tables.

When completing the RACI or the CRUD matrixes, most project managers recommend the responsibility of each role have a minimum assignment of "Informed." That way, team members or other interested parties receive project information on a regular basis and can access the details about the project if needed. Providing this "Inform only" role will maintain constant communication and provide a level of visibility for the stakeholders that helps overall project communications.

FIGURE 9.11

A responsibility matrix chart.

Responsibility Matrix Chart Example

Responsibility Codes

Responsible: Performs the work
Accountable: Ultimately accountable for delivery; maximum one per task
Sign-Off: Approval must be gained for deliverable to be acceptable
Consult: Review & provide feedback
Informed (blank) = not involved

	Customer	Upper Management	Proj Mgr	UAT Lead	Training Lead	Release Management	Sponsor1 (TBD)	Lead Analyst	Designer	Dev Lead	Test Lead	Tier 1 Rep	Release Lead	Operations Lead
Project Initiation/Kickoff														
Task A	R	I	R											
Work Product A	A	I												
Task C														
Business Requirements														
Task C	C	C	R											
Work Product A					I	I	C				C	I		
Work Product B									C					
System Requirements														
Task C	I	I	I				R							
Task D					I	I	C			R	C	I		
Work Product A			R, A						C					
Design														
Work Product A	C	I			I	I	C			R	C	I		
Work Product B			R, A						C					
Work Product C									C					
Build														
Task F	C	I			I	I	C			R	C	I		
Task G			R, A						C					
Task H									C					
Test														
Task 1	C	C	R											
Work Product A					I	I	C				C	I		A
Task K									C			C		
User Acceptance Approval Phase														
Task L			R	R, A	R									
Work Product A			A											
Task N			A											
Production Phrase														
Work Product A	I	I	I							R	R			
Task P	I	I				C	I			A				
Work Product B										A				
Post Production Support/ Warranty Period (if applicable)														
Task O	I	I	I							R	R			
Task P	I	I				C	I			A				
Task Q										A				

TABLE 9.3

Example of a CRUD Responsibilities Matrix

Task/Responsibility	Administrator	Power User	End User	Guest
Table A	CRUD	CR	U	R
Table B	CRUD	CRU	C	R
Table C	CRUD	R/A	C	R
Table D	CRUD	CRUD	C	R
Table E	CRUD	CRUD	D	R
Table F	CRUD	CRU	U	R

In some projects, team members may take on multiple role types for a particular task in the RACI matrix; for example, these team members will have Accountable and Responsible roles at the same time. Normally, when the role assignment is Accountable, the second role type added is Responsible. For example, the Test Lead is "Responsible" and "Accountable" in developing and approving the Software Test Plan. When there are multiple assignments to a particular team member, this often allows for a reduction of staff. However, in other situations, it may not reduce the size of the team at all, but it does spread the workload across various team members on the project. There are many examples of why team members take on multiple project type roles; more often than not it is due to the specific needs of the project, their expertise, lack of project funding, and lack of staff, to name a few.

Planning to use the responsibility matrix

When planning to use a responsibility matrix tool, the project manager must first understand the methodology that the project will utilize. That methodology will establish the framework for the Responsibility Matrix and will section the project out into manageable pieces for allocating work products. The next planning step, before utilizing a responsibility matrix, is to understand the various roles on the project and determine who will be working in those roles. Finally, the project manager should review previous responsibility matrices and go over the chart to get an understanding of where other projects utilized the various roles. This will provide the project manager with a better understanding of the roles and tasks, and when creating the responsibility matrix on their project, it can help improve communications with the team members. In the planning to prepare for using a CRUD matrix on a project, the project manager must understand the various application roles on the project, and the tables within the application. In understanding those two elements, the project manager can work with the customers and the database administrator to complete the CRUD matrix according to the level of access each role requires. In both cases, if the project manager has this information for creating the RACI and the information for creating a CRUD, then they have adequately prepared for using both of these tools on their project.

Before you can create the responsibility matrix tool, you must formulate a plan. In the questions and answers below, we have provided some initial thoughts and ideas as to how we would respond to each of the questions. Each of these responses will provide you guidance and start you thinking about how you would utilize the tool on your project. Planning on how to use the tool and thinking about where to use it makes sense. This is an effective way to plan and utilize this valuable communication tool.

Planning Questions

1 *When would you create or develop either the RACI or the CRUD tools?*
During the project-planning phase when selecting the project methodology the RACI is excellent to capture who is going to do what for the project, when reviewing security assignments in the design phase is best time to create the CRUD

2 *Who is going to use this tool, both from an input and output status?*
Project Manager, Team members, subcontractors or specific skill areas

3 *Why are you going to use this tool?*
Assign direct accountability and responsibility to project tasks and delivers. Prevent conflicts on who performs what tasks or creates the deliverables on the project.

4 *How are you going to use this tool?*
To track the accountability and responsibility of the work activities of the project team

5 *How will you distribute the information?*
Spreadsheet format, presentation format, e-mail, document control system

6 *How often will you distribute the information?*
At the beginning of the project, the team jointly develops the RACI and sends it to the team members. It is then stored in the document control system for reference and access by any team member.

7 *What decisions should you make from this tool?*
Decisions on the various accountably levels to assign to the roles on the project

8 *What information does this tool provide for your project?*
Assignment responsibilities, accountabilities, consultant roles, etc.

9 *What historical and legal information do you need to store?*
Lessons learned information, historical versions of chart and assignments

10 *What will be the staffing requirements (role type) to run and maintain these tools?*
Project manager, project team members, resource managers, upper management

Reporting using the responsibility matrix

The project manager owns the responsibility for developing the responsibility matrix. Once the team approves the chart, the project manager should obtain approval of it from the team members who were actively involved in developing it. If anyone rejects the document, the project manager should work directly with those team members to determine the problems or concerns that they have with the document or with providing approval; otherwise, every team member is required to sign and approve before starting work on the project. When the team members sign off on the chart, they are providing proof and ownership that they have seen the chart and have accepted the responsibilities and accountabilities the chart describes. No signatures often means no acknowledgment, and this allows project team members to not be as engaged as they should be, claiming they didn't know about the chart or never approved the tasks outlined for them. Project managers can avoid this situation and prevent it from ever occurring by ensuring every project team member signs and approves the responsibility matrix.

Depending on whether the project is also a software database project, during the design phase the project's Database Administrators may be required to create a CRUD matrix; however, it does not need creating until later in the project because it often requires more information and the technical details about the project that are not known in the beginning phase.

The responsibilities matrix does not contain the actual status of the project and therefore does not require regular weekly reporting. The project manager creates the responsibility matrix in a spreadsheet format and then stores it as part of the Document Control System for long-term archiving and accessibility by anyone interested. The responsibility matrix could be included in an automated scheduling system that the project is already using, and this would allow the simple updating of the matrix fields when adding new activities to the project, maintaining the ongoing currency of the responsibility matrix with minimum effort.

 See Chapter 15 to learn more about how to plan, create, and use this responsibility matrix.

Summary

The tools described in this human resource chapter assist project managers with managing and controlling their team members. As we all know, managing a project team can be challenging and something that takes practice and years of experience. Good project managers who are team focused and team driven are hard to find. Utilizing these tools will help you become a better communicator and a better leader for your team members.

This chapter includes tools such as critical chain method, human resource plan, responsibility matrix, and resource leveling. Out of all the tools, the one that sticks out is the Critical Chain tool because of the different mindset and the way of approaching projects. There is a lot of information on critical chain; review the Web, search the library, but find out as much as you can about it.

With tools like these, project managers and team members will have an easier time controlling project resources, driving successful projects, and keeping team members content.

Chapter 10

Defining Communication Tools to Manage Project Communications

Project communications is the most important aspect of project management. Communications management tools such as an issue management plan, communications management plan, and project presentations all leveraged best-practice techniques in performing project communications. Project managers should continually try to improve how they communicate with their customers and their team members. Utilizing these communications tools can enhance their communication efforts.

Some tools we mention in this chapter are familiar to you. Keep an open mind and look at these tools from a pure communication perspective so that you can utilize these tools in a more effective way. Sometimes the planning process of a tool will bring forth a new and better way to use the tool.

In this chapter, we also explore project communications tools in the managing of project information. These tools assist project managers in communicating effectively while managing and controlling the execution of the project. Using the tools in this chapter can help you become a better communicator.

Introducing the Communication Plan

The purpose of the *communication plan* is to determine, document, and plan the information needs for the project. The goal of the communication plan is to ensure that the correct audience is receiving the correct project information in a timely manner that is acceptable to them. At a minimum, the project manager will send a weekly project status report and a monthly newsletter; these two deliverables should contain enough information for the customers to understand the project and the overall status. The communication plan will establish a cadence or a rhythm for the project's communication by utilizing tools such as the status reports, budget spreadsheets, issues lists, and so on. Customers and upper management will anticipate and rely on this regular delivery of project information. As project manager, you should ensure you utilize a communication plan on every project, regardless of the size or complexity of the effort.

You also want to ensure your customers and team members approve the communication plan as early as possible in the lifecycle of the project. In gaining this approval, it lets you know that your customers have approved what information they want to receive, the format they will receive it in, and the timeframes for delivery. Project managers should ensure that their customers always feel that they have enough information and exposure to project information. The communication plan is one of the methods that project managers use to accomplish this objective.

CROSS-REF See Chapter 4 for more information on the project status report.

NOTE The Project Management Institute's knowledge area for this tool is the Communications Management area. This tool can be associated with the other knowledge areas, such as Integration.

ON the CD-ROM We have included a sample of this Communication Plan tool in the Communication Managing folder. Use this as a guide to create your own version of this tool.

TOOL VALUE The communication plan provides the direction and a process to follow for communicating project status and information. It is the communication roadmap for the project.

The project manager should review the communication plan periodically throughout the project to ensure that what they are communicating actually matches what was set forth in the plan. You may have documented something in the plan, such as producing a monthly newsletter, but never actually created and distributed them. It could be for many reasons why you decided not to deliver the newsletters, but regardless of why, you are not following the communication plan that you agreed and signed off on with your customers. On some projects, customers may hold you directly accountable for delivering every item documented in the plan. A periodic checkpoint of reviewing the current plan and the status information you are sending could prevent any confusion and ensures that you are delivering what you said you would in the communication plan.

Table 10.1 shows a table of contents from a sample communication plan. In this communication plan, you see two new tools called the communication requirements matrix and the people report matrix that are not part of any other communication plan you have seen before, but valuable to provide a complete picture of the information you're sending to your customers.

TABLE 10.1

Example of a Communication Plan Table of Contents

Section	Description
1	Communication Plan Overview
2	Project Communication Requirements Matrix
3	People Report Matrix
4	Method and Timeframes for Distribution
5	Lessons Learned (Previous Projects)
6	Historical Information (Examples/Samples)
7	Close Out

The most important components of the communication plan are the communication matrixes noted in Sections 2 and 3. These sections describe in detail who, what, where, when, and why project status information will be delivered for the project. All other sections of this example are valuable and important to the document as well, but as a project manager, pay special attention to these two sections. A communication plan could stand alone with these two sections and be thorough enough but not a complete plan.

CROSS-REF See Chapter 2 for more information on communication requirements matrix and the people report matrix to understand these two communication matrixes completely.

One of the components of a communication plan is the timeframe as to when customers will be receiving their reports. When establishing these timeframes in the document, you are also establishing the project's rhythm. These timeframes include the meeting cadence (rhythm of how often meetings occur, such as daily or weekly), team members' delivery dates (final status reports), and the project status report delivery dates to the customer. A project without any rhythm can struggle. Customers often see a project with a meeting cadence as a positive aspect of project communications and appreciate the continual and constant flow of information. An example of rhythm cadence and accountability could include the following:

- Monday: Status collection day
- Tuesday: Weekly status meeting
- Wednesday: Status report submission and compilation
- Thursday: Customer project status review meeting
- Friday: Final project status report submission and distribution

This rhythm provides an ongoing communication cadence on a weekly basis to the project team members and customers.

A communication plan helps anyone involved on a project understand what reports are delivered and when. For anyone receiving project information, the communication plan describes to them what, when, and how they will be receiving it. For the team members responsible for creating the project information, the communication plan describes the type of data, when to send it, and in what format. The communication plan is a win-win for the sender and the receiver because they both are obtaining information from a single document for two completely different purposes.

Planning to use a communication plan

When planning to use the communication plan, the project manager has to identify the various stakeholders on the project, identify the format and type of media for sending project communication, and identify who receives the information. These are the main components to any communication plan. You should also determine if there are any available lessons learned information from past projects and find, if possible, any historical reports that were helpful on previous projects for use on your project. When collecting this information and planning for the creation and use of a communication plan, the project manager would have the data he or she needs to be successful in planning to use the communication plan on their project.

Before you can create the communication plan tool, you must formulate a plan. Ask yourself the following questions.

Planning Questions

1 *When would you create, develop, and write the project communication plan tool?*
Planning phase of every project, when planning communication aspects of the project need updating

2 *Who is going to use this tool, both from an input and output status?*
Upper management, owners, executives, project manager, team member, subcontractors

3 *Why are you going to use this tool?*
To establish the communications on the project, to set a framework in place that allows team members, stakeholders to understand when and how communications will occur

4 *How are you going to use this tool?*
Upper management will use document to decide whether to proceed with project, determine cost estimates, determine schedule estimates, determine proposed solutions, and determine resourcing needs

5 *How will you distribute the information?*
Document format such as Microsoft Word, document control system, e-mail, in-person presentation

6 *When will you distribute the information?*
Once, to sell the project idea to upper management and customers

7 *What decisions can or should you make from this tool?*
Go/no-go on approving project, schedule, cost, resource and scope decisions

8 *What information does this tool provide for your project?*
Describes the project, provides an idea how long it may take, how much it may cost, identifies technical challenges, comparisons of similar projects if applicable

9 *What historical and legal information do you need to store?*
Decision on why it was approved or not, lessons learned information (around feasibility study creation and acceptance or rejection)

10 *What will be the staffing requirements (role type) to run and maintain these tools?*
Project manager, project analyst, possible project team members

Reporting using the communication plan

On most projects, the project manager and the team members jointly create the communication plan. The communication plan is an extensive document that will require help from the team members to complete all the details. Project managers should not look to try to create this document on their own. Because the project manager is responsible for communicating the project information, it makes sense that he/she also owns this document because it sets the foundation for those communications. In the creation of the document, one of the important factors to consider is the involvement and approval from the project customer. Project customers have to buy into what, when, and how often the project manager intends to communicate project information. That way, the customers will understand when they will receive project information from the project (specifically the project manager) and can establish their own rhythm for communicating or making project level decisions based on that information.

One of the newly introduced tools is the communication requirements matrix which displays the information for the customer by who, what, meeting types and frequency. By establishing this type of matrix, you can identify these requirements with your customer then work with them to ensure they are getting the project information they require.

Communication requirements plan matrix template

Table 10.2 is an example of a communication requirements plan matrix. It provides a summary of the customer information needs for the project. This matrix does not capture the scope of the project, just the communication needs of the customer.

TABLE 10.2

Example of a Communication Requirements Plan Matrix

Who	Information Needs	Types Meetings	Frequency
Project Manager and Team Members	Action Items Progress Reports Change Requests Issues Specifications	Team Meetings Status Meetings Staff Meetings Design Reviews One on One Contract Negotiations	Daily, Weekly, As Needed
Sponsor	Progress Reports Financial Reports	Financial Meetings Major Milestone(s) Phase-end / Go/No-Go Meetings Issue Resolution	Monthly
Client	Status Reports Ship Dates Specifications Change Notices	Design Reviews Change Requests	As Scheduled

As project managers become familiar with using a project communication plan, they each will have their favorite templates or examples that they will follow for use on their projects. Luckily, the project management profession has hundreds of different examples of communication plans for different project types, across different industries, so there are plenty to choose from on the Internet.

 **CROSS-REF** See Chapter 14 to learn more about how to create and use the communication plan.

Introducing E-Mail

The purpose of introducing the e-mail tool in a project environment is to describe how to communicate effectively with all project stakeholders. We all know that this tool has been around for many years — it's part of our daily lives. The objective of stating this tool is not from a how-to-use perspective, but from how to plan for and communicate the use of this tool.

E-mail has become the number one choice of communications across the world. From schoolchildren to professors, everyone is using e-mail on a regular basis. The challenging aspects of e-mail are not how to use the tool, or how to construct a simple e-mail; the challenge of this tool is how to communicate project information effectively. The complexity of communicating with e-mail is discerning what information is appropriate for sending in an e-mail. For example, if a project manager blindly sent an e-mail surprising his stakeholders and his management that the project is over budget $2 million, this would be an ineffective use of this tool. The reason for this is the project manager is surprising the customers with this information. What the project manager should have done was to bring everyone involved together in person and explain to them about this budget shortfall and the reasons why it occurred. Then, the project manager sends the e-mail as backup information. Alternatively, sending an e-mail to introduce a new team member is an efficient use of this tool.

 The Project Management Institute's knowledge area for this tool is the Communication Management area. This tool can be associated with all the other knowledge areas.

 E-mail allows quick, accurate written communications to anywhere in the world instantly.

The volume of e-mail that arrives in inboxes on a daily basis certainly proves that it is the most common method for project communications. If you count the number of e-mails compared to the number of phone calls you receive each day, you will quickly see how popular and integral e-mail has become in our day-to-day lives.

With the high usage of this communication tool, it lends itself to overuse — and sometimes misuse — quite easily. How many times have you received an inappropriate joke, or a message typed in ALL CAPS, which makes you think the sender is angry or did not realize that he had pressed the Caps Lock key. Whatever the situation, e-mail can be a powerful and dominating tool that can quickly work against someone at the press of the Send button.

Project managers must frame their e-mails carefully to ensure that every e-mail is stating exactly what they want it to state, carries the right tone they want it to carry, and is something that anyone could see. A common saying is "Do not write anything in an e-mail, that you would not want to be read in court." Those words could not be any truer.

Figure 10.1 is an appropriate e-mail sent from a project manager about the project budget information to his team leads. He had requested previously some budget information from all of them and now he is asking for them to double-check the numbers before submitting them formally for final review.

Using e-mail as a communication tool benefits every member of the team. For example, if the project manager sends out a task list by e-mail to a project team member, that team member can use that e-mail message as a check list for the work activities being requested by the project manager. This scenario is a great use of the tool and one that is helpful to both parties. The project manager can keep track of the request, and the team member can respond back to the project manger when the activities are complete.

As noted earlier, the challenge to using e-mail is how people are communicating with the tool. Often times, you read e-mail messages that should never have been sent, either because the tone was wrong, or because the message was insulting, and you find that the information being sent is not appropriate for sending over e-mail. With the challenges of off-shore virtual teams, that includes language problems, time zone problems, culture differences, communication problems, and work environments, it is becoming harder to communicate effectively when utilizing e-mail with those team members. Add the challenges of language barriers and different cultures, and time zones, an e-mail, in many cases, needs to become a work of art. E-mail is no longer that informal communication tool that everybody considered it as in the early days. As project managers, each must be aware that their image of leadership reflects how they communicate in their e-mail messages. The level of scrutiny that you have on your e-mail messages, compared to your team members, is completely different. Your messages set project direction, distribute project status, and set the overall tone of the project.

FIGURE 10.1

This is a typical project e-mail where the project manager is asking the team leads about project budget.

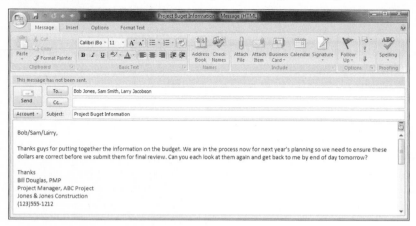

How does a project manager survive in this environment? How does he or she know what to put into an e-mail message or what to leave out? Many of these answers are simple, and you need to apply a level of common sense when creating and sending your project e-mails. Here is a list of dos:

- **Sending positive project information:** Such as new hires, team members leaving project, milestones hit, meeting agendas, meeting minutes, status reports, any kind of project successes are all well received.

- **Posting project help wanted:** Areas of the project where you need help, assistance or just do not have enough information, an e-mail is a good tool for those purposes.

- **Initiating thoughts and brainstorming discussions with team members:** A project manager could ask for group input on a problem or issue.

- **Initial contact to customers or management staff:** Using e-mail is a great way to introduce someone into the project environment. This person may be someone that you are dealing with from a project perspective. Sending an initial e-mail is a great icebreaker.

- **Tracking conversation follow-ups:** E-mail works well for following up on conversations or decisions made by individuals, by capturing and documenting in an e-mail for historical reference.

And here is a list of don'ts

- **Avoid trying to solve a conflict with e-mail.** Too many times sending an e-mail escalates the conflict and wastes time. Having a face-to-face meeting is a better way to solve the conflict.

- **Avoid negative tone in your e-mails.** The tone of your e-mail is important because people interpret information differently. It is important to re-read your e-mail messages before you click Send to ensure the tone is appropriate.

- **Avoid sending negative project information in an e-mail message without approval first.**

CAUTION Remember, everything you write in an e-mail may be retrievable. Even if your company is not involved in a legal dispute on a project you worked on, companies can access your information during litigation. There are high-tech companies that can extract information from your hard drive even after you have erased it!

Planning to use e-mail

The project manager has to set up rules for using e-mail messages. He must establish archiving processes for important e-mails and ensure that all team members have e-mail access. He needs to set up distribution lists for team e-mails and review and provide e-mail etiquette to the team members. In taking these necessary steps, the project manager will have gone a long way toward planning the use of e-mails on their project and possibly reducing problems in the future.

Before you can create and send an e-mail, you must formulate a plan. Ask yourself the following questions:

Planning Questions

1 *When would you create, develop, or write this tool?*
Ongoing process throughout the life of project

2 *Who is going to use this tool, both from an input and output status?*
Everyone involved in the project (all stakeholders)

3 *Why are you going to use this tool?*
To communicate project information, transfer files and drawings, and assign work tasks to team members, and so on.

continued

---

continued

4 *How are you going to use this tool?*

It is important to communicate carefully using this tool. Ensure that you protect sensitive information, and remember all communications could be open to the public.

5 *How will you distribute the information?*

Electronic e-mail tool, document format, presentation format

6 *When will you distribute the information?*

Throughout the life of the project (24 X 7)

7 *What decisions can or should you make from this tool?*

Information distributed via e-mail can assist in project level decision making

8 *What information does this tool provide for your project?*

The tool itself does not provide any information as it only transmits the information after generating it outside the tool

9 *What historical and legal information do you need to store?*

Most projects store e-mails for historical purposes and archiving, and possible litigation, lessons learned information

10 *What will be the staffing requirements (role type) to run and maintain these tools?*

IT resources to maintain the tool at corporate level only, possible project manager, team members, or company policy to set up rules for using e-mail

Reporting using e-mail

When reporting project information, e-mails are the standard method for most project teams. Specifically, the project manager is responsible for creating and sending the project e-mails to all relevant stakeholders and keeping them informed throughout the project. Those e-mails include Go Live announcements, major milestone announcements, staffing and resource announcements.

One of the tools project managers have to assist them in the auditing process is a feature in e-mail that assists in the tracking and capturing of customer and team member's acceptance or rejection. For example, the project manager creates and sends an approval e-mail, and the recipients send back their approval or rejection. The project manager then stores and archives those approvals or rejections for auditing purposes. This feature is popular in today's e-mail packages and called voting buttons. In most cases, internal auditors accept the voting button e-mails as notification of official approval. Without using e-mail and this specific feature, the project manager would have to obtain the actual signatures from each stakeholder manually. This is more time consuming and may be difficult if the approvers are not all located in the same physical location.

 See Chapter 18 to learn more about how to use e-mail.

Introducing Instant Messaging

The purpose of an instant messaging tool in a project environment is to communicate instantly with anyone involved with the project. This tool is undeniably popular; even kids are using it. In this section, we discuss the appropriate uses for this tool in a project environment.

The instant messaging tool is informal and, therefore, no one should use it as a formal information discloser. Information such as budgets, timeframes, and the hiring or firing of team members are all subjects that are inappropriate for this tool. Much like e-mail, the challenge of using instant messaging tool is not how to create a simple instant message, but rather how to communicate effectively and appropriately with such a powerful communication tool.

Instant messaging has some of the same characteristics as the e-mail tool; once information is sent across the company's servers, it can be retrieved. This information is stored on central servers internally or externally. Companies can retrieve this data, but it would require extra effort and extra costs.

The goal of any instant messaging tool should be to communicate quickly and informally with any member of the project team without worry that the information is formal or official. One of the main reasons people accept the information that way is the fact that the information is not saved and as soon as a person logs off the information disappears. The instant messaging tool is excellent for quick questions, light project information, or connecting with someone on the project. In most cases, the project team members use the instant messaging tool to initiate lighthearted or friendly conversations between the various team members assigned to the project. In that manner, instant messaging is an excellent communication tool to connect people all over the world.

Although there is a place for instant messaging in the communication process, it can easily become a distraction. Project team members can spend a great deal of time chatting and not doing their project work.

 The Project Management Institute's knowledge area for this tool is the Communication Management area. This tool can be associated with all the other knowledge areas.

 Instant Messaging is always available and used for communicating to anyone on the project globally and instantaneously.

Instant messaging allows for instant connections with co-workers or team members when needing to start an electronic conversation. Some of the caveats to using the instant messaging tool are that the computer needs an Internet connection and the software needs installing on your computer. Without those three items, the tool will not work. Some instant messaging packages allow for sending video as well as audio so it becomes more interactive, and you can see and talk to each other.

Project managers often use the tool to determine if their team members are online and available to start conversations. Many project managers also use the tool as an awareness tool to ensure that the team members are working during specific timeframes and generally available for the project. When team members are always offline or not logged into the tool, nowadays some people see them as not being team players or not working as hard as they could be for the project. Some could find this as a downside of the instant messaging tool, because they feel that the project manager is always watching them.

Figure 10.2 represents a sample instant messaging screen shot with a typical conversation occurring between the project manager and a team member. In this example, it is clear that the project manager should never send this type of information over this tool. Although only one person received it, the information sent was inappropriate for this type of tool. Imagine, if for example, there were multiple people reviewing Bruce's screen and saw this information come up. Imagine if Sally, Mary, or Frank saw it.

FIGURE 10.2

An example of an instant message exchange between a project manager and a team member about a project event

The instant messaging tool can be helpful to a project manager and team members because it allows for ongoing and instant access to everyone, regardless of their location. Project managers can have team members located all around the world working on their project, and when everyone is using the instant messaging software they are available to one another and can communicate as often as they would like. The instant messaging software brings all team members closer together and instantly available to one another for communicating.

In communicating with team members or project customers, it is always a good idea to have a list of the do's and don'ts for instant messaging in a business or project environment. It is important that project managers and team members understand the guidelines their companies have established for these tools.

Here are some tips and tricks, and rules on using instant messaging to keep you and your project out of court.

- Don't use instant messaging for personal use during work hours, keep tone and messages businesslike.

- Don't expect or assume that someone is always available to use the tool. Unless the team member approves it, nobody should contact him after hours.

- Consider differences in culture when communicating, including use of tone. Jargon may mean something in one culture and mean something completely different in another.

- Do not send official project information over instant messaging without following up with an e-mail or some other form of written documentation.

- Unauthorized, unrestricted instant messaging use is bad practice.

- Limit instant messaging access to only those team members with legitimate project need.

- Plan and use instant messaging policies and rules to provide clear guidelines for team members.

Planning to use instant messaging

As project managers start into their projects, one of the components of managing communications is to understand how they can use the Instant Messaging tool for effective project communications. In order to do so, project managers should plan to use this tool. There are few project managers who think about planning to use the Instant Messaging tools on their projects. You might even ask the question, why would you have to plan to use such a simple tool? You just pick it up and use it. This can be a mistake. The project manager should consider how he wants the team to use instant messaging and create guidelines and rules for using the tool. Doing so reduces any miscommunications later in the project on the way some team members and stakeholders may be using instant messaging. Before you can use an Instant Messaging tool, you must formulate a plan. Ask yourself the questions in the following section

---

Planning Questions

1 *When would you create, develop, or write this tool?*
Ongoing process throughout the life of project

continued

---

continued

2 *Who is going to use this tool, both from an input and output status?*
Almost everyone involved in the project

3 *Why are you going to use this tool?*
To communicate lite project information, transfer files and drawings

4 *How are you going to use this tool?*
Communicate on the fly project information

5 *How will you distribute the information?*
There is no distribution of this tool besides typing into the Instant Messaging tool

6 *When will you distribute the information?*
Throughout the life of the project

7 *What decisions can or should you make from this tool?*
There should be limited project information transferred via this tool, unless backed up by e-mail to confirm

8 *What information does this tool provide for your project?*
The tool itself does not provide any information; it only transmits the information after generating it outside the tool

9 *What historical and legal information do you need to store?*
None, there is nothing stated on instant messaging that should be stored for long-term storage, the nature of this tool is instant messaging between two parties. Any information that requires storage requires a different tool.

10 *What will be the staffing requirements (role type) to run and maintain these tools?*
IT resources to maintain the tool at corporate level only. Possible project manager, team members, or company policy to set up rules for using e-mail.

CROSS-REF See Chapter 18 to learn more about how to use the instant messaging tool.

Introducing the Project Calendar

The purpose of the *project calendar* is to display the major project events on a formatted document, which displays calendar days to allow for easy understanding of important and critical project dates.

The project calendar is not a *personal calendar*. It is quite different. Project calendars should store only project information, such as milestone dates, meeting events, current activities, and so on. The only personal information stored on a project calendar would be vacations or known personal events that would have an effect on the project, but would contain all the team members, not just a single team member as a personal calendar would. This is important to understand when there is a discussion pertaining to information on the project calendar, or carrying a project calendar around with you. The value in having this information about the project is priceless. Personal calendars are also valuable, but different. After the project calendar is fully loaded with key project dates and project information, it is a major benefit to the project manager, upper management, customers, and project team members. The project calendar brings everyone together to a common understanding of the project dates and deliverables, and raises awareness on any scheduling conflicts. There are many benefits to using a project calendar. For example, when a project has a major milestone delivery in the last two weeks of December, the project calendar displays for everyone's review and determination of the impact of this milestone in the holiday season. The team can then re-plan the milestone delivery if applicable. If re-planning occurs, another benefit of the project calendar is that it highlights the impact of moving the deliverable on the downstream activities. Yet another benefit of the project calendar is the ease of communicating project information to the customers or senior management. Carrying a fully loaded project calendar enables project managers to access project dates on demand. By having the information readily available, team members, customers, and upper management are reassured that the project manager appears to have everything under control on the project.

NOTE The Project Management Institute's knowledge area for this tool is the Communications Management area. This tool can be associated with all the knowledge areas.

ON the CD-ROM We have included a sample of this project calendar tool in the Communication Managing folder. Use this as a guide to help you create your own version of this tool.

TOOL VALUE The project calendar allows instant access to the project's schedule and is an excellent way to communicate schedule and project information. It is compact, portable, and easy to read and understand.

The project calendar is a helpful tool for any project manager, team member, or stakeholder trying to understand the major milestones of the project. The project calendar in an instant can provide high-level milestone dates to anyone asking, and if used correctly it will track the high-level status of the project as well. As the project manager monitors and controls the execution of the project, he should ensure the keeping of the project calendar is up-to-date for tracking status. As major milestones are completed, the project manager marks off the milestones as complete on the calendar and communicates that information to any interested stakeholders.

Figure 10.3 represents a typical project calendar from a project-scheduling tool. This project calendar represents a software project, showing both development and testing timeframes. As you can see, the development work spans over a three-week period and testing occurs over a two-week period. You will also notice the flow of the work, development and testing, respectively.

A project manager can use the project calendar tool to communicate project timelines, costs, and individual project activities. It is beneficial for project managers to add weekly status meetings, key review meetings, and other major project events to the calendar when initially setting it up. The project calendar shows all the project deliverables and is a great asset during the projects planning process. In the planning process, the project calendar communicates holiday schedules, vacation schedules, and time off for team members that could impact a project. For example, in the month of December, many projects avoid the last two weeks of the month due to holiday season and vacations, so during the planning process, the project calendar has these dates blocked off as nonworking time. In doing so, your project will not calculate these dates as workable days, when most people are not working during that time.

FIGURE 10.3

This is a project calendar of a typical software project.

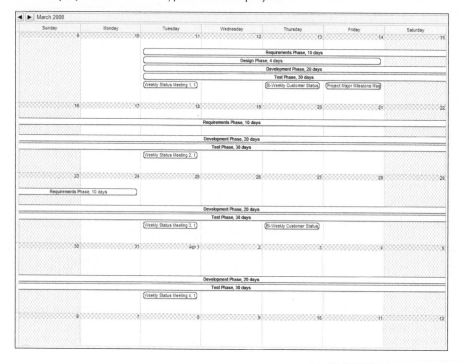

The project calendar is primarily for the project manager to use as a guide to the time lines, deliverables, and as a tool to ensure the project is executing to the schedule. The project manager uses the project calendar to communicate with team members as to whether or not they are going to make the major milestone dates on the project. The team members will use the project calendar as a graphical representation of their milestones and plan their work and other activities accordingly. If each team member has the project calendar printed out and at their desks, they can determine quickly when they need to allocate time to the project. It becomes an individual planning tool for each team member.

Project calendars come in different views depending on the needs of the project or organization. Here are some examples of various project calendars used in the industry today:

- **Long range calendars:** 5 years, 10 years, 15 years
- **Daily calendars:** Events of day
- **Monthly calendars**: Events of month
- **Multiple calendars:** One project is overlapping with another projects calendar
- **Hourly calendars**: Planning in 15-minute increments
- **Resource calendar:** A resource calendar is an individual resource calendars as an example for equipment such as cranes, trucks, bulldozers, concrete mixer
- **Individual resource calendar:** Created when assigning resources to a project

Planning to use a project calendar

In planning to use the project calendar, the project manager must first determine where and how a project calendar is going to be effective on their project. Utilizing a project calendars is better on smaller to medium projects. Large projects tend to have a project scheduling team in place to create a master project schedule, but project managers will still want to create their version of a personal project calendar. That way, they can have it on hand and be able to capture the project major milestone events on that calendar and then be able to watch and monitor the project progress from their calendar. For example, in a software project, you add the major events of the development methodology including the project phases such as project requirements, design, development, and test. After determining that the project calendar is still a viable tool for the project, the project manager will then work with the team leads to start them thinking about the duration of their components as well as getting started in utilizing a project calendar for their work effort. After receiving some initial dates from the team members, the project manager adds those high-level dates onto their project calendar tool. Having this information gives the project manager the basis to start discussions with the customer on the proposed project finish dates. The next step in the planning process is for the project manager (and team leads) to work with the customer and start discussing the proposed dates using the project calendar as a canvas in those discussions. This can lead to some great discussions as to what the team is proposing and what the customer is expecting as a project end date. The project manager would facilitate those discussions and ensure that in the end the project schedule has agreement by both parties. After agreement, the project manager then updates the master project schedule with the agreed dates. Upon performing these planning activities, the project manager is adequately prepared for using a project calendar on their project.

> **TIP** When using a manual paper calendar, buy plenty of correction fluid; project milestone dates change all the time, so you are going to need it!

Before you can create the project calendar tool, you must formulate a plan. In the following "Planning Questions" section, we have provided some initial thoughts to help you start thinking about how to utilize the tool on your project. Planning on how to use the tool and thinking about where it makes sense is an effective way to utilize this valuable communication tool.

Planning Questions

1 When would you create, develop, or write this tool?
During the life of the project

2 Who is going to use this tool, both from an input and output status?
Upper management, clients, project manager, team members, subcontractors, or specific skill areas

3 Why are you going to use this tool?
Upper level management reporting of project schedule information, detailed sub-area reporting on project schedule, project-planning discussions, communicating project deliverable dates

4 How are you going to use this tool?
To communicate high-level project schedule to customers and clients, upper management, team members, resource managers, and anyone interested in project

5 How will you distribute the information?
Dashboard format, electronic, plotter, document control system, e-mail, document format — printed, presentations

6 How often will you distribute the information?
Ad-Hoc, initially after creation, and as needed basis after that

7 What decisions can you make from this tool?
Schedule decisions, risk decisions, resource decisions

8 What information does this tool provide for your project?
Schedule information, resource allocation, phase overlapping, delivery dates, milestone dates, holidays, and vacation schedules, key project meeting dates

9 What historical and legal information do you need to store?
Historical calendars, lessons learned information

10 What will be the funding and staffing requirements to run and maintain these tools?
Project manager, project scheduler, team members, and subcontractors

Reporting using the project calendar

The project manager creates the project calendar tool on the project mainly as a tool for his/her own use. On larger projects where the project has a project planning and control group, someone in that group is responsible for developing the project calendar tool.

The easiest method to create a project calendar is via a word processing program or a project-scheduling tool. Each software application has the ability to create a blank monthly project calendar and therefore is the right tool(s) to use to create these calendars. There are two thoughts on the reporting of project calendars: do not report it and use it as a planning and executing tool only, or use the project calendar as a reporting tool and incorporate it as part of the official project reporting method. The decision on what method to use to report is the project manager's and the customers'. Mostly, it will fall to the project manager, but some customer may have their preferences and want the project calendar officially reported. The project manager may want to use the project calendar as an internal tool only; she could then choose other methods, such as the Gantt chart or Project Milestone list, to report the status of the project.

Figure 10.4 represents a typical project calendar using Microsoft Word. This calendar is blank to allow the addition of project level milestones through the planning process. Depending on the planning process, this blank sheet is perfect for starting the discussions of a high-level timeframe for the project.

 **Every project needs to have a graphical representation of its activities.**

There is no formal reporting for the project calendar. If the project manager decides that she wants to report with the project calendar, then they would be prepared on a weekly basis, or using the same reporting timeframes as the other project reports. Otherwise, the project calendar is more of a project manager's administration tool and then formal reporting is required in addition to the project calendar.

There are two formats for the project calendar — printed document and electronic. The most useful aspect of using this tool in a document format is that it allows you to write on it, carry it around, and have the information readily available. Using an electronic format also has its benefits, such as continuous and automatic updating providing real-time status of the project. When updating the project schedule, the updating of the project calendar is automatic.

CROSS-REF See Chapter 15 to learn more about how to use the Project Calendar tool.

FIGURE 10.4

This is a project calendar developed using an e-mail software package. Many different software packages are available to create project calendars.

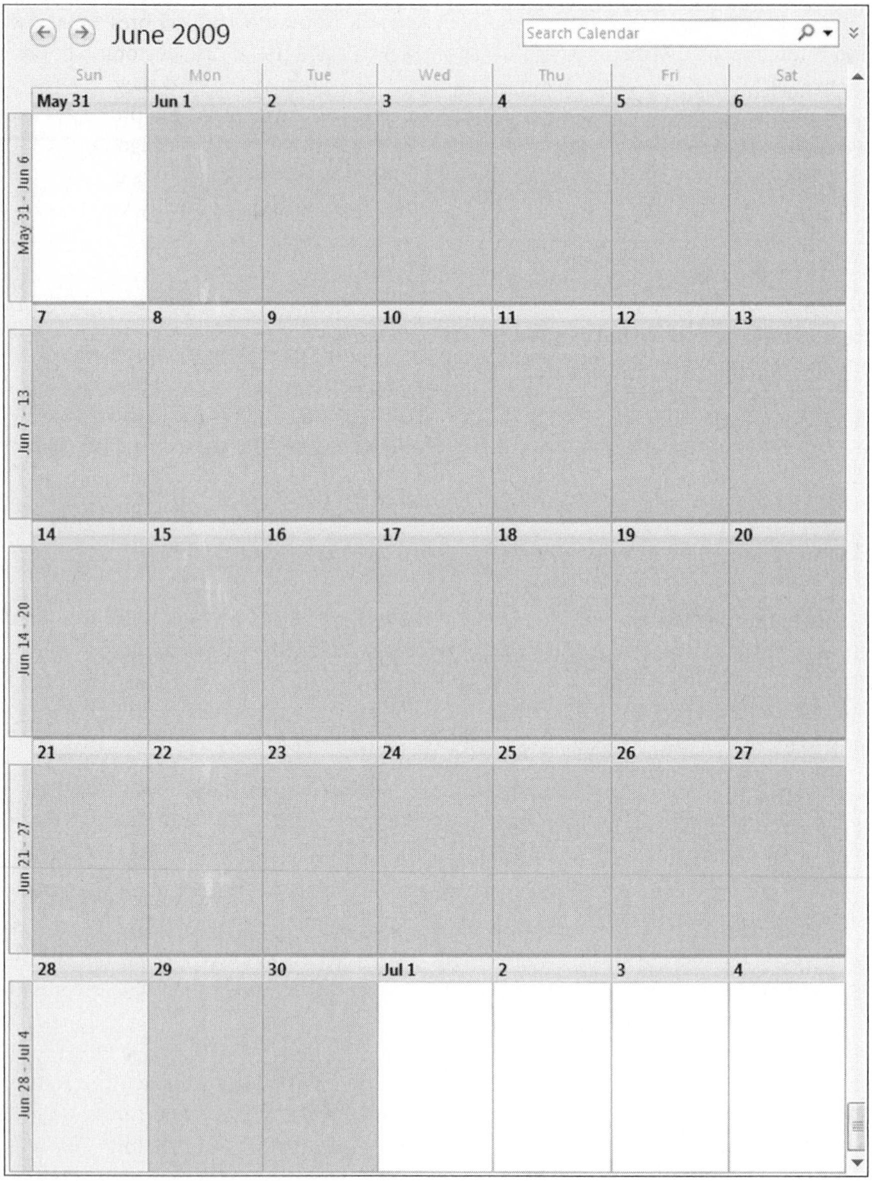

Introducing the Project Presentation

The purpose of the *project presentation* tool is to present project information in a formal and structured manner to customers, executives, upper management, and team members. Project managers must be careful and consider the story they want to present when creating a project presentation. If you do not put thought and consideration into the project presentation, then the customers could walk away feeling as if the project is out of control, unstructured, and possibly that they are wasting their time and money. This is a perception that customers could have toward the project manager because it is that project manager that presented the confusing and mixed messages to the customers. The project manager may struggle to change the customer's thinking if it is early in the project and the project manager is either new or has not yet built any creditability with that customer.

Project managers own their project presentations, which means that they are 100 percent responsible for the meeting, inviting participants, scheduling, the message to deliver, and every other aspect of putting together the presentation and the corresponding meeting event. Project presentations let the project manager show off their presentation skills and bring his or her project to the forefront for a project review with customers and upper management. There are thousands of project presentations on the Internet, and your company should have templates as well to start any project manager off with developing their project presentation. Regardless of the details within the presentation, there are templates for all types of messages, project types, milestone events (i.e., like project Go Live decisions) where each ranges from a granular level of detail to high-level summary presentation.

NOTE The Project Management Institute's knowledge area for this tool is the Communications Management area. This tool can be associated with all the Knowledge areas.

ON the CD-ROM We have included a sample of this project presentation tool in the Communication Managing folder. You can use this as a guide to help you create your own version of this tool.

TOOL VALUE Project presentations can communicate an abundance of project information to a large number of people. It is in a controlled environment, in which you have the control.

The project presentation tool is valuable when presenting project information in a formal setting normally to a medium to larger audiences. A project presentation is presenting relevant project information; it also provides an opportunity for project level decisions to occur at the meeting while all stakeholders are available and focused on the project. When everyone is in the same room and focused on the project and presentation materials, the project team members have the advantage of acquiring management-level decisions made at that meeting that affect the project. It also provides the opportunity for team members to speak to the customers when they may not normally get an opportunity to do so during normal working time on the project. Project managers need to ensure that they capitalize on this and get the decisions required at that meeting.

Figure 10.5 represents a typical one-page project status slide. This project presentation example represents the required fields and phases on a typical data warehouse software project. The fields and information captured provide anyone interested with a page-at-a-glance view of the project information.

The project presentation tool should be clear, concise, and easy to read. When developing the project presentation, ensure that all project information is at a summary level to meet the audience's needs. Customers and upper management audiences are different, so creating that right balance of summary level and detailed level information can be tricky. Most often, a project manager holds a project's presentation when the project team hits a major milestone, such as a software project's design complete, UAT complete, or a Go Live phase. At that time, you will want to ensure the material presented is a true and current representation of your project. The milestone checkpoints provide the confidence to the customers that the project is progressing either positively or negatively, but does give them the ability to determine for themselves how it is progressing. This is also a chance for project managers to shine by presenting the project in its best light and with the latest and most up-to-date information.

FIGURE 10.5

This is a typical one-page project presentation slide, specifically focusing on the status of the project.

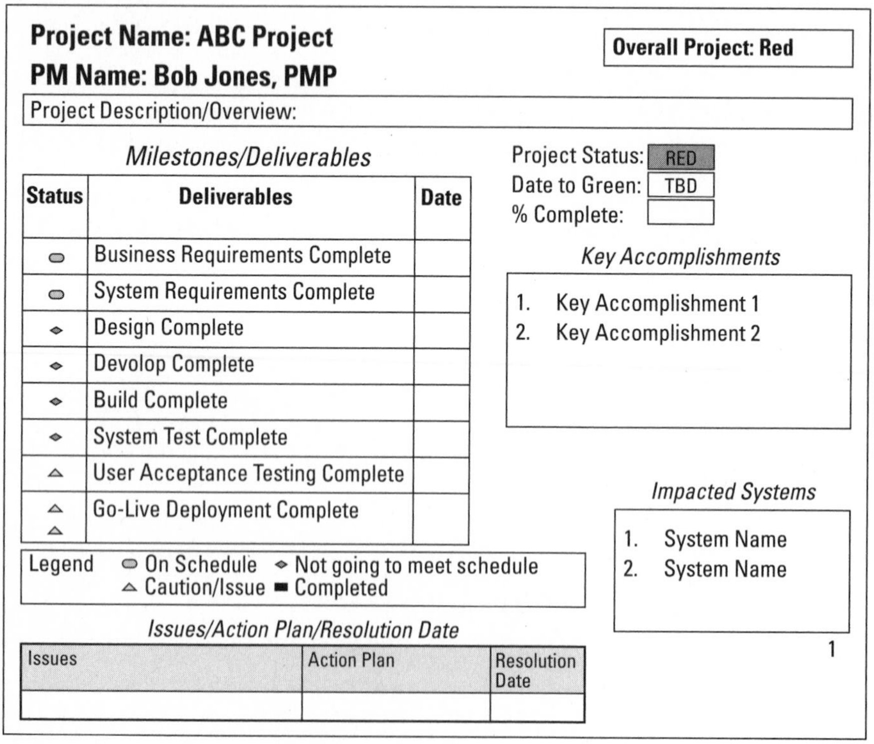

The project presentation is beneficial to all members of the project team, especially the project manager. The team members who in most cases report through different department leads tend to do everything possible to ensure their area of the project is complete before presenting the information to their management and customers. This is helpful to the project manager because it pulls all the information together and represents the most current and accurate picture of the project at one time. He or she knows exactly what is going on with the project, and can present the data with confidence. During the day-to-day work activities of a project, pulling status information and compiling it into a formal presentation is not a normal activity. Project presentations actually force the team members and project manager to come together to compile the information. It sets a stake in the ground as to the most current status of the project.

Project presentations are different from industry to industry. The format and information contained in the presentation can vary greatly depending on project size, complexity, industry, and the specific organization's requirements. The project presentation for a large construction project is going to vary from the presentation of a small software project. However, the core aspects of the presentation remain the same, but because the industries are so different, the project presentation is also different.

Planning to give a better project presentation

In planning for a project presentation, the project manager has to develop all project presentation material, align customers and team members that are presenting material, invite attendees, book the meeting room and any meeting equipment, gather the background for what deliverables are required for the meeting (such as compliance materials, audits complete, and so on). Finally, the project manager should send a reminder and follow-up prompt to the key meeting invitees to ensure they are attending. In doing these activities, the project manager would have taken most of the steps to adequately plan for preparing for his or her project presentations.

Before you can create the project presentation tool, you must formulate a plan. Ask yourself the following questions.

Planning Questions

1 *When would you create, develop, or write this tool?*
Beginning of project, through the life of project and specifically at the end of major phases, or when requesting additional funding, time, or resources

2 *Who is going to use this tool, both from an input and output status?*
Everyone involved in project

continued

333

continued

3 *Why are you going to use this tool?*

Present project information to various stakeholders and seek feedback from audience for project guidance

4 *How are you going to use this tool?*

Develop the presentation material, seek guidance on information from team members for additions to presentation, and deliver a story to the audience

5 *How will you distribute the information?*

Presentation format such as Microsoft PowerPoint (r), e-mail, document control system, in-person presentation

6 *When will you distribute the information?*

At actual project presentation meeting event, as required, or on-demand

7 *What decisions can or should you make from this tool?*

The purpose of most project presentations is to obtain a decision from the upper management, clients, or customers or team members on various areas of the project; one example would be the approval to move to the next phase of the project decision

8 *What information does this tool provide for your project?*

Depending on the presentation delivered, the information will vary. Generally, what a project manager presents is the key aspects of the project such as risks, issues, schedule, costs, and resources.

9 *What historical and legal information do you need to store?*

Previous versions of documents presented, lessons learned information, and relevant information that supported development of presentations

10 *What will be the staffing requirements (role type) to run and maintain these tools?*

Project manager, team members, communication manager

Reporting using project presentations

In most cases, the project manager creates the project presentations. This is excellent because they are responsible for the meeting and therefore should own the responsibility of compiling this material. On larger projects where the project has a project control group, quite often someone in that group is responsible for developing the project presentation working alongside the project manager. If this is simply a matter of compiling the information from various team members, anyone can do it, but the project manager should still be active in compiling the presentation. In the end, the project manager owns and has to present this information to their customers.

The following are examples of the various types of project presentations that project managers would make on their projects:

- **Media presentation:** These presentations can occur for both the announcement and closeout of the project and major milestones.

- **Project kick-offs:** A project kick-off is an initial meeting to bring everyone together for the project.

- **Requests for funding:** The project manager calls a meeting to present the request for additional funding to customers.

- **End of phase presentation:** The project reaches the end of a particular phase (design complete) and the project manager calls a meeting to close out that phase.

- **Weekly status meeting presentations:** Weekly status meetings often have a presentation component to them that requires developing a project presentation and presenting to the customers.

- **Technical presentations:** Technical presentations, such as a new design on a roof truss for the management, contractors involved in the roof. Technical presentations tend to be discussions as well as a presentation.

- **Lessons learned:** A project presentation that goes over lessons learned information on the project and addresses how future projects can benefit from lessons of the existing project.

- **Project closures:** A project closeout presentation, where the project manager gathers the stakeholders and obtains final approval on the team's efforts is normally the last one made.

Project managers formally report the project presentations during various times throughout the life of the project. The project manager creates a project presentation in presentation software packages, such as PowerPoint, and it is then stored in the document control system for long-term archiving and retrieval. Project presentations often have compliance aspect to them that requires formal approval and sign-off, and therefore they require the security of the document control system.

CROSS-REF See Chapter 19 to learn more about how to use this project presentation tool.

Introducing Prototyping

The purpose of *prototyping* is to provide to the customers models and test versions of the final product for demonstration and functional walkthroughs prior to the final design. The engineering and software development industries utilize prototyping as part of their standard development life-cycles, and both disciplines continually take full advantage of the powerful nature of this tool. The construction industry has been using prototyping for years and normally starts with smaller scale design of the structures to provide an insight for the customers on the look and feel of the project they are developing. The software industry has also utilized prototyping for many years from using basic screen designs on paper to the working versions of the applications. For example, in software projects, a prototype can be something as easy as a series of hand-drawn screen shots or as complicated as a working software application without all the functionally. In each case, the customer can acquire an understanding of what and how the final product will perform when it is finally developed and usable as a product.

Project managers should utilize prototyping whenever possible to allow their customers the early review of the product, which can lessen the need for change requests in the future. Prototyping enhances communication between all parties involved because it allows everyone to view the design of the final product, which solicits feedback on that design.

> **NOTE** The Project Management Institute's knowledge area for this tool is the Communications Management area. This tool can be associated with the knowledge areas: Time, Cost, Quality, and Risk.

> **TOOL VALUE** Prototype because it is a physical or three-dimensional representation of the product; it provides everyone involved with a much more in-depth understanding of the final product.

A prototype serves as a scaled replication of the final product. For example, in construction a prototype can be something as easy as a series of colored paint strips or as complicated as a working elevator albeit without all the functionally. The level of detail and type of prototype on a project is going to depend on the industry, size of the project, and specific methodology used to develop the product. Using prototyping is a smart approach because the upfront value to seeing an example of the final product is a great way to communicate the ideas behind the product at a relatively low cost. It makes sense to show your stakeholders early in the design process what they will receive when the project completes.

The goal of prototyping is to demonstrate the product to the customers before actual construction begins. Customers can evaluate immediately if they like the design and suggest changes to the design early in the project. Prototyping promotes discussions on ideas, concepts, and possible changes to the final product.

Project prototyping is helpful to all members of the project because it allows for ongoing communication between the stakeholders and the team members on the design of the final product. This process can be beneficial to all members because it opens primary lines of communication between stakeholders and team member that are not usually available on projects. Often, during these sessions the team members and customers establish good relationships that often continue throughout the project. The prototyping session brings a number of people together working on a common goal and forms a cohesive team, which is good for project communications and moral.

Figure 10.6 represents a typical project prototype of a concept car. In this prototype, you can see the look of the car, get into it, and test drive it. This type of prototype is common in the auto industry.

FIGURE 10.6

This is a typical prototype of a new smart car.

The quality assurance aspects of the prototype could eliminate potential design flaws discovered during the prototyping phase. When discovering flaws, the team can make product requirement changes, and making those changes early in the process saves time and costs to the project. Quality assurance is completed by working with the customers as they review the product and provide insight to their likes and dislikes, and this generally provides direction or changes they would expect to see. The process may take several tries and require the project manager to continue driving this testing with them. The quality assurance process is important on all projects, ensuring the highest level of quality a project can afford is a top priority for everyone involved.

Many different industries utilize the prototyping methodology. The following list covers some of these industries:

- **Architecture and engineering:** Prototypes include concept cars, skyscraper models, highway models, bridge models, and scale models of all kinds.

- **Mechanical and electrical engineering:** Prototypes include wiring diagrams, breadboard, model of an elevator, HVAC system in a model building, and scale models.

- **Computer science and computer software engineering:** Application prototype for a new time entry system, project dashboards prototype, screen shots, and user interfaces, to name a few.

- **Aerospace:** Prototypes include concept planes, wind tunnel models, cockpit mockups, full-scale cabin demo models, sometimes used for marketing.

CAUTION There are some disadvantages to using the Prototyping tool that includes unfinished subsystems, possibility of implementing the prototype product before all final designs, high expectation may not be able to be met, and often it has limited features and less flexibility then the final product.

Planning to use a prototype

When planning to use a prototyping process, the project manager must first determine if the project they are managing makes sense to use this methodology and determine how and who on the team will be engaged in the development of the prototype. Project managers must also work with the customers and gather their feedback, expectations, and success criteria for the prototype. They can then set up the development and timeframes for prototyping in the project schedule, develop a series of feedback loops for the project team, and identify costs or budget impacts for developing a prototype. In doing this planning work, the project manager has ensured that his or her project is ready for engaging in the prototyping process. Without taken these steps, the project manager or the project may not be ready.

Before you can create the prototyping tool, you must formulate a plan. Ask yourself the following questions.

Planning Questions

1 *When would you create this tool?*
Design stage of project, before development begins

2 *Who is going to use this tool, both from an input and output status?*
Upper management, owners, executives, project manager, team members, subcontractors, or specific skill areas, the media (TV, radio, newspapers)

3 *Why are you going to use this tool?*
Review and seek approval of the mockup of product from the clients or customers and to ensure agreement of the design of the final product

4 *How are you going to use this tool?*
To demonstrate the product's design and functionality to the client or customer in the early design phases and seek their approval on the design

5 *How will you distribute the information?*
Physical models, software, working prototypes, documentation, drawings

6 *How often will you distribute the information?*
As needed, many project methodologies take advantage of prototyping to allow the customers the chance to see the product in the early stages and may have multiple iterations

7 *What decisions can you make from this tool?*
Design decisions, quality decisions, risk decisions, schedule and cost decisions, go/no-go decisions

8 *What information does this tool provide for your project?*
Look and feel of final product, a view into limited product functionality, cost information, design areas, specifications, and three-dimensional representation of final product

9 *What historical and legal information do you need to store?*
Initial models, assumptions, constraints, lessons learned information

10 *What will be the staffing requirements (role type) to run and maintain these tools?*
Designers, engineers, craftsman, and architects

Reporting using a prototype

The engineering, design, and technical teams develop the prototype for the project. The prototyping phase begins after the design phase of the project has started. When the prototype is ready, the customers engage by working with it, testing it, and then communicating their likes and dislikes of it. This process generates a report that becomes valuable feedback for the project team to use when developing the next version of the prototype or the final product. Each report summarizes the impact to the project from the design change perspective. Impacts such as cost and schedule or scope changes may be possible fallouts of these design sessions. There can be multiple sessions for a particular project depending on size and complexity of the prototype and therefore multiple reports from this process.

The project manager reports from the prototype process weekly during the prototyping cycle. Prototyping can use hundreds of different formats, depending on project type. For any electronic versions of the prototyping, screens, and reports, they are stored as part of the document control system for long-term archiving and are accessible by any interested stakeholder on the project.

CROSS-REF See Chapter 15 to learn more about how to use a prototype.

Introducing the Work Package

The purpose of the *work package* tool is to create a document that describes all the work on the project. Work packages comprise the majority of the work breakdown structure dictionary. This is often a hard copy document created from a template or an electronic version of a document, or a combination of both. A work package also includes the reporting of progress for each work package as they complete. A work package in a *scheduling* tool is an activity or task of a project, and each one (work package, activity, or task) is a specific deliverable. Each should define all the effort, materials, equipment, risk, quality, cost, resources, duration, and scope for that deliverable. Because they are individual deliverables, by reporting progress on each one, as they are complete, the project manager can easily track progress and performance of the overall project. Because work packages are usually short in duration this also helps in your estimating and with the accuracy of reporting the remaining work. Because each work package identifies and defines specific work and deliverables, it helps control any scope creep.

 The Project Management Institute's knowledge area for this tool is the Communications Management area. This tool can be associated with all other knowledge areas as well.

 We have included a sample of this work package tool in the Communication_Managing folder. Use this as a guide to help you create your own version of this tool.

 Work package identifies and defines all the work for each deliverable on the project.

The work package tool benefits most members of the project by formally documenting the work completed and communicating the remaining work. As the various components of the project complete, the project manager checks off those components from the master list until the team delivers the entire project. This process is ongoing throughout the life of the project. If there are any questions or details about what was completed, who signed off, the date of completion, the project manager can use these work package forms to communicate that information. The project manager can communicate the individual work package form or summarize them to a higher level on the work breakdown structure (WBS) for the stakeholders. This lets them know exactly what the latest progress is and what tasks are remaining. Without the work package form, there may be less documented proof that a work deliverable was completed.

Figure 10.7 represents a work breakdown structure and the associated work packages for each level. The work package is the lowest level of the work breakdown structure. When reporting work package status, you are reporting at the lowest level of the project.

FIGURE 10.7

A typical work package sitting in a typical work breakdown structure.

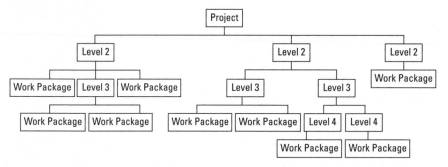

Project managers must be aware of the following work package characteristics:

- Any unnecessary project work should not have a corresponding work package because that work does not belong in the project.

- Every work package has a specific deliverable associated to it.
- Each work package should define all the effort, materials, equipment, risk, quality, cost, duration, and scope for the deliverable.
- Work packages and WBS do not logically link; they are in a hierarchical format.
- Each work package has a unique ID associated to it.
- Work packages help control change (scope creep).
- The work package description should have a verb and a noun.
- The work package is the bottom level of the work breakdown structure.

 Always document the completion of a deliverable.

Planning to use a work package

The main concern when planning to create and use a work package when developing a work breakdown structure is to make sure that you include all the work required to complete the project and do not include any work that is not required. You should have a clear understanding of what work will and will not be included in the work package. If any work that is required is missing, a delay in the project schedule and extra cost is likely when the missing work is included later in the project.

Before you can create the Work Package tool, you must formulate a plan. Ask yourself the following questions about a work package.

Planning Questions

1 When would you create or develop the work package tool?
During the planning phase and when a change request creates a new one

2 Who is going to use this tool, both from an input and output status?
Everyone on the project will want exposure or access to the work package

3 Why are you going to use the work package tool?
To plan, monitor, and report progress on individual tasks

4 How are you going to use this tool?
Identifies all activity information on a single task, such as costs, risks, schedule, and quality for updating and reporting. Plan and extract information from task and use it at appropriate times.

continued

continued

5 *How will you distribute the information?*

Document format such as Microsoft Word, WBS dictionary, document control system, e-mail, presentations, and potential dashboard information

6 *When will you distribute the information?*

After work break structure dictionary is complete, when change requests are approved

7 *What decisions can or should you make from this tool?*

Decisions on any activity information such as costs, risks, schedule, and quality

8 *What information does this tool provide for your project?*

All information about individual tasks or activities (work packages) on project

9 *What historical and legal information do you need to store?*

WBS dictionary, lessons learned

10 *What will be the staffing requirements (role type) to run and maintain these tools?*

Project manager, cost manager, risk manager, quality manager, schedule manager, and procurement manager

Reporting using a work package

The work package is not a period report. The work package can contain project status information, but the main use is for gathering information, not reporting on it. The work packages are included in the WBS dictionary and are available to anyone interested in those details.

There are probably as many ways to report progress on a project as there are projects. One of these many ways is to use the work package as the reporting document. When reporting progress using this method, as work completes, record it in a work package. The project manager determines the work completed and any remaining work. Then he takes this progress information and summarizes it to communicate the status of the project, usually on a weekly basis. The information documented in the work package describes the details around what work was completed.

The following is a list of items that can be included in a work package:

- Project name
- Project manager
- Description
- Finish date

- Responsible team members
- Cost variance
- Time variance
- Actual resource hours used
- Remaining hours
- Materials used

The completion of the work package results form is the responsibility of the individual team member who completed the work, or the team lead within that particular area of the project. If there are major project areas led by different team leads, those individuals are responsible for compiling the information for their areas and reporting the results. When using the work package methods to collect progress data, these forms are extremely helpful in understanding what data to collect. Without the form, team members would struggle with what information they should or should not collect. Because of the signatures on the document, if needed, they could also serve well in a court case where proof is required on formal acceptance. When presented in a legal dispute, it could sway an arbitration panel or court decision because it has signatures as to when a team member completed the work and any comments about the work. It is expected as the final documentation of the project is compiled, work package forms will be part of the overall work documentation and included with the WBS for long-term storage and lessons learned.

Figure 10.8 represents a sample work package progress form from the Fillmore Construction Project. The team lead (John MacDonald) completed this form when the work activity was finished. The information on this form provides documentation that the work is complete and approved by the stakeholders, as shown by their signatures.

There is no formal reporting of the individual work package forms to the customers based on the standard reporting process. These forms assist the project manager in monitoring and controlling their project and reporting to the stakeholders at a summary level only if applicable. If information at the detailed level is required, then stakeholders can review this detail individually on each work package form.

There usually is not a timeframe associated to reporting of work package result form. The work on a project completes at various times; therefore completing the work package form would also occur at various times. Therefore, reporting at regular intervals can be challenging. In some cases, project managers have gathered the week's forms and report them at the end of day on Friday. This is not a common occurrence, as these forms do not tend to lend themselves to formal reporting. Other tools do the reporting using the information from a work package. The work package document is stored as part of the project document control system.

CROSS-REF See Chapter 20 to learn more about how to create and use a work package.

FIGURE 10.8

This is a typical work package form.

Work Package Progress Form - Fillmore Construction Project

Project Name: **Fillmore Construction Project**	Project Manager: **Jack Smith**	Date Required: **May 14th, 2009**
WBS Code: **AJ.02.10.06**	Activity Summary Description: **Module 26 - North Wall Electrical box installation**	Actual Finish Date: **May 14th, 2009**
Responsible Team Member: **Charlie Wade**	Cost Variance: **−$645.00**	Time Variance: **+5 Days**

Completion Comments/Notes:
Wiring was installed with two circuts reversed and required an additional inspection. Task finished 5 days earlier, and under budget.

Approvals/Signoffs:	Team Lead Signature/Date:	Project manager Signature/Date:
Mary Jones	*John Macdonald* **May 9, 2009**	*Bob Allen* **May 10, 2009**

Summary

The tools described in this chapter help project managers and team members manage their project communications. As we all know, managing project communications is tricky and critical to the success of the project.

As you review this chapter, one of the tools that may make an impact on your day-to-day project management responsibilities is the *project calendar*. The *personal* calendar has been around for many years, but the *project calendar* is a relatively new concept. It is popular with its graphical format and easy-to-communicate characteristics with the team members, upper management, and the project's customers.

The chapter includes tools such as computer-aided design, communication plan, e-mail, and the work package tool. With so many tools at their disposal, project managers should have an easier time determining how to manage and communicate appropriately with their customers and senior management.

Chapter 11

Defining Communication Tools to Report Project Communications

I n this chapter, we explore project communications tools in the Project Communications Management concept area. This chapter covers the communication tools used to report project information on an ongoing basis.

Project communications management is the most important aspect of project management. In communicating to customers and upper management, project managers should use the appropriate communication tools. These tools report status, as well as provide the customers with the information they need to make project level decisions. Tools such as a stoplight report, budget spreadsheets, and dashboard reports all help customers obtain the information they need to make project decisions. These decisions range from adding additional budget to cover budget overage as shown in the budget spreadsheet tool to hiring additional team members because the stoplight report is showing the project is red (meaning in trouble) due to schedule.

In this chapter, we present the tools used to report project information to customers and upper management staff about the project. These tools help the project manager communicate more effectively and assist them in their management of the project.

Introducing the Daily Progress Report

The purpose of a daily progress report is to document the outcome of a daily progress meeting and assist the project manager and team members in their understanding of the project's status on a daily basis. The software development industry utilizes the daily progress meetings as part of a development methodology called SCRUM, which is used quite heavily in an attempt to make project team members accountable, share their project status on deliverables, and bring the team together as one unit. The daily progress report is the documented results of that meeting. The term SCRUM is taken from the game of rugby. As in rugby, it uses a small, cross-functional team to produce the best project outcome. Although Scrum's main intention was the management of software development projects, it has uses as well in running software maintenance teams, or as a program management approach: Scrum of Scrums.

Each day, after the team has the daily progress meeting, the project manager (or ScrumMaster) compiles the results of the meeting into a daily progress report. SCRUM teams that avoid or do not document the updates from the team members end up missing an excellent opportunity to communicate this information to a wider audience. We recommend that project managers, regardless of the industry and methodology they are using, implement the daily meetings and document those meetings using the daily progress report.

The communication aspects of having a daily progress report are beneficial to both the project team members and the project manager. Bringing the team together for 30 minutes at the beginning of each day allows the team to focus on the project and communicate the status, issues, concerns, highlights, and lowlights of the project. It also provides an atmosphere of togetherness for the team members.

 The Project Management Institute's knowledge area for this tool is the Communications Management area. This tool can be associated with all other knowledge areas.

 We have included a sample of this Daily Progress Report tool in the Communicating Reporting folder. Use this as a guide to help you create your own version of this tool.

 Daily progress reports provide a current snapshot of the project on a daily basis. No other tools bring team members together every day to talk about the project pertaining to their own concerns and needs of the project.

Using the daily progress report benefits everyone on the team. Not only project managers, team members, and upper management, but also customers can benefit greatly from hearing the status and the roadblocks the team the members are facing on the project. The meeting is short and the information from that meeting (daily progress report) is provided directly by each team member. This ensures that everyone involved in the project gets the information they need directly from the people doing the work. Project managers can work through roadblocks or issues with team members, and everyone can hear what the others are facing. Customers who sit in on the meeting or read the daily progress report can step in where they need to and help when appropriate. One important aspect of the daily progress report and the associated meeting is how simple the meeting actually is and how little time it takes. The process is as follows:

1. All team members gather in-person (or on a conference call) for this meeting.

2. The project manager then asks each team member the following questions:

   - What did you complete yesterday?

   - What do you plan to work on today?

   - What is stopping you from completing your activities?

3. A member of the team, or a scribe, can capture the answers from each team member into the daily progress report.

4. At the end of the meeting, the project manager receives the report from the scribe or team member, cleans up any formatting or something not looking right, and sends it out to the team, upper management, customers, and anyone else interested in the report.

5. The process continues daily until the project is completed.

One of the benefits the project manager receives from a daily progress report is a higher level of commitment and accountability from each team member. Because the project manager addresses each of the team members directly at the meeting, and they are accountable to provide status and state what they are doing, it provides an incentive for the team members to make as much progress as possible on a day-to-day basis. It allows them to show the project manager they are not slacking off and they are not letting the other team members down on the project. The information that they provide shows that they are providing value and demonstrating that value to the other team members. It is a very powerful human resource tool because it forces a sense of competition among the team members where everyone would be focusing on ensuring that the team members know they are valuable to the project.

Another important item to remember when communicating project status using the daily progress report is the differences between this report and the periodic reports. The two are different. The daily progress report provides a current status of the project each day, and the periodic reports summarizes a week's worth of information. The issues and risks, for example, on a periodic report can be weeks old, where the information coming directly from the team members each day is real time.

The aspect of daily progress reporting is not new — projects have been doing this for years when they are in trouble, or there are upcoming milestones that the team is striving to complete. When troubling situations occur, or the project is focusing on a milestone, the project members come together and discuss the problems or concerns until everything is resolved. If the team is focusing toward a milestone, the team will continue to meet daily until achieving that milestone. This normally happens throughout the project during the difficult times or the times when needing to focus on a milestone. After accomplishing either, the project team goes back to having weekly status report meetings and weekly reporting. Sometimes these highly effective team-focusing meetings occur for a short time only and the information is only effective for a short time on the project.

Planning to use a daily progress report

In planning and preparing to use a daily progress report, the project manager must first align with the team members regarding their participation and the value of these meetings. Initially, team members may resist the idea of having daily meetings. They will argue it is a waste of time, just another meeting, or does not add any value. Project managers should prepare for this resistance and insist that team members attend. The next area in the planning process that the project manager must stay on top of is planning for who will capture the various statuses provided by the project team members. The project manager needs to select a minute-taker for each meeting and determine a process for selecting that person. If no one takes the minutes, and the information is missing, the project manager has lost the ability to create the daily progress report. If the project manager notifies the team members that they have to rotate capturing the daily status, they are usually more accommodating when told ahead of time. As the project manager prepares to use this tool, he/she must talk to the customers and upper management to determine if they need copies of the daily progress report, or want to receive any additional communications from this meeting. In some cases, customers pass on receiving daily status and are satisfied with a weekly summary communication only. Customers may feel that obtaining daily information, while the project is progressing, may not be valuable; however, the project manager on the other hand, as noted above, may think the complete opposite and will value those reports immensely. After preparing and taking the steps for using this tool, the project manager has adequately prepared for its use on the project.

Before you can create a daily progress report, you must formulate a plan. In the following "Planning Questions" section, we have provided some initial thoughts to help you start thinking about how you can utilize the tool on your project. Ask yourself the following questions.

Planning Questions

1 When would you create, develop, or write this tool?
Daily and throughout the life of the project

2 Who is going to use this tool, both from an input and output status?
Project manager, team members, clients or customers, upper management

3 Why are you going to use this tool?
To determine the activities of the project team members on a daily basis; to determine where the project manager needs to help resolve roadblocks or issues team members are having; to determine the latest status of the project on a daily basis

4 How are you going to use this tool?
Gather the team members together on daily basis; capture their responses to the standard project questions and then assist in providing help to the team members with the blocking issues

5 *How will you distribute the information?*
Document format such as Microsoft Word, e-mail, document control system

6 *When will you distribute the information?*
Daily, after the daily progress meeting occurs

7 *What decisions can or should you make from this tool?*
Decide on what blocking issue is the most important and where the project manager needs to support the team members

8 *What information does this tool provide for your project?*
A daily status or update of project activities; work activities from project team members, blocking issues from preventing progress of team members

9 *What historical and legal information do you need to store?*
Previous versions of the daily report, lessons learned information

10 *What will be the staffing requirements (role type) to run and maintain these tools?*
Project manager, team members, clerk or administrative assistant

Reporting using a daily progress report

The project manager is responsible for creating the daily progress report. Although project managers may not actually capture the daily status in the meeting, they compile the information and communicate the information on a daily basis.

The daily progress report allows the project manager to hear the challenges and concerns on the project directly from each team member. If the minute-taker compiles or summarizes the information for the daily progress report, then the project manager would be aware of the issues, but not necessarily who stated it, or what team member it is affecting. This is not recommended. The minute-taker should capture the name of the team member who is having the issue, so the project manager can work with them to help resolve their issues. If the minute-taker summarizes all the information captured by the various team members, it lessens the value of the daily progress report. It would lessen its value because it is not providing the project manager with the detailed information he/she needs to help resolve the team's problems. As an example, if the minute-taker documented at the summary level, the project is $500,000 over budget. This statement does not tell the project manager where in the project there is this overage and therefore he/she would not necessary know where to start to resolve the problem. Whereas, if the minute-taker documents into the daily progress report that the finance manager stated that the design area is $5,000 over budget, the project manager would know exactly where to focus their attention.

The project manager compiles and sends the daily progress report to the team members, customers, and, in some cases, upper management. The value of getting this type of report each day provides the ongoing updates of project information to interested stakeholders immediately and allows complete exposure of what is occurring on the project. The report should be in a document format, distributed by e-mail, and stored long term in the Document Control System, archived, and accessible by anyone interested in the project.

 See Chapter 21 to learn more about how to use and create the daily progress report.

Introducing the Dashboard Tool

The purpose of the *dashboard* tool is to provide the project's customers and upper management staff with a real-time graphical view of the project's critical information. This information includes project schedule, costs, issues, and risks. Usually, project managers arrange for dashboards placed on a company Web site where customers and upper management can go directly to the site for the latest information. Dashboards are popular with customers and senior management because they can obtain current data from the project and then make decisions based on the data. Without a dashboard, those same groups would have to wait until the weekly status report to get the similar information. The communication aspects of using project dashboards are tremendous. After the project manager sets up the process to ensure the dashboard is loaded correctly every day, or develops a manual process to create the dashboard, few steps are needed to complete this process. When someone is interested or needs project information, the project manager directs them to the dashboard for the latest project status.

Dashboards are used mostly in multiproject environments, because rarely do companies want to spend the time and effort to develop and maintain them for a single project. The cost of ongoing maintenance and support rarely warrants a single project dashboard. They are expensive.

One of the powerful aspects of the use of a dashboard is the ability to roll up multiprojects into a consolidated view of all project information. Project dashboards are probably the most utilized project tool for senior managers to be directly involved with the information from the project.

 The Project Management Institute's knowledge area for this tool is the Communications Management area. This tool can be associated with all the other knowledge areas.

We have included a sample of this dashboard report in the Communicating Reporting folder. Use this as a guide to help you create your own version of this tool.

 Dashboards offer real-time access to project information for customers, upper and senior management, and team members. This real-time look can give customers the feeling of how well the project is progressing and whether they need to take action on any areas of concern.

Using a project dashboard has many benefits. The most important benefit is the real-time access to project information that is only obtainable in this type of format. For example, if the customer wants to track the status of the error counts during the testing phase, the project manager may create an error tracking report format and add it to the dashboard. As testing progresses, the customer has the latest information on the error counts. The other benefits of the dashboard are access to and the availability of project information in what looks or appears to be automatic.

Figure 11.1 shows a typical dashboard report. Companies use thousands of different dashboards. For example, the metrics listed in Figure 11.1 provide a graphical status of the project focusing on six different aspects. There is no correct number of project points to add to a dashboard. The needs of the customers and upper management determine what project points are displayed.

FIGURE 11.1

This dashboard report is developed in Excel and manually produced each week. It is either sent to the project stakeholders or posted to an internal Web site for their review.

Project Dashboard Report

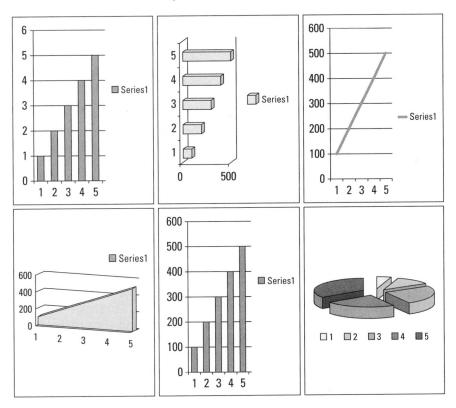

| TIP | The best type of information for adding to a dashboard report is summary-level information. |

Project teams often create dashboards that have the ability to pull detailed information and drill into capabilities. Initially, creating a dashboard with high-level project information solves the need for communicating project information, but more often than not, the customers or upper management will want to perform further analysis on the data, and perhaps look at the data behind the data. These "drill-through capabilities" are common on project dashboards and are a real advantage to using this tool. Customers can often select the data on the dashboard to open up further dashboard pages and see finer details behind the dashboard data. Tools, such as Microsoft Excel, are often used in the development and reporting of dashboard information, and are easily set up to allow drill-down capability print detail information. Databases, such as Oracle and Microsoft's SQL server, are also popular for storing and generating project dashboard data, and both have the drill-down features available for further analysis of the data.

Dashboard reports commonly have a number of different project points stored on them. The points include project costs, schedules, or other financial information. Other financial data can be details such as number of hours worked by team members, overtime costs, material costs, and so on. By creating these types of dashboards, you are catering to the needs of customers and upper management who tend to focus on these limited but important areas on the project.

Dashboards do have their limitations. Dashboards must have a meaningful value to the project, because keeping them current adds to the workload of the team members. Other challenges or limitations include adding too much information to the dashboard, which makes it hard to read, confusing, and a huge overhead to maintain. The challenge project teams have when creating a dashboard report is the ability to put all the project data points onto a single screen, or a single Web site, that is viewable in a format that is easy to read and understand. Some companies use a dashboard that represents a view of their projects from a program perspective. A program-level dashboard report provides a summary of many projects executing at the company into a single view. It is beneficial to be able to look across all projects occurring in the company.

Program level dashboards tend to focus on specific areas of the company. Larger companies have hundreds of concurrent projects, so adding all of them to a single dashboard would be difficult and hard to maintain over a long period. Normally, companies segment the dashboards and show in a single view a range of 10 to 15 projects. Doing so keeps the project list reasonable and the amount of data that requires generating, small. Having a program level dashboard provides upper and senior management with the ability to determine the pulse of their projects in one summarized view.

Planning to use a dashboard report

In planning and preparing to use a dashboard report, the project manager must first determine the role of dashboards in the company. Whether dashboards are common to all projects, or something brand new to the company, a project manager must determine where and how they fit the project. In some cases, there may be no automated solution for creating a dashboard, so the project manager will have to create a manual solution. When the company does have a dashboard capability, the project manager needs to determine the internal process to get a dashboard set up for his or her project. After determining that process, and the types of dashboards available for projects, the project manager should then determine who on the project team is on point to gather the data and add to the dashboard for the project. Usually, the project manager needs a couple of different team members to create the dashboard, so he/she needs to allow and plan for their team members to work on the dashboard as well as the time and affect it has on their other project work. The project manager and the team members responsible for developing the dashboard begin by working with the customers and gather their requirements for the dashboard. The goal of this meeting is to gather the customers' needs for the contents of the dashboard for their project. After taking these necessary planning steps, the project manager has adequately prepared for the use of the dashboard on his or her project.

Before you can create the dashboard report, you must formulate a plan. In the following "Planning Questions" section, we provide some initial thoughts to help you start thinking about how you can utilize the tool on your project. Ask yourself the following questions.

Planning Questions

1 *When would you create or develop this tool?*

The planning of the dashboard starts at the beginning of the project where the project manager works with the customers to determine what they want to include on the dashboard

2 *Who is going to use this tool, both from an input and output status?*

Executives, upper management, clients or owners and customers, project manager, subcontractor (larger projects), press (the media)

3 *Why are you going to use this tool?*

To provide upper management with a snapshot of the latest status of the project, without displaying all the details behind the numbers (user can drill down into data if they desire)

4 *How are you going to use this tool?*

To display various aspects of the project that will also allow upper management and executives to analyze and make decisions based on the data displayed

5 *How will you distribute the information?*

Dashboards reside on Web sites that allow you to retrieve the project information. Project managers can use spreadsheets to create and distribute dashboard reports on a periodic basis depending on the needs of the project.

6 *When will you distribute the information?*

Data is available all the time when using a dashboard report, but if it is a manual report, then the data should be reported monthly at the minimum.

continued

continued

7 *What decisions can or should you make from this tool?*

The objective of the project dashboard is to provide enough information for executives and customers or clients to make project-level decisions or request further details.

8 *What information does this tool provide for your project?*

Any high-level summary information concerning the project, such as budget, costs, schedule, and so on. Executives and customers may request information for the dashboard that they want displayed. Most often, executive managers request dashboard customizations for their specific needs.

9 *What historical and legal information do you need to store?*

Limited, because the nature of dashboards is to provide the latest project status, and therefore historical information is not in the nature of this tool. A dashboard only reports information from other tools. The other tools will have the historical and legal information stored in them.

10 *What will be the staffing requirements (role type) to run and maintain these tools?*

Depending on dashboard type, a full dashboard is going to require IT resources to create and maintain the site. When using a dashboard report, a project manager and team members are involved

Reporting using a dashboard report

The dashboard is a complex and technical communication tool and is not a tool most project managers can create by themselves. Because of the complexities of this tool, a project manager needs a team of software developers with the skills available to create and maintain the dashboard. The development team is normally responsible for the ongoing development and maintenance of the dashboard at least through the end of the project, and sometimes that same development team will continue to maintain the dashboard for as long as management continues to see value.

Manual dashboard report creation is the project manager or assigned team member's responsibility. Either person must enter the project data by using a spreadsheet tool and generate data points or calculations manually. The project manager or analyst would also continue this manual process monthly, if that is the agreed upon time with the customers until the end of the project. Alternatively, until the project manager can get the dashboard automated and a development team would take over the ongoing support of the tool.

CROSS-REF   See Chapter 18 to learn more about how to use a dashboard report.

Introducing the Pareto Chart

The purpose of the *Pareto chart* tool is to identify the highest priority item, or items, in a set of data. The Pareto chart is a unique form of a histogram and prioritizes which item to solve, and in what order. The chart actually helps the project manager and the team members focus attention and effort on the most important item on the chart. The chart provides the team with a starting point to solve the first problem identified in the chart, then the next, and the next, and so on.

NOTE Vilfredo Federico Damaso Pareto invented the Pareto chart, and Joseph M. Juran and Kaoru Ishikawa made it popular. The popular Pareto's law states that 80 percent of the problems stem from 20 percent of the causes. The Pareto chart is a communication tool that helps prioritize the problems in an easy-to-read format. This law originated when Pareto was observing a connection between population and wealth and noticed that 80 percent of Italy's wealth was in the hands of 20 percent of the population. He then carried out surveys on a variety of other countries and found a similar distribution applied in those countries as well.

Because the Pareto chart is a graphic representation of the most important issues or items to address on the project. Communicating this chart to customers or team members is relatively easy. Customers can determine immediately where the largest problems or concerns are, and then focus attention on those areas to achieve resolution. The project manager owns the responsibility of communicating these problem areas to the customers, team members, as well as to drive the resolution of each area.

NOTE The Project Management Institute's knowledge area for this tool is the Communications Management area. This tool can be associated with the following knowledge areas: Integration, Time, Cost, Quality, Human Resources, and Procurement.

ON the CD-ROM We have included a sample of this Pareto chart tool in the Communicating Reporting folder. Use this as a guide to help you create your own version of this tool.

TOOL VALUE Identifies the predominate problem in a set of data elements. It prioritizes the items on the chart, allowing customers and team members to understand what to address first, second, and third.

One of the benefits of the Pareto chart is that it assists the project manager and customers by identifying and ranking the major project problems to address. The chart has the ability to display graphically the results of the analysis and to focus the team on correcting the highest ranked issue first, then second highest, third, and so on. As the team members address the highest ranked issues first, doing so provides the most benefit to the project with the least amount of work, thus following Pareto's law. If the project manager takes advantage of using Pareto charts, they can increase the chance of success for their project because they are removing the largest problem areas that the project is facing first. Without a Pareto chart, it is possible to miss problems or issues, or not address them at all. This could have a negative effect on the project. Another situation on the project where the Pareto chart proves extremely helpful is at the point where project team members are working on lower priority problems without even realizing it. After creating the chart, the team may realize that they are focusing their attention on the wrong areas of the project, wasting time and effort on less important items. This could have a negative impact on the project. What the team should be doing is focusing on correcting the higher priority items highlighted on the Pareto chart.

Figure 11.2 represents a Pareto chart showing that 60 percent of the project problems are in the first two categories. That percentage jumps to 80 percent when the third category is included in the analysis. Therefore, if the project team resolved the first two categories, they would solve 60 percent of the project problems. If they work on the first three categories, they solve 80 percent of the project's problems. This process continues until all problems are resolved.

FIGURE 11.2

An example of a Pareto chart indicating various issues and factors of project delivery problems.

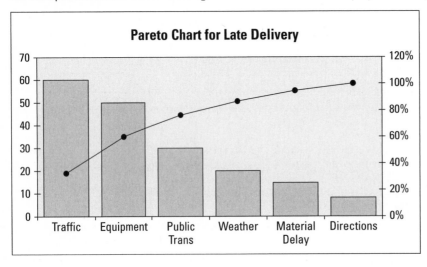

Figure 11.2 displays traffic congestion as the major problem for vendor late delivery on the project. It is also clear that equipment issues (either lack of or availability) are a project problem that needs resolution. To understand how the Pareto law works for this particular chart, you need to review the cumulative percentage line. This line goes across the top of the chart on a curve. In this line, you will see that the second point in the equipment bar column directly relates to roughly 65 percent of the problems on the project and the other problems represent the remaining 35 percent. Therefore, if the project team resolved the traffic and equipment problems, they would resolve 65 percent of the late deliveries. Imagine how easy it would be to create this chart for your project, and how valuable it would be to communicate to your customers and upper management the current project problems.

The following tips can help you read and understand a Pareto chart:

- Look for a breakpoint in the cumulative percentage line. This point occurs where the slope of the line begins to flatten. The issues located under the steepest part of the curve are the most important and are located on the left side of the chart.

- If there is not a clear breakpoint in the slope of the line, look for the issues that make up at least 60 percent of the problem. After you improve the predominate issues at the 60 percent level, recreate the Pareto analysis chart and find the new predominate issues. The project team needs to address these new issues.

- If the bars are all similar in size or more than half of the issues make up 60 percent, try a different breakdown of issues that might be more appropriate, or consider the issues addressed. The project team has solved the majority of the issues with the least amount of effort. If you want to continue, recreate the Pareto chart with the majority of the issues removed from the analysis.

Planning to use a Pareto chart

In planning and preparing to use a Pareto chart, the project manager must first define the major project problems that he/she wants to track using a Pareto chart. The project problem defined in Figure 11.2 is vendor late delivery of material to the construction job site, with the reasons for the problem broken down into subcategories (equipment, traffic, weather and so on). That same process occurs to determining what areas you want to track for the project in the planning phase, so the project manager can establish the Pareto chart as early as possible. This is not an easy task, and project managers must put some time and effort into thinking about what makes sense and what are the problems and the subcategories for their particular projects that require tracking. After the subcategories have been determined, the project manager should work with the team members to select someone who is responsible for creating the chart for the project. That chosen team member will own the Pareto chart and the maintenance of it throughout the life of the project. If no one is available to take on this task, the project manager is responsible and creates the chart. This is true in many cases. After determining the project team member responsible, the project manager then works with the customers to obtain their requirements for the Pareto chart. This may require the project manager teaching the customer about the chart, showing examples and explaining to them the value the chart brings. Customers may have their own unique requirements of what they want to see on the report. The customers could also have specific reporting requirements such as timeframes and frequency of reporting. After performing these planning activities, understanding the problems, and determining the customer's requirements, the project manager has adequately prepared for the use of the Pareto chart on the project.

Before you can create the Pareto chart, you must formulate a plan. In the following "Planning Questions" section, we provide some initial thoughts to help you start thinking about how you can utilize the tool on your project. Ask yourself the following questions.

Planning Questions

1 *When would you create or develop this tool?*

During the execution phase when project problems are being identified and possibly affecting the project

2 *Who is going to use this tool, both from an input and output status?*

Project manager, team members, clients or customers, upper management, risk manager, quality manager, purchasing manager

3 *Why are you going to use this tool?*

To understand where to focus the efforts of the team to resolve the biggest problems of the project, using the least amount of effort (80/20 rule)

4 *How are you going to use this tool?*

Analyze the project problems, chart the problems for communicating and visibility, and work with project team members and customers to resolve the most common problems

5 *How will you distribute the information?*

Chart format, presentation such as PowerPoint, e-mail, document control system, document format such as Microsoft Word

6 *When will you distribute the information?*

As project problems are identified and the chart is created, the project manager communicates and distributes the information.

7 *What decisions can or should you make from this tool?*

Decide the order of conditions to resolve, generally working on most prevalent condition, decide what level of effort to resolve the conditions at

8 *What information does this tool provide for your project?*

Rank the project's most prevalent conditions, categories of the conditions, and determine what problems to resolve

9 *What historical and legal information do you need to store?*

Historical versions of chart within presentations or reports, lessons learned information

10 *What will be the staffing requirements (role type) to run and maintain these tools?*

Project manager, team member, risk manager, quality manager, purchasing manager

Reporting using the Pareto chart

In most projects, the project manager is responsible for creating a Pareto chart, but other team members have taken on the responsibility occasionally. For example, the test manager is perfect for taking on the task of creating the Pareto chart because of their access to valuable test issues that can be charted for the project. The Pareto chart is an internal tool focused more on controlling how the project executes than delivering particular project status. Some other examples of how projects use a Pareto chart include:

- Safety violations charts (Quality/Human Resources)
- Project issue charts
- Bug defects in testing, by bug categories charts (Time)
- Cost estimating over-run charts

Every week the project manager reports the project's Pareto chart to the customers. The chart indicates the project problems and based on that information, the project manager assigns tasks to the team members to work on to resolve. The Pareto chart is an important aspect of project monitoring and controlling, and therefore should be included as part of the standard projects reporting cycle. The project manager uses a spreadsheet tool and the graphing capabilities of the spreadsheet to create and graph the Pareto chart. The Pareto chart is stored as part of the document control system for long-term archiving and is accessible by any interested stakeholder on the project.

CROSS-REF   See Chapter 21 to learn more about how to use this Pareto chart.

Introducing the Periodic Report

The purpose of *periodic reports* is to communicate project information on a regular periodic basis to upper management, customers, and anyone interested in the project. Creating periodic reports establishes a rhythm for the project and a cadence that is critical to the project's communications. Periodic reporting is common on all projects and only differs in the type of reports the customers want and what reports the project manager provides. The weekly status report is a common periodic report for most projects. The budget spreadsheet also falls into the category of common reports. There are a handful of reports that every project manager is aware of. They are common periodic reports and are required every reporting cycle.

Project managers own establishing communication rhythms for their projects, and the basis of those rhythms are the reports and information sent with the periodic reports. As noted, project status reports are just one of the many different reports included in the realm of periodic reports. Other common periodic reports include project schedules, issues lists, risk lists, and various resource reports.

NOTE   The Project Management Institute's knowledge area for this tool is the Communications Management area. This tool can be associated with all other knowledge areas.

ON the CD-ROM We have included a sample of this periodic report in the Communicating Reporting folder. Use this as a guide to create your own version of this tool.

TOOL VALUE Provide ongoing communications to project customers or upper management on a regularly scheduled basis. Establish a cadence of reporting that customers can come to expect and rely on when making project level decisions.

Periodic reports offer a number of benefits to customers, upper management, and team members on the project. It makes sense that project customers and upper management would benefit the most from periodic reports because of the wealth of information delivered in the reports and updated status they receive. On a weekly basis, the project normally makes progress and then reflects that progress in the latest periodic reports. The customers can make project-level decisions or course corrections based on the updated information.

Project managers can benefit from being involved and gathering the latest project information from their team members. Having this information enables the project manager to take ownership of the information that the team members are providing, and in doing so, they are getting a deeper level of understanding of the project. This allows the project manager to be closer to the project issues and quicker to resolve potential problems that may arise.

Table 11.1 shows a list of typical project periodic reports. There are hundreds of examples used on projects today, and this is a small sampling to generate ideas as to what is possible on your projects.

TABLE 11.1

Example of Periodic Reports

Type of Report	Delivery Timeframe
Foreman Report	Daily
To-Do List	Daily
Project Trouble Report	Daily/Weekly
Project Status Report	Weekly
Risk Management	Weekly
All Hands Report	Bi-Weekly or Monthly
Customer Report	Weekly/Monthly
Payroll Report	Monthly
Quarterly Project Report	Quarterly
Annual Project Review	Yearly

When determining what reports to include as periodic reports, the project manager must ensure that customers and upper management are part of that decision-making process. Many times companies have a standard list of reports that they encourage project managers to report with as part of their standard weekly reporting cycle. However, project managers and customers may also have reports that they deem important and want reported as well. Your project customers can have different reporting requirements that are specific to that project only that they will want to see in the list of periodic reports so project managers must be sure to work with them and obtain those requirements from them.

On most projects, distribution of standard project reports (periodic reports) are on a weekly basis and are significant for most project customers, but if the project is in trouble or has serious issues, the project manager moves to reporting daily, and the periodic reports still continue but are not as important as the pressing issues of each day. Depending on how long the issues continue, or if there are other major problems, the project manager will sometimes put the periodic reports on hold until the problems are resolved. This rarely happens.

In some projects, the periodic reports actually fall on a monthly basis. This scenario is applicable to only a small number of reports. A monthly actuals report for example, is a perfect candidate for reporting once a month. The reason is that actuals calculate monthly, and, therefore, weekly reporting data that does not change would not make sense. Showing three weeks of actuals data and no updates is less impressive than one monthly report with the most current data.

High-level management reports, staffing reports, time and cost reports, change request summary reports, monthly newsletters, and the project's WBS are examples of other monthly periodic reports. Another example would be the WBS report, It is likely to change over the month because some team members have left the project, and new members have come onto the project, therefore changing the actual work accomplished or not accomplished as well as the changing of skills on the project.

Some of the challenges of periodic reporting are the workload behind developing the reports and the team's ability to pull the information together in a timely manner. Communicating effectively with your customers may require producing a number of reports to ensure that you have all the information they need to make project decisions, change directions, solve issues and help guide the project to completion. Often, any additional reporting is extra work that the team members must complete over and above their regular activities. The challenging component of getting team members to work on items over and above their current workload can be difficult for the project manager. Project managers may need to work directly with team members to stress the importance of a task; or, in some cases, reduce other tasks they are working on to ensure that they have the time to work on these additional reports.

Planning to use periodic reports

In planning and preparing to use periodic reports, the project manager must first determine which reports the company requires on every project, and which reports are in their own toolbox that they produce for every project they manage. In planning for this list of reports, the project manager should have the list of periodic reports for the project, and after establishing the necessary reports the project manager works directly with the project customers or stakeholders to determine exactly their reporting needs and timeframes. In doing this, it establishes a rhythm and cadence for project reporting and allows the project manager to plan accordingly to produce those reports. Every project is different and every stakeholder is different, so discussing the various reports they want to see, and how they want to see them as part of their reporting cycle, is important and should help in ensuring the customers are getting the reports they need. Once these planning and preparing activities are completed, and the project manager has the list of periodic reports required by the customers, he/she has adequately prepared for the use of the periodic reports on the project.

Before you can create a periodic report, you must formulate a plan. In the following Planning Questions" section, we provide some initial thoughts to help you start thinking about how you can utilize the tool on your project. Ask yourself the following questions.

Planning Questions

1 *When would you create and develop periodic reports?*

Throughout the life of the project and as the project progresses, there will be different areas and aspects of the project that require ongoing communication; status, budget, schedule, staffing, and resources.

2 *Who is going to use this tool, both from an input and output status?*

Everyone involved in the project will have some involvement with periodic reports and the project information they each communicate. The press has a need and a requirement for periodic reports, and project managers and customers should determine their needs for project information as well.

3 *Why are you going to use this tool?*

To continually update and distribute project information on a regular basis to ensure customers and upper management are receiving regular project communications

4 *How are you going to use this tool?*

To gather project information from team members or appropriate parties, develop the specific report type, distribute project information to stakeholders of the projects, and in some cases receive feedback from information sent, such as project costs reports

5 *How will you distribute the information?*

E-mail, newsletter, document control system, presentations, document formats, spreadsheet formats, graphical formats. There are unlimited types of formats to send project information.

6 *When will you distribute the information?*

The timeframes for periodic reports are set by the company, the customer, or the project manager, depending on the information that needs reporting.

7 *What decisions can you or should you make from this tool?*
Unlimited project level decisions can be made from receiving project information on a periodic basis, such as cost and schedule decisions

8 *What information does this tool provide for your project?*
The information provided is based on the reports requested by clients or customers, and depends on the information sent in the reports

9 *What historical and legal information do you need to store?*
Previous versions of the various periodic reports are determined by the project manager as to whether long-term storage is warranted, lessons learned information

10 *What will be the staffing requirements (role type) to run and maintain these tools?*
There are no specific roles or staff called out, because depending on the project, anyone can use to generate a regular periodic report

Reporting using periodic reports

The project manager is responsible for ensuring the ongoing communications of the project's activities. To do so, the project manager relies heavily on periodic reports that he/she and the team members generate for the project. Depending on the type of report requested, it may not be in the best interest of the project manager to generate the report, so he/she may delegate to someone more appropriate and closer to the information.

Certain reports are contained in the periodic reports that project managers are responsible for reporting each week. The list of reports is going to be specific to the needs of the project and created during the planning stage of the project. Periodic reports use a variety of formats for creation, including word processing, spreadsheets, and presentation tools. These reports are stored as part of the document control system for long-term archiving and are accessible by any interested stakeholders on the project.

 See Chapter 21 to learn more about how to use a periodic report.

Introducing the Press Release

The purpose of a press release is to communicate project information worthy enough to warrant press exposure. A press release (news release or press statement) is a written or a recorded communications tool directed at members of the news media for announcing project information. The project manager has many different methods of getting press releases to the media. Typically, the project manager or the owner's representative mails, faxes, or e-mails some pertinent information regarding the project to newspapers, magazines, radio stations, and television stations.

If desired, the project manager or the owner can hire a commercial press-release distribution service to distribute the news releases. If project activities are going to impact the public in any way the project manager or a representative of the project needs to alert the press and provide the details of those activities. Sometimes news releases announce news conferences. The opening of a new bridge is a good example because it informs the public the bridge is complete and ready for use. The news conference includes more detail that the public may need. News conferences require much more preparation than a press release

A press release is different from a news article. A news article is a compilation of facts and opinions developed by journalists and published in the media, whereas the aim of a press release is to encourage journalists to develop articles on the subject.

NOTE   The Project Management Institute's knowledge area for this tool is the Communications Management area. This tool can be associated with all other knowledge areas.

ON the CD-ROM   We have included a sample of this press release tool in the Communicating Reporting folder. Use this as a guide to the first step in creating your own personal version of this tool. Your company or project may have specific requirements that will enhance this communication tool further; however, we believe this is a great starting point for the creation of this tool for your project.

TOOL VALUE   A press release is an inexpensive and timely way to inform the public about a project. The project management has total control of the subject matter released to the news media.

Because someone on the project staff writes a press release, it generally has a bias toward the objectives of the project. The use of press releases is common on large projects with high visibility. The aim is to attract favorable media attention for the project.

CAUTION   Although most projects can benefit from using a press release, it can also bring a level of exposure that may be harmful to the project if not managed correctly.

Depending upon the visibility of the project, the project manager must make the decision as to how much or how little information they are going to release to the media. The content of the material released is critical and all levels of responsible management should approve the release before sending it outside of the company.

TIP   It is a best practice to train the team members to refer a person from the press to contact the project manager or the owner's representative concerning any information about the project.

Planning to use a press release

The owner (customer) or the owner's representative is usually the driving force behind a press release. Most project managers would rather continue the progress being made on the project than take the time to prepare for a press release. However, if there is a request for a press release, the project manager must be involved. He /she is the one person who knows and understands the most about the project. The project manager is responsible for all released information about the project to any outside party, and if not responsible because there is a press release specialist on the team, the project manager still has a say in the released material. In planning and preparing to use a press release, the project manager should first review the section in the project management plan that pertains to the process of dealing with the media. This establishes the method to create the press release. The next step is to assess what project information to release and what information not to release. Because dealing with the media is not easy and requires a special skill, the project manager should hire a company that provides that service, and then work with the communications manager to train and provide the support for the press release specialist in order for them to be able to present an accurate press release. Then the project manager must review, modify, and approve the press release material for submission to the media. After performing these steps, the project manager has adequately prepared for the use of the press release on their project.

Before you can create a press release tool, you must formulate a plan. In the following "Planning Questions" section, we have provided some initial thoughts to help you start thinking about how you can utilize the tool on your project. Ask yourself the following questions.

Planning Questions

1 When would you create, develop, or write this tool?
During the initiation process to make an announcement on the project and periodically during the planning, execution, or construction phases, and at ribbon cutting or end of project

2 Who is going to use this tool, both from an input and output status?
Communication manager, project manager, customer or client, legal, and press.

3 Why are you going to use this tool?
To announce information about the project, keep public informed as an advisory and safety tool/ announcement

4 How are you going to use this tool?
Write press releases and send to media outlets, presentations, and interviews

5 How will you distribute the information?
Document format, TV/ radio announcement, newspaper, newsletter, personal interviews, project office control room

6 When will you distribute the information?
Major project events such as the beginning and completion, problems on the project that are public impacting, major catastrophes

7 What decisions can or should you make from this tool?
Decide to notify the press or not, decide what information goes into the release, style of release

continued

continued

8 *What information does this tool provide for your project?*
Supply information to project team members, public feedback, general official feedback or comments

9 *What historical and legal information do you need to store?*
Previous versions of press releases, lessons learned information, press detail information, names, and addresses

10 *What will the staffing requirements be (role type) to run and maintain these tools?*
Communication manager, project manager, legal team, clients or customers, owners

Reporting using a press release

The communication manager works alongside the project manager, upper management, legal, customers, and other staff to generate the project information for press releases. All parties must approve every press release generated for the project before sending it out for a wider release. Projects that require press releases are usually large and often have individuals involved that deal solely with the press and the high-exposure communications requirements for the project. The following sidebar is an example of a press release by an engineering firm for a project in San Francisco.

CROSS-REF See Chapter 19 to learn more about how to use a press release.

Introducing the Project Newsletter

The purpose of the *project newsletter* is to provide a high-level project status and other information about the project in a light and fun format for customers, upper management, and project team members. The project manager can use the format to distribute project information using "fun" colors and graphics, and he/she can distribute the newsletter in a more relaxed manner. Project newsletters have high visibility and describe the current activities for the people that work on the project. Most of the larger projects use project newsletters to communicate project information. Newsletters are usually distributed monthly to their audiences.

Most project managers enjoy using project newsletters on their projects because they can deliver project information in an enjoyable and lighthearted way. Customers appreciate getting information in this form and manner as it often breaks the monotony of the weekly status report. Even the most strict project manager can soften the news when presenting it in a project newsletter format. However, some information, such as certain personal team member information or detailed budget information may not be appropriate to send using this type of format. We recommend you chose wisely what you add into your project newsletter.

CH2M HILL and the City and County of San Francisco Launch Solar Energy Web Mapping Portal

By: Brad Jones
Source: CH2M HILL

SAN FRANCISCO, 20 June 2007 — CH2M HILL Enterprise Management Solutions (EMS), together with the City and County of San Francisco's Department of the Environment, today launched the first solar mapping Web portal of its kind. Officially introduced today during a press conference at San Francisco City Hall, the portal estimates the solar energy potential for commercial and residential structures in San Francisco.

Present at today's press conference were San Francisco Mayor Gavin Newsom, CH2M HILL EMS Senior Vice President Mike Underwood, and San Francisco Department of the Environment Director Jared Blumenfeld.

The portal, available at www.sf.solarmap.org, allows building owners to visualize the potential environmental benefits and monetary savings that would result from installing solar energy panels on their property.

Leveraging Google Maps as a visualization platform, users enter an address to see a map view of that location. With a simple click, users are then provided with:

■ The estimated amount of solar photovoltaic (PV) energy that could be installed on the roof;

■ The estimated amount of solar PV energy that could be generated at that site;

■ Potential electricity cost reduction resulting from the solar PV installation;

■ Potential carbon dioxide/greenhouse gas (CO_2) reduction as a result of installing a solar PV system.

NOTE The Project Management Institute's knowledge area for this tool is the Communications Management area. This tool can be associated with all other knowledge areas.

ON the CD-ROM We have included a sample of this project newsletter tool in the Communicating Reporting folder. Use this as a guide to create your own version of this tool.

TOOL VALUE A fun and light-hearted method of delivering project information. Although, in most cases the project newsletter contains the same content as a project status report, the method of communicating the information and the format and style in delivering the message are different.

In general, project managers and team member do not have the time to jazz up or add graphics or colors to their project communications; they just send the information out as fast as they can and do not worry about the colors or the formats of the data. A project newsletter changes all that as it allows the project manager to add colors and jazzed-up graphics. Most team members will be actively engaged in the project newsletter process. Some customers receive it and offer praise for the good work the team is doing, while others will reuse this information and forward the information to their superiors for exposure to the project, and possible intervention or support when necessary. Often, customers send project newsletters to executive staff that are not normally part of the project reporting cycle, or have anything to do with the project.

Figure 11.3 shows a typical project newsletter for a construction project. Note the graphics and easy-to-read format and layout.

For some reason, most small projects do not utilize project newsletters. The reason could be due to the size of the project, or that people may think project newsletters are not valuable. They also may think they know everything that is occurring on the project because it is a small project. In fact, by not utilizing project newsletters, the project teams are preventing themselves from communicating as effectively as possible to their customers. They are ignoring the importance of adding "Fun" to the project reporting that is often needed. In all probability, the main reason a small project does not create and distribute a monthly project newsletter is the fact that team member(s) do not have the time to create and maintain them for the project.

Projects today use hundreds of different formats and types of project newsletters and each one caters to the specific needs of the project. Most project newsletters should have the same basic project information, such as current happenings, help wanted, time lines, contact information, a biographical write up on a team member, and other applicable information. Project newsletters should contain high-level project information only, and rarely should they contain the specific details of the project.

There are few disadvantages of using project newsletters on projects. Some consider the extra work to create the project newsletter to be a disadvantage. However, creating monthly newsletters and the time involved is limited after establishing the first one for the project. Sometimes, customers may want to be involved in the project newsletter process, which can be time consuming to the project manager who is coordinating the newsletter information. Generally, having a customer engaged in the project newsletter process is a positive experience.

Planning to use a project newsletter

In planning and preparing to use a project newsletter, the project manager must first determine if there is a company standard format, style, or template required for use on projects. Knowing this information helps the project manager determine the most important aspect of the newsletter, such as content and format, and provides a starting point for the information that the project manager needs to collect on an ongoing basis. Then the project manager can work with the customers to determine their project newsletter requirements. The project manager will also track the reporting requirements of the customer. Customers may have their own requirements for project newsletters, such as who should receive it. The customer might want to put some of the information in the project newsletter into their company's newsletter to obtain exposure across the company. This could involve making modifications to the project newsletter that the project manager is propos-ing. Another important aspect of planning to use project newsletters is to communicate the cus-tomer's timeframe for newsletter reporting. Understanding the customers' project newsletter requirements in the project's planning phase allows the project manager to set the work activities for the team members as well as establishing a communication cadence with their customers. After preparing and understanding the format, the content, timeframe, and special requirements from the customer, the project manager has adequately prepared for using this tool on their project.

FIGURE 11.3

An example of a project newsletter.

APPLE ROAD CONSTRUCTION PROJECT
MONTHLY NEWSLETTER

Volume 1 • Issue 5 • June 2008

What's Happening?

As of July 10th. 2007 the project is currently on track and progressing towards, the August 10th finish date. There are no major issues or concerns, the project is on track and almost complete.

Highway Updates Related to Apple Road

- **ADA COUNTY**
  Interstate 84 Eagle westbound off-ramp rebuilding
  Construction started March 29 on a project to improve and widen the I–84 westbound off-ramp at Eagle Road. Improvements include a new off-ramp lane that will lengthen the ramp 1,600 feet.

- **Locust Grove Overpass construction**
  Work started in December 2006 on a new overpass that will connect Locust Grove and offer an extended route over Interstate 84 between Eagle Road and Meridian Road. Currently, Locust Grove Road south of Interstate 84 ends near the interstate.

Help Wanted!
- **Clean Up Crew wanted for open day clean-up**
  Jones Construction is hiring 10–15 clean-up workers for open day of Apple Road. If interested please contact Jones Construction @ 123-555-1212.

Links:
- Gov Cal Highway Standards
- Highway Safety Reports– 2006 – 2007

Key Contacts:
John Smith – Project Manager
Mary Jones, Communications and Media Contact
Jones Construction – Owners

To Unsubscribe:
If you do not wish to receive further updates on the project contact Mary Jones.

Project Timeline

NEXT MILESTONE/DELIVERABLE	DATE
Project Finish	08/10/2008

Before you can create a project newsletter, you must formulate a plan. In the following "Planning Questions" section, we provide some initial thoughts to help you start thinking about how to utilize the tool on your project. Ask yourself the following questions.

Planning Questions

1 When would you create or develop this tool?

Periodically during life of project, based on an agreed timeframe by the customer, often established by the standards of the customer

2 Who is going to use this tool, both from an input and output status?

Everyone on the project including the press (large projects) uses the contents of a project newsletter

3 Why are you going to use this tool?

To communicate project information such as new resources, milestones dates, happenings on the project in a light-hearted or fun way

4 How are you going to use this tool?

Develop and capture project information from project stakeholders and then compile into a project newsletters for distribution

5 How will you distribute the information?

Document format, document control system, presentation format, e-mail, project bulletin board

6 When will you distribute the information?

The normal timeframe for most projects is monthly, some go bi-weekly, and some are set at a longer duration.

7 What decisions can or should you make from this tool?

Limited project decisions should be made from a project newsletter. The information should be at such as high level that making decisions from a project newsletter is not recommended.

8 What information does this tool provide for your project?

Major project-related information, such as budget, timeframes, costs, resources, scope, and current happenings on the project. Information outside of project, but may impact your project.

9 What historical and legal information do you need to store?

Previous versions of the project newsletters, lessons learned, backup appropriate materials

10 What will the staffing requirements (role type) be to run and maintain these tools?

Communication manager, project manager, team members, clerk

Reporting using a project newsletter

The project manager has the ultimate responsibility for creating and distributing the project newsletter. If the project is large enough and has an administrative team in place, then a member (communications manager) of that team may be responsible for the creation of the project newsletter. The project manager can then work with that team member to ensure that he understands the contents and is comfortable with the information in the newsletter before sending it to the customers.

The project manager will report using the project newsletter on a monthly basis, not weekly, because they are more of a presentation-type report and focus on promoting the highlights and current happenings of the project at the monthly level, compared to containing the minute details of a status report. The project newsletter uses a document format for creation. It is stored as part of the document control system for long-term archiving and is accessible by any interested stakeholder on the project.

 See Chapter 21 to learn more about how to use a project newsletter.

Introducing the Spider Chart

The purpose of the *spider chart* tool is to present graphically the comparisons of a variety of information. Most team members use it to evaluate multiple alternatives based on multiple criteria. A spider chart, also known as a radar chart or star chart, is a two-dimensional chart of three or more quantitative variables represented on axes that start from the center of the chart. The relative position and angle of the axes varies and depends on the amount of data comparison. The chart looks like a spider web, hence the name spider chart.

NOTE The Project Management Institute's knowledge area for the spider chart tool is the Communications Management area. This tool can be associated with the following knowledge areas: Time, Cost, Quality, Human Resources, and Risk.

ON the CD-ROM We have included a sample of a Spider Chart tool in the Communicating Reporting folder. Use this as a guide to create your own version of this tool.

TOOL VALUE A spider chart is used to compare performance of different entities on a same set of axes.

Figure 11.4 shows a simple spider chart for the hours worked for five months (M) by Mr. Brown. **Note:** Months 1 through 3 are part time, and months 4 and 5 are full time. You could display several workers and identify quickly who worked the most and who worked the least. To keep the example simple, this spider chart only has one alternative. The spider chart is useful when you have relatively few alternatives (3-6) that you want to compare based on a few different criteria (4-8). If you have more data to compare, a different tool may be more useful.

FIGURE 11.4

An example of a spider radar chart.

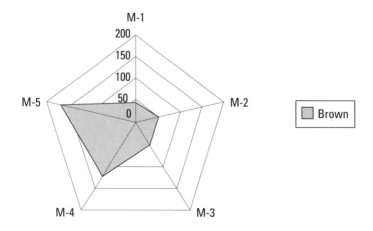

A spider chart is a great communication tool because it is visually compelling and easy to set up. It is also a quick and effective method of communicating project data to your customers. Projects have several different aspects where generating a spider chart is valuable, such as:

- Comparison reports
- Hours worked for team members
- Vendor comparison
- Cost and budget reports

The charts are quick and easy to create and provide a lot of information. The project manager communicates the project comparison data to the stakeholders of the project by using a spider chart. The chart compares project data, and the results of those comparisons assist with making project-level decisions. When utilizing spider charts on projects, the chance for exposing more information and potentially reducing issues are greater.

The spider chart is a graphical way to compare certain types of information on the project. The chart helps evaluate alternatives for the project depending on the data charted. A spider chart defines performance data and identifies strengths and weaknesses in that data. By using a spider chart, you no longer have to place data sets side by side to compare them. You can see variances or deviations in multiple types of information right in the chart. You can develop the chart by using a spreadsheet tool that has charting capabilities.

A spider chart is most useful when you need to see patterns in your data. It has multiple axes along which the data is plotted. On a spider chart, a point close to the center on any axis indicates a low value, and a point near the edge is a high value. In most cases, you place high marks near the outside due to the nature of what is measured. In other scenarios, you may want points near the center, or low values.

Planning to use a spider chart

In planning and preparing to use a spider chart, the project manager must first determine if solving the problem by using the spider chart format will be of benefit to the person or group receiving it. The data must meet the criteria of comparing different entities on a same set of axes. Most team members use this type of chart to evaluate multiple alternatives based on multiple criteria. When understanding these factors, the project manager should work to understand the criteria that he or she would set up to create the spider chart. The project manager will analyze the chart and then work with the customers so that they understand what the chart is communicating about the variables. After preparing these steps, the project manager has adequately prepared for the use of the spider chart tool on the project.

Before you can create a spider chart tool, you must formulate a plan. In the following "Planning Questions" section, we have provided some initial thoughts to help you start thinking about how you can utilize the tool on your project. Ask yourself the following questions.

Planning Questions

1 When would you create, develop, or write this tool?
On-demand throughout the life of the project

2 Who is going to use this tool, both from an input and output status?
Upper management, owners, clients or customers, project manager, team members, subcontractors, or specific skill areas

3 Why are you going to use this tool?
To compare project variables in a chart or radar format

4 How are you going to use this tool?
Report performance data, strengths and weakness reporting, detail analysis on data, project performance reporting, multiple variance reporting

5 How will you distribute the information?
E-mail, presentations, document format such as Microsoft Word, document control system

6 When will you distribute the information?
After completion and on-demand

continued

continued

7 *What decisions can or should you make from this tool?*

Comparisons of project data, value judgment (setting value data points). Determine limits or bounds, quality ratings.

8 *What information does this tool provide for your project?*

Comparisons information with varying categories on project

9 *What historical and legal information do you need to store?*

Older versions of chart within a document or presentation, lessons learned information

10 *What will be the staffing requirements (role type) to run and maintain these tools?*

Everyone involved in executing and controlling the project is involved in the development or adding value or information to the project spider chart.

Reporting using a spider chart

The project manager is most likely responsible for creating the spider chart for the project. If the project is large enough to have an administrative team, then a member of that team may be responsible, but in most cases, it falls to the project manager. The chart is a little hard to read and understand initially, but after you use it regularly, these charts become a regular in every project manager's toolbox.

Figure 11.5 shows a more complex example of a spider chart. In this example, two additional team members have been added to the previous example (see Figure 11.4), Jones and Smith, to create a more realistic chart. The idea is to compare the amount of work each team member worked each month. As you can see, Mr. Brown and Mrs. Smith work approximately the same amount of time each month, roughly half time (there may be a reason why both of them worked more in month 5). The chart shows Mr. Jones worked full time each month except the fourth month, in which he hardly worked at all.

Figure 11.6 shows an example of another spider chart. In this example, one of the unique aspects of this chart is the low temperature readings of Ice Land Springs. The display of this location is the small dashed circle on the chart. The data for this location is unique because of how little the variance in temperature is between summer and winter, especially when you compare it to the other two locations.

Notice the temperatures for Alice Springs. When you study the chart, you will see that Alice Springs is hot in January and cool in July. This data is opposite from the temperatures in the other two locations. This difference represents the northern and southern hemispheres. It appears Palm Springs and Alice Springs have the same temperatures but during opposite times of the year.

FIGURE 11.5

FIGURE 11.5

A more complex example of a spider radar chart.

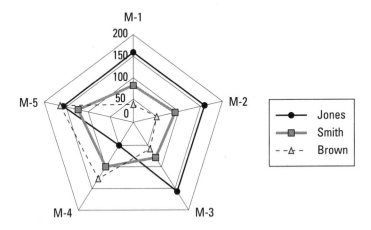

FIGURE 11.6

An example of a spider report.

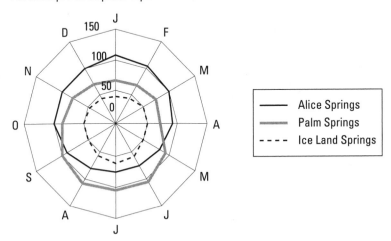

The spider report contains project-specific data that is constantly changing, so reporting it weekly or at least monthly is important. The spider chart is stored as part of the project's standard documentation and is always available to the project stakeholders and team members.

CROSS-REF See Chapter 21 to learn more about how to use a spider chart.

Introducing the Stoplight Report

The purpose of the *stoplight report* is to communicate simple project status information in a colored graphical format. Project schedules, mostly Gantt charts, use colored graphical balls of red, yellow, and green (stoplight colors) on each activity row on the project schedule to represent the status (schedule, cost, or both) of that activity. Most automated project scheduling tools have the ability to generate stoplight reports. These reports can become a common communication tool, without adding much cost or work to the project. The criteria for setting the parameters for each colored ball are often part of the project management office's (PMO) responsibilities and change slightly depending on the tolerance levels of the individual project manager. A risk tolerance level could mean how many days a project manager would let a task become late before switching the color of the stoplight (ball) from green to yellow or yellow to red. Alternatively, how much over budget can a task be before the project manager changes the color of the budget stop light (ball) from green to yellow? Both examples represent the risk tolerance level of the project manager and each example requires setting the limits before using the stoplight report. Some project managers are more tolerant than others are so the stoplight report's risk tolerance levels will vary from project manager to project manager.

Project managers who choose to utilize a stoplight report are being proactive in their project communications and are using a tool that requires little or no cost to share more information about their project with their customers. Because most project scheduling tools already have this existing functionality, the costs associated with creating the tool would equate to a small amount of time and effort to set up the criteria within the tool and make the stoplight report available. Once the report is set up, there is no additional cost to utilize it. The project manager communicates the stoplight report in the same manner as they would communicate a project schedule or a Gantt chart, with the only difference being that each activity has an associated colored ball on each row of the project schedule. Customers enjoy having the stoplight report because the colored balls allow them the ability to see the status of the project at a single glance, by individual task or activity. If the project manager chooses to roll up the activity, then the customers will be able to determine the status of the project, rolled up at the summary level.

NOTE The Project Management Institute's knowledge area for this tool is the Communications Management area. This tool can be associated with the following knowledge areas: Time, Cost.

ON the CD-ROM We have included a sample of this Stoplight Report in the Communication Reporting folder on the CD-Rom. Use this as a guide to help you create your own version of this tool.

TOOL VALUE The value of the Stoplight report is to communicate the status of the project at a glance using a series of colored balls (stoplights — red, yellow, and green) to show the severity level of each activity on the report.

There are many benefits to using stoplight reports on projects. One benefit is the low cost of implementing them. Because the tool is already available via the software-scheduling program (you must have an existing scheduling tool) the project manager only has to create the criteria for each colored ball, and then the project manager displays the columns in the tool with those colored balls. The stoplight report is complete and ready for reporting purposes. As the project manager updates the tasks on the project, the colored balls change colors appropriately based on the criteria established when creating the colors.

Another benefit of using the stoplight report is the ability to determine immediately the overall status of the project by reviewing the most dominating color on the project schedule. Therefore, if the project schedule is showing the majority of project activities as red (critical), the project for all purposes is in a red condition. Meaning it is either behind schedule or over budget, or both. There could be multiple conditions that generate a red status; budget and cost are just two big factors. If the majority of the project activities are yellow, the project is in a yellow condition, meaning it is in a potential problem state; green and the project is in a green state, meaning it is proceeding according to the plan. No other tool provides a high-level status of the project by showing colored stoplights (balls) for each activity.

Figure 11.7 shows a typical stoplight report created by using a scheduling tool. In this example, Task 7 has a dark (red) indicator associated with the *cost* column. This represents the costs associated to the task are significantly over budget. On Task 11, a red (dark) indicator in the *schedule* column indicates the activity is running behind schedule. In both cases, project manager, customer, or upper management can grasp the status of each activity at a glance and determine the status of the project.

FIGURE 11.7

An example of a stoplight report on a typical project.

	Task Name	Duration	Start	Finish	Schedule	Cost
1	⊟ **INITIAL PLANNING**	**24d**	**8/1/05**	**9/1/05**		
2	DECIDE THEME AND LAYOUT	7d	8/1/05	8/9/05	●	●
3	ARRANGE COVER PHOTO	10d	8/10/05	8/23/05	●	●
4	PLAN THE CHAPTERS	6d	8/10/05	8/17/05	●	●
5	ASSIGN CHAPTERS	11d	8/18/05	9/1/05	●	○
6	⊟ **WRITE CHAPTERS**	**38d**	**8/18/05**	**10/10/05**		
7	RESEARCH	16d	8/18/05	9/8/05	○	●
8	INTERVIEWS	15d	8/25/05	9/14/05	○	○
9	ARRANGE PHOTOGRAPHS	8d	9/15/05	9/26/05	●	●
10	WRITING	12d	9/8/05	9/23/05	●	○
11	PREPARE FOR FACT CHKRS	5d	9/19/05	9/23/05	●	●
12	ALL TO EDITOR	1d	9/26/05	9/26/05	●	●
13	CHECK SOURCES AND FACTS	7d	9/27/05	10/5/05	●	●

Project managers who set up the stoplight report for their projects will quickly discover the value of this type of reporting for themselves, the team, and their customers. Both the customer and upper management staff value having such an important communication tool available to them and being able to see exactly where the project is having issues and problems. In some cases, the customers or upper management will start managing and getting involved in the project where they are seeing the issues. Many times, their involvement is on an exception basis only. This allows them to focus their attention on the red and yellow activities and ignore the green ones that are tracking well. Exception-based management is a valuable way for executive and senior management to be involved without having to get into the details of the project.

> **TIP**   Managing by exception is fast and efficient.

When using a stoplight report on the project, in most cases two main data points are utilized. Those data points are for scheduling data and cost data. Although other data points are possibilities, most project managers tend to stick with these two major project drivers. They seem to be the most relevant and most popular for use with the stoplight report. They are also the most valuable to the project manager to assist him in managing and controlling the project. Sometimes a project manager will use a quality indicator.

There are few challenges in using a stoplight report, other than setting up and establishing the criteria for each indicator (red, yellow, green), and communicating that criteria to the customers. The customers may have their own opinion on what they want that criteria to be, so project managers should be prepared for that initial feedback and possible changes to the criteria. Adding the stoplight report to a project brings huge benefits for everyone involved, but the initial reports require communications and possible walkthroughs with the customers to ensure everyone is reading and understanding the information correctly.

Communicating with a stoplight report is easy but something that some project managers do not take advantage of on their projects. This could be because they do not see the value, or they simply do not know how to produce the criteria for the stoplight fields to create the report. Generally, it is just a simple task of the project scheduler teaching the project manager the criteria to enter for each of the stoplight indicators, and then teaching them how to create the fields in the scheduling tool to generate the report. In most cases, this is often simple and takes a limited amount of time. If the project has project schedulers associated with it, they would know how to create the criteria and the associated fields.

Planning to use a stoplight report

In planning and preparing to use a stoplight report, the project manager must first determine the performance criteria; either being the schedule or cost that is driving the customer on this project. When understanding this criterion, the project manager should work to understand the customer's risk tolerance level on each criterion and add that tolerance level to the criteria set for each colored ball in the scheduling tool. One example includes the condition that when the activity goes late by three days it displays a yellow indicator, but late by five days shows a red indicator for the schedule performance indicator. All that criteria is easily updatable, and the project manager can configure it where appropriate. The project manager during this planning cycle would then work with the customer to understand their reporting requirements for the stoplight report from both a timeframe and a delivery method perspective and plan their creation and delivery of the report accordingly. After the project manager completes these planning tasks, the project manager has adequately prepared for using the stoplight report on their projects.

Before you can create the stoplight report tool, you must formulate a plan. In the following "Planning Questions" section, we have provided some initial thoughts to help you start thinking about how you can use the stoplight report tool on your project. Ask yourself the following questions.

Planning Questions

1 *When would you create and develop the stoplight report?*
Created in the planning phase, but reported on during project execution

2 *Who is going to use this tool, both from an input and output status?*
Upper management, owners or clients, project manager, team members, subcontractors or specific skill areas, project scheduler, cost manager

3 *Why are you going to use this tool?*
To present graphically, the health of the project to clients or customers, upper management, and team members as it is a visually compelling and easily understood tool

4 *How are you going to use this tool?*
Develop the criteria for project conditioning and report out on the project activities with the red and yellow conditions to give full exposure to customers and upper management of the project issues.

5 *How will you distribute the information?*
Project server, e-mail, document control system, dashboard, project schedule report, and project cost report

6 *When will you distribute the information?*
Generally as part of the status reporting cycle

7 *What decisions can or should you make from this tool?*
Cost decisions and schedule decisions, resource decisions, dependencies. Decisions based on the condition of the activity.

8 *What information does this tool provide for your project?*
Health indicator for project focusing on cost and schedule performance indicators

continued

continued

9 *What historical and legal information do you need to store?*
Previous versions of the project stoplight report contained in a project schedule format, lessons learned information included and archived with project's status report

10 *What will be the staffing requirements (role type) to run and maintain these tools?*
Project manager, team members, project scheduler, cost manager, resource manager, subcontractor, and anyone else reporting progress on the project

Reporting using a stoplight report

On most projects, the project manager or the scheduling manager is responsible for creating the stoplight report. Because the project manager owns the development and creation of the project schedule, it makes sense that he would own the stoplight report as well. That way, if any one of the activities shows a color that is not green, the project manager will be aware of the situation and address it immediately. Sometimes, project managers are aware of particular project situations that are actually green, but are showing red and yellow status incorrectly.

When sending out the status of a project and the various colors associated to each of the activities, the stoplight report sends a loud message one way or another on the status of the project. A stoplight report full of green-colored performance indicators shows a project under control from a cost and schedule perspective. A red and yellow project shows one that could be on the edge of trouble, and the customers and upper management should review the project to determine if there are areas where they can turn around some of the conditions causing the red and yellow indicators. A project showing a stoplight report of all red indicates that there are serious project issues and upper management support is required immediately. Project managers should be cautious when using and reporting the stoplight report in an all-red status condition because of the high visibility that it will bring to the project. Project managers must understand before sending out the report the message they are trying to portray about their project and what reactions or support are they seeking. Sometimes, a project manager can communicate one message, but the stoplight report can show another.

Each week's stoplight report is part of regular project reporting. The stoplight report contains project-specific data that is constantly changing, so reporting it weekly is important. The stoplight report is stored as part of the document control system for long-term archiving and is accessible by any interested stakeholder on the project.

CROSS-REF See Chapter 21 to learn more about how to create and use a stoplight report.

Summary

In summary, the tools described in this chapter assist project managers in communicating the status of the project to team members, customers, and upper management. These communication tools help to get the right project information to the customers and upper management staff in order to ensure they have the information they need to make project decision, or change directions when applicable on the project. These reports include reports on cost, schedule, and resource information and custom reports.

As you review this chapter, the one tool that can make the biggest impact on your project is the dashboard report. The dashboard report is an advanced technique in project communication and an important tool in presenting up-to-date project status to your customers. If there is no company standard dashboard available, then project managers should consider creating a manual dashboard so customers are at least manually receiving the summarized project information on a recurring basis.

The chapter includes tools such as periodic reports, press release, project newsletter, spider chart, and the popular stoplight report to name a few. There are a number of great communication tools available and ready for immediate use on your projects. The great value of these tools is the ongoing basis they provide the stakeholders with the latest and greatest information about the project. With tools like these, a project manager has more than enough combination of ways to be successful in communicating on their projects.

Chapter 12

Defining Communication Tools to Manage Project Risk

Project managers manage risks by regularly monitoring them to ensure that they do not negatively impact the project. Project risks can include project going over budget, resources leaving, missing key milestone dates, and other external dependencies. Risks events may or may not occur; therefore, project managers work more aggressively on risk management to prevent as many risks as possible from occurring and impacting the project.

Project managers must be diligent in the tracking and managing of project risks to prevent them from becoming issues. In many cases, a project manager uses a risk assessment form to track and monitor project risks, because this form allows for sharing of project risk information with the customers, team members, and upper management. Project managers must track risks on at least a weekly basis and communicate all risk items to the team members. Many project managers review project risk events at the weekly status meetings to ensure everyone is onboard and understands the risk events. It is important they are actively pursuing their closure at all times.

In this chapter, we explore project communication tools in the Project Risk Management knowledge area. Managing project risk is an important aspect of project management.

Introducing the Decision Tree Diagram

The purpose of the *decision tree diagram* is to identify the best decision for the project from several options created in the diagramming process. A decision tree diagram is a graphical representation of the various outcomes possible to help solve a project problem. This tool is also a decision support tool that uses graphics to depict a tree tipped on its side with branches from left to right. A decision tree diagram branch represents a node of uncertain outcomes and each branch represents a decision. The decision tree diagram illustrates key interactions among decisions and associated chance events to the point that the decision maker understands them. This tool can help increase communication among team members and customers and can help explain how the project team members came to the conclusions they did to solve the project problems.

The communication aspect of using a decision tree diagram is beneficial to project managers. First, they can use it to explain how they made a decision, describe the decision made, describe the possible outcomes, and then show the customers the diagram of complete decision-making process. When laying out the decision process to customers and upper management, they may challenge some of the decisions made, which is beneficial because they can see exactly how the team came up with the final decision and the path they took to get there.

NOTE   The Project Management Institute's knowledge area for this tool is the Risk Management area. The tool cannot be associated with any of the other knowledge areas.

ON the CD-ROM   We have included a sample of a decision tree diagram in the Risk folder. Use this as a guide to create your own personal version of this tool.

TOOL VALUE   The decision tree diagram provides project team members with several options to choose from when making project decisions on uncertainty or unknowns.

There are two main benefits to using a decision tree diagram. The first is that everyone involved on the project can see why the team chose to take a particular path to resolve a project problem using the easy to read graphical format. The second benefit is the process that the decision tree diagram takes the project team members through when creating the diagram and the different options and solutions the team members come up with when trying to solve the problem. The process of creating a decision tree diagram is generally a good team bonding exercise that usually has long-lasting benefits for the project team members as well as the project.

Figure 12.1 is a decision tree diagram. In this example, the problem the team is trying to solve is to either rent or buy an office building. After researching real estate market values, it is determined that renting an office building would be $250,230 for a high-rise building and $60,300 if the building were located in a business park. If the decision was to buy a building, the price is $245,000 for a condominium complex and $80,000 for a building located in an industrial area. It was determined that to rent a high rise, the probability would be 40 percent, and if renting in a business park, it would be 60 percent. If the decision was to buy, it was determined the probability to buy into a condominium complex was 45 percent, and 55 percent to go into an industrial area.

FIGURE 12.1

This figure represents a Decision Tree Diagram tool diagram.

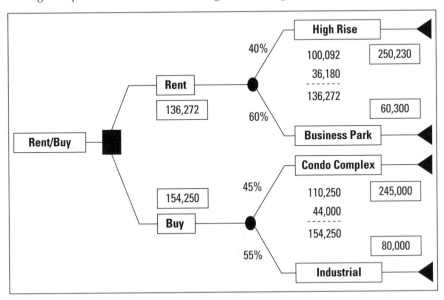

The business problem: The Jones Smith company needs to purchase or rent office space for additional staff members. The Decision Tree Diagram tool will support the answer for the decision to this business problem. In the Decision Tree Diagram tool above, the top branch (Rent) shows the value of the two options identified. When multiplying the cost of each branch times (x) the probability percentage for that branch it creates an expected value for each branch. Note, the value for the High Rise is $250,230 and the probability is 40 percent, multiplying the value times (x) probability gives an answer of $100,092 for that branch. In the business park branch you will see the calculations have changed; in this case, the value is $36,180 and the probability is 60 percent, and when adding the two branches, the expected monetary value for the branch is $136,272. Using the same calculations for the Buy branch, the expected monetary value is $154,250. The company can now determine if the difference between renting and buying ($17,978) is justified.

As you can see in this example, the team had a difficult project situation to resolve and came up with various decision paths to follow based on the results of each decision point. As an example, in the Buy decision point the two different branches of that were both Buy — Condo Complex, and Buy — Industrial. The team had to choose the better option of the two choices. When creating those decisions paths and associated decision points, the project team worked out the calculations and other factors to help them make a decision on which one to choose, and from these decision points there could be additional branches created on the decision tree diagram. In the end, the decision tree diagram enables the project team members to make educated decisions based on the different paths created, and as a team, select the correct path to follow for the project.

NOTE The decision tree diagram is not the only tool you can use to make project level decisions. Many other factors are involved in these decisions, and although the tool is great for helping in that process, it is not the sole contributor.

Industries such as software, aerospace, construction, and insurance are using decision tree diagrams. Here are some examples of how project managers can utilize the tool:

- Insurance: Actuaries use decision tree diagrams to calculate and segment customer patterns.

- Aerospace: Solving the probable cause of an airplane crash by identifying all parts on the airplane can be accomplished with a yes-or-no tree developed to determine the path or branch of the tree that most likely caused the accident.

- Real estate: Real estate planners use the buy/rent decision tree, shown in Figure 12.1, on a regular basis when determining future directions for their clients.

- Buying or leasing a fleet of company trucks.

NOTE Decision tree diagrams are versatile and easy to create. The decision tree process requires full team involvement to ensure that you are getting the best possible choices to the project's problem.

Planning to use a decision tree diagram

In planning and preparing to use a decision tree diagram, the project manager must first determine the project problems they need to resolve with the tool. The project could have a number of problems to resolve and using a decision tree is important; however, the project manager must determine if it is as important as the current work of the project. Creating a decision tree diagram requires the project manager to pull the project team members off their current tasks to help build this diagram. Before pulling the team away, the project manager should ensure that the problem is big enough to warrant the team's time spent away from their project activities. A project manager must consider those impacts first and determine if there are any that affect the project's schedule and budget. Therefore, in the planning process, it is important to ensure you are using the decision tree diagram for the right-size problem, and although this problem solving process works on smaller problems as well, the cost of pulling the project team members from their current activities to work on small problems may not be cost effective.

The next step in the planning process is to determine how you will bring together the project team members for the decision-making process and then setting up the logistics of the event. This can be a major event where team members come to a central location from around the world and work together to resolve the project problem, or it could be a smaller event where the project team members have a series of meetings to resolve the problem. After performing these two planning items, the project manager should be able to use a decision tree diagram on their project.

Before you can create a decisions tree diagram, you must formulate a plan. In the following "Planning Questions" section, we provide some initial thoughts to help you start thinking about how you can use the tool on your project. Ask yourself the following questions.

Planning Questions

1 When would you create, develop this tool?

At project initiation and planning phases when the team members have a major decision to make and it requires people coming together to resolve

2 Who is going to use this tool, both from an input and output status?

Upper management, owners, executives, project manager, team members, subcontractors, or specific skill areas

3 Why are you going to use this tool?

To assist in making major decisions on the project, to provide options to clients and customers on project decisions

4 How are you going to use this tool?

Bring the team members together to resolve a project problem and document each path of that problem on the decision tree diagram

5 How will you distribute the information?

Microsoft Word, plotter (graphics), document control system, e-mail, Visio, PowerPoint, a variety of different tools to use to create this tool

6 When will you distribute the information?

After the project team members have resolved major project decisions and the team, or the customers, need answers to the problems

7 What decisions can or should you make from this tool?

Cost decisions, schedule decisions, decisions based on various options, risk decisions

8 What information does the tool provide for your project?

A decision tree with enough information to make informative project level decisions

9 What historical and legal information do you need to store?

Results of the decision tree diagramming process, lessons learned information, and older decision tree diagrams

10 What will be the staffing requirements (role type) to run and maintain these tools?

Project manager, team member, risk manager, cost manager, resource manager

Reporting using a decision tree diagram

The project manager is responsible for creating the project's decision tree diagram. In most cases, the project manager drives major project decisions and, therefore, should be responsible for the decision-making process and hold the responsibility of creating this tool. Others on the team can certainly be involved, but it is important that the project manager drive all project problems to a resolution and in the end a creation of the diagram.

The project manager can generate many different reports with the decision tree diagram. Some of these reports include:

- Skill level decision report
- Buy or make decisions report
- Purchase or rent decision report
- Resource hiring decision report
- Vendor decision report

The project manager does not use the decision tree diagram to report status each week because it does not have project status information. The project manager reports the decision tree diagram one time only when the project problem has been resolved and there is a final decision to be made. If or there are changes to any of the chart data, the project manager reports this new information to everyone involved in the project. The decision tree diagram uses a document format for creation that is stored as part of the document control system for long-term archiving and is accessible by any interested stakeholder on the project.

CROSS-REF   See Chapter 17 to learn more about how to use and create a decision tree diagram.

Introducing the Expected Monetary Value Tool

The purpose of the expected monetary value (EMV) tool is to calculate a contingency value for a risk event. The EMV uses a mathematical technique to derive an average outcome of an uncertain event that could happen in the future. EMV is a mathematical formula that can help make comparisons between ranges of those uncertain outcomes.

If you could somehow determine precisely what would happen because of choosing each option in a decision, making project decisions would be quick and easy. You could simply calculate the value of each contending option and select the one with the highest value. On real projects, decisions are not quite this simple. However, the process of decision making still requires choosing the most valuable option — most valuable being, in this case, the option that has the highest EMV. Using modeling and model simulation for cost and schedule analysis instead of EMV method during risk analysis is better because there can be a bias in the EMV application. In addition, EMV uses decision tree analysis (see Decision Tree Diagram tool above in this chapter and Chapter 17).

The Project Management Institute's knowledge area for this tool is the Risk Management area. There is no other secondary area for this tool.

We have included a sample of an expected monetary value tool in the Risk folder. Use this as a guide to the first step in creating your own personal version of this tool.

The value of the expected monetary value is that it supports decision analysis and can calculate a contingency amount for a risk event or for the entire project.

The calculations from the expected monetary value provide for great cost communication on a project. They state exactly what contingency funds to allocate for the project. This can be done by the total project or each individual risk event. This allows the customers and upper management to be fully aware of both the calculations and needed contingency amounts for the project. The project manager works with the customers to ensure the additional funds are in the project for contingency purposes whenever possible. When doing so, and after a risk event occurs, the project manager could end up absorbing the impact of the event because he/she had planned for it and had the money available in case the risk event occurred.

Table 12.1 below, which has rain as the risk event, tracks the contingency value required based on the varying degrees of rain possible. This includes no rain to a downpour. For each risk event outcome, you must estimate a value and determine a probability of that outcome. In the example of rain, the probability can be determined by helping factors such as time of year, weather reports, and historical information. The calculated value of the rain event determines what actions would need to occur if it does rain. For example, does work stop when the rain occurs and therefore the value could be the worker's wages and the damage done to the concrete? Or, does the project have to purchase tarps and covers to prevent the rain from hitting the concrete (tarps for example cost money and would be included in the expense of the risk event)? All of these expenses would calculate the value of the risk event in the Expected Monetary Value formula.

Table 12.1 is an example of an Expected Monetary Value calculation based on the five rain events occurring and the impact it would have, should they occur. In this example, you can see that if a Gully Washer occurs, the project expected monetary value equals 45.

TABLE 12.1

Example of Expected Monetary Value (Rain on New Patio)

Outcome	Probability		Value if Risk Occurs		Expected Monetary Value
Drizzle	15%	X	0	=	0
Avg. Rain	10%	X	50	=	5
Hard Rain	5%	X	200	=	10
Gully Washer	3%	X	1500	=	45
No Rain	67%	X	0	=	0
Total	100%		Expected Value	=	60

Calculating the total expected monetary value provides the project with the monies required for emergency purposes (contingency) and using the EMV formula is a more of an accepted method to the customers or upper management then guessing and not knowing what to apply to the funding to allow for contingency.

The project manager benefits from calculating the expected monetary value of the project because it is providing a justification and reasoning behind the additional dollars requested to cover any unexpected risk events. When obtaining those additional dollars, it provides more of a buffer to the project manager when managing not only the budget, but the various risk events as well.

Every risk event has an expected value. The risk event's value is created by using the expected monetary value formula and is the estimated amount it takes to replace or fix the project should the risk event occur. You calculate the expected monetary value by multiplying the probability of occurrence by the value of the risk outcome. Every risk event has varying degrees of outcomes.

Generally, estimating the value of an outcome of a risk event is better than estimating the probability. Normally, probabilities are educated guesses at best, where the value is what it would cost to replace the item if the outcome of the event actually occurred.

The project management profession uses the following formula for calculating risk event's expected value. It is a standard formula used for many years in the industry.

Table 12.2 is an example of the Expected Monetary Value formula. This is the standard formula for multiple outcomes of a particular risk event.

TABLE 12.2

Expected Monetary Value Formula

Outcome	Event		Value if Risk Occurs		Expected Monetary Value
Outcome Event 1	Probability 1	X	Value 1	=	**Expected Monetary Value 1**
Outcome Event 2	Probability 2	X	Value 2	=	**Expected Monetary Value 2**
Outcome Event 3	Probability 3	X	Value 3	=	**Expected Monetary Value 3**
Outcome Event 4	Probability 4	X	Value 4	=	**Expected Monetary Value 4**
	100%				Total Expected Value

The biggest reason why any project manager would use the expected monetary value tool is so they can determine the value of the risk event(s) should it occur and to understand how much money they need in their budget to cover these events. Projects must have a contingency fund allocated to cover known risk events. To get an accurate estimate of how much money the project needs to cover the risk events, one of the most accurate methods is using the expected monetary value tool.

Planning to use an expected monetary value tool

In planning and preparing to use an expected monetary value tool (EVM), the project manager has a number of steps to accomplish before doing this analysis. The project manager must first perform a risk analysis identifying the risk events on the project. This includes the creation of a risk matrix (see the risk matrix tool in this chapter and Chapter 17) and then identifying the highest-priority risk events to apply the EMV analysis. Next, the project manager determines how low (how far down the list) on the risk priority list to calculate the expected monetary value. For every risk event, there is a trade-off on the value of knowing the EMV and the cost to acquire it. After the cut-off point is established, the team can start calculating the EMV by using the calculation shown in the previous section, for each risk event selected. This task is not difficult; it just takes time and effort from the project team members. How much time and effort is up to the project manager to decide. After all the risk events EMVs are calculated, the project manager sums them. This total is a percentage of the contingency for the risk on the project. Now the project manager must determine what percentage of risk remains and estimate that value. Combining the two values, the calculated EMV and estimated EMV, you have the total expected monetary value (contingency) for the project, and the project manager can set aside or request those funds in the budget.

One way to estimate the remaining EMV is to consider using the Pareto principal, the 80/20 rule. Assume the portion of the risk you identified is 20 percent of the risks and is 80 percent of the contingency value. That means 20/80 × the calculated value is the remaining contingency. Total the two contingencies and you have the total expected monetary value for the project.

CROSS-REF See the Pareto chart tool in Chapters 11 and 21 for more information.

Before you can create the expected monetary value tool, you must formulate a plan. In the following "Planning Questions" section, we provide some initial thoughts to help you start thinking about how you can use the tool on your project. Ask yourself the following questions.

Planning Questions

1 *When would you develop this tool?*
After generating risk events for a project, and as new risk events occur

2 *Who is going to use this tool, both from an input and output status?*
Project manager, team members, subcontractors or specific skill areas, risk manager, cost manager

3 *Why are you going to use this tool?*
To calculate the value associated to risk events and ensure that contingency funds are in the budget

continued

continued

4 *How are you going to use is tool?*

Calculate a risk cost for each risk event, summarize to generate a total contingency budget, estimate the contingency of project

5 *How will you distribute the information?*

Spreadsheet format such as Microsoft Excel, document control system, e-mail, presentation

6 *When will you distribute the information?*

After creating the contingency amount required for the risk events

7 *What decisions can or should you make from this tool?*

Cost decisions, risk value decisions, purchase or In-house development decisions (difference between purchasing off the shelf, and developing in-house)

8 *What information does the tool provide for your project?*

Costs associated with risk events and the expected value required for risk events

9 *What historical and legal information do you need to store?*

Lessons learned, decisions made based on tool, actual costs of risk events versus planned costs

10 *What will be the staffing requirements (role type) to run and maintain these tools?*

Project manager, team members, risk manager, cost manager

Reporting using an expected monetary value tool

The project manager is responsible for working with their team members to calculate the risk events expected monetary values. In working alongside the project team members, customers and other interested parties, the groups develop the values and create the contingency needs of the project. The project manager approaches the customers and upper management to request additional monies for the project. If the project is large enough and has an administrative team, then a member of that team may be responsible to work alongside the project manager to help coordinate the process and calculate the expected monetary values for the risk events. The expected monetary value is an excellent communication tool because it helps identify all the project risks and their associated values or costs to remediate.

Table 12.3 shows another popular example of calculating the expected monetary value by rolling a die. Each time you roll a die, you have one-sixth (.1666) of a chance of getting any one of the six numbers on the die. This is the probability; the number that you roll is the value. Therefore, multiplying the probability and the value you rolled, gives the expected value. Remember, the expected value of each outcome provides no real value for this calculation. The total of all possible values is your expected monetary value. In this case, every time you roll a die, you are averaging a 3.5

expected value. That means if you were playing a board game, every time you rolled the die you would average 3.5 squares forward; in other words, for every two rolls you would average seven squares forward.

TABLE 12.3

Example of Expected Monetary Value (Rolling Dice)

Outcome	Event		Value if Risk Occurs		Expected Monetary Value
Roll Die 1	.1666	X	1	=	**.1667**
Roll Die 2	.1666	X	2	=	**.3332**
Roll Die 3	.1666	X	3	=	**.4998**
Roll Die 4	.1666	X	4	=	**.6664**
Roll Die 5	.1666	X	5	=	**.8333**
Roll Die 6	.1666	X	6	=	**1.0**
	100%				**3.5**

Each week, the project manager and team members should calculate the remaining expected monetary values on the project's risk events as part of the regular management of the project. The project manager should include any reports from that process in the project's reporting. The easiest format for calculating the expected monetary value is a spreadsheet tool; however, the information is also captured and re-reported in various formats, such as PowerPoint presentations or on internal Web sites. The expected monetary value spreadsheets or presentations are stored as part of the document control system for long-term archiving and is accessible by any interested stakeholder on the project.

CROSS-REF See Chapter 17 to learn more about this Expected Monetary Value tool.

Introducing the Issues List

The purpose of the *issues list* is to track project issues to be able to stay on top of those issues, preventing them from negatively affecting the project. The issues list is a central repository for storing project issues. These issues are stored, managed, and controlled by the project manager throughout the life of the project. Project managers should monitor issues and risk events equally, although the focus should be a bit higher on issues because issues have already occurred and could be impacting the progress of the project. In some cases, issues need immediate resolutions; other times they can wait until the team has a chance to react to them appropriately. Issues can quickly become risk events if they are not controlled, and they can easily start to have a negative impact on the project. Some issues may be large and important enough where they end up becoming activities that require adding into the project schedule. This is a common process where an issue actually becomes something the team has to resolve quickly and work items go on hold to focus on the issue. The project manager adds the issue to the work activities so the team members address and work it immediately. When this occurs and the issue becomes part of the project, the project manager should generate a new work package in the WBS. (See work package in Chapters 10 and 20.)

One of the most widely used communication tools on a project is the issues list. A project manager communicates the issues list at least once a week ensuring that he/she continues to drive resolution on each item. All projects have issues, some small, some large, and project managers must be continually reviewing and working the issue list to increase their chances of a successful project. Without the issues list, the project manager can have project problems that he or she has no idea what they are about and in all likelihood they are putting the project as a whole in risk. Active issue management is one of the top responsibilities and priorities of a project manager and something that can really increase the chance of success.

NOTE   The Project Management Institute's knowledge area for this tool is the Risk Management area. The secondary area for this tool is Quality.

ON the CD-ROM   We have included a sample of this Issue List tool and the various tables listed in this chapter in the Risk folder. Use this as a guide to help you create your own version of this tool.

TOOL VALUE   A central repository for storing and communicating the project's issues while continuing to track issues in a consistent format.

The project issues list is beneficial to any project because it brings exposure to customers, team members, and upper management of all project issues. One benefit that the project manager receives by using an issue list is a greater depth of knowledge of the project issues and the possibility of understanding how they can help resolve each of them. There is a big difference when a project manager is engaged in issue tracking and resolution, compared to just being the ones to add issues to a list and not having the depth or the knowledge to understand them. Project managers can handle issue management either way, but benefit more when more fully engaged and actively working. The project manager must ensure that all issues statuses goes through them for updating or closing on the issue list. By having the issues status flow through the project manager, it provides him/her with a better understanding of each issue they are working. One of the project manager's main responsibilities is to track, monitor, and control project issues and therefore it makes sense that they manage and update the issue list at all times.

Table 12.4 is an example of a typical project issue list. In this example, the columns represent a basic set of fields required to actively report and resolve the issues. It is important that the project manager add as much detail as possible in the description field, so that anyone reading the issue understands it and the impact it has on a project. This example is one of thousands available on the Internet, or as part of your company's PMO processes and procedures.

Issue or a Risk?

Is it an issue or a risk? One important distinction that project managers need to be aware of, and sometimes gets confused with, is the difference between issues and risk events. The difference between a project issue and a risk event is that issues have occurred and have been identified, and a risk event is a possibility that something may happen in the future. The main attribute of a risk event is that it is in the future (a risk event cannot be in the past), whereas issues are able to be both in the past, in the present, and in the future. An easy way to look at this is issues are more in the present, whereas risk events are always in the future.

TABLE 12.4

Example of a Project Issues List

Issue Title	Type	Status	Description	Resolution
Project Funding	Budget	Open	Project is going to lose funding crossing fiscal years	Obtain dollars in second half of year
Resource Loss	Staff	Open	Project needs to hire two additional resources ASAP	Hire staff before fiscal year end

Another benefit of the issue list is the ability for the project manager to communicate the consolidated list of issues to the customers and upper management. If issues are stored in multiple places, such as people's e-mails, or in different spreadsheets, the project manager may have major problems trying to determine where they all are, and who is working or trying to resolve them. This could be a real mess for the project manager and it may end up projecting a low level of confidence to the customers or upper management that the project manager does not really have a good handle on their projects. The benefits of having a consolidated list is that it not only forces a project manager to engage in every project issue and know that there is a central place where they are all stored, but it ensures the project manager is keeping the information updated and current. An old or outdated issues list is not an effective way to manage a project.

> **TIP** A best practice is to communicate issues to customers, stakeholders, and team members on a weekly basis.

Table 12.5 is an example of an issue list. This example provides more details on each project issue. Project managers should use Table 12.4 as an example of the minimum set of fields to capture for an issue list, but use table 12.5 if they want an extensive version or something a bit more complex.

TABLE 12.5

Example of a Comprehensive Issues List

ID	Issue	Section	Impact	Probability	Owner Name	Date Open	Assigned to	Date Closed	Status	Res.
1	Platform problems	Construction	High	2	Bob Smith	12/4/ 2008	Joe Jones		Open	TBD
2	Resource left paving team	Staffing	Medium	4	May Douglas	10/14/ 2008	Fred Brown	11/28/ 2008	Closed	Hired new resource

When storing project issues, project managers should ensure that their issues are stored in a central location such as a document tracking system, or a spreadsheet tool, or any other application as long as there is an agreement that there is only one single location. This location should be available at all times and allow anyone to access it when they need to. Team members may be working on the issues, or customers may want to see what is happening on one issue or another, so establishing a central location, open and available, will satisfy everyone's requirements as well as open the communications on the project.

If the project's issues are truly problematic, the project manager may need to manage the issues on a daily basis, compared to weekly until the issue is resolved. Each issue varies, and the project manager must decide which issue to focus the majority of their time on resolving. At a minimum, project managers should review the issue list daily and determine which issues are the most project impacting and focus their attention on the highest impacting project issues first. If the issue is large enough, the project manager could turn the focus of the team to resolving the issue first, before continuing onto performing the project's activities. If the project manager does not address the project issues at least on a weekly basis, it can cause serious repercussions to the project.

Many methods are available to track issues. Several software packages are on the market that can manage and maintain lists. There are automated tools such as word processors or spreadsheets, and there is the old-fashioned manual method of pen and paper, which, although rarely used, is still a viable option. On a large project, it makes the most sense for projects to invest in a software package so that multiple teams can access the issues simultaneously, and the project manager can control and monitor the issues across a large group of team members. Large software packages often contain a knowledge base that includes information on each issue and stores relevant information to allow further details to be associated to each issue. Other times, project managers use document control systems as a place to create and store project issues. In either case, the actual software packages or the document control systems (an automated tool) are one of the best methods for tracking and controlling project issues.

Planning to use an issues list

In planning and preparing to use an issue list, the project manager must first determine what the structure of the list will look like and how many fields they will use. Some project managers use the same structure repeatedly regardless of the size or complexity of the project where other project managers use what the company directs them to use, or they select old issue lists from past projects. After determining what the issue list will look like, the project manager works with the customers and ensures the list is suitable for their purposes as well. The customer may suggest additional fields that the project manager has never considered; therefore, adding a checkpoint with the customer during this planning phase and confirming what they want to see on the issue list makes good sense. During these conversations with your customer on what the issue list should look like, the project manager should address the importance of how the customers would like to see the list and how often. Because the issue list is such an important communication tool that everyone relies on, it is important to ensure the delivery timeframes are set ahead of the project starting. After performing these planning activities, the project manager has adequately prepared to use the issue list tool on their project.

Before you can create the issue list tool, you must formulate a plan. In the following "Planning Questions" section, we provide some initial thoughts to help you start thinking about how you can use the issue list tool on your project. Ask yourself the following questions.

Planning Questions

1 **When would you create or develop the issue list?**
During the planning phase of the project, before any work activities begin and there have not been any Issues identified

2 **Who is going to use this tool, both from an input and output status?**
Project manager, team member, customer or clients, executives, upper management, subcontractor

3 **Why are you going to use this tool?**
Track and control project issues, store old issues for lessons learned

4 **How are you going to use this tool?**
Add issues to the list; work with team members to resolve issues, close issues when complete, report issues during reporting cycle

5 **How will you distribute the information?**
Document format such as Microsoft Word, e-mail, document control system, formal project presentations

6 **When will you distribute the information?**
Distribute issue lists during the regular reporting cycle

continued

---

continued

7 *What decisions can or should you make from this tool?*

Issues to resolve/work on, issues to remove, who is accountable for the issue, what issues require management or client support

8 *What information does this tool provide for your project?*

List of issues, who is responsible, timeframes for closure, impacts to project

9 *What historical and legal information do you need to store?*

Closed issues, lesson learned information, issue resolution documentation

10 *What will be the staffing requirements (role type) to run and maintain these tools?*

Project manager, team member, risk manager, document control administrator

Reporting using an issues list

The project manager is responsible for creating the Issues List on the project. Most often, the project manager is actively monitoring and controlling the issue list on their project so they should own the reporting of the issue list as well.

Communicating the issue list is one of the more important responsibilities for a project manager. The project manager should be working their project issues closely enough so that he/she can present them to the customers if required. A project manager who can only speak to issues at a high level will quickly find that they really have no idea what is happening on their project and therefore are not managing it as effectively as they should be. One best practice in communicating issues lists is to review the list during the weekly project status meeting. This provides the project team full exposure to the issue list and can give the project manager the updated information on how the issues are being resolved. As the project manager reviews the issues with the team members, he or she should ensure that the issues are being resolved as quickly as possible. Sometimes issues remain open for most of the project, which is okay, as long as everyone agrees the issue should remain open. The project manager must ensure there is a continual readdressing of that issue so it is not lost or forgotten. For example, a budget issue where the project is running over budget is likely to remain open for the duration of the project or until additional funding is added to the budget to cover the overage.

> **TIP** Every issue listed should have a team member as the owner. If not, the issue defaults to the project manager to own the issue until assigned to another team member.

Each week the project manager reports on the project issue list to both the project's team members and customers. The project manager uses a document or a spreadsheet to create the project's issue list. The issue list is stored as part of the document control system for long-term archiving and is accessible by any interested stakeholder on the project.

> **CROSS-REF** See Chapter 21 to learn more about how to use and create an issue list.

Introducing the Issue Management Plan

The purpose of the *issue management plan* is to document the process and procedures for managing and controlling project issues. A project issue has a distinct meaning across project management. It is an event or a project situation that requires a resolution. For example, an issue on a drug research project could include two pharmacologists disagreeing about how they should clinically test a particular drug. An issue management plan also has a distinct meaning; it provides a structured process for identifying and resolving project issues throughout the life of the project. An issue management plan is not an issue list. The issue management plan guides upper management, customers, and project team members with the directions of what to do with project issues once someone on the project raises them. The issues management plan covers issue management and escalation, tracking tools, resolution procedures, and issue closeout. Each of these areas of the issue management plan will focus on controlling and monitoring the project's issues, not identifying or resolving them. If a project team does not have an issue management plan in place or any processes to control project issues, the team can be quickly overwhelmed and not process the issue correctly. In the end, this could negatively impact the project.

Project managers should be proactive about how they communicate their issue management plan at the beginning of the project. This usually requires calling a meeting with the project team members to go over the process of managing project issues from beginning to end; including how to open issues, how to close issues, when to report issues, and what tools to use. By the end of the meeting, everyone on the team should understand how the project manager will drive issue management on the project. The project manager then works with the customers and walks them through the issue management plan as well, before any activities begin so they have the same understanding that the team members have on how the project manager will handle issue management. This plan provides customers with the foundation of how the project manager manages and controls project issues. The plan also sets expectations of the process they should follow to raise issues they discover on their own.

 The Project Management Institute's knowledge area for this tool is the Risk Management area. The secondary area for this tool is Quality.

 We have included a sample of an issue management plan in the Risk folder on the CD-Rom. Use this as a guide to create your own version of this tool.

 It provides guidelines to the project team members on the issue management and control process.

By using an issue management plan, the project manager can document and describe to those involved in the project how they are going to manage and control project issues. Without that understanding, team members and customers will have no idea how the project manager is driving the issue management process. For example, if a customer has an issue with a software application and has no idea how to raise this concern or bring exposure to the problems he is having, the customer can get frustrated and be unhappy with the project. The project manager must avoid that situation at all costs and ensure that even though there is no issue management plan or document in place, there is always an open communication between the customer and the project manager to allow either party to voice any concerns they are having on the project. Likewise, an issue management plan will have those steps documented as well, which allows customers to raise issues or concerns.

Table 12.6 is an example of an issue management plan table of contents. As you can see, this comprehensive document describes in detail the management and controlling of project issues. This document is thorough and provides clear direction to anyone involved with project-related issues.

Example of an Issue Management Plan Table of Contents

Section	Description
1	Introduction to Issue Management
2	Purpose of Issue Management Plan
3	Scope (Address issues consistently across projects)
4	Management and Escalation (How to manage, how to set issues priority, escalation procedures)
5	Issue Tracking Tools (Tools used to track issues)
6	Issue Process (Step-by-step of how to manage an issue)
7	Roles and Responsibilities (Who does what on an issue)
8	Resolution and Closeout

The issues management plan template highlights some key areas that project managers should address on their projects. The sections such as management and escalation, issues tracking tools (used for development of issues lists), and the issue process are areas that project managers must consider carefully when developing their project's issue management plan. For example one of the easiest sections of the issue management plan to complete, but which requires careful consideration, is the issue tracking tools section. The project manager completes this section with the details of what tools they want to use for tracking issues. The section contains details such as will it be a spreadsheet, will it be a more complex tool, or will it be an in-house developed tool?

NOTE   The methods used to track and control issues on a construction project are different from how they track and control a research project. However, the fact that both projects have issues means that both should utilize an issue management plan.

Another major area of the issue management plan that project managers should consider carefully is roles and responsibilities. In this section, the project manager describes the various roles in the issue process, and the responsibilities of each team member. For example, on some projects the analysts take on the responsibility of working and resolving project issues, whereas on other projects, the project manager drives resolution on all issues. Therefore, there can be big differences between how a project manager decides to handle roles and responsibilities from project to project. The project manager will update the document accordingly.

Advanced Issue Handling — Ranking Process

One challenge that project managers have in the issue management process is to understand how important the issues are on a project. Then once having the information on how important, the project manager needs to understand how much time and effort their project team should spend to find a resolution. The project manager needs to be able to prioritize and rank the issues. To help understand the importance and impact of the issue, a ranking process is required. *Ranking* is a technique for determining the importance of an issue on a project. The process of ranking includes comparing one issue against another issue, and letting the team decide what issue has a higher impact to the project. Before starting this ranking process, the project team members should establish the importance (factor) for the budget and the schedule. In order to understand this, the project manager needs to determine if the project is schedule or cost driven.

If the project is cost driven, the default value for the schedule factor, which is not the driving force of the project, is 1.

If the project is schedule driven, then the default value of the cost factor, which is not the driving force of the project, is 1

When setting these values to 1, you are establishing a base factor for the calculations, and these factors are setting the ranking criteria and the importance of either the schedule or the budget. Either the cost factor or the schedule factor will be 'one' in every calculation.

When determining the various severity levels of 1, 2, or 3, each level requires a description to understand what the value means. If your project is schedule driven, that is, it has a hard deadline to complete, to calculate the ranking level multiply the schedule impact by a factor value (set as either cost or schedule factor). With a schedule-driven project, this factor value could be 2, 3, 4, or even 5; it depends on how important the schedule is over the project's cost. For example, if the budget is three times more important than the schedule, and if you had an issue that had a medium budget impact and a medium schedule impact, the cost impact would be a value of two (medium) times three (three times more valuable than schedule) and the schedule impact would be two (medium) for the schedule value. When multiplying these two numbers together, you get an Issue rank of 12. When completing this ranking process for each issue on the project, sort from the lowest to highest based on their impact. Here is the exact calculation for creating an Issue rank (the Ranking process) as follows:

Ranking Level Value = (Budget Impact X Budget Factor) X (Schedule Impact X Schedule Factor)

The last section of the document, and the section the project manager must ensure they complete as correctly as possible, is the resolution and closeout section. This section describes such items as how the team resolved the issues, where the issues are stored long term, what approvals are required to complete an issue, and how the project manager or the systems will archive them once completed.

Table 12.7 is an example of an Issue Severity Level Ranking table. This table can guide the team to focus on working on the project's most severe issues first and then put them in order of priority.

TABLE 12.7

Example of an Issue Severity Level Ranking Table

Issue Severity Level	Description	Project Impact	Budget Impact	Schedule Impact
3	High: Immediate Resolving	Yes	High (3)	High (3)
2	Medium: Resolve before Project Launches	Maybe	Medium (2)	Medium (2)
1	Low: No Project Impact	Does not stop project	Low (1)	Low (1)

By putting issues up against one another and determining the impact on the project's scope, project team members can almost immediately identify where to focus their time and attention. If the issue ranks high enough, quite often the project team members will shift their focus to address the issue and leave the other project activities on hold until the issue is resolved. The ranking process becomes extremely valuable to the project manager when addressing project issues and determining where to focus the team member's attention to obtain the biggest impact to the project. The project manager will then know, based on the rank of each issue, where they should focus their time in controlling the project's issues and in what order.

 In cases where there is either a budget or a schedule factor, the remaining factor would be defaulted to one.

Table 12.8 is an issue ranking table. In this table the budget factor has a value of 1, and the schedule factor has a value of 3, making the schedule impacts three times more important (value) than the budget impact.

TABLE 12.8

Example of an Issue Ranking Table

Issue Description	Budget Impact (X Factor)	Schedule Impact (X Factor)	Ranking Level
Budget problems	2 X 1(Factor) = 2	1 X 3 (Factor) = 3	6
Resource leaving project	3 X 1(Factor) = 3	1 X 3 (Factor) = 3	9
Material delivery late on job site	1 X 1(Factor) = 3	3 X 3 (Factor) = 3	9
Union contract issues unresolved	2 X 1(Factor) = 2	2 X 3 (Factor) = 6	12
Scheduling issue has project 2 weeks over	3 X 1(Factor) = 3	2 X 3 (Factor) = 6	18

By using this formula you can create a ranking system where the higher the value in the ranking level the more severe the issue is on the project. The rankings range from 1 to 81 on a typical project. Once ranked, you can group the issues based on their ranking score and focus the team's efforts on resolving the issues first that are in the higher-ranked levels.

 **Budget and schedule impacts and associated ranges are project specific and determined by the project manager and team.**

 **In most cases, by group and ranking project issues, the project manager can create a Pareto chart based on this data to determine where he or she should focus the project team's resources.**

Planning to use the issue management plan

In planning and preparing to use an issue management plan, the project manager must first determine if there are any internal company processes in place for issue management, and if so, then determine how they will utilize those processes on their project. In some cases, these processes are generic enough and the company may have a template available that can serve as a good starting point for the project manager to use on their project. Next, the project manager should plan to discuss with the team the issue management process and determine if there are any special processes or considerations the team has for issue resolution that they want incorporated into the document. If there are processes the team members want added, the project manager will add the relevant information into the issue management plan directly. The final step in the planning process is working directly with the customers to determine if they have any processes or special requests they would like to see in the issue management process. The customer's ideas could include any reporting on issue resolution, approvals or sign-offs, or how they will be involved in the issue process. Knowing whether the customers have any special requests or not will provide the project manager the advantage of understanding how to engage with their customers when communicating issue resolutions. A project manager who has customers that are engaged and active in issue management will tend to be able to process and resolve issues faster. Other customers who are not as engaged can tend to let issues stay around longer and therefore there could be more work for the project manager. After performing these planning steps, the project manager has adequately prepared for the use of an issue management plan on their project.

Before you can create the issue management plan, you must formulate a plan. In the following "Planning Questions" section, we have provided some initial thoughts to help you start thinking about how you can use the issue management plan on a project. Ask yourself the following questions.

Planning Questions

1 *When would you create or write an issue management plan?*

During the planning phase of the project while developing the other documents, utilize for managing and controlling the project.

2 *Who is going to use this tool, both from an input and output perspective?*

Project manager, team members, subcontractors, customers

3 *Why are you going to use this tool?*

To document the process for managing and controlling project issues, provide guidance and direction to team members and customers on that process.

4 *How are you going to use it?*

To guide the project team members, and in some cases customers, through the process and procedures to open and close project issues, utilize issues tools

5 *How will you distribute the information?*

Document format such as Microsoft Word, document control system, e-mail, presentations

6 *When will you distribute the information?*

At the time the document is complete

7 *What decisions can you make from this tool?*

Decisions on the management and escalation of Issues process or procedures, decisions on roles and responsibilities, on issue management process, scope decisions, tool decisions

8 *What information does this tool provide for your project?*

Issue management and escalation, issue tracking tools, issue resolution and closeout procedures, issues process, issue roles and responsibilities, issue deliverables

9 *What historical and legal information do you need to store?*

Lessons learned Information such as what process and procedures worked or did not work, historical versions of the document itself

10 *What will be the staffing requirements (role type) to run and maintain these tools?*

Project manager, team member

Reporting using an issue management plan

On most projects, the project manager is responsible for creating the issues management plan. This is because issues are so important that the project manager has to be responsible for this activity or it could put the project in jeopardy. There are rarely any projects where the project manager does not take on this responsibility, but in those rare cases, at a minimum, the project manager assigns issue management to someone who has a similar level of authority to make project decisions and drive resolutions. There are some cases in which the project team leads each own respective issues lists in their own areas, and track their own resolution, but usually, those individual project area risks are promoted to the overall project issue list and brought to the attention of the project manager and the project customers.

The communicating and reporting of an issue management plan are limited mainly to team members and sometimes project managers. This communication is from a management and control perspective only, not necessarily a communication of status for providing updates of particular issues. Project managers will not have to provide ongoing communications regarding the issue management plan because after the customers and team members see the document originally, they are usually fine with the document and then move on. It is only when special processing or special considerations are required that the team members or customers engage more in the reviewing of the issue management plan.

The issue management plan uses a document format for creation and is stored as part of the document control system for long-term archiving and is accessible by any interested stakeholder on the project.

 See Chapter 16 to learn more about how to use and create an issue management plan.

Introducing the Risk Assessment Form

The purpose of the *risk assessment form* is to manage, assess, and evaluate potential project risks. Project risks are events that could occur on the project and potentially benefit or jeopardize the project. For example, the project does not have enough money in the budget to see it through to completion. If that risk event occurs, the project would have to stop until money becomes available or continues with management support to go over budget. The risk assessment form provides a view of the potential project risks, if the risks do transpire; it also documents and provides risk mitigation strategies to help reduce any negative impacts on the project. Risk assessment forms differ from project to project and company to company, but each is valuable to the project team in helping them manage and control their various project risk events. The ability to communicate the potential problems and impacts that the risk event could have on the project on one form, and to use that same form to work with the customers and upper management to resolve the issue, is invaluable. Each group can see exactly how the project is impacted and determine what they can do to mitigate or reduce the risk completely.

The communicating of the risk assessment form is something that will become a regular part of project reporting. The project manager has the responsibility each week to communicate the risk assessment information to the customers and management to bring full exposure of the project's risks.

NOTE   The Project Management Institute's knowledge area for this tool is the Risk Management area. There is no other secondary area for this tool.

ON the CD-ROM   We have included a sample of a risk assessment form in the Risk folder. Use this as a guide to create your own version of the tool.

TOOL VALUE   Assess and evaluate the potential impacts of risk events occurring on the project. The assessment and mitigation information stored on the risk assessment form provides a process to follow if the risk events occur. There are limited numbers of software tools that store risk mitigation information as well as a risk assessment form.

The most important benefit to using a risk assessment form is the actual listing of the project risk events in a central repository for anyone to access. The storing of the risks into one location allows anyone involved in the project to find the risk, evaluate the impacts, and in some cases actually work to resolve or mitigate the risk. When project managers store risks scattered on spreadsheets, Web sites, or in project status reports, it is more difficult to mitigate or eliminate the risks on the project simply because they do not know where to find them all. Other benefits of using a risk assessment form are the tracking of risk probability, budget impacts, scope impacts, or schedule impacts the risk event could have on the project. Tracking this kind of information for each risk event puts each of them into perspective as to how important they are to the project, or in other cases, how they are of little importance and therefore could drop off. The project manager and team members complete this assessment each week throughout the project.

Figure 12.2 is an example of a risk assessment form with one project risk event. In this example, the risk event describes a potential problem with an outside vendor on a construction project. The vendor is potentially going to deliver steel to the site one week late. The probability of that risk event occurring is low — about 10 percent — and the budget impact, if it does occur, is estimated to be $50,000. A contingency of $5,000 is set aside to cover the costs of the additional activities that must occur if the steel is late. This leaves a shortfall of $45,000 between the impact of the steel delivered one week late and the $5,000 set aside to offset this event. If this event were actually to occur, the project manager would set aside $50,000 from the contingency fund, to ensure there is no loss to the project. With the proper calculations of the contingency monies, there will be enough to cover this event. Further information about this example includes the schedule running one week late (if the event occurs) and the end date of the project pushing out one week later than planned. The project manager has established in the contract with the vendor that there is a penalty of $11,000 a day for delivering the steel late, which is payable immediately and noted on the risk assessment form. The penalty money should be paid right away to offset the loss from the project budget.

FIGURE 12.2

This figure represents a risk assessment form.

Identification		Probability (%)			Impacts					Mitigation	
							EMV				
WBS#	Description of Risk	Low	Medium	High	Budget Impact	(Contingency)	Schedule Impact	Scope Impact	Penalty		Possible Solutions
		10	50	100							
1234A	Vendor delivers structural steel, 1 week late	X			50,000	5,000	1 week delay	N/A	Yes, 1 1,000 per day		Mitigate Avoid Transfer Accept Retention

The process of completing the risk assessment form is simple but without considering the real impacts to the project, completing the form would not be that valuable. When completing the form, the project manager must have a good handle on the details around the risk events and the various impacts the risk events can cause if they do occur. For example, determining the probability and the budget impact of a risk event is rarely something project managers tackle on their own; this is something that team members jointly decide with the project manager. Both groups determine whether the event will occur at all, the chances of that occurring, as well as how much of the budget it would take to keep the project on track after the event occurs. This same process continues for each column in the risk assessment form where the team members and the project manager jointly evaluate the risk events to the different areas documented on the form and describe the impacts it would have on the project. The exception to this process is completing the contingency column and the dollar amount required for covering the project if the risk event occurs. This is the contingency fund that the project manager should put aside in anticipation of the risk event occurring.

The risk assessment process is complex and challenging. Another challenge in completing the risk assessment form is the process of risk quantification. Risk quantification involves evaluating risks for possible project outcomes. It evaluates the probability of a risk and its affect on the project. The end-result of that calculation is the amount contained within the expected monetary value (EMV). This term is familiar in the project management industry, and one that is common across projects in all industries. There are many formulas in the industry today for calculating risk assessments and especially risk quantification.

CROSS-REF See Expected Monetary Value tool located above.

Here is an example of a situation where project managers would apply the expected monetary value as it relates to risk assessment and quantification.

You are pouring a concrete patio in the backyard of your house. Your goal is to make it as smooth as possible and have it slope away from the house to limit any water problems. One of the risk events that might occur is the possibility of rain after pouring the concrete, which will ruin the finish of your patio. The objective is to understand how much money to set aside in case it rains, allowing you to cover the costs of refinishing the patio.

Table 12.9 shows the possible outcomes and expected values of this project. As you can see in the table, there are only three types of outcomes associated to this situation, and each has a calculated expected outcome value associated to them.

TABLE 12.9

Example of a Possible Outcome and Outcome Value Chart

Outcome	Risk Event Probability	Risk Event Value	Expected Outcome Value
Drizzle	0	0	0
Regular Rain Showers	5	$50.00	$2.50

Outcome	Risk Event Probability	Risk Event Value	Expected Outcome Value
Downpour	1	$1,500	$15.00
No Rain	94	0	0
Expect Monetary Value Total	100%		$17.50

After identifying a risk event, the project manager should break the event down into the possible outcomes. In this example identify the types of rain (drizzle, regular rain, downpour, and no rain), and then estimate the probability of each outcome; for example, the likelihood of it occurring. The next step is to estimate the value of the outcome occurring on the project, which can be difficult because understanding the value of a particular risk event is complex. To understand the complexity of the value of a risk event, a project manager will have to consider the following factors:

- Type of project
- Resources used
- An associated billing rate
- Amount of time
- Materials used
- Quality requirements

When reviewing and considering these factors, it provides a project manager the basis of estimating the value of the outcome if it actually occurred. The next step is to use the formula as noted above; multiply the outcome probability _ the outcome estimated value to create the expected outcome value. After obtaining these values, the project manager calculates and totals individual expected outcome values to create the total expected monetary value and enters that information onto the risk assessment form in the contingency column.

NOTE Most of the time there are varying degrees of an outcome for each risk event. For example, a snowstorm will cause a delay in the project. The varying outcome for a snowstorm is the amount of snow; it may snow 1 inch and cause no delay. It may snow 1 foot, 2 feet or 3 feet, with the varying outcomes producing a varying amount of delay on the project. There is also the probability that it will not snow at all, which is also one of the outcomes.

Planning to use the risk assessment form

In planning and preparing to use a risk assessment form, the project manager must first determine if any other risk assessment forms or processes are already in place at the company, and if there are, decide how to utilize that process on their project. If there is a form or process in place, the project manager should determine how to use it, or work with someone who already understands it.

The next step in this planning process is for the project manager to consider the risk assessment processes that the project team members will go through to assess project risks. This includes team members attending weekly meetings to go over the risk events, completing extra assessment work, and finishing any other activities that can help the project manager and team members assess the impact of the risk event. This is actual time on the project that the project manager may not have allocated for the team members. The project manager will need to consider this when planning the overall project schedule and provide extra time, if possible, for risk assessment and completing of the risk assessment form. After performing these planning activities and informing team members that they will have to work on the risk assessment process as part of their regular project work, the project manager has adequately prepared for the use of the risk assessment form on their project.

Before you can create a risk assessment form, you must formulate a plan. In the following "Planning Questions" section, we provide some initial thoughts to help you start thinking about how you can use the risk assessment form on your project. Ask yourself the following questions.

Planning Questions

1 *When would you create or develop the risk assessment form?*
During the planning process, the project manager creates the risk assessment form, and then it is updated and refined throughout the project.

2 *Who is going to use this tool, both from an input and output status?*
Project manager, team member, risk manager, quality manager, and anyone on the project focused on resolving project risks

3 *Why are you going to use this tool?*
Assess and track project risks, assign risks to particular team members for resolution, determine probability and impacts of the risk impacts

4 *How are you going to use this tool?*
To guide, assess, and evaluate the impacts of project risk events. It also has contingency dollars and mitigation strategies contained for each risk event to guide the team should the risk event ever occur.

5 *How will you distribute the information?*
Spreadsheet format such as Microsoft Excel, e-mail, document control system, presentations, complete in electronic format

6 *When will you distribute the information?*
Weekly reporting of the form allows for ongoing communications of the project risks.

7 *What decisions can or should you make from this tool?*
Project decisions based on risk events, probability decisions, impact decisions, mitigation decisions, contingency decisions

8 *What information does this tool provide for your project?*

Number of project risks, budget and schedule impacts, and contingency dollars required for risk events as well as any mitigation strategies to tackle the risk events

9 *What historical and legal information do you need to store?*

Historical risk events, previous versions of the risk assessment form, lessons learned information

10 *What will be the staffing requirements (role type) to run and maintain these tools?*

Project manager, team member, risk manager

NOTE   Research has shown financial benefits depend more on the frequency and how the assessment is performed than on the formula used to quantify the risk events.

Reporting using a risk assessment form

The project manager is responsible for driving the project's risk assessment activities, which include weekly meetings with the team members to go over every risk event and apply impacts and mitigation strategies for each event directly onto the risk assessment form. This also includes closing out risk events whenever possible and mitigating any potential risks on the project.

During these risk assessment sessions, the project manager should receive enough detail to communicate the issues to their customers and upper management. Part of the risk assessment process could be to have a customer meeting in addition to the weekly status meeting, and to go over the list of risks and the various assessments that the team members have assigned to the risk events. This weekly meeting provides the customers and everyone with the full understanding of the risks, and from a customer perspective, they can get involved whenever possible to help resolve the risk issues. It is beneficial to a project if you have customers who will engage and help resolve risks and actively participate in this process. Unfortunately, customers who do not engage in this process and leave the risk management completely up to the project team to resolve are decreasing the chances of being successful on the project. Weekly risk communication is an important part of keeping customers informed and aware of all project risks.

Project managers will use a spreadsheet for creating a risk assessment form. Often, the risk assessment form is re-reported using other various formats, such as PowerPoint presentations or on internal Web sites. The project manager will store the risk assessment form in the document control system for long-term archiving which is accessible by any interested stakeholder on the project.

CROSS-REF   See Chapter 20 to learn more about how to use and create the risk assessment form.

Introducing the Risk Management Plan

The purpose of a *risk management plan* is to document the process and procedures for managing project risks. Every project has risks, and most project managers deal with the risks based on a set of processes and procedures established within the risk management plan. Without these guidelines, the project manager or team members may struggle to address risks properly. The risk management plan is an internal guide for the project manager and team that help them manage the project's risk events. This plan is a thorough and detailed document, which acts as a comprehensive guide to risk management from initiation to closeout and lessons learned. The completeness of this risk management plan provides not only the process and procedures of risk management, but also a complete end-to-end process.

The project manager and team members are not the only ones who require guidance on the risk management process; customers also need to understand what they are doing and how to process and control project risks. Customers are quite often responsible for adding project risks and should be following the same process that project manager or the team members follow in this process. This is important because of how quickly the project can go badly and in different directions if customers are following one process and everyone else is doing something different. The project manager should be watching this closely, ensuring everyone follows one standard process for managing and controlling project risks. Everyone must agree to the process and the documentation in the risk management plan.

Communicating a risk management plan is an important aspect of project communications. Project managers should ensure that they communicate the risk management plan to everyone dealing with project risks. That way, when project situations arise and team members have problems, they can turn to the risk management plan as a reference guide to walk them through the process. The risk management plan is the project manager's method of tracking, controlling, and processing risk events. Therefore, the project manager should be generous in communicating the issue management plan as widely as possible. If the project manager is distributing it, team members will be aware of the processes and procedures and will try to help resolve the issues whenever they can. On the other hand, if the project manager does not make it as available as possible, the team members and customers can be stuck understanding how to control project risks and may struggle with the process.

 The Project Management Institute's knowledge area for this tool is the Risk Management area. There is no other secondary area for this tool.

 We have included a sample of a risk management plan in the Risk folder. Use this as a guide to create your own personal version of this tool.

 To provide the processes and procedures for managing and controlling project risks.

The biggest benefit for utilizing the risk management plan is the various processes and procedures documented in the plan that guide the team members and customers through the risk management process. These processes include everything from risk analysis, risk response planning, and risk communications. The risk management plan is complex and leaves literally no risk area untouched on a project. The process itself of completing the risk management plan will help the team members ensure that they are involved and thinking about risk management at all times. Without a risk management plan, project team members can tend to ignore risk management and not be as concerned about project risks as they should be. This is risky, because when all team members are actively monitoring and tracking risks, projects tend to go much smoother and have fewer problems. When they are not, the project often goes out of control and in many cases is unrecoverable. The risk management plan helps team members become more proactive on risk management; they will look to prevent or mitigate risk events rather than avoiding them or letting them become project-impacting issues.

Table 12.10 represents a sample table of contents for a risk management plan. This risk management plan should be applicable for most projects. The plan provides guidelines and procedures for the project manager and team members to monitor and control the project risk events. There are six major sections of this template, each covering a different aspect of risk management.

TABLE 12.10

Example of a Risk Management Plan Table of Contents

Section	Description
1	Risk Identification
	Conduct Formal Risk Identification Reviews
	Conduct Informal Risk Identification Reviews
	Document the Candidate List
	Validate the Candidate Risk
2	Risk Analysis
	Perform Risk Categorization & Prioritization
	Perform Impact Analysis
	Review Risk Against Risk Tolerances
	Risk Tolerances
	Review Risk Analysis and Ranking
	Risk Tolerances
	Review Risk Analysis and Ranking
	Acceptance of Risks
3	Risk Response Planning
	Plan Mitigation Activities
	Review Risk Action Plans

continued

TABLE 12.10	*(continued)*
Section	**Description**
4	Risk Event Plan Implementation
	Monitor Symptoms Events
	Execute Action Plan(s)
5	Risk Tracking and Controlling
	Report Risk Status
	Review Changes to Risk Profiles and Action Plans
	Retire Risk
6	Risk Communications
	Periodic Status Meetings
	Report Lessons Learned on Risks
	Escalate Risks

There are six major sections of a risk management template; each section covers an aspect of risk management. These sections are:

- **Risk identification:** Risk identification is the process to which a project manager or team member will identify, document, and validate the project's risk events. In this area, the project team identifies the source of risks and the risk events that may occur on the project.

- **Risk analysis:** Performing categorization and prioritization, risk impacts, risk tolerance review, risk analysis, ranking, and finally acceptance. In this area, the project team analyzes the various risks and assigns the risks to the event matrix.

- **Risk response planning:** Planning of mitigation, contingencies, and action plans. In this area, the project team determines the best method to lower the impact of negative risk events and identifies the advantage of positive risk opportunities.

- **Risk event plan implementation:** Monitor symptoms and warnings and execute the action plans. In this area, the person responsible for each risk event should look for symptoms and warnings that pertain to their risk event and communicate those warnings to the team. The team should then analyze the warnings to determine if the risk event is actually occurring.

- **Risk tracking and controlling:** Reporting status, reviewing changes to profiles and action plans, and closing off risks. In this area, the project team reports on risk events and impacts to the project, and the team members work their various risk plans to ensure the risk events do not impact the project. In the end, when the risks are resolved they should be tracked as closed or retired. The project manager should schedule time in the course of every project status meeting to review and go over the project risk events.

- **Risk communications:** Status meetings, lessons learned, and escalation procedures. In this area, the project team reports project risks to stakeholders/customers/owners on a periodic basis. The project manager tracks lessons learned on the specific risk events and escalate risk to upper management when applicable.

In the developing of the risk management plan, it is common to use terms and definitions throughout the plan when describing how to manage and control risks. Here are some common definitions and terms in the industry.

- **Risk event:** A discrete occurrence that may affect the project for better or worse
- **Risk identification:** Determining which risk events are likely to affect the project
- **Risk quantification:** Evaluating the probability of risk event occurrence and effect
- **Risk response control:** Responding to changes in risk over the course of the project
- **Risk response development:** Defining enhancement steps for opportunities and mitigation steps for threats

One of the key sections to the risk management plan is risk strategies the project team will use on the project. The five common risk strategies are:

- **Risk acceptance:** Accepting risks on project. The project team will take on the risk to resolve. In cases where mitigation is impossible and acceptance is the only option, the project team must accept the risk and deal with it.

- **Risk avoidance:** Avoiding or eliminating the occurrence of a risk event. The project team usually identifies the cause of the risk event and works to eliminate it. It is not acceptable to avoid all risks on the project. For example, when pouring concrete to build a new patio in your backyard, you can eliminate the risk of rain ruining the surface by constructing a temporary structure with tarps over it; therefore eliminating the rain from hitting the patio, or you could schedule construction for the summertime when no rain is expected.

- **Risk transfer:** Risk transfer means to move the liabilities of the risk from one party to another for overall management of the risk. Risk transfer does not remove the probability or liability of the risk, it just transfers it; for example, in the auto insurance industry, when people sign-up for auto insurance, it transfers the liability of the risk, minus your deduction, to your insurance company.

- **Risk mitigation:** Reducing the impact or the occurrence of the risk event. Address the risk event as early as possible in the project to avoid negative impacts; for example, having a fire extinguisher at arm's length in a lab where a fire can start any time, while ensuring that all staff has training on the use of the extinguisher to avoid the fire spreading.

- **Risk retention:** When the project manager makes a decision to self-insure any losses due to a risk event occurring, he is willing to accept the loss in time and cost. In some cases, where the costs of insuring small risks would be greater than the value of the risk event occurring, risk retention is the owner retaining the value of the loss of any risk event.

Risks events can fall into multiple strategies. Project teams must look at each risk, determine the best strategies for them, and then put that risk into the selected strategies. Although it is possible for risks to be in multiple strategies, in the end, they belong in just one.

Planning to use the risk management plan

In planning and preparing to use a risk management plan, the project manager must first determine how he/she will manage their project risks, and what processes already exist that will guide them through risk management processes. After determining what the project manager can and cannot do as it pertains to risk management, the project manager has a starting point from which to start generating the risk management plan. The next step in the planning process is where the project manager makes decisions in the risk management plan itself. Because the document is so complex and detailed, the project manager should review the template to determine what areas make the most sense to use on the project. There may not be a need for some areas outlined in the template because they are not applicable to the project, or the size of the project does not warrant the amount of information. The project manager will decide what they will use in the risk management template on their projects. The only caveat to that are the standards that the company may have when it comes to what they expect to be in each risk management plan. Those requirements are necessary to be in the risk management plan as a minimum for developing the company, and therefore the project manager must ensure they compile and document in the risk management plan. This is often the case, and the project manager must be aware of that when choosing what they will use within their risk management plan for their particular project.

The next area the project manager should focus on is how the team members will utilize this tool. Specifically, how will the team members be active in the risk management process, and how can they help mitigate risks whenever possible? In doing so, this will get the team members thinking about risk management in general, and how they plan to be involved to help resolve the project's risk events.

After the project team, the project manager should turn his focus to the customer. The project manager has to plan accordingly on how he/she can engage with the customers and determine their roles in risk management. Some customers will be engaged and take risk management seriously, where others will not want to be involved and will let the project manager handle the risks as part of his/her responsibilities. These customers will tend to want to engage only when the risk becomes a project issue and they have something they can resolve, rather than getting involved early and handling the issues ahead of time. After preparing and planning these activities, the project manager has adequately prepared for the use of this tool on their project.

Before you can create the risk management plan, you must formulate a plan. In the following "Planning Questions" section, we have provided some initial thoughts to help you start thinking about how you can utilize the tool on your project. Ask yourself the following questions.

Planning Questions

1 *When would you create or write the Risk Management tool?*

This tool is created in the planning process before work begins, which allows the project team to prepare for risk events on their project.

2 *Who is going to use this tool, both from an input and output perspective?*

Upper management, owners, customers, executives, project manager, team members, subcontractors, risk managers

3 *Why are you going to use this tool?*

Document the process and procedures for managing and controlling project risks, describe the identification, analysis, response planning, and communication aspects of risk management

4 *How are you going to use it?*

Guide customers or clients and team members through the risk management processes and procedure and use as a guidebook and training tool for anyone unfamiliar with risk management

5 *How will you distribute the information?*

Document format such as Microsoft Word, document control system, e-mail, presentation

6 *When will you distribute the information?*

This tool is one that is delivered once at the time of creation and then only randomly as required. This tool contains no status so it would rarely be communicated as part of regular status reporting

7 *What decisions can or should you make from this tool?*

Decisions on process or procedures for managing risks broken down by the subareas outlined in the plan, and as part of the risk management process, i.e., identification decisions, analysis decisions, planning decisions and communication decisions

8 *What information does this provide for your project?*

Risk identification, risk analysis, risk response planning, risk event plan implementation, and risk tracking and control

9 *What historical and legal information do you need to keep?*

Lessons learned Information, processes and procedures that were successful, and the actual risk management plan itself

10 *What will be the staffing requirements (role type) to run and maintain these tools?*

Project manager, team members, and risk manager

Reporting using the risk management plan

The project manager is responsible for driving the risk management process and therefore is responsible for ensuring that there is a risk management plan available for their project. Unless the project manager assigned a separate risk manager on the project, the project manager will also be responsible for creating the risk management plan as well. One of the main responsibilities the project manager has during this risk management process is to ensure that the team members and customers continue to drive risk awareness and risk mitigation strategies for the project. Putting a risk management plan in place at the start of the project ensures the project is heading in the right direction from the beginning of the project.

There is no regular project reporting of the risk management plan because it does not contain any project status information. The risk management plan does, however, require approval and sign-off from the customers, so the project manager must obtain that sign-off as soon as everyone is comfortable with it and before the project gets going. The risk management plan uses a document format for creation and is stored in the document control system for long-term archiving and is accessible by any interested stakeholder on the project.

CROSS-REF See Chapter 16 to learn more about how to use and create the risk management plan.

Introducing the Risk Matrix Tool

The purpose of the *risk matrix* tool is to create a communication tool that prioritizes and categorizes project risk events into an easy-to-read chart for communicating to team members and customers. The risk matrix is extremely flexible, and it is possible to produce multiple types of risk matrix charts using different categories on your project. For example, you could have a risk matrix that outlines all the risks in a specific category, such as time, cost, or quality. There could be three separate risk matrixes alone for the project. The value of having multiple risk matrix charts is to allow the project manager and the customers to approach risk management in a prioritized manner. It also allows the project manager to compare how risky each category is to one another and then focus the team members on the highest risk category first to resolve those problems.

Team members and customers can use the risk matrix tool to determine the overall risk level of the project. The *risk level* is a rating of how risky the project is to complete against a number of known and unknown factors. The most common factors used in risk assessment include schedule, budget, or scope.

NOTE The Project Management Institute's knowledge area for this tool is the Risk Management area. There is no other secondary area for this tool.

ON the CD-ROM We have included a sample of this risk matrix tool in the Risk folder. Use this as a guide to help you create your own version of this tool.

TOOL VALUE A simple and easy-to-read chart to assess the risk level of the project. No other tool with a single glance can help someone decide how risky a project is to complete.

The most important benefit of using a risk matrix is the immediate ability to assess and understand the project's risk level when viewing the chart. The project's risk level is important to know on any project because it allows project decision makers or executives to decide if the project should continue or stop immediately. It lets the project manager know where to focus resources to help reduce risk events, and the overall viability of the project. If the project continues to show a number of high-level risks week after week, management is likely to become involved, possibly terminating the project unless those issues can be resolved. The risk matrix tool can be beneficial on large or small projects because every project will have risk events and every customer will want to know how risky their projects are. The more risks on the project, the more comprehensive the risk matrix tool can be.

Figure 12.3 is a completed risk matrix of a typical project. Prior to creating this matrix, the team identified 35 risk events and ranked each with impact and probability ranging from low to high. The team then placed the number from 1 to 35 (risk events) in the appropriate cells in the table. At a glance, the project customer or team members can easily determine that this project is a high-risk project due to the number of risk events that fall into that area of the matrix. The higher the count of risk events within a certain cell determines the project's risk level.

FIGURE 12.3

This figure represents a risk matrix with project risk data points.

	Probability		
Impact	**Low**	**Medium**	**High**
High	Medium	High	Very High
Medium	Low	Medium	High
Low	Very Low	Low	Medium

When reviewing the risk matrix it is clear how risky the project is by the number of actual risk events located in the top-right corner and by the number of risks in general on the project. In this example, there are nine risks events assessed by the team as High Impacting and High Probability. This example illustrates an extremely high-risk project; anytime there are that many risks in the high area of the matrix, it lends itself to being a higher-risk project. The other risk events (noted by numbers) are scattered among the other cells, although they should not be ignored, they are simply not as important as the top nine noted in the highest cell. When customers or upper management staff review this chart, in most cases they will look directly at the top-right corner and start focusing on the nine risk events that the team has deemed to be High Impacting and High Probability. They will focus their attention on those risks to determine what they can help mitigate or eliminate. When that occurs, project managers can rest assured that they have successfully utilized this communication tool and have communicated and exposed the risk events properly.

When reviewing this example risk matrix, it is clear there are nine separate categories where a risk event can fall on a particular project. On the left side of the chart, there is the designation called Risk Impact, which ranges from High to Low. The top of the chart has a Risk Probability designation, which also ranges from High to Low. There may also be some variations to the chart. As project managers sometimes like to carry additional values in each of the designations, such as Very High and Very Low, making even more categories where team members can assign risk events. Regardless of the layout of the risk matrix tool, the fundamentals are the same and based on the two designations. The team members evaluate each risk event as to how it will impact the project, judging their impact against, scope, schedule, and budget, and they evaluate the same risk event based on the probability of it occurring. At the end of the process, after assessing all risk events, the project manager and team members complete the risk matrix.

CROSS-REF   See Chapter 17 to learn more about how to create and use a risk matrix.

TIP   Calculate the expected monetary value of each risk event per cell to determine the cost of risk on your project.

As noted earlier in this chapter, the risk matrix tool can have different formats and use various data-points. The expected monetary value calculation, first introduced in the Risk Assessment Form tool, lends itself nicely to plotting its data points on a risk matrix. Figure 12.4 shows an example of the expected monetary values calculations for the risk events per cell. This project has previously been determined to be of high risk, and therefore you would expect that monetary value amounts in the upper-right corner of the matrix to have the large values. In this case, the expected monetary value of the High-High cell is $92,425 and happens to be the highest of any of the other cell values. When reviewing the chart, notice the cells surrounding the $92,425 cell. They too contain high values, which further substantiates that this project is a high-risk project.

Upper management and customers will be able to determine quickly from using the risk matrix, just how risky the project is. If there is a high percentage of the risk events sitting in the High Impact and High Probability cells on the risk matrix, then the project as a whole is high risk. However, if the majority of the risks are sitting in the Low Impact and Low probability area, obviously the project is of low risk. The project manager and team members assess the risk level of the project based on where the majority of the risks fall on the risk matrix.

FIGURE 12.4

This figure represents an example of a risk matrix with expected monetary value calculated.

		Probability		
		Low	**Medium**	**High**
Impact	**High**	23, 26, 27, 30	High	1, 3, 4, 5, 7, 8, 21, 33
	Medium	18, 20, 24	9, 19, 35	6, 14, 17, 22, 32
	Low	25, 29	16, 28, 31	11, 13, 34

Planning to use a risk matrix tool

In planning and preparing to use a risk matrix, the project manager must first determine how he/she will handle their project's risk assessment. This process is going to be project specific and dependent on how the project manager wants to undertake this process. Some project manager's book additional meetings where they can focus the team's attention on the project risks; however, some project managers will handle this process as part of the regular status meeting. After determining the implementation of the process for risk assessment, the project manager will work with the project customers to determine their requirements and reporting needs for the risk matrix. Areas the project manager will cover in these customer conversations include the customer's involvement in the risk assessment process, their risk tolerance, their report requirements, and their role in the resolution and closeout of the risk. These are important areas for the project manager to understand when planning for using the risk matrix tool and determining how he/she will manage this process. After completing these planning activities, the project manager will have adequately prepared for the use of this tool on their project.

Before you can create a risk matrix, you must formulate a plan. In the following "Planning Questions" section, we provide some initial thoughts to help you start thinking about how you can use the risk matrix on your project. Ask yourself the following questions.

Planning Questions

1 *When would you create or develop the risk matrix?*

During project execution, and during the planning phase when only requiring the need to establish and set up the process for populating the data in the tool

2 *Who is going to use this tool, both from an input and output status?*

Upper management, owners, executives, project manager, team members, and subcontractors or specific skill areas, the media (TV, radio, newspapers)

3 *Why are you going to use this tool?*

To display project risks in a ranked and categorized structure allowing anyone involved in the project to understand the level of each project's risk

4 *How are you going to use this tool?*

To graphically present a project's risk level to customers and upper management staff and to determine where to assign resources to reduce potential risk events

5 *How will you distribute the information?*

Plotter, newsletter, document control system, presentation format, e-mail

6 *When will you distribute the information?*

This tool is reported during the project's reporting cycle, which in most cases is weekly. The only other time would be if the risk events change dramatically and the chart changes would be another time to redistribute the risk matrix.

7 *What decisions can or should you make from this tool?*

Risk decisions, schedule and cost decisions, go/no-go decision on project based on number of risks in specific categories, resource decisions (skills sets, availabilities)

8 *What information does the tool provide for your project?*

Risk ranking, risk categories, project risk level

9 *What historical and legal information do you need to store?*

Lessons learned information, risks that occurred

10 *What will be the staffing requirements (role type) to run and maintain these tools?*

Project manager, team members, risk manager

Reporting using the risk matrix tool

The project manager is responsible for driving the risk assessment process, and, therefore, drives the creation of the risk matrix tool. In working alongside project team members, the project manager adds the various risk events into the different categories on the project's risk matrix. The risk assessment process is a negotiation among all team members; however, when complete the project manager has the final say regarding where the risk event actually falls on the chart. In almost all cases, it will be where the team has placed it.

Communicating the risk matrix is also the responsibility of the project manager and something that should go no longer than one week between reporting. Risk events can prevent a project from succeeding, and the project manager must stay on top of the project's risks to increase the chance of being successful on their project. Communicating the risk matrix any longer than a two-week cycle is asking for trouble and can quickly see one-time project risks become project issues that will negatively impact the project. The project manager creates a risk matrix using a presentation tool such as PowerPoint and stores it as part of the document control system for long-term archiving purposes.

CROSS-REF See Chapter 17 to learn more about how to use and create the risk matrix.

Introducing the Risk Model

The purpose of a *risk model* is to generate a risk assessment, or a project risk score. Risk assessments and risk scores relate to the overall sense the project team has on the project's risk level, or an understanding that the team members would have in the likelihood of the project being successful. By answering a series of risk questions in the risk model, where each question has a value associated to it, the project receives a total risk score. Depending on how the project team jointly answers the risk questions, the risk score can go up or down, changing the risk level of the project dramatically. Companies use risk assessments and risk scores as scoring mechanisms to keep projects going, possibly allocating additional resources or funds, and as a method to keep the project under tight control. The risk modeling technique is a relatively new concept to the project management industry. Using risk modeling allows companies to concentrate on the higher-risk projects first before getting involved in the lower-risk efforts that may or may not need any attention.

The risk model is a good communication tool for communicating the project's risk score and the associated data on how the score is calculated. When communicating the risk model, the project manager can show the customer the various questions applied to generate the risk score and the total risk score itself. The risk model holds valuable information on what the project team thinks about the risk level of the project by the answers they have provided to the risk questions. Project managers should communicate the risk model as often as possible to their customers and upper management staff to ensure that everyone is fully aware of how risky the team thinks the project is, and what actions the project manager or the team members should take to mitigate or eliminate those risks.

NOTE The Project Management Institute's knowledge area for this Risk Modeling tool is the Risk Management area. There is no other secondary area for this tool.

ON the CD-ROM We have included a sample of this Risk Modeling tool in the Risk folder. Use this as a guide to help you create your own version of this tool.

TOOL VALUE The risk model provides a risk assessment of the project from the project team member's perspective. No other tool asks team members and customers a series of questions that generates their thoughts on the risk level the way the risk model does.

Risk models give you the ability to generate a project risk score that helps you understand how risky the project is and provides exposure to the team's answers to the various risk questions.

The unique aspect of the risk model is the fact that the project team completes it together and has not taken the results from an individual team member perspective, but aggregated across the team. The results from this process are from an overall team perspective, which is much more beneficial because one or two team members can skew the score based on what they personally think about the project.

The project manager and team members can benefit from the use of a risk model because it drives the creation of a risk assessment score on the project. Knowing your project's assessment score compared to other similar projects helps you, as the project manager, know how risky your project is and how much time and effort you should spend focusing on risk events. For example, if your project were a low-risk project you would spend only limited time on your project watching the risk events compared to a high-risk project. Generating a project risk score and an associated risk assessment spreadsheet provides the project manager the direction they need to understand how much time they will spend on the risk events.

More and more companies are starting to utilize risk models as approved mechanisms for project funding and resource commitments. The companies are actually compelling projects to go through the risk modeling process to achieve a final risk score, which allows management to determine across the company what are the higher-risk projects. When all projects complete the same risk model and assessment, the information from all risk models across the company is extremely valuable to upper management. It provides upper management and executives the risk assessment score across all projects going on now in the company. It allows the executives to make tough business level decisions such as canceling projects, adding additional funding, and pulling resources based on the project's risks scores and how they are comparing to the other project's risk scores.

TIP It is important to note that changing these questions for every project would be beneficial because no two projects are the same and the questions need adjusting accordingly.

Figure 12.5 is a typical project risk model. The questions on the risk model are specific to the type of project, and the scores associated to each question are project specific.

FIGURE 12.5

This figure represents an example of a risk model.

Risk Register

Risk #	Risk Category	Risk Description	Risk Probability (High/Medium/Low)	Risk Impact (High/Medium/Low)	Mitigation Plan (See Risk Breakdown Structure for Description)	Risk Owner	Status
A3481	Budget	The Engineering group is 200K over budget on the project.	Medium	High	06.01.03.02	Fred	Article
J4372	Schedule	Phase 2 late by more than two weeks.	High	High	05.02.02.01	George	Future
E0062	Economy	Interest rates become greater than 6%	Low	High	10.06.03.11	Sam	Past

The risk model is a spreadsheet containing a series of questions and scores associated with each question. When a user answers a question, the answer selected has an associated score. The total of all answers (all single scores) generates one risk score for the project. The risk model has questions based on the type of project and the associated industry; for example, it would be irrelevant to ask software type questions when assessing the project risks on a construction project. The two projects are too different, and the scoring from one of the projects would not be relevant against the other; therefore, there is not a single risk model applicable to all types of projects. Every person has the capability of updating the risk model questions and scores to reflect their specific type of project.

Updating the questions and answers is easy, but time consuming; however, project managers believe this is the only drawback to using the tool. Proactive planning and completing the risk model early enough in the project can prevent the maintenance and use of this tool from becoming overwhelming. The time-consuming aspect of using this tool troubles those project managers less who have set it up early and only require updating it when new risks come onto the project and new scores require calculating. The project managers who do not create the risk model early in the project and end up leaving it to a later stage of the project will tend to think the tool is harder to manage, when in fact it is the time pressure of the project, not specifically the tool.

TIP   Projects need a new risk assessment score when adding new risk events to the project.

In using a risk model, one of the important aspects of the tool is to learn how to read and understand the results of the tool. Use the following score chart to determine how to understand what a risk score means on the project. The project manager can update Table 12.11 to reflect specific needs of the project, and it is not meant to be a default table for every project.

Table 12.11 represents a risk score description chart. Use this chart to determine the risk score for your project. The score ranges and the score descriptions can vary from project to project and are up to the project manager, team members, and customers to decide on the values. Customers' roles will vary from project to project.

TABLE 12.11

Risk Score Chart

Risk Score	Description
1 – 35	Indicates your project has a low risk assessment score and your project is low risk.
36 – 72	Indicates your project has a medium risk assessment score and your project is medium risk.
72 or Higher	Indicates your project has a high risk assessment score and your project is high risk.

NOTE   The project manager should become knowledgeable with the specifics of their projects in order to generate an effective risk model.

The risk model in part uses a series of categories; the type of project and industry sets the specifics of the categories. The categories include budget risk, failure risk, and mission critical risks. The categories are unlimited, and the project manager along with the team members determine which categories they will use to track in the risk model.

Planning to use a risk model

In planning and preparing to use the risk model, the project manager must first determine if the company has a risk modeling process in place already. If so, the project manager will utilize that process and associated risk model for their project. In some cases, the project manager may have to attend training on the company's process or team up with someone who knows it already and determine how to use it on his/her project. Assuming that the company does not have a risk modeling process in place, the first step in the planning process is for the project manager to adapt the risk model template (shown in Figure 12.6 and located on the CD-ROM) for use on their project. This includes understanding the complex calculations and formulas in the spreadsheet as well as knowing each of the areas on the spreadsheet well enough to understand where specific risk events could occur; without that knowledge the project manager has limited ability to create an effective risk model. After ramping up on the process, the next step for the project manager is to determine how the project team would engage in the risk assessment process. This includes setting up various meetings to determine how team members are involved and what roles they will play. After establishing how the team members will engage and setting up the processes internally on the project, the project manager then works directly with the customer to determine their involvement in the risk modeling process. When discussing this with the customer, the project manager should determine their reporting requirements, and at what level they want to be involved in risk management. If the risk score generates and secures project approvals, or generates requests for funding, then most customers will want to be involved heavily in the process. After completing these planning activities, the project manager has prepared adequately for using the risk modeling technique on their projects.

Before you can create the risk model, you must formulate a plan. In the following "Planning Questions" section, we provide some initial thoughts to help you start thinking about how you can use a Risk Model tool on your project. Ask yourself the following questions.

Planning Questions

1 **When would you create or develop the risk model tool?**

During project planning phase initially, and then throughout execution while risks events are rolling on and off the project

2 **Who is going to use this tool, both from an input and output status?**

Upper management, owners, project manager, team members, subcontractors or specific skill areas, risk manager

continued

continued

3 *Why are you going to use this tool?*

Assess project risks and to generate a project risk score, compare risk scores among other projects to ensure that adequate funding and resources are working the project risks

4 *How are you going to use this tool?*

Answer risk questions to generate a risk score, update risk model with applicable questions for the project type, and share risk score with upper management, customers

5 *How will you distribute the information?*

Spreadsheet format such as Microsoft Excel, document control system, project presentations

6 *How often will you distribute the information?*

Distributing the risk model should be part of the regular project reporting cycle, which in most cases is weekly.

7 *What decisions can you make from this tool?*

Decide where to focus resource-based risk scores, evaluate, and decide if risk questions are applicable, decisions on budget and resources associated to project, based on risk score

8 *What information does this tool provide for your project?*

Project risk score, answers provided by team members to project risk model questions, overall assessment of project risk

9 *What historical and legal information do you need to store?*

Project risk model questions and answers, lessons learned Information, the document itself

10 *What will be the staffing requirements (role type) to run and maintain these tools?*

Project manager, risk manager (if applicable), project team members

Reporting using a risk model

The project manager is responsible for driving all risk mitigation on the project, which includes using risk models, risk assessment forms, funding toward risk spending, and all other areas involved in project risk. The project manager is also responsible for driving the risk modeling process, which includes the creation of the risk model. The project manager cannot do this activity alone and therefore need the help of the team members to complete this risk modeling process. With the team members involved answering the risk questions and coming up with the project's total risk score it allows everyone to get involved in the process and have the same understanding of the project's risk assessment.

The risk model and associated results from the modeling process require reporting on a weekly basis as part of the project's regular reporting. A week-to-week review of the project's risk scores allows for the project manager to perform trending analysis and for upper management to watch those trends closely to determine if progress toward reducing risks is occurring. If possible, you should report the risk model within the weekly status meeting; otherwise, report as often as you feel is appropriate for the project. The risk model is developed by using a spreadsheet and stored as part of the document control system for long-term archiving, and is accessible by any interested stakeholder on the project.

CROSS-REF See Chapter 15 to learn more about how to use and create a risk model.

Introducing the Risk Register

The *risk register* is the result of quantitative and qualitative risk analysis in the risk response planning. It contains all identified project risk events with their descriptions, causes, probabilities of occurring, impacts, mitigation plans, and updated status. The risk register is a section of the project management plan.

CROSS-REF See the project management plan in Chapters 4 and 14.

One of the purposes of the risk register is to document the risk mitigation strategies for all project risk events. Risk mitigation is the plans and actions taken to reduce or prevent harmful impacts to the project. Project managers utilize two tools with risk mitigation planning. The first tool is a risk register, which is a list of the project's risk events with a detailed mitigation strategy documented for each risk item. The second tool is the risk assessment form, which we cover earlier in this chapter that consists of a list of risk events for the project. Both tools are similar but have different purposes. For example, there is no expected monetary value in the risk register, but they are covered in the risk assessment form. The risk register carries information on mitigation steps, whereas the risk assessment form recommends a strategy only and provides little details. There are other differences between the two forms, with the biggest and most importance difference being risks events that have clear mitigation plans transferred from the risk assessment form to the risk register for resolution. The main difference is that the risk register focuses more on the details around the mitigation strategies whereas the risk assessment form uses calculations and focuses on the impacts (schedule, scope, and budget) and lists the risks events only. The two forms have similar characteristics but are quite different, and our recommendation is to handle them separately as two distinct tools. Risks without mitigation plans stay on the risk assessment form until plans are developed.

NOTE There is nothing stopping project managers or team members from combining the tools into a single comprehensive tool; that is definitely an option, but for the purposes of describing the risk register, it is important to keep them separate.

One method of working project risk mitigation is by selecting one of the predefined strategies for resolving the risk events. The project management profession has five major strategies for risks mitigation. They are acceptance, avoidance, transfer, mitigate, and retention. When working with strategies, the project manager and team members need to decide which strategy they will select for each risk event. In some cases, project managers choose avoidance for handling the risk events, which states they will not even try to mitigate the risk. For example, a team might use the avoidance strategy on some projects; the project manager has no authority or approval over project funding and therefore he/she can choose risk avoidance as an acceptable risk strategy.

Project managers should be active in communicating the risk register on their projects because of the information and work activities the risk register will store for all the risk events. For example, the risk register has mitigation steps documented for the risk events and the project manager or team members may be active performing these steps to resolve the risk if there happens to be changes or updates to those steps. Ongoing communication of that document is very beneficial to everyone involved. If there are project efforts that come from the mitigation strategies in the risk register, those efforts need to be included alongside the other project work activities that the team members are completing for the project. For example, if the project has four to five project risk events and the team members have chosen to mitigate each risk, then they now have additional work on the project. The project manager captures the work inside the risk register tool and then uses it as a method to track and monitor the work until it is complete. Communicating the use of the risk register tool is also important when it comes to highlighting how the project team is addressing the risks on the project. No matter which method the project team decides to use to handle risk mitigation, it is important to ensure the customers are aware and provide risk mitigation help whenever possible. Keeping the customers involved will tend to keep them supportive of the team working the risk events. Constant communications and ongoing updates of the risk register are beneficial to the project team members, customers, and upper management.

NOTE The Project Management Institute's knowledge area for this tool is the Risk Management area. There is no other secondary area for this tool.

ON the CD-ROM We have included a sample of this risk mitigation plan tool in the Risk folder. Use this as a guide to help you create your own version of this tool.

TOOL VALUE This tool is a single repository to communicate the risk mitigation activities performed on the project's risks. It is the single location to find risk information. It documents how the team is working to reduce the impacts or the risks on the project.

There are many benefits of using a risk register on your projects. The first benefit is that the tool is great to use when communicating with customers and upper management about how you are going to mitigate the project's risk events. The risk register tool displays the risk events and mitigation steps or comments, so everyone is on the same page on how each risk event is resolved. Secondly, as noted above, the tool highlights the mitigation steps for the team members and provides exposure to their work activities on these items. The project manager needs to be aware of what they need to be complete for closing out each risk event. Without the risk register tool, the project manager will have no mechanism in place to track specific work tasks associated to the risk events, and therefore may struggle to keep a handle on what the team members are actually doing to resolve the risks. If the team members focus on mitigation strategies only, and let the other project work activities suffer, the project manager can step in and help to course correct. The team members can be off resolving potential risk events, which in turn could waste time and money and impacting the deliverables of the project. The risk event may never come to fruition and working on preventing a risk event that is a low probability could have a negative impact on the project.

Figure 12.6 represents an example of a risk register on a typical project. In this example, three risk events have mitigation plans established. The other project risk events do not have mitigation plans and, therefore, have not been transferred from the risk assessment form to the risk register. In two of the risk events on the risk register, there are specific mitigation steps or statements about the risk events. Depending on the strategy chosen for the event, the migration steps differ from risk to risk. This risk register is easy to complete and, like the other risk communication tools, are excellent in communicating risk information to the project team members and customers.

In reviewing the risk register in Figure 12.6, you can quickly determine how beneficial this tool is to anyone wanting to learn more about the risk mitigation plans for the project.

The risk mitigation plan requires that there is a project-risk-mitigation process in place. The two tools mentioned (risk register and risk assessment form) are used more as a repository for storing risk information, but the mitigation process is different and important for a project manager to understand before they can implement it successfully on their projects.

The risk mitigation process starts with understanding the project risk events and the different impacts that each risk has on the project. After the team understands and lists the risk events in the risk assessment form, the team then decides if there is a mitigation strategy possible for each risk event. If so, the project manager moves the risk event from the risk assessment form to the risk register and then adds the mitigation steps to the risk event.

After the project team determines which risks they can mitigate and what risks they can't, the project manager only adds those events with clear strategies to the risk register. This then leaves the risk events that do not have clear mitigation strategies left in the risk assessment form, and the risk events that do are put in the risk register. When moving the risks between the tools, the actual mitigation strategies do not have to be solidified at the same time; the team only has to determine which ones could have a mitigation strategy. Once the risks are in the risk register, the project manager and the team members should decide on the mitigation strategy and then prepare and plan for executing that strategy if the risk event occurs.

As the team starts the assessment process, they may find they have moved some risk events prematurely to the risk register when they still belong on the risk assessment form. Some risks may not have obvious mitigation strategies so therefore would not move automatically to the risk register. In those cases, the risks are accepted as "as is." An example of this would be the project having a drop-dead date for completing. This is a non-mitigating risk event because the completion of the project is directly linked to a major opening of an international event. That drop-dead date would be an ongoing, unsolvable risk event that the project team would carry throughout the life of the project.

As the assessment process continues, it is normal for the project team to accept risk events as a normal course of action. Risk acceptance is normal when the project team determines that the risk is too low in probability, and the event does not warrant developing a formal mitigation plan. Most risks only require observation, and most often do not amount to anything. By accepting a risk, the project team should document and justify that acceptance for future reference and continue to watch the risk until the end of the project.

FIGURE 12.6

This figure represents an example of a risk register.

Project Risk Model			
	Total Project Risk Score		Component Risk Assessments
	Interim Score	1	
			Low Budget Risk
	Low Risk 1-35	Score	
		1	Low External Dependencies Risk
			Low Management Risk
	Medium Risk 36-72	Score	
			Low Mission Critical Risk
			Low Failure Risk
	High Risk >72	Score	
			Low Control Risk
	Question Number	Project Risk Question	Answer Lists (Note- when you click in each answer cell, a drop down list will appear)
Budget Risk	1	What is the estimated total project cost?	Project Cost is less than $150 thousand
	2	What percentage of the agency budget does the project represent?	The project is less than 2% of the agency budget.
	3	Have sufficient project funds been budgeted and allocated?	Minimum essential funding is budgeted and allocated.
	4	How much confidence is there in the experience and funding projections?	
	5	Is funding available for maintenance of the project deliverable after project closure?	
External Dependencies Risk	6	Is this project dependent on another projects deliverable?	
	7	Does this project require resources from other organizations?	
	8	Does this project require data from other sources?	

During the risk assessment process, the project team members have five mitigation strategies that they can choose from when determining how to resolve or mitigate risk events. When selecting a strategy for each risk event, the project manager must work with the team members to implement that solution for each event. The project manager will drive this process until each risk event is resolved and the project is complete.

CROSS-REF See the risk management plan located in this chapter for more information on the risk mitigation strategies and information on the five mitigation strategies.

Planning to use the risk register

In planning and preparing to use a risk register, the project manager must first determine the steps and processes around mitigating risk events. He must plan how he will direct the team members throughout the risk mitigation process, including determining the various project meetings he will hold to process risk events, and reviewing the risk register template to ensure it carries the information applicable to their project. The project manager must discover if there are any existing internal processes that must be followed to utilize the risk register. The next step is to work with the project customers to determine how they will be involved in the risk mitigation process. Some customers will want to be actively engaged in the process, attending meetings and wanting to be in on all decisions around the strategies selected for each risk event. In those planning discussions, the project manager will discuss and capture the reporting requirements from the customers as well, ensuring they continually receive information they need to be fully engaged in the process. After preparing and taking these necessary steps, the project manager has adequately prepared to use a risk register on the project.

Before you can create the risk register tool, you must formulate a plan. In the following "Planning Questions" section, we have provided some initial thoughts to help you start thinking about how you can use a risk register on your project. Ask yourself the following questions.

Planning Questions

1 *When would you create or develop the risk register?*
Risk assessment planning, after selecting the risk events that will have mitigation strategies assigned to them

2 *Who is going to use this tool, both from an input and output perspective?*
Owners, customers, executives, project manager, team members, subcontractors, risk manager

3 *Why are you going to use this tool?*
To document the mitigation plans for risk events and share those plans with anyone involved in the project. To plan work activities for project team members or customers while they execute the risk mitigation activities, and track work activities of project team members on various risk events.

continued

continued

4 *How are you going to use it?*

Develop the risk mitigation strategies for each project risk event that warrants a strategy. Develop the risk register and add mitigation steps to risk events that have the possibility of having mitigation steps, document probability estimates of risk events occurring

5 *How will you distribute the information?*

Document format such as Microsoft Excel, document control system, e-mail, risk register, weekly status reports, and project presentations

6 *When will you distribute the information?*

The project manager would utilize this valuable communication tool throughout the life of project.

7 *What decisions can or should you make from this tool?*

Risk mitigation decisions for each risk event, decisions to lower impact or risk probability factor. Decisions on future direction of risk events including elimination.

8 *What information does this tool provide for your project?*

Strategy for handling each risk event, risk probability, risk impacts, risk owners, risk status, risk cost and schedule impacts, and risk priority

9 *What historical and legal information do you need to keep?*

Risk register itself, lessons learned Information, actual costs associated to risk events, and actual schedule impacts based on risk events

10 *What will be the staffing requirements (role type) to run and maintain these tools?*

Project manager, risk manager, and team members

Reporting using the risk register

The project manager is responsible for driving risk mitigation planning and therefore owns the creation of the risk register on most projects. In most cases, the project manager owns the risk assessment form as well, so it makes sense that they would also own the risk register tool and have the responsibility of transferring project risk events from one tool to the other.

The project manager will use the risk register to report status every week to team members, customers, and upper management. Because the risk register contains the latest status of risk events and their mitigation strategies, reporting every week will provide customers and upper management with the exposure on the information if they need it. In most cases, the project manager creates the risk register using a spreadsheet, but it can be created as well using a table in a document.

The risk register is stored as part of the document control system for long-term archiving and is accessible by any interested stakeholder on the project.

 See Chapter 16 to learn more about how to use and create the Risk Register tool.

Introducing the Risk Simulation Tool

The purpose of the *risk simulation* tool is to provide the project manager with a method for determining the probability of the project completing on time and budget. The tool is an add-on package to most of the project scheduling applications on the market. This powerful risk assessment tool, considering risk, provides the ability to predict each activity's finish date and a project end date, or the final cost for each activity and the project, long before the project ever comes close to completing. The project manager can then make adjustments in the project based on the results he/she is seeing as results in the risk simulation tool, and those adjustments can enhance the chances of the project succeeding. As the project manager continues to re-run the simulations, even finer adjustments are possible. One of the more popular risk simulation tools on the market is the Deltek Risk+ product. This product works alongside Microsoft Project software, Deltek's wInsight product, and Microsoft Excel. Other products on the market perform the same functions as this one does; however, this product is very friendly and easy to use. You can find the products that perform risk simulations by searching the Internet. The Deltek risk simulation tool is one of the more popular tools on the market and is widely accepted in the project management industry.

Communicating the risk simulation results is possibly one of the easiest things a project manager has to do on their projects. The tool predicts the project's final cost and potential finish dates while still providing customers and upper management with a look at the future results of the project. If the risk simulation tool determines the project will come in $1,000,000 over budget at the beginning of the project, the customers or upper management staff can reduce scope, add more resources, or cancel the project. This is something that would not be possible without having this tool on your project. When advising customers or upper management of a $1,000,000 overage late in the project, they have little time to react.

NOTE The Project Management Institute's knowledge area for this tool is the Risk Management area. There is no other secondary area for this tool.

ON the CD-ROM We have included a sample of a risk simulation tool in the Risk folder. Use this as a guide to help you create your own version of this tool.

TOOL VALUE The risk simulation tool provides the ability to predict the project's final costs and potential end dates.

The immediate benefit of using a risk simulation tool is the ability to predict the project's end date early in the project's lifecycle. This is the number one reason why project managers use this tool. The second reason why this tool is so beneficial is that it calculates and predicts the project's final costs, as early as possible in the project. This provides an opportunity for the project manager and the customers to react accordingly with the predicted cost information. Both of those benefits provide very early planning information for the project manager, customers, and upper management and allows everyone to plan accordingly. For example, if you run the report and it shows the end date of the project is expected to be much later and the costs of the project are expected to come in under budget, the project manager may decide to hire more resources to allow the project to finish earlier while the costs of the project increase. This type of project level decision continues to increase the value of using the risk simulation tool.

The project manager benefits the most from the risk simulation tool. The tool reports a future state of the project from a budget and schedule perspective and therefore provides great benefit to the project manager from a planning and controlling perspective. If the project manager utilizes the tool and determines the project is never going to hit the targeted end date, then they can adjust the parameters on the project and re-run the simulation. Adjustments continue until the tool shows a more realistic date for the end of the project. After the simulation is accurate, the project manager makes the adjustments on the actual project to ensure that the project has the best chances of making the end date reported in the tool. When a project manager decides to use a risk simulation tool on their project, the What-If Scenarios are endless.

Figure 12.7 shows the results of the risk simulation run against a simple project. In this example, the risk simulation takes project activity durations and changes them through each pass; the software then recalculates a new end date for each activity. The tool runs the simulation for the number of passes specified when initiating the program. The simulation software used in this figure is the three-point estimate method covered later in this section.

 It is important to note that budget simulations are also possible and another major benefit of using this tool.

When reviewing the results of the tool, you can see how easy it is to read the chart and determine, based on project data, the more realistic finish date of the project. The probability ranges, aligned next to the finish dates on the chart, tell the reviewers what the chances are of completing the project at the specified date. In Figure 12.7, for example, there is an 80 percent chance the project will finish on 4/1/2009, and a 100 percent chance it will finish on 5/14/2009. When the customers or project manager sees these results on the risk simulation tool, they both can determine how the project is tracking toward its targets, and if necessary can make adjustments to get it back on track. This can include reducing scope, adding staff, and extending the project end date.

Figure 12.8 shows a three-point estimate spreadsheet. As you can see from the table there are three estimates provided for each activity on the project. These estimates come from the project team member doing the work, and then providing what they feel is the duration in days to complete the task. In order for the risk simulation process to work correctly, there is specific data needed in the tool to calculate the project's information. The project manager gets from each team member their Optimistic (feeling good estimate), their Most Likely (gut feel estimate), and their Pessimistic (negative, worst case) estimate, and compiles that information into this table.

FIGURE 12.7

This figure represents an example of a risk simulation results for a project. (*Courtesy of © Deltek, Inc.*)

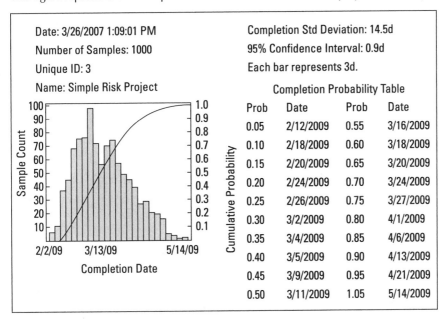

Date: 3/26/2007 1:09:01 PM

Number of Samples: 1000

Unique ID: 3

Name: Simple Risk Project

Completion Std Deviation: 14.5d

95% Confidence Interval: 0.9d

Each bar represents 3d.

Completion Probability Table

Prob	Date	Prob	Date
0.05	2/12/2009	0.55	3/16/2009
0.10	2/18/2009	0.60	3/18/2009
0.15	2/20/2009	0.65	3/20/2009
0.20	2/24/2009	0.70	3/24/2009
0.25	2/26/2009	0.75	3/27/2009
0.30	3/2/2009	0.80	4/1/2009
0.35	3/4/2009	0.85	4/6/2009
0.40	3/5/2009	0.90	4/13/2009
0.45	3/9/2009	0.95	4/21/2009
0.50	3/11/2009	1.05	5/14/2009

FIGURE 12.8

The three-point estimate spreadsheet required for the risk simulation software.

Project Name: ABC			
Activity Name	Optimistic	Most Likely	Pessimistic
Activity 1	3	5	7
Activity 2	5	8	10
Activity 3	8	10	14

In viewing the table, you will see the three estimated values of Optimistic, Most Likely, and Pessimistic. Here is a definition of each:

- **Optimistic:** Shortest reasonable duration the activity will take if everything goes right.
- **Pessimistic:** Longest reasonable duration the activity will take considering a large number of problems and issues on performing the activity.
- **Most Likely:** The most likely duration the activity will take, derived from historical information and experience.

The Expected Value calculation is common in the project management industry. This formula estimates a weighted value based on the Optimistic, Pessimistic, and Most Likely estimates. This formula is used in the simulation tool, Figure 12.8, to derive your expected value. Here is the formula to calculate expected value that the tool is using automatically on the tasks in the project. The formula is as follows:

Expected Value = Optimistic + 4 – Most likely + Pessimistic/6

In the collecting process, the project manager may find that the team members may not be comfortable with this process because they never created these three estimates for their projects before; and, therefore, they may require some coaching. Collecting this information in this format is new to most companies not utilizing the risk simulation tool. If your company is not already using it or creating estimates from the team members in this format, it can be quite an adjustment for team members to make. However, after the adjustment period is over and the team members start thinking in this manner, the payoff to using this tool is huge. The project manager drives this expectation on collecting hours at the beginning of the project, before any work activities begin so that team members get used to the idea of thinking about their work activities in this manner. If the project manager requests from the team members that they provide their estimates in this format, from the very beginning of the project, they are setting the expectations and providing the ability for them to be able to run the risk simulation throughout the project. The project manager then provides training to the team members so they know how to enter and think about the three different values and then enforce the team members to provide the data in that format throughout the project. Otherwise, if the team members refuse to provide any of the relevant data, performing risk simulations may be almost impossible.

One of the techniques that the project manager can utilize is using a spreadsheet to collect the three data points instead of having the team members enter it directly into the project. Using a spreadsheet makes teaching the team members faster and the learning process so much easier for them, while still getting the data in the format required by the software to run the simulations. There is no loss when collecting the data in this format for the project manager as the data can be loaded directly as it is into the risk simulation tool. However, because the concept is new to the team members, they may struggle to come up with Optimistic and Pessimistic estimates for their tasks. The one estimate they can provide is what they think is the Most Likely estimate, which in most cases is all that is required from them, because there are standard project management formulas that can create the Optimistic and Pessimistic values.

We have included a sample of a three-point calculator spreadsheet on the CD-ROM for use on your project. We have also included the risk simulation spreadsheet, the one shown in Figure 12.8 so you have the final format to load into the risk simulation software if required.

The project manager also has the ability to capture the three-point estimating data within a project-scheduling tool, such as Microsoft Project. When doing so, this data is automatically in the tool and has the ability to eliminate the manual process of transferring the spreadsheet data into the scheduling tool, and possibly avoids any data entry mistakes. Because the scheduling tool is tied directly to the risk simulation software, if it is possible, entering the three point estimates directly into the tools is a best practice. The spreadsheet is only a temporary measure to get team members thinking about this process and easing them into this new estimating process. Entering directly into the tool is the long-term plan for any project manager.

Figure 12.9 shows a typical project schedule configured to accept three fields required for the risk simulation software. Adding these three fields into the scheduling tool takes only a few minutes and provides the risk simulation tool with the data it requires to run the simulations.

When running the risk simulations, and using the valuable results from the tool, the project manager is increasing their chance of a successful project. In doing this, they are actually enhancing the critical path method of project scheduling and using the three-point method of project estimating and allowing a tool to simulate the outcome of the project based on the data within the individual work activities.

CROSS-REF See Chapter 6 for more information on the critical path method, under the Project Schedule tool.

Planning to use a risk simulation tool

In planning and preparing to use a risk simulation tool, the project manager must first determine if the tool is available for use on the project. If the tool is not available, then the project manager will need to purchase it, get it installed, and take training on how to use the tool. If it is available, and after confirming its availability, the project manager then starts to work on the challenges of the team's unfamiliarity with the three-point estimating method and their learning curve to get them all engaged in the process. It also requires that the project manager shift the company's thinking, moving from critical path model to three-point estimating model, which can be very challenging. After ensuring the team members are collecting their estimates in the right format and the software is in place for capturing the data, the project manager then works with the customers to understand what role they will play in the risk simulation process. It is important to understand where the customers feel they want to be involved or can provide support in this process. Communications between the project manager and the customers will also include any special reporting requirements that the customer may have, and how often would they like the risk simulations run on the project. Some customers want a weekly simulation run on the project, so they have a week-by-week comparison of how the project is tracking. Considering these customer requirements, the project manager has adequately prepared for the use of the risk simulation tool on their project.

FIGURE 12.9

A project schedule with risk simulation data loaded.

	Task Name	Start	Finish	Optimistic	Most Likely	Pessimistic	Jul 20, 08 S M T W T F S	Jul 27, 08 S M T W T F S	Aug 3, 08 S M T W T F S	Aug 10, 08 S M T W T F S	Aug 17, 08 S M T W T F S	Aug 24, 08 S M T W T F S
1	Project ABC	7/24/08	8/25/08	0 days	23 days	0 days						
2	Activity 1	7/24/08	7/30/08	3 days	5 days	7 days						
3	Activity 2	7/31/08	8/11/08	5 days	8 days	10 days						
4	Activity 3	8/12/08	8/25/08	8 days	10 days	14 days						

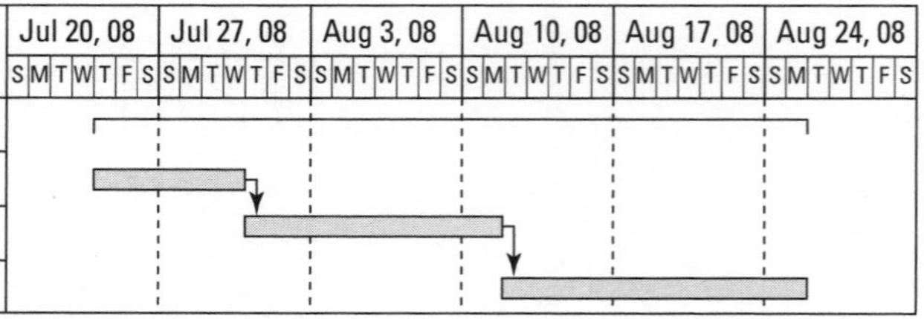

Before you can create a risk simulation for your project, you must formulate a plan. In the following "Planning Questions" section, we have provided some initial thoughts to help you start thinking about how you can use the tool on your project. Ask yourself the following questions.

Planning Questions

1 When would you run the risk simulation tool?
Throughout the project the project manager will run the risk simulation tool, and as the project progresses the project manager continues to re-run the tool.

2 Who is going to use this tool, both from an input and output status?
Upper management, owners, executives, customers, project manager, risk manager, and team members

3 Why are you going to use this tool?
To predict future schedule end dates and final project costs early in the life of the project

4 How are you going to use this tool?
Load cost and schedule information into the tool then run the simulation software to return the results

5 How will you distribute the information?
Project schedule report, project cost report, probability charts and graphics, e-mail, and project presentations.

6 How often will you distribute the information?
On-demand, and when project durations or project costs are changed

7 What decisions can you make from this tool?
Schedule and cost decisions, overall project go/no-go decisions, resource estimates on project activities

8 What information does this tool provide for your project?
Forecast end of project completion information, forecast probabilities of various end dates and cost values

9 What historical and legal information do you need to store?
Results of simulations both cost and schedule, lessons learned information

10 What will be the staffing requirements (Role Type) to run and maintain these tools?
Project manager, project scheduler (larger projects), risk manager, cost manager, and subcontractor

Reporting using a risk simulation tool

The project manager is responsible for completing the risk simulation tool on their projects. The project manager owns the end-to-end process of ensuring that team members are providing the three-point estimates they will run, the simulation software, and must analyze the results. Additionally, the project manager is responsible for communicating the results to the customers and upper management staff.

The risk simulation tool requires regular weekly reporting to the customers and upper management. The results of the simulation do not contain official project status, but do simulate the final cost for the project and its expected end date. Running this simulation weekly provides a more realistic view of the project, and when continually refining the data as the project progresses, those costs and dates forecasted come closer to reality. The risk simulation uses a project-scheduling tool to drive its creation. Historical copies of the simulation files and older versions of the project schedule are stored as part of the document control system for long-term archiving and are accessible by any interested stakeholder on the project.

CROSS-REF See Chapter 15 to learn more about how to use and create a risk simulation tool.

Introducing the Safety Report

On today's projects, it is vital for project team members, subcontractors, and consultants to respond swiftly to safety problems, accidents, and incidents to effectively resolve the situation and quickly set procedures to mitigate or eliminate them from happening again. The purpose of a *safety report* is to provide a record of those safety occurrences, infractions, and issues on a project. Safety reports are generally applicable to construction or hazardous work areas but can be applicable to any type of project.

Every project should have a safety program. Safety hazards exist on every job site, even in office environments. A safety program creates procedures to follow and is a circular process. The project manager establishes rules to guide the process, monitors the safety incidents, and then reports on the safety condition of the project. Depending on the number and severity of the accidents and safety infractions occurring, the project manager and safety manager reacts accordingly on their project. The safety program is a never-ending process. It is common to use a safety report to identify safety violations and keep statistics on the safety record of the project. Using safety reports to display the number of days without an accident, especially when a new record is close to being broken, can be a great reminder and motivator for the team members.

NOTE The Project Management Institute's knowledge area for this tool is the Risk Management area. The secondary knowledge area for this tool is Quality.

ON the CD-ROM We have included a sample of a safety report tool in the Risk folder. Use this as a guide to create your own version of this tool.

TOOL VALUE The safety report's calculations of the safety problems, accidents, infractions, and incidents summarized are what drive the ongoing safety program.

The safety report provides customers, team members, and upper management with project safety information. The safety report consists of accident information, risk and mitigation steps, training recommendations, budget, and violations compiled at the monthly level. It provides a clear picture of the safety environment of the project. The project manager works with the safety manager (they are normally two different people) and goes over the safety report together every month. Once compiling the report, the project manager sends that report to customers and upper management for review.

Table 12.12 is an example of a table of contents for a safety report. As you can see, there are only six sections of the report, and each section captures the important safety aspects of the project. The report is simple to create and important on the higher safety risk projects such as construction projects.

TABLE 12.12

Safety Report Table of Contents

Section	Description
1	Monthly Accident Incident
2	Monthly Safety Summary
3	Safety Risk Mitigation
4	Safety Training
5	Monthly Safety Budget/Cost
6	Monthly Safety Violations

When using a safety report on the project, it tends to benefit both the project manager and customers. Both groups are responsible for providing a safe and risk-free work environment for their team members and therefore both will want to be active in understanding how safe is the work environment the team members are working in as they execute the project. When the project employs a safety manager, who is tasked with completing safety reports, supporting safety compliance issues, and determining best practices around safety, it increases the chance of having a safe environment for the team members. Team members use the safety report to file safety events or lodge safety complaints; however, in most cases the safety report benefits the project manager and customers, because it provides that true understanding of the true state of the project.

A safety report exposes project team members to possible hazardous situations that could occur in their work environment. For example, a construction job site is a hazardous work environment where safety reports are a common practice that reported regularly, where safety issues could occur. An office environment is not as hazardous and does not require as comprehensive of a safety report. Most safety managers generate safety reports on a weekly basis and the reports are summarized.

NOTE For situations when someone is hurt, an accident report is used. Safety reports are summarized versions of accident reports, covering safety summary reports, safety risk areas, training, and budget reporting.

Safety reports are common to all industries and presented to the public frequently. For example, when you go into any warehouse-type store, in most cases, you will see the current safety record of that warehouse. It usually reads "No accidents in the last 45 days." This safety record is an important aspect of that working environment because the goal of everyone working in that type of environment is to get the maximum number of days without incident. It is a daily reminder to employees to take safety seriously.

The construction industry routinely uses safety reports. On construction projects, all new staff members must go through safety training classes. The safety manager assigned to the construction site conducts these classes. Quite often, companies provide safety training for specific skills. For example, if a new piece of equipment comes on the job site, the assigned skilled labor team member who is to use the equipment will be required to attend a safety session for that machinery to ensure they are qualified and can operate it. On construction projects, the owner, project manager, laborers, and possibly government (OSHA) receive the safety report on a monthly basis and provide all parties all the information they need on the safety aspect of the project. The report is always available in the job shack on the construction site for anyone's review.

Other industries that are safety conscious are research laboratories and manufacturing facilities. In the lab environment, it is quite common to see staff wearing safety glasses, gloves, overcoats, and protective clothing to ensure they are safe while performing their job functions. In manufacturing, it is common to have staff wear hardhats, safety glasses, and ear protection to protect them from their environment. Each industry is serious in their safety processes and procedures, and the expectation is that all the staff will follow these procedures.

Planning to use a safety report

In planning and preparing to use a safety report tool, the project manager must first determine if his or her company has a safety program. Without a safety program, there will be no safety reports. Most companies have a safety program with procedures, even if they are minimal. The project manager should meet with the human resource manager to go over and understand the company's safety program and safety rules. Whenever the project manager implements a safety procedure on the project (job site) it should tie directly to the company's procedure. A major responsibility of the HR manager is the support of your safety program on the job site; use that support to its fullest. The HR manager and team should be highly involved in the authorization and the guiding of the initial direction of the project's safety program. You should involve as many of the team members as possible as well as the customer and contractors. Doing this not only will create a better safety program, it also communicates an understanding of your desire for a safe project environment.

After creating the safety report, the safety manager enacts the safety program. The safety manager will involve all of the team members, customers, owners, and contractors in this step of creating a safety program. The safety manager should not expect to create the perfect safety program if it is the first time they have implemented one. These programs are an evolving process. The project's safety program continually improves through the life of the project. Another task the project's safety manager will complete is to identify and define the success criteria of the safety program to produce the safety report. Those criteria should describe all the procedures to be able to report all safety problems, incidents, infractions, and accidents on the project. Every safety incident must go through a step-by-step process in order to be reported, tracked, and analyzed to produce the safety report. These steps are as follows:

1. An accident, an infraction, a safety problem, or a safety incident occurs on the project.
2. A team member must respond and report the occurrence.
3. A lead investigator performs an investigation and determines a root cause for the event.
4. The safety manager implements an incident prevention action plan to avoid future occurrences.
5. The safety manager will continue to track each individual incident and analysis and determine root cause.
6. The safety manager and the project manager creates the safety report monthly and informs and continually improves safety processes on the project.

The safety reporting process should track all safety status using all the safety accidents, infractions, safety problems, or safety incidents that occur on the project; then consolidate it into the weekly safety report. The report can be a customized dashboard real-time review or distributed via a document or e-mail.

Before you can create the safety report tool, you must formulate a plan. In the following "Planning Questions" section, we provide some initial thoughts to help you start thinking about how you can utilize this tool. Ask yourself the following questions.

Planning Questions

1 *When would you create, develop, or write this tool?*
After a safety program is implemented, when a Safety infraction or accident occurs, during execution stage of project

2 *Who is going to use this tool, both from an input and output status?*
Project manager, safety manager, or owner

3 *Why are you going to use this tool?*
Keep track of safety infractions and accidents occurring on project

4 *How are you going to use this tool?*
Complete form when incident occurs, file with appropriate resources statistical analysis

5 *How will you distribute the information?*
Document format, spreadsheet format, complete online, e-mail, document control system, and in-person presentation

6 *When will you distribute the information?*
After accident or safety infraction occurs on project

continued

---

continued

7 *What decisions can or should you make from this tool?*

Analysis the accident data to provide to make decisions on preventing future accidents, decide on type of accident, and increase safety training for team members

8 *What information does this tool provide for your project?*

Provides multiple selections for detailing and describing accident events, provides number of safety violations and accidents to date on project, categories of accidents and infractions

9 *What historical and legal information do you need to store?*

Safety report itself, lessons learned information

10 *What will be the staffing requirements (Role Type) to run and maintain these tools?*

Safety manager, project manager, clerk, or administrative type assistant

---

Reporting using a safety report

The safety manager is responsible for developing the safety report. Large projects can utilize administrative personnel in the development of a safety report.

In the previous example, you clearly see the situations that have occurred on the construction site for the week ending 3/7/2008. The example in Figure 12.10 is a typical report with a small sampling of incidents on the project. In a real-life situation, the safety manager who develops the safety incident report reports multiple incidents on a weekly basis. Most companies will have a written form for the safety manager to complete, which is similar to this report. If there is no existing report, you can use this as a starting point for your project.

Figure 12.11 shows an example of an accident investigation report created by the Corp of Engineers. As you can see in the example, the accident report is detailed and captures all the information that is pertinent. A report like this evolves over a period of time and is updated and improved periodically. This example would represent a sampling of an accident report that could be used in any industry for any type of accident situation. Notice the amount of information that is captured and stored about the event. The wealth of information collected on the form allows for very easy communictions.

The project manager generates the safety report on a weekly basis but provides a summary to the stakeholders and upper management monthly. Some safety managers may decide to report the safety reports on a weekly basis, but it may become a level of overhead not necessary if there is little to report. The safety report has a variety of formats, where document and spreadsheets are the most dominant. The safety report is stored as part of the standard project documentation.

CROSS-REF   See Chapter 20 to learn more about how to use and create a safety report.

FIGURE 12.10

This figure represents an example of a safety incident report.

Week Ending: 3/7/2008

Safety Risk and Mitigation Report

Risk Event	Mitigation/Elimination Strategy	Date of Occurrence	Time	Reported to	Person(s) Violator
Boards with nails sticking up	Removed nails from boards, and stored board	3/4/2008	10:08 am	John Smith	Fred Green
Iron workers, not using safety line	Snapped on safety line	3/5/2008	1:35 pm	AJ Black	Bruce Baker
Insufficient ventalation in Paint area	Added exiting blower to the area	3/5/2008	3:32 pm	Sally Spiker	John Jones

FIGURE 12.11

This figure represents an example of an accident investigation report. (This is just a partial example of the accident report.)

(For Safety Staff only)	Report No.	Eroc Code Go	UNITED STATES ARMY CORPS OF ENGINEERS ACCIDENT INVESTIGATION REPORT		Requirement Control Symbol CEEC-S-8 (R2)

1. Accident Classification

Personnel Classification	Injury/Illness/Fatal	Property Damage	Motor Vehicle Involved	Diving
Government ☐ Civilian ☐ Military	☐	☐ Fire Involved ☐ Other	☐	☐
☐ Contractor	☐	☐ Fire Involved ☐ Other	☐	☐
☐ Public	☐ Fatal ☐ Other		☐	

2. Personal Data

a. Name (Last, First, MI)	b. Age	c. Sex ☐ Male ☐ Female	d. Social Security Number	e. Grade
f. Job Series/Title	g. Duty Status ☐ On Duty ☐ TDY ☐ Off Duty		d. Employment status at time of accident ☐ Army Active ☐ Army Reserve ☐ Permanent ☐ Foreign National ☐ Temporary ☐ Student ☐ Other (Specify) ☐ Volunteer ☐ Seasonal	

3. General Information

a. Date of Accident (month/day/year)	b. Time of Accident (military time) hrs	c. Exact Location of Accident	d. Contractor's Name (1) Prime: (2) Subcontractor:
e. Contract Number ☐ Civil Works ☐ Military ☐ Other (Specify)	f. Type of Contract ☐ Construction ☐ Service ☐ A/E ☐ Dredge ☐ Other (Specify)	g. Hazardous/Toxic Waste ☐ Superfund ☐ Derp ☐ IRP ☐ Other (Specify)	

4. Construction Activities *(Fill in line and corresponding code number in box from list - see instructions)*

a. Construction Activity	(Code) #	b. Type of Construction Equipment	(Code) #

5. Injury/Illness Information *(Include name on line and corresponding code number in box for items e, f, & g - see instructions)*

a. Severity of Illness/Injury	(Code) #	b. Estimated Days Lost	c. Estimated Days Hospitalized	d. Estimated Days Rest. Duty
e. Body Part Affected Primary	(Code) #	g. Type and Source of Injury/Illness		
Secondary	(Code) #	Type		(Code) #
f. Nature of Illness/Injury	(Code)			(Code)

Summary

The tools described in this chapter help project managers monitor and control their project risks. Risk management is challenging on most projects, and, therefore, if project managers can utilize tools that will help them in this process it will increase their chances of running a successful project.

As you read this chapter, the one tool that jumped out and made the biggest impact on risk management is the Risk Modeling tool. Risk modeling is a relatively new concept that is catching on quickly and becoming relevant in risk management. The risk modeling process allows project managers to work closely with their team members for a solid understanding of the project risks and exposes those risks to customers and upper management for possible resolution.

The chapter included tools such as decision tree diagram, issue list, risk assessment form, risk simulation, and safety report. Each of these risk tools can help you control the risks on your project, which should bring it to a successful conclusion.

Chapter 13

Defining Communication Tools to Manage Project Procurement

I n this chapter, we explore project communication tools in the Procurement Management knowledge area. The tools included will help project managers in the procurement area of their projects. Procurement management can be very difficult for project managers, especially when working with vendors or outside contracting companies; for example, when dealing with fixed-bid projects that have constant scope change requests by the customer. Procurement management is managing the relationships between the vendor company and your company, and keeping the relationship friendly when the vendor company continues to request additional funding to perform the extra work. Requesting funding every time there is a scope change, regardless of the size of the work, can strain the relationships between the two companies tremendously. If one company continues to drive change requests through the process and the other company is expecting payment for every additional work item requested, the relationship between the two parties becomes tense and the project manager must step in and manage the situation accordingly. This may not be easy.

In the following chapter, we present tools used to manage project procurement activities. These tools are critical to communicating the procurement activities on the project. Procurement is a very important aspect in project management and something that project managers need to be diligent about as they manage their projects. It includes contract knowledge and legal awareness.

Introducing the Document Control System

The *document control system* acts as a central repository for project information. This electronic filing system stores all the project files and acts as a security filter for project managers to apply on specific files to lock out certain people from making unwanted changes or seeing data they do not have the authority to see. The document control system can hold any type of electronic file the project is using, with the only limit being file size. Often, companies put tight restrictions on how large the files can be, and how many files the document control system can hold per project. It is common to store project schedules, budget spreadsheets, requirements documents, and design specifications. Anything you can create electronically can be stored as part of this system.

The document control system is not like other tools. One of the benefits and the great things about this tool is that the project manager does not report using the tool and it is not part of any regular reporting. It is not that kind of tool. Instead, people come to the tool for project files and information. Fortunately, this tool does not require the project manager to do anything special to communicate with it. Interestingly enough, it is one of the best communication tools available to the project manager and the project because it acts in itself as a repository and, therefore, provides unlimited information to anyone authorized to access the system. This is due to the system always being available and having the ability to store all project files within it. No other tool stores all project documents within itself while also being a single repository available at all times.

NOTE The Project Management Institute's knowledge area for this document control system is in the Procurement Management area. The secondary area that this tool could be associated with is Risk.

TOOL VALUE Stores all project documentation in a single repository and provides access to anyone involved in the project.

The benefits of using a document control system are tremendous. To begin with, having all project documents in one place allows a project manager to control and monitor their project documentation more effectively. No longer does a project manager need to worry about finding spreadsheets or looking for update budget sheets. Using a document control system helps to enforce the location for storing all project files on the project.

Most document control systems have check-in and checkout capabilities that keep documents locked, preventing unauthorized access. Here are some additional benefits of using a document control system.

- Create documents faster and more efficiently.
- Access documents faster and more efficiently.
- Boost stakeholder/customer satisfaction by providing full access to project documents.
- Improve security by controlling access when checking-in and checking-out project files.
- Reduce document overload. No need for multiple versions of same document.
- Become more productive since all project team members are using the same repository.

- Provide immediate online access to project documentation.

- Comply with auditing process and procedures where internal auditors have full access to the project documentation.

The document control system is an ideal tool for the multiproject environment where there is a need to pass information from one project to another. For example, if one project manager wants to see a design drawing from another project, all she/he would need to do is to access that drawing from the other project's document control system. The sharing of files occurs instantly, and everyone gets the information they require for the project. Long gone are the days of trying to find files on e-mail servers or personal hard drives when companies choose to implement document control systems for their projects and document management purposes.

 Managing and controlling project documentation should be a top priority for any project manager from the very start of the project through completion.

Project customers will find great value in being able to access project information at any time (24/7), knowing that the information they are accessing is the latest for the project. At any time, customers can pull up project schedules, budget reports, status reports, or any other project document. If project managers choose not to use a document control system, it can cause problems and uncertainty for customers trying to find information. It will portray a poor image to the customers that the project manager or team members are unable to keep their documents and the files straight, leading them to question how the project manager could possibly run a successful project.

Increasingly, companies are starting to utilize document control systems for storing not only project information, but also all company documentation. The following is a list of some of the more popular document control system packages on the market:

- Microsoft SharePoint Services

- Microsoft Groove

- Documentum

- KnowledgeTree

- FileHold

The biggest difference between the systems in the list is the functionality they have built into them. When selecting a document control system there are some key features that project managers' should be looking into to help manage and control their project's documentation. Following are some of the key features of a document control system:

- **Archival:** Ability to archive

- **Creation:** Ability to create material, such as documents, spreadsheets, drawings

- **Distribution:** Ability to send and receive both technical and administrative reports

- **Filing:** Ability to file documents manually or electronic

- **Retention:** Ability to hold documents for a specific period

- **Retrieval:** Ability to retrieve documents and access the information quickly
- **Security:** Ability to lock documents and limit access
- **Storage:** Ability to easily store documents and obtain additional storage if required
- **Workflow:** Ability to move documents among team members

> **TIP** All projects must have some form of document control. If you do not have a formal system, implement a manual workaround. A manual workaround for example would be putting a directory structure on a shared network drive and having all team members and customers save their files to this drive. This is a manual workaround because setting up the structures would be manual, setting up security would be manual, and nightly backups may need to be manual. It is not at all as robust as the full document control system solution but it works for small projects.

All projects, regardless of size, can utilize a document control system. Although smaller projects do not have the volume of documents generated that a medium or large project creates, the importance of creating an organized structure for storing and controlling project documentation is still applicable. On medium and large projects, the amount of documentation created is so large that the only method of keeping the files straight is to add it to a document control system in a structured and organized manner. Managing a large project without some mechanism of document control is almost impossible.

The document control system is a communication tool by itself. It stores all the project documentation, and customers can "communicate" with it at any time by accessing the information on the project. Most of the document control systems have alerts and messaging capabilities that can communicate to anyone interested on the status of files changing, or the addition and deletion of files in a particular folder. The document control system actually communicates on behalf of the project manager in those cases because it auto-generates messages and e-mails those messages out to anyone who has signed up to receive them. The different document control systems have a number of communication alerts and messaging features available within the tools. This brings a new level of communication for the project manager and team members to utilize on their projects.

Project managers utilize the document control system daily because this tool is important to help them manage and control their project's documentation. The project manager along with the document control specialist plans and designs the structure of the document control system in a manner that he/she feels will be easy to find project information, and will be easy to share with anyone with permission wanting project information. One of the document control system's biggest benefits is that a project manager can use it as a repository for storing sign-offs and approvals. The advantage of using a document control system for these purposes is the security it has built into the system. The project manager can take advantage of that security by storing the approvals he/she receives from the project's customers or upper management. If there is ever a time someone is looking for proof that something has been approved, the project manager can point them to the folder where the approvals are stored, and they can access it themselves. Without utilizing a document control system, the project manager or team members would waste valuable time searching through e-mails and looking on hard drives to find approvals that they may never end up finding.

In some cases, there may not be a document control system in place, and the project manager could be forced to implement a manual solution to simulate a document control system. To create a manual solution that would simulate an automated document control system, you are going to use tools such as e-mail, personal hard drives, or network drives in order to create a structure that would store the files. The project manager should consider the manual solution as a short-term fix that requires the immediate escalation to upper management to provide a better long-term solution. With the costs of projects today, and the relatively inexpensive document control systems available, companies have no excuse for having project teams deal with manual workarounds, especially when dealing with the risk of the deletion of important project documentation because it is stored on someone's laptop computer somewhere. Even the smallest companies running the smallest projects should have an automated document control system in place to store important project-related documentation in a safe and secure environment.

Planning to use a document control system

In planning and preparing to use a document control system, the project manager must first look at the type of project they are managing and determine how they want to manage and control the project's documentation. One of the most important steps in planning and preparing to use this tool is the setup and establishing of the project's directory structures. In this planning activity, the project manager should review the project's development and project management methodologies to be sure they set up the same structure as the methodologies within the tool. After creating and planning the project structure, the project manager should then work with the project team members and establish which project files they want to store and share. The team members normally have suggestions for the structure of the document control system that the project manager will need to implement after setting up the tool for the project.

After working with the team members, the project manager then works with the customers to determine if and how they want to get involved in the tool, what access they would like, what alerts they want to receive, and generally what their involvement will be in using this tool. These conversations can be very interesting, especially if a customer is not familiar with the options of the tool and does not realize that he/she could have access to all the project documentation. It is usually a difficult situation for the customers because they end up getting access to the project documents that, in most cases, they should not be accessing because there is too much detail. For example, most customers should not be reviewing the detailed test scripts developed by the testers on a software development project; however, those files will be in the document control system, and accessible by anyone who has access and the appropriate level of security to the files. However, if the project manager does not provide access to some of the project documents, it could look to the customers that they are hiding something, which is not beneficial to anyone, and it could look like the project manager is not organized or worse yet, hiding something. Either way, it is not good for a project manager to have the perception that they are hiding something on their projects; therefore, it is important that the project manager review the security setting in the document control system to ensure everyone has the right security level of access in the system. If not, you could have team members or customers trying to access project information and fighting the security problems along the way.

Before you can create the document control system, you must formulate a plan. In the following "Planning Questions" section, we provide some initial thoughts to help you start thinking about how you can use a document control system on your project. Ask yourself the following questions.

455

Planning Questions

1   *When would you create or develop the document control system?*

There are only a few companies that create document control systems, so in most cases, this is purchased and implemented at the company level, the project manager starts utilizing the tool for their project and sets up the appropriate structure.

2   *Who is going to use this tool, both from an input and output status?*

Anyone involved with the project will access the document control system.

3   *Why are you going to use this tool?*

To monitor and control project documentation, backup and archive documentation, save project approvals and sign-offs in secure location, and as a central repository for all project information

4   *How are you going to use this tool?*

To access all project documentation within the document control system, store project-related documentation and approvals into tool for safekeeping, point any compliance auditing teams to tool for accessing project information

5   *How will you distribute the information?*

The document control system is available for access on a continual basis and therefore does not actually distribute anything; people use it to access project data. However, it does have a built in messaging service, which would be the closest thing to distributing project information.

6   *When will you distribute the information?*

Distribution is not necessary as it is always available 24/7 and can be accessed by anyone interested in the project documentation.

7   *What decisions can or should you make from this tool?*

When all documents for the project are stored in the document control system, all project decisions that can be made from the information. Whether it be schedule, scope, resources, or budget decisions, having all the project documentation available makes the decision-making process much easier.

8   *What information does this tool provide for your project?*

All project documentation is stored in this tool, so all project information is available. The only limitation to this is the files that are secured and for limited viewing such as payroll data or personnel files; that information is available and provided by the tool, but to limited people.

9   *What historical and legal information do you need to store?*

All the documents stored for the project, therefore there is no specific legal or historical need calling out separately

Reporting using a document control system

The document control system stores project documentation and does not have a specific project status associated to it, nor does it store project status information contained in the tool. What it does store are the actual files that contain project status and scope information. If customers want the latest status, or want to pass files back and forth, they can do so by going directly to the document control system, finding the project and documentation they are looking for and then sending it to whoever needs the information. As the project progresses, more and more files go into the document control system providing even more valuable project information for the customers and upper management staff.

Another important note to take away when thinking about setting up a document control system is the tool's security setting. When setting up the document control system for the project, the project manager must ensure everyone has the appropriate level of security assigned. Project team members must be able to access the files needed to work with on the project, and in some cases this may mean locking out certain people from seeing project information that they should not be seeing. For example, resource rates and contract information may not be applicable for everyone to see, and the project manager should set security in place in the document control system to prevent that from occurring. Project managers often overlook security for one reason or another, but it is important to ensure security is correct for the project at the very beginning.

 See Chapter 15 to learn more about how to use and create a document control system.

Introducing the Formal Acceptance Document

The purpose of a *formal acceptance document* is to capture and store the customer's final approval and legal acceptance of the project. In most cases, the signing of the formal acceptance document closes out the project and tells the team they have completed their work; in other cases, the document acts as the input into the start of the closeout process. Project managers find this document to be one of the tools they create and use most on their projects. When customers sign the formal acceptance document they accept the work product(s), and the team is free to move on to other efforts. Without that signature, the customers have not accepted the project as delivered, and the project team may remain in place until the customer provides their approval. An important distinction between the formal acceptance document and the user acceptance document is that the formal acceptance document represents the approval of the project and not necessarily a particular project deliverable like the user acceptance document covers. When customers approve the formal accept-ance document, they are approving the whole project. At the end of the project, the project man-ager can send a final report to their customers summarizing all the project's activities. The final report should be stored and archived along with the other project documentation.

> **TIP**   Some project managers use a final report every time they complete a project. Consider using one for your projects as well.

From a communication perspective, the formal acceptance document is one of the most rewarding documents that a project manager can send. When the project manager sends out this document, there are usually many cheers, best wishes, and "job well done" e-mails sent to the team members. It is normally a great time for the project and the team members.

> **NOTE**   The Project Management Institute's knowledge area for the formal acceptance docu-ment is the Procurement Management area. There is no secondary knowledge area known for this tool.

> **ON the CD-ROM**   We have included a sample of a formal acceptance document in the Procurement folder. Use this as a guide to the first step in creating your own version of this tool.

> **TOOL VALUE**   The value of this tool is that it signifies the formal acceptance and legal approval that the project team has delivered the project to the customers.

There are many benefits of using a formal acceptance document on your projects. The first benefit is that it confirms the customers have signed off and approved the project. These signatures are beneficial if there are any questions or concerns around the evidence that the customer accepted the project. The evidence can be an actual signature on a piece of paper or an e-mail acceptance.

The second benefit is that the acceptance of the project officially transfers ownership and responsi-bilities from the project manager to the project customer. The project manager ensures he or she obtains the signature from all stakeholders designated to sign off on the project. If for some reason the project manager is unable to get signatures from the customers, it is the project manager's responsibility to address, not the stakeholders or owners. It would not be a good situation for the project manager if he/she is unable to get approval on the project because it is preventing the responsibility and transfer of ownership from him/her to the customer. Without that signature, the project manager could end up owning the project for longer than they ought to.

Another benefit of using a formal acceptance document is that it can be critical if needed in a court of law. This document, once signed, is a legally binding agreement between two parties. You can imagine on a multi-million dollar project how important the customer's signature is if in the mid-dle of a major lawsuit, the customer states that he never approved the project, and you have a signed piece of paper proving that he did.

Customers also benefit from using the formal acceptance document in legal actions; however, proj-ect managers must be aware of this double-edged sword. As the focus for the formal acceptance document is mainly for the customers to provide their approval and acceptance, the same holds true for the project manager. When the project manager signs the document, he or she states that the project team has delivered the scope of the project based on the customer's requirements. The document holds both parties accountable for the project, and if there is a legal case the project manager must ensure that she can stand behind the signed document.

Figure 13.1 shows a typical formal acceptance document. When the customer and the project manager sign on the signature line, it represents both parties' acceptance of the project.

In reviewing the formal acceptance document example in Figure 13.1, it is important to note the Client/Owner signature field. No formal acceptance document is complete without sign-off in that field. In today's electronically driven society, the formal handwritten signature is going away, and e-mail acceptance is now becoming the norm. Even when using the format in Figure 13.1, the project manager can still capture the customer's approval when they send it by e-mail; the project manager simply copies the e-mail directly into the document.

From a legal perspective, ensuring that the customer's signature and formal acceptance document are together is vital. If they are not, it might be harder to prove that signature is actually for the formal acceptance document and not something else. Therefore, because of the importance of the customer's sign-off of the formal acceptance document, it is the responsibility of the project manager to archive the document for future reference (legal cases) or in the event of internal company audits. In some cases, legal departments of some medium to large companies will obtain acceptance signatures from the customer, relieving the project manager of this task. The legal team stores those acceptances along with the other project documentation and may have its own process for archiving this documentation. Project managers should solicit help from the legal team when first creating the formal acceptance document. The legal team will also confirm that if there are any issues, they can cover the project if it gets into any legal trouble down the line.

One problem project managers face today is that they often forget to use the formal acceptance document on their projects because they are too busy or preoccupied working on other projects, or a project manager may consider the formal acceptance document unimportant or simply not want to take the time to create it. In some cases, if the project has not gone as planned, they may feel it is not appropriate to obtain a sign-off from an unhappy customer. In every project, regardless of how well it went, obtaining this sign-off is critical because, in some companies, the project literally cannot close out until the customer formally approves it. In some projects, customers may hold off providing their sign-off to delay the start of the project's warranty period. Project managers should not allow this delay to happen. Sometimes project managers do not know how to proceed when put in this position and therefore do not know what to do. For example, on a typical project after the project team finishes their work activities, they start the warranty period and fix any issues that arise during that time; however, if the project team finishes their work activities and the project customer has not approved the project, regardless of the reason, the project manager is in a difficult situation. If that situation occurs, project managers have a couple options they can take, each option having pros and cons, and each requiring the support of upper management before implementing. These options could include but are not limited to the following:

- Do they start on the warranty period, even though the project is not accepted?
- Do they stop and disperse the team to work on other projects?
- Do they sit idle and wait for the warranty period to start?

FIGURE 13.1

The formal acceptance document is an e-mail from a project sponsor to the legal team. The example, once signed, is a legal and binding document.

Formal Acceptance Form

Project ID/Num: _____ Project Name: _____ Acceptance Date: _____

Project Client/Owner Name: _____ Customer/Owner Department Name: _____

Project Manager Name: _____ Project Management Office Rep: _____

Project Acceptance or Information:

    Acceptance or Reject Delivery of project: Accept: _____ Reject: _____ (*)

    * If rejected please explain the reason:

_____

_____

Further Comments:

_____

_____

Project Detail information:

Planned Start Date: _____ Actual Start Date: _____

Planned Finish Date: _____ Actual Finish Date: _____

Actual Budget ($): _____ Final Costs ($): _____ Over or Under Budget: _____

Signatures/Approvals Section:

Project Manager Approvals: _____

                    Print Name

                _____

                    Signature

Project Client/Owner Approvals: _____

                    Print Name

                    _____

                    Signature

Regardless of the actions the project manager takes with the team members, do note that some customers will ride a situation like the aforementioned for as long as they can, which prevents warranty periods from starting. Project managers should have a back-up plan in place if this happens on their projects and engage their management as soon as possible to help resolve it.

Planning to use a formal acceptance document

In planning and preparing to use a formal acceptance document, the project manager must first work internally to determine if there is an acceptance process already used by the company, which may include standard templates, processes to follow, or methodology rules established that the project manager must adhere to for their projects. After determining if there is a formal acceptance document template available to use, the project manager then works with the project customers to determine what they want updated or changed on that template to suit their needs. It is important that the customer see the formal acceptance document long before requesting their sign-off on the project. At this point, the project manager is just looking for the customer's acceptance and approval of the proposed format, not the content in the document or the project itself. These conversations between the project manager and customer will help the customer be more willing to accept the document and sign off on it when the project finishes. After taking these steps, the project manager has adequately prepared for the use of the formal acceptance document on their project.

Before you can create the Formal acceptance document tool, you must formulate a plan. In the "Planning Questions" section, we provide some initial thoughts to help you start thinking about how you can use a formal acceptance document on your project. Ask yourself the following questions.

Planning Questions

1 *When would you create the formal acceptance document?*
In the planning phase of the project when the project manager is developing the tools to manage and control their project

2 *Who is going to use this tool, both from an input and output status?*
Project manager, executives, owner, or client, upper manager, legal team, team members

3 *Why are you going to use this tool?*
To obtain formal acceptance and approval of the project from the customer

4 *How are you going to use this tool?*
Send out document to obtain acceptance, as a legal document in the court of law and as a document to close out the project contract with a vendor or contracting company

continued

continued

5 *How will you distribute the information?*

E-mail, document format such as Microsoft Word, document control system, project closeout presentation

6 *When will you distribute the information?*

At close of project, when seeking to gain approval from the customer, and then after obtaining signatures as evidence the project has closed

7 *What decisions can or should you make from this tool?*

Decisions based on whether or not to accept the project

8 *What information does this tool provide for your project?*

Provides legal documentation that customer and project manager have accepted the deliverables of the project

9 *What historical and legal information do you need to store?*

The document itself, signatures of people responsible for closing the project

10 *What will be the staffing requirements (role type) to run and maintain these tools?*

Project manager, document control clerk, and legal clerk

Reporting using a formal acceptance document

The project manager is responsible for developing and driving the project's formal acceptance document. This includes the development and obtaining of signatures to close out the project. The project manager develops the document in the planning phase and then will utilize the formal acceptance document at the end of the project to capture the customer's acceptance. In most cases, this document can be very basic, providing the fields necessary to capture acceptance and approval only. If the document is complex, it may make it harder to obtain approval at the end of the project.

There is no weekly reporting of the formal acceptance document because it is a one-time document utilized at the end project and contains no project status information. The formal acceptance document is created using word-processing software and is stored along with all the standard project documentation as part of the document control system for long-term archiving, and it is accessible by any interested stakeholder on the project.

   See Chapter 22 to learn more about how to use and create a formal acceptance document

Introducing the Lessons Learned Document

The purpose of the *lessons learned document* is to capture and record the experiences and lessons that the project manager, team members, and customers learned as they executed and delivered the project. Capturing and collecting lessons learned data has one main purpose — to enable a project team to learn and grow from events in the past. The events on the project can be positive and provide information that the project manager can utilize on future projects, or negative, providing lessons to avoid in the future. The project manager captures lessons learned information based on everything that occurs on the project. In some cases, the project manager may want to focus the team's attention on just the main areas of the project, such as budget, schedule, quality, and scope. In other cases, the project managers may decide to capture everything. The project manager must have an agreement with their customers, that the information they are capturing will be valuable and that they will also provide lessons learned data throughout the project.

The project manager should communicate lessons learned information throughout the life of the project, from weekly status meetings where the project manager collects and discusses the lessons learned information, to the weekly status reports where the project manager adds the information to share with the customers. At the end of the project, the project manager will call a project-wide lessons learned meeting and present all the data collected each week and present it to the customers, team members, and upper management staff. The summarized lessons learned information is recorded on a day-to-day basis by capturing the happenings on the project. When recording the day-to-day events on the project, you end up missing capturing one of the most important aspects of the project, the feelings or the concerns of the team members and customers. Those types of responses come out during the actual lessons learned meeting, where the project manager asks for people's opinions at the meeting. A typical day-to-day event on a project could be anything that is negative or worth noting to possibly prevent it from occurring on future projects. There are also day-to-day events that are positive as well, and those require capturing. Typical examples include customers not signing off on a key document, or lack of communication occurring between team leaders causing problems in the deliverables or the project missing key dates. Any one of these events could have processes and procedures put in place to prevent them from reoccurring.

During the actual lessons learned meeting, the project manager will focus on what went right and what went wrong on the project, and could choose to cover those areas over the main project areas, such as scope, budget, and schedule, or possibly open it to the whole project. It just depends on what the project manager or customer agrees to cover during the meeting.

NOTE   The Project Management Institute's knowledge area for lessons learned documents is the Procurement Management area. There is no secondary knowledge area known for this tool.

ON the CD-ROM We have included a sample of a lessons learned document in the Procurement folder. Use this as a guide to create your own version of this tool.

TOOL VALUE Lessons learned information could prevent projects from wasting time and money on their efforts. Taking the time to review lessons learned materials before a project starts could save time and money on that project.

Future project teams can gain enormous benefits from learning how one project handled something, and either repeating it or avoiding it on their project. If project teams are aware of the mistakes on past projects, they can possibly prevent them from occurring on their projects. As long as future project teams are continually learning from past projects' mistakes, capturing lessons learned information is well worth it and will save time and money in the end.

Other benefits of collecting lessons learned information include:

- Identifying experiences that have occurred on the project to pass on to a future project.

- Ensuring teams are constantly aware of and identifying issues and risk events that occur on the project. In other words, the team is always looking for lessons learned information instead of allowing those details to pass them by and not capturing them for historical reference.

- Obtaining knowledge about new processes and procedures, how those processes were performed on the project, and using the data captured from lesson learned information to enhance the chances of success on the next project.

- Ensuring that the project benefits immediately by often making mid-project decisions that are based on what you have learned from prior weeks. By waiting until the end of the project and not capturing any information, you lose the valuable information gained each week by your team members.

Project managers can benefit significantly from utilizing and implementing the various results from the lessons learned information. Successful project managers learn the importance of this information quickly and whenever possible try to implement the best practices from those teachings onto their projects.

CROSS-REF See Chapter 1 for more information on the lessons learned process.

Table 13.1 is a table of contents for a lessons learned document or presentation material, and documents the four main questions asked of any team members, Areas of Success, Areas of Improvement, General Lessons Learned, and Final Thoughts. Once completed, the document is very comprehensive and extremely valuable for team member, customers, or future project managers.

TABLE 13.1

Example of a Table of Contents for Lessons Learned

Section	Description
1	Areas of Success
	Project Budget
	Project Schedule
	Project Quality
	Other Areas
2	Areas of Improvement
	Project Budget
	Project Schedule
	Project Quality
	Safety
	Other areas
3	General Lessons Learned Information
	Resource Assignments
	Working Conditions
	Overtime Issues
	Other Areas
4	Final Thoughts
	Failures
	Successes

The lessons learned process is one that actually starts from the beginning of the project, not at the end. A common mistake project managers make is waiting for the project to complete, or being close to finishing before starting to capture lessons learned information. Waiting until the end is too late in the process to start collecting this data, and because the majority of the team members have moved on to other projects, most of the time it is impossible to acquire this information. Even if it were possible, the team members would have a hard time remembering the majority of the lessons learned information from several months in the past. The lessons learned information is critical to collect as soon as it occurs and is fresh in the minds of the team members and customers working on the project.

Lessons Learned

The project manager decides at the beginning of the project to have bi-weekly team meetings that include lunch and drinks for the local team members and anyone who attends the meeting in person. Remote team members are welcome to come, but are not allowed to charge the project travel budget to get to the meeting. Team members that live in a different country are never going to get to the lunch meeting, and realize they are out of luck. After a couple of meetings, the local employees like the social aspects of the meeting and are really starting to become a good team. The remote employees, who make up 40 percent of the project team, feel left out. As the project manager starts to collect the weekly lessons learned information, the feedback from the remote employees is that they are not happy about this bi-weekly meeting and feel like they are missing out and are not part of the team because they do not get to be involved in the lunch or the social aspect of that meeting. As a project manager, when reading the lessons learned feedback, you now see that something you are doing on the project needs fixing immediately. You feel lucky you have collected the lessons learned weekly because you may never have had a chance to get that feedback from the remote team members. How productive do you think the remote team members would have been if the project manager did not fix this immediately, or had waited until the end of the project to collect the lessons learned feedback? The result would have been many lunches and many shunned team members working on the project who would have ended up resenting the project manager. This example is one of thousands where collecting lessons learned feedback throughout the life of the project paid off for the project manager and the team members.

The other advantage of collecting lessons learned information during the life of the project is to be able to make project adjustments based on what the team has learned from the project event. If there is an event on the project that occurs and is then captured as part of the lessons learned process, there is a high likelihood that the team will not repeat the same event on the project again. If it is a positive event, then the team will learn from that event as well and may repeat it if the outcome was beneficial to everyone.

The process of collecting lessons learned information is actually quite easy. Simply approach your team members and ask them what went right and what went wrong, and then document their responses. Capture the lessons learned information each week during the weekly status meeting when everyone is together and thinking about the project. Taking this approach is different than asking the team members to provide generic lessons learned information because they will not know what to provide, or have any idea where to start, or in general, be stuck on the question.

TIP   Some team members struggle if you do not frame the questions for them, and may end up giving random thoughts on lessons learned information that makes no sense. When framing this into the two questions, what went right and what went wrong; you should have no problem collecting the information.

It is also valuable to get specific examples and details from the team members or customers. For example, if a team member answers the "What went right?" question with "budget," this reply would not be specific enough because you are looking for both detailed and specific answers to these questions. Examples of "What went right?" replies that a project manager would want to capture are, "The budget was managed correctly throughout the project," or "I could tell every week how much of the budget we were spending, and how much we were projecting to overrun." These kinds of responses to the lessons learned questions provide real value to the project manager on what he or she did right on their project. The responses also provide tangible items that the project manager did on the project, and the team members liked and appreciated the project manager doing. When other project managers read this lessons learned information, and get an understanding on what types of events have gone well and what events have gone poorly, there is a good chance that it could change those project managers' opinions of how they run their own projects. When they see that the team members really liked something that the project manager did on the project, it may inspire them to do the same thing. The project manager would take the same approach and logic with the question "what went wrong?" The project manager should accept only detailed and specific answers to the question so they can use them that information as a learning experience, and possibly avoid repeating any mistakes.

> **TIP** It is wise to re-read the lessons learned at approximately 25, 50, and 75 percent of the way through the project.

Project managers should read the lessons learned documents of any projects that are similar to the project they are to manage, or if there are other lessons learned documents available, they should read and review them as well. If possible, once the project manager reads the lessons learned materials, he or she should communicate with the author of the lessons learned; who, in most cases, will be the project manager of the project, to get as much information as possible from them; Information that may not have been written, or documented, but valuable nonetheless. Many times, you can learn more information offline about what occurred on the project than you can ever learn from a series of documents. Set up face-to-face meetings and review the lessons learned materials or relevant project information to help you manage your project better. Most project managers who have worked on other projects would be more than willing to talk about their projects.

Planning to use a lessons learned document

In planning and preparing to use a lessons learned document, the project manager must first establish with team members and customers the process of collecting data throughout the life of the project. This process may be difficult for team members to adjust to because most of them are used to providing feedback at the end of the project only.

Collecting information from customers is usually an easier process than collecting from the team members — the customer will, in most cases, be quick to provide feedback on the positive and negative events of the project as often as you are prepared to accept it. The next step in this process is for the project manager to focus his or her planning efforts on what information they will collect, when they will collect it, and what format they will use to collect the data. Normally, the project manager uses the two-question format, but depending on the project, they may adjust that to suit the specific needs of the project. Some projects may gather more information than others, so the project manager should adjust their lessons learned process accordingly. Finally, the project manager needs to incorporate the lessons learned data into a final report or presentation. Often, project managers choose to collect and store the data weekly and choose not to report it, whereas other project managers report the information as part of their regular project status reporting cycle. After performing these planning steps, the project manager has adequately prepared for the use of the lessons learned document on their project.

Before you can create the lessons learned document, you must formulate a plan. In the following "Planning Questions" section, we provide some initial thoughts to help you start thinking about how you can use the lessons learned document on your project. Ask yourself the following questions.

Planning Questions

1 *When would you capture the lessons learned information?*
The project manager creates the template in the planning stages and as the project begins, the project manager captures the lessons learned information throughout the project.

2 *Who is going to use this tool, both from an input and output status?*
Everyone involved in the project will benefit from the lessons learned documentation and staff on future projects will benefit from lessons learned on previous projects

3 *Why are you going to use this tool?*
To capture the successes and failures on the project, improve the project during the lifecycle processes; increase the chances of success for future projects by learning from project successes and areas for improvement

4 *How are you going to use this tool?*
Capture the lessons learned information directly from the team members on what went right and what went wrong on the project; provide the lessons learned information to other projects to increase their chances of success

5 *How will you distribute the information?*
Document format, project presentations, document control systems, e-mail, and potential newsletter information

6 *When will you distribute the information?*
Distribution of the lessons learned information occurs at the end of the project when the project manager summarizes the information and compiles it for use after the project completes.

7 *What decisions can or should you make from this tool?*
Lessons learned information allows for project level decisions. If the project manager receives something that is troubling the team members, he or she can make immediate decisions to correct the situation.

8 *What information does this tool provide for your project?*

Provides ideas for improvements, and solutions for issues that arise on the current project and provide directions to all future projects

9 *What historical and legal information do you need to store?*

Document itself, references to the document, presentations of lessons learned materials and any correspondence relating to lessons learned

10 *What will be the staffing requirements (role type) to run and maintain these tools?*

Everyone involved in the project could potentially provide information to lessons learned information.

Reporting using the lessons learned documents

The project manager is responsible for capturing and collecting the project's lessons learned information. In most cases, this also means the project manager will capture the lessons learned information as part of the project's weekly status meeting and then compile the information into a format usable by the project team members or customers. The lessons learned information becomes a valuable feedback form to the project manager on how she/he is managing the project. This is valuable from a learning perspective because in some cases it can change how the project manager manages the project going forward.

A good assignment for a project communications manager is the lessons learned compilation each week. This information could go into the monthly newsletter as tips and tricks. Also, articles could be written about a particular lesson that would be of interest to the team members and of benefit to the project.

Reporting using the lessons learned data comes down to both the weekly reporting of information on a project status report, and a single meeting at the end of the project. A lessons learned presentation and meeting occurs when the project finishes and is closed out.

> **TIP** Schedule informal lessons learned meetings with your project customers so you can receive more constructive and valuable feedback than they would give at a large, all project postmortem meeting where they may feel shy and not ready to give the same kind of feedback. It is important to capture your customer's real feelings and concerns about the project during the project, not at the end.

> **CROSS-REF** See Chapter 22 to learn more about how to use and create a lessons learned document

Introducing Phase Closeout Document

The purpose of a *phase closeout document* is to capture the required signatures and approvals at the end of each project phase, ensuring that the phase is properly closed-out. The typical activities that occur in the phase closeout process include finishing remaining tasks, obtaining final signoff, performing project documentation audits, and performing quality assurance activities. Most of these activities are the responsibility of a project team, but the project manager drives each to its closure.

One important task that the project manager must perform is to identify who on the project can close out each phase and provide their approval for the project team to move on. Whether the phase is moving from design to development, development to test, or design to construct, each phase has a unique set of tasks and deliverables required to finish before the phase is officially complete. The project manager ensures throughout the phase closeout process that everything to be finished is actually complete. After confirming everything is finished, the team members can then move on to the next phase.

The phase closeout is an important process within any project development methodology. Each methodology has specific details as to what project deliverables are required for that phase. The methodology also has details on which roles can provide approval to close out a phase, so the project manager, by working with the methodology and the responsibility matrix they created during the planning process, should have a good idea of who needs to approve what for the project.

When a phase closes, some team members will move onto other projects. For example, when the project moves from the design phase to the development phase, the project manager releases most of the project's designers. This is important to remember, because after the project manager releases these resources, obtaining their services again can be challenging. The other factor to consider is the budget, as team members move on and take on other assignments, their charging toward the project ends immediately. The project manager should watch this closely and ensure that as team members leave, they also stop charging to the project's budget.

NOTE   There is an important distinction between the project phase closeout and the formal acceptance document. Project managers should be aware of this while executing their projects. Project phase closeout is the customer approving a particular phase of the project, not the whole project. The formal acceptance document is the customer accepting the whole project, including all phases required to complete the project. These are two distinct and very different documents.

Communicating the phase closeout document occurs with the same positive enthusiasm and good will as sending out the communications for the formal acceptance document. When completing a project phase and sending out notification that the team completed their work, the project team members deserve positive feedback and recognition for their hard work. Sending out the phase closeout document provides project managers with evidence that they have complied with the project's auditing and compliance requirements. Most of the time, the compliance teams must obtain signatures and formal acceptance from the project team members and customers, which is the main purpose of the phase closeout document.

The Project Management Institute's knowledge area for this phase closeout document is the Procurement Management area. There is no secondary knowledge area known for this tool.

We have included a sample of a phase closeout document in the Procurement folder. Use this as a guide to create your own version of this tool.

The phase closeout document captures and stores the customer's acceptance and approval on a particular project phase.

The main benefit of using the phase closeout document is to capture acceptance and approval either from the customers, or in some cases the team leaders, that the project phase is complete and the project team can move on to a new phase. The process of shutting down one phase, obtaining approval to proceed to another, and providing all the documentation can be demanding. The project manager works with each team member, ensuring that their deliverables are complete and then seeks formal acceptance from the customers and team leaders to move on to the next phase. Some project phases do not require acceptance from the customers, but do from the team leaders; therefore, the project manager needs the team leaders of those areas to sign off, allowing the project to continue forward and into the next phase of the project. On a software project, for example, when the project moves from development to test, these phases may not require the customer to approve or be involved in that process. There is nothing in particular in those two phases that the customers would need to approve or be involved in, and therefore those customers would not need to sign off or provide any approval for the phase. In this case, the project manager works with the team leads in the development and test group to obtain their sign-off and approval to close out the development phase.

Another benefit of using a phase closeout process is that it represents major break points in the project. These are good stopping points to check on the project ensuring the team is progressing and still on target for the project's budget. These phase closeout points are generally milestones within a specific methodology used for the project. At each major milestone, the project manager performs a checkpoint on how well the project is progressing and whether it is on target to complete on time and on budget.

Table 13.2 shows a table of contents for a standard phase closeout document. There are four main sections to this document and each should have enough detail to capture what has occurred to date on the project. The four sections outlined in the template represent standard deliverables and key components of the project. Project managers working alongside their project team members are responsible for creating a phase closeout document for the project.

TABLE 13.2

Example of a Phase Closeout Document Table of Contents

Section	Description
1	Milestone Presentation & Associated Meeting
2	Project Audits
3	Go/No-Go Decision
4	Sign-off & Approvals for Phase Closeout

In reviewing the table of contents for the phase closeout document, it is clear that for such a small document, there is tremendous value in capturing this information for the project. The following list describes each section.

- **Milestone presentation:** Normally part of any methodology used on projects. There are always specific milestones required by the project team members to complete at the end of each phase. This presentation and associated meeting is documenting the various deliverables and presenting them to the customers and upper management. The actual presentation or links to the presentation are contained in this document.

- **Project audits:** Many large organizations have auditing teams in place to ensure the project complies with the requirements of the development methodology. The audits and the results of the audits are stored in this document.

- **Go/no-go decision:** The go/no-go decision criterion is stored in this section of the document. This can include decisions based on schedule, budget, scope or resources.

- **Sign-offs and approvals:** All sign-offs and approvals for the phase are stored in this section. In most projects, this means actually copying e-mail approvals from the different sign-offs and approvers, and copying them into the document for safekeeping. This keeps the document and the sign-offs together to satisfy any auditing requirements, if needed.

One of the key components for every phase closeout process, and in software projects specifically, is the formal meeting and presentation required to obtain phase closeout approval. Closing down a project phase creates a lot of paperwork and requires the project manager to obtain formal approvals to complete it. The required documentation becomes a valuable part of the presentation created for the phase closeout meeting. The purpose of the meeting is to present the status of the project at a specific point and obtain approval or denial to move to the next phase of the project. The project manager includes upper management, stakeholders, and team members in this phase closeout meeting because their official approval is required to move on to the next phase.

More companies are utilizing phase closeout meetings as part of their regular project management lifecycle. If, as project manager, you are not completing phase closeout meetings and obtaining approval to move forward, you should start to adopt this process immediately. As you move from phase to phase meeting with customers and obtaining approval, you are gaining their support to keep the project going as well as complying with most project methodologies on the market today. In some cases, someone in upper management, or a customer, may not like the direction the project is heading. They may feel the project is not going to be worth the overall costs and effort in the end, and they could actually choose to shut down the project at the phase closeout meeting. Closing down the project is a viable option for them at these meetings. Most likely, it probably will not be done at the meeting.

After the phase closeout activities are completed, the project manager should document the work and place those documents in the project's document control system archives for future reference. Phase closeout documents, once completed, are great communication tools because they store specific and detailed project information at the time of the phase closeout.

Planning to use a phase closeout document

In planning and preparing to use a phase closeout document, the project manager must first determine what internal processes are already in place that can provide direction, templates, or process to guide the project manager in the phase closeout process. If there is no process or procedures in place that the project manager can utilize, the first step is to determine how to use the phase closeout document on their project. In this planning step, there are four major areas that require careful consideration before developing the actual document; the presentation, audits, go/no-go decisions, and finally sign-offs and approvals. The components that are in the milestone presentation, how auditing works, and who provides the go/no-go decisions, are all questions and answers the project manager needs to understand before the phase closeout meeting occurs.

After the project manager determines what to present at the meeting, the next step is to work with the team members to explain what they need to understand about what their role is in the phase closeout process. It is quite common for project team members to own certain stages of the project (design-dev, dev-test). In those examples, the customers are not involved at all, and therefore the project manager will be working some of the phase closeout meetings and presentations internally, and not require customer input or approval, or even their attendance at the meeting. In other project phases, the project customers will be very active in their involvement. During the planning process, the project manager should work with the customer directly to ensure they are engaged in the phase closeout process because it is important that they understand the phase closeout process, its purpose, and how the customers are involved in it. The project manager should ensure there are no concerns from the customer's perspective when the project actually moves to the point in the project where the actual phase closeout meeting occurs and they are required to provide input. After performing these various planning steps to plan and prepare for using the phase closeout document, the project manager has adequately prepared for its use on their project.

Before you can create the phase closeout document, you must formulate a plan. In the following "Planning Questions" section, we provide some initial thoughts to help you start thinking about how you can use the tool on your project. Ask yourself the following questions.

Planning Questions

1 *When would you create or develop the phase closeout tool?*

After the end of each phase is the best time to utilize this tool

2 *Who is going to use this tool, both from an input and output status?*

Project manager, client or customer, upper management

3 *Why are you going to use this tool?*

To confirm the acceptance of a particular project phase and as approval to move on to the next phase and confirm project compliance from the auditing staff

4 *How are you going to use this tool?*

Project managers work directly to obtain sign-off of the document and the project phase

5 *How will you distribute the information?*

E-mail format with approval buttons (approve or reject) as the acceptance of the phase. In some cases, the project manager seeks actual signatures in the document, and project closeout presentation.

6 *When will you distribute the information?*

Thoughts and ideas: At the end of the phase when documents require signatures and approvals to close out the phase

7 *What decisions can or should you make from this tool?*

Decide on proceeding to next phase of project, decide on the action to take that is preventing the customer's approval

8 *What information does this tool provide for your project?*

Acceptance and approval of the project phase, for example design complete is approved and signed off by customer, show remaining work to obtain approval

9 *What historical and legal information do you need to store?*

Historical copies of a phase closeout form

10 *What will the staffing requirements (role type) be to run and maintain these tools?*

Project manager, customer, team members

Reporting using a phase closeout document

The project manager is responsible for driving the phase closeout activities on the project. It is his responsibility to ensure compliance and approval of each project phase. Without approval, the project manager should stop the project until full compliance and approval are obtained from everyone involved. It is only after obtaining all approvals that the project manager should allow the project team members to proceed with the deliverables of the project. Stopping a project can be difficult, but when projects do not stop, and continue without approvals, in some cases they are opening themselves up for major lawsuits. Stopping a project can be difficult, but in the end it makes the most sense and is best for the project and sometimes the company. Because one of the major benefits of the phase closeout is getting everyone together and agreeing on the direction of the project, having these mini stopping points is beneficial to the project.

Reporting of the phase closeout document occurs at the end of every project phase and is not part of the regular project reporting cycle. Reporting provides the opportunity for the project manager to present the major deliverables for each phase to the customers, and in most cases upper management, to allow them to decide to move forward with the project. If the project is in an unrecoverable state, the decision of shutting down the project could occur at this time. Phase closeout documents come in a variety of formats and are stored as part of the document control system for long-term archiving and are accessible by any interested stakeholder on the project.

 See Chapter 19 to learn more about how to use and create the phase closeout document.

Introducing the User Acceptance Document

The purpose of the *user acceptance document* is to capture and store the customer sign-offs and approvals for the various project deliverables. User acceptance documents signify the *approval* of specific project deliverables, not the project phase, or the project itself. That is an important distinction to remember because the formal acceptance document, and phase closeout document, both cover very specific areas of the project but do not cover specific deliverables. The user acceptance document covers the subject of obtaining signatures and approvals for work deliverables. The project manager must be diligent to ensure that customers accept and approve the project deliverables, including requirement documents, design documents, and test plans, and user acceptance documents. The user acceptance document is stored for long-term purposes in case the project should ever be audited and evidence of signatures is required as proof that someone signed off on the deliverable. User acceptance documents are common across all industries. An important part of utilizing the user acceptance document is the project manager's role in communicating and gaining approval from the customer. As project team members complete the project deliverables, the project manager delivers to the customer the user acceptance document for sign-off and approval for that particular deliverable. The project manager drives the user acceptance process and is responsible for ensuring the customer approves all deliverables on the project.

NOTE   The Project Management Institute's knowledge area for user acceptance documents is the Procurement Management area. The secondary knowledge area known for this tool would be Quality.

ON the CD-ROM   We have included a sample of this user acceptance document in the Procurement folder. Use this as a guide to create your own version of this tool.

TOOL VALUE   A user acceptance document is a single source that project managers can use to capture the customer's approval. It is a legal document on the customer's acceptance of the project's deliverables.

The benefit of utilizing a user acceptance document is that it provides evidence that the customer has accepted the project's deliverables. Without that approval, the project team could be heading down the wrong path and may never recover. Because most of the project deliverables drive the end result of the project, customers should be actively engaged in approving these documents. For example, the customer is responsible for and develops the business requirements document on most projects. The project team members own and develop the technical requirements document. Because the technical requirements document theoretically translates business requirements into a technical solution, it is easy to see why project managers will want the customer's approval on this document; likewise, it is easy to see why customers themselves will want to approve it. In this case, the project manager delivers the user acceptance document and the technical requirements document to the customer to capture their approval on the technical document. The expectation is that the technical requirements document and the business requirements documents match and should capture the business requirements originally asked. In most cases, the author of the user acceptance document stores the acceptance and approval of the various project documents directly into the document itself.

TIP   Use the acceptance document's table of contents as a checklist for all the deliverables on the project.

Figure 13.2 is an example of a user acceptance document used in the software development industry. This type of form is usable by any industry and any type of project, not just software. The most important part of this form is the customer signature and the conditions and statements that they are approving when signing off on a deliverable. Because this user acceptance document is project specific, the ability to update it and change it to the specific requirements of the project is very beneficial.

The process of utilizing the user acceptance form is simple and easy. The project manager updates and changes the user acceptance form based on the deliverables created by the project team. The project manager then delivers the form and the deliverable to everyone required to sign off and approve that particular deliverable. A best practice is for this process to take no longer than one week. If it takes any longer, people tend to forget what happened on the project, or they tend to think it is not important. The project manager should continue to drive signatures and approvals until everyone required has signed off. After obtaining the signatures, the project manager holds the customers who have accepted and approved the project deliverables accountable to that decision and any issues that arise. If there is any question about whether a customer accepted a deliverable or a particular item on the project, the project manager will have the signed forms as proof that the customer approved the deliverable. The user acceptance document is an official project document; a document that lawyers could potentially call into legal proceedings to act as evidence that a customer approved a deliverable on a project. A project manager does not want their project to end in legal proceedings, but if it does occur, the user acceptance documents act as evidence to support that the customer did sign off and approve the deliverable.

 **TIP**   Make sure you obtain all signatures stored within the user acceptance documents. Remember, you may never see these people again, except in court.

The project manager may want to seek legal advice when creating the user acceptance document to protect the project from a court action. A legal team review provides the project manager with confidence that, from a legal perspective, the signatures (approvals) he obtains on the document will hold up in court. If the legal team suggests updates or changes to the user acceptance document, the project manager should implement those changes immediately and send the revised document back to the legal team for final approval. Only after the document has had final approval from the legal team does the project manager go over it with the customer for their approval of the document.

FIGURE 13.2

The user acceptance document's purpose is to obtain approval from the stakeholders to approve the specific deliverable on the project.

Date: _____

This acceptance form acts as formal document of the _____ deliverable on the _____ project.

By signing off on this document, you agree to the following terms outlined below.

Please approve each statement below:

____ The deliverable is of the highest quality the project can afford.

____ I have fully tested the deliverable (if applicable) and it passes my tests and is ready from my perspective to be moved into a production environment. If the deliverable is a document, I have read it and agree to the contents of the document.

Signature: _____

Printed name: _____

User acceptance documents come in a variety of formats; each one is different based on the deliverables created for the project. For example, the design document on a construction project looks different from a design document on a software project, and therefore the user acceptance document for both of these documents will be different. It is the responsibility of the respective project managers to create a user acceptance document for their specific projects.

Planning to use a user acceptance document

In planning and preparing to use a user acceptance document, the project manager must first determine if there are existing processes in place that they must follow for their projects. There may be standard templates, legal requirements, and project management office requirements that are already in place to guide a project manager through the process of obtaining the user acceptance from their customers. If not, the project manager must determine how they want to handle the user acceptance process themselves. This means planning for the different deliverables that require sign-offs, setting up the document control system for storing and tracking these approvals, reviewing the project's development methodology, and ensuring the project stays in compliance with other planning activities that are required to utilize this important tool.

The next step is for the project manager to work with the team members to determine how they will be involved in the user acceptance document process. This could mean aligning with them as they complete their project deliverables to ensure the customers are approving and providing sign-off for their work deliverables. After performing these planning activities, the project manager will have adequately prepared for the use of the user acceptance document on their project.

Before you can create the user acceptance document, you must formulate a plan. In the following "Planning Questions" section, we provide some initial thoughts to help you start thinking about how you can use a user acceptance document on your project. Ask yourself the following questions.

Planning Questions

1 *When would you create or write the user acceptance document?*
The project manager sends the form to capture approval from the customer throughout the project, as specific deliverables complete.

2 *Who is going to use this tool, both from an input and output status?*
Project manager, team members, executives, owner or client, upper manager, anyone who would is required for sign-off and approval on project deliverables

3 *Why are you going to use this tool?*
To capture approval and acceptance of the various deliverables of the project such as functional specification documents, design drawings, test plans, phase closeout, etc.

---

4 *How are you going to use this tool?*

Provide to customers to approve deliverables, then use as evidence that customers have accepted the specific deliverable

5 *How will you distribute the information?*

E-mail, document control system, document format such as Microsoft Word and project presentations.

6 *When will you distribute the information?*

When required to obtain approval from the customer on acceptance of deliverable

7 *What decisions can or should you make from this tool?*

Decide on whether or not to approve, possible of go/no-go situation/decision

8 *What information does this tool provide for your project?*

Provides the fact that the component/deliverable of phase approved/rejected

9 *What historical and legal information do you need to store?*

Document itself containing signatures, and reasons why

10 *What will be the staffing requirements (role type) to run and maintain these tools?*

Anyone on the project that would be involved in the user acceptance document

Reporting using the user acceptance document

A project manager is responsible for creating the user acceptance documents, and it is also the project managers responsibility to ensure compliance and approvals are gathered from each project customer or stakeholder required to sign off on the project. Without that approval, the project manager should stop the project until all customers have approved the deliverables. Although this would be a very bold move for a project manager to take, it would stress the importance of signing off on the deliverables required for the project.

The reporting of user acceptance documents occurs after the customers have accepted the work deliverables. This is not something that must occur at a specific time; it occurs regularly throughout the life of the project. The project manager should celebrate the sign-off of major documents and report to customers and team members on the accomplishment of the project team obtaining that approval.

CROSS-REF See Chapter 22 to learn more about how to use and create the user acceptance document.

Summary

In summary, in this chapter we explored the various project communication tools in the project Procurement Management knowledge area. Project procurement can be a very difficult area of your project to manage, especially when working with vendors and outside contracting companies. Most project manages know very little about the procurement field. In some cases, such as in contract negotiations, companies can be difficult to work with and require strict guidelines set up and followed between the two companies. When dealing with vendors or contracting companies, it is important to ensure that everything is signed off and approved before any work activities begin.

As you read this chapter, the tool that stands out as most important in the project Procurement Management area is the lessons learned document. This document will have the biggest impact on your project, especially when you are starting a new project and there is historical lessons learned information available from previous, similar efforts. The lessons learned document is beneficial to both future projects and project managers themselves to learn and grow from their project experiences.

In this chapter, we covered procurement-related tools such as the document management system, formal acceptance document, lessons learned documents, and user acceptance documents. Each document focuses on acceptance, from either the team members or the customer's point of view, and each is very valuable to manage and control your project.

Part III

Project Lifecycle Processes

Chapter 14

Using Communication Tools in the Initiating Process

In this chapter, we explore the communication tools project managers can use to plan the start up and initiation of their projects. These project initiation tools are easy to use but are critical to getting a project started correctly. Each tool enhances the information and communication the customers, team members, or upper management receive from the project, and are critical in communicating the status of the project during this initiation process. The tools included in this chapter can help you become a better communicator. During the initiation of your project, you must identify the tools you will use to communicate the information your customers need, and it is critical to understand that during the startup, your customers will want a regular project status to ensure everything is on track and progressing as planned. The project manager is responsible for this communication, not only at the beginning of the project, but throughout the life of the project; therefore, it is important to get off to a good solid start.

Mastering the Communication Plan

Before exploring the *communication plan* tool, you need to understand how this tool can assist and support you on your project. The following project scenario emphasizes the importance of the tool and reasons why the communication plan is critical to every project.

A medium-sized drug company wants to develop a brand-new application that tracks the testing status of their drugs at various locations around the world. They compile that information into one central location where everyone can have access to the test results. Each location has a project manager assigned to the project. The unique aspect of this project is that each location is different; and, although the development of the application occurs in the United States, there will be special localization changes required at each location. The necessary modifications include language changes on screens and reports, and keyboard mapping changes that could affect the application. The inclusion of the localization changes makes this project complex, and the communication between the different locations are even more difficult. Here is your challenge:

> How can you manage and control your communications with the different locations and their uniqueness on this project?
>
> How do you set up and control effective communication with the project managers around the world?
>
> How can you communicate project information over the various time zones?
>
> Do you expect all project managers to travel to the U.S.? Will you go to them?

These critical questions require answers before the project kicks off; otherwise, the project manager will have difficulty gathering statuses from the numerous locations around the world without having a plan as to how the information will be coordinated and compiled.

The solution is the development and use of a communications plan. A communication plan documents and describes in detail how project information will flow on the project. The communication plan documents the status meetings, status reports, and frequency of reporting, and all other aspects of communication on the project. A project of this size requires a robust communication plan — one that requires buy-in from all locations and all project managers in order to be successful.

CROSS-REF   We recommend that you review the Communication Plan tool's planning questions in Chapter 10.

Creating the communication plan

Project communication is critical on every project, but an up-to-the minute status on most projects provides little to no value and costs a tremendous amount of time and effort to collect this information. Setting expectations, such as daily reports or an ongoing up-to-the minute status, will set up the project manager to succeed in delivering the correct level of project communications to their customers.

The actual steps in creating a communication plan vary from project manager to project manager. Instead of providing step-by-step instructions on creating a communication plan, a better option would be for the project manager to complete the communication plan template. Here is the project communication plan template for your project. You can use this template if their company does not have one available for you to use on your projects.

ON the CD-ROM   We have included a sample of this communication tool in the Communication tools under the Communication Managing Subfolder on the CD-Rom. Use this as a guide to create your own version of this tool.

Example of Project Communication Plan

Section 1: Project Communication Plan Overview
Write a communication plan executive summary. Include the purpose, the goal, the who, what, where, why, and the how of the plan.

Section 2: Project Communication Requirements Matrix
Document and develop the communications requirements matrix of the document. Develop the communication requirements matrix to control who receives what information on the project.

Section 3: Role Report Matrix
Document the role of the people receiving the report, how often they receive it, and the type of report. This matrix is also new to the industry and becomes a valuable tool in understanding how the project information will flow. Develop this matrix with your project stakeholders early in the project it should prevent key individuals from missing valuable project information as your project progresses.

Section 4: Timeframe
Document when each report will start and how often it is distributed.

Section 5: Lessons Learned
Document how you are going to acquire the lessons learned. It is important to document the lessons learned each week at the status meeting.

Section 6: Historical Information
Identify and document the plan for retaining historical information on the project.

Section 7: Closeout
Document the plan for the final report, the formal acceptance document, lessons learned document, project archives, and the user acceptance document.

Using the communication plan

Prior to using a tool such as the communication plan, it is imperative to identify who on your project team will utilize this tool and for what purposes. Knowing who will use the communication plan helps determine the level of detail required, frequency of distribution, style, and format of the report and ensures that when you are communicating it, you are doing so at the appropriate level for your team members and customers.

Before utilizing a communication plan, it is important to review the planning section developed in Chapter 10 and refamiliarize yourself with the activities and tasks outlined in preparing to use this tool. Then follow these steps:

1. Ensure that your communication plan covers all areas of the project you want communicated. Are the right reports listed, are the timeframes reasonable, are the customers satisfied with the proposed reports, and so on. In this step, the project manager is also thinking about who are the recipients of the plan, including upper management, vendors, partners, and executives, and adjusting the communication plan accordingly.

2. Review lessons learned information from any past projects and update the communication plan with best practices from that valuable information. There could be very valuable information in other project manager's lessons learned documents and you should be taking advantage of this information if it is available.

3. Work with the customer to obtain approval on the communication plan. This step includes sending the communication plan and the user acceptance document to the customer for their approval and sign-off. You may have to call the team members and the customers together and go over the plan and do a walkthrough of the document. If the customer engages when the project manager is building the communication plan, then an additional walkthrough of the document with the customers may not be required. After you receive the approvals from everyone you requested sign-off from, the next step is to ensure you store the document and the approvals in the document control system for long-term storage, archiving, and retrieval purposes.

4. As the project moves from planning to executing, continue to review and update the communication plan based on your customer's ongoing requirements and the specific communication needs for the project. This is also the point in the project where you will start sending all the reports outlined in the communication plan. This is the implementation point for the communication plan and the best time to determine if the customers are getting what they need from the information.

5. Update and enhance the communication plan throughout the life of the project. Even near the end of the project there may be a new report created that the customer will want reported to them. Ensure you document that report as well in the Communication plan. The project manager drives to ensure all customers and team members approve and sign-off on the plan when applicable.

Mastering the Customer Requirements Document

Before mastering the customer requirements document, it is important to understand how this tool can assist and support you on your project. The following project scenario emphasizes the benefits that you, the project manager, can gain by using the customer requirements tool.

The companies finance department would like a new financial system developed to replace their old legacy 20-year-old system. The staff has asked for the ability to track people's actuals, their monthly forecasts, budget data, estimate to complete data, and any variances. The customers want the new application developed in four months, and the budget for the project is unknown. The project resources are still in question, but at this point, you, as project manager understand this is a top-priority project, so getting resources to work on your project will not be an issue. You are currently working in the finance department, and you are one of the long-time and most senior project managers in the department, so management asks you to manage this project. As you start into the project, you determine quickly that there are no requirements anywhere and nobody has documented anything. You ask the project analysts, customers, and no one person has written anything down. The fact that there is no documentation worries you; you are also wondering why nobody on the project has a clue as to what they are supposed to be working on and yet they continue to work every day and don't ask questions. This is a mess, and one of the first things you do is to call formal customer requirements gathering sessions, where you can actually document the customer's wants and needs from the project. As you start into those requirements gathering sessions, you have a number of questions for the customers about the project. The questions include:

What are you trying to accomplish?

What are the goals of the project?

What are your business needs?

What do you like about the existing system?

What are your dislikes about the existing system?

What are your critical success factors for this project?

To obtain the answers to these questions, the project manager should use a customer requirements document. The document covers all aspects of the wants and needs of the customer. Many times, these documents cover business-specific requirements and often require additional discussions and requirements sessions in order to understand them completely. All projects, regardless of size or complexity, will have some form of requirements from the customer.

 We recommend that you review the customer requirements document's planning questions in Chapter 5.

Creating a customer requirements document

Creating the customer requirements document on a project is a vital activity on every project. All project team members must understand and develop the project's deliverables based on the requirements captured and documented in the customer requirements document.

Creating and capturing customer requirements provides the opportunity for the project manager and team members to understand exactly what the customers are looking for; for example, what do they want from the project, what are their goals, and what are the specific business needs they are trying to fulfill? What are the project's success criteria? Having the full team involved in capturing this information allows for little or no confusion around what they are requesting and what they hope is the solution. Customer requirements gathering sessions are complex and the project manager must manage them effectively or they can end up being a big waste of time. Some customers ask for items that may be reasonable, but force the project team into awkward situations where delivery may not be possible. Therefore, the management of these requirement sessions is tricky and it is important for you as project manager to try not to promise the world to your customers, when you may only be able to deliver just a small piece of it.

Project managers should be active in the customer requirements gathering process to allow them the chance from the beginning to understand what the customer is requesting and why, and to ensure that they make the correct decisions. When the project manager oversees only and does not completely understand the project requirements it can end up hurting them when they run into difficult project situations and are unable to provide the deep knowledge level answers that customers or upper management will be asking during those situations. This is a difficult place for a project manager to be in on their projects.

Project customers play a big part of the requirement sessions and in the end have the responsibility to ensure that the project manager and team members understand all the requirements completely before the session's end. Because the customer's requirements are the driving factors that make up the project, it is important that everyone understands them and there is no confusion by anyone involved. If the project manager ensures early in the project that everyone is onboard and understands what is required of them, there is a great chance of eliminating any confusion that can usually cause impacts to the budget and time delays on the project. Many times, the project team is thinking one thing and the customer is thinking another, which leads to project failure and unachievable goals.

The actual steps in creating a customer requirements plan can vary from project manager to project manager and depend greatly on their favorite tools of choice. Instead of providing step-by-step instructions on creating a customer's requirements document, a better option would be for the project manager to complete the customer requirements plan template. Here we provide a customer requirements plan template for your project.

Customer Requirements Table of Contents

Section 1: Scope
Document the scope of the project. If there are clear out of scope items, it is important to add to the out of scope components as well.

Section 2: Customer Needs (Goals and Objectives)
Document the Goals and Objectives of the project. Add any specific detailed goals or objectives associated with the project as well.

Section 3: Policies and Procedures Definitions

Document any procedures or definitions specific to the customer requirements, these could be areas such as internal policies within the customer or client area that may impact the project. It is also important you add the procedures to the document, as they will have an impact on the final product of the project.

Section 4: Business Use Cases and Scenarios

Document use cases and any user scenarios. This is one of the main areas of the document so capturing this information can be critical to the success of the project.

Section 5: Business Unit Interactions (if applicable)

Document interactions the customer groups have with other areas of the company or if applicable, outside the company, to the final product of the project. Recognize the interactions in this document to ensure you consider them when designing the system.

Section 6: Deployment Requirements

Document the project's deployment requirements. If there is anything special about deploying the final product, then use this section to capture that information.

Section 7: Output Reporting Requirements

Document any reporting requirements. Reporting requirements could range from the type of data required (software development projects) to a specific report created when the product goes live. Rarely are there reporting requirements for projects other than software.

Section 8: Operational Requirements

Document any specific operational requirements such as ongoing support, backup and recovery options; anything required for ongoing support and maintenance of the product. Operation requirements are generally software focused, but are also applicable in other industries.

Section 9: Testing Requirements

Document the specific testing requirements customers will want to be involved in for the project. The requirements can vary from project to project or industry to industry, but this section will provide the opportunity to capture those specific testing needs.

Section 10: User Documentation and Training Requirements

Document any specific user documentation or training requirements the users have for the project. Projects can vary greatly, but the users may have specific training requirements for the project that require capturing and documenting in the requirements document. This can range from training users all around the world, to using a "train the trainer" model.

continued

continued

Section 11: Requirements Priority Matrix

Document the customer requirements onto a priority matrix to ensure there is a priority associated to every requirement listed in the document. This matrix is important to allow the project team members an understanding of what order to work the requirements. This matrix also provides input to scope discussions allowing items to potentially fall out of scope based on how high they are on the list of priorities.

Section 12: Assumptions, Risks, and Constraints

Document any assumptions, risks, or constraints associated with the project. The tracking of this information is important because it allows team members to understand exactly what the parameters of the conversation are, and what they will be involved with on the project. Having knowledge of this information will be beneficial to the project team members.

Section 13: Participating Markets

Document any markets associated to the project. There may be projects implemented in different markets. If that is the case, this section of the document will contain the information associated with those markets.

ON the CD-ROM We have included a sample of this tool in the Communication tools, under the Scope Subfolder on the CD-Rom. Use this as a guide to create your own version of this tool.

Using a customer requirements document

Prior to using a customer requirements document, you must identify who on your project team can utilize this tool. Doing this determines the level of detail required, frequency of distribution, style, and format of the report. This ensures the project manager is communicating the appropriate level of detail to the project team members, customers, or clients.

Before using a customer requirements document, review the planning questions section in the customer requirements document section in Chapter 5 and refamiliarize yourself with the activities and tasks outlined when preparing to use this tool. Then follow these steps:

1. Ensure the document is complete and captures the requirements of the customers correctly. You must meet with the customer and the analyst together to ensure that they both agree on the contents of the document. After you obtain this agreement, obtaining approval from the customers should be easy.

2. Seek approval from the downstream users of the customer requirements document. For example, on a software project, the downstream users could be testers, developers, and designers. Each of these groups must be able to use the document for their portion of the project, and if not, the project manager must ensure the document gets the information to make it usable to them.

3. Send out the customer's requirements document and the user acceptance document to obtain the official project approval.

4. After you receive the approvals, store the document in the document control system for long-term storage, archiving, and retrieval purposes.

5. When the project team and the customers have approved the document, facilitate the technical components of the project from the customer requirement document.

6. As the project moves out of the initiation process and into the planning process, start the communications between the customers and the project team members on the document. As the team becomes clearer on the requirements and they start to translate those customer requirements into technical requirements, the customer requirements document becomes more of a supporting document now on the project and rarely used.

As the project moves into the executing phase, there are rarely any updates or changes to the customer requirements document. The only exception is when the customer introduces change requests into the project, which forces changes to the customer requirements documents, then, directly into the associated technical requirements.

Mastering the Feasibility Study

Before investigating the feasibility study, you must understand how this tool can assist and support you on your project. The following project scenario emphasizes the importance of the tool.

The staff in the marketing department would like a new system that scans computers, to determine the most popular and most used software application that runs on the company's computers. The marketing department has an idea that if the majority of the company's employees were using a particular software application, then the rest of the world would want to use that same software as well. It was just a hunch, but they believe it would pay off. After the marketing department has the information from the employee's computers, they will develop various worldwide marketing campaigns to promote the most used software. The marketing group has contacted you to manage the effort and lead your team into the process of building this scanning software. The problem you thought about immediately when approached with this project is how can you obtain the data from everyone's computers, and how feasible is this idea in general. You realize this is going to be a tough project to manage and before you send your team down the path of even trying to generate scanning software, you start to ask some questions to the marketing department about the project. Your questions include:

What is its long-term value of knowing this data?

What kinds of marketing plans do you have once receiving the data?

How often do we scan the employee's computers?

To obtain the answers to these questions the project manager should refer to the marketing department's feasibility study that they created to get the project approved. The feasibility study captures the answers to these simple questions and provides management with the information they need to decide whether to proceed with the project. The project manager taking on the project would be looking for some of the same information.

CROSS-REF   We recommend that you review the feasibility study's planning questions in Chapter 5.

Creating a feasibility study

The project customer creates the feasibility study document to justify why the company should initiate a project and how it might positively affect the bottom line. After the customer creates the feasibility study, upper management has the opportunity to approve before it officially authorizes the idea as a project. A feasibility study, and the corresponding idea, is not a project until it has management's official approval. It is important to note that although most feasibility studies do receive approval to proceed to a project, the process of completing this document generates some initial discussions and provides an opportunity for the groups doing the work, something to estimate the size of the project with to determine if it is even feasible. The feasibility study is also a mechanism that many companies use to provide management an opportunity to shut down the project before spending large sums of money on a project that may never be profitable. A feasibility study is more of a scapegoat for management to make decisions on ideas or proposals that they may not be comfortable with turning into a project. In most cases, if a company is going to have a business group work on an idea and create a feasibility study, there is a high probability of approving the project and it is going to proceed. But, there are times when ideas are bad, and some proposed projects are just not feasible. These normally never make it past the initial stages with management and hardly ever become projects. The feasibility study and associated process saves a company time and resources from starting on a project that may never get off the ground.

The actual steps of creating a feasibility study can vary from project manager to project manager and depend greatly on their favorite tools of choice. Instead of providing step-by-step instructions on creating a feasibility study, a better option would be for the project manager to complete the template The following is a sample feasibility study template for your project.

Example of Feasibility Study Table of Contents

*S*ection 1: Executive Summary
Document the executive summary for the project. Document the high-level value the project will bring in.

*S*ection 2: Background Information
Document the background information on why the company is requesting the project and what values will it bring if the project is to go forward.

---

*S*ection 3: Description of Current Situation/Problem

Document the current situation or problem the project will address or resolve. In some cases, the situation or problem may not be bad enough, and therefore it may not warrant the creation of a new project. This is where the author of the document will have to "sell" upper management on the feasibility of the project.

*S*ection 4: Description of Proposed Idea

Document the proposed idea of the project. This is the opportunity to really sell the idea and tell what the project is.

*S*ection 5: Project Time Lines

Document the proposed time lines of the project. Add any hard dependencies or deadlines into this section of the document. Create a rough schedule.

*S*ection 6: Feasibility Review Board

Document the roles and responsibilities of the Feasibility Review Board. What will they do, how long will it take to provide an approval, who are they? Document the input and approval process for the project to get in front of the Feasibility Review Board.

*S*ection 7: Go/No-Go Decision

Document the go/no-go decision and associated criteria of the document. This will provide the formal capturing of approvals on the project, as well as any criteria around that approval. For example, if there is a hard budget, that should be documented as well.

ON the CD-ROM   We have included a sample of this tool in the Communication tools, Scope Subfolder on the CD-Rom. Use this as a guide to create your own version of this tool.

Using a feasibility study

Prior to using a tool such as the feasibility study, it is imperative to identify who on your project team will utilize this tool so that you can determine the level of detail required, style, and format of the report. Having this information ensures that the project manager is communicating the appropriate level of detail to the project team members, customers, or clients.

Before utilizing the feasibility study, review the feasibility tool planning section in Chapter 5. Then follow these steps:

1. Read the feasibility study to understand the proposed project. This includes sitting down with the requestor or the author of the document and going over the idea or suggested project. Getting the correct understanding of the project before it ever starts is going to be extremely beneficial to you.

2. Then, although the customer did not initially write the feasibility study, you should work with them or the author to obtain approval on the document. This is the responsibility of the customer not the project manager, but the project manager may be involved in the process. After obtaining approval on the feasibility study, the customer directs the project manager to initiate a new project.

3. Store the feasibility study and all the approvals in the document control system for long-term storage, archiving, and retrieval purposes. As the project moves into the planning process, the project manager may not utilize the feasibility study that often and it may remain untouched in the document control system for the rest of the project.

There are rarely any updates or changes to the feasibility study when the project moves into the executing phase of the project. The only exception would be customers reviewing the document as the project nears completion to ensure it is matching as close as possible with the original request. Even in those cases, rarely is the feasibility study document ever updated; it would not be the right place to put the updates in most cases.

Mastering the Human Resource Plan

Before mastering the human resource plan, you must understand how this tool can assist and support you on your project. The following project scenario emphasizes the importance of the tool and the reasons why the human resource plan is critical to every project.

A large construction firm in New York City has just won the construction contract to build the latest "Jones Tower." Samuel J. Jones is famous for a number of beautiful high rises in New York and has buildings and construction activities all over the world. The Jones name is world renowned for stunning buildings and the use of gold throughout his buildings. As you can imagine, winning a contract like this is huge for the construction firm and this one job, if done successfully, it can put the firm on the map. The pressure is on for the company to succeed. With a project of this size, you can only imagine the number of skill sets required and the large teams necessary to complete this project. You, as a young project manager, get this assignment and must get the project under way as soon as possible. You know you have $15 million dollars alone allocated to the top project resources, but you have no plan, no process, and at this point no one on your project team. You have many questions that you need to ask your management that include:

Where do I do hire some resources?

How do I get a handle on the resources needed for such a large project?

What about resource costs, do I have enough money to hire who I need?

What are their roles and responsibilities?

To obtain the answers to these questions, the project manager should immediately create and utilize a human resource plan. The human resource plan covers all aspects of the project's staffing requirements, which range from the different skills required, resource training needs, roles and responsibilities, resource assignment timeframes, and any estimates that are used for bidding or writing contracts. Everything documented about the project's resources are included in the human resource plan. A human resource plan is critical to every project regardless of the size, because even a small 3- to 5-person project has the same staffing needs as a larger 40- to 70-person project.

CROSS-REF We recommend that you review the human resource plan tool's planning questions in Chapter 9.

Creating a human resource plan

Creating a human resource plan is an important aspect of any project because it defines and documents all aspects of the resources needed for the project. This staffing information is critical in managing, maintaining, and controlling the project's resources. The human resource plan is a comprehensive document detailing many areas of project staffing. Some of the critical areas of the human resource plan areas include project timeframe, project staffing requirements, skill sets needed, roles and responsibilities, and resource qualifications, to name a few. All projects, regardless of their size, require human resource plans. The value of the plan is not just on larger efforts, but the control and structure it enforces on all projects. All sizes of projects require resources, and regardless of the number of resources or the length of time, planning their use on the project is essential.

The human resource plan is valuable when capturing the project's materials requirements as well. In this case, both the staffing requirements and the material requirements are located in a single document. Materials and equipment requirements can range greatly, depending on the industry, and the type of project. In the construction industry, the human resource plan captures equipment needs, such as cranes, trucks, and bulldozers. In the software industry, the project manager adds any computer hardware or software-specific requirements into the human resource plan.

We recommend that project managers develop the human resource plan as early as possible in the project's planning phase so that they can request their project's staffing requirements through the proper channels as soon as possible. Without a proper team and skill sets to perform the project's work, the project may struggle to be successful.

Project customers are not involved in the creation or development of the human resource plan. However, because the customers are ultimately responsible for the project's budget, they will want to watch the hiring or resources very closely to ensure that the project manager stays within the budget allocated for staffing and materials.

The actual steps of creating a human resource plan can vary from project manager to project manager. Step-by-step instructions for creating a human resource plan are not necessary because a better option is for the project manager to complete the template. Here is the human resource plan template for a project. Project managers can utilize this template if their company does not have one available for use on their projects.

Human Resources Plan Table of Contents

*S*ection 1: *Project Introduction*

Write a summary introduction for the resource plan. (This is for the reader of the human resource plan, such as functional managers, team members, or the owner of the project.)

*S*ection 2: *Project Background*

Give a brief history and background on how the project was established. Review the feasibility study and the project charter.

*S*ection 3: *Project Timeframe*

Document the high-level schedule of the project. Show the major milestone dates.

*S*ection 4: *Scope, Goals, Objectives*

Describe the scope of work needed to carry out the resource plan. Include the goals and objectives.

*S*ection 5: *Staffing Plan*

Describe the staffing plan for the project. What staff members, when needed, resource skills if applicable, and so on.

*S*ection 6: *Project Staffing Requirements*

Describe how you are going to acquire the resources needed to complete the project. Document the staffing requirements for the project.

*S*ection 7: *Type of labor skills needed*

Identify the skills that will make up the project team.

*S*ection 8: *List of Resources (Equipment/Hardware/Building)*

List and describe the non-human resources that will be required on the project.

*S*ection 9: *Roles and Responsibilities*

Describe the roles and responsibilities for the project. Create a responsibility assignment matrix (RAM), and in addition, you may want to create a RACI chart. (See Chapter 9.)

*S*ection 10: *Resource Qualifications*

Identify the necessary qualification each skill will need for a successful project.

Section 11: Training Needs

Document and list any activity that will elevate the skills and competence of all the team members. This is more than technical training; it should include interpersonal skills, teambuilding, and management skills.

Section 12: Staffing Counts

Determine the number of team members it will take at any time on the project.

Section 13: Staffing Timeframes

Determine when each team member will be needed and for how long.

Section 14: Material Needs/Other Resource needs

Identify the material and equipment over the life of the project needed to complete the project.

Section 15: Resource Company Information

What resource company will you use to hire the resources you do not have, but require for the project?

Section 16: Bidding and Contract Terms

Understand the bidding and contract, then document how you are going to disseminate that information so all team members understand it.

Section 17: Summary

Write an executive level summary of the resource plan.

We have included a sample of the Human Resource Plan Table of Contents in the Communication tools, Human Resources Subfolder. Use this as a guide to the first step in creating your own personal version of the plan.

Using a human resource plan

Prior to using a human resource plan, the project manager must identify who on the project team will utilize this tool because this determines the level of detail required, frequency of distribution, style, and format of the document. When determining who is going to use the human resource plan, you are ensuring you are communicating the appropriate level of details to your project team members, customers, or upper management.

Before utilizing the human resource plan, we recommend that you review the planning section developed in Chapter 9 to refamiliarize yourself with the activities and tasks as outlined when preparing to use this tool. Then, follow these steps:

1. Review the human resource plan to determine if all staffing and resource requirements are in the document properly. Before you can start using this document, you should ensure that the known roles or resource types are in the document. Many times, the project manager may not be the one who creates the human resource plan, so checking the document for this information is a safe way of ensuring the document is accurate before using it officially to ask for resources.

2. After you confirm the human resource plan is correct and does reflect the proper staffing requirements or materials required for the project, then work with the resource managers and communicate your project's staffing needs to them. This ensures that the functional managers have the information that they need to find you resources for your project. When providing the human resource plan to the resource managers early in the project, they should have the time they need to prepare and free up (or hire) resources for your project. Approaching resource managers late in the project will usually result in scrambling to find resources and in some cases not being able to find staff available at all.

3. Work with the customers when they are needed for the project. You should ensure that your customers have committed to being involved in the project and will be available at the time in the project that they are required. If not, you should ask them if they could provide others who would be committed at the time they are needed on the project. You can use the human resource plan to show the customer the timeframes that they are expected to be involved in and determine if that timeframe will work for them. If not, the two groups can work together to make sure they can find an agreeable timeframe and in some cases shift the dates of the project around to make it work for everyone.

4. Compare the staffing and materials requirements and their potential costs to your resource budget and determine if there is a delta. Review the staffing and equipment needs to complete the project and ensure that the funds allocated are enough. If the funds are insufficient, then show the justifications that you outlined in the human resource plan and the budget spreadsheet showing the potential overage, and then let management decide whether they want to proceed. In some cases, management stops the project because it is projecting over budget. If you map the budget to the actual resources and determine the differences early in the planning process, the customer and upper management will be aware of the potential overage the project will have on funding long before the project progresses too far along. If the project does proceed with the resources outlined in the human resource plan, it will be up to the customer or upper management to determine how they will handle any potential budget shortfalls.

5. As the project moves into the planning process, start working with the resource managers to obtain the project team members you require for the project. You would also work with the procurement group and start to purchase the materials you need as well for the project. Both the staffing and materials needs are documented in the human resource plan, so to initialize this process, the information should all be available to the project manager.

During the executing and controlling processes of the project, the project manager is continually updating and revising the human resource plan based on the needs of the project. This updating to the plan will include the project manager comparing budget allocations with ongoing staffing requirements, rolling vendors on and off the project, and updating the human resource plan based on project changes continually occurring on the project. The human resource plan is a document that project managers should update and use throughout their project to ensure they are managing and controlling their project resources.

Mastering the Project Charter

Before learning how to use the project charter, you should understand how this tool could assist and support you on your project. The following project scenario emphasizes the importance of using the project charter and the reasons why the project charter is critical to every project.

The sales department has asked the information technology group to create a new application. They want the application to be usable worldwide. The IT group says creating the application should take about six months, and provided a project estimate of $1,000,000. They have no idea what the real costs of the project will be because it is so early in the requirements phase, so they took a guess at this estimate. The IT group has very little idea about the scope, goals, objectives, critical success factors, start or finish dates, or resources requirements. The sales team has not documented anything about the project start-up information to date. As project manager, you know how important this documentation can be and require it to get your project started and kicked off. You are the most senior project manager in the department, and management decided it would be best that you manage this project for the company. The problem is, without the startup information you certainly have some catching up to do, and you need it before you can go much further into the project. You have some questions about how you are even going to get this information, and the questions you are asking yourself include:

How will I get this information?

Where do I start?

What contacts do I have in the business to obtain this data?

To obtain the answers to these questions, the project manager should have utilized the project charter document. This document has the information about the project he/she was looking for. The project charter includes the main aspects of the project including project purpose, general scope, budget, timelines, resources, critical success factors, and expected benefits, to name a few. This information will provide the project team with the information they need to get the project started. Without a project charter, the project manager or the team members will have no idea why they are involved in the project, or what the objective is they are trying to achieve.

CROSS-REF　We recommend that you review the project charter's planning questions in Chapter 4.

Creating a project charter

In most cases, the customer or sponsors of the project create the project charter document. Project managers and team member will support the creation of the document, but are not normally involved in the process. The project charter starts as the responsibility of the customer, but ends up being what the project team has to execute for the project. The project charter describes many aspects of the project and is the single source of information that anyone involved in the project can use to understand the project, and what the goals of the customer are, and what they are trying to achieve.

One of the aspects of the project charter is its flexibility and how useful the document is for any size project. The sections covered in the project charter are applicable for any project, across most industries. All project charter documents have the same basic sections including project purpose, scope, budget, schedule, deliverables, critical success factors, and resources. Project managers should ensure that the main areas of the project are also in one form or another covered in the project charter document. Budget, for example, is one key area of the project charter that the project manager will monitor closely throughout the project.

Project customers should be active in the creation of the project charter. Customers are responsible for many aspects of the project charter and should be a driver of this document to ensure it captures what they want and expect from the project. A project scope item that is captured incorrectly or is simply wrong can send a project in the wrong direction, and the customer would not be happy with the results. The project charter captures the wants and needs of the customer, so their role in the creation, acceptance, and reporting of the document is critical to the success of the project.

The actual steps in creating a project charter can vary from project manager to project manager. Instead of providing step-by-step instructions on creating a project charter, a better option would be for the project manager to complete the template. Here is an example of the project charter table of contents for your project. Project managers can utilize this template if their company does not have one available for use on their projects.

Project Charter Table of Contents

Section 1: Introduction
Introduction of document, purpose, revisions, general information on contents of document

Section 2: Overview of the Project
Document the overview of the project, customers involved, and business reasons

Section 3: Purpose of the Project
Document the purpose of the project, why it is so important, who is involved

Section 4: Objective and Goal
Document the objective of the project, what are you trying to achieve

Section 5: Business Need or Opportunity

Document the business need or opportunity this project can provide for the company

Section 6: Financial Benefits of the Project

Document the financial benefits to performing this project. It is important to include both hard and soft financial benefits this project will bring to the company.

Section 7: Expected Benefits

Document any other expected benefits to the project that don't fall under financial, but are still important enough to document.

Section 8: Scope

Document the scope of the project; document what are both in and out of scope

Section 9: Project Budget

Document the current budget allocations for the project. Document all constraints and assumptions.

Section 10: Project Start and Finish Dates

Document the proposed start and finish date of the projects. Make sure that you document all constraints and assumptions along with any other major milestones.

Section 11: Major Deliverables

Document the major deliverables of the project; normally this is in line with the methodology you selected for the project. Each methodology will have its own set of deliverables for the project,

Section 12: Resources

Document the resource requirements of the project. Cover areas such as skill sets, timeframes, training, and all other aspects of project resources.

Section 13: Critical Success Factors of Project

Document the critical success factors to the project, what the customers feels the project should have and still be successful.

Section 14: Assumptions and Constraints

Document any project assumptions or constraints worth noting in the charter document.

Section 15: Sign-offs

Document the customers and project team members who have signed off on the project charter document.

 We have included a sample of the project charter tool in the Communication tools Integration Subfolder. Use this as a guide to create your own version of this tool.

Using a project charter

Prior to using a project charter, you should identify who on your project team will utilize the project charter document. When you determine this, and understand the level of detail required, frequency of distribution, style, and format of the document, you will be able to ensure that you are communicating the document at the appropriate level of detail to your project team members, customers, or upper management.

Before utilizing the project charter tool, review the project charter's planning section in Chapter 4. Then follow these steps:

1. Work with your customers and review the project charter together, and that way you can ensure the document has everything necessary to initiate the project. If it does, then the project manager will accept the responsibility for the project and start the project initiation activities.

2. Send out your project charter document for final sign-off from your customers and upper management. This includes sending a copy of the project charter and the user acceptance document to your customers for approval. After obtaining approval, the project manager then stores it in the document control system for long-term storage, archiving, and retrieval purposes.

3. Start the hiring process to build your project team. This includes working with the resource managers and obtaining internal resources where applicable.

4. Hold your project's kick-off meeting and present the project charter to your team members. This meeting is the first time that the project team reviews the project charter. A follow-up meeting with the team members may be necessary.

As the project moves into the planning process, the project manager or team members will usually utilize the project charter document as a general guide only and will rarely use it to drive the activities of the project team members. There are little or no updates to the project charter document in the executing phase of the project.

Mastering the Project Kick-Off Meeting

Before investigating the project kick-off meeting, you must understand how this tool can assist and support you on your project. The following project scenario emphasizes the importance of the tool, and the reasons why the project kick-off meeting is critical to every project. Here is the scenario:

The design of the Olympic tennis stadium is complete. A large construction firm has just won a major contract to construct the tennis stadium for the upcoming summer Olympics. The construction firm decides to take some shortcuts to save some costs and starts immediately into the construction phase. There are no meetings, little communications, and the construction firm just decides to go full steam ahead. The firm includes no one else in this decision, and immediately starts to build the tennis courts, player facilities, and adjoining gift shops and museums. The project manager in the construction firm believes that bringing all the subcontractors together at the beginning of the project is a waste of time and money, and would only cause delays to the construction of the project. Therefore, the construction firm decides to forgo the project kickoff meeting and figures the project team members can meet at any time. As the project progresses, there is little communication between the construction firm and any of the other subcontractors. Suddenly, the construction firm hits a major roadblock in construction phase and requires the assistance of the subcontractors before they can proceed. The construction firm now needs the other subcontractors, such as the Olympic design team, and the United States Tennis Association team to assist them in getting over a design hurdle on the tennis courts. Because the construction firm has left the subcontractors completely out of the loop until this point, it is going to be difficult to have them jump in now and be able immediately to help with the situation. Because the subcontractors have not been in the loop or communicating with the construction firm, they have little understanding on their role and responsibilities or how they can offer help. The subcontractors at this point do not feel like they are part of the project yet.

Think about this situation from your perspective as the project manager leading this effort. What would you have done differently? Then ask yourself the following questions:

How important would a project kick-off meeting have been in this situation?

How could the various subcontractors and the construction firm have learned the design requirements for their tennis courts?

What about the United States Tennis Association, what requirements do they have on court sizes, locker rooms, balls, and nets?

What would have brought each of the groups together to help them form better relationships and start the project off with high morale?

To obtain the answers to these questions, the project manager should have called a project kick-off meeting. A project kick-off meeting would have prevented the situation above from ever occurring in the first place and would have kept the various subcontractors communicating more effectively and being able to provide more support and potentially eliminating the problem and save cost. The customer and upper management should have insisted that the project manager hold a project kick-off meeting and not use the excuse of costs to prevent this meeting from occurring. A project kick-off meeting would have saved two to three months of lost work, and thousands in cost to the project budget. Because nobody planned this work, it immediately affects the project costs, which may jeopardize the project as a whole. Project kick-off meetings are critical communication tools on every type of project that help drive toward a successful project.

CROSS-REF We recommend that you review the project kickoff meeting tool's planning questions in Chapter 4.

Creating a project kick-off meeting

Having a project kickoff meeting can motivate a team like no other meeting. The anticipation of kicking off a project, forming a project team, and coming together to accomplish a goal is exciting. Bringing everyone together at the start of the project and providing them with the scope, goals, objectives, and project background is priceless. The team is going to know from the start all about the project. Project managers should not take on the responsibilities of the meeting themselves; they need to ensure that the customer also steps up and is involved in driving components of the meeting. It is important for project team members to hear directly from the customers what their thoughts and perspectives are on the project and what they want to see as the end result. When project team members gain the inside knowledge directly from the customer, they feel connected to the customer and they will want to engage faster on the project.

There are plenty of topics to cover in a typical project kickoff meeting. The project kickoff meeting is an opportunity to share project information with the customers and team members at the same time, and is often a highly charged and energetic meeting for everyone involved.

Project kickoff meetings can vary in length; normally they will last a full business day, but there are always a number of agenda items to cover. Therefore, it is important to have the right agenda to ensure that the message you want delivered is correct and the right people are at the meeting to receive and understand that message.

Project managers and customers who co-host the meeting need to spend time creating an agenda that is going to energize and excite the team members. The agenda must have both a project message and a management message — both messages are critically important to get across at this early stage of the project.

The stakeholders or customers should attend the project kickoff meeting to provide everyone on the project their perspective of the project. Their attendance at the meeting provides a level of enthusiasm to the meeting that the team members will embrace. The fact that the team members can have the ability to hear directly from the customers their thoughts on the scope, goals, and objectives for the project is priceless.

You should think about the following items when considering your stakeholder's attendance and requirements for the project's kickoff meeting:

- **Identify and define stakeholders.** Determine who the key project stakeholders are and ensure that they are on the invite list for the meeting.

- **Conduct a stakeholder analysis.** There are two levels of stakeholders on every project: the first are the customers, clients, owners, or upper management themselves, and the second level are the project team members. A stakeholder analysis determines the wants and needs of each stakeholder on the project.

- **Identify the key stakeholders.** Identify the names of the key stakeholders to ensure that they are invited; then verify they will attend the meeting. When identifying the key stakeholders, it is beneficial to explain to them what their roles in the meetings will be and what materials they will cover.

- **Determine the information needs of the stakeholders.** Communicating the information needs of the stakeholders at the project kick-off meeting allows everyone to have the same understanding of what is required to keep everyone informed of the project status.

- **Determine project team member roles.** If team members are unclear of their roles they will need to work directly with the project manager to address any concerns or issues they have. In this case, the project manager may be able to identify the tasks assigned to the team member or will be able to point the team member to a team lead for direction.

- **Include company-specific tasks.** Perform any activities the company has outlined specifically for the kick-off meeting.

At the end of every project kick-off meeting it is a best practice for you, as the project manager, to accomplish a set of tasks to ensure that proper documentation of the meeting occurs, and everyone achieves what they need from that meeting. The tasks include the following:

- **Document agreements and distribute them to the team.** The meeting minute's taker, usually a member of the administrative team, documents the meeting and sends minutes to the meeting attendees within two days.

- **Clearly identify action items.** The project manager should highlight and identify any assignments or action items during the meeting, then follow up in the meeting notes.

- **Establish clear expectations.** If there were any expectations identified during the meeting, the meeting notes will capture those expectations, and the project manager will then ensure that they meet the expectations of the team members and customers during the life of the project.

- **Communicate requirements and deadlines.** Project manager will communicate the specific needs, or any associated deadlines, with the customer.

- **Answer questions brought up during the meeting.** Often there are questions that the project manager cannot answer at the meeting and has to follow up later with a response. The project manager owns the responsibility of getting those questions answered and following up by sending the answers out to the meeting attendees.

- **Provide additional information.** If there is any information that comes up at the project kickoff meeting that needs tracking, or more research, the project manager either will be responsible for performing that work or will delegate it to a team member for resolution.

The actual steps of creating a project kickoff meeting can vary from project manager to project manager and will depend greatly on their favorite tools of choice. Instead of providing step-by-step instructions on creating a project kickoff meeting agenda, a better option would be for the project manager to use the project kickoff meeting agenda template here in this chapter, or grab the template from the CD-ROM and use that as a starting point for your projects.

ON the CD-ROM We have included a sample of the project kickoff meeting agenda in the Communication tools Integration Subfolder. Use this as a guide to create your own personal version of this tool.

Example of Project Kick-Off Meeting Agenda Table of Contents

Section 1: Project Goals, Objectives

Document the goals and objectives of the project. The customers or owners may provide their specific goals and objectives, as well as adding the project team's goals to this section.

Section 2: Project Scope

Document the project's scope

Section 3: Project Out of Scope

Document the projects out-of-scope components. It is important to call out what items the project will not complete so the customers and team members are clear on this at the beginning of the project.

Section 4: Risks/Issues

Document the project's project risks and issues. At this point, the project may not have many risks and issues, but it is important to track and note any at this time.

Section 5: Budget Estimate

Document the project's budget estimate. At the project kick-off process, the estimate provided will be at a tolerance level and an established variance level; having a refined estimate at this stage of the project would be difficult.

Section 6: Project Schedule

Document the schedule of the project. The schedule will be a milestone level only and will match to the major deliverables of the project. The methodology selected will drive the deliverables.

Section 7: Methodology Deliverables

Document the various methodology deliverables. Depending on the type of project and the methodology chosen, this section will include all the relevant deliverables for this project.

Section 8: Requirements Deep Dive

Document the detail requirements for the project.

Section 9: Design Deep Dive

Document the detail design information for the project.

Section 10: *Development Deep Dive*
Document the development details for the project.

Section 11: *Test Deep Dive*
Document the detail testing information for the project.

Section 12: *User Acceptance Criteria Deep Dive*
Document any specific user acceptance type testing for the project.

Using a project kick-off meeting

Prior to using a tool, such as the project kickoff meeting, it is imperative to identify who on your project team will be involved in the meeting; it will allow you to determine the level of detail required at the meeting, meeting style and format, length of meeting, location, and level of executives to invite.

Before utilizing the project kickoff meeting, review the planning section for this tool in Chapter 4 Then follow these steps:

1. Work with the customer to schedule a project kickoff meeting. This may require a great deal of coordination and time to ensure that remote team members (if applicable) are coming in for the meeting, and to ensure that any executives who are involved in the project have plenty of time to free their calendars and be available to attend. The coordination of the room, food, equipment for presentations, and giveaways prizes requires plenty of time to complete before the meeting. Book it early!

2. Meet with your team members and your customer to finalize the kickoff meeting presentation material. It is important that long before the meeting event, the project manager must have presentation materials to present at the meeting. Some projects have pre-scrub meetings where the project manager presents the meeting material to upper management early to allow them to scrub the material to their liking before the team members and customers see it. The project manager, after those meetings, will change the meeting materials based on feedback from upper management. Doing this is a best practice to ensure that management approves all presentation materials before presenting them to the customers or executives. Another best practice is for the project manager to call a "pre-scrub" meeting with the customers and allow them to see the materials before the official meeting. Again, if there are any problems from the customer side, the project manager should resolve them before the meeting. In taking this extra step, you have prepared your management, you prepared your customers, and the official meeting becomes a rubber stamp meeting. We highly recommend the processes outlined in this step as they have proven to be successful.

3. Hold your project's kickoff meeting. At that meeting, the project manager presents the materials to the team members, customers, upper management, and in some cases, executives. This is normally a joint effort between the project manager, the customers, and the team members that provided supporting materials for the meeting. Each customer and project is going to be different, so the project manager will have to adjust accordingly.

4. Complete the meeting follow-up activities. You should store all project kickoff meeting material within the document control system for long-term storage, archiving, and retrieval purposes.

After the project kickoff meeting, the project then moves into the planning process. In that process and subsequent processes, there are no additional steps for the project manager to complete for the project kickoff meeting, and generally the project manager stores the materials and puts them away for long-term storage.

Mastering the Project Management Plan

Before you can master the project management plan, you must understand how this tool can assist and support you on your project. The following project scenario emphasizes the importance of the tool and the reasons why the project management plan is critical to every project.

A large construction company is building a bridge over an expansive river. The bridge is 2 ½ miles long and is expected to take three years to build. The schedule is not yet final, and is not expected until late fall before it will be ready. This is a large project, and to be successful the project requires the coordination of state government, local government, and environmental groups to work together. As project manager, you understand that this is going to be a large project and you will need many control documents to ensure the success of the project. You have never completed such a large project, and your firm is giving you the chance to prove yourself on this project. You know this has to go right, and you struggle with a number of questions as to what to do next. These questions include:

Where do you start on the project?

What should you do to add some rigor to your project?

To obtain the answers to these questions, the project manager will use a project management plan that will contain the various management plans required to manage and control the project. A project management plan is a great starting point for any large project where it requires a level of discipline and structure to be successful. The project management plan includes many project control documents, such as scope management, schedule management plan, cost management plan, quality management plan, process improvement plan, staffing management plan, communication management plan, risk management plan, and the procurement plan. These various plans all add specific processes and procedures to their particular areas of the project that, when used correctly, provide structure and rigor that a project team can follow on their projects.

CROSS-REF We recommend that you review the Project Management Plan's planning questions in Chapter 4.

Creating a project management plan

The creation of the project management plan is a best practice on all projects regardless of industry, size, or type and the only caveat to this would be the project's size. A small, one-month or less effort would not need a management plan necessarily because the time and cost of producing the various documents for such a short project outweigh the value of the documents themselves. Project managers must determine when to use project management plans on their smaller projects, and still have it be cost effective for the project. Project manager will tend to utilize the plans regularly on their medium to large projects.

NOTE It is important to add that the same rigor and process is required on all projects; however, not to the same degree on smaller projects.

The project management plan is the overall master document that guides the execution and control of project deliverables. The project management plan is a series of other management documents that help the project manager manage and control their projects. Without having a management plan in place, the project manager would not have controls or procedures to help guide them as they run their project. The various issues such as scope, budget or schedule could all impact the project negatively if the project manager does not have plans in place that provide them the direction of handling these issues when they arise on their projects.

Project managers are often the authors of the project management plan and are responsible for its ongoing maintenance and upkeep. Project managers often have an interest in developing and implementing the project management plan on their projects.

Customers should be active and engaged in the creation of the project management plan and be aware of the process and procedures established for the particular projects. Because there are so many process and procedures within the project management plan, it is important that the customer understands these procedures and abides by them when working on the project. A good example of this is the risk and issue management process contained in the project management plan. If there are processes and procedures established to create and track issues and risks, the customer must be engaged and be sure to follow this process closely to eliminate the chance of derailing or disrupting the project team members. A customer who feels that he has an important risk can stop a project if they feel the project manager is not handling it properly.

The actual steps of creating a project management plan can vary from project manager to project manager and depend greatly on their favorite tools of choice. Instead of providing step-by-step instructions on creating a project management plan, a better option is for a project manager to complete this template. Here is the project management plan for use on your projects.

ON the CD-ROM We have included a sample of this tool in the Communication tools Integration Subfolder. Use this as a guide to create your own version of this tool.

Example of Project Management Plan
Table of Contents

Section 1: Introduction

Document the introduction information on the project management plan. Any information specific to the document itself belongs.

Section 2: Project Description

Document the description of the project; specifically what the project is trying to achieve, and what the project team members will accomplish.

Section 3: Application

Document how you will apply and use the project in the company.

Section 4: Scope

Document the scope of the project.

Section 5: Constraints and Assumptions

Document any constraints or assumptions of the project.

Section 6: Risks

Document the project's risks.

Section 7: Issues

Document the project's issues.

Section 8: Relationship to Other Projects

Document the project's relationships or dependencies on other projects. This is important to note, especially if the project is stuck waiting on other efforts and is unable to proceed.

Section 9: Mission Statement

Document the project's mission statement for customers and team members. This should be a one- or two-line statement on the overall mission of the project.

Section 10: Project Objectives

Document the objectives of the project. This can include both the objectives of the project owners or clients and the project team members themselves.

Section 11: Project Team Members

Document the project team members. This should include both the team member's names and contact information.

Section 12: Project Roles and Responsibilities

Document the roles and responsibilities of the team members. This will include all customers, clients, and active members of the team.

Section 13: Project Plan Management

Document how the management and controlling of the project management plan will occur. The main areas will contain frequency of updates, responsible person(s), and the notification tree, once updates occur, .and so on.

Section 14: Project Approach

Document the approach to managing and controlling the project. There are many different project management styles and approaches and it is important to document the approach used, and any expectations the project manager has for the project. It ensures everyone is in-line at the beginning of the project.

Section 15: Conflict Management

Document how to manage and control conflicts on the project.

Section 16: Project Administration

Document any administrative type activities for the project.

Section 17: Project Tasks, Deliverables, and Milestones

Document the major tasks, deliverables, or milestones at the highest level. Document the lower-level detail in the project schedule, not in the project management plan.

Section 18: Planning Approaches/Methodologies

Document the selected methodology for the project, including the reasons behind selecting the methodology.

Section 19: Key Deliverables

Document the major deliverables for the project. Lower level or sub-deliverables will be included in the project schedule.

Section 20: Major Milestones Dates

Document major milestone dates for the project. These dates will depend on the methodology used, as well as selected milestones for the project.

continued

continued

Section 21: Scope Management

Document the management and controlling activities of the project's scope. Areas that you might cover are scope strategy, scope planning, scope definition, scope verification, and scope change control.

Section 22: Issue Management

Document the management and controlling activities of the project's Issues. Areas covered include, purpose, strategies, or process and procedures.

Section 23: Risk Management

Document the management and controlling activities of the project's risks in this section. Areas covered include purpose, strategies, or process and procedures.

Section 24: Problem Management

Document the management and controlling activities for any problems or concerns that arise on the project. Areas covered include purpose, strategies, or process and procedures.

Section 25: Financial Management

Document the management and controlling activities of the project's finances. Areas covered include purpose, strategies, or process and procedures.

Section 26: Communications Management

Document the management and controlling activities of all communications on the project. Areas covered include purpose, strategies, or process and procedures.

Section 27: Summary

Document the summary project information not covered in the other sections. Approvals and signatures are important items that are included.

Using a project management plan

Prior to using the project management plan, you must identify who on your project team will utilize the document so you understand the level of detail required, frequency of distribution, style, and format of the document itself. In doing this, it ensures that you are communicating the appropriate level of details to the project team members, customers, or upper management.

Before utilizing the project management plan, review the project management plan's planning section in Chapter 4. Then follow these steps:

1. Make sure that the project management plan is complete. Go over the document with your project team members and customers to ensure that it captures all areas of the project correctly. This step includes ensuring that the various project management plans are included in this document, or that there are pointers (or links) to the management documents if they are stored as separate documents. For example, when reviewing the project management plan, you will quickly know whether the risk management plan for example is included in the document completely or does it just have a link to another document that has the risk management information in that document. This layout and structure of the document is important for you to understand how you are going to maintain and update the document throughout the project.

2. Send the project management plan to your team members and customers for their acceptance and approval. Send the project management plan along with the user acceptance document for official project approval.

3. Store your project's project management plan and the acceptance documents in the document control system for long-term storage, archiving, and retrieval purposes.

4. Implement and enforce the use of the project management plan and associated process on your project. This step includes utilizing the management plans as a project situation arises. For example, the project manager utilizes the issue management plan when the first issue comes onto the project. The project manager utilizes the procurement management plan when the first vendor is hired or the first contract is required. As the project moves into the executing processes, the project manager and team members use the different management plans that are specific to the project situation that occurs.

   As the project moves into the planning phase, and then into the executing phase, the project manager and team members can expect to perform ongoing updates and enhancements to the various management plans required for the project. This process continues throughout the life of the project.

After completing each of these four steps, the project manager should fully understand and be able to utilize the project management plan on their projects.

Mastering the Project Organization Chart

Before mastering the project organization chart, you must understand how it can assist and support you on your project. The following project scenario emphasizes why project organization is critical to your projects.

A large software company would like to replace its in-house developed accounting system with one of the larger software applications on the market today. The in-house developed system has been around for many years and has a large number of subsystems involved that either sends data to or receives data from this homegrown system. To replace the system with an off-the-shelf version is going to require a large team. A team member from each subsystem needs to be part of this core project team to ensure that they continue to receive the data they need after the off-the-shelf version goes live and into production. There are 15 subsystems involved in this implementation, so there must be at least 15 people on the team alone, not counting the implementation team; and, because this is a large project team, you are going to need a process in place to control these resources. You have many questions on the management and controlling of these resources including:

What will you do to gather all these people together?

How can you tell what and who is working on which system?

What open positions has the project not yet filled?

This scenario is a perfect example of when a project organization chart would be beneficial to the project manager in controlling and understanding his or her project team. Project organization chart is also valuable for the team members so they know the organizational structure of their project and where other team members are working. The amount of information that an organization chart provides is helpful to the project manager and the team members in understanding who is working on the team.

CROSS-REF We recommend that you review the project organization chart's planning questions in Chapter 4.

Creating a project organization chart

Creating an organization chart is an important step on every project. The ability to map the project role to the person performing the task is essential to a project manager in their understanding whether they have the right roles for the project. Project organization charts take little time to produce, but can make a huge difference to the communications and the overall structure of the project.

An advantage to using an organization chart is viewing the project's staffing shortfalls. The ability to view, at-a-glance, how large or small the size of a team is that is working on an area of the project is invaluable. When the project manager keeps the project organization charts current, the ability to determine exactly where the project's staff has gone, and what job openings are current, is clear. When a team member leaves the project, the project manager should update the project organization chart to reflect the change and highlight that there are openings on the project that require filling. Those openings could be critical and affect the critical path of the project. When project managers show that information on the project organization chart, it makes it much easier for them to drive the message home and highlight the risk to the project that those resources are project impacting. In addition, project organization charts indicate a level of risk based on the team size. For example, when the project loses team members over a short duration, there is a resource risk on the project that is apparent to the customers and upper management and is highlighted showing the openings on the project organization chart.

The actual steps to create a project organization chart vary from each project manager. The following steps can help you get started if you have never created this tool before. We have also created a template for you as a starting point for your projects. This template will require updating based on your specific project needs and requirements but is an excellent guide to get you going.

ON the CD-ROM We have included a template of the project organization chart in the Communication tools Integration Subfolder. Use this as a guide to create your own version of this tool.

1. Create a blank organization chart for the project in one of the popular software packages. Initially, you can add your name, and your customer's name to get the project organization chart started.

2. Gather the names of the various roles and team member names for the project. If there is a project role and responsibility matrix created at this point, this would be an excellent starting point for finding names and roles on the new organization chart.

3. Fill in the names and roles from the responsibility matrix. This can be a time-consuming task, but something very important to get all the project roles included in the project organization chart.

4. Send your new organization chart to your project team members for review. You can also send it to the customers for their feedback, but you do not require their approval.

5. Post your project's organization chart into the document control system for long-term archiving, storage, and retrieval. You should also post the organization chart on the project communication board or your project Web site to bring exposure to who is working on the project.

6. Continue to refine the project organization chart and update it as various team members roll on and off the project.

Using a project organization chart

Prior to using a tool such as the project organization chart, you must identify who on your project team will utilize the chart so that you can determine the level of detail required, frequency of distribution, style, and format of the chart. One example of this may be the project manager who has a high-level project organization chart.

Review the project organization chart planning section in Chapter 4 and then follow these steps:

1. Use your project organization chart or org chart, as supplemental material to the human resource plan. The project manager will ensure the project organization chart and the human resource plan match with the project's roles and its current openings. For example, if the project organization chart states that there is a need for ten developers on the project, then the human resource plan should indicate ten developers as well or at a minimum have the actual name of the person or a "To be hired" listed in the boxes. It is important for these to match because if a customer questions the need for ten developers for example, the project manager would have written the justification and details already in the human resource plan, and therefore the project manager would just provide it to customers to help resolve their questions.

2. Present the project organization chart introducing the project team to your customers and your upper management. This presentation allows the team members to receive exposure at a management level that they may not normally receive and allows them to feel like they are part of a team.

3. As the project moves through its lifecycle, you should be posting and presenting your project organization chart onto Web sites, newsletters, and status reports so everyone is aware of who is working on the project. You should be looking to provide exposure to the team members as much as possible and highlight the good work they are doing on the project. This allows all the team members and outside individuals not on the project to understand who is working on what area of the project, and who can provide information on those different areas when questions come up. If any team members or customers have questions, they would be able to go directly to the person in charge of that area to resolve.

Mastering the Project Proposal

Before using the project proposal, you must find out how this tool can assist and support you on your project. The following project scenario emphasizes the importance of the project proposal, and the reasons why it is critical to every project. If we take a typical construction project where project proposals are relevant and used continuously on the project, it will explain why these communication tools are so important. Here is a scenario:

The Alaska State's Highway Engineering Department needs to construct a new railway crossing on one of the major highways in the state. The railway crossing is due by October 10 before winter storms hit. This is because sometimes working in northern Alaska the weather can become quite difficult for the workers and can shut down the projects for weeks. The engineering department has 12 employees who work in the railway department and perform this type of work, but they are already working on other projects and unable to make this tight deadline for this new project. The engineering department must install this crossing as soon as possible and before the cold weather comes into the area. The engineering department has asked you to be the project manager for this project. You have been working on railroad projects for many years and jumped at the chance to manage this effort. You need to get this project started as soon as possible and you have a number of questions that need answering before you can get going. These questions include:

How do you get this project started?

How do I write a contract for this work?

How much money is in the budget?

To obtain the answers to these questions, the project manager should use a project proposal document to document the needs and requirements of the project. Using that project proposal document, which contains all the relevant project information, the project manager can then go to outside companies and bid the work to them for this project. In this case, since the engineering department did not have enough staff to install the crossing in time, the project manager had no choice to develop a project proposal document and send it to various construction companies for bidding purposes. If the company matches the conditions of the contract and meets all the criteria, they usually win the project.

 We recommend that you review the project proposal's planning questions in Chapter 4.

Creating a project proposal

Creating a project proposal is a large undertaking for any project team. The legal aspects of these proposals are important, especially for projects that are going through the bidding process. Most project proposals are for bidding purposes only, and some company's rarely use them internally on their projects because their focus is toward hiring outside contractors, not for internal use. Therefore, the legal side of project proposals can be difficult, and project managers without a lot of legal experience or legal training could get the company into some trouble without even knowing it. The project manager's or contract manager's first job is to ensure every company bidding on the work is treated and handled exactly the same way. For example, providing some key project information to one company and not offering the same information to all of them can cause legal issues, and in some cases, lawsuits of unfair business practices. Can you imagine if a company offers inside information to one company on a multi-million dollar contract, and leaves the other companies out in the cold? When the project is in the bidding process it, if possible, obtains legal representatives for support, especially if there are any concerns or uncertainty in what you are doing. Otherwise, you could be putting your company, and the project, in jeopardy.

In creating the project proposal document, it is critical to add everything possible about the project in the document to ensure there is nothing that the bidding companies are missing. It would be unfair to any company to leave out known issues or concerns about a project that might affect their delivery of the work. Companies that leave out work intentionally are setting up the project to fail. A common practice that bidding companies take advantage of is to add a certain level of contingency (or padding) into their bid estimates to allow for any uncertainty or unknowns on the project. Most companies can expect those additional costs included and factored into the project proposal submissions and usually allow for that in the budget.

Project proposals act as the basis for contracts between the two companies and therefore need to be ironclad. Anything missing can end up as a series of change requests, which if not managed correctly, can derail a project, making it run over budget or run late and miss a component of the project schedule.

The actual steps of creating a project proposal can vary from project manager to project manager. Instead of providing step-by-step instructions on creating a project proposal, a better option would be for the project manager to complete a project proposal template. In the project proposal tool, the project manager may leave some of the sections in this document blank, noting that those sections are specifically for the bidding companies to complete. For example, when a section describes asking for the creation of a work breakdown structure, this section would be for the bidding company to complete, not the project manager originally writing the document.

ON the CD-ROM We have included a sample of this tool in the Communication tools Integration Subfolder. Use this as a guide to create your own version of this tool.

Example of Project Proposal Table of Contents

*S*ection 1: Introduction

Document the specifics of the document. Prepared by, revisions by, and document purpose.

*S*ection 2: Proposal Submissions Deadlines

Document the project's submissions deadlines. It is important to call out this information so bidding companies do not miss this important information.

*S*ection 3: Terms and Conditions

Document the contract's terms and conditions. The terms of a condition can vary from project to project, so it is important to add the appropriate information with the document.

*S*ection 4: Pricing

Document the project's submissions deadlines. It is important to call out this information so bidding companies do not miss this important information.

*S*ection 5: Warranty Coverage

Document any specific warranty information on the project. This is not applicable to all projects, but where it is, it is important to document completely.

*S*ection 6: Mandatory Conditions

Document the project's mandatory conditions. One of the most important aspects of contract management is ensuring companies follow and adhere to the mandatory items, so it is important that the hard requirements of the project are located. Mandatory items are that the project must finish on a specific date, or must finish under budget.

*S*ection 7: Mandatory Evaluation Criteria

Document the project's mandatory criteria based on the conditions outlined in the previous section.

*S*ection 8: Background and Current Practice

Document and provide a description of the background and current practices of the enterprise.

*S*ection 9: Project Description

Document the project's description.

*S*ection 10: Project Overview

Document and provide a description of the proposed project and outline the expected results. Create a brief outline of what the project will aim to achieve and list the main project targets. Identify the success criteria of the project.

Section 11: Requirements Section

Document and provide a description of the projects requirements. This section will include all the details the bidding company will require to successfully bid on the project.

Section 12: Project Structure – Roles & Responsibilities

Document the organization structure of the existing project, including the roles and responsibilities for each of those roles. If possible, include an actual project organization chart. This will allow the bidding company to understand how large the project team is and where there could be interactions between the groups. Note: This section is for the bidding company to complete.

Section 13: Technical Requirements

Document and provide any technical information about the project of the document. Capture any technical aspects that the bidding companies need to be aware of, or may have to find staff for, in this document.

Section 14: Critical Success Factors

Document the critical success factors for the project and document what the customers will deem as critical, allowing the bidding companies an insight into what, and how, they can succeed on the project.

Section 15: Project Plan Management

Document and provide an overall project management plan and a detailed work breakdown structure. Note: This section is for the bidding company to complete.

Section 16: Deliverables

Document and provide a list and brief description of all the tangible project deliverables. It is important to ensure that you capture the deliverables in the WBS at the work package level.

Section 17: Work Packages, Tasks, Activities, and Milestones

Document and develop a brief description of all work packages with durations for each package. Provide a list and brief description of all project milestones and when they are expected to finish; e.g., third week: A milestone is a task with no duration (zero time) and identifies a significant event in your schedule such as the completion of a major deliverable. Note: This section is for the bidding company to complete.

Section 18: Project Cost Control

Document and develop project cost estimates for each work package. This should include all labor, equipment, and materials for each package. This is an important part of the proposal, as the total project cost determines the sum of all work packages. Note: This section is for the bidding company to complete.

Section 19: Integration with Other Projects

Document and develop an integration plan detailing how the proposed project will integrate with other projects in the organization.

Using a project proposal

Prior to using a tool such as the project proposal tool, you must identify who on your project team will utilize this tool so that you can determine the level of detail required, frequency of distribution, style, and format of the document. Since the main users of the project proposal document are outside vendor or contracting companies, the level of detail for the document will be the same for everyone. Project managers can get into serious legal problems if they do not provide the same information to all companies at the same time throughout this bidding process.

Review the project proposal planning section in Chapter 4. Then follow these steps:

1. After creating your project proposal document, set up review meetings with your customers to ensure the proposal is correct and matching their needs. Always have a review meeting with the legal department. After obtaining official agreement that the document is ready, send the project proposal and the user acceptance document out for official project approval.

2. After your receive official sign-off and approval, store both the project proposal and the user acceptance document in the document control system for long-term storage, archiving, and retrieval purposes.

3. Initiate project discussions with outside vendors and contracting companies. There is a process called the "RFP" or request for proposal process. Companies that are heavily project focused are normally very involved and engaged in this process. You should follow the guidelines established by the procurement group and contact a number of companies to bid on the project work.

4. After starting this process work with your team members, customers, and upper management to respond to the various vendor companies, proceed through the bidding process until selecting a winning company.

5. After completing the bidding process, use the project proposal document as the basis for developing the project's contract. Much of the same information from the project proposal will go directly into the contract as the legal agreement between the two companies.

6. Initiate the project with the winning company by creating the contract and having both parties sign off and agree.

7. As the project moves into the later phases of the project, you will utilize the project's contract more often than the project proposal document because the contract is the legal document and the winning company should be working toward satisfying the contract, not the project proposal. In this role, you act on behalf of the owner and represent in all contract negotiations.

Mastering the Quality Management Plan

Before exploring the quality management plan, you must understand how this tool can assist and support you on your project. The following project scenario emphasizes the importance of the tool and reasons why the quality management plan is critical to every project.

A medium-sized pharmaceutical company was planning to put a new drug on the market by fall, but the tests continue to fail. In clinical testing this drug is causing allergic reactions to eight out of ten patients. It is unsafe for general release to the public. Most of the company's resources are focusing on this one drug, and its failed test results are now trying to get it resolved as fast as possible. This failure has had a huge impact on the company, and this problem must be resolved as soon as possible. As the most senior project manager on the project, management chose you to run the SWAT team to resolve this issue. Your mission is to eliminate the allergic reactions, get the drug re-tested, receive approval from upper management, and get it out the door for final approval from the Federal Drug Administration. You have one month to do this or the company is going to miss the launch date due to manufacturing backups. Missing the launch will mean the loss of hundreds of thousands of dollars in lost sales.

As leader of the SWAT team, one of the first areas you look into is the testing and quality levels applied to the drug throughout its development cycle; where are the results of the testing, what was the level of quality used, where is the quality metrics or quality management plan? You are seeing some real concerns that these documents are either missing or not available for one reason or another. After further investigation, you find the issue and know why people are having these allergic reactions — you are relieved and the end is in sight. You can see that the allergic reaction is due to a new drug added to the drug formula at the last minute. This new drug is a pain reliever, but does not mix well with the other drugs. Initial tests showed some abnormal results, but the test team ignored them and the drug continued to the clinical-testing process. You have a number of questions before you move forward. These questions include:

What do you do now?

Whom should you tell the problem to?

Where was the quality level for this project?

What testing occurred?

To obtain the answers to these questions, the project manager should have created a quality management plan. You saw in your early analysis of the issue that no quality management plan ever existed, and there was no mention about how quality was covered. The quality management plan covers areas such as quality planning, assurance, control, and standards. The quality management plan is critical to all projects to ensure that a level of quality is in place, and the labs are obtaining the best possible results with the highest level of quality.

 We recommend that you review the quality management plan's planning questions in Chapter 8.

Creating a quality management plan

The quality management plan documents the processes and procedures for managing quality and ensures a project does not have quality issues in the future.

Project managers are responsible for the development and execution of a quality management plan on all their projects. Regardless of the project size, every project must have some quality checks in place to ensure that the team implements the highest level of quality possible. Project managers need to ensure that they keep their teams thinking about quality on all aspects of the project, not just in single areas on the project that involve the team members themselves. It is unacceptable to have quality in development, but have no quality in the testing aspects of the project. It is the project manager's job to ensure the highest level of quality possible on the project at all times.

Project customers should be looking to use the quality management plan on their projects. They should realize that if the project team is not using the plan, then quality most likely is not of the highest priority for them. This problem should alert the project customers that quality might be an issue on the project. The customers should also be involved in the various quality levels set for the project and what quality will mean to the project. The project team may have one definition of quality and the customers may have something different. It is important that both agree to the level of quality for the project, and the quality management plan should include the level of quality that the team members and customers have agreed to so there are no surprises as the project executes and different quality scenarios or concerns arise.

The actual steps of creating a quality management plan can vary from project manager to project manager, Instead of providing step-by-step instructions on creating a quality management plan, a better option is for the project manager to complete the quality management plan template.

Example of Quality Management Plan Table of Contents

Section 1: Quality Management Approach

Most quality management approaches base their work on the International Organization for Standardization (ISO). This general approach uses tools such as Continuous Improvement, Design Reviews, Six Sigma, TQM, and Effect Analysis.

Section 2: Project Overview

Write a short, descriptive overview of the project.

Section 3: Quality Standards

Define the level of quality you want to set as a standard. State the metrics that will be needed to maintain the quality standard.

Section 4: Quality Tools

Choose the tools you will need to support the quality effort. You can use many tools such as control charts, cause and effect diagrams, Pareto charts, scatter diagrams, statistical sampling, fishbone diagrams, and risk simulation. There are also quality audits and inspections to consider when developing this section on quality tools.

Section 5: Quality Planning

Identify and enforce the level of quality expected on the project. To ensure everyone maintains a level of quality throughout the life of the project, project managers need to discuss and plan for the level of quality with customers and stakeholders early in the project.

Section 6: Quality Assurance

Document the tasks that make sure that the project team processes the necessary requirements to meet quality assurance. Document how you are going to set up and maintain quality assurance.

Section 7: Quality Assurance Procedures

Document the process that implements quality assurance for the life of the project. Do not forget continuous process improvement.

Section 8: Quality Assurance Roles and Responsibilities

Identify the team members that will be assigned to QA and document their roles and responsibilities.

Section 9: Quality Control

Document the plan to monitor and control project task results that determine if they meet with the quality standards established by the project.

Section 10: Quality Control Procedures

Document the process that implements quality procedures for the life of the project.

Section 11: Quality Control Roles and Responsibilities

Identify the team members who will be assigned to QC and document their roles and responsibilities. Create a quality roles and responsibility matrix for the team.

ON the CD-ROM We have included a sample of this tool in the Communication tools Quality Subfolder. Use this to help you create your own version of this tool.

NOTE Please note, in the defining portion of the quality management plan, Chapter 8, there are a number of quality tools mentioned that are worth considering for your project. Tools such as the Pareto chart, control chart, risk simulation, and histograms are all excellent communication tools for managing the quality level of your project.

Using a quality management plan

Prior to using a tool such as the quality management plan, you must identify who on your project team will utilize this tool so that you can determine the level of detail required, frequency of distribution, style, and format of the report.

Before utilizing the quality management plan, we recommend that you review the quality management planning section in Chapter 8. Then follow these steps to use the plan:

1. Hold a meeting so that the team can review and verbally approve the plan.

2. After receiving verbal approval, distribute the quality management plan and the user acceptance document for official project approval.

3. After receiving approval on the quality management plan, store the quality management plan and the user acceptance document in the document control system for long-term storage, archiving, and retrieval purposes.

4. Implement the various quality processes established and documented in the quality management plan.

As the project moves into the planning phase, and then into executing, you must continually update the various quality processes (based on the results of the project) and adjust the quality management plan accordingly. These updates and adjustments occur throughout the life of the project. Approval and sign-offs are required every time changes are made to the quality management plan.

Mastering the Scope Management Plan

Before mastering the scope management plan, you must understand how this tool can assist and support you on your project. The following project scenario emphasizes the importance of having a scope management plan.

A small software company has decided to develop their own time tracking system to replace the aging manual process they have in place today. The company has a number of departments, and because time tracking is so important to every staff member, it makes sense to add a leader from each department onto the project to provide advice and training in their respective areas; therefore, leads from Marketing, Sales, Finance, IT, and Human Resources are all part of the advisory/training team. As the project manager, one of your first tasks is to work with each of the leads and develop the scope of the project. Because you know how important and critical scope is to the project and how important it is for company leaders to approve it, you decided to meet with each lead and gather each department's requirements separately. After collecting the scope items from each leader and compiling the information, the leadership team signs off and approves the scope management plan. The project is now able to move onto the next process. As the project moves into the design process, the leadership teams are starting to see sample screen shots. Unfortunately, they are unhappy with what they are seeing. The leadership team is now concerned with the application and starts asking for a series of changes to the scope, additional functionality, and new reports not in the original scope. As the project manager, you want to do what is right for the application, but also realize you have a tight timeframe and a tight budget. The leadership team is unhappy and you need to figure out what to do. You have a million questions and are not sure where to turn for help. Some of your questions include:

How should you have managed and controlled scope?

Where do you create and document the change request process and procedures for the project?

Where are the scope verification procedures documented for the project?

Where were the scope definition process and procedures documented that the project manager followed when first gathering the project's scope items?

To find the answers to these questions, the project manager should have created and used a scope management plan at the beginning of the project. The scope management plan covers the critical areas of project scope control and the process and procedures around managing the scope. Areas such as planning, definition, WBS, verification, and control are all included in this document. If the project manager had created a scope management plan initially for the project, when any change requests hit the project, there would have been a process and procedure to follow to ensure that the project stays on track, avoiding the confusion the project manager faces in the scenario. Scope management is an important aspect of project management, and the scope management plan is a document to help manage and control that aspect of the project.

 **CROSS-REF** We recommend that you review the Scope Management Plan's planning questions in Chapter 5.

Creating a scope management plan

Creating a scope management plan provides the project manager with a better handle on how to manage and control project scope changes.

Regardless of whether the project is large or small, some scope management and control is required on every project or it can have some serious consequences. Mismanaging scope will impact quality, schedule, and costs on the project.

Project scope control is the most important aspect of the scope management plan. However, it is not the only aspect worth noting. The scope management plan also contains the work breakdown structure (WBS) of the project that outlines all the activities and deliverables of the project. This process and the procedures documented in the scope management plan make it easy to understand and process change requests. If any changes to the scope are not already included in the WBS when the customer and team members approve the scope management plan, the project team considers these as additions to scope and therefore they need to go through the change control process and be processed accordingly. The project manager compares the two documents, determines that there is indeed new scope, and develops a change request document for customer approval. Scope management plays an important role in the project not only when adding or removing scope, but when comparing scope items newly requested that may or may not already be in the document.

Project managers should ensure they are using a scope management plan on all their projects, and should ensure they have a plan in place before the first scope change hits, to reduce any impact to the project. Larger projects should always have a scope management plan in place to ensure scope does not get out of control or derail the project. Without a scope management plan, the various change requests could negatively affect the project in ways that may be hard to recover from, which could lead to disaster and completely derail a project to the point of cancellation. Can you imagine if you were working on a highway project and someone suggested adding a new lane right in the middle of the project? What if the team stopped working on their current work and started construction on the new lane? It would cost millions of dollars in impact to the project, let alone to the schedule.

Project customers must have a good understanding of the scope management plan so that they are fully aware of the scope change process and procedures. When they request scope changes, they are going to understand how the project manager and team member will respond to the request.

The actual steps of creating a scope management plan can vary from project manager to project manager. Instead of providing step-by-step instructions on creating a scope management plan, a better option is for the project manager to complete the scope management plan template.

Example of Scope Management Plan Table of Contents

Section 1: Project Overview
Document the overview of the project. Note any specific highlights or interesting aspects of the project here.

Section 2: Scope Planning
Document the results from the scope planning meeting. After working through the various scope planning meetings and determining the project scope, the project manager will add that scope to this section.

Section 3: Scope Definition
Document the scope of the project. This information comes from the scope planning meetings.

Section 4: Work Breakdown Structure (WBS)
Document the work breakdown structure. This includes everything in the WBS, including the contents and items in the work package.

Section 5: Scope Verification
Document the process for verifying the scope of the project. This could be something as simple as working with the customers and ensuring you have obtained sign-off for the project, and then documenting that process.

Section 6: Scope Control
Document the process for managing and controlling project scope. The process of ensuring change requests is complete.

 We have included a sample of this tool in the Communication tools Scope Subfolder. Use this as a guide to create your own version of this tool.

Using a scope management plan

Prior to using the scope management plan, you must identify who on your project team will utilize the plan so that you can determine the level of detail required, frequency of distribution, style, and format of the report. The scope management plan is normally a high-level document that sets process and procedures in place to help the manager determine project scope.

Before using a scope management plan, review the scope management planning section in Chapter 5. Then follow these steps:

1. Ensure that the team members have read and understood the plan, by requesting a project team meeting and going over the plan with all relevant stakeholders in the project. Project managers need the team members engaged and in agreement with this process in order for them to be successful on the project. The minute that a team member deviates from managing the scope as documented in the plan, the project can run into big trouble.

2. Communicate the scope management plan to the customers. This is an important step to ensure customers are aware of the scope management process and the various tools to use when asking for additional scope items.

3. Obtain sign-off and approval from management and the customer on the scope management plan. This includes sending the scope management plan along with the user acceptance document for official project approval.

4. Store both documents and approvals in the document control system for long-term storage, archiving, and retrieval process.

5. Implement the scope management plan on the project.

Summary

The communication tools that we described in this chapter are some of the best choices for the project's initiation process. The initiation process is the first process in the project lifecycle, so establishing a communication rhythm and understanding how to create and use the tools early in the project is important.

One of the important take-away items from this chapter is how the project manager will use each tool through the initiation, planning, and executing processes. The project manager drives the use of the communications tools on their projects, and having them available to use provides the project manager a mechanism to effectively communicate their project information.

Chapter 15

Using Communication Tools in the Planning Process

I n this chapter, we explore project communication tools in the project planning process. The planning process assists project managers in planning the execution and delivery of their projects. The tools in this chapter assist the project manager with this task.

During the planning process you must identify what communication tools you are going to use to effectively plan and manage your project. The tools we cover in this chapter can help you become a better communicator on your project. We highly recommend that the first tools you consider in the planning process are the scheduling and cost control tools; paying particular attention to the project calendar and the risk simulation tools, because they are excellent communication tools and ones that will help you understand your project dates more thoroughly.

We can now explore the communication tools necessary to help you plan your project. The primary communication tools include Project Calendar tool, Estimating tool, Resource Leveling tool, and the Work Breakdown Structure tool. Each of these will aid in the successful communication and execution of your project.

Mastering the Delphi Method

Before you can use the Delphi method, you must understand how this tool can assist and support you on your project. The following project scenario emphasizes the importance of the tool, and the reasons why the Delphi method is critical to trying to address and resolve large-scale problems on your projects.

A large-scale software company whose headquarters is in St John's Newfoundland, Canada, and has offices located around the world, has decided to replace their old billing system. As the most senior project manager, you have been chosen to lead this project. As you start into the project, one of the challenges you recognize immediately is that you must work with all the offices located around the world and gather their requirements for this new billing system. Doing this is critical to the success of the project, especially if you expect those offices to use the system once it is implemented. The Information Technology Department (IT) designed the current billing system using their own requirements and did not take into consideration any of the user's specific requirements. This was a biased approach to designing and from your lessons learned, you do not want to duplicate that mistake on this new system. The problem you face is how do you obtain everyone's requirements, and not let one group such as IT, who has dominated the discussions of requirements and design in the past, do the same thing again on this new effort. The other challenge is that management will not approve travel expenses for off-site staff to travel to your headquarters location and partici-pate in the requirements gathering sessions. This is a major setback for the project, and you are uncertain about how to approach this problem. You have a number of questions, including how you are going to bring everyone together to capture the requirements of this new billing system in a timely and cost-effective manner. Some other questions you have are:

How do I capture worldwide requirements?

What mechanism do I have at my disposal?

How do I coordinate people in the various time zones?

How do I prevent one particular group from dominating the requirements gathering sessions?

To obtain the answers to these questions, you should use the Delphi method tool. The Delphi method is a process for obtaining solutions for large-scale problems from a group of individual experts. The technique uses a process of allowing each individual the opportunity to provide his or her expertise in the solution of the problem. This technique or method has the advantage of keep-ing the bias out of the process as the individuals make their own decisions on the problem.

The Delphi method could be a useful process in these scenario described above. The project man-ager would have reached out to each of the worldwide offices, gathering their requirements and consolidating their information into one final requirements document. Regardless of what the indi-vidual groups ask for in their requirements, the Delphi method eliminates dominant groups from challenging or influencing other groups or individual team members.

 We recommend that you review the Delphi method's planning questions in Chapter 8.

Creating the Delphi method tool

Creating and developing a Delphi method session and report is a multifaceted process, and although it can be done on smaller scale problems should the need arise; it is mainly tailored to larger-scale problems. Difficulties occur when you try to assemble a team of experts on a timely basis due to the demands on their time to be able to participate in the Delphi method process. When planning or scheduling this process, plan it well in advance and keep in mind the timeframes required and allow adequate time to work through the process and reach the solution. The main objective of this method is to gather and analyze information and reach a consensus without any bias. The Delphi method process enables each expert to work alone, preventing his or her personality from dominating the outcome of the solution.

The project manager can play many roles in the Delphi method process, such as the facilitator of the process itself, or as an active team member. It depends partially on his or her skills.

The project customer should be actively involved in the Delphi method process. They introduce the problem, which the team is trying to resolve, and offer financial and budgetary support for this process. At the end of the Delphi method process, the customer can evaluate and most likely select the solution the team has agreed upon and implement that solution.

The steps to create the Delphi method are the same steps in using the Delphi method. Because the Delphi method is a process, the steps are already included in the process. This tool is unlike any other tool we cover in this book. There is no physical method of creating the Delphi method; when you use the process it creates the tool.

Using the Delphi method

Prior to using the Delphi method, you must identify whom on your project team will utilize and be involved in this process. You must have *subject matter experts* (SME) involved in this process.

Before utilizing the Delphi method, review the Delphi method planning section in Chapter 8. Then follow these steps:

1. Identify the problem you are trying to resolve. Make sure this is the only problem because this method produces one solution at a time.
2. Develop a scope for your problem. This should include the deliverables, assumptions, and constraints as well as the technical information available.
3. Assemble a team of qualified SMEs in fields related to the problem. Then set the requirements for time and schedule with these experts and identify the budget.
4. Send the scope documentation defining the problem to the experts for their first attempt at a solution. Have the experts identify the problem and develop their best solution.
5. You then receive and analyze the first solution from the team of experts.
6. Summarize the experts' solutions and present them to the team for further comments and ideas. Merge all solutions received, summarize, and compile them into a single document.
7. Send the updated process documentation. This documentation includes information from all experts from the first attempt and second attempts at the solution.
8. Receive updated solutions based on the next round of feedback.

NOTE Repeat Steps 6, 7, and 8 until reaching a consensus between the team and the project manager.

9. After the team reaches a consensus, you then call a face-to-face session that includes everyone involved and determine the final and best solution to the problem.

10. Establish the best-recommended solution for your problem.

11. Create solution document for review and approval, including scope, schedule, and budget.

12. Implement solution based on approval to proceed.

Mastering the Design Specifications

Before mastering how to use design specifications, you must understand how this tool can assist and support you on your project. The following project scenario emphasizes the importance of the tool.

The construction of a large facility project is just getting underway; the foundations are complete, and the framing has just begun. The project has 52 instances where the drawings and specifications are unclear, missing, or just plain wrong. These errors have resulted in requests for information (RFI) from the architects asking for additional clarification, revision, or changes. Each instance has caused a delay in the schedule and increased costs, resulting in change requests and a request for a schedule extension as well as more cost to the project. The team is anticipating numbers 53 and 54 soon. As the project manager on this construction job, you need to understand how to approach this problem. There are many questions that you need to answer immediately. These questions include:

How could you have prevented this from happening?

How are you going to get the project back on schedule?

How will you ever be able to make up the cost overruns?

To obtain the answers to these questions, you can use a design specifications tool. The design specifications documents clear and complete specifications of a product with the intent of building that product. On construction projects, the design specifications are the plans (drawings) by the engineering and architectural groups working on the project. In software, the design specification document will include what screens and reports will look like.

 We recommend that you review the design specifications planning questions in Chapter 8.

Creating design specifications

The design team creates the design specification on most projects, regardless of the industry. For example, in the software, construction, and research industries there are design teams who design the components of the product. On construction projects, the team may consist of an architect, engineer, and an analyst. On software projects, the design team consists of lead developers, lead designers, and lead testers. Design specifications are complex documents that require the technical knowledge and the expertise to be able to write and clearly articulate the information into a usable format for the designers and developers to develop the project. Developing clear, accurate, and complete design specifications documents is imperative to the success of creating any product. It is one of the success criteria for the project.

To be successful, project managers must communicate the information in the design specifications document to their customer. The customers can review the document, suggest changes, and understand the fundamental details behind the design of the product. Normally, design specifications include visual representations, drawings, and layouts of the product. Whenever applicable, add drawings to the document. When team members review the design specifications document, they can easily see the end result; or, if there are visual drawings in the document, they can see what the result will look like. Preventing clients from accessing any design specifications or simply ignoring their input will only lead to their frustration and make them unhappy with the final product; seeking their advice and suggestions early in the project is one the smartest things you can do. The design specifications document is the tool to share with your customer for their early acceptance and their long-term acceptance of the product.

Project managers must ensure that the design specifications document has the approval of the customer before considering it final. If you are waiting for approval, it could indicate that your customer is having some issues with the design that is preventing them from accepting the document or the overall software design on a software project. To assist with the acceptance, the design details contained in the document must be available for the client to review at all times. The project team should be available to answer any questions or address any concerns. Project managers should host a series of design specifications review meetings with the customer to analyze the document so they can understand what the team is developing. At the meetings, the customer has access to any team member and can discuss the details of the product directly with a specific team member if they desire. When you have open communication between everyone on the project and especially the customer, it normally provides the customer with the confidence that they are guiding the project and it is heading in the right direction and satisfying their needs.

Design specifications are often so broad in content that it would be impossible to create a valid sample for the multiple industries we cover in this book. In Chapter 8, we provided a software design specification template that is the basis of developing this tool for your project. Here are some basic steps in creating a design specifications document.

1. After the customer creates the concept for the product and delivers the customer requirements, you then work with your design team to create the preliminary design specifications based on the customer's requirements. Preliminary design would consist of enough engineering to develop conceptual layout, a primary specification listing, work breakdown structure, conceptual budget, and schedule. The specification evolves initially from the creation process.

2. Then your project team members review the preliminary design concept specifications developed by the design team. A preliminary review is mandatory to ensure the design addresses the scope of work. During that review, additional ideas and concepts most likely will develop and the project designer will add these to the design specifications document.

3. Then lead your project team, specifically the designers, in the development of a draft design specifications document based off the template provided on the CD-ROM or supplied by your company.

4. After creating the draft document, your project's lead design analyst will distribute it to other team members and the customer for initial review and input.

5. Once the team members and the customer have given input and feedback on the draft document, you ensure that feedback is incorporated into the final version of the document.

6. Enforce the use of the design specification document on your project.

ON the CD-ROM   We have included a sample of this design specification tool in the Communication tools Quality Subfolder. Use this as a guide to help you create your own version of this tool. This template is (c) Copyright of Construx Software Builders, Inc., used with permission from Construx.

Using design specifications

Before you can use a design specifications tool, you must identify who on your project team will utilize this tool so that you can determine the level of detail required, frequency of distribution, style, or format of the report. Normally, this tool captures very detailed level requirements within this document.

Before using the design specifications document, review the design specifications planning section in Chapter 8. Then follow these steps:

1. The first step in this process is to ensure the customer and team members sign off and approve the design specifications document. This includes sending the design specifications document, along with the formal acceptance document, to every team member and customer for their approval.

2. Once the team members and customer approve and send their approval to you, store it in the document control system for long-term storage, archiving, and retrieval purposes.

3. After gaining approval, and as the project moves into the executing process, you will enforce the use of the design specifications document with your team members to design the final-product. This includes calling design sessions based on the document, answering team member's questions, and ensuring that the team is utilizing the document to create the design of the final product.

Mastering the Document Control System

Before creating and using a document control system, you must understand how this tool can assist and support you on your project. The following project scenario emphasizes the importance of the tool and the reasons why the document control system is so critical to every project.

There is a large construction project under way in Toronto, Ontario, Canada. You have managed the project for the last couple of months and everything is progressing well, the project seems to be on track, and is expected to finish on time and on budget. The project team members are developing reports, documents, charts, graphs, and a number of other documents. The floor plans are also progressing well and the information on the project is flowing. Suddenly, the project hits a problem and is now in trouble. There are questions flying in from all directions, and people want to start finding project documents and reports. The customers are asking questions, the team members are scrambling to find answers and everyone is demanding information from you. There is a generic theme to the questions, they want information such as status reports, budget reports, and cost spreadsheets. People just want to find information about the project. You are asking yourself questions as well, and your questions seem to be around getting people the project information they need to make decisions during this difficult time. Your questions include:

How can you get the information to everyone in a timely and controlled manner?

How can you provide the information quickly without overwhelming everyone?

Where is the information stored?

What system should we use to meet all these requests?

To help keep a scenario such as this from happening, the project manager requires a document control system for storage of the project's documentation. The document control system is a repository of project information in a file folder system that creates a structured and organized approach to storing and finding project information. The document control system can save time and effort finding and retrieving any project information. On smaller projects, you do not necessarily need to automate the document control system; a manual filing system may be adequate. However, the project manager must create the same project structure in a manual system as he would for an automated tool to ensure that team members and customers can find the information when they need it.

On medium and large projects, there tends to be the need to create many documents, and vast amounts of information are available. The only solution in those cases is to keep the project documents in an organized and structured location if you want any chance of finding project information in the future.

Automated solutions in this chapter refer to specific software packages, such as Microsoft SharePoint Services, Microsoft's Groove, Documentum, and KnowledgeTree. However, there is a host of other storage and retrieval products on the market as well. These software packages are almost useless unless someone (normally the project manager) sets up and establishes an organized structure for storing project's documents. This system allows team members or the customer to find project information immediately and provides everyone involved with the confidence that they can obtain the information they need for the project.

CROSS-REF We recommend that you review the document control system's planning questions in Chapter 13.

Creating the document control system

It is common for smaller companies that do not have an automated document control system in place, to set up directory structures on their internal networks and use that structure as the document control system. When controlling and organizing project documents, rarely does a manual solution work as well as an automated packaged application. If possible, the project manager should look to use the more robust applications for their projects and have their company purchase these company-wide solutions for use on their projects. Once purchased at the company level, all projects can share the costs and everyone can benefit from the features of these powerful tools.

Project managers should use a document control system for all projects whenever possible. The software applications provide an opportunity to share project information and offer a location for long-term and secure storage of those files.

TIP As project managers face stricter internal audit requirements, they need to have better control over their documents, and are encouraged to put any documents in a controlled environment where project information is available for quick and easy access by project teams or any persons who may be auditing the project.

A document control system also stores project approvals and formal signoffs in a safe and secure location. If there is ever the need to retrieve evidence of an approval, it should be easy and quick to find within the document control system.

Project customers can also access project details and other information about the project within the document control system. They can add and update documents that they own and are responsible for on the project. However, if the customers get too much information there is a chance they could derail or sidetrack a project by digging into project documents that they don't really have the business of reading or seeing. For example, if a customer reads a design document and they disagree with the design, in some companies, they would have no right to question a design and therefore could cause major problems on the project challenging something that they "found" when looking in the tool. On the other hand, if the team members and customer are not accessing the information, the project manager will need to be continually providing regular updates, wasting time and effort that could be spent managing the project. There needs to be a happy and workable medium for this situation and is handled on a case-by-case basis. This can be time consuming and something that project managers may not have time to do, especially when the information is in the document control system and readily available to everyone involved in the project.

Because the document control system is an automated tool, there are no detailed steps available for creating the tool. Information technology staff would have been available to install and set up the tool for the company and depending on the package, the installation steps can vary greatly. Individual project managers would rarely have to do more than create a project instance and start storing project files.

The following steps outline how to create a manual document control system for companies that do not have an automated system in place, but still want to take advantage of this valuable communication tool. To creating a manual document control system, follow these steps:

1. Find a shared network drive where all your team members have read/write access. Most companies have a common drive, or a network drive that is sharable across multiple groups; you will create the manual document control system on that shared network drive. Worst-case scenario is you will use your own hard drive or buy a portable drive for team members to access. This is really the worst case, but may be required depending on the situation.

2. Establish a file format and structure based upon your project's established WBS. This includes developing and publishing a standard naming convention for files, and setting processes and procedures for the document format structure.

3. Create the top-level directory using your project's name.

4. Then, create subdirectories based on major categories of your project. This is going to vary from project to project; but across the different industries, these should be relatively the same. Suggestions for subcategories include:

   - Administrative documents
   - Financial documents
   - Drawings
   - Project schedule
   - Project costs
   - Issues and Risks Documents
   - Project Management Documents

5. After you completely set up each of the directories, the next step is establishing the security rights on each folder. This may or may not be possible and you may need help from the security team.

6. Finally, communicate the new directory structure to your team members and customer and train them on how to use it.

Figure 15.1 represents the directory structure for a document control system. The directory structure provides a sampling of folders for a single project but can vary depending on the type of project you are managing.

FIGURE 15.1

A sample of a document control system.

Manual Company Document Control System
- 1. Administrative Files
  - New Hires Files
  - Payroll
  - Project Startup Files
- 2. Financial Files
  - Project Budget
- 3. Project Schedule
- 4. Requirements Files
  - Design Specification
- 5. Technical Files
- 6. Issues and Risk Files
  - Issue Files
  - Risk Files
- 7. Quality Files
- 8. Reporting
- 9. Team Resource Files
- 10. Misc Files

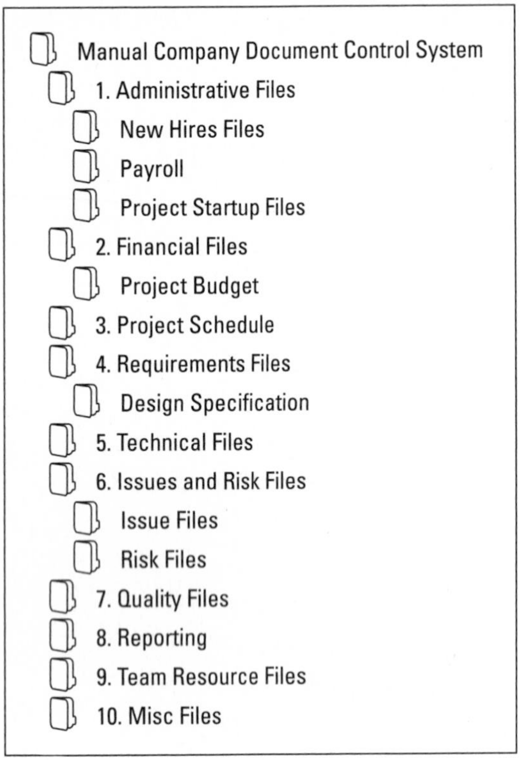

Using the document control system

Prior to using a document control system, you must identify who on your project team will utilize this tool to determine the level of detail required, style, how you will store the information. Use of this tool ensures that the project manager is communicating the project information to their customers and there is open access to the project documents where applicable.

Before utilizing the document control system, review the planning section in Chapter 13. Then follow these steps:

1. Ensure that your project team member's and your customer are fully engaged and aware of how to store project documentation. This could mean setting up additional training sessions, or one-on-one session(s) to ensure the team members know how to store their project files. Unlike most tools, the document control system is not something that requires approval or sign-off from anyone on the project; this is because it is an internal project management tool used mainly by you and your team members. It generally has no affect on the outcome of the project.

2. After you have confirmed that your project team members and customer are storing their project documentation in the document control system, the next step is for you to ensure that they will continue to use it on an ongoing basis to store documentation and important project files. You will continually remind and monitor this usage throughout the project.

3. As the project moves to the executing process, continue spot-checking to ensure everyone is putting the project documentation in the document control system. You should be looking for the project's key deliverables as well as signatures and approvals for each document. The reason for doing this is to prepare the project and yourself for internal audits or anyone else looking for key documents on the project. It is important that you ensure your project documents are stored in the document control system or they could fail their audits and suffer other consequences.

Mastering the Estimating Tool

Before you can use the estimating tool, you must understand how it can assist and support you on a project. The following project scenario emphasizes the importance of the tool.

The project team has been working on an estimate for over six months. The project is for the seven-year construction of a natural gas pipeline from the northwest shelf off the coast of Australia, coming ashore at Port Hedland, and then down to Perth. Just north of Perth, there are plans to build a large, natural gas refinery at Wanneroo, Western Australia. The estimating team is having a difficult time justifying the project's estimated cost to the natural gas board. The previous review of the estimate by the board resulted in criticism toward the estimators who had not taken into account all aspects of the project and future labor costs. The board members consider the estimates of the estimating team as insufficient. The team has broken the work down to a detailed level that they feel comfortable with in developing their estimate. As the project manager leading the estimating team in this effort, you have a number of questions that you want answered. These questions include:

How can we scrub this estimate to reveal any deficiencies?

What is the variance in the estimate?

Does the team have any other saving techniques to reduce the costs?

Should we create the WBS now and estimate at the work package level?

To obtain the answers to these questions, you should use a forecasting tool to address future labor, material, and equipment costs. Forecasting is a technique used to determine future costs to a project. Normally, a professional forecaster is brought-in to assist in this process on large projects like the one in this scenario, and with their findings, they can predict the costs of the project based on future trends in the industry. In this scenario, a professional forecaster would have been invaluable to the process of producing the estimate for the pipeline. Because of the seven-year duration of this project, it is not too late to do so.

CROSS-REF   We recommend that you review the estimating tool's planning questions in Chapter 7.

Creating an estimating tool

A professional forecaster has the training and the understanding of how to read future conditions and can create project forecasts. Forecasters have the ability to look at trends, determine how they will affect the project, and inform the project manager, team members, and customer of the impacts. A forecaster can gather information on a project or a subject area that requires a forecast, such as labor rates, materials, and equipment. For example, a forecaster will know what union contracts to include for increases in labor rates for the local area. The forecaster will also know working conditions and can extrapolate those effects on future rates. In addition, by understanding economic effects, supply and demand on materials, and concurrent projects, the forecaster can estimate potential material costs as the project progresses. World events, such as a local or even global war, can have an effect on prices. Government and environmental regulations can also have a major impact on future prices. The end-result of a forecaster's work is to provide the forecast information to the project manager or the project team for creating the project estimate. The project team when providing their cost estimates in the creation process should rely on the forecaster to provide this data when applicable. Project managers need to be involved in the estimating process and should ensure the estimators include rate changes and inflation, especially if the project is more than two or three years in duration, into their forecasts to be confident that they have come as close as possible to the real costs of the project. When it comes to changes or updates to the project's budget or schedule, project managers will also be involved in estimating and will provide updated information based on the changes and adjust it accordingly.

Although the estimating process is often complex, the end-result is a projection of the real costs of the project. This projection is important for the customer in their determination of whether to proceed with the project or make the decision to shut it down immediately.

Creating a forecast

Even though this section is the *creating an estimating tool*, one of the support professions is forecasting. The following steps explain what a forecaster performs when creating a forecast.

1. The forecaster identifies what to forecast and why to forecast it; this is normally material, labor rates, and equipment.

2. The forecaster gathers information and data to complete the forecast.

3. The forecaster then analyzes data and information and validates all informational resources.

4. The forecaster derives the forecast for the project, and any impacts via the project cash flow.

5. The forecaster distributes the forecast information and estimates.

6. Finally, the forecaster gathers information to make their forecasts as accurate as possible on labor rates, material, and equipment costs.

As project manager, you should understand exactly what these steps are and how you can help the forecaster do their work. You need to know how long the process is going to take, the cost impacts of him/her doing the work and the impact to the project. We recommend highly you are active in this step and work closely with your forecaster on your project team. It will give a much better understanding of future trends in the industry.

Creating a project estimate tool

The following steps explain what an estimator would do to create an estimate for the project.

1. Assign an estimator to your project. This could be the project manager or a separate team member focused solely on estimating.

2. Ensure the estimator understands the scope of work and what to base the estimate on.

3. Work with the estimator as they review design specifications (i.e., construction industry drawings), and identify areas in the specifications to perform the estimate. Answer any questions where appropriate.

4. Work with the estimator as they perform the estimate for the project.

5. Present the estimate to your customer or upper management. In construction for example, this turns into a bid.

6. Store your project's estimate and associated documents in the document control system for long-term storage, archiving, and retrieval purposes.

Using the estimating tool

Prior to using the estimating tool, you must identify who will use this tool so that you can determine the level of detail required, frequency of distribution, style, and format of the report. Project estimates are generally very detailed in nature so there is no confusion as to what the expected costs of each component would be on the project.

Before using the estimating tool, review the estimating tool planning section in Chapter 7. Then follow these steps:

1. You must apply the cost estimate or labor hours to the budget creation process. For example, if you have an estimate from a vendor or contracting company, they can take that estimated value and determine how close it is to the project budget.

2. Depending on whether it is over or under budget, you should react accordingly, which means you may have to ask for additional money from your customer, or ask the customer to reduce scope and try to reduce costs.

3. At the end of this process, store all your relevant documents in the document control system for long-term storage, archiving, and retrieval purposes.

Mastering the Project Calendar

Before you can use a project calendar, you must understand how this tool can assist and support you on your project. The following project scenario emphasizes the importance of the tool.

A large manufacturing company in Denver, Colorado, has decided to implement a new human resource management system to replace their current system. The current system can no longer keep up with the demands from the personnel department; and, therefore, the system must go. Management has assigned you to be the project manager of this project, and you have already started to delve into the details. Your customer in the personnel department is demanding and wants to ensure that you stay on top of the project's schedule and communicate the project schedule to them weekly. Unfortunately, the personnel department staff is not especially computer literate; and, therefore, if you send them the weekly project schedule, it would likely be meaningless because they would not know how to read it. You could develop various reports from the scheduling tool that would be helpful, but it may be difficult for the staff to grasp the actual project timeframes; you are frustrated and do not know what to do. As the project progresses, management is hearing complaints that the customer is not getting the status on the project schedule they have been asking for, and that you have not found a way to provide it to them. Upper management is asking what you are doing about providing the project schedule to the customer because they too are hearing complaints from the customers. Upper management is asking the following questions:

What are you doing about reporting the project's schedule?

How can the customer access the project schedule today?

Is there a manual way you can provide a project schedule to the customer?

To obtain the answers to these questions, the project manager should utilize a project calendar. The project calendar communicates the high-level timeframes of the project directly to the customer and is a valuable communication tool for every project manager. The project manager can print out the calendar and hand write the project timeframes, or produce an electronic version using the built-in calendar view in most scheduling tools. This provides the customer with a high-level picture of the project's timelines. Using a project calendar allows the project manager the ability to sit down with the customer and plan the project schedule together and jointly planning the key milestones on the project. With the dates in front of the customers you are able to negotiate and talk with them about what the project will look like from a schedule perspective. For example, if there is a scenario where the project schedule shows the project's development phase occurs over a major holiday, the project manager and customer can agree to move those dates to a more appropriate timeframe, knowing that leaving it during a holiday adds a level of risk to the project. In those cases (moving a major project milestone date), the project manager and customer can look on the calendar and determine the downstream effects to moving that date. The project calendar is a graphical tool that provides a great picture of the project's major milestone dates and is one of the best tools a project manager can utilize on their projects.

CROSS-REF We recommend that you review the project calendar's planning questions in Chapter 10.

Creating a project calendar

Having a project calendar at your side at all times is helpful to provide answers on-the-spot about the project's schedule. Another benefit of the project calendar is that it displays the high-level schedule of the project's deliverables across the months of the year; providing a yearly look at the project in graphical format, making planning the project much easier. When reviewing the different project milestone dates, the customer may see overlaps or impacts to their business processes, such as month-end reporting, quarterly reports, or year-end reporting. If this is the case, you should work with the team members and try to adjust the project schedule accordingly.

TIP Add multiple projects to a single calendar to get a multiple project schedule view. You can quickly see any timeframe overlaps on the projects.

The easiest way to create a project calendar is to print out a blank copy of a project calendar template (month-by-month view). When you have a paper copy of the project calendar, you manually enter your project's major deliverable dates into the specific dates on the calendar. If you are managing multiple efforts, then create a project calendar for every project you manage and potentially an overall project calendar to track any overlaps between projects, if applicable. After the team approves the timelines, then create multiple paper copies of the calendar. That way you can provide them to your team members and customers to be able to utilize throughout the project.

You can also use a project-scheduling tool, such as Microsoft Project, to create a project calendar. After entering the tasks on the project schedule, you can change the view in the tool to "Calendar," and it creates a project calendar. Print the results to have a paper copy of the electronic calendar and you will be ready for those on the spot questions about project timeframes.

Figure 15.2 is a project calendar created by using a project-scheduling tool. The calendar in this example illustrates high-level phases only, but is enough to plan and communicate the activities of the project to anyone interested.

Using a project calendar

Before you create and use a project calendar, you must identify who on your project team will use this tool so that you can determine the level of detail required, style, and format of the report. A project calendar tends to be more of a high-level tool for higher-level conversations about timeframes and dates. Adding too many details to a project calendar can get messy and potentially hard to manage. We recommend you use this tool as a high-level tool with high-level information only.

FIGURE 15.2

A project calendar created by using a project scheduling tool.

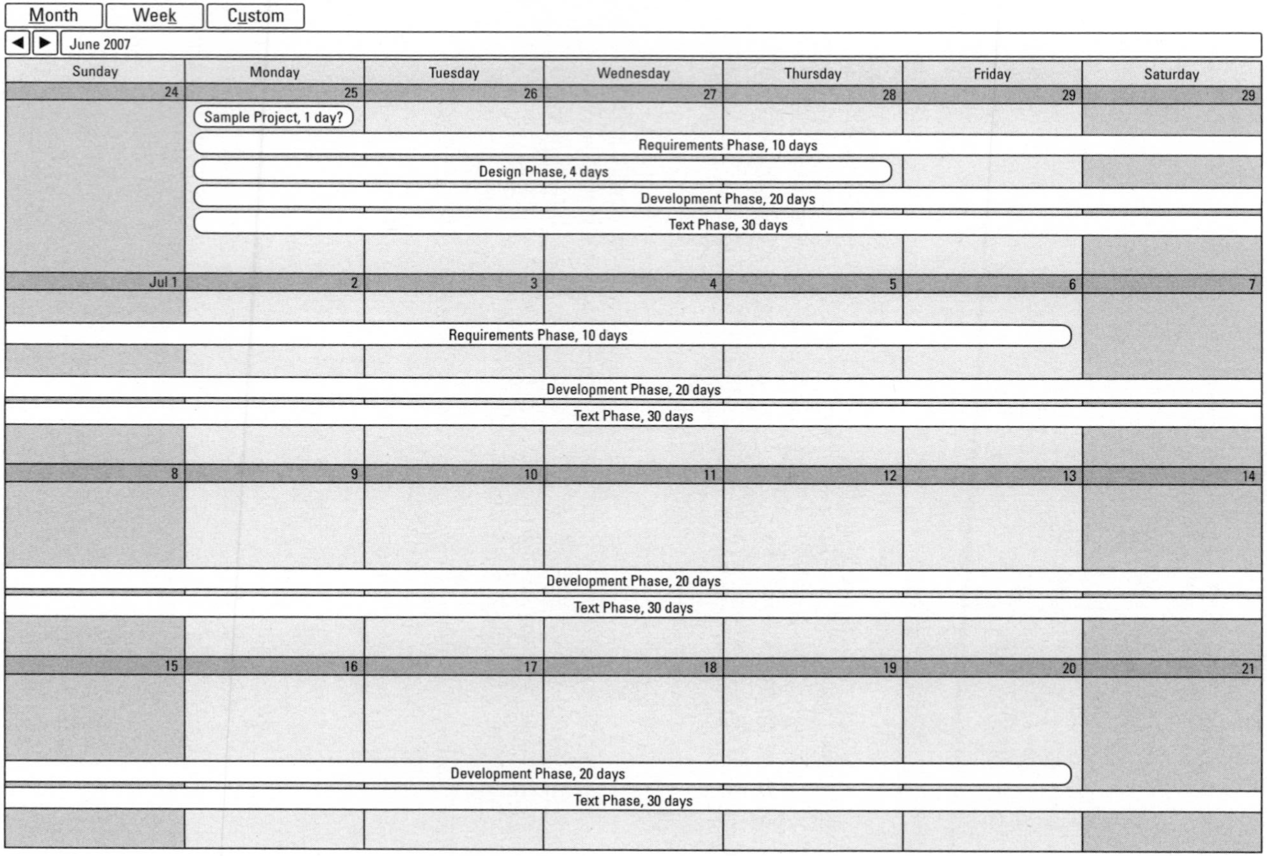

| | Month | Week | Custom |
| | June 2007 | | |

Sunday	Monday	Tuesday	Wednesday	Thursday	Friday	Saturday
24	25	26	27	28	29	29
	Sample Project, 1 day?		Requirements Phase, 10 days			
		Design Phase, 4 days				
			Development Phase, 20 days			
			Text Phase, 30 days			
Jul 1	2	3	4	5	6	7
		Requirements Phase, 10 days				
			Development Phase, 20 days			
			Text Phase, 30 days			
8	9	10	11	12	13	14
			Development Phase, 20 days			
			Text Phase, 30 days			
15	16	17	18	19	20	21
		Development Phase, 20 days				
			Text Phase, 30 days			

Before using a project calendar tool, review the project calendar planning section in Chapter 10. Then follow these steps:

> **NOTE** The steps assume you are working on a small project and have to create the schedule working with the team.

1. Choose the format that you will use on your project. We recommend you add holidays and company slow periods into the project calendar as well. Add holidays and team member days off immediately to the calendar. That way, when you add dates for project tasks, you can see how the new dates fall on the existing calendar with the holidays already included. If the project calendar shows a major section of the project occurring during a slowdown period (Christmas), it is letting everyone know that it would be a project risk to try and do that work over that period; therefore, it requires that portion of the project be moved.

2. Communicate to your customers how project deliverables sit on the calendar. You should develop the project schedule with customers and team members anyway, so once you get approval, then the official project schedule is complete. The project calendar works great as a communication tool for working the project's rough dates and negotiating with the customer. Eventually, after working out the rough schedule, you enter the tasks and dates into automated scheduling tool for project execution.

3. After reviewing the calendar with your customer and obtaining approval from the team members that the dates are workable, add these dates to the master project schedule and manage to the dates everyone has agreed to.

4. As the project moves into the executing phase, continue to utilize the project calendar. You should always have a project calendar on hand and be able to provide key project dates to anyone requiring project schedule information. It is best practice to update the project calendar manually first on the paper calendar and then make the official updates on the project schedule on a weekly basis. This ongoing process continues throughout the life of the project.

5. When you use a paper version of the project calendar, it is impossible for you to add it electronically to the document control system. These hardcopy project calendars are perfect working documents that the project managers may discard at the end of the project. However, the information from the project calendar is stored directly in the electronic project schedule and therefore none of the information is ever lost. At the end, the project schedule is stored in the document control system for long-term storage, archiving, and retrieval purposes.

Mastering Prototyping

Before using the prototyping tool, you must understand how this tool can assist and support you on your project. The following project scenario emphasizes the importance of the tool.

A large motorcycle plant has an idea to design and develop a brand-new model of their Sport Touring bike. As the lead project manager for the company, management decides you are best suited for this project. You are now the project manager; and as you initiate the project, management begins to direct questions to you concerning details around the design of the motorcycle. The design schedule allows for another nine months, but management is pushing hard for answers to their questions, such as

> How can we tell if this motorcycle is going to run at the performance requirements we want?
>
> How heavy will the motorcycle be?
>
> What kind of gas mileage will it get?
>
> How well will it race?
>
> Will this be a racing motorcycle or a day riding motorcycle or a combination of both?

To obtain the answers to these questions, the project manager should create a prototype of the new motorcycle. A prototype is a method by which the customer has access to a modified or reduced version of the final product before the full development process begins. By creating a prototype, the customer can see what the final-product will look like, without going through the full development cycle. For example, software developers utilize prototyping heavily to allow clients to see sample reports with sample data and sample screen shots. This gives the customer a chance to approve or recommend changes to the reports or screens based on what they are seeing in the prototype. The advantage of prototyping for the customer is that it allows them to provide input into the final design of the product during the planning and design phases, and it builds an understanding between the customer and the project team on what the final product's design, look, and feel will be. The other advantage of prototyping is the time and money it saves on making design decisions early in the project, compared to later.

Prototyping comes in many different variations. Paper prototypes are common on software developments projects by creating screens and reports on paper and allowing customer to approve the layouts and designs with little or no development expense. Other prototyping includes miniature versions of a product such as a model car, a construction project, buildings, and bridges; using a variety of materials to create smaller versions of the actual facilities. Finally, there are working prototypes that represent a final version of the product but with less functionality than the finished product. These prototypes have enough functionality built into them to provide the customer an understanding of what they will receive as the final product.

CROSS-REF   We recommend that you review the prototyping tool's planning questions in Chapter 10.

Creating a prototyping tool

The prototype methodology is beneficial on projects that generate a final-product. A project that has no tangible product at the end will not utilize the prototype or prototyping tool. For example, a project that creates produces a service offering, such as a new health insurance offering, would not have the need to utilize a prototype. However, many project types can utilize the prototype process if they wanted too. Motorcycles, jackets, televisions, and radios are some of the thousands of examples of possible prototype projects. Many different methodologies incorporate prototyping into their lifecycle. Certain architectural and construction projects favor prototyping, as well as software development and research projects. Each industry has a unique approach as to how they include prototyping within their development methodologies, but the result is the same.

Project managers must remain active during development of the prototyping deliverables created for their projects, but will not normally be involved in the actual creation of the prototype. Project managers who utilize prototyping should ensure that they get their customer involved in the creation of the prototype as early as possible so they can provide the team with feedback on the design of the product and the project team can know they are hearing the requirements directly from the customer. The goal of any prototyping process is to have the customer approve the prototype; that way it speeds up the time for development and allows the development activities on the project to officially begin.

Using prototyping

Prior to using a prototype, you must identify who on your project team will utilize this tool so that you can determine the level of detail required, frequency of distribution, style, and format of the report. Generally, prototypes tend to focus toward the needs of the customer, so the level of detail required can vary greatly. This is a very specific project-related requirement.

One important aspect of using the prototyping process is the development methodology that incorporates prototyping within it. This methodology allows for a specific timeframe in the lifecycle to allow the prototyping process to occur and allows for time in the development cycle (which may include multiple sessions and the customer review sessions) to complete. One of the advantages that project managers have when entering into projects that incorporate prototyping is that management has already agreed that they can allocate enough time in their project schedule for the prototyping process to be done correctly. The customer and senior management must be supportive of this process or the project manager will have a hard time succeeding. It would be difficult for a project manager to squeeze a prototyping process into a normal development lifecycle process; in most cases it just does not work. A development methodology that includes prototyping and one that does not are two different and distinct methodologies.

Before you can use a prototyping tool, review the prototype planning section in Chapter 10. Then follow these steps:

   1. Set up review sessions for your customers to look at the prototype and provide feedback. This requires setting up meetings, getting the right people involved, and ensuring the customer has plenty of opportunity to go over the prototype and provide their feedback. Another important step in this process and a best practice is to set a prototype limit. Doing this includes setting the number of times your project team will enhance the prototype, and how many chances your customers will get to review and provide feedback. Setting this limit as early as possible in the process is important, or the prototyping process will continue longer than expected, and may not ever complete. The important item to stress to the customer is that it is just a working model, and not the final product.

2. After your customer reviews the prototype, gather their feedback, expectations, and success criteria on the model. Then you should work with your development team to incorporate that feedback into the next version.

3. Set up new timeframes for customer review of the prototype.

4. Have your project team members demonstrate the prototype again to the customer and gather their next round of feedback. This process continues until you complete the set number of review sessions as agreed to in Step 1.

5. Where applicable, you should store any documentation, comments, and feedback into the document control system for long-term storage, archiving, and retrieval purposes.

Mastering Resource Leveling

Before you can master a resource leveling scheduling program, you must understand how this tool can assist and support you on your project. The following project scenario emphasizes the importance of the tool.

You have accepted the project management position in a project office in Stavanger, Norway and have been working on a project for the last two weeks. The project is a hookup and commission for one of the Norwegian offshore oilrigs in the North Sea, located 20 miles off the coast of Norway. Not only is there a maximum limit of workers that can be on the rig, but you have the added pressure of ensuring the rig is running at no less than 98 percent capacity. You have heard that the welding superintendent (there are several superintendants for each trade) on the rig has requested an additional 47 welders. Because the rig is limited to a specific number of workers, the 47 additional welders would go over that limit. Therefore, you must work directly with the scheduling team to reduce the rig by at lease 32 workers in order to accommodate the new request for welders and not go over the maximum limit of worker on the rig. This is going to take some creative thinking by the scheduling team. However, after analyzing the request they come up with the following solution: remove ten painters, seven technicians, nine instrumentation installers, and six boilermakers. For this immediate request, the resource leveling process works well in the coordination of workers leaving the rig and the new welders that are arriving on the rig. As project manager, you realize that ensuring a 98 percent capacity on the rig at all times is going to be a challenge, and you must implement some process to stabilize these ongoing requests. You have a series of questions you are asking yourself. Those questions include:

How am I going to keep the work flowing at a constant rate?

How can I resource allocate the various skills required in advance of requests?

How can I support the rig's resources to ensure they are working at maximum capacity?

You can use resource leveling to answer these questions. Resource leveling is the technique used when you are constrained by a maximum number of resources on the project at any one time. This can be for short periods of time or for the entire length or the project. The limit could be only for a specific resource or for the total resources on the project, such as the oil rig in the scenario.

By using a resource-leveling scheduling program, you can achieve a resource-loaded project schedule where each activity has the proper resources assigned and there are no over-allocations of resources. In the previous scenario, if the project manager works closely with the resource allocations, he /she will be able to determine the future requirements of the resources and understand exactly what is next. The random pulling of resources on and off the rig is avoidable by ensuring the superintendents and project managers follow the staffing levels established in the resource leveling process.

CROSS-REF We recommend that you review the Resource Leveling tool's planning questions in Chapter 9.

Creating resource leveling

One of the most challenging aspects of project management is resource leveling. Creating the resource-leveling charts and determining the right staff allocations for a project can be difficult. Many factors determine resource levels across a project. One of the primary considerations in the leveling process is the current and future workload of each individual project team member.

Creating true resource leveling for all resources across the enterprise is difficult and often not handled correctly or efficiently. The critical chain tool (See Chapter 9 for more information on critical chain) challenges the resource leveling method and whole idea of assigning project team members to multiple projects. It considers resource allocation and scheduling simultaneously, and then automatically resource levels during the scheduling process. The critical chain method believes that team members should be on one task until they complete that task and therefore resource levels resources to work on one task at a time.

Project managers need to understand and comprehend the value of resource leveling early in the project to be able to keep the project team members successful and continually working on their project activities. Resource leveling is an ongoing process that takes time to perform correctly. As the project moves from phase to phase, and as resources come and go, their project allocation hours go up and down. Project managers should be looking at resource allocations at all times to ensure that the individual resources have the appropriate allocations on the project.

TIP It is a best practice to resource level no more than two weeks into the future when executing a project. The reason being the project resources change during those two weeks and you have to resource level again anyway.

A project customer will have little knowledge of the resource leveling process because their involvement provides little value, or may actually end up being harmful to the process. Normally, project managers and resource managers complete the resource leveling process with the scheduling team alone, and reflect the outcome of the process to actual assignments on the project schedule. In rare cases, if the results of the resource leveling process determine additional resources are required, it would be beneficial to review the data with the customer and request additional funding for the project to obtain those resources if the project would be over budget by adding those resources. If not, then the customer would not need to be involved in that process.

ON the CD-ROM We have included a sample of a resource leveling tool in the Communication tools Human Resources Subfolder. Use this as a guide to help you create your own version of this tool.

The following steps provide you with how to level project resources:

1. Assign your project resources to the activities you want to resource level. A good method for accurate resources leveling is to assign only one resource type per activity.

2. Set the maximum limits on your resources and create your resource leveled project schedule. Analyze it for any over allocation of resources. You should review the various resources that are allocated and determine an action plan to remove the over-allocations whenever possible.

3. Set an allocation maximum value for each type of resource. This provides the maximum levels for each type of resource that you have on your project. This also limits the number of resources that are scheduled.

4. Run the leveling process within the project-scheduling tool to level your project resources accordingly.

NOTE Best practice is to ensure the project has a schedule baseline set to compare back to the original resource assignment and the newly created leveled resource assignments

5. Reanalyze the results of the resource leveling process within the project schedule. You can set a number of parameters in the scheduling tool to control the resource leveling process. The initial run and results generated by the resource leveling process most likely will not meet your expectations. You and your project schedulers must take the time to analyze the results and then change the parameters to benefit the project and the leveled team member.

   Figure 15.3 shows an example of an over-allocation report from a Scheduling tool. In this report, you can see just two of the many team members, but you will notice that one team member has many activities on his plate. A project manager running this type of report will see a desperate need for running the resource leveling process.

6. Update or implement options or changes to your project's resource assignments, based on the results of leveling process and Figure 15.3 the "over-allocated report." Depending on the results, there are multiple options available such as assigning additional resources, overtime, change schedule dates, analyze, or reschedule portions of project. It is advisable to do some manual leveling because the automated leveling cannot make assumptions where you can. You might consider changing the logic relationships between the activities so the resources that are scheduled simultaneously are scheduled in series, not in parallel.

7. Go back to Step 3 and re-run the leveling process until satisfied with results. This process continues throughout the life of the project.

TIP Resource level every week to ensure there are no resources continually being over-allocated or burning out.

FIGURE 15.3

FIGURE 15.3

An overallocation report from a popular scheduling tool.

ID	●	Resource Name			
1	◆	**Bill Downs**			

ID	Task Name	Units	Work	Delay
35	Complete Initial "DRAFT" SRD	100%	8 hrs	0 days
36	Schedule SRD Walkthru and send out SRD	100%	8 hrs	0 days
40	Make necessary changes to SRD	100%	8 hrs	0 days
41	Send out SRD for Signoff	100%	8 hrs	0 days
4	System Proposal complete and Signed off	100%	8 hrs	0 days
7	Close SDF Gate 9 by sending System Proposal to Release team	100%	8 hrs	0 days
8	Assign Analysis	100%	8 hrs	0 days
10	Send out for Review Initial BRD	100%	8 hrs	0 days
12	Create Initial Project Plan	100%	8 hrs	0.5 days
13	Create T&C (0) +-100%, send to customer and Release team after reviewing complete	100%	8 hrs	0 days
15	Send out Project Plan to Project Team	100%	24 hrs	0 days
16	Negotiate and Complete Appendix B	100%	24 hrs	0 days
17	Setup Weekly Status Meetings	100%	28.8 hrs	0 days
19	Hold kickoff Meeting	100%	8 hrs	0 days
20	Prepare BRD for walkthru	100%	32 hrs	0 days
21	Walkthru of BRD with Customer	100%	8 hrs	0 days
22	Identification of source system, new data elements	100%	8 hrs	0 days
23	Determine amount of data, size of data, frequency of data	100%	8 hrs	0 days
24	All Other for completion of BRD for walkthru	100%	8 hrs	0 days
25	Make necessary changes to BRD	100%	16 hrs	0 days
26	Send out BRD for Inspection	100%	8 hrs	0 days
27	BRD Inspection	100%	8 hrs	0 days
28	Make necessary changes to BRD based on inspection	100%	8 hrs	0 days
29	Get BRD Signoff from everyone	100%	8 hrs	0 days
30	Send Baselined BRD to Release Team	100%	8 hrs	0 days
31	SQ8-1 Business Requirements Doc. Baselined (WP02.1)	100%	8 hrs	0 days
32	Close SDF Gate 8 by sending inspection paperwork, inspection minutes, BRD, BRD	100%	8 hrs	0 days
42	Receive Sign-off for SRD	100%	8 hrs	0 days
43	Send Baselined SRD to Release Team	100%	8 hrs	0 days
44	SQ7-1 System Requirements Doc. Baselined (WP03.1)	100%	8 hrs	0 days
45	Close SDF Gate 7 by sending walkthru'd SRD to Release Team	100%	8 hrs	0 days
69	Create UAT Plan	100%	16 hrs	0 days
71	Get all Files for System Test	100%	8 hrs	0 days
73	Close SDF Gate 3 (email for software build for Sys Test env)	100%	8 hrs	0 days
77	Provide Test results to Customer	100%	8 hrs	0 days
87	Close SDF Gates 1 & 2 (emails for Sys. Test & UAT Complete, Test Results Asses	100%	8 hrs	0 days
99	Close SDF Fate 0 (emails for Sev. 1/2 MR's Resolved, Installation complete) to R	100%	8 hrs	0 days
102	Lessons Learned	100%	8 hrs	0 days
103	Customer Survey (Optional)	100%	8 hrs	0 days
104	Monitor Post Implementation Results	100%	8 hrs	0 days
37	Receive HIGH LEVEL DESIGN ON Project*	100%	8 hrs	0 days
38	Finalize SRD document with HIGH LEVEL DESIGN and then send to team for review	100%	8 hrs	0 days
65	Close SDF Gate 4 (email from ETL team indicating that the Kit is complete and s	100%	8 hrs	0 days

ID	●	Resource Name			
2	◆	**Bob Callan**			

ID	Task Name	Units	Work	Delay	Start
5	Project Prioried and WISDEM Resources available	100%	8 hrs	0 days	3/4/02
6	Identify Project Team	100%	8 hrs	0 days	3/4/02

Using resource leveling

Before you can use resource leveling, you must identify who on your project team will utilize this tool so that you can determine the level of detail required, frequency of distribution, style, and format of the report. The resource leveling process is a detailed process so the information in the resource leveling report is detailed in nature. This allows the project manager and the team members to understand the tasks the project resources are assigned to.

Before you resource level, review the resource leveling planning section in Chapter 9. Then follow these steps:

1. Review and analyze your project's resource leveling reports coming from the project scheduling system or any manual reports you may have generated. It is an ongoing process for you to run these reports throughout the life of the project and try to avoid and prevent any over allocation or burning out of your resources.

2. Check with your team members weekly and determine how their attitude is; are they hitting their deliverables, or feeling overwhelmed? The reports can indicate how under- or over-allocated resources are, one way or another, but you still need to care about your resources and check in with them personally. You will want to ensure that they are working effectively.

3. Depending on the results of those conversations, adjust your team member's workloads accordingly. If there are any other resource issues, they will also need to adjust the workloads of team members.

Mastering the Responsibility Matrix

Before mastering the responsibility matrix, you must understand how this tool can assist and support you on your project. The following project scenario emphasizes the importance of using a responsibility matrix.

A mid-sized insurance company in Dallas, Texas, has decided that it will develop a new payroll system to replace its current manual application. You decide that you want to be involved in the project, and management assigns you the role of scheduler and cost control manager. The project is already three months into the planning process, so you are a little behind when you start, but have full confidence that you can catch up quickly and start to add value to the project. You are not familiar with the other team members, so the project manager introduces you to 11 team members on your scheduling team, and 5 members of your cost team. After a week on the project, you are finding it difficult to acquire information you need regarding who does what on the project. You have requested a project organization chart, but the project is so large it only shows group titles, and therefore it is not providing you with the information you need. You need answers to a number of questions to determine who is responsible for what area of the project. Your questions include:

Do the team members know what their responsibilities are on the project?

What groups are involved in the project?

Who should be the consultant on what deliverables are on the project?

Who is accountable to producing what on the project?

To obtain the answers to these questions, the project should use a Responsibility Matrix tool. The responsibility matrix provides all the information about who is responsible for performing what activities on the project. In the case of project deliverables, it also documents who creates what deliverable on the project. When new project team members join the team, they can utilize the responsibility matrix immediately to understand who is working on what, and what groups are involved in the project. The responsibility matrix, is sometimes nicknamed RACI (Responsible, Accountable, Consult, Inform), or called a responsibility assignment matrix (RAM).

CROSS-REF We recommend that you review the Responsibility Matrix tool's planning questions in Chapter 9.

Creating a responsibility matrix

When creating a responsibility matrix, it is important to bring the project team members to the same understanding immediately on who is responsible for what on the project. The responsibility matrix is especially important on projects where team members are located in different organizations or the project has a large vendor (consulting) presence; it ensures that no one is working on tasks not meant for them.

In software development projects, specifically database technology projects, there is a responsibility matrix called the CRUD matrix. The CRUD matrix stands for Create, Read, Update, and Delete. These are different security access levels which are granted to particular roles in a software application. For example, one role in the software could have only an "R" access assigned to it. In that case, it would mean it could only "read" data from the tables, it could not "create," "update," or "delete" records from that table.

The project manager should make sure that there is an accurate responsibility matrix on every project they manage, regardless of how large or small the project. The responsibility matrix should be developed and approved before any work activities begin. When the project manager uses a responsibility matrix, it helps to ensure that the project team will at least know what activities they are responsible for and should prevent team members from overlapping or duplicating any work efforts. It also allows any team member who may have preconceived ideas of their project assignments to look at the RACI and know exactly what their project assignments are. Developing a responsibility matrix can be a long process, but it is critical to obtain agreement with team members before any work activities begin. You cannot be halfway down a project lifecycle and then decide to put a RACI in place. The responsibility matrix eliminates confusion and miscommunications on who is responsible for what project tasks or deliverable.

Project managers must be diligent in obtaining sign-off and approvals on the responsibility matrix from both project team members and respective management. It should be stressed that the responsibilities matrix or CRUD can, and should, only be revised using a definitive process with all team members engaged. The project manager uses the formal acceptance document to obtain the sign-off and then stores both in the document control system for long-term storage and retrieval.

The project customer may play a small role in the creation of the responsibility matrix from the perspective of being involved in the resource assignments on the project. Project managers should ensure that the customer is aware of their roles and agree to those roles during the initiation of the responsibility matrix; and if they cannot take on a role, assign someone who can. It is the customer's responsibility to account for and ensure completion of their assigned activities.

The actual steps of creating a responsibility matrix vary. If you have never created this tool, the following steps can help you get started.

The following steps are guidelines for project managers to utilize when creating a responsibility matrix.

1. Define the template that you will use for this process. If your company has one then use that, otherwise use the template located on the CD-ROM.

2. Gather your team members together and go over the template. Explain to each team member the legend and what the R, A, C, I means and the different layout and format of the chart.

3. Guide your team through adding the deliverables to the template by major project milestone. This would include all the deliverables in the project initiation phase, design phase, and test phase. Add deliverables directly to the template.

4. After entering all your project deliverables within each of the major milestones, you should add all the project roles in the columns across the top forming a matrix.

   As a team, add the responsibility code for each role to each deliverable on the project. This is where discussions can be quite challenging and as project manager, you will need to drive these discussions to what makes sense for the project. This step includes adding, for example, a letter R to the project manager for the task of creating an end-to-end project schedule. This can be a long process and may cause the team members concern. The biggest problems the team members will have is to take on assignments that they do not believe are theirs, or that another team member is working in their area of the project. The responsibility matrix discussion can be uncomfortable and requires a strong project manager to ensure all team members are onboard and ready to complete the tasks assigned to them. Some project managers will initially have the customer involved in this discussion, and other project managers will leave it until after the project manager and team members have completed the matrix and presented it to the customer.

5. Continue the process until you and your project team members are satisfied with the results.

6. After you have completed this process, send the RACI to the project team members and your customer for their approval. This is a critical step in the process because of how importance it is to have your team members and customers approve what they will be accountable for on the project.

7. Update when changes occur. Keep it current.

Figure 15.4 represents an example of a responsibility matrix template. This blank template is ready and available for the project manager to complete. The updates to the template are project specific and include particular project roles and project phases that differ from project to project. Project managers are to update this responsibility matrix accordingly.

FIGURE 15.4

A responsibility matrix

Responsibility Matrix Chart Example

Responsibility Codes:

Responsible: Performs the work
Accountable: Ultimately accountable for delivery; maximum one per week
Sign-Off: Approval must be gained for deliverable to be acceptable
Consult: Review & provide feedback

Informed
(blank) = not involved

	Customer	Upper Management	Proj Mgr	UAT Lead	Training Lead	Release Management	Sponsor1 (TBD)	Lead Analyst	Designer	Dev Lead	Test Lead	Tier 1 Rep	Release Lead	Operation Lead
Task C														
Work Product A														
Work Product B														
System Requirements														
Task C														
Task D														
Work Product A														
Design														
Work Product A														
Work Product B														
Work Product C														
Build														
Task F														
Task G														
Task H														
Test														
Task 1														
Work Product A														
Task K														
User Acceptance Approval Phase														
Task L														
Work Product A														
Task N														
Production Phase														
Work Product A														
Task P														
Work Product B														
Post Production Support / Warranty Period (if Applicable)														
Task O														
Task P														
Task Q														

ON the CD-ROM   We have included a sample of a responsibility matrix in the Communication tools Human Resources Subfolder. Use this as a guide to create your own version of this tool.

Using the responsibility matrix

Before you can use a responsibility matrix tool, you must identify who on your project team will utilize this tool so that you can determine the level of detail required, frequency of distribution, style, and format of the report. A responsibility matrix is a very detailed tool with respects to assigning the four letters to each task or deliverable on the project. Before utilizing the responsibility matrix tool, review the responsibility matrix planning section in Chapter 9. Then follow these steps:

1. Work with your team members to review the contents of the responsibility matrix to ensure everyone is in agreement with how the responsibility codes are allocated on the form. This includes working with everyone involved in the project and discussing as a team and a single group, the various roles and responsibilities of each team member.

2. After everyone agrees with the contents of the responsibility matrix and you have obtained everyone's approval and sign-off, then the document is locked unless there are major project updates. The actual use of the document becomes something that you utilized at the beginning of each project phase as a checklist to go over with your team members. You want to make sure they re-review and are comfortable with producing the deliverables they have signed up for in that particular phase.

3. As the project moves into executing process, you should continually review the responsibility matrix to ensure your team members are creating the deliverables they have agreed to create. As the project continues through its lifecycle, continually check progress of the deliverables assigned to your team members until everything is complete and the project closes out.

Mastering Risk Models

Before mastering the risk models and modeling tool, you must understand how this tool can assist and support you on your project. The following project scenario emphasizes the importance of the tool.

A small design and construction company, in Tacoma, Washington, has hired a risk management consulting company to analyze the risk events among five software projects. The owner of the design and construction company, who is also the owner of the five software projects, is extremely risk adverse. When it comes to risk on a project, she is fidgety and likes to be well aware of all the possible risk events. She wants to know which of the five projects has the most risk, and what she can do to prevent those risk events. Due to a poor business cycle, she needs to cancel one of the projects because there is not enough budget for all projects. She feels that if she assesses all the projects and then determines which is the riskiest, she may be able to cancel just one. As senior project manager at your risk consulting company, you have offered to take on and manage the task of determining what project(s) to cancel, and will recommend from the risk analysis that your team performs, which project or projects, to shut down. You start your activities by running a risk analysis and creating a risk matrix for each one of the five projects. You discover a pattern for each project, but three of the matrixes were so similar it is hard to tell which one has the highest risk. The owner is not pleased. She was looking for a more definitive answer because she must cut at least one project from the five. She wants to see some method, with simple and understandable justification from you. You try to explain the matrix values, but this makes the owner even more confused and angry.

You understand what the owner wants, but do not have the correct tools to create the results.

How could you have avoided this situation?

How can you solve this dilemma?

To obtain the answers to these questions the project manager should use a risk model. There are many types of project risk models, but most of them are in-house and customized using a spreadsheet, and some are computer programs designed for a specific task. The risk model tool is perfect for this scenario. In generating a risk model, you create a project risk score wherein the elements, which you can measure and compare, are consistent across all other projects. This gives you metrics that are reliable when comparing one project to another. You create the metrics for the model and have total control over them and their associated scores. However, the owners or customer must approve the metrics before you run the model.

CROSS-REF We recommend you review the risk model's planning questions in Chapter 12.

Creating a risk model

Creating and updating a risk model for each project is one of the project manager's primary responsibilities. As the project changes, the risk score will also change. Therefore, the project manager needs to update the risk model to generate a new risk score and a new risk assessment for the project. It is important for every project manager to understand the project risks, the overall assessment of those risks, and the level of severity associated to them. The risk score concept for project managers is relatively new, but helps tremendously with uncovering the real risk assessment for a project. Without it, project managers do not truly know their risk impacts relative to other projects. Some project managers and team members assess risks as, low risk, medium risk, or high risk, and make these assessments on personal feelings, not facts. Rarely does high, medium, or low ever have enough detail to explain the meaning behind an assessment, and often project managers or owners are leaning on their experiences from past projects to clarify what they really mean. A risk score eliminates this situation and forces projects through the same assessment ratings to generate it and base it on the same criteria applied to the same types of projects. In the end, the higher risk score project is the riskier project.

Project managers can create a risk score on all of their projects by using a project risk modeling spreadsheet, and after doing so project managers will quickly become accustom to using these risk scores on their projects and rely on that information to assist them in making project decisions. Some of these decisions might include assignment of contingency in forecasting, staffing allocations, schedule adjustments, and risk aversion planning or anything related to the project and the overall assessment of risk.

Project customers should be active in the risk modeling process. In project situations where the project manager is risk adverse and the project client is more of a risk taker, the project's overall risk score should reflect both parties' opinions in how they answer the questions. It is critical that the project does not report a risk score skewed by the dominant opinions of one or two people — the consensus of the whole team is required for this process to be reliable and successful.

Figure 15.5 shows an example of a risk model.

 We have included a sample of this risk model in the Communication tools Risk Subfolder. Use this as a guide to help you create your own version of this tool.

FIGURE 15.5

A risk model.

Project Risk Model Example

Total Project Risk Score			Component Risk Assessments		
Interim Score		0			
			Low Budget Risk		
Low		Score			
Risk		0	Low External Dependencies Risk		
1 – 35					
			Low Management Risk		
Medium		Score			
Risk			Low Mission Critical Risk		
36 – 72					
			Low Failure Risk		
High		Score			
Risk			Low Complexity Risk		
> 72					
	Question Number	Project Risk Question	Answer Lists (Note–when you click in each answer cell, a drop down list arrow will appear)		
Budget Risk	1	What is the estimated total project cost?			
	2	What percentage of the agency budget does the project represent?			
	3	Have sufficient project funds been budgeted and allocated?			
	4	How much confidence is there in the expenditure and funding projections?			
	5	Is funding available for maintenance of the project deliverable after project closure?			
External Dependencies Risk	6	Is this project dependent on another projects deliverable?			
	7	Does this project require resources from other organizations?			

To ensure all projects are calculating their risks using the same methodology, organizations should adopt the use of a risk score template on all projects. Doing this ensures that the criteria for assessing risks are identical for all projects, and when making the assessment between the projects, the various scores assigned will reflect the true risk scores of the project.

Using a risk model

Prior to using a tool such as the risk model, you must identify who on your project team will utilize this tool so that you can determine the level of detail required, frequency of distribution, style, and format of the report. Risk models are detailed in nature and allow anyone trying to make a risk assessment on the project the information they need to make that assessment.

Before using a risk model, you should review the risk model planning section in Chapter 9. Then follow these steps:

1. Open your project's risk model spreadsheet. Use the template if your company did not already have one in place.

NOTE The developer created this tool in Microsoft Excel, so using Excel or a software package that can read Excel files is desirable.

2. Modify each risk question to make it more applicable to your project type. The risk model spreadsheet comes with a variety of standard risk questions applicable to most projects; however, because the questions are generic, they may or may not be 100 percent applicable to your project. Therefore, you, your team members, and customer should develop the questions together, adapting them to their particular project. In doing so, the true risk score of the project will be created and will allow for a much better representation of the project's risk level.

3. Modify, if applicable, your risk scores associated to answering the risk questions. In the same way you modified the risk questions, there is a good chance you will need to change the score ranges as well. Note: You will see there are a number of columns and rows hidden on the spreadsheet, and you may need to adjust some of those hidden columns and score ranges to reflect the specific needs of your project. We recommend you do this at the company level, making the range wide enough for use on all projects. At the end of this step, the risk model should be available for use on the project.

4. As the project moves into the planning process, enforce the use of the risk model on your project. This consists of you calling your project team members together to answer the risk questions and calculating new project risk scores periodically.

5. Then report the results of the risk model, specifically the risk score, to your customer and upper management. Store a copy of you project's risk model in the document control system for long-term storage, archiving, and retrieval purposes. Depending on the results and the discussions from the customer or upper management, you may need to make decisions and adjustments on your project.

6. As the project moves into the executing process, call your project team together once a month and re-run the risk model to generate a new risk score.

7. After every run, a new risk score is created, and you should present the results to your customer and upper management for review. If applicable, you should make project changes or adjustments based on your customer's review of the risk score.

8. At the end of the project, after running your last risk model, you should provide the last version to your customer, and then store it along with the other versions within the document control system along with your other project documentation.

Mastering the Risk Simulation Tool

Before mastering the risk simulation tool, you must understand how this tool can assist and support you on your project. The following project scenario emphasizes the importance of the tool.

A midsized software project in San Diego, California has just kicked off a new project. The project is under a strict time constraint. You and your team have planned for, and implemented, task acceleration procedures in order to hit the first three milestones on time. You have been working in conjunction with the client and have been closely monitoring the 17 milestones that are driving the project, but unfortunately, even with the accelerated procedures you have put in place your project has failed to meet the first 3 critical milestones. You are concerned that the project will miss another milestone and then slip the completion date entirely. You have analyzed the remaining schedule and noticed that a specific task for completion on the overall milestone was running behind schedule for the first 75 percent of its duration. As project manager, you should have been aware that the path on your network logic diagram was causing the delay in schedule, but for some reason you missed it. Upper management has started asking scheduling questions and wants answers immediately. Their questions include:

Can you forecast schedule problems like this in advance?

What can you do differently to prevent this from occurring again?

How can you predict the future state of the project by the information you are already tracking?

What impact will these slips have on the budget?

To answers these questions the project should use a risk simulation tool. The risk simulation tool will process the project information multiple times to create a future-state view of the project. This view can be either a schedule review or a cost review, depending on the needs of the project. In the previous scenario, the risk simulation tool would have worked perfectly to produce a schedule view of the end of the project, determine the dependencies, and show schedule impacts. The risk simulation tool shows the range of finish dates and the probability of making those dates for each activity contained on the project. When reviewing the latest finish date of the activities converging on the milestone, you will have the critical path that most likely will need shortening to make the schedule for that milestone.

Using the risk simulation tool for understanding where the budget will be at the end of the project can be extremely valuable. The risk simulation tool answers questions on the probability of making the budget and the expected final cost of the project.

CROSS-REF   We recommend that you review the Risk Simulation tool's planning questions in Chapter 10.

Creating a risk simulation

Creating the project's risk simulation is easy after you have the software in place and the data collected to drive the simulation software.

Creating data points that the risk simulation software needs to process for each of the project tasks can be a bit more difficult and time consuming when project team members are not familiar with the format or have never collected estimates in that format before. These data points are defined as Optimistic estimate, Pessimistic estimate, and a Most Likely estimate. Project team members must provide those three values on each project activity to allow the risk simulation tool to calculate the schedule and cost estimates. See Chapter 12, Risk Simulation tool, to understand more about the three-point estimating spreadsheet. This may involve a learning curve for some team members. The learning curve on the methodology should be minimal. The name of the methodology is three-point estimating — it has been around for many years. Many companies use this three-point estimating as a standard practice in capturing estimates for their projects, so it is not tied solely to needing this data for a risk simulation tool.

If the company is already using the three-point estimating system to capture the optimistic, most likely, and pessimistic values for estimating projects, then the risk simulation software has the data it needs to simulate the project. Project managers should embrace the three-point estimating model because it holds a new level of accountability to the team members. When obtaining three possible durations for a single task from the team member, the project manager has the ability to work with the team members and hold them accountable for making at least one of the durations they provided, even in the worst case, the pessimistic estimate.

The steps to creating a risk simulation tool depend greatly on the software package available to the project manager. In the following example, we use Deltek's Risk+ package.

NOTE   If you have not done so, it is important that you purchase a Risk Simulation software package such as Deltek Risk+ or @Risk, a risk analysis systems for Microsoft Project, and install and configure the software package, ensuring it works correctly before starting this process.

To create a risk simulation for your project, follow these steps:

1. Open the project-scheduling tool. Ensure you have purchased and preinstalled a risk simulation add-on package.

2. Create the project activities with relationships. You should be familiar with this process already; this is a standard activity when creating project schedules.

3. Create three new columns in your project schedule. Label the first column optimistic, the second column most likely, and the third column pessimistic.

    Figure 15.6 is an example of the three new columns added to the project schedule.

FIGURE 15.6

The project schedule and the data needed for a risk simulation.

	Task Name	Start	Finish	Optimistic	Most Likely	Pessimistic
1	⊟ **Project ABC**	**7/24/08**	**8/25/08**	**0 days**	**23 days**	**0 days**
2	Activity 1	7/24/08	7/30/08	3 days	5 days	7 days
3	Activity 2	7/31/08	8/11/08	5 days	8 days	10 days
4	Activity 3	8/12/08	8/25/08	8 days	10 days	14 days

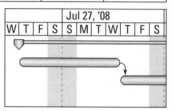

NOTE   The actual data values (3 days, 5 days, and 8 days) entered and shown in Figure 15.6 are not associated with these step-by-step instructions.

4. Enter the data values into the Optimistic, Most Likely, and Pessimistic columns for every activity on your project. Your team members working on the project tasks should enter their three estimates directly into the project schedule, or provide the data to you so you can enter it on their behalf. These values are required for the tool to create the risk simulations on cost and budget.

5. Then activate the add-on risk simulation tool to create the risk simulation results chart for the project.

6. Evaluate the results from the simulation. If there are any problems, tweak the data and re-run the simulations. In this case, you have the option of doing risk simulation on portions of the project, and you do not have to include the whole project.

7. Communicate your project's risk simulation results to your customers, project team members, and depending on the results, upper management.

8. Depending on the results, adjust your project accordingly.

Using a risk simulation

Prior to using a risk simulation tool, you must identify who on your project team will utilize this tool so that you can determine the level of detail required, frequency of distribution, style, and format of the report. Normally, the risk simulation produces canned and generic reports that are often at the summary level, but this depends greatly on the software selected.

Before using the risk simulation, review the risk simulation planning section in Chapter 12 and then follow these steps:

1. Analyze the results of the risk simulation on your project such as reviewing the graph and the different end dates for individual activities, phases, or the entire project.

2. Make project level decisions based on the dates or the budget from the simulation report. The possible decisions are to report to upper management when the dates are much later than expected or accept the dates as reality and adjust your project going forward. The same decision and analysis will occur when reviewing the budget information. The budget report could be way over budget, or come in under budget. In either case, you will have to adjust your project based on the results of the tool if those results are unfavorable.

3. When accepting the schedule the risk simulation tool produces, apply the new durations that the tool suggests in the simulation process, to your project's work activities. Apply this same process to your project's budget.

   After applying these dates to your project's schedule, you will have a new schedule and therefore should create a new baseline schedule for your project. Make sure you always keep a copy of the original baseline schedule for historical references.

4. Repeat this risk simulation process throughout the life of the project. This is not a one-time process and as the project changes and moves through the lifecycle, continuing to re-run the simulation will only increase your chances of success.

5. Store the risk simulation materials in the document control system for long-term storage, archiving, and retrieval purposes.

Mastering the System Requirements Document

Before using a systems requirement document, you must understand how this tool can assist and support you on your project. The following project scenario emphasizes the importance of the tool.

A large log home manufacture, in Seattle, Washington, has decided to replace their payroll system with an updated application developed internally by its IT department. As fast as the company is expanding, and with the number of new employees recently hired, the existing system has quickly become outdated and can no longer serve its original purpose. Management selects you to be the project manager for this effort. As the project progresses, the first step is for the project's analysts to collect the business requirements from the customer. After collecting those requirements and obtaining approval from the customer, the project team focuses on the technical requirements of the project. The challenge is determining where to create and store these technical requirements. The project's analysts have concerns on what information to collect, and where to document the project's technical requirements. The analysts are asking some tough technical questions that include:

Which legacy systems will feed this new application?

What conversion activities are required?

What will the User Interface look like?

Will the new application be adequate for the company's future growth?

To obtain answers to these questions, the project manager will enforce the use of a system requirements document on their project. A system requirements document contains the technical details of the project that provide the development and design teams with information they need to develop the product. The software industry uses the system requirements document as a standard deliverable on almost every project. A system requirements document is an excellent communication tool because of all the technical information contained in it and the information it provides about the actual details of how to develop the product.

CROSS-REF   We recommend you review the system requirements document's planning questions in Chapter 5.

Creating a system requirements document

Creating a system requirements document on any software development project is often complex and is generally the responsibility of an analyst assigned to the project. These analysts have the training and technical background to turn the business requirements into technical requirements, which can be challenging in their own right. The project manager is seldom involved in the details of the development of the system requirements document because of the technical nature of the document, and their roles are generally not technical in nature.

Systems requirements documents are going to vary from industry to industry and have a multitude of different names that all mean literally the same thing. The concept behind the document is to map the business requirements or customer requirements to a technical solution. For example, if the customer has a requirement to store a large amount of data on an hourly basis, the system requirements of this request could be a database.

Project managers must ensure that the systems requirements document is complete and accurate for the downstream users of the document in order for them to build their portions of the project. For example, the designers and developers of the project are the two main users of the system requirements document, and therefore the project manager must ensure that these two groups are actively engaged in the creation of the document and approve it before the project begins either one of those phases. If the project manager does not manage and control this process, there could be problems on the project and you can have either group not agreeing to the contents and therefore not creating the deliverables based on the details in the document. It can be quite disrupting for the project and may negatively impact the project.

In some projects, the customer wants to be involved with the creation of the system requirements document. If a customer is technically inclined they can review and comment on the system requirements document. Other customers will have little or no involvement in this document and are simply not interested in all the details. Project managers will need to manage this process closely, and if the customer is asking technical questions or needs to review the system requirements document the project manager needs to provide technical resources to back up the document and respond to the customer. When the customer becomes involved, the project manager must add additional time and possibly cost to the schedule for the extra work.

You can use the following system requirements document template for your project. The template is located on the CD-ROM for use if your company does not already have a template. The table of contents provides the major sections of the document and will be handy when the document is completed and you are looking for some particular information.

Example of System Requirements Table of Contents

Section 1: Document References
Document all initial document items, such as author, contact name and date, revision history

Section 2: Sign-off Section
Document all staff who signed off on this project. This includes the sign-off of actual signatures, or copies of e-mails containing signatures.

Section 3: Document Conventions
Document any conventions associated to the document. These conventions can include items such as Business Processes (BP##), Operational Requirements (OPR##).

Section 4: Business Procedure Mapping
Document any business procedure mapping. This would include procedures that the business has that are relevant to the project activities or deliverables.

Section 4.1: Business Requirements Identification
Document the business requirements of the project.

Section 4.2: Business Process Analysis
Document the specific business processes to the business process description, and map the business processes to the business requirements document. This mapping is easier if created in a table format, and easier to read.

Section 4.3: Initial System Requirements Summary
Document the mapping between the system requirements and the business requirements. The project analyst creates a mapping table to provide traceability between system and business requirements.

Section 5: System Description
Document the description of the system. This can be a high-level description containing functionality of the system.

continued

continued

Section 5.1: System Overview

Document the overview of the system. This is normally just a high-level overview of the system that is under development.

Section 5.2: System Objectives

Document the objectives of the system, from a technical perspective. This will clearly state what the objectives are for the new application.

Section 5.3: System Process Specifications

Document the mapping between the process names and the process descriptions and their mapping back to the system requirements. This provides the traceability between the System Process and their mapping to the system requirements.

Section 5.4: System Constraints

Document any system constraints. System constraints could be a variety of items such as applications that need to work together, database space, or availability, etc.

Section 5.5: System Risk/Impacts/Assumptions

Document any risk, impacts, or assumptions. This is important to document the system risks associated to the project. Impacts to the risk events occurring or any assumptions.

Section 5.6: System Interfaces

Document the interfaces your system will have with other systems, including the information that is important because it allows technical team members to look at both systems and determine any impacts or changes required to each system. If the project manager misses the new application, they could have major problems.

Section 6: User Interface Designs

Document the details around the user interface design. These details will include look and feel to screens, sample screen shots, usability expectations, etc.

Section 7: Source System Model

Document the details around the source systems, if applicable. If the project has a source system or reading information from a source system, those details belong.

Section 8: Functional Processes

Document the step-by-step functional processes to generate the system. Document as much detail as possible for the technical staff on the project. The project analyst completes this process using a table of process names, process descriptions, and process steps, and describing each in detail.

Section 9: Functional Process Model

Document the step-by-step functional process in a series of diagrams, allowing the technical staff consuming the information to understand the processes using a series of diagrams. These diagrams may assist the project team members in understanding the processes, and therefore make their coding or development cycle easier.

Section 10: System Operational Requirements

Document the operational procedures (step-by-step) to move a system into a production environment in the company.

Section 11: System Deployment Requirements

Document the deployment requirements, where these steps include the deployment process to production, and then the steps after production implementation. This includes communications to the users that the application is ready for production use.

Section 12: Context Diagram

Document the context diagram of the application. Normally, this includes a picture, of the diagrams, tables, databases, etc.

Section 13: Conversion/Migration Needs

Document any conversion or migration activities. It is important to cover all details of the conversion or data migration work here so the project team members involved in the process can understand exactly what they must do for the application.

Section 14: Data Communication Requirements

Document any Data communication requirements for the application. This will include notifying the users of any data changes, data availability times, and any other data-related items.

Section 15: Inter-Project Dependencies

Document any dependencies the project has with other projects. Dependencies can include other project launching, data dependencies, or anything else that connects projects together.

Section 16: Testing Requirements

Document the various testing requirements for the project. This can be as high level as the steps to perform the testing only, to the detail level of specifics around test cases. This is going to depend on the needs and requirements of the project.

Section 17: Report Requirements

Document the report requirements for the project. If the project requires special reports, the project analyst documents the details here for everyone to review.

ON the CD-ROM   We have included a sample of the system requirements in the Communication tools Scope Subfolder. Use this as a guide to create your own version of this tool.

Using a system requirements document

Before using a system requirements document, you must identify who on your project team will utilize this tool so that you can determine the level of detail required, frequency of distribution, style, and format of the report. In this case, this document is very detailed and quite complex. It provides the actual details for designers and developers to create their portions of the project so there should be no high-level content at all in this document.

Review the system requirements document planning section in Chapter 5 and then follow these steps:

1. After the project analyst completes the system requirements document, it is best for you to arrange for a team review of the document to ensure everyone is onboard with the system. The project should not go much further until the project team completes their reviews of the document and provides their approval that the system can be built from the details described in the document. As the system requirements document is the basis for what the project team will produce, it is important that the team members review the document and understand what they need to deliver. You need to engage and ensure those discussions and approvals occur with your team members.

2. After obtaining the approvals on the document, including using the formal acceptance document, store the approvals into the document control system for long-term storage, archiving, and retrieval purposes.

3. As the project moves into the executing process, you must ensure your team members are using the system requirements document. The different team leads on your project should take the system requirements document and create the deliverables noted in the document. Your project team members will utilize the document throughout the life of the project until they have completed all their deliverables.

Mastering the Work Breakdown Structure

Before mastering the work breakdown structure, you must understand how this tool can assist and support you on your project. The following project scenario emphasizes the importance of the tool.

A midsize design and engineering company, in Fairbanks, Alaska, has just won the contract for a small project supporting the mega Panama Canal expansion effort. The entire project schedule for this enormous effort is to be continuous from 2005 to 2025, but your portion of the project is targeting for only two years in length. The overall project has a $5 billion dollar budget. You are the project manager, and your budget is $3 million. When you arrive in Panama and begin to start work on the project, you find you are busy in the initial project startup activities. One of your first activities would be to hire and build a project team, which you do and complete in two weeks. As the team engages, and the project progresses into the requirements phase, there are more and more questions coming from your team members. These questions include:

What zone is dock No. 2?

What is the budget for module 6?

Who is responsible for the layout of surveying of the West Bank?

What are the risks on the project?

To obtain the answers to these questions, the project manager should use a work breakdown structure tool (WBS). A WBS is a tool that breaks down the work activities on a project in a hierarchal order to reach a level of activities that is manageable. A WBS identifies *all* the work on a project. A component of the WBS is the WBS dictionary. The WBS dictionary catalogs information for easy access. In the scenario, if you had created a WBS to address the questions asked by the team members, you could have directed those team members to the WBS dictionary for the answers. This would have eliminated a lot of confusion and questions from the team members involving the components of the project.

 We recommend that you review work breakdown structure's planning questions in Chapter 5.

Creating a work breakdown structure

Project managers, design teams, project controls staff, and construction managers should all be involved in the development of the WBS. The WBS must reflect all tasks necessary to complete any given project, including everything from inception to completion. The tasks and subsequent subtasks should be in a descending order, with groupings by work type. The tasks should have an associated coding structure and should use work codes, schedule activity codes, budget/cost, and contract codes. These codes are used to sort, select, group, and summarize the tasks on the project. The WBS is the ultimate reference point and tool for all detail of the project and its management. It has an associated dictionary wherein lies the descriptions of the particular WBS elements and associated codes.

The creation of a WBS, especially on large projects, takes days or weeks and many meetings with the various stakeholders, and even the owner of the project should be involved with this process. Remember the WBS includes all the work to be completed on the project in detail. The creation of the WBS by all stakeholders is extremely beneficial for two reasons: it creates a detailed understanding of the project work, and it acts as a bonding tool and motivator for the team.

You can also use an automated scheduling system such as Microsoft Project to create a WBS. By indenting the activities in the schedule, you automatically create the WBS without even realizing it. Microsoft was the first to present this feature in a scheduling system and now all scheduling products have this much-needed capability.

The project manager uses the WBS throughout the entire project's life from initialization to close-out and beyond. The WBS is involved in every aspect of the project. On most projects after approval the WBS changes very little, but on occasion there are change requests that require the WBS to be updated.

The WBS is graphical in nature, and because of that it is best practice to use a plotter to draw it and hang the printout on the wall in the project office. That way, everyone can review and provide comments on the WBS. The other half of the WBS is the WBS dictionary. The dictionary is the detailed presentation of the WBS, and it documents every element of the WBS in written terms.

The project customer should be involved in the development and approval of the WBS, including all subsequent revisions, and may wish to have input into the elemental breakdowns, coding structure, retrieval process, and specific requirements from their Operations and/or Financial Groups.

The actual steps of creating a WBS can vary from project manager to project manager and depend greatly on their favorite tools of choice. Make sure of the following:

- The project team and other stakeholders participate in the development of the WBS.
- The functional leads and managers are involved.
- The WBS must make sense from the point of view of how the organization does business.
- The descriptions of each element are obvious.
- All products are identified and all deliverables are in the work breakdown structure.
- The sum of the work is represented by all the Level 2 elements, which must add up to 100 percent of the work on the project (i.e., 100 percent of the scope).
- The sum of the work represented by all the child elements under each parent element must add to 100 percent of the work of the parent.
- The integrative elements, where necessary, are assembly-type work.
- The work packages are reasonable in size (the amount of work).
- The WBS element numbering is in a logical manner and if possible, related to other projects and organization numbering schemes.
- The description of each element is understandable in terms of what it represents.

Basic rules or guidelines to follow when you are creating a WBS

There are rules you should follow in order to create a work breakdown structure. These rules or guidelines are a standard through out the project management profession. Use the following guidelines to create your WBS.

- Each WBS element should represent a single tangible deliverable.
- Each element should represent an aggregation of all subordinate WBS elements listed immediately below it.
- Each subordinate WBS element must belong to only one single parent WBS element.
- The deliverables require decomposing to the level that represents how they are produced.
- Deliverables must be unique and distinct from their peers, and decomposed to the level of detail needed to plan and manage the work to obtain or create them.

- Deliverables require clear definition to eliminate duplication of effort within WBS elements, across organizations, or between individuals responsible for completing the work.

- Deliverables should be limited in size and definition for effective control, but not so small as to make the cost of controlling them excessive, and not so large as to make the item unmanageable or the risk unacceptable.

Identifying functional levels of the WBS

When you create a WBS, there will be many summary levels (parents) above one level of detail elements. Below the top level, you can have many varying levels under each one of the elements. That is, you can have four levels under one top-level element and seven levels deep under another top-level element. There are four main levels of a WBS.

- **Project level:** Charter and project scope
- **Major level:** Major components, assemblies, subprojects, or phases
- **Mid-levels:** Subassemblies
- **Bottom level:** Work package, task, activity

There are many different ways to create a work breakdown structure: you can use the top-down method, the bottom-up method, or the build it a piece at a time method.

 When creating the WBS, it is important to include all the work on the project and not any work that is not on the project.

One of the most popular ways to develop a WBS is to get the project team and stakeholders involved in the process. Before the group meets, everyone should read the preliminary scope and have an understanding of the objective of the project. You are going to need a roll of butcher paper or plotter paper, several packages of sticky note pads, and some pens or pencils. The following are the steps in applying the *top-down method to create your WBS*:

1. You should schedule a large room (conference) with a long table for a WBS meeting.

2. Explain what everyone will do, and hand out the sticky note pads and pens to everyone in the room.

3. Then, you should roll out the paper and put the project description in an element (box) at the center-top.

4. You then facilitate the group in creating the next (major) level, which will be the major categories of the project. Make sure there is an element (category) for project management, usually drawn on the far left.

5. Identify the elements under each element on the major level. You are now starting the mid-level elements for your project.

6. Continue working this process until the project team breaks the work into smaller elements.

7. Then break the work down to the work package level. Make sure each *work package* description is a verb and a noun for clarity when creating them.

8. After breaking your WBS down to the work package level fill in the appropriate information into that work package: Cost, Start and Finish Dates, Resources, Risk, and Quality.

9. Then store all your WBS materials in the document control system for long-term storage, archiving, and retrieval purposes.

ON the CD-ROM We have included a sample of this work breakdown structure in the Communication tools Scope subfolder. Use this to help you create your own version of this tool.

Using a work breakdown structure

Before you can use a work breakdown structure, you must identify who on your project team will utilize this tool so that you can determine the level of detail required, frequency of distribution, style, and format of the report.

Review the work breakdown structure planning section in Chapter 5. Then follow these steps:

1. Place a graphic representation of the work breakdown structure on the project wall in the project war room, on a central project Web site, and in the document control system for easy access by the team members.

2. Describe to your customers the overall work breakdown of the entire project using the work breakdown structure graph. Only go to the lowest level the customer wants. This allows your customer to understand the project's structure and overall work activities.

3. Work with your team members and describe their project tasks using the work breakdown structure. Go over the specifics of the team member's tasks, any interdependencies, as well as where the task fits in the project.

4. Use your project's work breakdown structure to gather information dealing with schedule, costs, resources, risks, issues, purchasing and quality aspects of the project. This step includes all aspects of managing the project when using the work breakdown structure. As the project is in progress, you can identify completed tasks by each work package and report progress on the project.

5. Store the work breakdown structure in the document control system for long-term storage, archiving, and retrieval purposes.

WBS Bottom-Up Method

Another method for creating a WBS is the bottom-up method. Start out the same as the top-down method (above) with the roll of butcher paper and sticky notes. Each stakeholder writes a description (at least a verb and a noun) of a *work package* on the sticky note and places it on the table. When everybody thinks they have written enough descriptions and the ideas are exhausted, the project manager then gathers the work packages. Identify with the group members all the identical work packages and keep only one of the duplicates. Gather all the remaining work packages and place them into groups based on the most applicable categories. For example, if you were working on a construction project, these categories would include mobilizations, earthwork, and foundations. You will find during the grouping process that the project team members will order these categories from left to right in the order of accomplishing the work. You will find mobilization, earthwork, starting at the left-hand side of the butcher paper, and the ending group (far right) as closeout activities. The team members in the grouping process end up setting the order of the tasks automatically. You will find that the project management activities such as scope, planning, cost estimating, etc., will be placed in it's category in the far left. These work packages fall into the administration category of the project.

Summary

The tools described in this chapter are some of the more common communication tools known to project managers for planning their projects. The planning process is one of the most important for project managers to complete correctly, because it establishes how the team members execute the projects deliverables.

The tools in this chapter include some of the very popular tools such as the document control system, responsibility matrix, estimating tool, and the very important work breakdown structure. These tools are very common to project managers today and used across almost every industry. The other tools that some project managers may not be as familiar with, but will value greatly are the project calendar, Risk Modeling tool, and the Risk Simulation tool. As project managers gain experience using these three tools specifically, they will become part of the project manager's toolbox in no time.

Using the reporting communications tools identified in this chapter will benefit both the stakeholders and the project team and enhance their project communications. The tools and reports are simple, easy to create, and informative in presenting the information to the various parties.

Chapter 16

Using Communication Tools in Administrating the Planning Process

I n this chapter, we explore project communication tools in the project planning process specific to assisting the project manager. When project managers start planning for a project, they rarely look at the tools they will use because their focus is elsewhere — on the budget, schedule, scope, and resources.

The tools in this chapter are will guide and direct the project manager in thinking about how they will administer the project in the planning and executing processes. These tools give project managers a head start at managing and administrating the planning process and will also make them aware of tools they may not be familiar with and can start using immediately.

Mastering the Budget Spreadsheet

Before mastering the budget spreadsheet, you must understand how this tool can assist and support you on your project. The following project scenario emphasizes the importance of and reasons why the budget spreadsheet is critical to every project, especially the cost-driven ones.

A large real estate firm has decided to overhaul its computer sales application to bring it into the 21st century. The current system has been in use in every sales office all over the country for many years. Replacing the sales application is not going to be easy — it is going to take a lot of coordination with all the sales offices to ensure success. You, the most senior project manager at the company, are stepping up to lead this project. You understand that the project is going to be big and realize that there are a number of different

IN THIS CHAPTER

Mastering the budget spreadsheet

Mastering the change control tool

Mastering the comprehensive test plan

Mastering the critical chain

Mastering the earned value analysis tool

Mastering the issue management plan

Mastering quality metrics

Mastering the risk management plan

Mastering the risk register plan

Mastering the schedule management plan

areas you will be working in. You also realize that working on such a large project is going to be expensive, but you really do not know just how expensive. You have a number of questions that include:

> How do you track the costs and budget on such a large project?
>
> What mechanisms will you use to control and monitor costs?
>
> What is your budget?

By using a budget spreadsheet, you can answer these questions. The budget spreadsheet captures and manually tracks the costs and expenses on the project, and the project manager uses the estimates provided by the various groups to request funding from the customer and proceed with the project.

 We recommend that you review the budget spreadsheet tool's planning questions in Chapter 7.

Creating a budget spreadsheet

A budget spreadsheet is an important tool for any project. Project managers must ensure that they have a complete control on the project dollars at all times. Hundreds of different types of budget spreadsheets are available, and most companies have templates or examples for use on their projects. In addition, most experienced project managers also have a version of a budget spreadsheet that they like to use on their projects.

Project managers must ensure that they understand and can track the dollars closely on their projects. If for some reason a project manager feels uncomfortable with the calculations, or unfamiliar with how to allocate dollars across the project, they should work with the finance department and clear up any confusion they have. On most projects, project managers are responsible for the dollars allocated to a project, and without detailed and weekly tracking, the project can quickly get out of control.

One of the most complicated aspects of budget spreadsheets, and budgets in general, is the handling of project forecasts. In creating budget spreadsheets, forecast columns must be created for each project to track the forecasts of the project. Budget forecasts are the expected rate of spending of monies on the project, and project managers must watch forecasts closely to provide an understanding of how close the project is tracking to the budget. For example, if the forecasts come in at $500,000 for a $700,000 dollar project, the project manager quickly determines at a glance if the project is tracking correctly. This is just a high-level glance from the cost component of the project and does not factor in any other aspects of the project. It is important to understand that monies alone do not provide the current status of the project; they are only one aspect of it.

The challenging aspect of the budgeting process is watching the forecasts swing on a week-to-week basis. Forecasts can move significantly every week, throwing the project budgeting process into emergency planning in order to understand what has happened and why it has changed. This emergency planning is an important part of the budget management customer review process because as forecasts shift each week, that shift in dollars requires an explanation. Customers want to understand why the dollars change on a weekly basis, and if the project manager only tracks budgets monthly, she will miss the week-to-week swings, and the budget and forecast amounts could alarm the project manager or customer. Project budgeting is best captured and reviewed on a week-to-week basis, and the project customer who in the end is responsible for the dollars spent on the project, should be active and accountable to the creation of the budget spreadsheet. The customer must hold the project manager and team members accountable to the project to ensure that they know what the project manager is doing with the money and that they are spending it wisely on the project.

The actual steps of creating a budget spreadsheet can vary from project manager to project manager and will depend greatly on their favorite tools of choice. Table 16.1 is an advanced monthly tracking budget spreadsheet; this is a good spreadsheet to use when tracking monthly hours (actuals and estimates) from the individual team members.

TABLE 16.1

Example of a Budget Spreadsheet (Hours/Project Costs)

Name	Emp Rate	Contactor Rate	Jan Act	Jan Est	Actual Total Costs per Month	Est. Total Costs per Month	Hour Var	Cost Var
Employee 1	$45		2	2	$90	$90	0	0
Contractor 1		$96	5	5	$480	$480	0	0
Employee 2	$35		2	3	$70	$105	-1	-35
Employee 3	$25		5	1	$125	$25	4	100
Employee 4	$44		6	6	$264	$264	0	0
Contractor 2		$100	10	6	$1,000	$600	4	400
Employee 5	$22		2	2	$44	$44	0	0
Employee 6	$45		10	15	$450	$675	-5	-225
Employee 7	$65		2	2	$130	$130	0	0
Employee 8	$45		15	5	$675	$225	10	450
			==	==	========	========	=====	===
Totals			59	47	$3,328	$2,638	12	690

This budget spreadsheet is easy to create and is something any project manager should be able to accomplish. Use these steps to create your own budget spreadsheet for your project. We have included the template on the CD-ROM as a starting point.

1. List your project team member's names in the Name column. Regardless of how many people are on the project, you should document the first and last name of everyone in this column.

2. Determine your team member's burn rate (burn rate is the standard cost of employees per year) and add that rate to the column named EMP Rate. You should be able to obtain these rates from the Finance Department. After obtaining this information, enter the rates for each employee into the budget spreadsheet. These could be different for each employee and the roles they play. Be careful, some of this information can be deemed very sensitive.

3. Complete this same process for the contractors and vendors that are on your project team. The rate will differ depending on the contract and vendor's costs, but again, should be easily obtainable.

4. Fill in the Actual Hour's column and the Estimated Hour's column (in Table 16.1, these columns are noted as Jan Act and Jan Est. columns). You have two different methods of obtaining this data. First, you can work with your team members and obtain both values from them; otherwise, you can obtain this data from your company's financial system. Since this process is completed monthly, it does not take a great deal of time and is relatively easy to be able to get the team member's monthly hours.

TIP   Estimates and forecasts often change from week to week, so project managers should go into the financial system weekly to determine if there are any changes to the team members' monthly estimates.

NOTE   An important note for the project manager to consider is the above example (Table 16.1) shows only one month. The project manager will enter two columns for each month of the project, Actuals and Estimates, and depending on how long the project is projecting, there could be up to 12 additional months, or 24 different columns. When creating a budget spreadsheet like this, the only available data a team member can provide early in the project is the estimates per month, and although rough, those estimates should be enough to clarify the expected costs of the project.

5. After entering your team member's Actuals and Monthly Estimates on the budget spreadsheet, the formulas already in the template will automatically calculate your spreadsheet totals.

6. Review the data and make adjustments where appropriate, and the budget spreadsheet is then complete and ready to use. You will continue this process through the life of the project.

ON the CD-ROM   We have included a sample of the budget spreadsheet in the Communication Tools Cost subfolder. Use this as a guide to create your own version of this tool.

Using a budget spreadsheet

Before using a tool such as the budget spreadsheet, you must identify who on your project team will utilize this tool so that you can determine the level of detail required, frequency of distribution, style, and format of the report.

Review the budget spreadsheet planning section in Chapter 7.

1. Ensure your budget spreadsheet data is as accurate as possible at all times. This means establishing a process to utilize your budget spreadsheet on the project, including the work you perform to compile and report information, and the tasks your project team members complete to enter their estimates on a monthly basis. You will need to develop these processes and work closely with your team members to ensure they know what to expect.

2. After establishing the process for data entry and updating your budget spreadsheet, work with your customer to determine their reporting requirements on the budget spreadsheet. Understanding how often customers wants to see the budget spreadsheet is important to establishing a good communication rhythm with them.

3. As your project moves into the executing process, you will continue this constant updating of the budget spreadsheet by gathering the actuals from the financial systems each month, and adding and updating team member's estimates. After each monthly update, a copy of the budget spreadsheet is stored in the document control system for long-term storage, archiving, and retrieval purposes, and the master budget spreadsheet will be used in project cost and budget discussions.

4. As the project finishes, store your final budget spreadsheet in the document control system.

Mastering the Change Control Plan

Before you master the change control plan, you must understand how this tool can assist and support you on your project. The following project scenario emphasizes the importance of and reasons why a change control plan is critical to every project.

A large telephone company has decided to replace its human resource system with a new off-the-shelf application. Because the new application relates to capturing and storing human resource data, certain precautions must be taken to protect that data from getting into the wrong hands. These precautions require input from different groups in the company as to how data in the new application will be displayed and still protect the employee's personal data. The legal department and/or the employee's union representatives will want to ensure they understand who has access to what data, and who is controlling that access. You, as the top project manager for the company, are now leading this effort, and one of your first tasks is to create the customer requirements for the project. An analyst is assigned to your project to work with each group and determine their requirements for the system; you capture their requests in a business requirements document. After your analyst finalizes the document and obtains everyone's approval, he then locks down the document from any changes going forward. He believes that he has captured everyone's requirements, since they all signed off, and believes he has everyone's personal data fully protected in this new system. As the project moves into the design phase, the leadership team has seen some of the screen designs, and they also see screens and reports displaying personal information; this is not good and they are not happy. Your analyst thought he was clear when he wrote in the specifications document to show only limited personal information fields on screens or reports. However, because he said limited, and did not specify exactly, the development team is now requesting a change request to eliminate all personal information fields. This was not specified clearly in the requirements document, so the development team made some assumptions. You agree this was a mistake on your analysts' part. You have a number of questions that require answers, and these questions include:

How can you control this project change?

What process or procedures do you follow?

How do you control costs and schedule changes associated to this change?

What happens if we get 25 or maybe 50 change requests in one week?

To obtain the answers to these questions, the project manager should use a change control plan. A change control plan can establish and document the processes and procedures to control changes on the project. Changes on projects occur all the time, and projects that have clearly defined and established change control processes can usually prevent changes from negatively influencing the project.

CROSS-REF We recommend that you review the change control plan's planning questions in Chapter 4.

Creating a change control plan

Establishing a change control plan is critical to every project, regardless of the size or industry. Scope changes can easily derail projects possibly shutting down projects completely. Change control is a serious aspect of project management and something that project managers should manage and control very closely throughout the project.

Project managers need to establish a project change control process as early as possible in the project to ensure that all parties, team members and customer, agree to utilize this process. The best time to create this process is before any work activities begin, thereby reducing the chance that a change request will occur. When everyone agrees to employ this process and changes start appearing on the project, it ensures that everyone will follow the change control process.

Project managers must stay on top of change requests, if they do not keep a tight control over them, they can easily run into major project issues. The costs and schedule impacts from a large change request are sometimes too much for the project to absorb. Therefore, the project manager may need to go back to the customer to obtain more time or more money to include the extra work. When project managers are managing projects that have contractors and vendors on their teams, they must be aware of the contract that hired those team members. The change control process can play a large part in what work the "hired" vendors or contractors working on the team will do for the project. The contract could have the team members being hired to do one task, and you want them to do something completely different, and therefore you may have difficulty getting them to do anything more than their originally agreed to.

For fixed-bid projects where both companies have agreed on a single cost to perform the work, any changes introduced on the project will most likely result in a change request for the additional work, and involve costs to the project. The project manager must process these requests through the change request process and procedures established and documented in the contract.

 If a project manager handles change requests in any other way than a rigid change control process, they are asking for trouble, and this could end up hurting the project.

The actual steps of creating a change control plan can vary. Use the template we provide to create a change control plan for your project. The template is located on the CD-ROM for use if your company does not already have one. The table of contents provides the major sections of the document and will be helpful when the document is completed and you are looking for particular information in the document.

Change Control Plan Table of Contents

Section 1: Change Control Board, Roles and Responsibilities

Document in this section the roles and responsibilities of the Change Control Board. This includes: the purpose and direction of the board, what they are responsible for, what they can and cannot approve, etc.

Section 2: Change Board Impact/Considerations Review

Document in this section the impacts and considerations that are different about this Change Control Board that may not be the same as on other projects. Some projects have different aspects and handle Change Control Boards differently; this section would have all that documentation.

Section 3: What Process Must the Requestor Follow to Initiate a Change? What Is the Flow?

Document in this section the flow of how a change request is initiated and how it flows through the change control process. Include the Change Control Board presentation, the change request documentation to complete, timeframes, approvals, etc.

Section 4: Change Board Timeframes and Response Expectations

Document in this section the timeframes and expectations the Change Control Board has on their responses. For example, if they need to make a decision on the change request in one week, document the timeframe here. If there are any expectations on timing, document those exceptions here as well.

Section 5: Change Request Documentation and Expectations

Document the Change Request documentation in this section. Normally, it would be only a change request form, but if there is any additional documentation based on the special needs of the project or the specific change request form, then document those specifics here also.

Section 6: Any Additional Information on the Change Control Plan or Process

Document any additional information on the change control plan or process here. Any special considerations, such as process for emergency change requests would go in this section. Change Control Boards are usually standard, but is important to capture any different processes in this section.

continued

continued

Section 7: Mandatory Change Process

Document in this section how the Change Control Board will handle any mandatory changes. This includes internal audit findings, government laws or regulations changes, or any company processes that are forcing changes onto the project.

Section 8: Approvals and Responses from Change Control Board

Document in this section any approval expectations and possible responses from the Change Control Board, including any "canned" responses the Change Control Board responds with such as; denied as being too costly, outside the scope of the project, having significant schedule impacts, Approved, with cost impacts that need understanding, and acceptance by the executive team.

ON the CD-ROM   We have included a sample change control plan tool in the Communication tools, Time subfolder. Use this as a guide to your own version of this tool.

Using a change control plan

Before using a change control plan, you must identify who on your project team will utilize this tool so that you can determine the level of detail required, frequency of distribution, style, and format of the report. Review the change control plan's planning section in Chapter 6 and then follow these steps:

1. Ensure that your customer is aware of the change control process, including the change control plan for the project. In this step, you will be working with the customer early in the planning process to review the change control plan and ensure they understand the process. This could include a training session; a lunchtime meeting, a one-on-one meeting, or whatever it takes to ensure your customer knows how to use change requests on the project.

2. When your customer is comfortable with the project and the associated change control plan, ask them for formal sign-off and approval, and ensure your team members provide their approval as well. Obtain this approval by sending the change control plan and formal acceptance document to your customer and team members.

3. After receiving both your customer's and team members' approval, store them both in the document control system for long-term storage, archiving, and retrieval purposes.

4. Next, you should enforce the use of the change control plan on your project. This requires that you work with your team members and customer and, as they suggest changes, you can ensure they follow the change control process.

5. As your project moves into the planning process, ensure you establish a change control board for your project, selecting members from upper management, the customer group, and executives to be part of it. In the process of getting the board members set up and on

the team, ensure that they are comfortable with the change control plan by reviewing it with them. This may include making changes to the plan based on the board's input, or making adjustments along the way. If the plan changes, you must distribute it to your customer and project team member's for reapproval. Also, ensure you set up weekly change control board meetings to review the change requests for the project.

6. As the project moves into the executing process, and after you establish the change control board, all project change requests go through this change request board for processing. This includes helping your customer develop change requests, booking the change control board meeting, and walking your customer through the process. This process continues throughout the execution of the project.

Mastering the Comprehensive Test Plan

Before you master the comprehensive test plan tool, you must understand how this tool can assist and support you on your project. The following project scenario emphasizes the importance of the comprehensive test plan and why it is critical to every project.

A large software company has developed a new telephone device that some say will change the world. The company has promoted the new telephone device for months, and it is now ready for launch in the United States and Canada. Thousands of customers are excited about the new phone and have been standing in line for days ready to purchase it. Clearly, advertising works and the worldwide hype is enormous on this new product. Management has asked that you be the project manager for the launch of this incredible new device. You gladly accept, as this is the kind of project that can help your career tremendously if you succeed. The expectations are great and the product is sure to be a success, or is it? Being the project manager, you are afraid that the success of this phone is riding solely on your back, so the pressure is on. Your upper management team has a number of questions for you:

How will you ensure the device will work out of the box?

Will customers be able to make their first, second and hundredth call?

What will you do to ensure the reliability of the product?

What are the required tests that will ensure the successful launch of this phone?

To obtain the answers to these questions, the project manager must use a comprehensive test plan. The project manager uses a test plan to ensure the appropriate rigor and structure to the testing process that will all but guarantee the successful launch of the project.

NOTE It is important to understand that simply having a test plan does not guarantee things will not go wrong; however, it will significantly reduce the chances of major problems occurring on the project, and that alone is worth the effort to produce this valuable tool for your project.

CROSS-REF We recommend that you review the comprehensive test plan's planning questions in Chapter 8.

Creating a comprehensive test plan

Creating a comprehensive test plan is critical for every project, regardless of the project type or industry. Some form of testing must be completed on every product, and the testing performed on a project sets the quality of the project. When project teams do limited product testing, it often leads to major quality problems. Project managers must be active in the creation of the comprehensive test plan and work closely with the test team to ensure that when creating the plan, it is high quality and the test cases are as complete as possible. As the project moves into the testing phase, the project manager must ensure that the testers execute each test case thoroughly, and the results are as expected. Otherwise, the project will continue the process of fixing bugs, retesting, re-fixing, and retesting until everything is resolved and the project is ready to launch; often this process takes months. Depending on the problems, the only way this process completes is when the comprehensive test plan states specifically "the project can launch when there are specific numbers of errors at certain severity levels." For example, a project can launch if there are only two severity level bugs, but cannot launch if there are four or more.

A project customer demands high-level quality applications and stability in the products they are purchasing. From cars rolling out of auto plants to denim jeans coming off the assembly line, each has its own level of quality and testing applied to it before releasing it to the public. Today, consumers are less tolerant of cheap toys on the market and are expecting better durability than they once did.

Using a comprehensive test plan is critical to ensuring that testing has a level of organization and structure, and helps to ensure that customers receive the highest quality in their products.

The actual steps of creating a comprehensive test plan vary. Use the template we provided to create a comprehensive test plan for your project. The template is located on the CD-ROM for use if your company does not already have one. The table of contents provides the major sections of the document and will be handy when the document is completed and you are looking for particular information in the document.

Example of a Comprehensive Test Plan Table of Contents

Section 1: Test Plan Identifier

Document any identification information about the document, such as naming conventions, revision history, etc.

Section 2: Introduction of Testing

Document the testing required for the project. Document high-level requirements, expectations, and the goals of the testing for the project.

*S*ection 3: *Test Items / Test Cases and Scripts*

Document the items required for testing; normally, this is a high-level list of items, and you will also want to add the test cases and test scripts to be run during the testing phase.

*S*ection 4: *Testing Risk & Issues*

Document any specific issues and risks associated to testing. Many times, the risks and issues are associated to the testing activities only and not the total project issues or risks.

*S*ection 5: *Features to Be Tested*

Document the features in the application required to be testing.

*S*ection 6: *Features Not to Be Tested*

Document the features that will not be tested.

*S*ection 7: *Approach*

Document the testing approach. Document any special circumstances, including how testing will occur, methodology used, and any other information applicable to testing.

*S*ection 8: *Item Pass/Fail Criteria*

Document the pass/fail and fail criteria for testing. Often a customer has specific testing criteria that they want applied to the testing, and it is important to have that noted here.

*S*ection 9: *Entry & Exit Criteria*

Document the entry and exit criteria for testing. Often testing teams have an established criterion they want applied to the project and those details would be in this section. One example of a common exit criteria is the number of bugs remaining before the project goes live. The criterion is that, if there are less than three bugs remaining in testing, the project can still go live with those bugs.

*S*ection 10: *Test Deliverables*

Document the various testing deliverables for the project and document what and who is responsible for what testing deliverable and the times frames for each task.

*S*ection 11: *Environmental Needs*

Document any environmental needs for the project. Document the space, security, hardware and any other environmental factors for the project.

continued

continued

Section 12: Staffing and Training Needs

Document the staffing needs of the project. Document the roles required, any special training needs or requirements for the testers assigned to the effort.

Section 13: Responsibilities

Document the specific responsibilities of the testing team members, test lead, and, if applicable, test manager. This section will have details of each member, their work responsibilities, and any other relevant information. It is important to understand what each of the roles will perform on the project.

Section 14: Schedule

Document the test schedule associated to the testing portion of the project. All testing deliverables, staff assignments, and timeframes are documented in this section. It is best practice to copy the testing schedule into this section directly, providing the most current project testing information.

Section 15: Contingencies Plans

Document any test contingency plans within this section and ensure that the plan has all relevant items, timeframes, and other relevant information in this area. It is important to document this in case there are any problems and the project needs to draw upon these contingencies.

Section 16: Approvals

Document the approvals and staff members who have signed off on the test document.

ON the CD-ROM We have included a sample comprehensive test plan tool in the Communication tools Quality subfolder. Use this as a guide to help you create your own version of this tool.

Using a comprehensive test plan

Before you can use a comprehensive test plan, you must identify who on your project team will utilize this tool so that you can determine the level of detail required, frequency of distribution, style, and format of the report.

Review the comprehensive test plan's planning section in Chapter 8 and then follow these steps:

1. As the project moves out of the initiation process and into the latter stages of the planning process, and before the team actually needs to utilize the comprehensive test plan, you should ensure that your team members and the customer have signed off and approved the document. Due to the importance of the project, and the fact that your customer is engaged in the testing process, it is essential that they sign off and approve the test plan long before testing begins. You must ensure you send the comprehensive test

plan document, along with the user acceptance document, to the customer and team members for their sign-off and approval.

2. After receiving approval and sign-off from your customer and team members, store the document in the document control system for long-term storage, archiving, and retrieval purposes.

3. As the project moves into the executing process you will ensure your project teams utilizes the comprehensive test plan, and that the test lead you assigned to the project enforces the actual testing processes using the details, processes and procedures outlined in the plan. You may need to step in and help your test lead if you determine they need assistance in making decisions or need help with the test process. However, you are not responsible for driving this process; that will be the test lead's responsibility, but offer support when needed.

4. You will assist your test lead in executing and enforcing the use of the comprehensive test plan throughout the testing phase. This may include updates and changes to the comprehensive test plan (requires re-sign-off), or anything else that may occur as testing is executed on the project.

Mastering the Critical Chain

Before you can master the critical chain tool, you must understand how this tool can assist and support you on your project. The following project scenario emphasizes the importance of the critical chain tool.

A large software development company has on average 20 to 40 projects occurring at one time, and individual project team members have 4 to 6 projects assigned. The constant pressure of producing something for each project will impact the output of each team member. The project managers in charge of each project demand two to five hours per week from each team member. You are working at this company and are one of those project managers. In reviewing the whole staffing situation, you can see that a team member must switch their work efforts on a continual basis to keep up with the demands placed on them. Your team members are burning out quickly and management is starting to ask you some tough questions. These questions include:

How can you help your team members manage the pressures of performing the work and not burnout?

You are losing your most valuable employees on a regular basis, how can you stop it?

How many projects are you asking your team members to be on at one time?

To obtain the answers to these questions, the project manager should use the critical chain methodology on their projects to ensure the project team members are focused on one project at time, reducing their chances of burnout. The use of the critical chain methodology is becoming popular in planning and helps to prevent the issue described in the aforementioned scenario from ever happening. So often in multiproject environments with shared resources, project team members face constant pressure to complete multiple tasks at the same time. The result is frequent task switching by the resources, also known as multitasking. Frequent task switching drains productivity and can be resolved by applying the critical chain method.

CROSS-REF We recommend that you review the critical chain planning questions in Chapter 9.

Creating a critical chain

Creating and using critical chain methodology is a fundamental change in the way businesses work today. The ideas and concepts behind reducing multitasking and allowing staff members to focus on single items is a paradigm shift that not all businesses are ready to make. There is a perception that when staff members are not constantly busy, they are wasting time and money and should be getting real work done. However, that is a misconception, and one that more and more companies are starting to realize. As quality on products continues to drop and multitasking is becoming a way of life, many companies are suffering.

A project customer rarely is involved in creating critical chain reports but should support the process and provide help wherever possible. The customer should buy into the concept of no multitasking for their project team members so they will gain the project benefits of using this methodology. The customer must support this methodology by understanding that team members who are not working actively on a particular area of the project are still valuable and not wasting time. These same team members could be supporting or helping another area of the project unbeknownst to the customer.

The actual steps of creating a critical chain report can vary, but here are some simple steps to help you get started.

1. Open your favorite project management scheduling tool. This can be any project-scheduling package you are using today on your project.

2. Confirm that the status date for the schedule is correct, and that only completed work is before the status date, and only remaining work is after the status date. You may need to add Actual Start, Actual Finish, and Remaining Duration columns to your project schedule. The Actual Finish column will be a quick and easy way to determine the tasks that are still open.

3. Run the reports according to the instructions in your critical chain add-in or critical chain project management software. The instructions will be different depending on yours, or your company's, software tool of choice.

4. Analyze the results of the reports and adjust your project accordingly.

Figure 16.1 is a sample resource critical chain report. A tremendous amount of information is displayed in this resource chart; however, the most important information is what task to complete next. The report provides details on project name, resource names, start dates, and durations, and provides a status of the project's current resource assignments.

FIGURE 16.1

A sample resource critical chain report

Project Name	Resource Name	Task Name	Task Prioritization Metric	Open Preds?	Expected Start	Remaining Duration (Days)	Task ID	Notes
MYouth Center2	Builder[2]	HVAC	1.09	No	10/28/2003	2 days	24	
MYouth Center2	Builder[3]	Drywall	1.09	No	11/11/2003	3 days	34	
MYouth Center1	Builder[2]	Paint Touch-up	−0.14	Yes	11/4/2003	2 days	52	
MYouth Center4	Builder[4]	Sitework	0.79	Yes	10/29/2003	2 days	5	
MYouth Center1	Builder[2]	Final Cleaning	−0.14	Yes	11/6/2003	3 days	53	
MYouth Center4	Builder[6]	Foundation	0.79	Yes	10/31/2003	5 days	6	
MYouth Center1	Builder[2]	Final Inspection	−0.14	Yes	11/12/2003	3 days	54	
MYouth Center4	Builder[6]	Structural Steel	10	Yes	11/13/2003	4 day	14	

Using a critical chain

Before you can use a critical chain, you must identify who on your project team will utilize this tool so that you can determine the level of detail required, frequency of distribution, style, and format of the report. Review the critical chain planning section in Chapter 9 and then follow these steps:

1. Distribute your critical chain reports at least weekly. The reports will go to the system owner, the project management director, the resource managers, and the resources working on your project. These reports should be distributed a day before the buffer management meeting.

2. Based on the information in the reports, you and your resource managers will decide on a plan of action to address the issues; and if possible, implement the plan.

3. Work with your system owner/operator and conduct the buffer management meeting. Ask the three golden questions:

   - What's going on? A simple request for clarity.

   - What are we doing about it? This will ensure that the outcome of the meeting is buffer management, not buffer watching.

   - What are we doing to prevent this in the future? With this question, a process of ongoing improvement is embedded in the organization.

4. Work with your resource managers and implement any additional actions directed by the system owner/operator.

5. Finally, work with your project team to report progress for the next reporting cycle.

Mastering the Earned Value Analysis Tool

Before you can master the earned value analysis performance tool, you must understand how this tool can assist and support you on your project. The following project scenario emphasizes the importance of the tool.

A large research company, in Dallas, Texas, is working on a new bio-energy product that will transform water into a form of gas. Management has asked that you be the project manager for this new project, you accept and are ready to get started. The project you are working on has a planned schedule of 25 months. The executive management team has reviewed and approved the budget of $2,000,000. You have received approval to spend $120,000 per month until the project is complete, and everyone agrees this is a reasonable budget expenditure rate for this type of project. The owner, and the project team, fully expects to stay within the cost limits of $120,000 per month for the life of the project, and everyone is excited to get the project under way.

At the end of the first month, you present a glowing performance report to the Executive Management team showing the actual costs spent for the first month were only $90,000, which is under the planned budget by $30,000, or 25 percent. All the stakeholders were happy until one of the financial officers asks if the project is on schedule and *performing* according to the $120,000 budget rate, and not the $90,000 expenditure. You quickly assure the financial officer that the project is on schedule, and just as quickly the financial officer shoots back a number of questions, including, how you know if the performance equals the expenditure rate? No one in the room can answer the question. The last statement made in the meeting came from the Chief Financial Officer: "I want the performance answers by the next progress meeting." No one said a word. The financial officer speaks up again asking some tough, but fair questions. These questions include:

Have you performed according to your schedule?

What amount of the $90,000 have you actually earned?

What is your cost performance index?

To obtain the answers to these questions, the project manager should utilize the earned value analysis techniques on his/her project. Without using the earned value analysis technique, it is difficult to integrate cost and schedule data to create a performance report. Without those performance reports, project managers or executives would have a difficult time understanding the true performance of the project team. In today's project environment, and especially on large projects, it is common for one group to create the project schedule, and an entirely different group to estimate and track the project costs. Therefore, the cost and the schedule are rarely integrated, making it difficult to determine the performance rate of the project.

CROSS-REF We recommend that you review the earned value analysis performance's planning questions in Chapter 7.

Creating the earned value analysis tool

Creating the earned value analysis process is becoming more popular on projects today because it integrates scheduling and costs on the project into a single view. Earned value analysis creates both a tabular and graphical presentation of reports for customer and team members to utilize. When creating earned value analysis reports, it is important that the project manager ensure that there is a project schedule created and maintained on the project. The second step is to ensure that the project manager cost loads (monies or labor hours) the original project schedule. Finally, the project manager creates a baseline schedule from the original schedule, and once the project starts, the project is ready for performance reporting.

CROSS-REF Turn to Chapter 6 to learn more about the Baseline Schedule tool.

Before creating earned value reports, ensure you are comfortable with the terms and the calculations. We have covered some of these terms previously (see Chapters 6 and 7 for more details on these terms), but it is valuable to re-review them before creating the earned value reports.

The earned value calculations consist of the following:

Cost formulas for measuring cost performance

The following items are the cost calculations for the earned value reports.

Cost Variance (CV)	$CV = EV - AC$
Cost Performance Index (CPI)	$CPI = EV / AC$

Earned Value Analysis Terms

Earned Value: At the time of calculating the report, earned value is 2, or 2 percent complete for the task, multiplied by 5 percent that is expected to be complete for the task.

Planned Value: At time of calculating the report, the planned value represents how much work was expected to be completed at this time, however, the task should have been 5 percent complete, and was only 2 percent complete.

Cost Variance: At time of calculating the report the task was 2 percent complete, showing the task is $108 over what it was estimated to have cost at 2 percent complete.

Schedule Variance: At time of calculating the report, planned value was 5 percent, the task was 2 percent complete; therefore it shows the task as behind schedule.

Cost CPI: At time of calculating the report, cost CPI is 0.02 for this task, which indicates from a cost perspective that the task is over-running due to over spending, and is actually completed at this time.

Schedule SPI: At time of calculating the report, SPI is 0.40, which means the work rate is performing at 40 percent of what was expected.

Schedule formulas for measuring schedule performance

The following items are the schedule calculations for the earned value reports. Here are the two calculations:

Schedule Variance (SV)	$SV = EV - PV$
Schedule Performance Index (SPI)	$SPI = EV / PV$

 **The first variable in each of these calculations is the earned value (EV) variable. In the schedule variance calculation, EV is the earned valuable variable.**

Figure 16.2 shows an extensive earned value performance report displaying various performance data values for each activity in your project schedule. As you can see, the chart shows not only the three earned value fields, planned value, earned value, and actual cost, but also the cost and schedule variance fields, and the performance fields cost and schedule performance indexes. This type of report, along with the S-curve graphics report, provides all the information you need for performing performance analysis on your project.

FIGURE 16.2

A sample of an earned value performance report

Activity Description	% Complete	Planned Value (Budget)	Earned Value	Actual Cost	Cost Variance	Schedule Variance	Cost CPI	Schedule SPI
Preliminary Plan	2%	100	2	110	–108	2	0.02	0.02
Final Plan	100%	250	250	210	40	0	1.19	1.00
Move Out	100%	300	300	265	35	0	1.13	1.00
Remodel	70%	1200	840	1300	–460	–360	0.65	0.70
Move Back In	1%	250	2.5	10	–7.5	–248	0.25	0.01
Total	55%	2100	1395	1895	–500	–705	0.74	0.66

Figure 16.3 shows the earned value S-curve chart that displays the trend of your project showing actual values, planned values, and finally, earned values are all up-to-date. These represent the condition of the project that can be trended to display an estimate at completion if necessary. It is clear from this example that the project is performing behind schedule and is significantly over budget.

FIGURE 16.3

An S-curve chart showing a sample of the performance of the project.

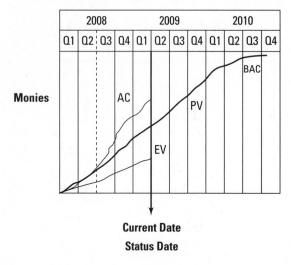

The following steps can help you get started in creating your earned value analysis reports.

1. Establish immediately that you will use the earned value analysis (EVA) technique to report progress and performance on your project, including determining what reports to create. It takes a lot of thought and planning to run a project using EVA, but the benefits will significantly outweigh the time and effort involved to create and maintain it. Use the work breakdown structure to help plan the development of the project schedule; the process works best if the entire team and the customer are involved. Your customer will provide ideas from an executive point of view and their buy-in involvement, which is extremely important and will create a better final product. During the planning for earned value analysis, you will want to assign specific team members to be responsible for the status and performance of each activity on the project.

   You must make a decision at this point on how your team members are going to estimate each activity and how to collect actuals. The easiest way to do this is to use labor time sheets because it is an efficient means of keeping track of the hours that team member's work on each activity. It is harder to acquire actual costs because actual costs may not be available in a timely manner; they could come in two or three months late with their posting.

2. Create you original project schedule.

3. Cost load (monies or labor hours) your project schedule. This is not an easy task; each activity requires an estimated cost applied to it and this cost can be monies or labor hours, or both. If you are having trouble estimating the cost of the activity, you may be more comfortable breaking it down into several smaller pieces that are more manageable, but be sure to do this before recording any progress. Using the project's work breakdown structure can significantly help you with this process.

CROSS-REF Turn to Chapter 5 to learn more about the Work Breakdown Structure tool.

4. Forward your original schedule to your customer and your team members for approval. This includes sending the original project schedule and the user acceptance document to your team members and customer to gain their approval. In most cases, you will call a project schedule review meeting with the team members and customer to review the schedule, ensuring everyone understands it, and providing them with the confidence that they will sign off on it.

5. After obtaining the sign-off and approval, create your baseline schedule.

6. After the first reporting cycle begins, the earned value analysis carries throughout the life of the project. The information needed to create the variety of performance reports is the actual start of an activity, the percentage complete, or the actual finish of the activity if it is 100 percent complete. Update every activity on your project schedule that is in progress, and establish an actual finish date for activities that have completed since the last reporting cycle.

7. Gather actual costs for each of your project activities that have reported progress. The calculation can be completed in many ways, for example, actual costs could be labor hours to date per activity, hours times labor rate, or gather actual costs by monies, totaling the expenses on each activity. Each of these calculations will depend on how the project manager created the estimate originally.

8. You now have all the information you need to create the earned value reports, by updating the performance report, applying the new progress information to your scheduling system, and creating the performance reports. The performance reports can be tabular or graphical with the plan value (PV), earned value (EV), and actual cost (AC) curves. The report would be created each month automatically during the reporting cycle. The reports should consist of the following:

   ▪ S-curves showing the Plan Value (PV), Earned Value (EV), and Actual Cost (AC) curve

   ▪ Cost and schedule variance reports

   ▪ Cost performance index (CPI) and the schedule performance index (SPI)

   The earned value reports are now ready for distribution.

9. Maintain your baseline schedule and keep it current with approved change requests each reporting cycle. Every time you add value or remove value from a project, you must include it in the baseline schedule. If an approved change order adds 1,000 hours to the current schedule, the project manager should add the 1,000 hours to the baseline schedule. Without the baseline change, the performance reports will be undervalued or overvalued, and this will give the appearance of being either underperforming or over performing.

ON the CD-ROM We have included a sample earned value analysis performance tool in the Communication tools, Cost subfolder. Use this as a guide to help you create your own version of this tool.

Using the earned value analysis tool

Before you use the Earned Value Analysis Performance tool, you must identify who on your project team will utilize this tool so that you can determine the level of detail required, frequency of distribution, style, and format of the report.

Review the earned value analysis performance tool planning section in Chapter 7 and then follow these steps:

1. Distribute your earned value reports after each reporting cycle or on demand, when applicable. You will send these reports to your owner, client, team members, subcontractors, and in some cases, the media.

2. Host a number of status meetings to review the earned value reports with everyone involved in the project. Your first meeting is strictly for team members to become current on the project's performance, the second meeting is for the customer to become current on the project's performance. In each of these meetings, action items could result for either you or your team members from reviewing and discussing the project performance. If that is the case, adjust your project accordingly.

3. Ensure you continue to focus your team members' work efforts on the results and outcomes of those performance report meetings. This could include a variety of areas on the project that require updating to improve the project's performance. Examples include adding staff, reducing scope, and moving activity timeframes.

Mastering the Issue Management Plan

Before you can master the issue management plan, you must understand how this tool can assist and support you on your project. The following project scenario emphasizes the importance of the tool.

A large hardware company has decided to create a new computer keyboard. The new keyboard will be affordable, wireless, and come in a variety of colors. As project manager you immediately kick off the project and get the team working on the planning process; however, in one of the areas you find a high number of issues which is unsettling, because the project is just getting going. These issues include staffing, hardware issues, technical issues, and budget issues, to name a few. You need to get control on these issues immediately or your project may be in trouble. You notice that there is no process setup for controlling or managing issues on the project, so you have no idea how to handle all these project issues, you are confused and need some guidance. You have a number of questions including:

What do you do to resolve these issues?

How do you manage and control project issues that do not need immediate resolution?

What can you do to stop an issue from derailing a project?

What are the roles and responsibilities of the team members in the issue management process?

What plans or procedures do you have for issue management?

To obtain answers to these questions you should use an issue management plan. An issue management plan covers all aspects of issue management and control, including escalation, tracking, resolution, roles and responsibilities, and all deliverables associated with issue management. The issue management plan prevents issues from derailing the project, and as issues arise the project manager and team members will have an established process to follow.

CROSS-REF We recommend that you review the issue management plan's planning questions in Chapter 10.

Creating an issue management plan

Creating an issue management plan is important on projects and is often overlooked. Many project managers look at issue management plan documents as overhead that provides no real value to the project; however, that could not be further from the truth. The issue management plan is critical to managing and controlling project issues.

Project managers should use the issue management plan as a supporting document to help them with their risks. As team members or a customer raises project issues, the project manager needs to know how to track and monitor these issues. Without the guidance that the issue management plan provides, how would a project manager begin to tackle these issues and prevent them from negatively affecting the project? Project managers must be diligent in watching and controlling project issues, and ensuring that when a project team member or customer raises an issue, the project manager watches it closely until it is resolved. To track an issue, the project manager must ensure that the issue has an owner assigned, and a status, priority, and due date associated to it; these fields are the minimum needed to track each issue, and without these fields the issues will be difficult to monitor. The project manager should manage and control the continual evaluation of each issue on a weekly basis, and if issues are of a high priority and could harm the project, the project manager and the customer must resolve them as quickly as possible.

A project customer must be active in assisting with the creation of the issue management plan. The customers must have a good understanding of how to initiate a project issue because they will be responsible for creating many throughout the project.

CAUTION It would be a negative impact to the project to have the team immediately shifting their attention to every project issue the customer raises; however, using an issue management plan with its associated processes would prevent that from occurring.

In some cases, project issues actually become risks and require tracking as risks. Not all issues that come up are project issues, and therefore require review before the project manager can determine whether to track them as issues or as a risk, which may be more appropriate. If tracked as a risk, the process and procedures outlined in the risk management plan will track it.

CROSS-REF   See Chapter 12 for more information on the risk management plan.

The actual steps of creating an issues management plan vary. Use the template we provided to create an issues management plan for your project. The template is located on the CD-ROM for use if your company does not already have one. The table of contents provides the major sections of the document and will be handy when the document is completed and you are looking for particular information in the document.

Example of an Issue Management Plan Table of Contents

Section 1: Document Identification

Update this section to include the date created and author, and any documentation identification information.

Section 2: Introduction

Write a brief introduction at a summary level for the reader and upper management.

Section 3: Purpose

Describe the purpose of issue management.

Section 4: Scope

Write the scope of the issue management plan; how the plan will be defined and how you are going to control the process.

Section 5: Management and Escalation

Describe the process and rules that would escalate an issue for management to resolve.

Section 6: Issue Tracking Tools

Identify and describe the tools used for issues management, such as a flow chart or issues management list.

Section 7: Resolution and Closeout

Describe the format and rules for resolution and closeout of an issue.

Section 8: Glossary

Define the terms used in issues management

Section 9: Issues Process
Identify and describe the process of issues management.

Section 10: Roles and Responsibilities
Describe the roles and responsibilities needed to manage issues on the project.

Section 11: Configuration Items
Identify and describe the configuration items for the project.

Section 12: Deliverables
Identify all deliverables and make sure they are in the WBS at the work package level.

Section 13: Support Tools
Identify and describe the tools needed to manage the project issues

Section 14: Communications
Document the process for managing and controlling project issue communications; this will include types, frequency, etc.

ON the CD-ROM We have included a sample issue management plan tool in the Communication tools, Risk subfolder. Use this as a guide to help you create your own version of this tool.

Using an issue management plan

Before using an issue management plan, you must identify who on your project team will utilize this tool so that you can determine the level of detail required, frequency of distribution, style, and format of the report. In the case of the issues management plan, this is a detailed document that team members will utilize to determine how to manage project issues. This document is rarely produced at the summary level.

Review the issue management plan's planning section in Chapter 12. Then follow these steps:

1. In using an issue management plan, you should ensure that your project team and your customer has signed off and approved the document. This may require you to schedule review meetings and review the document with your customer so they understand it and can ask questions if necessary.

2. Distribute your project's issue management plan and the user acceptance document to the team members and customer for their sign-off and approval. Before obtaining signoff, it may be necessary to hold walkthrough meetings to ensure everyone understands the processes and procedures within the document and are more comfortable in signing.

3. After obtaining approvals, store the issue management plan, and the associated approvals, in the document control system for long-term storage, archiving, and retrieval purposes.

4. As the project moves into the planning process you should start to utilize the issue management plan, and the process and procedures associated with issue management, on your project. Issues come and go on the project, so as soon as the project begins, you should immediately follow the procedures outlined in the plan.

5. As the project moves into the executing process, ensure you enforce the continual use of the plan to drive issue resolution and closeout through the end of the project.

Mastering Quality Metrics

Before you can master the quality metrics tool, you must understand how this tool can assist and support you on your project. The following project scenario emphasizes the importance of the quality metrics tool.

A large manufacturing company has been developing nuts and screws for years and has been so successful in the marketplace that they have decided to expand their product line to include a new type of screw. The company is excited about the new screw, and market tests have proven that this screw will be successful. The company president was approached by NASA who is interested in the screw as well, and asked if it could perform "special" tests on the screw. This is exciting for the company — it is hoping to secure a long-term contract with NASA, so they happily accepted the NASA request. Your assignment, as the most respected project manager at the company, is to work with the NASA test team to ensure they are getting everything they need for this testing. This is your moment to shine, but as the testing progresses, results come back that are unfavorable and the NASA test team is not happy. They are about to give up on the project and you do not know what to do. The NASA team is asking some specific questions about quality. Question that include:

What level of quality is acceptable for the screw?

What numbers did you agree to before testing started?

How large are the test results?

What area of testing is failing?

What is an acceptable level of failures per thousand?

To obtain the answers to these questions, the project manager should use quality metrics. Quality metrics ensure the quality on any project by enforcing that the team members hit a specific level of quality established by the metrics. In the case of the NASA scenario, if 2 screws out of 200 fail, is this acceptable? It is unlikely, but possible, based on the rigor that NASA applies to all their testing. The project manager leverages the quality metrics tool defined at the beginning of the project to ensure the testing meets or exceeds that level established, in this case, for the two failures. If it does not, then the NASA team is correct and is justified in getting out of the project unless something changes immediately.

CROSS-REF We recommend that you review the quality metrics planning questions in Chapter 8.

Creating quality metrics

Quality metrics are levels of rigor and control applied to the testing and results of the product. The testing results completed for each quality metric comes from a series of testing limits, upper and lower, and determine the pass or fail quality criteria.

Project managers must be active and understand how quality is determined and judged on the project. Quality metrics ensures that the project team is adding a level of rigor and process to their testing and work results to achieve the highest possible quality for the project. Quality metrics are applied to various aspects of the project in the managing and controlling of the project. For example, in the software industry, a popular quality metric included for code drops is how often did the team develop new code for the test team to pick and test, how many bugs were found in the code, and how long did it take between code drops.

In developing a quality metrics, it is important to utilize a standard process each time to ensure that the metrics is consistent across all tests. The industry has a well-known process called the Shewhart Cycle. The Shewhart Cycle Chart has four main areas:

1. **Plan:** Improve results by designing or revising the process components.
2. **Do:** Implement the plan and measure its performance.
3. **Check:** Evaluate and report results to stakeholders.
4. **Act:** Make a decision on possible process changes for improvement.

Using the Shewhart Cycle requires an ongoing circular process through the four main areas of the cycle. It is critical to complete these areas in a circular motion, starting from the plan and moving through to the Act area, and when you finish the Act area you move back to the Plan area and proceed though the cycle back to act. It is a continuous cycle. When creating the quality metrics, it is important that you utilize the Shewhart Cycle. This allows for a standard method of creating any given quality metrics on the project.

A project customer must be active in defining and understanding what level of quality is acceptable to them. For example, some customer may have a higher tolerance level of accepting risks, and therefore will agree to a larger number of product failures than other customer might. Project managers must be aware of that level of tolerance, from customer to customer, and ensure the project is driving toward that level to ensure the customer is satisfied with the released product.

The steps for creating a quality metrics can vary. We have provided some guidelines in creating your own quality metrics below.

For the purposes of getting started and learning how to create quality metrics, we have a simple scenario for you to follow. You can adjust or modify this scenario for your project.

Scenario: We want to track the number of software errors by severity level on a software project for every release that goes into the user acceptance environment. There are five possible release cycles that will go into the user acceptance phase that can be counted and are possible to generate metrics from. The metrics that the team is judged on would be the last metric. This metric is as follows: zero severity 1 bugs, less than 3 severity 2 bugs, and less than 5 severity 3 bugs. If the project team members can hit their quality metric on the bug counts, then the project is at an acceptable level of quality and can be released into production.

1. Work with your project's test lead and ensure they understand and define the metrics that they will be testing and tracking towards. This metric should be based on the overall quality metrics defined for the project. The test lead notifies their testers of the metrics and you notify your customer. Then work with the test lead and develops the quality metrics tracking table to store the metrics once the testing process gets started. See Figure 16.4 for a sample of this table. The test lead will take ownership of capturing and reporting this information going forward and throughout the testing process.

2. As the project releases its first round into the user acceptance environment, you will then work with your test lead to track the results of the testing effort and count the software errors based in the different severity categories (Severity 1, Severity 2, etc.). Once complete, enter those results into the new created quality metrics table for reporting purposes.

   Figure 16.4 shows a sample of a quality metrics from the first round of testing in the user acceptance environment. Because this is the first round only, the project team has time in the schedule to recode and retest in order to bring the error counts down. This chart is good for tracking toward the overall metrics for the project.

FIGURE 16.4

A sample of quality metrics after the first release into the user acceptance environment.

Bugs by Status and Severity Levels					
Status	Sev 1	Sev 2	Sev 3	Sev 4	Total
Active	5	22	5	0	32
Resolved	0	0	0	0	0
Closed	0	55	22	5	82
Total	0	77	34	34	145

3. After the values are in the quality metrics table, compare the results of the testing to the quality metrics defined for your project. Remember, those metrics were zero severity 1 bugs, less than 3 Severity 2 bugs, and less than 5 severity 3 bugs. In Figure 16.4, it is clear the development team has some work to do to be able to hit the metrics they need to achieve on this project.

4. Continue this process until the project testing phase completes and the project testing team has achieved the quality metrics established for the project. Otherwise, the project should not be considered complete or at an acceptable level of quality.

ON the CD-ROM We have included a sample quality metrics tool in the Communication tools, Quality subfolder. Use this as a guide to help you create your own version of this tool.

Using quality metrics

Before using a Quality Metrics tool, you must identify who on your project team will utilize this tool so that you can determine the level of detail required, frequency of distribution, style, and format of the report. In this case, quality metrics are often described and reported with detailed information. It is important to capture the details because the team members need this detail in order to create the metrics they are trying to achieve. Quality metrics documented at a summary level would not be valuable to the project.

Review the quality metrics planning section in Chapter 8. Then follow these steps:

1. As the project moves into the planning process, the first step in using quality metrics is to obtain approval and sign-off from your team members and customer. The project team works hard to obtain a level of quality outlined by quality metrics, and before the team spends the time and effort to achieve those goals, you must ensure everyone signs off and approves the metrics. This may require meeting with your customer and team members to ensure everyone agrees on the metrics and are comfortable signing-off on those metrics.

2. After everyone consents to the quality metrics, distribute them for approval and sign-off. This includes combining the user acceptance document with the quality metrics that the customer has previously approved and agreed to sign.

3. After approvals and sign-offs are received from your customer and team members, store the information in the document control system for long-term storage, archiving, and retrieval purposes.

4. As the project moves into the execution process, you must ensure your test team is working towards those quality metrics within the testing phase. This includes ensuring that your test lead is capturing the testing results, reporting and communicating those results, and driving their test team in hitting those defined quality metrics.

5. Continue to drive your project's testing phase to ensure all metrics are achieved and the level of quality is deemed acceptable to the customer.

Mastering the Risk Management Plan

Before you can master the risk management plan, you must understand how this tool can assist and support you on your project. The following project scenario emphasizes the importance of the risk management plan.

A small construction firm has just won a contract to design and build four high-tech racing sailboats for the next America's Cup, the world's most prestigious sailboat race. The firm, well known in the industry, has always wanted this big contract but has lost out five years in a row. This year the firm has the opportunity to prove how good they really are. If they can pull this off, this small firm will become an overnight success, so the pressure is on to build the first prototype boat as quickly as possible, ensuring the highest level of quality, while being considerate of the price. For the past year, you have been the lead project manager in boat design and construction for the company, so management thought it made sense for you to lead this effort and this is now your project. As the project progresses, risks and issues come and go affecting the project; but you are on top of each issue and risk, and nothing is affecting the project at this time. Then, all of a sudden, the project loses one of its top resources to another company. When it appears things cannot get any worse, the America's Cup design team calls to inform you that they are coming next month to review the prototype of the boat. The schedule just moved up two months. The funding expected to come in last month is going to be two to three months late which impacts the ordering of materials for the racing boats. Finally, upper management has started to ask some hard questions as to how you plan to get this project on track. The questions include:

What are you doing to control the risks hitting your project?

What plan do you have for these risks, and how do you plan to handle them?

Where are you storing the risks so we can see the progress on them?

Are they risks or issues? How are you making that determination?

Where is the risk event planning?

To obtain the answers to these questions, the project manager should use a risk management plan. The risk management plan is the documentation that describes the process of managing and controlling risks on the project. Areas covered in the plan include risk identification, risk analysis, risk response planning, risk event plan, risk tracking and control, and risk communications. If the project manager had used a risk management plan document in the scenario, it would have provided the project manager and the team members the processes and procedures to manage the project risks.

 We recommend that you review the risk management plan's planning questions in Chapter 12.

Creating a risk management plan

A risk management plan helps in managing and controlling project risks. This plan should be required on all size projects, across all industries. Risk management is complex, and if not handled carefully, risks can quickly become issues and immediately affect the project.

Project managers must be diligent in managing project risks to prevent them from becoming issues, and the risk management plan is important because it describes in detail the process and procedures for managing risks on the project. A project customer must be fully aware of the risk management process and ensure they know how to raise project risks correctly without derailing the project team. The project customer is often instrumental in discovering project risk, so it is important that they understand the risk management process in order to add risks to the project without negatively impacting the project team.

The actual steps of creating a risk management plan vary. Use the template we provided to create a risk management plan for your project. The template is located on the CD-ROM for use if your company does not already have one. The table of contents provides the major sections of the document and will be handy when the document is completed and you are looking for particular information in the document.

Risk Management Plan Table of Contents

Section 1: Risk Identification
- Conduct Formal Risk Identification Reviews
- Conduct Informal Risk Identification
- Document the Candidate Risk
- Validate the Candidate Risk

Document the risk identification sections of the document. This includes the various risk reviews, documenting, and validating the risk candidates.

Section 2: Risk Analysis
- Perform Risk Categorization & Prioritization
- Perform Impact Analysis
- Review Risk against Risk Tolerances
- Risk Tolerances
- Review Risk Analysis and Ranking
- Acceptance of Risks

Document the various risk analysis details. This includes prioritizing the risks, determining impacts, establishing tolerances, and ranking risks events.

Section 3: Risk Response Planning
- Plan Mitigation Activities
- Plan Contingency Activities
- Review Risk Action Plans

Document the risk response planning details, this includes any mitigation activities, contingency activities, and any applicable action plans.

continued

605

continued

Section 4: Risk Event Plan Implementation

- Monitor Symptoms Events
- Execute Action Plan(s)

Document the implementation details; for example if there is any special monitoring on events or any action plans if the events do occur, that are documented in this section.

Section 5: Risk Tracking and Controlling

- Report Risk Status
- Review Changes to Risk Profiles and Action Plans
- Retire Risks

Document the risk tracking and controlling details in this section. How will the project track risks, tools to use, various statues, etc.

Section 6: Risk Communications

- Periodic Status Meetings
- Report Lessons Learned on Risks
- Escalate Risks

Document how to communicate risk event tracking; when are the meetings, what is covered, who is responsible.

ON the CD-ROM We have included a sample risk management plan in the Communication tools Risk sub-folder. Use this as a guide to help you create your own version of this tool.

Using a risk management plan

Before using a risk management plan, you must identify who on your project team will utilize this tool, so that you can determine the level of detail required, frequency of distribution, style, and format of the report.

Review the risk management plan's planning section in Chapter 12. Then follow these steps:

1. Obtain sign-off and approval from your team members and customer on the risk management plan. This signoff confirms that they agree with the process and procedures established, and as risks arise on the project, they will follow the processes outlined.

2. Distribute the risk management plan along with the user acceptance document to your customer and team members for approval. After receiving the approvals, store both documents in the document control system for long-term storage, archiving, and retrieval purposes.

3. After receiving the approvals from your customer and team members, and while the project is still in the planning process, enforce the use of the risk management plan on your project. This includes setting up the risk identification process, establishing risk meetings, and defining risk tools. All the processes established and documented in the risk management plan require that you set up and establish them on your project. If you don't set them up, chances are no one else will.

4. As your project moves into the executing process, continue to enforce the use of the risk management process and procedures on your project. This process continues throughout the life of the project.

Mastering the Risk Register

Before you can master the risk register tool, you must understand how this tool can assist and support you on your project. The following project scenario emphasizes the importance of the tool and reasons why the risk register tool is critical to every project.

A large, world-renowned health agency has decided to implement a new health care program in a number of impoverished countries around the world. The new health system will provide sorely needed medicines to people in these countries, saving many lives; this application is long overdue. Drug and prescription information will be readily available to doctors when the system goes live. You are a lead project manager in the health care industry and want to head up the implementation of the new system. You are excited and ready to get going, but you also realize that a number of risks are surfacing that need immediate attention. Your management team is asking you a number of questions on the different risks—and risks are starting to appear from everywhere. The questions that management is asking include:

> How do you manage the project risks?
>
> What strategies did you develop for the risk events?
>
> What mitigation plans do you have in place for each risk?
>
> What risks are current on the project?

To obtain the answers to these questions the project manager should use a risk register. The risk register provides a tracking and status mechanism for controlling and reporting project risks. The risk register is often identified as a risk list. The risk register should provide project managers with everything they need to effectively manage and control project risks.

CROSS-REF We recommend that you review the risk register's planning questions in Chapter 12.

Creating a risk register

Risk mitigation is one of the most important categories in the risk register. Risk mitigation is the method of trying to ensure that project risk events do not stop or derail a project, also known as risk response planning. The upfront analysis and strategies chosen for the project risk events can prevent or reduce harm to the project and in some cases avoid the risk event completely. The development of alternative courses of action, or workarounds for each risk event, will provide a better mechanism for handling them if they do occur on the project. The project manager must drive these strategy discussions with the customer to ensure everyone is onboard with the risk mitigation process.

One risk mitigation technique is to bring the customer and team members together to examine the project's risk events and document how to react to the risks should they occur. The time taken upfront in selecting a strategy for risk events can save the project team time if risk events do occur.

NOTE It is important that the project manager continues to re-address risk events throughout the project and suggest strategies for those events as they arise. As the project progresses through the lifecycle, the risk events and strategies once selected as applicable can quickly change and may no longer work. It is common for an early strategy to be changed and updated based on the new ideas and directions of the project. This introduces new risks.

The risk register is a relatively new tool for many project managers and one that will assist in the risk mitigation of any project. The project manager should create the risk register at the beginning of the project and enter the project risks into the tool as soon as possible. The project manager can use the risk register and the risk assessment tools to assist her in managing and controlling risks. The risk register is an important tool in the reporting of project risks, and the customer and project team members should review it at least on a weekly basis. Many times risks are being resolved in the background as part of the project work, and the project manager sometimes finds this out later. Reviewing the risk register on a weekly basis prevents that from occurring. The project manager learns which project risks are completed at the next meeting.

Project managers should be actively creating risk mitigation strategies for the project, and should work closely with the customer to ensure they are in the loop and suggesting ways to resolve project risks with the project team. Project teams may have one idea of how to resolve the risks, and the customer may have something completely different. This miscommunication between the project team members and the customer requires immediate resolution. The project manager should drive this to a conclusion.

The actual steps of creating a risk register can vary. Instead of providing step-by-step instructions on how to create a risk register, a better option would be for the project manager to utilize the template that is included on the CD-ROM with your specific project details. Project managers could utilize this template if their company does not have one available.

1. Add the risk events that have a risk response plan onto the risk register spreadsheet. There may be several risk events listed on your project that may or may not be candidates for creating a mitigation strategy, so only add the actual events that have mitigation strategies. It is up to you and your team members to determine what risks warrant a mitigation strategy, and it is only those events that move onto the risk register.

2. Next work with your team members to identify a strategy for mitigating the risk events. Risk mitigation includes the following risk strategies to use on your projects:

   - Risk Acceptance

   - Risk Avoidance

- Risk Transfer
- Risk Mitigate
- Risk Retention

3. At this point, work with your team members to select a risk mitigation strategy for every risk event that warrants it. When selecting the mitigation strategy for the risk event, vote or have a discussion as a team about why that strategy makes the most sense for the risk. The first strategy selected may not make sense, but as a group, you will likely come to a consensus on which strategy is the correct one for the risk event.

4. Finally, communicate the completed risk register to your customer, upper management, and team members.

 We have included a sample risk register tool in the Communication tools Risk subfolder. Use this as a guide to help you create your own version of this tool.

Using a risk register

Before using a risk register, you must identify who on your project team will utilize this tool so that you can determine the level of detail required, frequency of distribution, style, and format of the report.

Review the risk register planning section in Chapter 12. Then follow these steps:

1. As the project moves into the planning process it is important that you obtain sign-off and approval from your team members and customer on the mitigation strategies outlined and documented in the risk register. This sign-off confirms agreement with the strategies selected for mitigating the various project risk events.

2. Distribute the risk register along with the user acceptance document to your customer and team members for their approval. Once approved, store both documents in the document control system for long-term storage, archiving, and retrieval purposes.

3. As the project moves into the executing process, you should actively monitor the risk events in the risk register and activate the risk mitigation strategies selected for the different project risk events that actually occur. This includes weekly risk register reviews, driving the mitigation strategies selected, and ensuring the team focuses on the high-level risk events.

4. Ensure you drive this risk mitigation process and risk strategy throughout the life of the project. Once the project reaches close out, and all risk events are resolved, store the final risk register into the document control system for the final time.

Mastering the Schedule Management Plan

Before you can master the schedule management plan tool, you must understand how this tool can assist and support you on your project. The following project scenario emphasizes the importance of the tool.

A large software company has just announced the creation of a new operating system that they feel is going to change the future of computing. The whole company is abuzz about what this new operating system can do, and news about it is sending the stock price through the roof. Management selects you as the project manager, and you get started immediately. As you develop the master schedule for the project, you quickly observe that there will be at least 25 different project schedules involved in the creation of the new operating system, and each will require its own separate project schedule and timeframes to complete their portion of the project. This is a massive effort and one where you will be spending a lot of time controlling project schedule changes and working closely with each group on what has changed and why. As the project gets underway you become concerned. The project leaders in each of the areas of your project are changing their schedules on an hourly basis and are not informing you they are doing it. They are trying to sneak changes in without you knowing. To ensure that everyone stays coordinated, your master project schedule requires continual updates based on the changes that the team leads are making. You have specifically asked each group to notify you when changes occur so you will know exactly what to change on the master schedule to keep all the schedules coordinated. Clearly, because the different group leads are changing their project schedules on a whim and not considering the downstream impacts of those changes, you may never get the master schedule coordinated with the other schedules; it may be a losing battle. Your management starts asking you how the project is coming and what is the latest status? Other questions they are asking include:

How are you controlling the project schedule changes?

Who is responsible for making project schedule changes in each of the areas?

What constraints and assumptions is the project schedule under?

How are you integrating all the group schedules and does one impact the others when they make a change.

To obtain the answers to these questions, you should use a schedule management plan. The schedule management plan documents the processes and procedures for making project schedule changes. The schedule management plan contains the process details to create the project schedule, the responsibilities of who updates and owns the plan, and the parameters and constraints on the schedule.

The schedule management plan is not one of the most widely used project communication tools, but provides tremendous value when it is used, and is a mechanism that will track and control project schedule changes like no other.

CROSS-REF We recommend that you review the schedule management plan's planning questions in Chapter 6.

Creating a schedule management plan

A schedule management plan is an important tool, regardless of who is updating the actual project schedule. It represents a sense of project schedule control and management that many projects never achieve. It also adds rigor and control to the project schedule, eliminating unnecessary changes and ensuring that agreed upon dates are maintained, and team members are working toward making those dates for the project.

Project managers often do not create a schedule management plan for their projects, mostly because they are solely responsible for making changes to the schedule and question why they should add an extra level of process that they do not consider necessary. That is a huge misconception, because although the actual updating of the schedule is important, it is not the only aspect of the document. The schedule management plan consists of who is responsible for creating the schedule, specific reporting requirements for the project, any schedule parameters, and assumptions and constraints on the schedule worth noting. Each section of the schedule management plan is important and can play a factor as to whether your project needs a schedule management plan or not. For example, the schedule reporting section is an important aspect of the project schedule management plan document because it notifies when the project manager will report on the project schedule during the course of the project. If the customer is asking when the project schedule is reported, timeframes, and how often, the project manager can point them to the schedule reporting section for all the details. If the customer wants changes or updates, they can go directly to the section and work with the project manager to update appropriately.

A project customer will not utilize the schedule management plan as part of the regular project process, but may want to review it more from an understanding of what and how the schedule changes occur.

The actual steps of creating a schedule management plan vary. Use the template we provided to create a schedule management plan for your project. The template is located on the CD-ROM for use if your company does not already have one. The table of contents provides the major sections of the document and will be handy when the document is completed and you are looking for particular information in the document.

Example of a Schedule Management Plan Table of Contents

Section 1: Schedule Management Plan Overview

Define how you are going to create, maintain and close out the schedule on your project. The schedule management plan should include detailed documentation on all the elements of how the schedule was developed. This process must incorporate report generation and include a baseline schedule for reporting project performance. A statement should define when various updates to the plan should occur. This involves controlling the schedule as well as the resources assigned to each activity. Identify what level of detail you will go down to, and how often you will update and report the project schedule.

Section 2: Schedule Management Responsibilities

Identify the resources required to manage the schedule and document who will be responsible for planning and creating the baseline, and updating, maintaining and closing out the project schedule. This section of the schedule management plan should identify who will generate the performance reports for each reporting cycle and also identify the person responsible for data entry and the scheduling tools.

continued

continued

Section 3: Schedule Baseline

Describe the details and approach to creating a schedule baseline for your project.

Section 4: Schedule Parameters

The schedule management plan should include any constraints, assumptions, and schedule limitations on the project.

Section 5: Schedule Change Control

There will always be changes to a project plan, therefore there must be change control procedures documented in the schedule management plan to control various changes. The document should include details on how, when, and why the schedule was modified and the process for approval for those changes. Describe how the baseline schedule will change when a change request affect the schedule.

Section 6: Schedule Reports

Determine what reports you will create for your project and how often they will be used.

ON the CD-ROM   We have included a sample schedule management plan tool in the Communication tools Time subfolder. Use this as a guide to help you create your own version of this tool.

Using a schedule management plan

Before using a schedule management plan, you must identify who on your project team will utilize this tool so that you can determine the level of detail required, frequency of distribution, style, and format of the report.

Review the schedule management plan's planning section in Chapter 6; then follow these steps:

1.   As the project moves into the planning process, you must obtain sign-off and approval from your team members and customer on the schedule management plan. This sign-off confirms that they agree with how you will manage the project's schedule.

2.   Distribute the schedule management plan along with the user acceptance document to your customer and team members for their approval. After receiving the various approvals, store both documents in the document control system for long-term storage, archiving, and retrieval purposes.

3. Once you receive the approvals, and as the project moves into the executing process, you must enforce the use of the schedule management plan on your project. This includes ensuring you are effectively managing and controlling the project schedule. This includes creating and managing a schedule baseline, driving and working with any schedule parameters, setting up and establishing a schedule change control process, and schedule reporting based on the schedule outline in the plan. The project manager carries out the schedule management process throughout the life of the project.

Summary

The tools we described in this chapter are the best choices for managing and administering your project in the project's planning process. Without proper administration of your project, you will quickly lose control and not accomplish the desired goals and objectives the customers are expecting.

Project managers and team members must understand how important the administration of a project is to ensure successful completion. The development and maintenance of the communication tools covered in this chapter may seem time consuming, but the value you will receive from utilizing them is priceless. For example, without a change control plan and procedures document in place, a simple change request could send team members scrambling and completely derail the project, yet that one tool could prevent this from occurring. Other tools such as the risk register, comprehensive test plan, and the critical chain tool are all valuable to your project in the planning and executing process.

Use of the reporting communications tools outlined in this chapter will benefit the project manager, customers, and project team members. The reports are simple, easy to create, and informative in presenting information to the various parties.

Chapter 17

Using Communication Tools in the Planning Process for Reporting

I n this chapter, we explore project communication tools in the project's planning process. The tools focus specifically on the reporting and communicating to the customer, team members, and upper management staff on the project's planning.

There are many different tools in this chapter. Some of the tools create the information that drives the deliverables of the project, such as the baseline schedule and the logic network diagram, where other tools are purely for reporting purposes, such as the project milestone list and scatter charts. Here is an excellent mix of tools that should help the project manager become a truly effective communicator during the planning process.

Mastering the Baseline Schedule Tool

Before you can master the baseline schedule tool, you must understand how this tool can assist and support you on your project. The following project scenario emphasizes the importance of the tool.

Your company is working on a prestigious subcontract for the Burj Dubai (BD) in Dubai, United Arab Emirates. The Burj Dubai is the tallest building in the world. Your company has about 25 percent of the job complete, and it is on time and within budget. The BD project manager has scheduled a meeting with your company to acquire an update on your progress. He is asking you for a comparison report between the original planned finish dates and the actual finished dates for the activities your company has completed or is working on. He also wants to see a performance chart to evaluate your progress against what you had planned to accomplish. You are showing the BD project manager the schedule and explaining that at this time your team is two days ahead of schedule. He understands, but patiently repeats his request for a variance report on the project's finish dates. The BD project manager stands up, says that producing variance reports are in the contract, and wants the two different variance reports (cost and schedule) on his desk first thing in the morning. You inform him that the task normally takes three days and therefore it may not be possible. You unfortunately did not create a baseline schedule when you originally started the project because you simply never thought you would need it. You neglected to read the part of the contract that defined the scheduling requirements. The current schedule has had five changes and creating a baseline schedule from it will be difficult. You have many questions that you are asking yourself, such as:

> How can you go back in time, recreate the original schedule without compromising the current schedule, and have the requested reports ready by morning?
>
> Is there a schedule saved that does not have progress on it?
>
> Is that schedule accurate? How will we know if it is accurate?

To obtain the answers to these questions, you should have used a baseline schedule tool. However, the answers to this scenario are twofold. You must first recreate the original schedule by removing any progress and the changes that are in the current schedule. Then by using the original schedule, you can create a baseline schedule. Once created, the cost and schedule variance reports will be relatively easy to produce using any automated scheduling tool.

CROSS-REF   We recommend that you review the baseline schedule's document planning questions in Chapter 6.

Creating a baseline schedule

Creating a baseline schedule is a best-practice technique for all projects. Even if you do not plan on using one, it is so simple you should create one anyway, just in case you need it. More than likely there will be several occasions on the project where the project manager will use a baseline schedule, so having it will be beneficial. Some examples include reviewing date and cost variances, analyzing schedule and cost performance indexes, monitoring estimates at completion, and reporting on remaining estimate to complete. Any of these scenarios would not be possible without creating the baseline schedule.

Project managers should create a baseline schedule for the project as soon as possible after the approval of the original schedule. This establishes the baseline. Every time there is an approved change request, the project manager should update the baseline to keep it in sync with the current schedule. Otherwise, there will be a false variance between the current schedule and the baseline schedule.

A project customer quickly learns how beneficial the baseline schedule is when they can see the project's performance information. The customer can compare the current budget and the baseline budget, current schedule to the baseline schedule, and so on. When the project manager creates a baseline schedule, many performance reports are available.

The actual steps in creating a baseline schedule are straightforward; however, it does depend heavily on the project-scheduling tool the project manager uses. The steps in creating a baseline schedule depend entirely on the scheduling system you are using, because each product will have a slightly different process for creating a baseline. To create a baseline for your project, follow the instructions of your project management software system.

 Ensure there is no progress reported on any tasks when creating a baseline schedule.

Using a baseline schedule

Prior to using a baseline schedule, you must identify who on your project team will utilize this tool so that you can determine the level of detail required, frequency of distribution, style, and format of the report. Review the baseline schedule planning section in Chapter 6 and then follow these steps:

1. The project manager when using a baseline schedule reviews the baseline dates and compares those dates to the current dates of the project. This is actually done quite easily using a scheduling tool and referring to the graphical time line portion of the tool, or through a series of reports. In any case, the project manager in this step is reviewing, analyzing and determining where the project currently stands, and comparing those dates to where it was suppose to be. The project manager would then report and act upon those variances accordingly.

2. The next step in this process is for the project manager to review the project's current costs to the baseline costs and report that information to the customer and upper management. Complete this through a series of reports internally in the Project-Scheduling tool.

3. The project manager would then review the labor hours from the current project to the baseline labor hours and report on those variances accordingly. Complete this through a series of reports internally in the Project-Scheduling tool.

4. The last step in using a baseline schedule is for the project manager, after completing the variance analysis work, to report the total project variance to the customer and upper management. Depending on the impacts and the different variances, the customer may have the project manager make course corrections to the project.

Mastering the Cost Estimate Report

Before you can work with a cost estimate report, you must understand how this tool can assist and support you on your project. The following project scenario emphasizes the importance of this tool. A large marketing firm has decided to replace their sales information system with an in-house developed application. The existing system has about six months left before it starts to fail continually and become unusable. The company is under pressure to ensure the new system is up and running within the six-month period, including a period of transition from old to new system. You are the project manager, and upper management has given you unlimited funding; however, they still expect you to continue to monitor and control the budget closely, just as you would for any other project. As you start into the project, the first area you start to look into is what systems and what other areas of the company are impacted by this existing application. Who uses the system today? In your research, you find that there are at least five different applications that are connected to the existing sales system. Each of these systems needs to be retired or somehow reconnected to a new sales system. You know that this is going to be a challenging project because of all the interdependencies, and you are expecting this to be quite costly. You then start to work with each group that is using the sales system currently and collect their costs to reconnect their system to the new system. You ask for each of the groups to e-mail you their initial cost estimates. As the estimates come in, you can see immediately you have a major problem. One area of the company sends the estimate in hours, the next sends it in dollars, another area sends it in man-weeks or man-months, and the last group refuses to send it at all. You have no idea what the project is going to cost and management is now asking for an up to date total cost estimate. You have a problem and you need help resolving it. You have all sorts of questions yourself that you need to address immediately. These questions include:

How are you going to get these estimates in one standard format?

How are you going to get everyone talking, communicating the same so you can easily compile and get the total back to management?

What billing rate is each of the groups using to calculate their costs?

What level of effort is it for each group? What are man-weeks?

To obtain the answers to these questions, the project manager should use a cost estimate report. The cost estimate report is a standard spreadsheet set up to consolidate information into an easy-to-read format that automatically calculates the estimates of a project. Most companies have specific versions of the cost estimate spreadsheet available to projects, and in some cases, project managers themselves have versions they like to use on every project. In this scenario, the project manager could have used a cost estimate spreadsheet to collect the estimates from the different groups, and if everyone were using the same tool correctly, the project manager would not have had any problems getting the information in the same and consistent format.

CROSS-REF We recommend that you review the cost estimate report's planning questions in Chapter 6.

Creating a cost estimate report

Creating a cost estimate report for a project is an important aspect of the budget/cost management process. Every project has costs associated with it and providing management an estimate of those costs before starting the project will let them choose whether to continue the project or shut it down immediately. When completing a cost estimate report, remember that these are estimates only and most companies will have a tolerance level for these estimates. Tolerance levels are percentage points that the project can be over or under and still be acceptable. For example, after the project finishes the product design phase, the project team should be able to give a +- 25 percent estimate of project costs. That means the team is expecting to be +25 percent over the total or -25 percent below the total. The below estimate rarely occurs, but the upper limit provides a hard boundary for the project team to strive to achieve. This also allows the project team some flexibility in their estimates and does not hold the team down to the dollar, which is impossible to do on most projects. Rarely, can a project team estimate exactly the costs of any project during the budgeting phase. Because the estimating process is normally done too early in the life cycle, and there are not enough details of the project, using a variance approach provides the teams with an ability to come close to providing the true costs of the project within a specific range.

 **A single point estimate is never exactly accurate. It is better to report a range between which the estimate will most likely fall.**

Project managers should be active in the development of the cost estimate report for many reasons. The first and most important reason is that the project manager is normally responsible for putting together the total budget for the project; and, therefore, must be involved in how the dollars are derived for the task. When working to compile the estimate, the project manager can work closely with each group, ask questions to have each group justify their costs, and ensure that the dollars are as close to reality as possible. If the groups realize that they are accountable to a single person when providing those numbers, it becomes harder for them to throw random numbers at a project without justifying them.

Another important aspect of compiling a cost estimate report is so that the project manager can understand the expected size and number of groups in the project. Even if the project manager does not understand all the details that each of the different groups has to do, when the cost estimate report indicates that there are a large number of systems involved, the project manager can start his/her planning process in dealing with a large project. If the cost estimate report shows just a couple of systems involved, then the planning efforts should adjust them accordingly.

The actual steps of creating a cost estimate report can vary. Use the template we provided to create a cost estimate report for your project. The template is located on the CD-ROM for use if your company does not have one.

Table 17.1 is a typical cost estimate report for a software project. This table shows the possible impacted systems down the left side, and the Size/Scope/Complexity across the rows.

TABLE 17.1

Cost Estimate Report

Project Name	Complexity Breakdown					Date:
Project Name: **ABC Software** **Development Project**	Size/Scope/ Complexity					**Earliest Possible** **Start Date**
	Very Low	Low	Medium	High	Very High	
System A	$	$	$	$	$	99/99/99
System B	$	$	$	$	$	99/99/99
Project Team (Resources)	$	$	$	$	$	99/99/99
Project Hardware and Ongoing Maintenance	$	$	$	$	$	99/99/99
Bundling Systems	$	$	$	$	$	$

1. The first thing you have to do when creating the cost estimate report is to obtain a blank template from the CD-ROM or use the company's template that is applicable for your project.

2. After creating the template and revising it so that it is specific for your project, you will work with the various impacted systems groups and describe the project to them. The goal to having these conversations is to ensure that the systems groups understand what the project is about and acknowledge if they are impacted by it. You will set up meetings, share requirements documents, and provide whatever information you can to bring all the groups up to speed to determine if they are impacted; and if so, allow them to determine those impacts by asking questions and getting answers. After the teams have the understanding of what the project is all about, you must wait until the impacted systems groups review the project information and send their impacts back to you for consolidation into the cost estimate report.

3. The impacted systems groups then enter their size and complexity into their version of the cost estimate report, to calculate the estimated cost for that application's effort. You will notice in the spreadsheet that there is a Size/Scope/Complexity area where each system can determine how complex their portion of the project is. Examples of the complexity will be very low, low, to very high for each application. After completing this information for the project, each impacted system will send the information to you for consolidation into the final spreadsheet. The different application leaders should also complete the section in the spreadsheet that says "earliest possible start dates" for their systems. This allows you to create an initial high-level project schedule from all the impacted systems and be able to tell immediately if that is going to be a problem for the project's end date.

620

4. After obtaining the impacts, you compile the information into the cost estimate spreadsheet. Once completed, the spreadsheet creates a cost estimate report automatically. Th consolidating of the cost estimates from the different groups is an important step for y to complete because it provides you with the knowledge and understanding of the le of effort from each of the groups involved. If a particular group comes back with a l effort, low complexity, then it is likely that group is not going to require a great deal time or effort paid to them on this project. Whereas high complexity, high effort gr may require an additional level of effort for you to work with them on the project.

5. Once completed, you provide this estimate to the customer and upper manageme their approval and directions on the next steps for the project.

 We have included a sample Cost Estimate Report tool in the Communication T subfolder. Use this as a guide to create your own version of this tool.

Using a cost estimate report

Before you can use a cost estimate report, you must identify who on your project team this tool so that you can determine the level of detail required, frequency of distributi format of the report.

Review the cost estimate report planning section in Chapter 6; then follow these ste

1. As the project moves into the planning processes, the first step you shoul ent the cost estimate report to the customer and upper management for ceeding with the project. This process can vary greatly from company to even from department to department. You must be aware of how to pre accordingly.

2. You then present the information to the customer formally. After doin wait to answers questions and for the go/no-go decision from the cus have reviewed and analyzed the data. Since the project is just movin process at this time, if the customer wanted to stop the project, it w impact to the company overall. The project customer and upper m decision to proceed or shutdown the project.

3. Depending on the results of the go/no-go decision, the project eit ately or shuts down and follows a modified version of the closeo responsible for managing and controlling both processes to their

Mastering the Decision Tree Di

Before you can master a decision tree diagram, you must understand h support you on your project. The following project scenario emphasiz

A large steel company has decided to expand its operations and is cu mercial real estate. The company has been doing extremely well for decided to expand its main office to be able to take on more busines

largest steel company west of the Mississippi River. Selecting additional real estate and
ompany's location is a large project for any company, and management has selected
lead in this effort. You begin by looking at the real estate ads in the local news-
l an existing building, you can move the existing operations into the new building,
complete. After a couple weeks of searching there is nothing that even comes
re looking for and now you are thinking this project is going to be harder than
ide to look at another option — building. This is a business decision. Building
ould mean that you are expanding your existing location to accommodate
machines. Buying means finding an existing plant where your existing
mediately and still have enough room to add additional machines and
mplex and one that you cannot make alone. You have a series of ques-
t that you need to know the answers to immediately. Your questions

f decision for the company?

ve?

s, the project manager can use a decision tree diagram. A
of questions to help you generate responses, and in the
ct. In working the diagram, you actually generate various
questions. The decision tree diagram is an excellent
ument exactly why the team has made the selection

decision tree's planning questions in Chapter 12.

often as they should because of the per-
e decision tree diagram is a challenging tool
it becomes one of the favorites of most
produce a decision tree are complex;
etter understanding of the complete
does not really help with an under-
ice for the more difficult problems.

e tool because of the value and
manager working with the cus-
ed with the public at the time
ct manager in an excellent
age it more effectively by
standing exactly when and why
brace the use of a decision tree tool on

e
ou
rel
w
of
ups

nt for

ols, Cost

can utilize
on, style, and

ps:
d do is to pres-
approval on pro-
company and
sent it and adapt

g so, you would
omer after they
g into the planning
ould have little
anagement make the

er ramps up immedi-
t process. You would be
respective conclusions.

agram
w this tool can assist and
es the importance of the tool.

rently in the market for com-
many years and has finally
s. After the company expands,

621

their projects to help them think through the different decisions while making a major project decision. The information and questions asked of them in the creation process allows them to think about the advantages and disadvantages of the various selections on the decision tree.

The steps for creating a decision tree diagram can vary, but you can use the following steps to create a standard decision tree:

1. You work with the customer and define a business problem/issue you are trying to resolve. There must be two or more options in the tree. If the problem only has one decision, it is not suitable for the decision tree method. You then create the template or find a template from the CD-ROM and make it available for use.

2. You create the decision tree by calculating the branches and determining the probability of and the values of each branch. This sets up the foundation for the decision tree to be able to perform a backwards calculation to arrive at multiple values (one per branch) to make a decision. Do not use this one data point to make your final decision because it is only one piece of information to help that decision-making process.

3. You work with the customer to set a range for the values that you would expect from each branch. You would create a high and low range for each branch. There could be mid-values at the end of the branch that will merge into one. You will always have a minimum of two values, and in some cases, you could create many values at the end of a branch; for each end of the branch is a possible outcome of the decision-making process.

4. You calculate each branch by taking the estimated value and multiply it by the probability. The results of this calculation determine the value of that part of the branch. This is the normal calculation for expected monetary value used in the industry.

5. You complete these calculations for each branch. Total the sum of the branch to provide the answer for the next branch in the tree. Continue this same process on all branches. These calculations will eventually reduce the decision tree to the number of options that you have established in the beginning. If you set up two options, after completing all the calculations, the final two options will be available to determine the final decision. When setting up the decision tree, it is not limited to just two options, as in a (Buy/Build) scenario. A third option, for example, could have been lease. Therefore, the tree would look like the following: Buy, Build, Lease, giving the tree three major options and three major branches.

6. The decisions tree diagram is complete and ready for customer and management review.

ON the CD-ROM We have included a sample decision tree diagram tool in the Communication tools, Risk subfolder. This is a guide to the first step in creating your own personal version of this tool. Your company or project may have specific requirements that will enhance this communication tool further; however, we believe this is a great starting point for the creation of this tool for your project.

Using a decision tree diagram

Before you can use a decision tree diagram, you must identify who on your project team will utilize this tool so that you can determine the level of detail required, frequency of distribution, style, and format of the report. Review the decision tree diagram planning section in Chapter 12 and then follow these steps:

1. You should determine the business problem the team and the customer is trying to solve. This understanding is going to be fundamental to the success of determining the solutions to the problem.

2. Present the results of the decision tree process to your customers to make the official decision. Whoever is responsible will make the project decision during this step and you will adjust your project accordingly.

> **TIP**   The project manager should not rely solely on the decision tree diagram for making the final decisions on a problem. There is a lot of uncertainly to the decision tree diagram method; therefore, do not use the decision tree diagram method as the only tool in your decision-making process.

Mastering the Expected Monetary Value

Before mastering the expected monetary value tool, you must understand how this tool can assist and support you on your project. The following project scenario emphasizes the importance of the tool.

The project you are working on is trying to choose between two vendors. You must make a decision between the two. The two vendors that the stakeholders have narrowed the bidding competition to are close on their bids. JJ Blink's bid is $400,000 and GA Jake, LLC is at $380,000. Your team has done some research and found both vendors to be equally qualified; however, they found that both vendors do not always deliver on time. Five percent of the time, JJ Blink delivered 10 days late. GA Jake, LLC had a record of being late 25 percent of the time and by 60 days. You know for every day that there is a delay, your company will spend an extra $2,000 on operating costs. The team has chosen GA Jake because they are the low bidder, but you are questioning this decision and have a number of questions you need answered. These questions include:

What if GA Jake, LLC is 60 days late?

Would you like to find out exactly what is at stake here?

If the project takes the delay time into consideration, will it change the outcome?

How much money will you have to set aside if the vender is late?

To obtain the answers to these questions, the project manager should use the expected monetary value. The expected monetary value calculates a contingency value for the project's risk events in case of the event occurring. The expected monetary value can be used to obtain the value of the risk event(s) should they occur. By calculating the expected monetary value, the lowest bidder in the above scenario in the end turns out to be the most expensive.

> **CROSS-REF**   We recommend that you review the expected monetary value's planning questions in Chapter 12.

Creating an expected monetary value tool

In the process of creating the expected monetary value (EMV), you as the project manager can get a better understanding of the value of the project and you can learn more about percentages and probabilities for some of the project's risk events. It is easy to come up with the EMV, all you have to know is the value of a risk event if it did occur and the probability of it actually occurring. Normally you could estimate how much it would cost to replace a part of the project or how many days delay a risk event would cause. However, trying to determine the probability if the risk event would actually happen is more difficult. For example, say that a wire shorts out in one room in a new building you are constructing and starts a fire. The fire only consumes the room and part of the hallway. You estimate it will cost about $122,500 to repair the damage, but what were the odds (probability) of the wire starting a fire in that room at all? When you are working with risks and especially EMV you must be able to accurately estimate the probability of the risk event occurring. If you cannot, someone else can — such as your insurance company. The probability of a wire starting a fire in a new building is less than 0.0001 of a percent. The point is it takes a lot more effort than just multiplying two numbers together. You must know what those two numbers represent in these calculations.

Many large construction projects use expected monetary value as standard procedures in the management and controlling of their project risks. The construction project managers have realized just how important and valuable this tool is to the project. The time and effort that the project manager and team members expend to produce the expected monetary value pays off greatly in the end. The communication aspects of this tool are remarkable and one that project teams and customer can utilize throughout the project.

Calculating the EMV formula provides the project with the dollar amount required for emergency purposes. Using this formula is a more accepted method than guessing and not knowing really what to apply.

The steps of creating an expected monetary value tool vary. The following steps can help you get started.

1. Before you can calculate an EMV, you have to work with the team members, perform a risk analysis, and identify the risk events of the project.

2. You should then identify the risk events that may happen on the project. The project team would then give each risk event a probability of occurring and the impact on the risk if it did occur.

3. Next, you would create a risk event matrix and identify the project's top risks. This will identify low, medium, and high risks.

4. Take the top risk events and calculate an EMV (contingency) for each risk event. You then select the top risk events using the risk matrix and calculate the EMV for the selected risk events. This identifies the highest risks on the project.

5. You then estimates the remaining contingency value required for the project. To do this, you may want to use Pareto's rule.

6. The next step is to add the values from Step 5 and Step 6 together to create the expected monetary value for the project. The EMV provides you with the amount of money required to cover any reasonable project risk events that could occur on the project.

7. The next step is to create a Contingency report and distribute it to the customer, team members, and upper management staff. You develop the report describing how he or she derived the total expected monetary value for the project.

> **TIP** Do some research and find out what the average contingency is for the type of project you are working on in your location. If there is a large difference between your contingency value and the average, you may want to re-evaluate how you derived yours. If your contingency is correct, then explain the difference in the report.

Using an expected monetary value

Before you can use the expected monetary value, you must identify who on your project team will utilize this tool so that you can determine the level of detail required, frequency of distribution, style, and format of the report. Review the expected monetary value planning section in Chapter 12 and then follow these steps:

1. Monitor and control the expected monetary value throughout the project. This will include understanding how much contingency is used, how much is remaining on the project, identify outstanding risks, and estimating the remaining contingency values. As the project executes, monitor the value of the risk events that are occurring and compare them with the estimated values you calculated and make corrections if necessary.

2. When risk events occur, you then estimate the cost of the risk event and apply it to the contingency money to cover the amount of the risk events. You continue this process throughout the project.

3. As the project closes, you evaluate the remaining funds in the contingency fund (if there is any) to move them into the project's main funding bucket for distribution. It is at this point that the project manager would initiate lessons learned process to track how the project managed the contingency funds against the associated risk events.

4. As the project finishes and closes out, you store all the expected monetary value estimates and associated documentation in the document control system for long-term storage, archiving, and retrieval purposes.

Mastering the Flow Chart

Before mastering a flow chart tool, you must understand how this tool can assist and support you on your project. The following project scenario emphasizes the importance of the tool.

A medium-sized window company has just won a major contract to supply the windows for a 45-floor high-rise apartment building in the center of Hong Kong, China. The company now has to hire up to 75 additional installers to take on this work. Because the company has won the contract, it is not a matter of if the company can hire the people, it is how fast they can bring them onboard and get them trained on this new contract. Management has hired you as the project manger to run just the staffing and hiring portion of the project. As you get into the hiring process, and as staff comes on board, one of the most complicated processes that you find is the number of different groups a person has to go through to become an employee at the company. Because you are a contractor and not an employee yourself, you are interested in learning the process as well. Here is the list that shows you what a person has to go through: HR paperwork, health care sign-up documents, company badge applications, immigration, and Social Security processing. At the end of all the paperwork, a new hire must sit through a half-day general orientation and company meeting. Your manager has just approached you and wants to get up to speed on the hiring process, and is planning to send 40 people through on Monday, so it is critical that the team members know exactly what to do. You have a number of questions that you need answered on the hiring process that you must find out before the people arrive to be hired. Those questions include:

How do your prevent 40 people from getting stuck in one area?

Will you have to walk each person through each step of the hiring process?

Are the various groups ready to take on the people?

How can you direct them to the next area?

What documentation is in place to get people from one area to another?

To obtain the answers to these questions, you should use a flow chart. A flow chart in this case will document the hiring processes and graphically show each new employee the steps they need to take to be hired. In this example, if the human resource department had set up a series of flow charts to help the 40 people through the hiring process it would allow the process to go much smoother. It could prevent the project manager from needing to be in many places at one time and provide the newly hired staff the directions and instructions they need to get through the hiring process.

CROSS-REF We recommend that you review the flow chart's planning questions in Chapter 8.

Creating a flow chart

Creating a flow chart is easy and used in a number of industries today to show a process or procedure. Quite often project teams overlook flow charts as being too simple or too basic providing no value to the project. Flow charts are not valued properly or recognized for how important they really are. Because flow charts are so basic and easy to learn, they become a powerful communication tool and the project manager may never realize it. Can you imagine how easy it would be to learn from the flow charts the current business processes, compared to learning from written instructions?

Project managers, customer, and team members must realize the value of teaching a business or project process by using flow charts. Many times, project teams review written business processes and still require the assistance of the customer to help them understand that information. If the customer develops that same business process information using flow charts, then the project team members will find it much easier and quicker to understand the processes.

The actual steps of creating a flow chart can vary. Use the template we provided to create a flow chart for your project. The template is located on the CD-ROM for use if your company does not already have one.

Figure 17.1 is a basic flow chart created in Microsoft Power Point. This example describes some of the definitions of each flow chart.

FIGURE 17.1

A flow chart that defines some of the common elements that make up a flow chart.

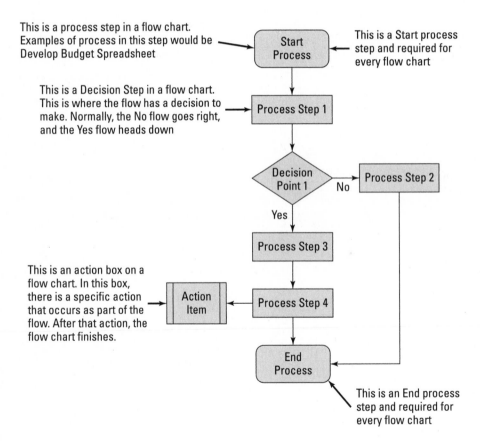

We have included a sample flow chart tool in the Communication tools, Quality sub-folder folder on the CD-ROM. This is a guide to the first step in creating your own personal version of this tool. Your company or project may have specific requirements that will enhance this communication tool further; however, we believe this is a great starting point for the creation of a flow chart for your project. The CD contains the flow chart from Chapter 8, the basic shapes and processes for documenting a process or procedure on a project. Use this basic flow chart as a starting point for the project.

Using a flow chart

Before you can use a flow chart, you must identify who on your project team will utilize this tool so that you can determine the level of detail required, frequency of distribution, style, and format of the report. Review the flow chart planning section in Chapter 8 and then follow these steps:

1. Ensure your customers and team members who will use the chart, understand it, and can follow the process. Since flow charts are great for teaching, you should have an easy time showing people how to read and understand this tool.

2. After you are comfortable your team understands the flow chart, you can continue to promote and drive its use on your project. Depending on the process outlined in the flow chart, you should be active in communicating it to your team members, customer, or upper management throughout the life of the project.

3. Store your project's flow charts in the document control system for long-term storage and archiving and retrieval purposes.

Mastering the Logic Network Diagram

Before you can master the logic network diagram tool, you must understand how this tool can assist and support you on your project. The following project scenario emphasizes the importance of the tool.

A large aerospace company has just announced the design of a new plane to be added to their commercial airplane division. This is an exciting announcement for the company and the aerospace industry — it is expected to become No. 1 in commercial airplane sales. The company is buzzing with excitement, and everyone is thrilled with the design of this new plane. As the most senior project manager in the company, upper management asks you to be the new program manager. As you start into the project, you understand that this is no easy task, and the first order of business you must complete is to determine the different groups involved in this effort and the order in which they are to perform their work efforts. Once you realize the various groups you have to work with, you can start to gather the list of tasks each group is required to perform to design and build the airplane. For a large commercial airplane, you realize that this is going to be an enormous list and the dependencies between the various groups are going to be complex. Each of the groups promptly reply to your request of their tasks, and you end up with thousands of tasks and no idea how they are all going work together, let alone how they will fit together to build a plane. The number of tasks you receive overwhelms you quickly and you have no idea where to start. You have a number of questions on where to go and where to start. These questions include the following:

What are you going to do?

Where do you start?

Is there a starting point anywhere among all these tasks?

What are the predecessors of these tasks?

What are the successors?

How much of a staff will be needed?

To obtain the answers to these questions, you should use a logic network diagram. The logic network diagram's purpose is to sequence and logically order all the tasks on a project. It is an easy-to-use tool and graphically shows the logic of each project activity. In a complex scenario such as building an airplane, using a logic network diagram makes perfect sense and allows the project team to group and move tasks around to get them in the correct order. When you begin a project, the ability to see the logical dependencies among project activities is priceless. The logic network diagram tool is one of the only tools that enable you to do this.

CROSS-REF We recommend that you review the logic network diagram's planning questions in Chapter 6.

Creating a logic network diagram

Creating a logic network diagram at the beginning of a project provides a number of benefits that many project managers today may not fully appreciate. It provides or displays visually the project's logical sequence of events. By doing so, it generates the various relationships needed and outlines where the main contact points are for each area. It easily displays activity convergence. This is where many activities converge into a single activity of milestone. These convergent activities tend to be at a higher risk. Anyone generating the diagram can update the tasks sequence using the tool. This sequencing is strictly a project-specific discipline and anyone involved in the project can review, update, and in some cases delete the sequencing if necessary.

 Project managers should be diligent and active when sequencing tasks during the creating of the logic network diagram. It is important to ensure communications and the relationship between the dependent groups continues to grow. It is important, as a project manager, to encourage the various groups discussing the order of the tasks and the dependencies.

Project owner/customer may be active in the creation and understanding of the logic network diagram for the project. The diagram allows them to understand in what order each task is drawn and where they are involved in the project. Often, due to constraints of other project considerations, the customer may need to reorder tasks where they see a conflict; the logic network diagram will show the impacts of that reordering to the project.

The actual steps of creating a logic network diagram can vary. The following steps can help you get started.

1. Open the Project-Scheduling tool.

2. Enter the tasks for project. For the purposes of this example, create activities called Test 1 to Test 20, on your project schedule.

3. Select Views ⇨ Network Diagram from the drop-down menu. This is a built in view to the tool (MS Project); and, therefore, once selecting that view, the tool auto generates the project's Logic Network Diagram tool.

4. Connect/link the activities with predecessors and successors.

5. After working with the various groups involved with the project, and some of the team members, the project's logic network diagram is complete.

Figure 17.2 shows a logic network diagram using a Project-Scheduling tool. This is a simple example but is created automatically by the scheduling tool.

FIGURE 17.2
_____

A logic network diagram.

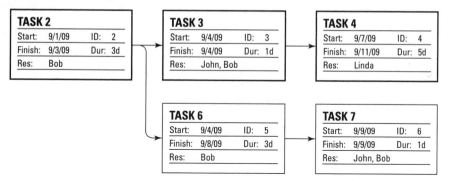

ON the CD-ROM We have included a sample Logic Network Diagram tool in the Communication tools Time subfolder. Use this as a guide to help you create your own version of this tool.

Using a logic network diagram

Prior to using a tool such as a logic network diagram, you must identify who on your project team will utilize this tool so that you can determine the level of detail required, frequency of distribution, style, and format of the report. Review the logic network diagram planning section in Chapter 6 and then follow these steps:

1. As your project moves out of the initiation process and into the planning process, you must ensure your team members and customer signed off and approve the logic network diagram. Since the diagram is so important to the logical order of the work activities, it is important that they sign off and approve the logic network diagram before work actually begins. Send the logic network diagram document along with the user acceptance document to your customer and team members for their sign-off and approval.

2. After obtaining approval and sign-off from both groups, you should then store the documents in the document control system for long-term storage, archiving, and retrieval purposes.

3. As the project moves into the executing process, enforce the use of the logic network diagram on the project. As your project team members are organizing the project's layout, they will utilize this diagram to help them with this planning process. You should communicate the use of the tool externally as well, so if there are external groups that have critical pieces on the project they should be aware of the logic network diagram as well.

4. One of the advantages you have in using the logic network diagram is to display the order in which your team will complete the project's tasks, and it allows you to create a straw man on generating a project schedule. In this process, you first create task boxes in the tool and add project tasks into their own box. Then using the tool, work with your team members and arrange the task boxes in logical order. Once complete, you are able to create a master project schedule based on the logic and order within the diagram. This process is easier to complete in the logic network diagram then it would be in a Project-Scheduling tool.

5. Continue this process until the project close out process where you finally store the final version of the logic network diagram in the document control system for long-term archiving and retrieval purposes.

Mastering the Project Milestone List

Before you master the project milestone list, you must understand how this tool can assist and support you on your project. The following project scenario emphasizes the importance of the tool.

A small drug research company has just landed the approval from the Food and Drug Administration (FDA) to produce a new cancer drug. The company expects this drug will reduce cancer in men between the ages of 45 to 65 and drop the number of new occurrences every year. This cancer drug has the potential of saving thousands of lives a year. The company is excited about the drug and feels that if it is a success, it can be profitable for many years. As the most senior member of the management team, you have volunteered and taken on the responsibilities for the communications between your company and the FDA to ensure everything goes smoothly. As you start into the project, it becomes apparent that the relationship between your company and the FDA is critical and more challenging than you expected. As the project kicks off and as the drug discovery phase begins, you start to document a number of questions for the FDA that need addressing immediately or else the project's time lines could be in jeopardy. Those questions include:

What does the FDA want to see with the drug?

When do they want to see it?

What approvals are required at each stage?

What are the various stages within their release cycle?

To obtain the answers to these questions, you should use a project milestone list. One of most popular methods of reporting the various milestones of any project is the project milestone list. The project milestone list displays high-level stages of a project and associated time lines. In this scenario, one of the most important questions your company has for the FDA is on their release process and the various milestones they have in testing and releasing a drug to market.

CROSS-REF We recommend that you review the project milestone list's planning questions in Chapter 6.

Creating a project milestone list

Every project has a methodology that guides its execution. In every methodology, there are major phases or activities that represent major events (milestones) of the project. Those milestones are points in time, when the project and its team members can pause, perform a self-check, and ensure that everything is still on course. Project managers must communicate the project milestone list early in the project to obtain buy-in and support from the customer. The project milestone list provides a road map of how the project proceeds through its lifecycle and gives senior management and customers the ability to verify at each milestone checkpoint and ensure that the project is on track. If not, the project may be given the top priority to get back on track, or in some cases, a decision is made to cancel the project.

Project customers and owners are fond of project milestone lists because they provide a list of key events on the project, giving them a roadmap into the future of how the project should deliver. The events include the phase name, start, and end dates. Once the customer has the information, it allows them to hold the project team accountable for making these milestone dates. Without a project milestone list, the customer would have no idea when various part of the project will deliver. After the customer approves the dates on the project milestone list, they generally remain for the remainder of the project. If there are changes, process them through the change request process. Once locked, the customer can then plan around those dates and make over all business decisions with that information.

The steps for creating a project milestone list can vary. Use the following steps can help you get started.

1. Determine the major milestones of your project's methodology to be able to tell what are going to be used on your milestone list. This process will vary from project to project and industry to industry.

2. Once determining the steps in your development methodology, create your project's milestone list from one of the available templates or in a tool of their choice. Using a template is the smarter choice because it saves time and provides a starting point.

3. Once the template and the specific milestones are complete in the tool, then work with your team members and your customer to define the actual delivery dates for each phase. This will allow your team members to engage in the process and determine when specific events will complete.

4. After filling in the events and the dates, the project milestone list is complete and ready for you to include it in your project reporting.

ON the CD-ROM We have included two samples of the project milestone list in the Communication tools, Time subfolder. Use this as a guide to help you create your own version of this tool.

Using a project milestone list

Before using a project milestone list, you must identify who on your project team will utilize this tool so that you can determine the level of detail required, frequency of distribution, style, and format of the report. Review the project milestone list planning section in Chapter 6 and then follow these steps:

1. Ensure that your team members and customers have signed off and approved the project milestone list for the project. Since this list is displaying the project timeframes and the major milestones, it is important that everyone signs off and approves it before work begins. Send the project milestone list along with the user acceptance document to your customers and team members for anyone who has not yet provided their sign-off and approval.

2. After receiving approval and sign-off from both parties, store the document in the document control system for long-term storage, archiving, and retrieval purposes.

3. After receiving approval on the project milestone list, you will then use the project milestone list within all your major project communication channels. This includes weekly status reports, project Web sites, newsletters, and any external communications. Since this is graphical in nature, it lends itself to being valuable in project presentations, newsletters, and Web sites. A very common usage of this tool is in the project meetings where you can present it to your customers as a graphical time line of the project. You will use the project milestone list quite heavily throughout the life of our project.

CAUTION Do not use this tool specifically to drive the project team members as they have the master schedule, but more of an ongoing communication tool for the project manager, customer, and upper management.

Mastering the Project Schedule

Before you can master the project schedule tool, you must understand how this tool can assist and support you on your project. The following project scenario emphasizes the importance of the tool.

A large software company has taken on the development and implementation of a large payroll system. The present off-the-shelf system is not keeping up with the current needs or demands of the employees. After searching through the existing software packages on the market, the company used a decision tree diagram and ended up rejecting the decision to buy. They have decided to develop the next version of the software in-house. As the company's most senior project manager, you are excited to get started and under way. You feel the project will be challenging, with many different groups in the company involved. As you start the project, one of your first tasks is to gather work activities from each department and any dependencies they may have. As you work with each of the groups, and start to document and capture this information, you quickly become overwhelmed. Capturing and recording this information on paper and then trying to determine the different dependencies between all the activities are almost impossible for one person. You realize that there is no way to capture all this information and understand how to link it together without some help. As you ponder what to do next, upper management is starting to ask questions. The questions they are asking are as follows:

What tasks are required to complete this project?

What tasks are related?

Who is working on what task?

Are there any dependencies between any groups?

What date does the project expect to finish?

What are the costs associated to the design phase of the project?

To obtain the answers to these questions, the project manager should use a project schedule. A project schedule allows for the mapping of all the project activities into a single plan and establishes both timeframes and resources for each activity. On most projects, the project manager loads costs into the schedule associated to each activity. When costs, resources, and timeframes are contained in the project schedule, the project schedule becomes valuable to the project manager and their customer. Very few projects can go forward without using a project schedule.

CROSS-REF We recommend that you review the project schedule's planning questions in Chapter 6.

Creating a project schedule

A project schedule is one of the most popular tools in a project manager's toolbox. The creation of a project schedule can be quite complex, especially when you resource load — cost load, determining durations, and adding dependencies between the different activities. Figuring out the dependencies between the tasks can be challenging and a very time-consuming aspect of schedule management. The maintaining and monitoring of the project schedule becomes a major responsibility of the project manager (in most cases) and occurs throughout the life of the project. Whether or not the project manager is physically updating the project schedule, it is the project manager's responsibility to ensure that the schedule is complete and up to date at all times. On large projects, many project schedulers may be assigned to a project. They update the project schedule to keep it current at all times. The project manager works with the different project schedulers directly to ensure the plan is accurate.

Project managers should utilize the power of the project schedule and use the information it provides for providing status and updates about the project. Many project managers tend to use the

635

project schedule as a task list only, which really provides limited value to the customers and to themselves. The project schedule is a lot more than a simple task list.

> **TIP** If you are going to create a project schedule, create it properly and load the resources, costs, and add dependencies. In doing so, it provides a nice picture of the exact status of the project.

The project customer is involved in creating and using the project schedule, and will often scrutinize the contents of the plan to ensure that they are getting what they need from it. If project managers decide that the project schedule is nothing more than a task list, then they may have a difficult time answering questions from the customers who are demanding more information.

The steps for creating a project schedule tool vary. Use the following steps to help you get started:

1. Open the Project-Scheduling tool and create your project activities. A best practice in naming the activity descriptions (not the summary activities, but work package bottom level) is ensuring they each have a verb and noun. This is important to ensure that all bottom level activities on a project have in their name, that verb and noun combination so readers reviewing the schedule will understand exactly the description and information about the particular activities. For example an activity with the name of cover photo could mean a million different activities or tasks to a photographer. Using a name like *Arrange Cover Photo for Final Take* for the activity makes sense and provides a descriptive that will allow anyone reviewing the schedule more information on the task.

2. Working with your team members, estimate the duration of the activity. This is a critical task because estimating durations is a difficult process and one almost everyone struggles with for his/her project. Estimating durations is a process to which the team members who are required to complete the work provide their best expertise as to how long the task will actually take them. You need to guide your team in this estimation process with each activity requiring at least a best guess durations entered at this point.

3. Identify the predecessors and successors (logical relationships). This is a challenging process and requires careful consideration when establishing links among the tasks on your project. Once the project schedule has established links between activities, it is important to remember that any changes to any of the dates will adjust the other dates accordingly. Establishing the predecessors and successors requires you and your project team to be involved in this linking process and understand how important these dependencies really are.

4. At this point, your project has a project schedule. It would be a basic project schedule at best, but it would offer at least a starting point. Take this starting point schedule and work with your team members to ensure that they captured the tasks and assignments correctly, and if there are any dependencies between the tasks that are incorrect. If so, correcting those links immediately should be your top priority. This is a good time to review the linking between all the areas of the project created in Step 3.

5. Update and maintain the schedule as the project progresses. Ongoing project updates and maintenance will be one of your regular activities and one where your project team will need to be actively involved throughout the process. Your team members must keep you aware of their task status; and when they finish actual work tasks, they notify you and you then update the project schedule. This may be done on a weekly basis.

> **NOTE** The following steps are optional, but highly recommended for every project schedule. The two steps (resource and cost loading) are important when it comes to utilizing the full benefits of the Project-Scheduling tool.

6. Assign people and materials/equipment resources to the project activities (resource loaded). Resource loading can be complex but important because it ensures that someone is directly responsible for each individual activity on the project schedule. Resource loading is also important when it comes to workload management and determining how many activities an individual project team member can work on and still be successful.

7. Apply costs to project activities (cost loaded). Cost loading schedules is also a difficult task, but once completed, pays off tremendously for the project. The ability to determine exactly what individual activities will cost and what the overall project is going to cost is beneficial for the planning and executing of the project. Cost loading involves loading resource costs and other costs into the schedule. When assigning resources onto a task, those associated costs apply directly to the task itself. The difficult nature of associating costs to an activity is determining the activity hours, the rate for the various skill sets, the costs for materials per task, and finally costs for the equipment used on that task, onto every task on the schedule. For a hundred or two hundred line schedule, this is a time-consuming process. For 1,000 or more activities it takes a team of schedulers. Equipment costs are also difficult to estimate when applied across the project schedule activities. Project schedulers must spread the larger equipment costs (such as a crane on a construction project) across all the activities involving the crane. This can be challenging because the costs and the actual work may not spread easily among the activities. To simplify this, construction projects create a single activity called crane, and apply all the tasks and timeframes to that single activity. This allows the relationship of one activity to one cost unit to remain intact.

> **ON the CD-ROM** We have included a sample project schedule in the Communication tools Time sub-folder. Use this as a guide to help you create your own version of this tool.

Using a project schedule

Before you can use a project schedule, you must identify who on your project team will use this tool so that you can determine the level of detail required, frequency of distribution, style, and format of the report. In this case, the project schedule can be used at the highest level, or include very low level detail. The choice of the type of detail will be up to the project manager to decide and how he/she is trying to display project information. Review the project schedule planning section in Chapter 6 and then follow these steps:

1. As the project progresses into the executing process, you must ensure that your project team and customers have approved and signed- off on the project schedule. This may require several meetings with the team members and customer to ensure everyone agrees, but you are ultimately responsible for ensuring everyone signs off on the document.

2. Once you receive approval and sign-off from both parties, then store those approvals in the document control system for long-term storage, archiving, and retrieval purposes.

3. Enforce the use of the project schedule on your project. Some project managers track and monitor the project daily using the project schedule, some weekly, and others will have their own specific timeframes to which they update the project schedules. You have to make a decision as to how often you want to report progress because there is no right or wrong way of handling the updating of the project schedule as long as you update it in time for the company's cutoff (normally weekly). It is best practice that the project manager goes no later than a week to update their project schedule.

4. As the project progresses into the executing process, you should enforce the use of the project schedule, from adding tasks, adding, and removing resources, changing dependencies, and adjusting costs. The project schedule management is one of your core responsibilities on every project.

5. As the project completes, then store your project's final project schedule into the document control system for long-term storage, archiving, and retrieval purposes.

Mastering the Risk Matrix

Before mastering the risk matrix tool, you must understand how this tool can assist and support you on your project. The following project scenario emphasizes the importance of the tool.

A large manufacturing plant has decided to update one of its most important and critical machines with a newer and faster model. The current machine, even though it has been successful for many years, is unable to process the steel fast enough, which is slowing down production in the plant. You as the lead manufacturing project manager for all plant-related projects have decided to head up this machine replacement project. You are excited about the fact that the plant will produce the steel much faster with the new machine, but you are worried about the risks of replacing such an important machine and one that has worked so well for many years. One of the first activities you perform on the project is gathering the team together to come up with list of risk events. In that process, you determine quickly that there are many risks, but struggle to understand how important each is to the project. You also have no idea of the probability or the impacts to these risks, which makes it difficult to establish how risky this project really is. You have several key questions that need addressing immediately. These questions include:

What is the risk level of this project?

How many risks does the project have?

What is the general impact of the risks?

How does one estimate probability of a risk occurring?

To obtain the answers to these questions, you should use a risk matrix tool. A risk matrix is a table that documents the probability and the impact of each risk event. When mapping the risk events to the risk matrix table, the project manager and team members identify and determine immediately how important and critical the risk events are to the project. Based on the impact and probability determination of each risk, the risk falls into the appropriate cells on the chart (table). The end result is a risk matrix for your project. At a glance, anyone should be able to see the project's risk level. After project managers start to use this tool and they get their project team members involved in the risk assessment process, everyone using the tool will quickly learn to adopt it as one of their favorite tools.

CROSS-REF We recommend that you review the risk matrix's planning questions in Chapter 12.

Creating a risk matrix

Creating a risk matrix is a great way to bring the team together and focus on one aspect of the project. In doing this, the team as a group decides the probability and impacts of every important risk event. This exercise also has a bonding effect on the team. After creating the list of risks and their probability and impacts, the project manager plots the risks in the matrix, and the process is complete. Project managers, who use the risk matrix on their projects, will be able to monitor and control their risks more effectively and have a better understanding of impact and probabilities of each event. This risk matrix also provides the project managers the information they need to help the team members focus on resolving risk events much sooner, thereby preventing negative impacts to the project.

A project customer should be involved in the creating and assessing of the project risks. Each customer has a different tolerance for risk events; and, therefore, the probability and impact decisions will differ from customer to customer. In addition, project team members might assess a risk differently. Bringing the two groups together and deciding on one assessment for the risk event is beneficial.

Many large construction projects use the risk matrix as a standard procedure in the management and controlling of project risks. The time and effort that project managers and team members spend to produce this tool, has an incredible payoff in the end. The ability to provide to both the customer and upper management the risk level of the project at a single glance is priceless.

The steps of creating a risk matrix tool vary. Use the following steps to help you get started.

1. Open a new risk assessment matrix template for your project. We have a template to use immediately on your projects.

2. Meet with your project team members and document the project risk events. This process is the same for every project and no different when developing a risk matrix.

3. Number each of your project's risk events 1, 2, 3.... Once the risks are determined, assign each risk a numerical value. There is no significance in the number assigned to each risk; it is mainly for tracking purposes and is required for placing onto the risk matrix.

4. Determine both the impact and probability for one of your project's risk events, and add them to the appropriate box.

5. After assigning the risks in the appropriate cells on the risk matrix, this process is complete. As noted earlier, it is important to have your customers and team members both involved in this process when determining the probability and impacts of each risk event. This allows both parties to see the assessment assigned to the risk event and can either agree or disagree at that time. This brings the groups together in the understanding of the risk events, and it allows both groups to hear why each of the risks were assessed at a particular level. It also provides the group as a whole to understand and set the tolerance level for handling risk events. It is important, as you manage your project, to understand that level of tolerance of the customer and be able to assess the risk events with that information.

> **ON the CD-ROM** We have included a sample risk matrix in the Communication tools Risk subfolder. Use this as a guide to help you create your own version of this tool.

Using a risk matrix

Before you can use a risk matrix, you must identify who on your project team will utilize this tool so that you can determine the level of detail required, frequency of distribution, style, and format of the report. Review the risk matrix planning section in Chapter 12 and then follow these steps:

1. Ensure your project team members and your customer agree on the risk events and where they were assigned in the risk matrix. This includes understanding how the team made the assessments and where each risk event fell on the risk matrix. To gain approval, you may need to gather everyone and go over the risk matrix together to make sure everyone is onboard and comfortable.

2. Once gaining everyone's approval on the assessment and placement of the risk events in the risk matrix, you then start to drive the resolution or the risk mitigation steps for each of the risk items in the high probability, high impact cells. For example, if there are a number of risk events in the high – high cell of the matrix, the project manager will want the project team to work on mitigation steps and techniques to reduce those risks events should they occur. The project team members do not generate risk mitigation steps for every risk on the project; it is not worth it and sometimes too expensive (both in time and cost), they would only generate them for the higher-priority risk events. It would be a risk to the project schedule if the project team members impacted and tried to mitigate each and every project risk event.

3. Once your project team members determine the higher-level project risks, then drive the mitigation step activities and procedures to reduce those project risks. This includes anything from eliminating the risk, to transferring it to another area of the company or a third party, to ignoring the risk all together. Whatever strategy the team selects for the risk event, you need to drive that resolution through your project team members.

4. Throughout this process, you will be continually presenting the risk matrix to your project customer and upper management. This is an important step because it keeps everyone involved with the project's risks events. It is also important to understand how your team members resolve the risk events. When presenting the risk matrix to your customer, it is important for you to understand the background of each risk event. It is also important for you to know why your team members placed the risk event in one box (cell) compared to another. If your upper management or customers were not involved in the assigning process, then they will be interested in that background and history on how the assessment process performed so be prepared to answer those questions.

5. The risk matrix and assignment process continues through the life of project. It is important to note this is an ongoing process and one that continues regular assessment throughout the project. It is a best practice to review the risks once a week.

Mastering the Scatter Chart

Before you can master the scatter chart, you must understand how this tool can assist and support you on your project. The following project scenario emphasizes the importance of the tool. You are nearing the end of a three-year project, which has had its difficulties. The project customers think that the project has always been behind schedule and over budget. You know this is not the case. In fact, you know the majority of the time the project has been on schedule and close to staying on budget. You have shown the customer the schedule and budget reports each month. Try as you may, the reports have too much detail to identify a trend, and the customer becomes frustrated even trying to figure it out. You ask yourself the following questions in the hope of trying to find a way to get the information to your customers:

What can you do to convince the owner the project was on time and within budget?

Can you create a report or chart that displays the project being on time and within budget most of the time throughout the project?

To obtain the answers to these questions, the project manager should use a scatter chart. A scatter chart tool can display both schedule and cost performance on the same chart. A scatter chart plots the schedule performance index (SPI) and the cost performance index (CPI) for each month of the project.

Figure 17.3 is a scatter chart that displays that the majority of time the project was on schedule and within budget.

CROSS-REF We recommend that you review the scatter chart's planning questions in Chapter 8.

FIGURE 17.3

A scatter chart diagram.

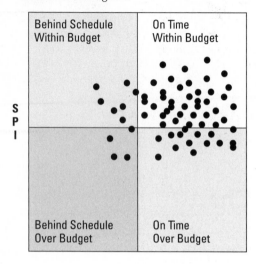

Creating a scatter chart

When you have two variables and want to evaluate if there is a relationship between them, then the best tool to use is a scatter chart. As one variable goes up, the other goes down or vice versa; the scatter chart will identify this for you. Alternatively, as in the case of the scenario, to show a grouping of the data to prove an assumption or make a point. You would usually use a scatter chart in preference to a line chart when you have two variables that are independent of each other. A scatter chart has two value axes, showing one set of numerical data along the x-axis and another along the y-axis. It combines these values into single data points and normally displays them in uneven intervals, or clusters.

With a scatter chart, you use an independent variable plotted on the x-axis and dependent variable plotted on the y-axis. When you add a trend line, you may see the relationship between the variables. For example, you might see a linear relationship between the concentration of a compound in solution and its reflective color. To be successful with certain sets of data, project managers should consider using the scatter chart tool. When you arrange your data for a scatter chart, place X values in one row or column and then enter corresponding Y values in the adjacent row or column. The x-axis and the y-axis of a scatter chart can only be a value axis. This means that the chart only displays numeric data on each axis. To display this numeric data with greater flexibility, you can change the scaling options on these axes.

The types of information you may want to display are comparisons of various groups. The groups usually have some kind of relationship with each other. If you want to show the trend of the project's performance, you can compare the SPI against the CPI, similar to what we did in the scenario.

A project customer may request scatter charts from the project manager but will rarely be involved in creating them. These reports are more project manager or project team focused, and the customer does not tend to get too involved in their creation. The customer will find great value, though, when the project manager creates and uses them on the project.

The steps of creating a scatter chart tool vary. Use the following steps to help you get started.

1. Collect the data for your project's scatter chart.

2. Open a spreadsheet tool that has a scatter chart graphing functionality.

3. Pick two of your project's variables to plot on the scatter chart. For this example, select and enter the same values as represented in Figure 17.4. This step includes the entering of all the data in the spreadsheet to match the chart.

   Figure 17.4 shows two variables selected to create a scatter chart. This example shows the variables to create a weight versus height scatter chart.

FIGURE 17.4

A scatter chart sample data showing the relationship between a person's height and their weight.

Weight	250	145	176	199	320
Height	6.1	5.5	6.9	6.2	6.9

4. Select the data for your scatter chart. Highlight all the data just entered including the weight and height labels on the spreadsheet.

5. Next, you should select *insert a new chart*, and select scatter chart as the chart type.

6. The spreadsheet tool produces the chart, and it is complete and ready for use on your project.

Figure 17.5 represents an example of a weight and height scatter chart built from this data in Step 3.

FIGURE 17.5

A weight and height scatter chart.

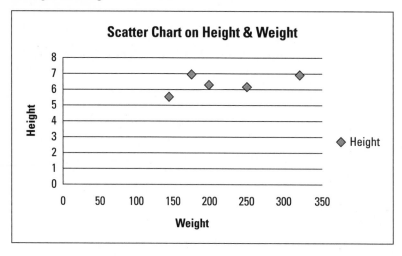

ON the CD-ROM We have included a sample scatter chart tool in the Communication Tools Quality sub-folder. Use this as a guide to create your own version of this tool.

Using a scatter chart

Before you can use a scatter chart, you must identify who on your project team will utilize this tool so that you can determine the level of detail required, frequency of distribution, style, and format of the report. Scatter charts tend to have more detail level data, and that allows anyone analyzing the data to have the details they need for that analysis.

Review the scatter chart planning section in Chapter 8 and then follow these steps:

1. Analyze the scatter chart and determine if patterns in the data look like they require attention and if they do, then react accordingly. There can be up to five correlations (positive, negative, possible positive, possible negative, no correlation) on any scatter chart that you need to be aware of and understand how those conditions are defining the data. As you are reviewing your scatter chart, look for those conditions and determine if there is any correlation between the two variables. There may be situations where easily adjusting the data would impact the project positively and other situations where the data is much more challenging to adjust and may negatively impact the project.

2. Continually gather and monitor your project's data and add it to the scatter chart. As you complete that process, the project manager moves to Step 1 to reanalyze the data. This is a continual process through the life of the project.

3. As the project completes, the project manager stores the scatter charts in the document control system for long-term storage, archiving, and retrieval purposes.

TIP Scatter charts can also assist the project manager in identifying trends in the performance of the project such as Figure 17.3 where the scatter chart displayed the cost performance index against the schedule performance index.

Mastering the Scope Definition Document

Before you can master the scope definition document, you must understand how this tool can assist and support you on your project. The following project scenario emphasizes the importance of the tool.

A large design company has recently won the contract to design a new bicycle manufacturing plant in Paris, France. You have been chosen to manage this project. As you start into the project, you quickly discover there are many aspects of the project that are yet to be determined. The area of the project where you find the biggest issue is in the allocation of the budget, where at first glance you see that the project funding is projecting 50 percent over budget. It appears that the owners do not understand that this is going to be a high-tech design and construction effort, and the old methods of construction are no longer acceptable or used in today's bicycle market. Therefore there is a big disconnect on the budget. The new environmental restrictions alone have added 30 to 35 percent increase to the budget, something that was not expected by the older managers. The project time lines are also problematic. The owner wants to move forward quickly, timing the opening of the plant prior to the next Tour De France for marketing reasons and the fact that some of their bikes are expected to be in the race. This is a huge marketing opportunity, which is adding additional outside influences to the project that were unknown to you when you accepted it originally. This also increases the risk of the project. As you report some of these concerns to management, they too have a series of questions and concerns that they want answered by you immediately. Their questions include:

What is the vision of the project?

What needs is the customer trying to fulfill?

Why are the environmental activities so expensive?

What is the scope of the project?

To obtain the answers to these questions, you should use a scope definition document. This document sets the common understanding of the project's scope and provides a starting point for the project manager to monitor and control the project. If the work is not in the scope definition document, it is not included in the project. The exception to this is getting scope items added through the change request process. The scope definition document covers all aspects of the project ranging from vision and scope, to risks, quality, schedule, budget and assumptions, and dependencies. When there are aspects of the project missing or not yet documented, the project manager needs to acquire that information as soon as possible.

CROSS-REF We recommend that you review the scope definition document's planning questions in Chapter 5.

Creating a scope definition document

Creating a scope definition document is critical to every project. The information within the document covers all the major areas of the project so anyone utilizing it understands the scope of the project. The document is rich in content, and initially looks like it took a tremendous amount of work to create; however, because it is so valuable, the amount of work is worth the effort. In order to be successful, project managers should develop and create a scope definition document on every project. Regardless of the size and the perceived overhead in developing the document, the rigor and processes the document covers is an excellent source for managing and controlling the project. The areas covered in the document include scope, goals, risks, quality, communications, budget, time lines, priorities, assumptions, constraints, and dependencies, to name just a few.

A project customer should be active in requesting and ensuring that the projects they are involved in have a scope definition document. Because of the structure and amount of information within the plan itself, it provides the project manager and team members a solid foundation and direction to manage and work on the project; a foundation any customer would be happy to have on the project and would expect to have on their projects. Customers must weigh the size of project and the overhead to create the scope definition document to the benefits they receive from it, and in most cases, they will see the payoff.

The actual steps of creating a scope definition document can vary. Use the template we provided to create a scope definition document for your project. The template is located on the CD-ROM for use if your company does not already have one.

The table of contents provides the major sections of the document. It will be handy when the document is completed and you are looking for particular information in the document.

Example of a Scope Definition Table of Contents

Section 1: Overview
Document the overview of the project in this section.

Section 2: Vision Statement
Document the vision of the project. This is normally a senior management-level statement about the project. What it is trying to accomplish, or what is the goal for the effort.

Section 3: Business Environment and Justification
Document the business environment and any environmental factors of the project. The business environment can have so many different things such as groups spread around the world, different cultures, relationship issues, and so on. You should also document the justification for the scope to ensure anyone involved in the project has the complete picture on the scope of the project.

Section 4: Business Opportunity

Document the business opportunity. This opportunity should align with the scope requested. Idea or suggestions could include, developing of under-utilization staffing report that could drive another business areas reduction of staff, as an example.

Section 5: Business Risks

Document the business risks for the project. These risks should be specific in how they relate to the business requesting the project.

Section 6: Customer or Market Needs

Document the customer needs and request for the project. There are times when the project may help resolve particular market needs and therefore, capturing those requirements is important for the project team to understand and execute on the project.

Section 7: Scope Statement and Purpose

Document the scope statement for the project. This scope statement will include the purpose of the project and any other high-level information about the project.

Section 8: Success Criteria

Document the success criteria of the project. Many times, this is often a directive from the business, but the project team themselves and may or may not have their own level of success criteria that should also be included.

Section 9: Project Background and Objectives

Document the project's background and main objectives. This background is great for communicating to the customer, clients, and the project team the reasons behind the project.

Section 10: Project Description

Document the description.

Section 11: Major Features

Document the major features for the project. Regardless of the type of project, every effort will have a list of features to accomplish, and listing those features in this section allows everyone the same understanding of what the project will accomplish in the end.

Section 12: Scope and Limitations

Document any limitations to the scope of the project. If the scope requires 50 completed reports at the production launch and the team's capacity is only 10 reports, that limitation requires documenting in this section to ensure a call out and known well ahead of time.

continued

continued

Section 13: Scope of Initial Release

Document the scope items list launched at the initial release of the project in this section. In the case of the reports, the scope could be 10 out of the 50 reports will be ready at launch.

Section 14: Scope of Subsequent Releases

Document the scope items released at subsequent releases of the project. In the case of the 50 reports required at launch, not all of them may be possible to launch, so there will be only a release of 10. In this section, the remaining scope and the different release dates are noted. Documenting this will provide a complete plan for the whole scope of the project and the associated timeframes.

Section 15: Limitations and Exclusions (Out of Scope)

Document the out-of-scope items. This is important to call out to ensure everyone understands exactly what is not going to be in this round of the project's delivery.

Section 16: Work Breakdown Structure

Document the work breakdown structure in this section of the document.

Section 17: Scope Items Defined (In Scope & Out of Scope)

Document the out-of-scope items.

Section 18: Risk event items

Document the known project risk events.

Section 19: Quality procedures

Document the quality policy and procedures. Pay special attention to any quality processes or procedures that the customer is requesting.

Section 20: Communication plan

Document the communication plan. This should include the standard communication items such as who, when, how, why communications will occur.

Section 21: Resource Assignment

Document the individual resource assignments. Document the names and roles and any contact information if possible. It would be beneficial to also document any associated timeframes that allocate the resources are expected to the project.

*S*ection 22: *Project Budget*

Document the budget for the project. It is important to note that this may or may not align with the actual estimate for the project, but just represent the funds allocated to the effort.

*S*ection 23: *Timetable/Schedule*

Document the timeframes or schedule for the project. The dates can be high level only and represent the major milestones of the project. There could be a situation where there are hard deadlines imposed by the business, and if so, they need to be added to this section of the document.

*S*ection 24: *Stakeholder Profiles*

Document the stakeholder profiles where applicable to the success of the project. In general, the higher the profile of the stakeholders, the higher the profile of the project. In general, if the stakeholders on the project have a high profile, then your project may have a high profile. If you are building a new house for a sports celebrity, your project has a high profile, but if you are building a house for the average person, the project will have a low profile. Write something in the scope that raises the risk of the project due to it being a high profile and under a microscope.

*S*ection 25: *Project Priorities*

Document the priority of the project in this section. If this project has a high priority, document it in this section to ensure that the project has the proper attention it needs to be successful.

*S*ection 26: *Operating Environment*

Document the operating environment of the project. Document any environment type of issues that team members, customer, or clients will have to be aware of for the project.

*S*ection 27: *Assumptions, Constraints, and Dependencies*

Document the project assumptions, constraints, or dependencies. This will allow a level setting to occur with everyone involved in the project as to some of the constraints and dependencies of the project.

ON the CD-ROM We have included a sample scope definition document in the Communication tools Scope subfolder. Use this as a guide to create your own version of this tool.

Using the scope definition document

Prior to using a scope definition document, you must identify who on your project team will utilize this tool so that you can determine the level of detail required, frequency of distribution, style, and format of the report. Review the scope definition document planning section in Chapter 5 and then follow these steps:

1. As the project moves into the later stages of the planning process, you must ensure your team members and your customers have signed off on the scope definition document. This document defines the work of the project and it is therefore critical that everyone agrees on the scope before any project activities begin. The project can become cluttered full of change requests if there is not a full agreement and approval on the scope of the project. To obtain this approval, send the scope definition document and the user acceptance document to your customer and team members for their sign-off and approval.

2. Once receiving approval and sign-off from both parties, store both of the approvals in the document control system for long-term storage, archiving, and retrieval purposes.

3. Once obtaining all approvals and sign-offs, you should enforce the use of the scope definition document on your project. This includes having your team members work on the scope that is included in the document only, and if other scope items come in, you should drive that work through the change request process.

4. You will continue to manage and control the scope throughout the project, until project closeout. Scope management is an important part of your responsibilities.

5. At the end of the project, store the final version of the scope definition document along with your other project documents in the document control system.

Summary

The tools that we described in this chapter are the best choices for creating, disseminating, and reporting status on your project within the planning process. Most tools span the executing and closeout processes as well, but initializing these tools will be used in planning.

Tools such as the project milestone list and project schedule both allow stakeholders to determine, at a glance, when the project will deliver on key components, and will allow them to plan for the project accordingly. The cost estimate and the logic network diagram are two more tools that make sense in the planning processes to help everyone involved in the project plan the project accordingly.

Use of the reporting communications tools outlined in this chapter will benefit the project manager, customer, and project team members. The reports are simple, easy to create, and informative in presenting information to the various parties.

Chapter 18

Using Personal Communication Tools in the Executing of a Project

IN THIS CHAPTER

Mastering the dashboard report

Mastering e-mail

Mastering instant messaging

In this chapter, we explore personal project communication tools used in the project executing and controlling process. Specifically, these are individual communication tools that support the project manager and team members during the project lifecycle.

These tools are informal and at the discretion of the individual. The tools help to keep track of your daily activities on the project. One of the most overused personal communication tools is e-mail. The project manager can receive hundreds of e-mails a day, which can be distracting and cause him or her to spend more time managing e-mails than managing the project. The other personal communication tool worth mentioning that most project managers never even consider when managing their project is the instant messaging tool. IM has now become invaluable to project communications. The ability to contact a team member instantly to ask a question or obtain project status is important in the continually ongoing effort to improve project communications.

Mastering the Dashboard Report

Before you can master the dashboard report tool, you must understand how this tool can assist and support you on your project. The following project scenario emphasizes the importance of the tool, and the reasons why the dashboard report is important to every project. Here is a scenario:

A large software company is interested in consolidating their project reporting. Every year the company works on 20 to 25 different projects and employs hundreds of staff. The projects span multiple project types including software development, hardware upgrades, implementation, and package solutions evaluations. Each project uses a standard project management methodology, and incorporated in this methodology are a set of project characteristics that are common across each project. These characteristics include, but are not limited to, quality, status, risks, issues, and finish dates. It is important to note that even though the projects are different, they each have the same basic characteristics. You as the project manager need to consolidate the information from each project into a format that is easy to read and understand by your upper management. The information must be ready for executive management to review by 8:00 a.m. each day, and you are on the hook to provide it.

The challenge you have is senior management is demanding a dynamically generated status, and no longer wants to wait for you to compile and send a manual report. You know that anything automatically generated can have problems, and because it is for your upper management, you must be extra careful. You are concerned and have some questions on how to move forward with an automated solution. Your questions include:

How do you consolidate this information?

What information is standard across all projects for grouping and reporting?

How will you automate this so it does not become a support nightmare?

What tools are available for this process?

To obtain the answers to these questions, you should use a dashboard report for all upper management's consolidated reporting. Project dashboard reports are quickly becoming a favorite management reporting tool and are becoming standard in most large companies enterprise project management. A project dashboard combines data from multiple projects into a single view, normally stored on a company Web site. When combining multiple project data into a single dashboard, the company can determine the status of all their projects, not just a single project. Comparing one project against another is one of the biggest advantages a dashboard produces. Upper management and customers will benefit from using the project dashboard across multiple projects because of all the information it presents and the summary view of the project information it displays.

CROSS-REF   We recommend that you review the project dashboard planning questions in Chapter 11.

Creating a dashboard report

Creating a dashboard report is one of the best methods of communicating project information throughout the organization at every level. Dashboard reports are becoming quite common on today's projects, providing upper management with a consolidated view of all project's status and issues. One of the factors to consider when creating a dashboard report is the long-term expenses and the cost of maintaining the system for the company. Creating a dashboard report is not a one-time activity because they take time and effort to produce and you should look at them as tools supplying project information that will be around for many years. Dashboards require updating and enhancing on a regular basis as more project information is developed or as more projects initiate at the company. Some dashboard reports report data real time, which also requires a support mechanism to be able to produce the data.

In some cases, project managers may want to provide a dashboard report, but are unable to create an automated version so their only choice is a manual solution. Producing a manual dashboard report, with a consolidated view of the status of the project, is better than not producing one at all. The simplest dashboard report available is a series of charts created in a spreadsheet tool, such as Excel. Excel has amazing charting capabilities, and a series of six or more charts, side by side is the purest most basic form of a dashboard report possible. For example, the project dashboard in Chapter 11, created in Excel, offers a tremendous amount of project information to the customer reviewing it. An automatically generated dashboard created at the beginning of the project will provide a level of visibility of project data throughout the life of the project and beyond.

The project customer should be involved in determining what information will reside on the dashboard report. The data should provide real value to the customer which will allow them to make project decisions. Project customers should be diligent in selecting the right data for the dashboard and work with the project team to determine the timing of that data so they are fully aware when the information is updated. A dashboard report is practically useless if you do not update the data regularly, or when the data becomes stale. At a minimum, the dashboard requires weekly, if not daily, updating of the project data.

The actual steps in creating a dashboard report tool vary. Use the following steps to help create a manual dashboard:

1. Select a tool that has charting capabilities within it. We recommend Excel or a similar spreadsheet capability. The goal is to produce the structure of the dashboard and then move to automating the data entry. It is important that the customer finds value in the data you are presenting on the dashboard, so do not spend a lot of time creating complex charts; produce some basic charts and obtain the approval of the customer first, then later you can try creating fancy charts.

2. Work closely with your customer, then manage and control the selection of the charts for the dashboard report. Choose the most relevant and important project data for your charts, such as cost charts, resource hours charts, change request charts, performance charts, and estimating and forecasting charts. Some of the more technical savvy project customers will have their favorite chart types that they may want to use on the dashboard display.

> **TIP** Ensure you can produce the chart your customer is requesting. Do not walk away promising the customer you can produce it, when really you have no idea how. It is possible you may not be able to produce it.

3. After selecting the chart types, create the table of data for each chart in the spreadsheet. Remember, this has to be meaningful data and relevant to the customers or they are not going to care about using the dashboard. Your customers will only want to see data they care about, and anything else will seem irrelevant to them.

4. Continue this process and create data tables for each chart type and add them to your project's dashboard report. It is common for only six charts to represent a dashboard, especially if using a spreadsheet. You can use up to nine separate charts, but depending on the charts, this is not always that valuable because there may be too much information and it would be difficult to read.

TIP   Remember, you are creating a single chart for a single row of data. Therefore, if you have cost data in the one table and resource hours in a second table, you must create two separate charts. Do not combine the charts; it would defeat the purpose as each chart as they should be single focused.

5. Align all charts together, three across and two down on the spreadsheet. You can use Figure 18.1 as a guide for placing the charts in the dashboard report.

6. Once you finish aligning the dashboard charts, you are ready to implement the dashboard report on your project.

Figure 18.1 represents a spreadsheet version of a project dashboard report. Dashboard reports come in all shapes and sizes and are specific to project type and customer needs.

FIGURE 18.1

This is a sample spreadsheet version of a dashboard report.

Project Dashboard Report

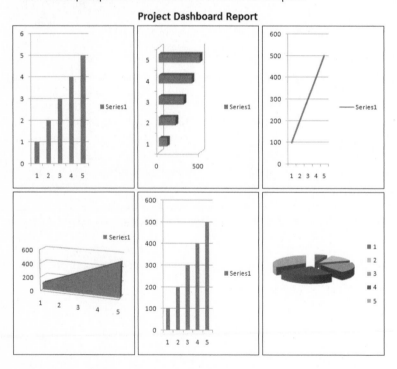

ON the CD-ROM   We have included a sample dashboard report tool in the Communication tools Communication Reporting folder. You can use this as a guide to create your own personal version of this tool. We believe this is a great starting point for the creation of this tool for your project. The tool on the CD-ROM has a basic dashboard displaying six different charts, each representing a different area of the project. For example, the number of schedule changes, number of change requests, resource hours, project costs, number of project risks, and number of project issues, to name a few.

Using a dashboard report

Before you can use the dashboard report, you must identify who on your project team will utilize this tool so that you can determine the level of detail required, frequency of distribution, style, and format of the report. In most cases, the main users are upper management or executive types and the information is displayed generally at a high management level. This will depend solely on the customers or upper management who will guide you in creating these reports.

Before utilizing a dashboard report, you should review the dashboard report planning section in Chapter 11. Then follow these steps:

1. Ensure that the project customer is satisfied and that the project dashboard is delivering the information they need to make project decisions or to learn more information about the project. The first mistake you can make is to add a dashboard report that provides no value to the customer. It wastes their time and effort and will set a bad impression with them about the project.

2. After receiving approval of the dashboard format, enforce the use of the dashboard report on the project. This includes working with the customer and determining the information for adding to the report, or tweaking information on the report, changing the timing on receiving data files, or adding more users. On manual dashboard reports there are many different areas you can work to ensure it is suitable for the customer. This includes moving it into an automated format, introducing new data, and chart types.

3. Throughout the executing process of your project, the dashboard report will have the latest project information at all times and be online and available to your customers or upper management. If the dashboard is manual, you will need to distribute it to your customers on a weekly basis. It is important that you communicate with your customers on a regular basis and ensure they are receiving the dashboard data they want to see and use. There can be hundreds of different methods of distributing these dashboard reports such as sending the dashboard out as a spreadsheet, in e-mail, or in a formal presentation.

4. After creating the project dashboard report, you should store the document within the project's document control system for long-term storage, archiving, and retrieval purposes.

A printed dashboard report can be the first step toward a full-blown automated enterprise-wide dashboard on every manager's computer. An automated dashboard allows any manager to bring up project information on their screen in any way they want. If they desire they can drill down to the lowest detail. Many consulting companies in the market today create enterprise dashboards.

Mastering E-Mail

Before you can master the e-mail tool, you must understand how this tool can assist and support you on your project. The following project scenario emphasizes the importance of the tool.

A small family-operated lumber company in Hornepayne, Ontario, Canada has been running successfully for many years. Hornepayne is located roughly 12 driving hours north of Toronto, Ontario, and therefore electricity, phone lines, and some of the more common amenities of a big city are not available in all areas. The lumber company is 30 miles north of Hornepayne's city limits and has electricity and a phone line, but limited Internet access.

The lumber company has decided to expand operations and open two additional sites. Each of the new locations will be operated by one of the sons, and the owners (father and mother) will continue to run the main operations. The owners have decided to hire a project manager to oversee the construction and opening of the two new locations, and after weeks of searching, they found you as the project manager and instantly offered you the role. One of the first areas you must tackle is project status reporting. You meet with the owners and both sons and ask them about their reporting needs. The father has one demand — he wants a written status report by the end of the business day on Friday, including a financial summary page and the backup report. He also wants to ensure that both sons receive the same report at roughly the same time; you agree, and the project progresses into the first week.

As the first Friday arrives, you know it is status report day so you go ahead and prepare the reports for distribution at the end of the day. As the day progresses, everything is going well until one of the suppliers in town calls you to an emergency meeting. The meeting ends at 4:25 p.m., and you are roughly 30 minutes away from the lumber company, leaving only 35 minutes to get the first status report to the owners and their sons. You are under incredible pressure and cannot miss this first deadline, but you also know that the owners and their sons are almost certainly in three different locations, and so even if you drive and make it to the first location in time, you will most likely have to drive to the other two locations as well to hand deliver the status reports to both sons. The pressure is on and you start asking yourself a number of questions. These questions include:

How do I get the three status reports out on time?

What tool would be appropriate to use in this case?

Is there an automated way to distribute the reports?

Will I need to drive to the different locations every Friday for the life of the project?

To obtain the answers to these questions, the project manager should have e-mailed the status report to the owners and both sons from somewhere in the town. Email provides a simple and effective method to communicate project information to multiple people simultaneously. E-mail is a popular communication tool and an effective method of getting project information to project team members or customers. E-mail is often the standard form of project communication and widely used on most projects.

CROSS-REF   We recommend that you review the e-mail planning questions in Chapter 10.

Working with e-mail

We know everybody knows how to send, receive, and use e-mail. Our goal in this section is to get you to think about how powerful e-mail can be to enhance your overall project communications. Appropriate project e-mail messages include status reports, issues, risks, and budgets. E-mail has taken over as one of the best methods to communicate project information on today's projects, so you must be proficient when sending your e-mails, and make every e-mail count.

In some cases how you communicate through e-mail messages can make or break your project. If you continually send e-mails that are demanding, demeaning, or negative you can cause major project problems that may end up preventing you from ever finishing the project. When sending these types of e-mails, you will quickly determine that very few people respond well when being communicated with on a negative basis, and therefore when creating e-mail messages it is important for you to consider your recipient's reaction to how they will read and interpret the message.

E-mail also offers another extreme that is important to note — the ability to communicate project information in wide distribution allowing multiple people to get the same message at the same time. It offers the ability for project managers to offer praise and send out messages of good work, congratulations, and thanks for a job well done. It is very encouraging for a team member to receive a personal thank you e-mail from their project manager or upper management staff member for the good work they are doing; most team members save those e-mails indefinitely.

Imagine if a project manager sends "thank you" messages regularly during the project offering the team support and encouragement and telling them how proud they are of the work that the team is doing. The morale of the team will be high, and team members will appreciate that you took the time to send an e-mail expressing appreciation and encouragement to them.

As noted previously, appropriate project e-mail usage is quite different from personal usage. Project managers will utilize project e-mail in the following categories:

- Sending and receiving project information. Send most project information by e-mail rather than producing paper copies. In most cases, the only limitation of what e-mail you can send is the size of the material.

- Scheduling and establishing meetings, calendar events, and reminders. Set up and establish meeting events, reminders, and some task-list items using e-mail and the calendar tool.

- Capturing and receiving formal sign-off and approvals. To capture the official approval of your team members, customer, or upper management use e-mail as a method and the tool. Also use e-mail when asking to approve a particular deliverable or phase. This formal acceptance from the customer provides legal evidence that the deliverables are signed off and approved.

- Communicating among team members, customers, or upper management staff. Project managers, team members and customers will communicate generally by e-mail. This allows relationship building and stronger bonds among people working together.

- E-mailing and communicating for project decision making. Send your formal project decisions via e-mail to team members, customers, or upper management. This allows you to communicate important project decisions in a clear and concise manner and if required to obtain a quick turnaround on decisions or approvals.

- Communicating and aligning the virtual teams. When you have a virtual team working around the world, you can use e-mail as a tool to ensure everyone is communicating and receiving project information on a regular and ongoing basis. This allows virtual team members to feel connected to your project even when they are not in the same physical location.

- Using and working with the Delphi method. The e-mail tool is a good solution for the Delphi method when communicating with the subject matter experts, and timing is critical in this process.

- Communicating with the press. Sending press releases and answering question via e-mail is very efficient way to work with the press and other media.

CROSS-REF   Turn to Chapter 8 to learn more about the Delphi Method tool.

Project customers can actively use e-mail throughout the project. Project customers and clients must also be aware of when and how to use e-mail when it comes to communicating project information as well and therefore it may require the project manager to spend time with the customers and ensure they are communicating the right information at the right level for their audiences.

Using e-mail

When using e-mail on a project, the project manager must be aware of the positive and negative uses of this tool. Before utilizing e-mail, review the e-mail planning section in Chapter 10.

List of positive uses for e-mail

The following list describes positive uses for e-mail.

- Storage of formal approvals and sign-offs from customers, team members, or upper management.

- Project information storage. E-mail often is a tool that project managers use to store project information files for backup or quick reference. For example, a budget spreadsheet can be stored in e-mail, and if the project manager or customer would like access to it, they can easily obtain it from their e-mail system.

- Communicating lessons learned information from the team members, customers, or upper management.

- Announcing a major milestone to the press can communicate to the project community and environs.

List of e-mail tool avoidances:

The following list describes specific avoidances for this tool.

- Avoid innuendoes, regardless of your personal relationship. Any e-mail sent should be professional and businesslike.

- Sending inappropriate jokes or sexual material over e-mail.

- Sending negative personal attacks on a team member, customer, or upper management that brings down the team morale.

- Never start false rumors about the project or people.

Mastering Instant Messaging

Before you can master the instant messaging tool, you must understand how this tool can assist and support you on your project. The following project scenario emphasizes the importance of the tool.

A small plumbing company in Manchester, England has been in business for the last 100 years. Initially the company had 2 employees but has grown to 20 and still occupies the same space. The employees are falling over each other and clearly, it is time to move to a larger building. The owner decides to open a second location across town, expanding operations and allowing the employees more working space to do their jobs. During the initial move and the set up of the new office, the relocation project runs into difficulties with the installation of telephones. The phone company has indicated they will schedule all communication infrastructures for the location, such as Internet, radio dispatches, and satellite, for next week; however, installation of the telephone connection will be one to two months. As the project manager, you are responsible for the relocation project and it is your job to figure out a way to communicate via the Internet or another way, due to the phones not working, and keep the ten plumbers working steadily. You have a number of questions on how the two offices will communicate. Questions such as:

> How can you get a message from one location to another or one co-worker to another?
>
> How can you send job information informally and still get it real time?
>
> How can two or more people communicate (chat) online and ensure the two locations are always talking?
>
> How can I get customer information such as name and address to plumbers based in the second office?

Using an instant messaging tool is the answer to these questions. The instant messaging tool allows for instant access among all project team members, regardless of where they work. In this scenario, by setting up instant messaging between the office managers at the two locations, the offices will continue to functional fully until the phones are functional. Using instant messaging may not be the best option, but is one that will work on a temporary basis, allowing the company to continue operations.

 **We recommend that you review the instant messaging planning questions in Chapter 10.**

Creating an instant message

Creating an instant message is easy — log into the tool, find a friend or co-worker, and start typing. Creating the correct instant message is tougher. Project managers and team members must choose their words (in text) wisely before ever hitting the send button. It is important to ensure that anything sent regarding the project is as informal as possible. The project team members should keep the communication light and direct.

If instant messaging conversations last longer than a couple of minutes, than either party should pick up the phone and call the other; unless that is not possible. Project managers should be careful with their tone when communicating using instant messaging, regardless of whom they are sending to; tone can be challenging and the message can come across as totally opposite to what you were trying to convey.

Project customers can be active in the use of the instant messaging tool on the project. Therefore, when communicating to your customers, again be careful about the information you send. If the customers are asking informal questions, provide them with informal answers; never send messages that would shock or surprise them over this instant messaging tool.

There is little value in covering how to create an instant message for this audience because it is already such a popular tool; however, we offer some do and don'ts of instant messaging. Some popular instant messaging tools are MSN Messenger, Yahoo Messenger, and AOL Messenger.

Using an instant messaging tool

Review the instant messaging tool planning section in Chapter 10 and re-familiarize yourself with the activities and tasks outline when preparing to use this tool.

List of positive uses for the instant messaging tool:

Use an instant messaging tool to do the following:

- Start an initial conversation with a project team member
- Send a positive note or message about a job well done
- Arrange project type activities such as team lunches, fun surprise, etc.
- Ask a quick question about the project
- Socialize and stay connected to project team members
- Share information with virtual project team members all over the world
- Brainstorm and hold discussions with virtual team members
- Confirm a meeting's date and time

List of instant messaging tool avoidances:

Avoid the following when using the instant messaging tool:

- Do not spy on your project team members. Just because they do not respond does not mean they are not working. One of the worst things a project manager can do is use the instant messaging tool to determine the availability of a member or to see if a project team member is working on a project.
- Be careful sending or receiving official project information over instant messaging. For example, never quote project team estimates over an instant messaging tool without following up with an e-mail or phone call to make sure the information sent was correct and was received.

■ Avoid sending personal type information over the tool. Personal information is too sensitive for instant messaging and is inappropriate to send over this type of tool.

■ Be aware of the time instant messaging can take. This tool can be a real time waster and something that can become compulsive quickly. Keep you messages brief and watch your time.

■ Avoid having multiple conversations going at once. Having multiple sessions open and typing to a number of people simultaneously can get confusing and could lead to sending an inappropriate message to the wrong person.

 **See Chapter 10 for a list of tips and tricks on using the instant messaging tool.**

Summary

The tools that we describe in this chapter are the best choices for personal communications while working on a project. This chapter illustrates only three tools, but these tools will be critical on your project and are important enough to address with everyone, especially project managers.

In this chapter, we discovered communication tools that are both project and personal related; tools such as dashboard reports that are excellent examples of a management reporting tool, and once implemented can be a popular and powerful method to communicate project status. Other tools, such as instant messaging, tend to be informal and used by the individual team member only for communicating informally on the project.

Use of the reporting communications tools outlined in this chapter will benefit the project manager, customers, and project team members. The reports are simple, easy to create, and informative in presenting information to the various parties.

Chapter 19

Using Project Communication Administration Tools in the Executing Process

In this chapter, we explore project communication tools in the executing and controlling process of a project. In this process of a project, the manager focuses his time on the management and administration of the project work.

The management and administration of some projects can be challenging, and without proper tools a project manager can be limited in his or her ability to succeed. While in the executing process, the project manager's top priority is to constantly report status and ensure that stakeholders are receiving the information they need to make decisions and to be involved in the project.

The tools covered in this chapter — change request forms, project newsletters, and project status meetings — all support the project manager by helping him successfully manage his projects.

Mastering the Change Request

Before you use a change request tool, you must understand how this tool can assist and support you on your project. The following project scenario emphasizes the importance of the tool and reasons why the change request tool is critical to every project.

A large mattress company in Jefferson City, Missouri, recently designed a new king-sized mattress that they call the King Plus because it is the largest and most luxurious mattress on the market. The company is receiving more and more requests for something larger than the California King bed, and they have decided to step up and meet the demands of the customers. As the senior project manager at the plant, management has asked that you lead this project. You accept and are excited about getting started immediately. A couple of months pass, and the project is moving along nicely. You complete the design phase and begin the prototyping phase. Upper management has seen some of the results from the prototyping. They are commenting on the size, feel, and comfort of the mattress; this is exactly what prototyping is all about, so you are very glad they are providing their input. As testing continues, upper management is starting to complain and becoming more negative about the mattress. You are starting to think this whole idea was a big mistake. Some customers who are testing the prototype mattress are calling upper management and complaining as well. Those customers want to see a number of changes, and the only thing that people like about the mattress is the size. Upper management knows that they must get the mattress design correct before it hits the market because it will be widely scrutinized, and any bad press will hurt the company. As the prototype phase completes, upper management requests a series of changes to the mattress that are outside what they originally wanted in the King Plus concept. You must get a handle on and control over everything they are requesting to make sure the mattress, in the end, meets management's needs. You are quickly becoming overwhelmed with all the changes that everyone is requesting and must get a handle on the situation fast or your project will spin out of control. You have a series of questions that need answering to determine how to get the project under control but you have no one to ask. These questions include:

How do I track and control these changes?

How do I report and keep a handle on these changes?

What process can I set up?

How does upper management or the customer document a change for this project?

To obtain the answers to these questions, the project manager will use a change request form and a change request log for tracking and controlling all project change requests. A change request form is the official paperwork to introduce change requests into a project. Change request forms contain the relevant information to determine what is the change being requested and has enough detail for the project manager and team members to investigate the impacts to make the change. To store the entire list of change requests, the project manager utilizes a change request log. A change request log is a central repository for all the change requests. It serves as the central spot where anyone can go to report on the number of changes, capture descriptions, or any other information about the project changes. Both approved and rejected change requests are stored in the change request log for long-term storage and historical reference. A best practice is to keep all change requests, regardless of their status, so that they will always be available to anyone who wants to see them.

CROSS-REF   We recommend that you review the change request planning questions in Chapter 6.

Creating a change request

The tracking of change requests is critical to keeping the project under control. When project managers do not have a formal change request process in place, the project manager is at risk of not being able to know all the changes requested on their project. The project manager has a difficult time trying to react to all the work the customers are requesting and has no process in place or method of controlling all the different requests. Without a rigid change request process, there is no stability for the team members, and they tend to be a little apprehensive and are not clear on what they need to work on next. The team members get into a mode of constantly reacting to changes and not progressing on their project activities.

To be successful, project managers must be diligent about processing change requests correctly on their projects. Not every small change requires a change request because there is a level of good will between the customer and the project team that should include "extra" work. On the other hand, that extra work must be very small and not affect the delivery of the project. If it does, then the extra work becomes a formal change request and the team should process it accordingly. The project manager defines what extra work means and decides what should and should not be a change request. When managing fixed-price projects for example, work items that arise during the execution of the project, which are not in the original contract (scope), in most cases become project change requests. Project managers need to watch this closely to ensure that the project does not run over budget. On fixed-price contracts, it is very easy to overrun budgets with the extra change requests that the customers are requesting. The costs quickly add up as change requests pile up on a typical project. The cost of these change requests are added to the baseline costs.

Project customers need to be active in the change request process, especially when it comes to changes or updates to the project schedule or the project costs. Customers should use the change request process themselves to ensure that they are providing the information the team needs to evaluate their requests properly. They should also be fully aware of the cost impacts of each of their changes. If there are any costs or schedule impacts, the customer must approve those respective changes before the team proceeds to work on the change request. Once the project manager obtains approval on the change request, the project team can make the appropriate adjustments to the project (schedule or cost) and then continue project execution. Without the customer's approval, if the change request is going to cost more, the project manager will be unable to proceed. If they do, then they are responsible for finding the additional dollars to account for the change request by the customers. This could put them in a difficult position, and one that they may not be able to fix themselves.

A change request log is the formal tracking and reporting of the project's change requests. The items captured on the change request form go directly into the change request log spreadsheet for formal tracking and reporting. The change request log does not contain details like the change request form would, but it does provides an excellent summary of all the change requests for reporting and discussion purposes.

The actual steps of creating a change request can vary. Figure 19.1 displays an example of a change request form for use on any project. There are many different versions of change control documents, and every company may have their own unique version for project managers to use. The following provides a typical example of a change request form.

FIGURE 19.1

A change request form is a standard document across all industries, differing only by project type.

Name of Project:	Project manager:
Change Request #	Change Request Date:
Change Requested By Name:	Current Project Phase:

Description of Change:

Scope Impact:

Schedule Impact:

Cost Impact:

Quality Impact:

Possible Risks:

Reviewed By: Position: Date:

Recommended Action: Approve Or Reject:

The following are some guidelines in creating a change request tool. These steps include:

1. Establish a Change Control Board.

2. Identify the project change and complete a change request form.

3. Submit completed form to the Change Control Board.

4. If approved, assess project impacts and include the project in work activities. Update project schedule, project costs, and work assignments.

5. If rejected, project customers should be able to determine the reason for rejection and update the form for resubmission, if applicable. The Change Control Board will re-review the change request once the team has made the changes based on the reason for cancellation. The team has to prove they are adopting the changes recommended within the project; an example of that includes the adoption of a new billing system.

ON the CD-ROM We have included a sample of this Change Request tool in the Communication Tools Integration subfolder folder. Use this as a guide to create your own version of this tool.

Using a change request

Prior to using a tool such as the change request, you must identify who on your project team will utilize this tool so that you can determine the level of detail required, frequency of distribution, style, and format of the report. The change request form will generally have as many details as possible in the document so the end users (team members expected to do the work) can understand what the change is that the requestor is asking for.

Before utilizing the change request, you should review the change request planning section in Chapter 6. Then follow these steps:

1. As the project moves out of the planning process and into the executing process, you must ensure that the project team members have approved the change request form and are comfortable that the form provides what they need to assess the work requested. Meet with the team members to go over the change request form and ensure it meets their requirements. If the team requests a change, then you should make those changes to the form, and once the change request form is acceptable to everyone, then the form is ready for use.

2. After the team agrees that the form is correct and functional, the next step is for you to meet with the customer and determine if they want any additional changes to the form. This is generally a quick conversation, because the customer will have completed this form when requesting changes and, therefore, will be less likely to want to add additional fields to it. However, they may want to delete what they feel are unnecessary fields, and this is where working with the customer ahead of time pays off. You can explain to your customer why the fields are important and why the team members need them. You should then explain to your customer that they must provide this information or your team members cannot properly assess the change request for them, and they will have to wait until they do provide the information on the form. After discussing this with your customer, you should then attempt to obtain their approval that the form is acceptable, and that they will use it when creating a project change request.

3. Most of the changes occur on the project when the project moves into the executing and controlling process. This is when you will send the change request form to your customer or requestor requesting a project change. Sending it to them early may have them losing the form and not having a copy when they actually need it.

4. After receiving the approved change request form from the customer, you then follow the steps outlined in the change control process established in the project planning process.

5. The process of using the change request form moves into the change control process, and, therefore, the change request form use stops at this point.

CROSS-REF Turn to Chapter 6 for more information on the change control plan.

Mastering the Phase Closeout Document

Before using a phase closeout document, you must understand how this tool can assist and support you on your project. The project scenario emphasizes the importance of the tool and reasons why the phase closeout document is critical to every project.

A small construction company located in Toronto Ontario, Canada has decided to replace their existing customer information system with a new system. The construction company must hire a contracting firm to complete the work because it has no information technology (IT) resources and, therefore, no one able to produce the system internally. As one of the most senior project managers working for the construction company, you would like to manage an IT project for the experience and, therefore, ask management if you can run this new project. Management agrees, and you are selected as the project manager. Fortunately, there is some time before the project starts, and you have a chance to study and learn more about the technology used in the new system.

As the IT consulting company comes onboard, you work with them to finalize the details of the contract. The one thing about the contract that you notice is that the IT company has its own method of developing the new software. Having the experts on the team that know the methodology well and can implement it for your project is going to make the project run a lot smoother. You are delighted to see that because you know there is nobody at your company with those same skills. As you start really getting into the contact, the one item you find missing is the transition periods between the different phases and what must occur when one phase completes and the other is about to start. Knowing the construction field well, you know that there are approvals at each phase closeout, but not knowing software, you are unaware if there is that same rigorous process. You have a number of questions for the consulting company before you are willing to sign the final contract and get the project started. These questions include:

What happens at the end of each phase in a software development project?

Who needs to sign off and approve the work?

What deliverables do you create when you close out a phase?

What must occur before the start of a new phase?

What meetings occur?

To obtain the answers to these questions, you can use a phase closeout document that covers the activities and tasks that occur at the end of each project phase. Regardless of the industry, there are formal processes and procedures required by the project manager to shut down a project phase. The phase closeout document contains that information every project manager needs to help them through the process. Shutting down one phase and starting another phase often includes formal presentations, sign-offs, compliance audits, and the official approval to proceed. It is beneficial to both the project team and the customer to handle phase closeouts correctly and not rush to the next phase. In this example, if the IT consultants had shown you the phase closeout document, you would have known exactly what will happen and would have signed the contract immediately.

CROSS-REF   We recommend that you review the phase closeout document's planning questions in Chapter 13.

Creating phase closeout material

Creating the phase closeout material is an important part of a project manager's responsibilities. The most important deliverable from a phase closeout is the customer's approval. Customer approval is usually a signature on a document, or a formal e-mail request that signifies to the project manager that the project can move forward to the next phase. The phase closeout process occurs several times in a project, depending on the methodology selected, and how many different milestones are in that methodology. Regardless of the number of milestones, at every phase closeout point, the project manager must apply the same rigor to every project and ensure each project is managed using the same processes each time. When project managers do not use a structured or formal process, they tend to get into trouble; an example of this could be not capturing all sign-offs, not finishing all documents or deliverables, or not confirming the schedule and budget. Using a structured sign-off process every time you complete a project phase provides the customers with a level of comfort that the project manager has everything under control.

The phase closeout process is very structured and has a series of steps the project manager must complete to officially shut down a phase. The project manager completes the phase closeout process outlined in the different methodologies used today. From construction projects to IT projects, each will use a methodology that has different phases described, and each will have some form of closeout or shutdown processes that the project team must follow on their projects. The software development methodology called SCRUM (see Chapter 11, daily progress reports for more information on SCRUM), for example, has a phase called sprints. Each sprint has a cycle, or a time period to which it has a set number of days. If a project has 11 sprints, so the phase closeout process occurs 11 times for a single project. In each case, the project manager must ensure that he/she performs the same tasks, receives the same approvals, and allows the project to proceed to the next phase or sprint. Other methodologies in software projects can have on the average four to five phases, and the phase closeout process would occur at the end of each phase. Formal closeout processes are a common process across all industries.

Project customers are also involved in the phase closeout process and work closely with the project manager to ensure that they are receiving what they need to close out the particular phase. Without the support of the customer, the project manager may struggle to close down each phase. In some cases, the project manager should put the project on hold and leave it there until the team members deliver all the outstanding tasks or deliverables. For example, if the customer refuses to sign off or approve a deliverable, the project manager should put the project on hold until the customer officially approves that deliverable. When customers refuse to sign off on a task or deliverable, the project manager may need to work closely with the customer, understand what their issues are, and try to resolve them as quickly as possible. The goal of the project manager is to ensure the customers have what they need and are satisfied and will approve the task or deliverable they are being requested to sign off.

The actual steps of creating a phase closeout can vary. The following phase closeout template can help you complete project phases on your projects in a structured and organized manner. Project managers should utilize this template if they do not have one from their company, or they feel this version is offering more than the company's existing template. This template is a great starting point for any project.

Phase Closeout Document Table of Contents

Section 1: Milestone Presentation

Every methodology will have specific deliverables required at every milestone. Develop the milestone presentation that includes project budget, timing, resources list, project deliverable list, risk list, issue list, etc. This should be a robust and comprehensive presentation.

Section 2: Audits

Document the various audits the project has completed, and the results of those audits. This provides customers and management with the knowledge that the project has gone through the internal steps required at this point in the project.

Section 3: Go/no-Go Decisions

Document the go/no-go decision points. This should include any caveats or assumptions; for example, at this phase of the project, the budget is running by $500K, but we have approval to proceed because management will find dollars to cover the overage.

Section 4: Sign-off & Approvals Obtained and Stored in Document Control System

Document the sign-offs and approvals. This includes the names of the staff that signed off, expected to sign off, and any of the user acceptance documents or other approvals.

ON the CD-ROM We include a phase closeout in the Communication Tools Procurement subfolder. Use this as a guide to create your own version of this tool.

Using a phase closeout document

Before using a tool such as the phase closeout, you must identify who on your project team will utilize this tool so that you can determine the level of detail required, frequency of distribution, style, and format of the report. In this case, the document should be as detailed as possible allowing the customer who is signing the document as much information as possible to understand fully what they are approving when closing out a phase. Review the phase closeout planning section in Chapter 13. Then follow these steps:

1. First you should understand the company's internal requirements for closing down project phases. There may be specific tasks or deliverables that the company imposes that the project manager must complete when closing down project phases. Once you have that information, make any necessary changes to the phase closeout document to ensure that information is captured and the project can react accordingly.

2. As the project moves through the executing process, you will be actively managing and controlling the phase closeout process at the end of each project phase. As your team members announce they have completed their deliverables for one phase, you should start to initiate the phase closeout procedures and start shutting down that phase.

3. After developing all the phase closeout documentation and facilitating the phase closeout meeting, you then send out the user acceptance document to the customer and team members to obtain official project approval that the phase is complete.

4. After receiving all approvals, you then store the documentation in the document control system for long-term storage and archiving purposes.

Mastering a Press Release

Before you can use a press release effectively, you must understand how this tool can assist and support you on your project. The following project scenario emphasizes the importance of the tool and reasons why a press release can be important to every project.

Your company is overseeing the construction of a new high-rise building in downtown Seattle, Washington. The excavation is almost complete, and the forms will be arriving soon for a large concrete pour. The estimate is a continuous concrete pour of 16,000 cubic yards for approximately 16 hours straight. Many issues will arise with a pour this large, and you are in charge of it. You need to block off two major intersections downtown for the entire time of the pour, so you have decided to schedule the pour on a weekend so that it will cause the least inconvenience to the downtown area. This project is going to be exciting and stressful all at the same time. You need some help from your upper management and the customer to continue to move the project along. The questions you have that require answering include:

How are you going to let the public know the pour is going to take place?

Will the media understand what we are doing?

What are you going to state what the duration will be? Will you say 16 hours, or will you give the pour some slack time, even though you do not want to disrupt traffic a minute longer than you have to.

A press release is the answer to all these questions. Assuming that you have all required permits and have hired city law enforcement for safety and traffic control now is the time to inform the public. In addition to a press release, you might consider, about a week before the pour date, you should schedule interviews with the local TV stations. After the interview, follow up by sending written notices to the TV stations on the progress of the event.

CROSS-REF We recommend that you review the press release's planning questions in Chapter 11.

Creating a press release

Only two types of press releases exist. A good press release shows the project in a good light, and a bad press release shows the project in a negative way. If the project is not highly visible and is on time and within budget, the odds of the media wanting a story are quite low. If the project is behind schedule or over budget, and a major catastrophe has hit it, then you may not be able to keep the press away. Although this generality applies mainly to construction projects, it can be true for other types of project as well. For example, when a large software project falls behind schedule, you will see many more news releases about it in comparison to when it is on schedule and going to hit the market on time.

Project managers should always notify the owner of the project and get their approval before releasing anything to the press. When giving a press interview or writing a press release, it is important to keep it as simple as possible. Unless you are an expert at crafting press releases, try not to put a spin on it. Professional journalists know how to spin a story better than anyone does. As a project manager you may want to set up a room dedicated to the media where the press has full access at all times and can obtain as much project information as is available to them. This is often a best practice technique for larger construction type projects, like a new football stadium, where the press constantly requires updates and the latest status of the project. This media room creates a trusting relationship between the press staff and the project staff, as long as the information is constantly accurate and available to them.

Project customers and owners should control press releases around the project as much as possible. A single person should be responsible for all project press releases to the media to ensure they are consistent. In most cases, it should be the decision of the owner to disseminate a press release, although this is not always possible. The press can release a story on the project at any time, and when this happens, it is usually not in the best interest of the project.

The steps for creating a press release can vary and depend greatly on the favorite tools of choice of the project manager or the press manager who is responsible for providing the press with information. For example, some press managers will choose to use radio for releasing project information, some may choose TV, others will use print ads. Press releases come in all shapes and sizes, and the method to release this information tends to be up to the press manager.

The following are some guidelines in creating a press release tool. These steps include:

1. First you should work with your customer and decide what information to include in the press release. This normally occurs during major project events like phase closeouts, openings, major milestones, and ribbon-cutting ceremonies. Identify and define what information you want to include and what information you should not include in the press release.

2. Then gather the information related to the press release from your team members, your customer, and potentially you would ask management if they wanted to add anything as well.

3. Create your project's press release document. This could include using sample templates or from scratch. You should ensure your information is put in logical categories and emphasis the main point that you are trying to get across to the public.

4. Obtain approval from the owner or customer, or any manager responsible for providing information, the legal department, and (potentially) upper management or stakeholders. You should be sure to inform and gain approvals from everyone involved in the press release process before distributing it.

5. Identify the types of media that you will distribute the press release to, such as newspapers only, and not television. You might consider putting the press release into the local community monthly magazines. Then, distribute the press release to the media that you have chosen.

6. Finally, you should follow up on all questions or issues raised by the press release. There can be many questions coming in from the public that will require your follow-up. Ensure you do so in a timely manner.

Using a press release

Before sending a press release, you must identify who on your project team will utilize this tool so that you can determine the level of detail required, frequency of distribution, style, and format of the report. Review the press release planning section in Chapter 11. Then follow these steps:

1. Determine the appropriate time in the project's lifecycle to release information to the media. The timing of the information may be critical; for example, releasing information on closing a street the day before it closes it is too late and becomes useless information.

2. Work with your customer and decide which information is appropriate and necessary to share with the press. When developing press releases, it is important to identify the information to release to the press and plan carefully the data that you will share. It is important to consider the order in which you will disseminate the information to the press. Remember, press releases are controlling expectations of the project that if communicated correctly are very beneficial to the project manager.

3. An important step in this process is for you and your customers to identify the information you will release for your project. There may be some information that is company proprietary and against company policy to release. There is some information that projects should not release due to the privacy concerns of individuals; and information such as cost, especially fixed cost contracts, is not appropriate to divulge to the press either.

4. The next step is to decide how to present the information. A press release in a written format is fine as long as that is the correct method for presenting it. For example, a written format would not work for a press conference but would be okay for sending to hundreds of newspapers around the country at one time.

5. The next step is for you and your customer to decide the time, place, and presenter of the press release.

6. The next step in using a press release is for you to present the press release to the media and any interested parties. After delivering the press release, you should then go through a lessons learned process. Press releases never go as planned so this is a critical step after presenting; the more press releases you perform, the better you will get at them.

7. Lastly, file the press release and any relevant information in the document control system for long-term storage and archiving purposes.

Mastering a Project Newsletter

Before you begin to master a project newsletter, you must understand how this tool can assist and support you on your project. The following project scenario emphasizes the importance of the tool and the reasons why the project newsletter is important to every project.

A large insurance company in downtown Sidney, Australia has decided to replace their main insurance software program in the next six months. The software has simply outlived its usefulness and needs replacing as soon as possible. As the most senior project manager in the company, you have elected to take on the role and manage this replacement project. You are excited about this project, because you were the project manager on the original project many years ago. As you get started on the project, you quickly realize that you need to find a way to provide project information to upper management and the various customers at a high level, without them needing to go into all the details of the project status report. The information should provide status information but should not overwhelm everyone with too many details. You need to come up with a way to get this data to them. Some of the questions you have are the following:

How do I get regular project updates?

How do I make the information interesting to read and still be informative?

What is an effective communication tool to provide summary of the project?

How do I communicate high-level project information only?

To obtain the answers to these questions, the project manager should use a project newsletter. A project newsletter is an excellent tool to communicate your project's information in a presentation-type format. It is easy to read and, if created correctly, can generate enthusiasm for the project. Project newsletters are most valuable on a monthly basis, but some projects have created them weekly when the project warranted it. However, more frequently than once monthly can become just a fancy status report, which defeats the purpose of the project newsletter.

CROSS-REF   We recommend that you review the project newsletter's planning questions in Chapter 11.

Creating a project newsletter

Project newsletters are useful, especially for upper management and the customers, because the reader does not have to sift through a lot of unneeded information to get the status of the project. Project newsletters create enthusiasm and a light-heartedness about a project that a project status report does not. Project managers often overlook creating a project newsletter for their projects because they do not have time, do not see the value, or do not want to do it. This is a huge mistake because project newsletters are one of the easiest communication tools available, and after the initial creation, it is one of the best tools to use for disseminating project information. Updating comes down to simply making a few updates on a month-to-month basis until the project completes. The minimal effort it takes to produce the project newsletter pays off greatly throughout the life of the project and provides customers and executives ongoing project information, in an easy-to-read, light-hearted format that offers a level of fun to the project.

Quite often project customers will drive the use of project newsletters on the project for their own status reporting. In some cases, the project customers use project newsletters to report through their management channels where their high-level management can obtain project information for their projects their teams are requesting. This is a great way for your customer's management to get involved in the project. They can pull project information out of the project newsletter that they may never have been able to find in a regular project status report.

Although the steps can vary, the following guidelines can help you create a newsletter.

1. You should create or define the template you will use for the newsletter. This would include using desktop publishing software, or one of the Microsoft Office tools to create the actual template for your newsletter. You should look at any internal company policies on templates and work with the customer to gain approval of what they would like to see in the newsletter as well. Your customers may have very distinct requirements that they want to see in a project newsletter.

2. You must work out the administrative aspects of the project newsletter long before sending out the first version. The administrative aspects include who will develop the newsletter going forward, where will the content come from, how often will it be produced, who are the recipients, what format and styles will be used, and so on.

3. After working out the administrative logistics, you are ready to create the first version of the project newsletter for the project.

ON the CD-ROM We have included a sample of a project newsletter in the Communication Tools, Communication Reporting subfolder. Use this as a guide to help you create your own version of this tool.

Using the project newsletter

Before using a project newsletter, you must identify who on your project team can utilize this tool so that you can determine the level of detail required, frequency of distribution, style, and format of the newsletter. In most cases, project newsletters will be very high level information about the project, presenting highlights, and positive information about the project.

Before utilizing a project newsletter, you must review the project newsletter planning section in Chapter 11. Then follow these steps:

1. Set up a rhythm for the project team members and customers to provide data for the project newsletter. You then need to determine the amount of time needed to compile the project newsletter, and determine a timeframe for distribution. This will be on a recurring basis, normally monthly, and driven by the needs of the customer. In this step, you should be looking as well to see if there are other newsletters going out that share the same timeframes as your newsletter and see if there is any duplication of project information.

2. Work with the customer to establish an official timeframe and approval that it is OK to send out the project newsletter on a recurring basis. This important step ensures everyone understands when the project newsletter deadlines are due and that you have the support of the customer to send this type of project information on an ongoing basis.

3. After obtaining that approval (no sign-offs are necessary) the project manager works with the agreed upon timeframe. The communication staff collects the project information, compiles it, and sends out the project newsletter.

4. The next step is to incorporate any feedback or issues you receive after sending the project newsletter to your customer, upper management, and any relevant stakeholders. You will take this feedback and update and improve the newsletter where applicable. This process continues throughout the life of the project. Make updates and adjustments to the project newsletter based on the customer feedback.

Mastering Project Presentations

Before you can begin to master a project presentation, you must understand how this tool can assist and support you on your project. The following project scenario emphasizes the importance of the tool.

A large software company has decided to implement a software project in a brand-new area of the company. The company has been around for many years and has a strong software development methodology in place. As an experienced project manager with a 15-year work history with the company, you decide to take on the project for this new area of the company. This area has new executives and new customers that no one in your group has worked with. You are both excited and nervous because you will be teaching the new group how projects are run in the company. As you start into the project, your best course of action is to work with the new group leaders and teach them the methodology you will use on the project; the methodology is simple and straightforward if you have done it before, but it is complex and overwhelming if you are new to it. As you start teaching the methodology to the group leaders, you see they have many questions about obtaining status, status reports, and generally where and how to get project information. Questions from the group leaders include:

How can I get a feel for the project status?

What phase of the project just finished?

How is the project budget tracking?

How is the project schedule tracking?

What are the current risks and issues on the project?

To help answers these questions, the project manager should create and use project presentations in order to provide the latest status about the project to include in the training. Project presentations are formal presentations to the project team all the way up to senior management and customer or owner on the status of the project. Project presentations can be a simple one-page document or multiple-page documents, where the project manager compiles as much information about the project as possible.

CROSS-REF   We recommend that you review the project presentation's planning questions in Chapter 10.

Creating project presentations

On most projects, there are two main types of project presentations utilized. One option is to give a one- or two-page presentation. The project manager summarizes the major components of the project for review by upper management and the customers. The project manager e-mails the simple project presentation to the customers for their review. In this case, this is a very informal manner in presenting the project presentation information. This type of presentation contains high-level summary information only. Customers can review and understand at the high level what is occurring on the project without getting unnecessary details. Another method of presenting a project presentation is in a more formal manner and consists of a large presentation and a team meeting to go over the presentation in detail. Project managers call these formal project presentation meetings for many reasons, such as phase closeouts, major project milestone reviews, and budget, risk, issue, and schedule reviews. In most cases, these types of project presentation occur when a project manager requires the customer's formal approval on a particular deliverable or project phase. In creating these presentations, the project manager should get the team leads involved and ensure that they are actively participating in developing content for the presentation and that they will be at the meeting to answer questions or concerns from the customers. What project managers do not want to do is take the information from the team members to put into their project presentation and be on the spot answering questions from the customers on that content.

A project presentation is a representation of your project at a major milestone, and it is critical in representing the status of the project at that time. Any open risks, issues, or roadblocks are included in the presentation material for resolution by customers or upper management staff. Project managers should realize that these presentations are opportunities to get support and approval from upper management and customers on project-level decisions that need resolution at the time of the presentation.

Project managers should play an active role in creating and preparing project presentation materials, because they are generally responsible for providing the information during the meeting. While compiling the information with the project team members, the project manager becomes familiar with the details in each area covered in the project presentation so that she/he can answer most of the tough questions raised at the meetings.

TIP Project managers should hold "preview" meetings for both the team members and the customers before the actual meeting. These meetings provide both parties a sneak preview of the materials before the formal meeting. If there are any issues or concerns, the project manager can address them with a smaller audience and in most cases take care of them before the meeting.

Rather than providing step-by-step instructions on how to create a project presentation, a better option for the project manager is to complete the template applicable to the presentation they need to deliver. The following steps provide you with how to work with and complete a project presentation template:

1. Determine the appropriate template to use. The project manager should establish if there are company templates they could use; and if so, the project manager will work with the customer, and if necessary, change it to meet their needs. It is important the customers approve the template and are happy with it before presenting it officially. The project presentation template will depend on what you are presenting at the specific stage the

project is currently; it may sound simple, but many times project managers do not realize that for every stage of the project, you use a different project presentation template. For example, a project kickoff presentation is going to be completely different then a lessons learned presentation. Project managers must select the right template for the type of presentation that they are to present.

2. Work with your team members to gather the information needed to populate the presentation material. In most cases, the project manager requires the team members to provide information to populate the project presentation template; this is because the team members are doing the work and are, therefore, much closer to the project and can provide the latest and most accurate status.

3. Create the project presentation keeping the audience in mind, use the information gathered, and put it into the template selected for this type of presentation. At this point, you are now ready to use your project presentation.

ON the CD-ROM We have included a sample of a project presentation in the Communication Tools Communication Managing subfolder. Use this as a guide to help you create your own version of this tool.

Using project presentations

Prior to using a project presentation, you must identify who on your project team will be involved in creating and delivering the project presentation to the customer, upper management, or other stakeholders. Knowing this can help you, as project manager, work closely with those team members and jointly develop the presentation together; that way, keeping the message consistent as to how you want it presented to your customer.

Before utilizing a project presentation, review the project presentation planning section in Chapter 10. Then follow these steps:

1. Determine if there are company standards or processes that you must follow before spending any time or effort creating and then presenting a project presentation for their customers. This will depend on the rules of the company; for example, the budget has to be a certain percentage of accuracy when presenting, the project has to pass internal audit, the project has to have a budget over $1 million. You must be aware of company policies and adjust the presentation process accordingly.

2. After determining the processes, then focus your team members on preparing the content for the project presentation. This includes arranging for the meeting event, hosting the preparatory meetings if there are any, and creating the content of the project presentation itself.

3. The next step is to call the meeting and present the materials.

4. After the meeting concludes, you then send any action items and meeting minutes to the presentation audience.

5. Finally, store the project presentation materials in the document control system for long-term storage, archiving, and retrieval purposes.

Mastering the Project Status Meeting

Before you can master the project status meeting, you must understand how this tool can assist and support you on your project. The following project scenario emphasizes why project status meetings are critical to every project.

A large automobile company in Niagara Falls, Ontario, Canada is in the beginning phase of its next new SUV production and the project manager is bringing the team together to kick-off the project. This project will have many different groups, and each group has its own roles and responsibilities. The groups consist of designers, engineers, and quality inspectors, to name a few. One challenge of this project is that the new SUV will have parts created all over the world but shipped to the Niagara Falls, Ontario's main manufacturing plant for final assembly. One of the challenges for the project manager is to ensure that all the different locations manufacturing the various parts are constantly communicating throughout the lifecycle of the project. The project manager must make sure that no one group is holding up another group, preventing them from completing their work. The project manager is depending highly on the groups to communicate effectively with one another throughout the project. In order to do so; he or she will have to play a big role in this communication. With all the groups and different companies involved around the world, the biggest concern for the project manager is how to keep the groups effectively communicating. The project manager is thinking about the varying ways to solve or manage the project's communication issues. He/she has some immediate questions that include:

> When do I get an opportunity to gather status from each team member?
>
> What will each of the groups cover in the status meetings and how will that information help the other groups?
>
> Who needs to attend these meetings?
>
> What information should be included in the report, and will each group have different information to report? If so, what will it be?
>
> How often does this meeting occur?

Having a project status meeting is an excellent way to bring the project team together to discuss the status of the project and work out any project issues and risks. The project manager can use the project status meeting in a number of ways including ensuring the team is tracking to the schedule, budget, and project scope. Other ways include encouraging and praising team members for their good work and holding cross-group discussions so everyone can share information.

CROSS-REF We recommend that you review the project status meeting's planning questions in Chapter 10.

Creating the project status meeting event

The project status meeting provides the opportunity for the project manager to bring together team members and sometimes customers to talk about the status of the project and to address any issues or concerns the team is facing. This may be the only time the project team gets together, either in a room or on a conference call, and focuses all of their attention on the project. During the rest of the week, the team members focus on their own project activities and tend not to interact with anyone else unless they have to. In the event the project has many issues or problems, we recommend the best practice of creating a daily project status meeting. This situation is usually temporary until the project is back on track and then status meetings return to the weekly cadence. In some projects, having a daily status meeting is an excellent way of keeping the project on track and marching forward. It can be a very informal checkpoint, but provides enough of an opportunity for the project manager to get together with the team members and discuss any high-level issues they are having.

CROSS-REF   Refer to Chapter 11 for more information on the Daily Progress Report tool.

When it comes to planning your project status meetings, we recommend that project managers hold two separate meetings: one with team members and another one with the customer (owner). Having two meetings allows project team members to have conversations and get into the deeper details of the project that would not be relevant for a customer or upper management to listen in. At the customer-focused project status meeting, the project customer can dive into details around budgets, time lines, and resources that would not be applicable or relevant to most team members. Project status meetings are the one opportunity where a customer can discuss details that are unclear and require more information than they see in a status report or other project e-mails that occur during the day-to-day operation of the project. Project customers should utilize these status meetings, ensure they are happy with the progress, and are available for removing roadblocks or any other concerns the project team may have at the time.

We suggest using the following template to help you create a project status meeting agenda and actual meeting event.

Project Status Meeting Agenda and Meeting Event

*A*genda 1: *Review Last week's Minutes*
The project manager will cover any action items from the last meeting as well as any relevant meeting minutes.

*A*genda 2: *Review Current Action Items*
This agenda item covers any current action items that the project team members are working on. The team members will individually speak to their respective action items.

*A*genda 3: *Review Project Schedule*
This agenda item covers the project team reviewing the project schedule and ensuring the team is tracking. The team members will each speak to their respective areas of the project schedule.

Agenda 4: Major Area Updates

This agenda item covers receiving a particular project status update from the project leads. Depending on the type of project, a design lead, engineer lead, test lead, etc., would all provide status. The team leads will each speak to their respective areas and provide updates on issues, risks, or other concerns that they are encountering.

Agenda 5: Review Current Budget Information

The project manager will cover the budget and cost review on the project.

Agenda 6: Review Project Risks

This agenda item covers the team reviewing the project risks. The team members will each speak to any risks that they are dealing with on the project.

Agenda 7: Review Project Issues

This agenda item covers the team reviewing the project issues. The team members will each speak to the issues that they are dealing with on the project.

Agenda 8: Lessons Learned (Right/Wrong)

This agenda item covers the team providing any lessons learned over the last reporting period to the project manager. The project manager captures what has gone right, what has gone wrong, and whatever is important to capture for lessons learned information from everyone involved and working on the project.

Agenda 9: Walk-ons

This agenda item covers any additional items that the project manager or team want to call to the attention of the project manager or other team members.

ON the CD-ROM We have included a project status meeting agenda in the Communication Tools Integration subfolder. Use this as a guide to create your own version of this tool.

Facilitating the project status meeting

Before you facilitate the project status meeting, you must identify whom on your project team will be involved in the meeting, what role they will play, what materials they will present, and generally how will they be involved in the meeting. Knowing this information is going to help you run a more effective meeting because you will understand exactly how to utilize your team members.

Before utilizing the project status meeting, review the project status meeting planning section in Chapter 4. Then follow these steps:

1. You should establish a cadence for your project status meetings. This cadence is going to depend highly on when the company requires project managers to report their respective projects statues. This is because the project status meeting is an excellent way for you to collect project information to use in creating the project status report.

2. Set up internal status meetings. Establish and set up both the internal team meetings and the customer status meetings on everyone's e-mail and professional calendars. One of the best practices is for you to consider these as separate meetings, one internal team meeting and another separate customer status meetings. It is important to set a day's lag between these meetings to allow information to be updated from one meeting before presenting at a different meeting. For example, if the project status for the company is due on Friday, then project team members' meetings should be held Tuesdays and customer meetings should be held on Thursdays. You can then send the project status report on Friday, the day it is due. This provides a day between the internal meeting and the customer meeting, and a day between the customer meeting and the submission of the final report.

3. Call the project status meetings. During the meeting you facilitate it by promoting conversations and go through the agenda items defined in your agenda.

 Collect lessons learned information from team members during this meeting.

4. Send the minutes to the attendees and then store them in the document control system for long-term storage, archiving, and retrieval purposes.

Summary

The tools we described in this chapter are the best choices for managing the administration component of the project while in the execution and controlling process. As you know, this is the process of the project where the project is in full swing so management of this project at this time is critical.

The tools outlined in this chapter can help you manage your project more effectively and communicate project information regularly.

Use of the reporting communications tools outlined in this chapter can benefit the project manager, customers, and project team members. The reports are simple, easy to create, and invaluable in presenting information to the various parties.

Chapter 20

Using Communication Tools to Monitor the Executing and Controlling of a Project

I n this chapter, we explore project communication tools that can help the project manager monitor and control their projects during the executing and controlling process. The communication tools in this chapter are specific to helping the project manager monitor project activities, and using tools such as issues lists, control charts, and project meeting minutes will help him/her with that process. These tools all help project managers keep a tighter control over the project as it moves through its different lifecycle processes.

One of the most widely used project tools in this chapter is the issues list. Without the ability to track and monitor issues on a regular basis, they can negatively affect the progress on your project. A project manager can utilize issue lists as one of their main project communication tools; it will engage the team members, customers, and in some cases upper management in helping to resolve the issues on the project.

Mastering the Control Chart

Before you can master the control chart, you must understand how this tool can assist and support you on your project. The following project scenario emphasizes the importance of and reasons why the control chart can be helpful on every project.

The Department for Transport in London, England has decided to implement a Motorway Safety Project that determines the average highway speeds on the M6 over a 72-hour period. The goal for this project is to determine how to lower the accident rate on a particular stretch of the highway that last year alone had eight fatalities. The transport department needs to make this a priority to prevent additional casualties. As the lead project manager for the Department for Transport, you ask to manage this effort. Management agrees, and you start working on the project. As the project begins, the first things you should do is establish a team, collect traffic data, and find the reasons behind all these fatalities. You realize you need to get out to the site so you are able to see what is happening first hand. You gather the survey equipment and take your crew to the site for data collection. As you begin the collection process, the data starts pouring in and your upper management staff starts to ask questions about the data. They too are interested in getting this resolved as soon as possible so are anxious to get answers from you. Management's questions include:

What is the upper speed limit in your sampling data?

What was the lower speed limit in your sampling data?

What is the average speed limit in your sampling data?

What timeframe did the highest speeds hit that portion of the highway?

To obtain the answers to these questions the project manager should use a control chart to present the data findings in a usable format from the test results. A control chart is a graphical report that displays the upper and lower control limits on a sampling of data. It uses a sample mean line that sets the average or the middle points for those control limits. The objective of the control chart is to determine how many data points are above the upper limit, how many are under the lower limit, and the percentage of the total outside the limits, both high and low. For example, in this scenario, we could have 100 cars of which 2 cars exceeded the upper limit, and 1 car was below the lower limit. This indicates 3 percent of the cars were outside the limits of that test.

CROSS-REF We recommend that you review the control chart document's planning questions in Chapter 8.

Creating a control chart

The creation of a control chart report is simple and easy to do. To create a control chart, each chart must have some common elements. Those elements include a central line, an upper control limit, a lower control limit, and process values plotted on the chart. A control chart is not applicable on all projects, but when data points are available, they are great communication tools.

Project managers should utilize control charts as often as possible as a mechanism to control the quality aspects of their project. There are many examples in which control charts are used, such as in manufacturing in counting the number of failures in a batch, and in software, counting the different severity level bugs hitting a threshold. To enhance the quality of the project, project managers should look for areas of the project to map data points onto a control chart.

To ensure success on projects, the project manager and customers need to promote and manage quality at all times. Using a control chart to graph the different data points ensures the team is focusing on quality and is continually working to improve the results. A control chart does an excellent job of displaying the project's quality issues and provides evidence of where the team needs to focus.

The steps for creating a control chart vary. The following steps can help you get started if you have never created this tool before. We have also created a template for you (located on the CD-ROM) as a starting point for your projects. This template will require updating based on your specific project needs and requirements.

The following steps will walk you through creating a control chart for your project. These steps will create an initial chart, and then you can update the chart with your own project information. If, at any time, you are unsure of how to enter the data, either go to the CD-ROM and use the sample that is on the CD-ROM or refer to Figure 20.1. It shows you exactly what the data will look like to create the chart.

1. Open a spreadsheet tool. (We used Microsoft Excel.)

2. Create your time-related data and title it Date. For this example, we took a sampling of three days. Enter these three days into the three separate cells going down the spreadsheet.

   ▨ 3/1/2008

   ▨ 3/2/2008

   ▨ 3/3/2008

3. Then create the sample-related data; create these samples for this example. Enter these three samples going down the spreadsheet and in the same row as each of the dates.

   ▨ Sample 1-1 (Row 1) = 2

   ▨ Sample 1-2 (Row 2) = 6

   ▨ Sample 1-3 (Row 3) = 5

4. Then create a second sample (Sample 2) column of data; create these samples for this example. Enter these three samples going down the spreadsheet and in the same row as each of the dates.

   ▨ Sample 2-1 (Row 1) = 4

   ▨ Sample 2-2 (Row 2) = 3

   ▨ Sample 2-3 (Row 3) = 4

5. Then create the Mean Data (Daily Average); create these samples for this example. This mean data is the average data for your sampling. Again, simply use three rows of data to get familiar with creating these charts. Enter these three samples going down the spreadsheet and in the same row as each of the dates.

   ▪ Mean (Row 1) = 3.0

   ▪ Mean (Row 2) = 4.5

   ▪ Mean (Row 3) = 4.2

6. Then you create the Sample Mean Data (Average of all Means). Create these samples for this example. *Note this is a constant for all rows of data. The Sample Mean data is your zero point data for the chart. Enter these three samples going down the spreadsheet and in the same row as each of the dates.

   ▪ Sample Mean (Row 1) = 4.50

   ▪ Sample Mean (Row 2) = 4.50

   ▪ Sample Mean (Row 3) = 4.50

7. Next, you would create the Lower Control Limit; create these samples for this example. Enter these three samples going down the spreadsheet and in the same row as each of the dates. Lower Limit 0.24

8. Then create the upper control limit; create these samples for this example. Enter these three samples going down the spreadsheet and in the same row as each of the dates. Upper Limit 6.08

9. Finally, your last step is to chart the data. Control Charts are Line Charts; select Line as the best option for this chart type, then select the data in the spreadsheet for charting purposes.

   1. Select the Time Sheet data. In Figure 20.1, select the data in the Date column.

   2. Select the Mean data. In Figure 20.1 select the data in the Mean (Daily Average) column.

   3. Then select the Sample Mean data. In Figure 20.1, select the data in the Sample Mean (Average of All Means) column.

   4. Select the Lower Limit data. In Figure 20.1, select the data in the Lower Control Limit column.

   5. Finally select the Upper Limit data. In Figure 20.1, select the data in the upper control limit column.

10. Your control chart is complete.

Figure 20.1 represents the sample data selected for the control chart. As you can see, the data represents 14 days and has an average mean of 4.50. The lower and upper limits have a large range. To calculate the average means, add the mean daily average data and divide it by the number of data points or rows.

FIGURE 20.1

The sampling of the data entered through the creation steps

Date	Sample 1	Sample 2	Mean (Daily Average)	Sample Mean (Average of all Means)	Lower Control Limit	Upper Control Limit
3/2/2008	2	4	3.0	4.50	0.24	6.08
3/3/2008	6	3	4.5	4.50	0.24	6.08
3/4/2008	5	4	4.2	4.50	0.24	6.08
3/5/2008	7	5	6.0	4.50	0.24	6.08
3/6/2008	6	0	3.0	4.50	0.24	6.08
3/7/2008	6	3	4.5	4.50	0.24	6.08
3/8/2008	5	5	5.0	4.50	0.24	6.08
3/9/2008	5	1	2.1	4.50	0.24	6.08
3/10/2008	6	3	4.5	4.50	0.24	6.08
3/11/2008	2	4	3.0	4.50	0.24	6.08
3/12/2008	7	0	1.5	4.50	0.24	6.08
3/13/2008	4	3	3.5	4.50	0.24	6.08
3/14/2008	5	0	2.5	4.50	0.24	6.08
3/15/2008	5	1	3.0	4.50	0.24	6.08

Figure 20.2 represents the control chart created by the sample data in the creation steps. As you can see, the values on the chart range from 1.5 to 6.0 and everywhere in between.

ON the CD-ROM We have included a sample control chart in the Communication tools Quality subfolder. Use this to help you create your own personal version of this tool.

FIGURE 20.2

A sample of a control chart.

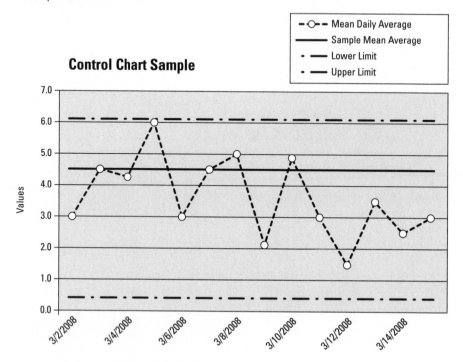

Using the control chart

Before using a tool such as the control chart, you must identify who on your project team will use it so that you can determine the level of detail required, frequency of distribution, style, and format of the chart. Review the control chart planning section in Chapter 8 and then follow these steps:

1. Analyze the data on the control chart and determine how it affects the test results. When you review the data, determine the initial steps to take and then, with the team members, dive into the details of the test results for further actions on what you can do to address them. You may need to call a series of meetings to get through all the data points and determine the best course of action.

 **TIP**   When reviewing the chart, you and team members must have an understanding of the upper and lower limits

2. Next, you should analyze the test results on the chart and determine if they are acceptable. If the data is acceptable, then you should decide if further testing is required and potentially stop testing at this point.

3. If the results are not acceptable, then you will require further analysis of the data. This could result in further testing or modifying the parameters (upper and lower limits) or simply re-run the tests.

4. After completing all the test cases, the test manager documents the test results and distributes them to you, your team members, and your customers.

5. After testing is complete, store all of your testing materials in the document control system for long-term storage, archiving, and retrieval purposes.

Mastering the Issues List

Before mastering the issues list, you must understand how this tool can assist and support you on your project. The following project scenario emphasizes the importance of and reasons why the issues list tool is critical to every project.

A large aerospace company has just announced that it is developing a new airplane for military use. This plane will take five to seven years to produce and should be released in 2016. This plane will be one of the largest and will be able to fly around the world with just two refueling stops. As a project manager, your assignment is the cockpit construction and design for the project. You have been involved in the production of many planes before, so to you this is just another construction project. Because of your background and knowledge in plane design, you are familiar with the various risks and issues associated with building planes, and you share your concerns with the project team. You know the cockpit has many dependencies with the other sections of the airplane construction project and therefore you will be responsible for driving each dependency to resolution. Without a cockpit, the plane cannot fly. Therefore, your portion of the project is critical. The challenge you face is how to expose project issues in a manner that other members of the team, customers, or upper management can review the issues for your area of the project. Other questions that surround your specific project issues include:

How do you capture and track issues for your area of the project?

What information should you capture about the issues?

How can you bring management exposure to your particular issues?

What tool should you use to discuss issues during a project status meeting?

To obtain the answers to these questions, the project manager should use an issues list on their project. The issues list is a critical communication tool, and one that every project should have regardless of the size or complexity. In the previous scenario, you would create and display an issues list that would be accessible by anyone, and add your specific areas issues. Many times the issues in one area of the project are related or resolved by other areas, so maximizing the exposure of your issues to everyone can help drive resolutions faster.

CROSS-REF We recommend that you review the issues list document's planning questions in Chapter 12.

Creating the issues list

An issues list is one of the easiest tools available for the project manager. In some cases, the basic issues list consists of six columns: issue ID, title, status, priority, owner, and due date. Large complex projects will have intricate issue tracking systems in place to capture numerous details around each issue and ensure that the project manager or owner of the issue is tracking it diligently. Larger projects need to share issues across multiple groups, so issue tracking systems become more relevant on those types of projects.

Project managers must be diligent in tracking and managing project issues. In some cases, issues can halt a project completely until they are resolved. Issues can range from simple to complex, and project managers need to manage and monitor them to resolution. The project manager reviews project issues each week with the team members and customers until they are resolved. After they are complete, the project manager moves the issue to the closed issues list for historical purposes. At this time if there are any lessons learned from the issue it should be documented in the lessons learned tool.

Project customers may be active in the resolution of project issues, and the more active they are in issue management the less likely issues will negatively affect the project. Customers have an amazing ability to reduce a project issue from something the team feels is large to something small and workable.

The actual steps of creating an issue list can vary from project manager to project manager and will depend greatly on their favorite tools of choice. Instead of providing step-by-step instructions on creating an issues list, a better option would be for the project manager to complete the template provided on the CD-ROM. Here is the issues list template for your project. Project managers would utilize this template only if no others were available for use on their projects and may have to make updates to this list for their project.

Table 20.1 shows the issues list for use on a project. This list provides the relevant fields for issue tracking, and you can use them for most projects. Project managers can update and enhance the issues list according to the needs of their projects.

TABLE 20.1

Sample Issues List

ID	Issue Description	Impact	Severity	Originator	Date Opened	Assigned to	Target Resolution Date	Status	Resolution
1	Platform problems	High	2	Bob Smith	12/4/2008	Joe Jones		Open	TBD
2	Resource left paving team	Medium	4	May Douglas	10/14/2008	Fred Brown	11/28/2008	Closed	Hired new resource

ON the CD-ROM We have included multiple examples of an Issues List in the Communication tools Risk subfolder. Use this as a guide to create your own version of this tool.

Using an issues list

Prior to using an issues list, you must identify who on your project team will utilize this tool so that you can determine the level of detail required, frequency of distribution, style, and format of the report. Issues lists can be very detailed so that team members can use them to understand as many details as possible or at a very high level so the customers can use the issues list for their purposes.

Before utilizing an issues list, review the issues list planning section in Chapter 12 and then follow these steps:

1. Ensure that your project team members or your customers have filled in correctly the issues on the issues list form. If there is any missing information on any of the issues, you are responsible for finding that information and filling it into the form. You and your team members may struggle to work on an issue with limited information or with missing pieces; therefore, it is important to have all relevant information entered on the issues list.

2. Arrange weekly review sessions with your project team members to ensure they are responding to the issues. This normally occurs in the project's weekly status meetings, but some project managers may want separate meetings to review issues.

3. Hold at minimum a weekly status meeting with your customers to allow them the opportunity to examine the issues list and ask questions. This normally occurs during the customer status meeting, but you may choose to hold a separate status meeting to go over the issues by themselves.

4. You should manage and force the use of the issues list on your project. This means adding and removing issues, all issues reporting, and the overall management of all the project's issues.

Mastering Project Meeting Minutes

Before you can use meeting minutes on your project, you should understand the value that meeting minutes bring to your project. The following project scenario emphasizes the importance of and reasons why creating project meeting minutes is critical to every project.

A large lumber company, in Vancouver, BC, Canada plans to replace their inventory system. This system keeps track of all the lumber mills, the daily production, inventory levels, and purchasing information for all the various mills in the company. As you can imagine, this was an important system, and a replacement project like this requires full support from both management and team leaders at each of the mills. There are 55 mills located around the world, and each expects to use this new inventory system. Because company headquarters will be the staging area for the project, it is critical that communications between headquarters and the various mill locations are ongoing.

Without it, the project is doomed to fail. As one of the most senior project managers in the company, your management asks you to lead the project. You accept, and then call the core team together and ask everyone to provide updates and obtain statuses on the project. Your first challenge is finding a time during the week when 55 people are free and available for a one-hour meeting, and to add to that challenge, you must factor in time zones from all around the world. This is a feat in itself, but you finally find a time, and everyone agrees to attend and participate in the meeting. As the project progresses, each week all 55 locations show up, and everyone obtains the latest status on the project. What surprises you is how well things are going; then, as the project moves into week 12, something happens and the 55 locations all dialing in and attending your status meetings drop down to 36 locations. The next week, it drops from 36 locations down to 28 locations, and then as you start sending e-mails requesting people to start attending, it works temporarily and the attendance goes up to 40. The project that was going along so well and had such great participation has lost the support of the project team members and, for one reason or another, the project managers in the different locations can no longer attend those critical status meetings. Because many of the team members are missing the meetings, they are not hearing the discussions, action items, and decisions made on the project. This is critical to the success of the project. At this point, you have no idea how to get the team's interactions and determine whether the decisions being made in the meetings are going to have any impact at all on the different locations. You need every project manager at every location on these calls! People are growing frustrated and asking many questions about what has happened at the meetings because they are not able to attend. Their questions include:

What happened last week on the project?

What are the action items from the meeting?

Who made what decisions?

What is the status of the project?

How is the yellow issue on costs tracking?

Did you capture any lessons learned information and what are they?

Project meeting minutes would answer all these questions and keep the project managers working in the different locations up to date on the project. In the previous scenario, if the project manager had captured and distributed meeting minutes, the team members in the different mills would have an update on the status, decisions, and action items each week of the project. The meeting minutes will capture this information, and anyone interested can review the minutes and be brought up to date on the project.

 We recommend that you review the Project Meeting Minutes tool document's planning questions in Chapter 12.

Creating project meeting minutes

Project managers should assign someone to capture the minutes for them — it's difficult to run a meeting and capture the minutes. Project managers should rotate the responsibilities of taking minutes among all the team members, or if possible, assign an administrative staff member to take the meeting minutes at every meeting.

Project managers should ensure that project meeting minutes capture all aspects of the discussions and action items that take place in the meeting. Some projects have agendas focused on capturing a lot of information and status, whereas other agendas are much looser and not designed with that in mind. In either case, the project manager should ensure whoever is taking the minutes is capturing the right information so the project meeting minutes are usable by anyone needing them after the meeting adjourns.

A best practice technique for project managers is to use action items within the project meeting minutes template and discuss the project's action items at every meeting until they are each completed. As the project status meeting begins, the project manager reads the action items from last week's minutes and ensures each item was completed or addressed in the previous week. If an action item is incomplete, it stays on the list and the project manager reviews the item with the responsible team member to determine why it was not completed or how long it will take to complete.

TIP No action items should go longer than a week's duration if the project status meeting's cadence is weekly. Anything longer than a week should become a task on the project schedule and not an action item for weekly project tracking. For example, hiring a resource could come up as an action item for a team lead at a project status meeting, but because it will normally take longer than a week to complete, the project manager will add it to the project schedule as a project activity.

Project customers are active in reviewing and acquiring project information from project meeting minutes. They want to review project decisions, action items, next steps, and the progress of the project captured in the project meeting minutes. With some project meetings the customers will be involved, and others they will not need to be. In those cases where the customer does not join or does not need to be involved, the project manager should still provide access to the project information to them. It allows the customers the feeling of having the information they need on the project and enhances communications between the two groups. This provides the customers with the information to ask questions, dive into details, and obtain the information they feel they need to be successful.

The actual steps in creating project meeting minutes can vary. We recommend that you use a project meeting minutes template for your projects.

ON the CD-ROM We have included a sample of a project meeting minutes tool in the Communication tools Integration subfolder. Use this as a guide to create your own version of this tool.

Using project meeting minutes

Prior to using a tool such as the project meeting minutes, you must identify who on your project team will utilize this tool so that you can determine the level of detail required, frequency of distribution, style, and format of the report. In most cases, project meeting minutes are very detail oriented and therefore there is an expectation that you add as many details as possible to the project meeting minutes document when creating.

Review the project meeting minutes planning section in Chapter 4 and then follow these steps:

1. The first step you should do is to create a storage location on the document control system to store project meeting minutes. In that location, you can place a blank meeting minutes template so anyone taking minutes has a format to follow.

2. The next step in this process is for you to identify a project team member, or administrative assistant team member, who is willing to attend every meeting and capture the meeting minutes. You need to secure this position long before the meeting event so the person knows, going into the meeting, that they are accountable for taking the minutes. Make sure you have a backup in case the first team member cannot attend a meeting. It is your responsibility to ensure the meeting minute taker has the template for each meeting.

3. After the meeting, store your project's meeting minutes in the document control system for long-term storage, archival, and retrieval purposes and send to all invitees of the meeting.

4. The final step in this process is for you to utilize the project meeting minutes to manage the various aspects of the project. The information covered at project meetings is valuable to you and the team in running the project. For example, when you capture action items in project meeting minutes it helps to drive deliverables of the project.

Mastering the Risk Assessment Form

Before you use the risk assessment form, you must understand how this tool can assist and support you on your project. The following project scenario emphasizes the importance of and reasons why the risk assessment tool is critical to every project.

A famous real estate tycoon has just announced his newest project in Nashville, Tennessee — a brand-new 18-hole golf course, hotel, and casino project. The project will take three years and will be the largest casino in the Nashville area. The budget for this project is $400 million. As a trusted advisor and leading project manager for this tycoon, he has chosen you to manage this massive project. As the project progresses through the various stages of the lifecycle, project issues and risks start pouring in. As you are leading all three projects and are managing over 900 risks, you are starting to feel overwhelmed, and you have no idea how to handle all these risks. You have no idea if these risks are going to affect the project. You do not know their potential impacts to the project. You are also struggling how to track them effectively, as there are just too many to handle. Upper management, and especially the world famous tycoon, are asking many tough questions about these risks and expect that you have a better handle on them. The questions include:

How risky is each project?

What is the expected monetary value of each risk event?

What is the probability of each risk event?

What is the risk score for each project?

What is the total budget impact to all risk events, across all three projects?

To obtain the answers to these questions, the project manager should use a risk assessment form for tracking and managing project risks. The risk assessment form captures and assesses project risk events, and as the project manager completes the form, it calculates an overall risk score for the project. Many projects do not calculate a risk score or perform proper risk assessments and therefore run into problems on their project. When they choose to ignore or simply not complete a risk score, it makes it difficult for upper management looking at a wide range of projects to determine which one is riskier and which one requires more of their attention. Companies that capture risk scores and assess risks properly allow management to focus on the higher-risk projects where they need to spend their time and not worry as much about the less risky ones.

CROSS-REF We recommend that you review the risk assessment form's planning questions in Chapter 12.

Creating a risk assessment form

Creating a risk assessment form is critical for every project, regardless of the size or complexity of the project. Every project has risks, and these risks require tracking and assessing by the project team members on a continual basis. By adding the risks to a risk assessment form, it provides the team members with the knowledge and head's up of a potential risk event that may have impact on the project. It is the project team's responsibility to control project risks, and especially the project manager, who is responsible for ensuring that the risk events do not negatively affect the project. The risk assessment form provides the project manager and team members with an overall assessment of each project risk, and from there they can determine how to mitigate the risk appropriately.

Project customers use the risk assessment forms but are rarely involved in the creation. Many times customers have risks associated to them directly and, therefore, keeping them actively engaged in this process ensures that they are aware and responsible for resolving their risks.

The actual steps of creating a risk assessment form vary. The following steps can get you started if you have never created this tool before. We have also created a template for you as a starting point for your projects. This template will require updating based on your specific project needs and requirements.

1. Create a risk assessment template for your project. This could be using an existing company template, referring to the template on the CD-ROM, or starting from scratch. Once you create the form, enter the project risks. Depending on the template chosen, it is a best practice for the project manager to enter the project risks into categories. The type of project determines these categories, and there are some sample categories already in the template the project managers can use immediately. Categories are also industry specific, so the project manager will update the categories as well, depending on the industry they are working in.

2. After entering all the risks onto the risk assessment form, then you should call a meeting with your team members and assign three values to each risk event. Those values include probability, impact, and exposure. The legend in the form provided on the template will guide you in what value to provide to each. This legend may need updating for your project.

3. After entering values for each risk event, the form will auto generate a project risk score. This is an automated number calculated from the numbers entered in each of the fields, once again if using the template attached on the CD-ROM. If not, then your company's template may have their own calculations or you may have to copy the formulas in the template provided on the CD-ROM. The most important aspect is to ensure your project has a risk score regardless of the template used to generate the number.

ON the CD-ROM We include a sample risk assessment form in the Communication tools Risk subfolder. Use this as a guide to create your own version of this tool.

Figure 20.3 shows an example of a risk assessment form. This form generates a risk score for the project when you enter the three factors of probability, impact, and exposure. The risk assessment form is easy to use and a powerful communication tool for your project.

Using a risk assessment form

Prior to using a risk assessment form, you must identify who on your project team will utilize this tool so that you can determine the level of detail required, frequency of distribution, style, and format of the report. Most of the times, we recommend that you add as much detail as possible into the form to allow anyone who is reviewing it to understand the risk event and determine if they can help or offer any assistance to potentially mitigate the risk. Capturing risks at a high level usually provides little value to anyone using the form and will tend to generate more questions than if the project manager or team members entered with as much detail as possible.

Before utilizing a risk assessment form, review the risk assessment form planning section in Chapter 12 and then follow these steps:

1. Your first step is to communicate the project risk score to the customers, upper management, and executive staff, where applicable. This includes distributing the risk assessment form to everyone involved, scheduling risk meetings to go over the risks, and storing the risk assessment form in the document control system.

2. Your responsibility throughout the project is to continue updating and assessing project risk events. This includes maintaining ongoing communications of the risk score to everyone involved with the project and the ongoing management of the risk items. You should go over all project risks at the weekly status meeting so everyone is fully aware of the potential risk items and can add and remove risks as appropriate.

3. At the end of the project, the final risk assessment form goes into the document control system for long-term storage, archiving, and retrieval purposes.

FIGURE 20.3

A sample risk assessment form.

Project Risk Model Example

Risk Category	Risk Owner	Probability	Impact	Exposure	Risk Score	Mitigation Plan	Action Item
Application		0	0	0	0		
Communications		0	0	0	0		
Functionality / Usability / Performance / Controllability		0	0	0	0		
Environment		0	0	0	0		
Legal		0	0	0	0		
Process		0	0	0	0		
Technology		0	0	0	0		
Work Breakdown Structure		0	0	0	0		
		0	0	0	0		
RISK SCORE TOTAL					0		

	Probability %	Negative Project Impact	Exposure: How many aspects of project are impacted?
	Chances of risk occurring in	3: High	5: All activities (80–100%)
		2: Medium	4: Most Activities (60–80%)
		1: Low	3: Many activities (40–60%)
			2: Some activities (20–40%)
			1: Few activities (1–20%)

Other Risk Categories to Consider

Requirements
Staffing
Costs/Resources
Quality/Features
Management
Customers
Time/Schedules
Staffing
Environmental including legal
Regulatory etc

Mastering the Safety Report

Before you can master how to use a safety report tool, you must understand how this tool can assist and support you on your project. The following project scenario emphasizes the importance of, and reasons why, a safety report is critical to every project.

A large warehouse store has just opened in Butte, Montana, and has hired almost the whole town to work in it. Everyone is excited about the store, as they know it will have a positive impact on the economy and has a reputation for treating its employees well. They hired you for the position of safety manager in the warehouse. The management of the store thought you could handle the job even though you have only worked on one large project in the area of safety. That project you worked on had one of the best safety records of a project of that size. One of the first tasks you start with is to have the company put up their large notice board at the store's entrance to display the store's accident-free safety record. The safety board will state the number of days that the store workers have had an accident-free environment. You have seen the board used on previous jobs and feel its presence provides an incentive for the employees to work safely. You also feel it is good for the public to see this board so they know how long the store has gone without accidents, which gives them a level of comfort that management cares about store safety. You then put the board up, and on the first day set the count to zero. As the days go by, you keep increasing the number on the board. Not only are you proud of it, but the whole store is proud of going so long without any accidents. You are planning a celebration at the 30-day mark, pizza, and soda for all the warehouse employees. You are thinking in the back of your mind, this job is a breeze, until a new employee is hired that changes everything. A new employee named Andy Smith joins the store as a new warehouse worker. Andy seems to be very accident-prone and has major mishaps on a weekly basis. This once accident-free store can no longer get past the seven-day mark with Andy around. You as safety manager are starting to feel the pressure because your once safe store is now having accident after accident and there is one main cause—Andy Smith. Upper management is now starting to ask you a number of questions about the accidents. Why they are occurring and what are you doing about it? Their questions include:

> What accidents occurred this week in the store?
>
> What was the main cause?
>
> Was anyone seriously hurt?
>
> Was it Andy again?
>
> Did any vendors get hurt?

To obtain the answers to these questions, you, as the safety manager, should use a safety report tool. The safety report provides a record of safety occurrences on the project in a store environment. The safety risk and mitigation report describes in detail the event, elimination strategy, date, time, reported to, and violator name on a single report. The safety report provides an accident report stating what occurred, who was involved, and who took ownership to resolve the issue. Safety reports are common on construction projects and other jobs where large groups of people work together.

CROSS-REF We recommend that you review the safety report document's planning questions in Chapter 12.

Creating a safety report

There are two types of safety reports for projects. One is a basic accident report that you normally complete with the accident information using a pre-canned template or form. These accident reports are generally simple forms that capture the details around the actual event. With these forms, you will provide an assessment of the situation. How the accident occurred and then, how possible it is to avoid it in the future. The accident report is not normally project related because it focuses on the specific details of the accident only and has nothing to do with a project.

The second safety report offers a summary of safety information at the project level. Creating this report provides upper management and customers with an understanding of what occurred and the state of the project from a safety perspective. Construction project teams have full-time safety managers whose role is to ensure the job site is as safe as possible for all workers. One of their main responsibilities is to create a project-related safety report that shows the safety conditions of the project for the owners, customers, insurance agency, and various government agencies.

If a project is small enough, the project manager is responsible for documenting and communicating all safety events occurring on the project. The project manager works closely in the creation of the report to make sure that he can understand the safety events. He will direct the team members in ensuring that safety always comes first when performing their project activities. Carelessness can be dangerous on a construction site, and if the project manager hears of these types of situations, he will work directly with the safety manager and with the team members to put a stop to it immediately.

Project customers, such as the owner, team members, inspectors, the media, and the government, will be active in reviewing and assessing the various safety issues and concerns on the project. As safety reports come in for review, customers will assess the project's safety situation and determine if, and where, they can provide assistance. The riskier the project, potentially the more insurance and higher risk the project is, so it is beneficial for the customers to stay involved and active in understanding the overall safety level of the project.

The steps to create a safety report vary. Below are some simple steps for starting if you have never created this tool before. We have also created a template for you as a starting point for your projects. This template will require updating based on your specific project needs and requirements.

1. The first step for you during the process of creating a safety report is to find the safety report template on the CD-ROM. The company may already have their own version of a safety report, so the project manager in most cases should use the company's version of the report.

2. The next step is for you to work with your safety manager, if applicable (you may be your project's safety manager) to complete the template with the relevant safety infraction information. This will include all the safety hazards, any accidents that occurred, or other situations that occurred.

3. Finally, you or your safety manager will analyze the safety reports on a weekly or bi-weekly basis to determine any trends or recurring safety-related issues.

ON the CD-ROM We have included a sample of a safety report in the Communication tools Risk sub-folder. Use this as a guide to create your own version of this tool.

Using a safety report

Before you can use a safety report, you must identify who on your project team will utilize this tool so that you can determine the level of detail required, frequency of distribution, style, and format of the report. In this kind of report, we recommend you add as much detail as possible about the safety incident.

Before utilizing the safety report, review the safety report planning section in Chapter 12 and then follow these steps:

1. Complete the safety report with the relevant safety-related information.

2. Extract information from the safety report to identify trends and upper limits on accident or incident data.

3. Analyze the data and make project adjustments accordingly. This could include training for team members, different processes, or placing the "Andy Smiths" into roles that will reduce the safety occurrences.

4. Store the safety report into the document control system for long-term storage, archiving, and retrieval purposes.

Mastering the Work Package

Before you can use a work package tool, you must understand how this tool can assist and support you on your project. The following project scenario emphasizes the importance of and reasons why the work package tool is critical to every project.

You, as the senior scheduling manager, have been working on the construction of a luxury hotel in Belize on the Gulf of Honduras for the last two years. The project is approaching completion and everyone on the project is excited because the president of the hotel chain is coming next week to dedicate the hotel at the grand opening. There will be much celebrating. The project manager and the cost manager are gathering documentation to calculate the final cost of the building and the amount of remaining work. As the senior scheduling manager, you are busy planning and scheduling the remaining work that you must complete in order to turn the hotel over to the owners. The project manager comes to you and wants to know how many labor hours it took to complete the electrical work in the theater; he wants the hours broken out by standard electrical construction work and the specialized electrical work for the theater system. You only have the work breakdown structure identifying standard electrical work and now must subdivide the electrical work into the two categories. You have all sorts of questions, including:

How are you going to meet the owner's request, while getting your own work completed?

What could you or should you have done, when?

When was the best time to develop the WBS to meet not only this request but also others that may arise on the project?

To obtain the answers to these questions, you should use the work package tool. It would have been easy at the beginning of the project to have the WBS work packages identify the two different types of electrical work; after all, they are two individual subcontractors, and you could have easily separated them. Now you have to go back and break the electrical work packages into the two subcontractors and report the results. This will now take quite a bit of time.

CROSS-REF We recommend that you review the work package's planning questions in Chapter 10.

Creating a work package

Before you can gain any value from the work package tool, you should have created the work breakdown structure to the level of detail necessary to track all the work on the project. The work package can identify the resources, cost, schedule, and any other information the project manager wants to track during the life of the project. The work package results are the actual labor hours, start and finish dates, actual cost, lessons learned, and so on that occur as the work package progresses toward completion.

To use and take advantage of the work package tool, project managers should create a WBS with the information they want to track, control, and report, and they must establish various structures to break out the work in order to report on schedules, costs, and labor hours. After the project starts, it is time to collect actual data occurring on the project. Each work package has planned information, and that information will have actuals, as the work accomplished on the work package is complete.

Project customers and owners should understand how important this tool is for reporting. Without planning and tracking the information in each work package, it would be difficult, if not impossible, to know what the status of the project really is.

Although the actual steps of creating a work package tool vary, the following steps can help you get started.

1. Create the WBS during the planning process. By creating the WBS, you are creating the work packages at the lowest level of the WBS. See Chapter 10 for more detail on the work breakdown structure.

2. After the final WBS is approved and operational, you should establish a baseline schedule for the project. This baseline creates all the information the project will need to make a comparison after the project has started. You will be able to compare the original start and finish dates with the current start and finish date; this will allow you to determine how far ahead or behind schedule you are, and you will also be able to do this with cost

and labor hours. It is difficult to create a baseline after you have started the project because you would have to remove all the changes made to the project and all the reported progress.

3. After the project starts, you can track the actual work on the project and report the progress of each work package, reporting actual start dates and actual finish dates. If a work package has started but has not finished, report the start date and the percentage complete. In addition, report actual costs and the actual number of hours worked on each work package. This information creates the reports produced in each reporting cycle.

4. You create reports from the work package. After you have included the progress information for a reporting cycle it is time to generate the various reports that the stakeholders will want to analyze. You can produce many types of reports if you have planned for them before the baseline was established. The Gantt chart tool is a standard weekly report with start and finish dates and duration with graphic bars for each activity. The work packages should include a description of work package, scope, scheduling data, cost, resources, quality, risk, procurement, contract requirements, constraints, and assumptions.

5. At this point, the work package is created and ready for you to use on the project.

Using a work package

Prior to using a work package, you must identify who on your project team will utilize this tool so that you can determine the level of detail required, frequency of distribution, style, and format of the report. We recommend when creating the work package, add as many details as possible so everyone fully understands what each work item includes. Work packages are your activities on the Gantt chart.

Before utilizing a work package, review the work package planning section in Chapter 10 and then follow these steps:

1. You should identify when to accomplish the work, including determining the dates, equipment, and materials to complete the work and identifying if there are any restrictions to completing the work. For example, noise restrictions on construction projects that would prevent work from starting before 8:00 a.m. or ending after 7:00 p.m.

2. Next, you should prepare for the work activities, including the acquisition of equipment and materials, possible permits, acquiring resources, evaluating risks and issues, reviewing the project schedule to ensure tasks are on track, identify any possible safety issues, and ensuring quality checks or processes are in place.

3. Instruct the team members to complete the work activities.

4. Check and inspect the work completed. This process requires you or the team leads of the respective areas to review the work deliverables and ensure it is high quality and that the tasks complete on time. In construction, this could involve building inspectors, plumbing inspectors, electrical inspectors, and safety inspectors.

5. Approve the work completed by the team members and report progress on the various work packages completed or in progress.

6. Store all relevant documents in the document control system for long-term storage, archiving, and retrieval purposes.

Summary

The tools we have presented in this chapter are the best choices for monitoring the project though the executing process. When the project is in the executing process, the tools in this chapter are invaluable in helping the project manager communicate project information effectively to customers and upper management.

The tools outlined in this chapter, such as control chart, issue list, risk assessment form, and work package, can help communicate the key components of the project. For example, the issue list and the risk assessment form are tools that help a project manager stay on top of their project throughout the life of the project, and the project meeting minutes tool keeps a project manager driving action items and monitoring the process of the project.

Use of the reporting communications tools outlined in this chapter will benefit the project manager, customers, and project team members. The reports are uncomplicated, easy to create, and informative in presenting information to the various parties.

Chapter 21

Using Communication Tools in the Executing Process for Reporting

In this chapter, we explore project communication tools in the project executing and controlling process; specifically, the tools in this chapter focus on reporting the project status.

Reporting during the execution and controlling process is paramount in order to keep on schedule and within budget. The communication tools selected for this chapter support the needs of the project manager and team members in reporting of project status. The common factor in these reports is the utilization of each, after the project is in the executing process and work activities are occurring. Each communication tool is progress and performance related and, therefore, is more important in this stage of the project than in the early stages.

Mastering Daily Progress Report

Before you can master the daily Progress Report tool, it is important to understand how this tool can assist and support you on your project. The following project scenario emphasizes the importance of the tool.

A large software company has decided to implement a brand-new software methodology called SCRUM into their development cycle. Although this methodology is new to the company, the software industry has used it for many years. You as a senior and experienced project manager want to learn this new methodology and decide to take on the responsibility of managing the project. Management has agreed, and you begin working on the project. By using the SCRUM methodology, you see immediately how much work the project team is going to be able to complete in such a short time and feel that this is going to be a beneficial methodology for use on this project. You believe this is a win-win for everyone involved, especially for the team members involved in the project. You are excited about getting started. Management on the other hand is not so excited because they are not familiar with this new methodology. Their biggest worry, besides the back room programmers, is obtaining updated project status for the projects that use the methodology. Some of management's biggest questions are:

How will they obtain status using this new methodology?

Who is working on what items?

What roadblocks could prevent the team from moving forward?

How can we help move the project forward?

To obtain the answers to these questions, the project manager uses a daily progress report that captures the answers to these three questions from each project team member. The questions are, what did you complete yesterday, what do you plan to work on today, and what is preventing you from completing today's activities?

After answering these questions, the project manager and project customers complete the status of the project. At the daily progress meeting each team member states what they have completed, what they plan to work on, and any issues they may have. This allows team members to hear from each other and offer assistance where they can. The software industry and the construction industry both utilize the SCRUM methodology of daily progress reports for their projects, and it is rapidly spanning across other industries.

 We recommend that you review the daily progress report's planning questions in Chapter 11.

Creating a daily progress report

By capturing status information on a daily basis, the project manager can determine how much progress is being made, and has been made, so that they can follow up with the team members on any outstanding items. The project manager can also assist in removing roadblocks where applicable. Capturing status information also allows project managers to hold team members accountable while reporting their status. If a team member plans to do something one day, and the next day reports that it was not done, the project manager has the previous day's information and can question the team member on why it was not completed. Without capturing status information on a daily basis, the progress of the team member would be lost and unrecoverable.

Project customers should encourage their project managers to use a daily progress report for all their projects. The time it takes to pull the team together and hear the latest project status is beneficial to everyone, especially the project customers and upper management staff. This report provides a first-hand view from project team members themselves on issues and concerns they are having on the project, and where they need help. Daily progress reports and associated standup meetings provide customers with levels of detail not normally obtained on a regular basis. It also ensures a greater level of communication between all parties.

The actual steps of creating a daily progress report vary. To get started, follow these steps:

1. Establish a daily progress report meeting with your project's team members. Customers can also attend this meeting, but the focus is to obtain information directly from team members.

2. Elect a member of your project team to capture information from other team members and store the information directly in the daily progress report. This task is important for any team member but can be time consuming, so you should rotate this responsibility among all team members.

3. Hold daily progress meetings and have each of your project team members report on the three standard questions about their work activities. The minute taker captures the information in the daily progress report.

4. At the end of each meeting, the minute taker sends you the daily progress report for your review and any final updates or corrections. Once that is complete, this information should be forwarded to everyone involved in the project and stored in the document control system for long-term storage, archiving, and retrieval purposes. This creation process continues throughout the life of the project.

ON the CD-ROM We have included a sample daily progress report tool in the communication tools Communication Managing subfolder on the CD-ROM. Use this as a guide to help you create your own version of this tool.

Using a daily progress report

Before you can use daily progress reports, you must identify who on your project team will utilize this tool so that you can determine the level of detail required, frequency of distribution, style, and format of the report.

Review the planning section in Chapter 11 and then follow these steps:

1. Ensure that you capture and store project information from each team member in the daily progress report. Even if a team member has no updates or misses the meeting the minute taker must capture that information from those individuals after the meeting. It is important to hear and track what each of your team members are doing, even if they are ill, regardless of how much or how little work they have accomplished, or if they attend or miss the meeting.

2. Review the daily progress report and act upon any action items that your team members provided at the meeting. If you hear that a team member cannot move forward, you should work directly with that team member to help them resolve their issues, or if you learn that a team member is currently not working on anything, assign them work or have them work on tasks with another team member. The daily progress report provides project information daily that will allow you to make those kinds of responses and project decisions, keeping you on top of your project.

3. Store the daily progress report in the document control system for long-term storage, archiving, and retrieval purposes.

Mastering the Gantt Chart

Before you can master the Gantt chart, you must understand how this tool can assist and support you on your project. The following project scenario emphasizes the importance of the tool.

A large moving company just won a major contract to move music equipment for a large band during their international tour of Canada, the U.S., and the U.K. The band will be touring for ten months. The moving company will move all stage equipment, music equipment, and other materials, from city to city, and country to country. This moving company has never worked with a band before, so it is thrilled to start on this project. As the most senior project manager at the moving company, and a music lover, you decide this will be a perfect project for you. As you kick-off and start on the project, you begin by meeting with the band and manager to ask a number of questions that need addressing immediately. Questions such as:

> When does the tour start?
>
> What cities are we going to and on what dates?
>
> What equipment needs moving?
>
> In what order do you set up the equipment?
>
> What is the budget for moving expenses?
>
> How many resources are working on this tour?
>
> When does the tour end?

To obtain the answers to these questions, the project manager should use a Gantt chart to track the project activities and costs. A Gantt chart documents the tasks and time lines of the project and acts as the main repository for the project schedule, resources, and task-related information. All projects should use a Gantt chart to track their project activities, or project managers will have a difficult time keeping control over their project.

 We recommend that you review the Gantt chart planning questions in Chapter 6.

Creating a Gantt chart

Creating a Gantt chart is easy to do and is something every project manager should have some knowledge of how to create. A Gantt chart helps a project manager stay on track with their project and the project's time line. The Gantt chart may be the only project communication tool used on the project, especially on a small project.

When creating a Gantt chart it is important to use the correct fields for reporting purposes. Popular fields to display are description, resource name, percent complete, total float, duration, start and finish dates, predecessor, and successors, to name a few. Each project manager chooses the fields to display in the Gantt chart.

The steps of creating a Gantt chart tool will vary greatly with each project manager because of the versatility of the tool and will depend on their favorite tools of choice. Use the following steps to help you get started:

1. Identify the information you want on the Gantt chart. This includes your project activities, rolled up or summary levels, the resource names, and percent complete. This step defines the look and feel of your project Gantt chart on the tabular section, or left-hand side of the report.

 NOTE There are two sides to the Gantt chart, a tabular side where the tabular columns display data, and a graphical side where the timescale and calendar information displays.

2. After establishing the initial look and feel of the Gantt chart, create a baseline schedule if you have not done so.

3. After establishing the baseline, add additional information to the graphic portion, on the right-hand side of the Gantt chart. The graphic, or time line side, has a tremendous amount of information available for reporting, and it depends highly on the project manager or scheduler's skills.

CAUTION Never connect logic relationships to summary tasks, only to detail tasks. Let the detail tasks drive the summary tasks.

4. The Gantt chart is now complete and ready for reporting.

Figure 21.1 is a basic Gantt chart. This example is simple but is a great starting point in the creation of your project activities. The dependencies and summarized view of the project, along with the Gantt chart view, provide an excellent representation of the timeframes of the project.

ON the CD-ROM We have included a sample Gantt chart tool in the communication tools Time subfolder on the CD-ROM. Use this as a guide to help you create your own version of this tool.

Using a Gantt chart report

Before you can use a Gantt chart, you must identify who on your project team will utilize this tool so that you can determine the level of detail required, frequency of distribution, style, and format of the report. The Gantt chart is going to be one of the charts that can be very detailed in nature. Project managers can always summarize the Gantt chart for reporting or printing purposes, but the real value of the Gantt chart is to track that detail and be completely aware of the project activities.

FIGURE 21.1

Sample of a basic Gantt chart report

		Task Name	Duration	Start	Finish	Predecessors
1		Sample Bar Chart	19 days	6/18/07	7/12/07	
2		Task 1	10 days	6/18/07	6/29/07	
3		Task 2	5 days	7/2/07	7/6/07	2
4		Task 3	4 days	7/9/07	7/12/07	3

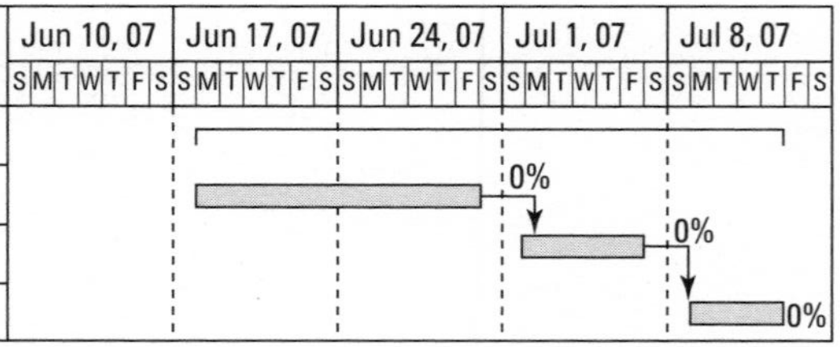
Jun 10, 07
Jun 17, 07
Jun 24, 07
Jul 1, 07
Jul 8, 07
S M T W T F S S M T W T F S S M T W T F S S M T W T F S S M T W T F S
0%
0%
0%

Review the Gantt chart planning section in Chapter 6 and then follow these steps:

1. Determine the information your customer would like to see on the Gantt chart. Because the Gantt chart is so powerful, you must determine the various characteristics such as cost, schedule, resource, WBS, and performance that your customer would like you to display.

2. After determining the needs of your customer, update the Gantt chart to satisfy those requirements, and present it to them for review. Once your customer is happy with the chart, not only the look of it but also the key milestone dates, seek their approval and sign-off on the chart. To do that, send the Gantt chart and the user acceptance document to the customer for their approval.

3. As the project starts, instruct your team members to use the Gantt chart to report progress. This includes having them enter the actual start, actual finish, actual work hours, actual cost, and remaining duration fields for each activity they have started and worked on.

Mastering the Histogram

Before you can master the Histogram tool, you must understand how this tool can assist and support you on your project. The following project scenario clarifies the importance of the tool.

A large furniture plant in Little Rock, Arkansas, decides to replace its ten-year-old inventory system with the most recent version. You are the project manager, and as the project progresses, you realize that the large number of staff working on the project is causing the budget to explode. You start asking questions about who is working on the project and why the costs are so high. You must find the underlying cause or you will never complete the project on budget. Upper management is watching the budget closely and wants detailed reports based on the resource hours and allocations for the project. Upper management's questions include:

How many hours this week did the staff work on the project?

What are the cumulative hours of the office staff?

Who worked the most hours in the group last month? Who worked the least?

To obtain answers to these questions, you can use the histogram. Histogram charts are powerful in their reporting of both cost and resource management data because they display information using stacked bars on the chart, which enhance the data and make reporting easier. In the above example, if the project manager had used a histogram report, upper management would have received the information they requested.

CROSS-REF We recommend that you review the histogram's planning questions in Chapter 9.

Creating a histogram

Creating a histogram is easy to do and beneficial for a project in communicating project information. Project managers will find histogram reports invaluable in helping them execute and control their projects because of how well they help monitor resource and cost areas of the project.

Once exposed to this type of graphic report, customers will expect the histogram on an ongoing basis because of how much information it displays and how easy it is to read and understand.

The actual steps of creating a histogram vary with each project manager. It will depend greatly on their favorite tools of choice. If you have never created this tool before, here are some simple steps to help you get started. We have also created a template for you as a starting point for your projects. This template will require updating based on your specific project needs and requirements.

1. Open a spreadsheet tool; this can be any spreadsheet application. We have used Microsoft Excel, but any tool with graphical capabilities will work.

2. Create the first row of data as the title row. In this basic example, we are using Resource Name, Wk1, Wk2

3. Create the second to fifth rows of data as represented in Figure 21.2. This data represents hours worked per resource across the various weeks. Figure 21.2 displays an example of what the hours would look like for this work group across five weeks.

    Figure 21.2 represents the data for this simple histogram report. This sample data provides an understanding of how to develop the report so it will immediately be helpful for your own project.

FIGURE 21.2

A sample of the data to create the histogram.

A	B	C	D	E	F
Resource	Wk 1	Wk 2	Wk 3	Wk 4	Wk 5
Sam	36	40	30	21	70
George	40	33	44	60	38
Fred	32	38	36	40	36
Bill	22	55	20	75	40

4. Highlight all rows of data to create your chart. This technique of highlighting the row may be different from application to application; however, if it is a Microsoft product, the highlighting process will be the same in every tool.

5. With the highlighted data, go to Insert ➪ Select Chart, select Column, and then select Stacked Bar chart as your chart type. The Stacked Bar type creates the histogram report because it adds multiple values of data into one column (each week).

Figure 21.3 represents an example of a histogram report based on the data you have entered so far in the example.

FIGURE 21.3

A sample of the histogram report based on the sample data.

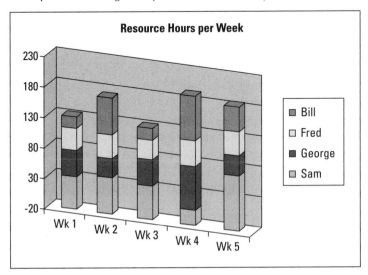

We have included a sample histogram in the communication tools Human Resources subfolder. Use this as a guide to help you create your own version of this tool.

Using a histogram

Prior to using a histogram, you must identify who on your project team will utilize this tool so that you can determine the level of detail required, frequency of distribution, style, and format of the report. The histogram is a chart that can display data at a summary level. Anyone looking at the chart that needs further detail will be required to view the source data that created the chart. You may have to create several detailed histograms.

Review the histogram planning section in Chapter 9 and then follow these steps:

1. Determine an internal process within your project team to obtain the data for a histogram. This step may have an effect on when you can produce the report and what actions will be required to obtain this data. Depending on the type of report, you may chose to collect this information automatically, and some may choose to collect it manually. The key to producing an ongoing histogram is to be able to know you can continually acquire the data to create the report.

2. Ensure your customers are comfortable with the report and can understand it. This is normally not a problem but is something you should confirm. This step will ensure that your customers know you are not generating reports for the sake of reporting, and that you want them to obtain real value from the reports. Discuss the histogram's reporting periods, and the frequency they want to receive the report. In most cases, your customers will be looking for weekly reporting as part of the periodic rhythm of the project, but you will never know until you ask.

3. Enforce the use of the histogram on the project. This includes generating the report, delivering it to the customers, and potentially setting up separate review meetings to discuss the information. Depending on the type of histogram reported, the customers or upper management may have a number of questions for you on the data behind the report. Resource histograms can be valuable in providing the team member's work hours either on a weekly or on a monthly basis. Depending on the results, the project manager can make adjustments accordingly.

4. Store the histogram in the document control system for long-term storage, archiving, and retrieval purposes.

Mastering the Pareto Chart

Before you can master the Pareto chart, you must understand how this tool can assist and support you on your project. The following project scenario demonstrates the importance of the tool.

A large construction firm has won the contract to construct two large skyscrapers in downtown Buffalo, New York, during the summer. They decided to use the "just in time" inventory method, a method that reduces the burden of carrying too much inventory, to save costs. During the building phase, the crew notices that the materials expected no later than 7:00 a.m. each workday are missing that deadline and arriving later and later each day. It is getting so bad that at times the crew is stopping work due to lack of materials. As the project manager, you need to get control of this situation as soon as possible because waiting for materials is not only affecting your budget, but also the morale of the crewmembers who are sitting around — or playing around — and someone could get hurt. As you start investigating why the materials are arriving late each morning, you turn up more questions than answers. Your questions include:

How many categories or possible reasons could we have for this late material?

What is the percentage of issues across the categories?

What percentage could we lower the issues, working on two, three, or four categories?

What is the number one reason for late materials?

To obtain the answers to these questions, the project manager should use a Pareto chart report to be able to determine how the materials are being handled on their project. A Pareto chart is a histogram chart with the data arranged in ascending order, from largest number of occurrences to lowest number of occurrences. The Pareto chart is a popular chart that a project manager can utilize to focus and resolve project issues in an order of priority. Without a Pareto chart, determining what the order of importance is, and the impact each issue has on the project, would be almost impossible.

CROSS-REF We recommend that you review the Pareto Chart tool planning questions in Chapter 11.

Creating a Pareto chart

A Pareto chart is priceless in determining the most dominant project issue in a set of issues, and it allows project team members to focus on those areas of concern. Project managers often use Pareto charts for charting the number of occurrences of a particular issue, number of bugs, types of risk events or safety occurrences.

When project managers realize how powerful this tool is and how much it will benefit them, they may want to use Pareto charts on all their projects. For example, in a software development project, Pareto charts based on bug types are a huge benefit because they allow the team to determine the specific category in which most of the bugs are occurring, and focus their attention there. This is beneficial to the project, and without it the project could be randomly fixing bugs with little or no idea how it will affect the project overall.

Project customers love it when project managers use a Pareto chart because of the graphical nature of the tool, which makes it so easy to read and understand. Customers will appreciate seeing the project's dominant issues and will want to see how the team is reacting to them.

To fully capture and control risks on your project, we suggest creating both the Pareto chart and a risk matrix. In doing this, it provides the most coverage and the best management of project risks. Creating a risk matrix chart identifies the highest risk events into the most predominate categories for charting purposes. For example, when creating a risk matrix, the process of creation includes the team members working together and adding risk events to the tool in categories of High-High, High-Medium, and so on. After this process is complete, you can take the results and create a Pareto chart.

CROSS-REF See Chapter 12 to learn more about the risk matrix tool.

The steps of creating a Pareto chart tool vary. To get started, follow these steps:

1. Select and analyze the issue or problem you are attempting to resolve and compare. This will identify the categories of risks for charting.

2. Open any spreadsheet application to create the Pareto chart. This can be any spreadsheet tool; however, the one used in this example is Microsoft Excel.

3. Determine the unit of measure for your project's Pareto report. In this example, we have used number of occurrences of percentage of change requests by category type.

4. Create the first row of data as title data. In this example, add these titles: Change Request Category, # of Occurrences, % of Change Requests, and Cumulative.

5. Create four columns of data under each of the titles just created. The data will fall under these categories: Change Request Category, # of Occurrences, % of Change Requests, and Cumulative. When creating these categories, the information is dependent on the type of project you are managing. In some cases, categories can be difficult to determine; in other cases, it will be easy, such as the number of software bugs across the different areas of the application. For example, the Pareto chart would display the number of bugs (problems in software code) by different sections within the application. For instance, number of bugs in reporting, number of bugs in data entry, number of bugs in the interface.

6. Enter data into the spreadsheet using the three different categories. In Figure 21.4, the data indicates the project team has submitted 50 change requests for this project. The two new columns, % of Change Requests, Cumulative %, are auto calculated in the table, and therefore do not require data entry. It is important to understand the meaning of each column. The % of Change Requests column is a calculated field based on the number of occurrences divided by the Total # of requests. Therefore, in this example, 50/167 is 30 percent. The Cumulative % column is also auto calculated, and based off the addition of the % of Change Request column and the Cumulative % Column. In every chart, the first row of data will carry the same value in the Cumulative % as the % of Change Requests column because there is no preceding Cumulative % and the first row acts as a starting point for the rest of the data. However, for additional rows use the Preceding Cumulate % amount, plus the current % of Change Request amount to calculate that row of Cumulative %.

7. Figure 21.4 shows the Project Team's Cumulative % of 30 percent to the Engineering's value of 26 percent for % of Change Requests to total the Cumulative % value of 56%. Enter 56% in the cumulative percent column on the engineering row. Continue this calculation for all rows of data. For an easy way to review and understand this calculation, refer to the actual spreadsheet on the CD-ROM.

FIGURE 21.4

A sample of data required to develop a Pareto chart for change requests.

Change Request Category	# of Occurrences	% of Change Requests	Cumulative %
Project Team	50	30%	30%
Engineering	43	26%	56%
Construction Errors	32	19%	75%
Customer	30	18%	93%
Wrong Equipment	12	7%	100%
Total # of Requests	167		

* Note all total issues have to add to 100%

8. Create your project's Pareto chart by selecting all the data in the table and then Insert ➪ Select Chart, select Column for the chart type. Once created, the chart is ready for use.

9. Create your chart's percentage line (originally, this was a column type) and convert it to a line chart by selecting the column of data representing the cumulative percent of defect on the spreadsheet, and change the chart type to represent a line chart. The results will change the cumulative percent into a line and it will display across all categories.

10. Once complete, assign a name to your chart, and your Pareto chart is ready for project reporting and presentation. At this point, you should store the Pareto chart in the document control system for long-term storage, archiving, and retrieval purposes.

Figure 21.5 is a Pareto chart for your project. In this example, the chart covers the various reasons and percentages as to why a project contractor is always late delivering materials.

FIGURE 21.5

A sample Pareto chart.

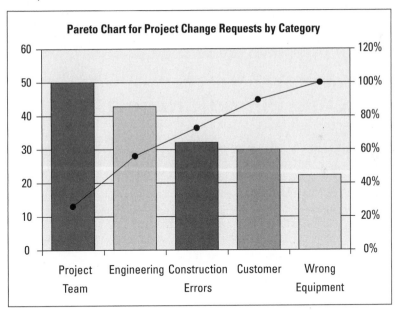

We have included a sample Pareto chart in the communication tools Communication Reporting subfolder. Use this as a guide to help you create your own version of this tool.

Using a Pareto chart

Prior to using a tool such as the Pareto chart, you must identify who on your project team will utilize this tool so that you can determine the level of detail required, frequency of distribution, style, and format of the report. The Pareto chart displays higher level and or summary level data, and if there are any questions about the chart, the project manager will have the background data to support how it was developed.

Review the Pareto chart's planning section in Chapter 11 and then follow these steps:

1. Ensure that your customers and team members are comfortable with reading and understanding the Pareto chart. This may require you scheduling a series of review meetings to ensure everyone understands the chart, or you may need to work directly with anyone who is struggling to understand the information; this is an important step before implementing the Pareto chart on the project.

2. Encourage the use of the Pareto chart on your project. First, you will need to determine how to acquire the data for the chart on a continual basis, then set up ongoing team meetings to create the chart and deliver it to the customers. Internal meetings with team members can occur during regular weekly status meetings where team members go over risks and issues, or separate meetings also work where you focus on just creating the Pareto chart.

3. Schedule customer meetings to go over your Pareto chart with them. It is possible too that you can update or change existing meeting agendas to discuss the Pareto chart with the customers as well.

4. Ensure you store all versions of the Pareto chart in the document control system for long-term storage, archiving, and retrieval purposes.

Mastering Periodic Reports

Before you can master the Periodic Reports tool, you must understand how this tool can assist and support you on your project. The following project scenario emphasizes the importance of the tool.

A small appliance shop in Tokyo, Japan wants to replace their customer database with a new system that will enhance their ability to market and target new customers. Because this shop is small and has no information technology (IT) experience, the shop owners determine quickly that they need to hire an IT contracting company to execute this project for them. As the lead project manager in the contracting company, you decided this would be a good project to lead. Part of your responsibility will be to lead the IT project team as well. As the project progresses, the shop owners' inexperience in IT becomes evident in their communications with you. Their biggest focus and concern is on the status of the project. They want to know how and when they will get their reports. Some of their questions include:

What types of reports will this project generate?

How often do you expect to run the reports?

What daily reports will we receive?

When can we see the budget reports?

To obtain answers to these questions, the project manager should use a series of periodic reports. Periodic reports consist of a variety of status reports that the project manager or team members produce at regular intervals for the project. These periodic reports include status reports, issues report, budget reports, and quarterly reports, to name a few. Periodic reports set the reporting rhythm of the project, and the project manager should inform the customer of this rhythm to ensure it is in line with their requirements. This rhythm is something project customers will come to expect as a way of receiving project information.

CROSS-REF We recommend that you review the periodic report planning questions in Chapter 11.

Creating periodic reports

Periodic reports are an important part of overall project reporting because they provide an ongoing status of the project directly to the customers. Establishing the time lines for periodic reports early in the project is important, and project managers should do this before any activities begin. The project manager or the team members should develop periodic reports until project completion.

Most project managers are responsible for determining the project's reporting time lines. This includes what reports are required, time lines, frequency, and any other special reporting needs of the customers. Most project reports use a weekly cadence, with the most popular report being the project status report. There are other reports where the project manager and customers work together to determine the delivery timeframe. For example, a project cost report may be valuable on a monthly basis only because few changes occur on it weekly.

A project customer plays a large part in the creation and use of periodic reports on most projects, and project managers should be working with their customers to determine their exact needs. Most customers expect a weekly status report; however, some may want a daily status report, and a weekly budget report. There are as many combinations as there are customers, so project managers must gather these requirements from the customers.

NOTE There are no single steps for creating periodic reports because periodic reports are not a single report, but a series of multiple reports. Therefore, it is impossible to provide step-by-step instructions for creating periodic reports. We recommend you review each tool in the book and follow the steps for creation for every tool.

Using periodic reports

Before you can use a periodic report, you must identify who on your project team will utilize this tool so that you can determine the level of detail required, frequency of distribution, style, and format of the report. Review the periodic reports planning section in Chapter 11 and then follow these steps:

1. The first step in using periodic reports is during the planning process when you will work with your customer and determine which reports are applicable for the project. In those discussions, use the tools outlined in this book to produce a list of standard reports for your customer.

ON the CD-ROM We have included a master list of all the tools in this book in the communication tools folder on the CD-ROM.

2. Create a project periodic report list and distribute it to your customers and team members. There is no sign-off or official approval of the periodic report list as it only acts as a guide for customers allowing them to be aware of which reports they are receiving for the project. In some cases, you can decide to drop some reports off the list, especially if they are not providing value, or depending on the needs of the project, you may add new reports to the list report. It is your responsibility to manage this list throughout the life of the project and control what reports go on and off the list.

3. Add time into the project schedule and allow your project team members time to create the periodic reports, because you will be responsible for creating most of these reports and finding time in your schedule may be challenging.

4. Deliver the periodic reports to your project customers. This includes setting up various meetings, delivering the reports, answering questions, and creating a location in the document control system for long-term storage, archiving, and retrieval purposes.

Mastering the Project Status Report

Before you can master the project status report, you must understand how this tool can assist and support you on your project. The following project scenario emphasizes the importance of the tool.

A tourism coordinator in a small town in Ontario, Canada has come up with a new idea to celebrate this year's Canada Day holiday that is going to make the whole country stand up and take notice. The goal is to place a Canadian flag on the lawn of every home in the small town, making this small town the most patriotic in Canada by flying more flags than any other city or town per capita. The tourism coordinator, who is a project manager in her own right, decides to take on the challenge and lead this project. The mayor of the town is a little unsure about the idea, but has decided to take a chance and has allocated a small budget for the project. This money is to be used for TV advertising, radio, and print media to get the idea communicated and help this little town achieve its goal. "Fly your Flag, Fly your Flag" is the town's new motto. The tourism coordinator is thrilled that both the mayor and the townspeople are excited about the idea, but she also is aware that she will be under pressure to provide ongoing status to the city council members throughout the life of this project. The one area she is struggling with is the understanding of what project details the city council members will want to see each week. She has a number of questions about how to provide them status, and the city council members have their own questions as well. Their questions include:

What did the project accomplish last week?

What are the current issues and risks?

How is the project progressing?

What is the progress on the project?

How many flags are in people's front yards out of the total number of front yards?

To obtain answers to these questions, the tourism coordinator should use a project status report. The project status report provides the latest project information. It contains a summary of the details of each of the major areas of the project and is the latest information at that point in time. The timeframe for this type of reporting is usually weekly for most projects, and continues until the project is complete. There are thousands of examples of project status reports across thousands of industries and millions of projects. Companies often have a standard template for projects. In the previous example, the city council members would have benefited tremendously from having a project status report generated by the tourism coordinator on a weekly basis.

CROSS-REF We recommend that you review the project status report planning questions in Chapter 4.

Creating a project status report

Creating a project status report is critical for all projects, and most companies expect project managers to create a project status report weekly on their projects. The project status report is the most common communication tool on projects today, and one of the only tools that project managers will create willingly due to their own requirements and the ongoing pressure from customers and upper management to provide status.

NOTE On larger projects where an administrative team is in place, it may not be necessary for the project manager to create a status report personally; but it is best practice that the project manager at least understands project status reports so that he or she can speak to it if needed.

Project managers must ensure that they create a status report and work with their customer to determine the reporting cadence early in the planning process. Some customers want daily status reports, but most want weekly reports, as established by the company's standard policies and procedures. Weekly status reports seem to work the best because enough time has passed on the project that the team members have completed additional work activities, and issues that have arisen in that time need addressing.

The creation of a project status report is straightforward; the project manager completes the project status report template and communicates it to the customer, team members, and upper management. However, creating a project status report that provides value to the customer is much more challenging. Normally, a project manager creates a generic project status report based on the company's template and sends it to the customer with no regard as to how it will serve the needs of the customer. The project manager in many cases is not aware if the customer has even read the project status reports. Therefore, it is critical when creating a project status report, the project manager takes the time to work with the customer to ensure the report offers what they need for the project; otherwise, the project manager could be wasting time producing a report that no one will ever read except himself or herself.

The contents of the project status report are the responsibility of both the project manager and the customer. A project customer should be involved in the project status report process to ensure they receive the information they need on the project. Rarely is a customer involved in the actual creation of the project status report. A report that does not contain the information the customer wants is of no value to them. Work with the customer to make sure that they receive the information they need.

The steps of creating a project status report tool vary. You can get started by following these steps:

1. Work with your customer and determine if the project status report template contains the fields they require on their project. Some customers are particular about the fields they would like to see and those they do not want to see on the report. This information sets the foundation for all status reports delivered to that customer going forward and is an excellent starting point for creating the report. You must also determine when your customer would like the project status report: weekly, monthly, or daily. The project status report is generally a weekly report, but some customers may have different requirements. Some may like to see it more often than weekly, whereas others would prefer a monthly report.

2. Develop an internal process on your project where your team members help you collect and compile project information for the project status report.

4. Create the project status report, including compiling the information, completing the template, and creating the actual report.

5. Distribute the project status report via e-mail and create a location in the document control system to store the report for long-term storage, archiving, and retrieval purposes.

ON the CD-ROM We have included a sample of this project status report in the communication tools Integration subfolder on the CD-ROM. This is a guide to the first step in creating your own personal version of this tool. Your company or project may have specific requirements that will enhance this communication tool further; however, we believe this is a great starting point for the creation of this tool for your project. There are hundreds of project status reports on the Internet, and three real-life reports on the template. Project managers will often be required to use the company standard report, but should work closely with their customer to ensure they are receiving the information they need.

Using a project status report

Before you can use a project status report, you must identify who on your project team will utilize this tool so that you can determine the level of detail required, frequency of distribution, style, and format of the report.

Review the project status report planning section in Chapter 4 and then follow these steps:

1. Enforce the use of the project status report on your project. You can refer to it for project information, to manage project deliverables, and respond to concerns from customer and team members for project status. Ensure that you carry the project status report with you at all times and have a printed copy available to refer to if required. The project calendar is another tool that you should always have with you to be able to answer any questions on the project schedule.

2. Use the project status report to provide project information to your project customer. This includes scheduling meetings with the customer to review the project status report with them. Establish this meeting when setting up the cadence of the project. We recommend that when you host the project status meetings, you have copies of the project status report available for your customer to refer to and make notes where applicable.

TIP Send out the project status report the day before the project status customer review meeting. Your customer will appreciate you being proactive and they will be able to review the materials ahead of the meeting.

3. Work with your team members and drive the project deliverables based on the status of the report. This includes checking on status, resolving issues or risks, and removing any roadblocks. You should be driving much of your project work from the project status report.

4. Store the project status report into the document control system for long-term storage, archiving, and retrieval purposes.

Mastering the Spider Chart

Before you can master the spider chart, you must understand how this tool can assist and support you on your project. The following project scenario emphasizes the importance of this tool.

A large computer manufacturing company has announced the latest in laptop design and is planning on a fall delivery to customers across North America. The company is excited about the new laptop because of its advanced features, and especially because the extended battery life has tested at an unbelievable four days without requiring a charge. This laptop and battery will change the world of mobile computing. You are the project manager on this project and as you review the details of the project, you discover that a number of resources are charging to your project, and you do not know whom they are, or what they do. This information is worrisome because the largest part of the project's expenses is associated to labor dollars, and without correcting or getting control immediately, the project will not stay within its budget. Upper management is watching this closely and wants to make sure this new laptop gets out to the market on time, and on budget. Upper management is starting to see the hours and associated resource dollars rising each month and feel they need to step in to help resolve the situation. Upper management is asking a series of questions that you are unable to answer. These questions include:

How many hours did Mary work last month?

What about Alice — how many hours did she work, considering she is part time?

What are the total hours of all resources?

Who worked the least amount of hours, and are they still contributing to the project?

To obtain answers to these questions you should use a spider chart tool. The spider chart provides a graphical method of presenting and comparing project information. Initially, the spider chart tool appears difficult to read, but after building and utilizing them a couple of times, you will quickly become accustomed to them and find them invaluable when comparing project data. It is also the responsibility of the project manager to teach project customers how to read and use the spider chart, and they too will come to love this tool.

CROSS-REF We recommend that you review the spider chart planning questions in Chapter 8.

Creating a spider chart

Creating a spider chart is valuable on any project when making comparisons of project data. For example, resource hours or project costs per group are areas where project managers will want to compare data points and graph them; the spider chart is the perfect tool for this purpose. Initially, the customer may find it confusing and hard to read the chart. You can teach the customer how to read it, and they will come to understand the value of the report.

Project managers quickly learn how beneficial a spider chart can be in helping to manage and control various aspects of their project. For example, spider charts can be beneficial when comparing different project areas and their associated costs. The spider chart is excellent for answering questions, such as how much does the analyst group cost each month compared to the design group. Alternatively, how many hours a week is one project team member working compared to another. This is all valuable information when managing and controlling your project.

The steps of creating a specific spider chart tool vary. You can follow these steps to help you get started.

1. Open any spreadsheet tool to create your project's spider chart. Any spreadsheet application should work, and in this example we used Microsoft Excel

2. Create the first row of data as your title row. This process is common for creating project charts in a spreadsheet application.

3. Enter title data (i.e., Hours, Jones, Smith, and Brown) onto the spreadsheet for the spider chart.

   It is important to understand that the data for a particular project resource will go down a column instead of across the columns. The goal is to have multiple values of data in the spider chart across various months.

4. In this step, the project manager enters the data for each column.

   Figure 21.6 represents the data to enter into the spreadsheet columns. This data represents hours worked for the various staff members across the month.

FIGURE 21.6

Sample data for the spider chart.

A	B	C	D	E
	Hours	Jones	Smith	Brown
	M-1	110	80	40
	M-2	162	110	50
	M-3	120	80	60
	M-4	40	100	120
	M-5	154	120	160

5. Select the data in the cells, and then go to Insert ⇨ Select Chart.

6. Select Chart Type Radar with Markers (when using Microsoft Excel).

7. The spider chart is now complete. If needed, you can apply any formatting or chart titles to improve the look of the report.

8. Store your spider chart in the document control system for long-term storage, archiving, and retrieval purposes.

   Figure 21.7 represents a spider chart of employees' working hour data, created by following these steps.

FIGURE 21.7

A sample spider chart.

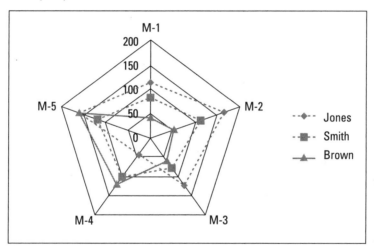

ON the CD-ROM We have included a sample of the spider chart tool in the communication tools Communication Managing subfolder. Use this as a guide to help you create your own version of this tool.

Using a spider chart

Before you can use a spider chart, you must identify who on your project team can utilize this tool so that you can determine the level of detail required, frequency of distribution, style, and format of the report. The spider chart is summarized and provides high-level project information; however, if a customer, team members, or management have questions or concerns, the project manager will have the data that was used to produce the chart. Review the spider chart planning section in Chapter 11 and then follow these steps:

1. Analyze your project's spider chart to determine the state of the project. This includes breaking down data, checking for boundaries, anomalies, data spikes, etc.

2. After completing the analysis of the project data, you can make project level decisions based on your findings.

3. Present the spider chart findings to your customer and upper management for their review and input.

4. Depending on the customers or upper management decisions, update the information on the spider chart accordingly. This could include updating additional time data points (months, years) or additional categories on the chart.

5. Store all versions of the spider chart in the document control system for long-term storage, archiving, and retrieval purposes.

Mastering the Stoplight Report

Before you can master the stoplight report, you must understand how this tool can assist and support you on your project. The following project scenario emphasizes the importance of the tool.

A large automobile framing plant, in Barrie Ontario, Canada has just announced their latest design in truck frames, which they anticipate will change the design of trucks for years to come. This automobile frame, developed using a completely new combination of steel and aluminum, will lighten the overall weight of the vehicle by almost 300 pounds. For the auto industry, a lighter truck means higher gas mileage, and therefore this frame is going to be important to every automaker around the world. As the plant's leading project manager, you have decided that this is something you would love to take on for the company. Management agrees, and you start working on the project's activities immediately.

As you start into the project, you discover early that because of its importance to the industry, this project has a high level of management overhead that includes ongoing project status reporting. Senior management is focusing on the schedule status and cost status. However, because there is such a high demand for this new truck frame, and due to the number of automobile companies that are lined up to purchase it, to be successful, this project must hit both its schedule and budget targets. The automobile companies will not tolerate a delay on the frame because of the downstream impacts to their own production lines, and the negative press it will get if it is late. As project manager, you need a way to effectively control all aspects of time and cost per project task, and ensure at-a-glance that you are able to focus immediately on trouble areas to keep the project progressing on time and on budget. You are struggling to find the best way to report information that allows for tight management and control of the project's activities, as well as upper-level dashboard type reporting to satisfy management and the project's customers. As you continue to work the project activities, management staff starts to ask questions about schedule and cost, and that increases the pressure to provide a report that answers their questions and provides that high-level, at-a-glance reporting they require. The questions upper management is asking include:

What is the current schedule status of the project?

Is the design phase on time and budget?

What is the current cost status of the project?

To obtain the answers to these questions, the project manager should use a stoplight report. A stoplight report provides anyone reviewing the report with an updated status of the project by using color indicators to represent the progress of each task. At a single glance, upper management and customers gain an understanding on the overall status of the project by seeing the most dominant color on the report; for example, an all red report indicates a project in serious trouble. A report that is showing all green indicates the project is on track. A stoplight report takes little time to create and implement on the project schedule but proves to be popular and useful for project reporting purposes.

CROSS-REF We recommend that you review the stoplight report planning questions in Chapter 11.

Creating a stoplight report

A stoplight report is one of the easiest reports to create for your project. A small amount of time spent determining the calculations and associated indicators offers a huge benefit in communicating project status. Anyone looking at the project schedule can tell if the project is in a red, yellow, or green status. All project managers should be reporting their project schedules using these color indicators.

Before you can benefit from a stoplight report, you must complete three items on the project schedule:

- Project schedule must have a baseline
- Project must be currently under way and have tasks actively working
- Project schedule must have reported progress

These three activities, at a minimum, must occur on the project schedule before using a stoplight report.

NOTE If you are unfamiliar with how to create a schedule baseline, refer to Chapter 17 for more information.

The stoplight report is a variance report; variance reports calculate the discrepancy in project information. The schedule variance shown on a stoplight report calculates the difference between the current finish date and the baseline finish date. In this case, it takes the actual finish date of a task and subtracts the original finish date (baseline finish date). For the cost variance calculations, the color indicators represent the actual costs minus the baseline costs (budget). When tracking the schedule or the cost variance, the color indicators on each of the activity rows allow the project manager to focus directly on where the project is in trouble and directs the team to focus on that area.

A project customer will heavily utilize the stoplight report but will rarely be involved in its creation. They will be able to determine, at-a-glance, the schedule and cost status of a project within each of the major areas, without necessarily having to review the details. If there are additional details needed, such as why one section shows areas of concern (yellow or red), then the project customer can work with the project manager and determine what has gone wrong and if there are any possible resolutions.

The actual steps for creating a stoplight report vary. You can follow these steps to help you get started:

> **NOTE**   You must set a schedule baseline before this formula will work. Ensure that there is no progress recorded before setting that baseline.

1. Open your project's scheduling tool. In most cases, you will be adding the stoplight report conditions to your existing project schedule. For this example, we used Microsoft Project to create the stoplight report.

> **NOTE**   You must have tasks in the schedule to display the stoplight indicators. Enter one or two temporary tasks to test that the stoplight indicators will display the correct color when you create the formulas.

2. Create a field that will store the two stoplight report calculations. To complete this task, create Custom Fields by selecting Tools, Customize, and then Fields on the MS Project menu system. (Short cut: Right-click on any column in MS Project, then select Customize Fields.) Each scheduling tool will have their own version for creating Customize fields if that feature is available in that particular tool.

3. Select Number for the Field type. Be sure to name the custom fields you are creating. You will be required to use that name again, so please write it down during this step. For this example, use SV for Schedule Variance and CV for Cost Variance as your new custom field names.

4. Pick the formula button and then create a new Formula for Schedule Variance. Within the Formula box, select the Field drop-down box, select Date, select Baseline Finish, and then in the [Finish] field enter a minus sign, and repeating the same steps, select the Field drop-down box, select Date, and then select the [Baseline Finish] field. After completing the formula, click OK. If a box comes up that asks you about overwriting the field, click OK. Here is the formula:

   ```
   [Finish] - [Baseline Finish]
   ```

5. Select a Graphical Indicators button (stoplight) for ranges of variances. Use the graphical indicator and then select the indicator color based on the tolerance range. Select the first box in the first row and enter the following Tolerance Ranges for Schedule Variance (days): Refer to your online help if you are unclear in this section.

■ If Schedule Variance is less than 1, the indicator is green. If you are on schedule or ahead of schedule, your indicator is green.

■ If Schedule Variance is within 1 and 5, the indicator is yellow, meaning the activity is within five days of the original schedule (Baseline).

■ If Schedule Variance is greater than 5 the indicator is red, in this case the activity is more than one week behind schedule.

Continue this process until the entering of all three rows is complete. Then click the OK button to save your work. Figure 21.8 shows the Microsoft Project version of what the graphical indicators look like when complete.

FIGURE 21.8

Graphical indicators.

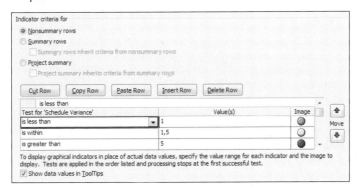

6. The project manager repeats the process for the Cost Variance formula. Select the Cost Variance field. Select the Formula box. Within the Formula box, select the Field drop-down box, select Costs, Baseline Costs, and Baseline Costs field. The project manager then enters a dash (-) and selects the Field drop-down box again; select Costs, and then the Actual Costs field. Click OK, and then click OK again when the box comes up asking you if you want to overwrite the field. If the box does not come up, continue. The formula should look like the following:

```
[Baseline Costs] - [Actual Costs]
```

NOTE   Name the Custom Field Cost Variance and remember the name because you will need to use it in the steps below.

7. Select a Graphical Indicators (Stoplight) for your range of variances. In this step, use the graphical indicator and select the indicator color based on the tolerance range. Enter the following criteria as you did in Step 5 and enter it now for the Cost Variance Field. The typical tolerance ranges for cost variance (days) include:

- If Cost Variance is less than or equal to 1, the indicator is Green.
- If Cost Variance is within 2 to 99, the indicator is Yellow.
- If Cost Variance is greater than 100, the indicator is Red.

NOTE   **Project managers are able to create their own ranges. The ranges shown here are just examples.**

After entering all three rows, click OK, and then click OK again to enter back into the Project-Scheduling tool.

8. The project manager then inserts both of the new custom fields into the project schedule by highlighting any column, and then choose Insert ⇨ Select Column, select Drop Down on Field Name, and find the new Custom field you just created. In this case, select Schedule Variance first, and repeat the process for Cost Variance.

9. The report is complete, and as long as there are one or two tasks in the project schedule, the indicators will display the stoplights. If you are using existing indicators on your project, it will represent the latest status of those activities. Tasks must be in the schedule for the stoplight indicators to show. Enter one or two temporary tasks now.

NOTE   **The Cost Variance indicator will not show up until costs are loaded on the project schedule.**

Figure 21.9 represents a project schedule showing the schedule variance stoplight indicators only.

To create a cost variance report, insert the Cost Variance custom field (CV) you created.

Figure 21.10 represents a project schedule showing the cost variance stoplight indicators only.

When creating both the Cost Variance and the Schedule Variance Report, insert both fields into the report.

Figure 21.11 represents a project schedule showing the cost and schedule variance stoplight indicators. Most project manager wants this type of view showing both indicators on their projects.

One of the most powerful features of this tool is the use of multiple levels of stoplight indicators on your schedule to represent the true status of your project (shown in Figure 21.11). Using a single indicator such as cost variance is good, but provides only one portion of the status. The stoplight report is important for any project manager to utilize because it draws attention to activities on the projects that are over or under a predetermined value. Also because the stoplight report is so graphical, it is easier to understand the areas of the project you should focus on immediately to re-establish control and return to the original plan.

FIGURE 21.9

A sample stoplight report with a single schedule variance indicator.

	Schedule Variance	Task Name	Dur	Start	Finish	Cost	Dec 23, 07	Dec 30, 07	Jan 6, 08	Jan 13, 08	Jan 20, 08
1		Sample Project	16d	1/2/08	1/23/08	$1,780					69%
2		Task 1	5d	1/2/08	1/8/08	$80			100%		
3		Task 2	3d	1/9/08	1/11/08	$400				100%	
4		Task 3	1d	1/14/08	1/14/08	$500				100%	
5		Task 4	5d	1/15/08	1/21/08	$400					40%
6		Task 5	2d	1/22/08	1/23/08	$400					0%

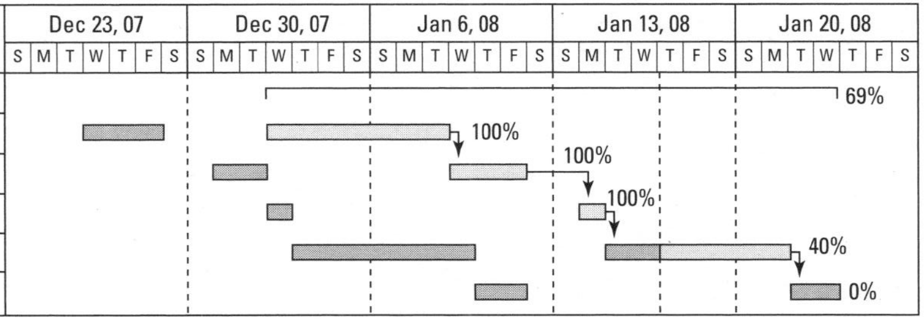

FIGURE 21.10

A sample stoplight report with a single cost variance indicator.

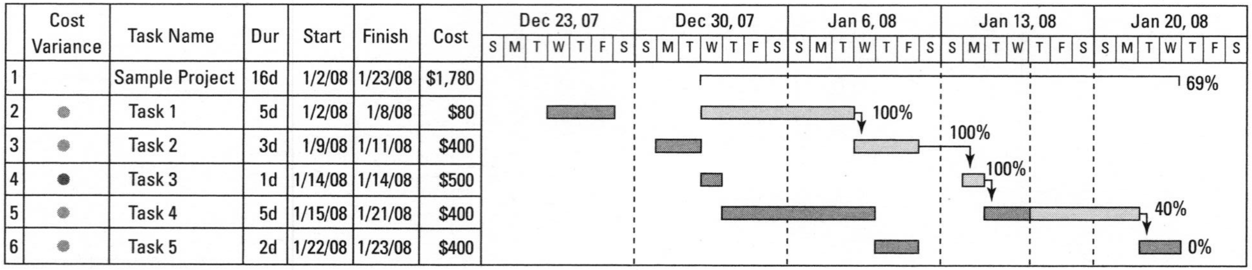

	Cost Variance	Task Name	Dur	Start	Finish	Cost	Dec 23, 07	Dec 30, 07	Jan 6, 08	Jan 13, 08	Jan 20, 08
1		Sample Project	16d	1/2/08	1/23/08	$1,780					69%
2	●	Task 1	5d	1/2/08	1/8/08	$80			100%		
3	●	Task 2	3d	1/9/08	1/11/08	$400				100%	
4	●	Task 3	1d	1/14/08	1/14/08	$500				100%	
5	●	Task 4	5d	1/15/08	1/21/08	$400					40%
6	●	Task 5	2d	1/22/08	1/23/08	$400					0%

FIGURE 21.11

A sample stoplight report with both the cost and schedule variance indicators.

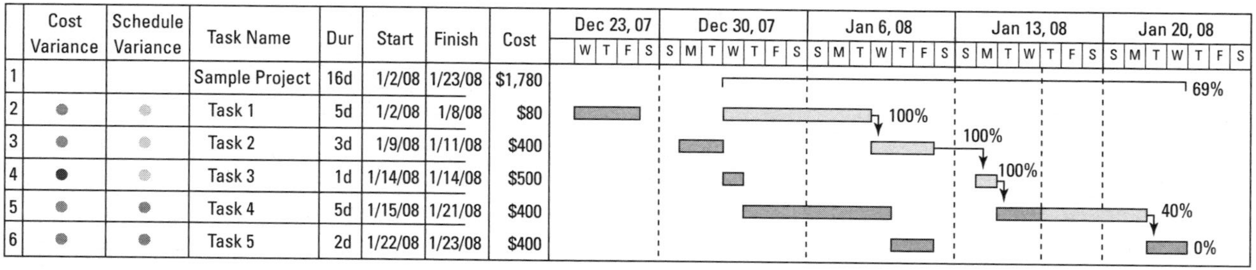
Cost Variance
Schedule Variance
Task Name
Dur
Start
Finish
Cost
Dec 23, 07
Dec 30, 07
Jan 6, 08
Jan 13, 08
Jan 20, 08
W T F S S M T W T F S S M T W T F S S M T W T F S S M T W T F S
1 Sample Project 16d 1/2/08 1/23/08 $1,780
2 Task 1 5d 1/2/08 1/8/08 $80
3 Task 2 3d 1/9/08 1/11/08 $400
4 Task 3 1d 1/14/08 1/14/08 $500
5 Task 4 5d 1/15/08 1/21/08 $400
6 Task 5 2d 1/22/08 1/23/08 $400
69%
100%
100%
100%
40%
0%

ON the CD-ROM We have included a sample stoplight report tool in the communication tools communication reporting folder. Use this as a guide to help you create your own version of this tool.

Using a stoplight report

Before you can use the stoplight report, you must identify who on your project team will utilize this tool so that you can determine the level of detail required, frequency of distribution, style, and format of the report. Review the stoplight report planning section in Chapter 11 and then follow these steps:

1. Incorporate the stoplight report into the weekly project status meetings with your team members. Review the report with your team members confirming the colors of the project and the tasks, and make adjustments where applicable. This allows you to confirm with the team members the various project colors and project statuses on a weekly basis. It also provides project team members with information on the color for their portion of the project, and if they are in Red or Yellow, they will know they need to work harder or smarter to get the project back into a green status.

2. Present the stoplight report to your customers and upper management. The stoplight report is easy to demonstrate because of the colors in the report and the fact that those colors represent the project's true performance. You may choose to schedule a separate meeting or present at a currently scheduled meeting; in any case, you will want to speak to each of the colors and talk specifically to why a task is red, yellow, or green on your project.

TIP One of the best practices project managers can utilize during the initial reporting of the stoplight report is to explain the criteria used to create each of the reports. This lets the customer know what the various colors mean, and if they have concerns on the criteria, they have the opportunity to change it early in the reporting cycle. If a project manager chooses to hide the criteria, or share it too late in the reporting cycle, the project manager may find he or she is in a situation where what they are reporting is incorrect because the stoplight report could be showing a green status when the project customer believes it is red. It all depends on the limits.

3. Focus on project work activities that are in red or yellow and determine where and how to get the activities into a green status. This process will occur throughout the life of the project.

4. Store the final stoplight report in the document control system for long-term storage, archiving, and retrieval purposes.

Mastering the Team Charter

Before you can master the team charter, you must understand how this tool can assist and support you on your project. The following project scenario emphasizes the importance of the tool.

A large software development company is in the process of creating a new word-processing application and expects it will rival the number one competition on the market. The company is ready to take on the challenge and has all resources ready to get into the word-processing market. As one of the more senior project managers in the company, management has decided that you will manage this project.

As you start into the project, you decide you need a project team consisting of resources from inside your company, but outside your work area. You are also going to require the resource managers to assign them to your project. You understand that working with resource managers is an important step in the resource assignment process. The resource managers ask specific questions around the details of your project and the type of resources you require. These questions include:

What type of resources do you need?

How long are the resources needed?

Do you have budget allocated to hire project resources?

Where is the list of names and roles working on the project?

To obtain the answers to these questions, you should use a team charter tool. Part of the team charter is the detail staffing plan of the project that describes the various aspects of staffing on the project. Areas contained in the team charter include resource timeframes, resource roles, budget amounts, team lists, interfaces, and any assumptions or constraints on the resources. The team charter provides the in-depth picture of the project resources working on the project.

CROSS-REF We recommend that you review the team charter planning questions in Chapter 4.

Creating a team charter

Creating a team charter document is no easy task, and a project manager needs time to understand the project and determine exactly the roles required to complete the work. When creating a team charter, the project manager must consider the following information about the resources needed, including resource start and end periods, resource roles, resource budget, resource skills and training requirements, and finally any resource assumptions or constraints. After acquiring this information, the project manager can create a team charter document.

A project customer may not utilize the team charter document very often, mainly because they normally are not involved in the details around utilizing resources. The only area where the customer will be involved with the team charter is the budget and the costs of the resources. If the project manager sees the budgets are too high, or it looks like there are too many resources on the project, the project manager may step in and start to question the resource requirements and the associated costs.

You can use the following team charter document template for your project. The template is located on the CD-ROM for use if your company does not already have one. The table of contents for the team charter document provides the major sections of the document. It will be helpful when the document is completed and you are looking for particular information.

Example of Team Charter Table of Contents

Section 1: Project Name
Document the name of the project or any associated internal project numbers.

Section 2: Team Charter Description
Document the description of the team charter and describe the direction of the team for this project.

Section 3: Purpose/Goals of Project
Document the purposes, goals, and objectives for the project from the customer and the team members' perspective. The team may have specific requirements that are important to record as well in the Purpose/Goals section.

Section 4: Resource Time Period (Start and Finish)
Document the time periods associated to each resource working on the project. This includes start and finish dates, and any skill sets or training requirements.

Section 5: Project Resource Roles
Document the roles required for the project and the corresponding names of the team members if available. It is important to capture the names to ensure there are no missing resources.

Section 6: Project & Resource Budget
Document the budget associated to the resources for the project.

Section 7: Team Members List
Document the list of team members associated to the project. Minimum fields to capture are; names, emails, and phone numbers.

Section 8: Project and Team Interfaces
Document any interfaces or connection points the team members may have on the project. Document all interfaces so team members know immediately where they will be working and with whom.

Section 9: Assumptions and Constraints
Document any assumptions and constraints associated to the project.

Section 10: Approvals
Document all approvals, and any conditions for those approvals on the project.

ON the CD-ROM We have included a sample team charter in the communication tools Integration sub-folder. Use this as a guide to help you create your own version of this tool.

Using a team charter tool

Before you can use a team charter, you must identify who on your project team will utilize this tool so that you can determine the level of detail required, frequency of distribution, style, and format of the report. Review the team charter planning section in Chapter 4 and then follow these steps:

1. Ensure the information for your project's roles are accurate and current because you will use this information to request resources and forecast project costs. It is critical that you keep the team charter document current at all times. The document is semiformal in nature, and does not require sign-off or approval from anyone on the team, or the project customer, but does require that the project manager keep it as accurate as possible.

2. Work directly with the resource managers to request your project staff, and use the team charter document in these discussions to set timeframes, work efforts, and roles and responsibilities of the requested staff. Discussions with the resource managers on staffing will occur throughout the life of the project.

3. Store the final team charter document in the document control system for long-term storage, archiving, and retrieval purposes.

Mastering the Team Lead's Report

Before you can master the team lead's report, you must understand how this tool can assist and support you on your project. The following project scenario emphasizes the importance of the tool.

A large manufacturing company is implementing a project portfolio system to replace an old database application they have used for many years. The database system was adequate, but the company's requirements have changed. The company plans to implement a new enterprise-wide system that is multiuser based and allows for cross project reporting. This is the latest application on the market and provides companies with a major advantage over other companies in managing and controlling their project portfolios. You are excited about this project because as soon as it completes you will utilize it in your new role as a project portfolio manager. You begin the project by reviewing the work activities immediately. In building the project team, you determine there is staff required in the following areas: analysis, design, development, testing, and implementation. After assigning the team leaders, it will be the responsibility of those leads to hire staff for their individual teams. Your normal working relationship will be at the team leader level only; rarely will you work with the team members. As the team builds up, you turn your attention to status reporting. The goal is to understand how you will gather project status reports from the different project areas, and because there are five different areas, trying to combine the information into one report is going to be difficult. You also need to ensure that team leaders send their status in a consistent format so you are able to combine the data easily. You also have questions about the individual project areas and the overall status for each area. Your other questions include:

How do you ensure the data sent by each group is the same?

How do you compile the information into a single format?

What are the particular issues in the design group?

What is the budget for training?

How is the user acceptance plan progressing?

To obtain the answers to these questions, you should use a team lead's report. A team lead's report is a status report that caters to one specific area of the project. In this scenario, the team leads from the engineering, design, development, testing, and release areas create their own specific project status report. The specific team leads report allows project managers to drill into the details of that area of the project specifically, working with the team leads directly on their portion of the project. The format of a team leads report is the same as the project status report, allowing the project manager to compile the information from all the reports into the project's final status report for the week with relative ease. There is no concern that formats will conflict or the project manager will not get the information he needs from each team lead; if the team leads are completing the template correctly, the information will be in the report.

CROSS-REF   We recommend that you review the team lead's report planning questions in Chapter 4.

Creating a team lead's report

Creating a team lead's report is critical for most projects because it allows the project manager to see the updated status from each area of the project. The individual team leads have the responsibility for creating their status in the same format as the overall status report, for easy compiling and data manipulation. The project manager creates the team lead's reports at the beginning of work activities for each area of the project, and the team leads continue to create it until all work in that area is complete.

Project customers utilize the team lead's report on the project in the same manner as they utilize the regular project status reports. Some customers may have specific interest in different areas of the project over others and may ask for a project status report from that particular area. A team lead's report satisfies that requirement from the customer and covers just the project status of that one area.

The project manager does not create a team lead's report, the individual team leads create their own reports. This is one tool that the project manager would struggle to create, and should not even try, because the value of the report is the fact that it is coming directly from the team leads that are engaged and running their areas. The project manager's only role is to ensure the team leaders are creating their respective reports in a timely manner and in the format used for consolidation into the overall project status report. The steps outlined below are for the project manager to follow to ensure team leads are creating the specific team lead's reports for their project.

1. Ensure that each of your project's team leaders has the template to create the team lead's report. In order for this to occur, each team leader will utilize the standard project status report template and rewrite their individual report using that template.

2. Establish an internal project process for receiving the information from each of your team leaders. This process will depend upon when the company requires its project status reporting, and how long it will take you to compile the information. After determining the most appropriate time, send that deadline to your project's team leads and drive them to complete the reports on time.

3. Set up a location in the document control system for your team leaders to store their team lead's reports. This will make the information available to you and others interested in their specific areas of the project. This is an important step to enhance project communications because it establishes a common repository for team members to retrieve the information they need, and it promotes communication sharing and open dialog between everyone involved in the project.

4. Enforce the use of the team lead's report on your project. Work closely with each of your team leaders to ensure they complete the report on time and store it in the right location. This process continues throughout the life of the project.

ON the CD-ROM We have included a sample team lead's tool in the communication tools Integration folder. Use this as a guide to help you create your own version of this tool.

Using a team lead's report

Before using the team lead's report, you must identify who on your project team will utilize this tool so that you can determine the level of detail required, frequency of distribution, style, and format of the report. The team lead's report focuses on providing the project manager with project information for one area of the project only. The team lead's report is very detailed in nature and will contain little to no summary information.

Review the team leads planning section in Chapter 4 and then follow these steps:

1. Gather individual team lead's reports from each team leader and compile them into the overall project status report. You will want to establish weekly meetings with the individual team leaders to go over the information they have documented in their report.

2. After reviewing the team lead's report, work with the team leads to resolve any issues or dependencies across the group or in some cases across the projects, and address the specific issues for that work group.

3. Compile the information from the team lead's report into the overall project status report. Asking the team leaders questions about their project status will increase the accuracy of your project's status report. This process continues throughout the life of the project.

Summary

The tools that we describe in this chapter are the best choices for reporting the project's performance and status information.

The communication tools in this chapter span a wide variety of project reporting, including daily progress reports, periodic reports, and project status reports, which are generally delivered weekly. Project managers will find reporting with the tools in this chapter beneficial because each tool brings its own benefits and reporting perspective.

Use of the reporting communications tools outlined in this chapter will benefit the project manager, customers, and project team members. The reports are simple, easy to create, and informative in presenting information to the various parties involved on the project.

Chapter 22

Using Communication Tools for the Closeout Process

I n this chapter, we explore project communication tools in the project
closeout process. Specifically the communication tools in this chapter
will focus on closing the project and ensuring that everything is complete, approved, and achieved to the customer satisfaction.

There are two aspects of the project closeout process. The first is the technical closeout that focuses on delivery of the product, and the second is the
administrative closeout. The technical closeout is where you close out and
archive all technical documents, files, and paperwork, for long-term storage.
This means you would put away or shut down anything that the team used
to build the project since the team no longer needs it. The administrative
closeout focuses on closing contracts, purchase orders, budgets, staffing reallocations, warranty period terms, payroll, and any legal issues and conditions. It is important for the project manager to understand how critical it is
to communicate effectively during both of these closeout processes. If the
project manager handles it incorrectly, or improperly, there could be legal
ramifications.

The communication tools included in this chapter consist of the formal
acceptance document, lessons learned document, and the user acceptance
document.

IN THIS CHAPTER

**Mastering the formal acceptance
document**

**Mastering the lessons learned
document**

**Mastering the user acceptance
document**

Mastering the Formal Acceptance Document

Before exploring the formal acceptance document, you must understand
how this tool can assist and support you on your project. The following

project scenario emphasizes the importance of the tool and reasons why the formal acceptance document is critical to every project.

A large shoe manufacturing company, based out of London, England, has just launched a project to create a brand-new shoe inventory system in their stores worldwide. Because the shoe manufacturing company produces shoes, not software, they decided to contract the work and hired a local consulting firm to manage and develop the inventory system. You, as the project manager working for the software consulting company, decided you could manage this project. After a yearlong effort, you have successfully implemented the project around the world and the customer is thrilled. You are now in the closeout process of the project and are ready to take on your next challenge. However, you have just realized that you neglected to obtain the customer's final approval on the project. You made sure that you captured the go/no-go decision to release the application into the production environment, but never followed up by obtaining the formal acceptance document. Your management is excited about the launch and happy everything is going so well; however, after three weeks into the production environment, the application starts to fail. The application opens in one store, but then immediately shuts down. In another store, the application refuses to let anyone login, so the staff are unable to use it. You have a real mess on your hands, and your upper management wants some answers. They are asking you for the customer's formal acceptance document that accepted the software as complete and ready for worldwide implementation. The customers are also asking their own questions, such as how are these problems going to be resolved, who is paying for them, how long to fix them? Questions are coming in from all over the place including:

How could you have captured formal approval from the customer?

What could you have used to prevent this situation from occurring?

The answers to these questions lie in the project manager using a formal acceptance document when releasing the inventory system to the stores around the world. A formal acceptance document is the document that transfers ownership at the end of the project from the project manager and team members to the customer of the project's product. The formal acceptance document is usually a single-page document, sometimes handled by e-mail, that is mandatory on all projects as evidence that the customer accepted the project.

CROSS-REF We recommend that you review the Formal Acceptance Document tool's planning questions in Chapter 13.

Creating the formal acceptance document

The formal acceptance document is simple and easy to create and requires little to no effort from the project manager. In most cases, the formal acceptance document is one page in length, or it may be an e-mail that includes Approve/Reject buttons; anything really, that provides the evidence that the customer accepted and approved the project. Even a single-page document can provide enough basic information that the person signing it understands exactly what they are accepting. Developing the document with limited information, or in a manner that allows customers to avoid any responsibility, can cause serious issues for the project manager or the company. You should always have the legal department overlook the acceptance document.

Successful project managers must ensure that they are diligent in using formal acceptance documents with their customers. Lawyers can use the formal acceptance document in lawsuits and court cases as evidence that the customers accepted and approved the work, therefore getting companies and project managers specifically out of trouble if their projects ever go to court. The formal acceptance document also provides a mutual agreement between two parties that the job is complete and both are satisfied with the results. Project managers need to ensure all customers approve and sign off on the project's formal acceptance document. If this means stopping the project dead until everyone signs off, the project manager may have to take those dramatic steps to do so. In this case, this could mean the project manager does not turn over the project to the customer. The project manager should ensure at the beginning of the project that everyone agrees on who will have final approval on the project, and then those individual(s), at the minimum, will sign off on the formal acceptance document. If the project manager does not get sign-off from everyone on the sign-off list, from an auditor perspective, the project is not signed off because everyone on that list must provide his or her approval.

Project customers play an important role in the formal acceptance process and should work diligently with the project manager to provide approval and acceptance of the project when it is complete. Ultimately, the project is not a success unless the customer signs the formal acceptance document. Customers should understand exactly what they are accepting when signing off on the formal acceptance document; with that signature, they are acknowledging they have accepted the responsibilities of the project. Rarely do customers have anything to do with the creation of the document, other than reviewing it and agreeing to what fields and information is on it and providing their agreement that they will sign off the document when it comes time to do so.

The actual steps of creating a formal acceptance document can vary from project manager to project manager. Instead of providing step-by-step instructions on creating a formal acceptance document, a better option is for the project manager to complete a formal acceptance document template.

Figure 22.1 is a sample formal acceptance document. As you can see, creating this document is simple — just use a template, and fill in the blank areas. This example shows a document seeking customer approval for the delivery of the project. The project manager is responsible for changing the document, depending on the needs of the project.

ON the CD-ROM We have included a sample of this Formal Acceptance Document tool in the Communication tools Procurement subfolder. Use this as a guide to create your own version of this tool.

Using the formal acceptance document

Before using a tool such as the formal acceptance document, you must identify who on your project team will utilize this tool so that you can determine the level of detail required, frequency of distribution, style, and format of the report.

FIGURE 22.1

A sample of a basic acceptance document.

Formal Acceptance Document

Project ID/Num: _____   Project Name: _____   Acceptance Date: _____

Project Client/Owner Name: _____   Customer/Owner Department Name: _____

Project Manager Name: _____   Project Management Office Rep: _____

Project Acceptance or Imformation:

        Acceptance or Reject Delivery of project: Accept: _____   Reject: _____ (*)

        * If rejected please explain the reason:

_____

_____

Further comments:

_____

_____

Project Detail information:

Planned Start Date: _____   Actual Start Date: _____

Planned Finished Date: _____   Actual Finished Date: _____

Actual Budget ($): _____   Final Cost ($): _____   Over or Under Budget: _____

Signatures/Approvals Section:

Project Manager Approvals: _____

        Print Name

        _____

        Signature

Project Client/Owner Approvals: _____

        Print Name

        _____

        Signature

Before using the formal acceptance document tool, review the formal acceptance document planning section in Chapter 13 and then follow these steps:

1. You must ensure the customer agrees they will sign off on the document when you request their signatures at the end of the project. You should work with the customers early in the project so that they are comfortable and agree with what is stated in the formal acceptance document and have no problems signing it when it comes time to obtain their signatures.

2. Next, you should distribute the formal acceptance document for approval at the end of the project to the appropriate stakeholders. When the project is complete, the project manager sends the document to everyone on the formal acceptance approval list.

3. On the last step, you should store the formal acceptance document, once signed-off and approved by all parties, in the document control system. This includes ensuring that team members have security rights and that the formal acceptance document is ready to use immediately by anyone on the team.

Mastering the Lesson Learned Document

Before exploring the lessons learned document, you must understand how this tool can assist and support you on your project. The following project scenario emphasizes the importance of the tool, and the reason why the lessons learned document is critical to every project.

A large software company decides to launch a brand-new software operating system that will change the way businesses utilize tablet computers. The software company is promising amazing new features and capabilities that hardware companies have never seen before. The company predicts that when the tablets hit the shelves, "they are going to sell like crazy." As one of the most senior project managers in the company, you are asked to be involved in the project and lead the effort. Because this is a new operating system and expectations are so high, you want to be involved in it from the start and contribute to its success. Management agrees that you are the best person to lead the effort, so you quickly begin planning the project's activities. As the project progresses, everything seems to be going along nicely and there are no major issues until you approach the software development phase. Your two top developers have run into some problems that are preventing them from moving forward. You investigate the situation, and it turns out to be a minor misunderstanding between the two developers; your work resolves the situation and the project continues. Then another situation arises between the two developers, and you step in again, resolve it, and put the incident behind you.

As the project moves into the test phase, a couple of minor problems occur; they are quickly resolved and the project continues. Again, you do not capture anything formally for the project on the test situation because you were thinking that it was minor, and there is nothing to worry about. As the project moves into the user acceptance phase, a major problem occurs and the project stops dead in its tracks. The users are unable to use the software, and the issues that the two developers were discussing back in the development phase, which you decided to ignore, have just derailed your project. You are trying to remember what the disagreement between the two developers was about but your memory is just not what it used to be. You are wondering now if that was the major warning sign that you should have taken more seriously. You call the two developers into a meeting, but so much time has passed they cannot remember what the issues were about either. Upper management is applying a lot of pressure to get the user acceptance testing phase going again. While the issues remain unresolved, the project is losing thousands of dollars a day. Upper management is trying to get into the details of the issues that occurred during development, and are looking for documentation to understand how they can help resolve the issue. Upper management is asking the following questions:

What happened during the development phase?

Who was responsible?

How was it resolved back then?

Who took ownership of that resolution?

What was the resolution?

Who approved the resolution?

To obtain the answers to these questions, the project manager should have used a lessons learned document. The lessons learned document captures the lessons everyone learned while involved in executing and working on the project. The lessons learned document provides a wealth of project information that only a project team member working on a project can provide because they are the ones working on the project and experiencing the events as they are occurring. It would be impossible for an outsider to provide the same level of information that someone working on the project can provide, especially if they are not part of the team. Every project should have a lessons learned document so they are able to provide best practices and lessons learned information to other projects or to other interested parties wanting to ensure they do not repeat the same mistakes.

 Collect lessons learned information during the life of the project and do not wait until the end. A best practice is to capture this data during the project's weekly status meetings.

 We recommend that you review the Lessons Learned tool's planning questions in Chapters 1 and 13.

Creating a lessons learned document

The creation of the lessons learned material occurs during the lifecycle of the project. A common mistake project managers make is that they wait until the end of the project to collect this data when the team has long forgotten it or has since moved on. Chances are slim that team members will remember from the beginning of the project what went right and what went wrong about the key questions to capturing lesson learned information. Asking someone to remember the details of something that happened six months ago is not realistic; people are so busy that they generally cannot remember that far back in time. The recommended approach for collecting and compiling lessons learned information is to capture it continuously during the life of the project.

 **TIP** Lessons learned in most cases are better than a daily log.

Project customers should be involved in providing lessons learned information throughout the life-cycle of the project. A project customer who is active on a project will be part of the events and situations that occurred, so you should capture their thoughts on the events as well for inclusion into the project's lessons learned information.

The actual steps of creating a lessons learned document could vary from project manager to project manager. Instead of providing step-by-step instructions on creating a lessons learned document, a better option would be for the project manager to complete a lessons learned template.

ON the CD-ROM We have included a sample of this lessons learned document in the Communication tools Procurement subfolder folder. Use this as a guide to create your own version of this tool.

Example of Lessons Learned Table of Contents

*S*ection 1: *Areas of Success*
Document in this section the areas on the project that were successful, such as budget, schedule, quality, human resources, and general project management.

*S*ection 2: *Areas of Improvement*
Document in this section the areas on the project that needed improvement, such as budget, schedule, quality, human resources, and general project management. Generally, anything the project team, customers, or project manager felt needed improving would go in this section.

*S*ection 3: *General Lessons Leaned Information*
Document the project's lessons learned information not falling in other categories, such as resource assignments, working conditions, and overtime issues.

*S*ection 4: *Final Thoughts*
Document any other thoughts or recommendations you have in this section.

Using the lessons learned document

Before using a tool such as the lessons learned document, it is imperative to identify who on your project team will utilize this tool. This will determine the level of detail required, frequency of distribution, style, and format of the report. This ensures the project manager is communicating the appropriate level of detail to the project team members or customers.

Before using the lessons learned document, review the lessons learned document's planning section in Chapter 13 and then follow these steps:

1. You should ensure there is a process in place for collecting lessons learned data during the lifecycle of the project. This includes adding time to weekly status meetings, setting up generic template forms, or Web sites to collect this information for your project.

2. After establishing that process, you need to collect the lessons learned information on the project. This process is best utilized during the weekly project status meetings when team members are together and you can provide the necessary information. You can also hold separate meetings to collect lessons learned information. You can also collect it in casual conversations with the team members or the customer.

3. After you collect and compile the lessons learned information throughout the project, you should create a lessons learned presentation for an end of project meeting. This presentation will provide everyone involved a summarized view of the areas of success and areas of improvement on the project.

4. Call a lessons learned meeting and present your project's lessons learned materials. This process includes not only presenting what was collected during the project, but also collecting new material presented at the meeting. In some cases, project team members or customers will wait until that meeting to voice their concerns or present lessons learned information. In these situations, all you can do is collect the new information, compile it with the other information, and discuss it as part of the meeting.

5. Store the lessons learned materials in the document control system for long-term storage, archiving, and retrieval purposes. This allows you to store all your project information in one location; this lessons learned information being just as important and relevant to store for the project.

Mastering the User Acceptance Document

Before mastering the user acceptance document, you must understand how this tool can assist and support you on your project. The following project scenario emphasizes the importance of the tool and reasons why the user acceptance document is critical to every project.

A large manufacturing company decides to update and enhance their current performance appraisal system. The company has grown from 20 employees in four years to 158 employees and is still growing. This is a substantial increase in staff, and the current system is unable to handle the load that the finance department puts on it. The employees feel the method by which management is appraising their performance is outdated, no longer valid, and long overdue. An updated system with new rules and policies for appraising employees is required immediately and management knows it. Management did a feasibility study and agrees. They approve the project. You as lead project manager for the finance group think that this project would be fun to manage and have asked if you can lead it. Management again approves, and you immediately start working on the project.

As you begin the start-up activities, you determine the methodology that the project is going to use, who and what customers will be involved, and the overall layout of the project. You are excited because this is going to be a typical project, but the end result will personally benefit every person at the company. You could be a hero in everyone's eyes. As you start the first phase of the project, the customers provide their requirements and you jointly develop the business requirements document. The customer signs off on the business requirements document, and you store the document and approvals in the document control system. The project then moves into the technical phase, and the same process occurs — the customer reviews the documents, approves them, and the project moves onto the design phase. As the project completes and moves into the production environment, something goes terribly wrong. The screens and the user interface for the new application are not usable. One of the biggest problems is that it is hard to input data into the application. The reports do not print correctly and on many reports the data does not fit onto the page — the application is a complete disaster and the company has wasted hundreds of thousands of dollars. You, as project manager, made the biggest mistake of your professional career, and management is looking for someone to blame. Management wants to understand who approved such a terrible, unworkable product for final delivery. As you scramble and look back over the course of the project, you review the information in the document control system and find that the customer only provided their approval for the first two phases of the project. After that, you have the documents that you sent to the customers for approval, but realize now, they were never returned as approved. You search and search but you quickly realize you forgot to secure the customer's approval on the project phases after the technical phase. You know the mistake you made, but you still have management asking some tough questions, such as:

What formal documentation should the project manager have used to capture the customer's signatures?

What process and procedures would the project manager have followed to prevent the project from moving into the next phase?

To obtain the answers to these questions, the project manager should have used a user acceptance document and followed through to ensure all customers signed them before moving on to the next phase of the project. User acceptance documents capture the customers' formal acceptance and approval at each phase of the project and have formal processes and procedures tied to them that allow a project manager to follow those processes. The user acceptance documents are critical for project audits when project managers seek approvals between project phases. Auditors request evidence of approval at a specific stage in the project and require approval on the project itself. These two approvals are very different. If project managers use the user acceptance document and ensure at every phase that there is a sign-off process, then they are doing their due diligence.

CROSS-REF   We recommend that you review the User Acceptance Document tool's planning questions in Chapter 13.

Creating a user acceptance document

The creation and use of the user acceptance documents is critical on all projects, and project managers must ensure that customers are happy with the product or deliverable from each phase of the project. Whether a construction, software, manufacturing, or research project, the customers play a vital role in the overall success and adoption of the product and therefore their approval is important. If the customers do not like the product or deliverable created, they may never approve it or never end up using it. For example, on a construction project, it is in the best interest of the contracting company and the design companies to ensure that the owners are as happy as possible with the building before turning it over to them. If there is a chance that the owners are going to want to build another building and/or give your company future project work, it is best to ensure they have a good relationship with the owner to secure future projects. A happy owner will most likely want to work with the same construction company again in the future.

Project customers should be active in the user acceptance process, but are rarely involved in the creation of the user acceptance document. Expect each customer to provide his or her signature on the user acceptance document at the end of every project phase or each major project deliverable. Without that approval, the project manager should stop the project until obtaining all approvals on the document. Because it is important to keep the project moving, upper management may choose to allow the project team to proceed without everyone's approval but will expect the project manager to continue to drive the process of obtaining the sign-offs. There could be valid reasons, such as holidays or vacations, that prevent a project team from obtaining approval on the exact date requested, and upper management will make the decision to stop or continue the project. If this does occur, upper management is taking the responsibilities of continuing the project without those approvals.

NOTE   It is important to note that from an auditor's perspective, this breaks all auditing rules; most projects state that without the sign-off of all parties, the project does not move forward.

The steps for creating a user acceptance document can vary from project manager to project manager. Instead of providing step-by-step instructions on creating a user acceptance document, a better option is for the project manager to complete a template.

Figure 22.2 is a sample user acceptance document. As you can see, creating this document is simple — just use a template, and fill in the blank areas. This partial example shows a document seeking customer approval for a project deliverable, not a project phase. The document is easy to update when seeking customer approval on a phase and not a deliverable. The project manager is responsible for changing the document depending on the needs of the project.

 We have included a sample of this user acceptance document tool in the Communication tools Procurement subfolder folder. Use it to help you create your own version of the User Acceptance tool.

FIGURE 22.2

A sample of a basic user acceptance document.

Date: _____

This acceptance form acts as formal document of the _____ deliverable on

the _____ project. By signing off on this document, you agree to the following

terms outlined below.

Please approve each statement below:

_____ The deliverable is of the highest quality the project can afford.

_____ I have fully tested the deliverable (if applicable) and it passes my tests and is
ready from my perspective to be moved into a production environment.
If the deliverable is a document, I have read it and agree to the contents
of the document.

Signature: _____

Printed name: _____

Using a user acceptance document

Before you can use a user acceptance document, you must identify who on your project team will utilize this tool so that you can determine the level of detail required, frequency of distribution, style, and format of the report. Before utilizing the user acceptance document, review the user acceptance document planning section in Chapter 13; then follow these steps:

1. You must ensure the customer agrees to sign off on the user acceptance document when the project completes a particular phase. To ensure this, the project manager will literally stop all project activities until everyone signs the document. You should work with the customers so that they are comfortable with the contents of the document. You usually do this in the project's planning process, when you receive their buy-in and approval that they will utilize this document when approving project deliverables.

2. You then enforce the use of the user acceptance documents with your team members as you go from project phase to project phase. This includes each team leader working with the project manager and generating a user acceptance document for their phase. For example, from the design phase to the build phase in a software project, the lead designer

may create a user acceptance document for the customers to sign and approve for the design phase of the project. The project manager will enforce the use of these documents with their team members by adding this as a formal step in the phase closeout process.

3. Store your project's approved user acceptance documents in the document control system after obtaining official sign-off from the customers. This includes ensuring that team members have security rights and the system is set up and ready to use immediately by anyone on the team. This may require you as the project manager asking the security team to validate your team member's access to the document control system to allow them complete access to the project files.

Summary

In summary, the tools that we describe in this chapter are the best choices for closing out and obtaining final approval on the project. The closing of a project should be something a project manager handles carefully. Normally, there is almost no time between when a project manager finishes one project and starts the next; and many times, because of that, project managers miss important tasks such as sign-offs, obtaining approvals, or other closeout activities that are critical for every project.

One of the most important tools in the project closeout process is the lessons learned document. You normally collect lessons learned in the closeout process of a project, but as we have discussed in this chapter, project managers should collect this data throughout their project and present it to customers and upper management at the end of the project.

Use of the reporting communications tools outlined in this chapter will benefit the project manager, customers, and project team members. The reports are simple, easy to create, and informative in presenting information to the various parties.

Part IV

Appendixes

Appendix A

What's on the CD-ROM?

This appendix provides you with information on the contents of the CD that accompanies this book. For the latest and greatest information, please refer to the ReadMe file located at the root of the CD. Here is what you will find:

- System Requirements
- Using the CD with Windows, and Macintosh
- What is on the CD-ROM?
- Troubleshooting tips

System Requirements

Make sure that your computer meets the minimum system requirements listed in this section. If your computer does not match up to most of these requirements, you may have a problem using the contents of the CD.

- PC running Windows 98 or later or a Macintosh running Mac OS X
- An Internet connection
- A CD-ROM drive

Using the CD

To access the content from the CD, follow these steps.

1. Insert the CD into your computer's CD-ROM drive. The license agreement appears.

   Note to Windows users: The interface won't launch if you have autorun disabled. In that case, click Start ⇨ Run (For Windows Vista, Start ⇨ All Programs ⇨ Accessories ⇨ Run). In the dialog box that appears, type D:\Start.exe. (Replace D with the proper letter if your CD drive uses a different letter. If you don't know the letter, see how your CD drive is listed under My Computer.) Click OK.

   Note for Mac Users: The CD icon will appear on your desktop, double-click the icon to open the CD and double-click the "Start" icon.

2. Read through the license agreement, and then click the Accept button if you want to use the CD.

   The CD interface appears. The interface allows you to install the programs and run the demos with just a click of a button (or two).

What's on the CD

The following sections provide a summary of the software and other materials you'll find on the CD.

Author-created materials

The author-created materials include various spreadsheets, charts, and examples that will help the project manager, team members, customers, and upper management in communicating more effectively on projects. Regardless of your role on a project, there is a tool on the CD-ROM that you can utilize.

After you read about each communication tool in the book, you can go to the CD-ROM to find the example tool. Or you may want to open the tool as you are learning about it to be able to try new things, add or enhance the tool, so that you can use it on your projects.

Most tools are created using the Microsoft Office products, such as Word, Excel, PowerPoint, MS Project, and MS Visio, which are common applications in today's business world. Otherwise, if you do not have those applications, there should be converters and other methods of reading these tools.

Applications

The following applications are on the CD:

- Adobe Reader

  Adobe Reader is a freeware application for viewing files in the Adobe Portable Document format. For more information, visit

  www.adobe.com/products/reader.

■ Mindjet MindManager Pro – link only

The Mindjet MindManager Pro tool accelerates and improves project planning. An easy to use brainstorming tool integrates with Microsoft Office.

`www.mindjet.com/us/`

■ Primavera PertMaster Project Risk – trial version

These tools will address full lifecycle risk management for your project using the advanced Monte Carlo analysis for cost and schedule analysis.

`www.pertmaster.com/`

■ Milestones Professional 2006 and Milestones Project Companion – trial versions

Milestones Professional 2006 focuses on making it very easy to set up a project and produce the standard Gantt chart, and has many presentation enhancement features. These tools are used to create presentation reports using Microsoft Project.

`www.kidasa.com/pc/index.html`

■ Innate Timesheets – demo version

This software assists in managing resources across projects. There are four main aspects of this software; Resource Management, Timesheets, Billable work, and Project Management software. Web based timesheets with an optional approval process track how time is being spent. You can compare planned vs. actual effort and measure performance against project plans and budgets. It is very easy to operate, with low overheads and automatic alerts that drive the timesheet process.

`www.innate.co.uk/`

■ WBS Chart Pro – demo version

WBS Chart Pro is a tool used for project planning. It breaks a project schedule down into a chart showing how a project is organized. There are multiple views and it allows project managers, team members, and customers to review how the project is organized.

`www.criticaltools.com/wbschartprosoftware.htm`

■ PERT Chart Expert – demo version

Pert Chart Expert is a tool that is also used for project planning and breaks down the project schedule by dependencies. This graphical tool allows project managers, customers, or upper management to graphically view the dependencies of the project tasks and adjust where applicable.

`www.criticaltools.com/pertchartexpertsoftware.htm`

■ Project KickStart – trial version

Project KickStart is a project planning application that focuses on small to medium size projects. The software includes steps for brainstorming and organizing a project plan. It focuses on planning a project, creating a project schedule, and making it easy to manage.

`www.projectkickstart.com/`

- EPK-Suite – demo version

  EPK-Suite is a resource and capacity planning, project and portfolio management, collaboration, and timesheet system, utilizing the Microsoft SQL Server and Windows SharePoint Services platforms. It features integration with Microsoft Office Project for major projects, and a browser based planning capability for less complex projects. The following functions are available: reports, portfolio management, resource management and collaboration.

  www.EPKGroup.com

- WSG System's Empire Suite – demo version

  The Empire Suite provides the solution to gain complete control of resource management and the planning, tracking, accounting and billing of your project deliverables. The applications in the Empire Suite provide solutions at every step of the project development life cycle: best practices, project planning, estimating, resource management, time and expense tracking and billing/chargeback.

  www.wsg.com

Shareware programs are fully functional, trial versions of copyrighted programs. If you like particular programs, register with their authors for a nominal fee and receive licenses, enhanced versions, and technical support.

Freeware programs are copyrighted games, applications, and utilities that are free for personal use. Unlike shareware, these programs do not require a fee or provide technical support.

GNU software is governed by its own license, which is included inside the folder of the GNU product. See the GNU license for more details.

Trial, demo, or evaluation versions are usually limited either by time or functionality (such as being unable to save projects). Some trial versions are very sensitive to system date changes. If you alter your computer's date, the programs will "time out" and will no longer be functional.

eBook version of the Project Management Communications Bible

The entire text of the *Project Management Communications Bible* is available on the CD-ROM as a PDF document. You can find any tool or any additional information. Any Acrobat viewer 7.0 and above can open the PDF file and view the contents.

To search the embedded index, open the Search panel (Shift + Ctrl+ F) and type a word in the first text box. Acrobat automatically uses the embedded index to find searched words.

Troubleshooting

If you have difficulty installing or using any of the materials on the companion CD, try the following solutions:

- **Turn off any anti-virus software that you may have running.** Installers sometimes mimic virus activity and can make your computer incorrectly believe that it is being infected by a virus. (Be sure to turn the anti-virus software back on later.)

- **Close all running programs.** The more programs you're running, the less memory is available to other programs. Installers also typically update files and programs; if you keep other programs running, installation may not work properly.

- **Reference the ReadMe:** Please refer to the ReadMe file located at the root of the CD-ROM for the latest product information at the time of publication.

Customer care

If you have trouble with the CD-ROM, please call the Wiley Product Technical Support phone number at (800) 762-2974. Outside the United States, call 1(317) 572-3994. You can also contact Wiley Product Technical Support at `http://support.wiley.com`. John Wiley & Sons will provide technical support only for installation and other general quality control items. For technical support on the applications themselves, consult the program's vendor or author.

To place additional orders or to request information about other Wiley products, please call (877) 762-2974.

Appendix B

Planning Project Communications in a Foreign Country

Whether it is negotiating a project budget or listening to your team member's personal problems, a project manager must always be an effective communicator regardless of the situation she is in. This skill set is also very valuable when traveling to different countries. In today's environment, project managers are traveling on assignments all over the world, and if they are not effective at their project communications, they are never going to be successful. When traveling abroad, you need to learn the cultures and customs of the country where you will be working and living, so that you can effectively communicate.

> **TIP** Be prepared for international travel. Spending upfront time learning the culture and customs of the country you are visiting will go a long way in establishing a great relationship with your new co-workers.

Business Travel

If you are lucky enough to win a project management assignment on a foreign project, we advise you to learn the customs and cultures of the country you will be working in before you travel there. By doing so, project managers learn how to act to avoid offending anyone with their actions.

Preparation

The time required to prepare varies from person to person. The project manager should determine the amount of time he is going to be in the country as a guide. A week-long trip requires a lot less preparation than someone going to stay for months or years. Most of the time if you are assigned to a long-term project in a foreign country, your company usually gives you enough time to prepare for the trip and in most cases helps you or pays to get you prepared to leave. If your project assignment is longer than a year, you may consider taking a class in the local language of that area so you can be a little prepared. Learning a second language will help project managers communicate with team members already living in that area. The team members will appreciate the extra effort you have taken to learn their language and will often be very gracious when you attempt some of the words when trying to communicate to them.

Dual-language business cards

In most countries, exchanging business cards at a first meeting is good business manners. It is best to carry business cards printed (front and back printed) both in English and in the language of the country you are visiting. When receiving the card from your foreign counterpart, for example in Japan, if you pocket it immediately, without spending any time reviewing it, that is considered rude and bad manners. It is acceptable to ask questions or make comments about the card after you have reviewed it.

TIP   Even though English is the international business language, getting business cards made in dual languages is a great idea for anyone working in a multinational company. Even if you are at home and staff from your international offices visits you, it would be a nice gesture for you to use your dual language card if possible.

Many times, international airlines can arrange to have these cards printed and ready for you when you arrive. It is imperative when visiting Japan or China that you do have dual language business cards. This is a standard practice for these cultures.

Culture

Learning the cultural differences between your country and the foreign country is important for a project manager. Individuals should familiarize themselves with basic cultural traits, such as hand signals, street signs, basic courtesy on tipping, and specific rules for women in the Near East countries, when looking to live and work in a different country. Project managers require flexibility and cultural adaptation before looking at working aboard. They and their team members traveling abroad for the first time will be very surprised by how much business manners, customs, religion, dietary practices, humor, and dress can vary dramatically from country to country. Be very alert and observant of the local customs. The quick way for project managers to get an overview of the country they are going to work in is to purchase a travel guide for that country or get a guide or a friend who lives there to show them around.

Understanding cultural differences is important to having a successful experience when working in a foreign country. The lack of familiarity with etiquette, social customs, and cultural norms of the country practices can hurt a project manager's creditability with the local team members. In some cases, it may slow them down from being motivated to work for you at all. If the project manager comes in and makes some major cultural blunder, it may affect the overall team's morale and put the project manager in an awkward position with them. It could take a long time to correct this situation if it does occur.

It is very important to have knowledge of the culture, management attitudes, and customs before traveling abroad. Project managers should research, read books, obtain training, and read personal interviews to learn as much as possible about the culture. Wiley & Sons has a number of books on the subject that would be a perfect companion for you to read and prepare yourself for the trip. Some examples are:

- *Essential Do's and Taboos: The Complete Guide to International Business and Leisure Travel*
- *Doing Business Anywhere: The Essential Guide to Going Global*
- *Doing Business in China For Dummies*

Greetings

Traditional greetings may be a handshake, a hug, a nose rub, a kiss on the cheek, placing the hands in praying position, or various other gestures. When cultural lines cross, something as simple as a greeting can become misunderstood between the two people and cause issues. Project managers need to be fully aware of the countries' accepted form of greetings or it could lead to awkward encounters with your foreign stakeholders.

Gifts

Gift giving is a common custom in China. When project managers are traveling to China, expect to bring a gift for your host. That gift should be from your home country or even better your home area. It does not have to be expensive, just considered carefully. Failure to bring a gift is an insult in some countries and in others presenting or offering a gift is like bribing someone. In sharp contrast, exchanging gifts in Germany is rare and is not usually an appropriate thing to do. Gift giving is not a normal custom in Belgium or the United Kingdom either, although in both countries, flowers and wine are a suitable gift when invited to someone's home. Again, know the customs of the country in which you are going to work.

Significance of gestures

A misunderstanding over gestures is a common occurrence in intercultural communication. A misinterpretation along these lines can lead to a big laugh or it could lead to working through the issues and social embarrassment for that person. Project managers who are working around the world need to be careful when using body movements or gestures to convey specific messages because some gestures that are common in their culture may not be common in the other culture and may end up offending someone.

- Putting hands on your hip in some cultures is an indication of challenge or a combative attitude.
- Crossing your arms in front of someone indicates that you do not agree, or are skeptical of them.

Negotiating styles

Project negotiating is a complex process even between parties from the same nation. It is even more complicated in international transactions because of the potential misunderstandings that stem from cultural and language differences. It is essential to understand the importance of rank in the other country, to know who the decision makers are, and to be familiar with the working style on a foreign project. It is also important to understand the nature of agreements in the culture. That way, project managers who are negotiating agreements understand what that means and will have a better understanding of how everything all fits together.

Differences in business styles

The project manager must pay attention to the different styles in accomplishing a project's objective. In some countries, team members have a very direct style and in others, they are much more laid back and not that aggressive. For example, in Germany project team members are very serious and generally get right down to business when they are working. There tends to be no small talk that could interrupt the performance of the project. Most folks from Germany feel that the work environment is very serious and should keep everything at a professional level.

Discovering etiquette

The following tips are a guide for some of the popular business travel counties. It is possible your next assignment could be in any one of the countries, so this list should have you thinking about how to prepare for that next major move. However, as you can imagine, every situation will be different, and the following tips may not work in every specific situation. The project manager must be aware and adapt the various tips to each situation as it occurs.

 Not all countries are listed here, just some to guide you in your preparation for your travels.

United States of America (U.S.)

Acceptable in most cases:

- In general, tipping is not included is the bill or tariff and a 15 percent tip is considered average.
- When in a crowd, always stand up when the national anthem is played.

Unacceptable in most cases:

- Americans tend to be very proud of their country, so do not disrespect it or make disparaging comments.
- Slang is unacceptable in business and project communications.

Belgium

Acceptable in most cases: Greeting someone with three kisses on the cheek, alternating from one cheek to the other. This is also a custom in France and Greece.

Unacceptable in most cases:

- Yawn, sneeze, or blow your nose in the presence of others.

- Place your hands in your pockets while talking to someone. By doing this, you are showing a lack of interest.

- Point your index finger at somebody. Pointing in most European countries is impolite and frowned on. If you need to point at something, you simply gesture in that direction. Most of the time a nod of the head will work.

China

Acceptable in most cases:

- Address a person using their family name. For example, use Mr. rather than Raymond Li. For business purposes, it is traditional to call a Chinese person by their surname along with their title, such as Director Li or Doctor Shi.

- Look at the business card from your Chinese business associate and note the name and position in their company this person holds. This is very important in China. Always put their business card in a front pocket, not a rear pocket when putting away the card. It would be an insult to put it in a back pocket. Also, remember to take or receive the business card with both hands if possible.

- Start all business meetings with small talk and avoid getting into the business topic too early.

- Always bring a gift to your host.

Unacceptable in most cases:

- Even though you start meetings with small talk, do not become too friendly too fast. The Eastern culture frowns upon quick informality.

- Do not be boastful and overbearing. A simple nod, or better yet a slight bow, and in some cases a mild handshake are all proper greeting protocol during introductions.

France

Acceptable in most cases:

- For business communications such as e-mail, or letters, use a very formal and business-like format.

- Avoid calling your business associates' personal phone (home or cell) for business-related topics. If you must make the call, make it before 9:00 p.m.

Unacceptable in most cases:

- Arriving late for meetings.
- Using first names during a business meeting. The French people are proud of their cultures and require a formal business atmosphere. Even if you are a friend, you should still use their last name and title (i.e., Director Brisard).
- Delay business discussions until the small talk is finished in a dinner or meeting environment. Jumping right into business discussions is considered rude.
- A man should never ask a woman what she did over the weekend.

Germany

Acceptable in most cases:

- Always knock before opening a closed door regardless of the door.
- Always be punctual whether a business meeting or a dinner. It is rude to be late to almost any engagement.
- Minimize small talk in business situations.
- Always use the title and family name of your local team members.

Unacceptable in most cases:

- When meeting someone, shaking his or her hand with your other hand in your pocket
- Being late for a business meeting

Italy

Acceptable in most cases:

- When greeting each other, you may kiss each other's cheeks and offer a long handshake.
- It is also acceptable to shake with both hands.
- Hire an interpreter if you are not fluent in Italian.

Unacceptable in most cases:

- Refusing repeats on your plate if offered.
- Being late for meetings or appointments is considered rude. Especially in northern Italy, they consider time the same as money.

Indonesia

Acceptable in most cases:

- If you are being introduced to several people, always start with the eldest or most senior person first.
- Titles are important in Indonesia as they signify status. If you know of any titles be sure that you use them in conjunction with the name.

Unacceptable in most cases:

- Crossing your legs when you are sitting and showing the sole of your foot.
- Women wearing short skirts is unacceptable. Women should dress conservatively, ensuring that they are well covered from ankle to neck.

Preparing and Planning for Foreign Project Communications

As project managers work on different projects around the world, it is important that before they head to the foreign country they spend the time and become aware of its religions, cultures, and customs. There are many different customs across many countries, so read up on the country you are going to work in. You do not want to get into a situation that is acceptable in your country, but unacceptable anywhere else. For example, in a Muslim country you do not sit with your legs crossed and your soles showing. Be aware of these types of common everyday situations that are problems in the foreign country. Project manages have to be overly aware of their environment and ensure they are being sensitive at all times to their environment.

When projects are short on staff and cannot find local resources, they quite often look abroad for talented individuals. In this case, if the project manager hires team members from a different country, those new team members need to be aware of the different cultures of the country they are working in. The team members should prepare as much as a project manager would prepare to work and travel aboard. Even if the new team members continue to work in their home country but are part of a team that is located in a different country, they still need to know the cultures of the country they are working with regularly. For example, if a group of individuals from China are working on a team based in the Canada, the team in China should understand Canadian customs, and the team from Canada should know the customs or cultures from China. Especially if there is travel between the two countries, this information is very important to learn before doing that travel.

The project manager should instill in the team members the customs and the cultural differences between the new members coming onboard. Taking time away from the team member's current activities and allowing them time to spend learning the culture differences of their newest team members is time well spent. It will help in the team members accepting the new team members and will help in the overall morale and teamwork. If each team member spends the time up front learning the different customs, you are going to build a very strong team and the new team member will feel accepted.

In some cases, project managers go to work in a foreign country where the two countries (the project manager's home country) and the new country, for many different reasons, are hostile toward one another. Project managers need to be very careful in these types of situations and, when managing their projects, need to be alert to the environment and political unrest of the country. If you are selected and opt to take a project on in that part of the world, then working very closely with your advisors at the company on security, protocols, and other procedures could be life saving!

Tool Breakdown Structure Diagrams

In this appendix, we provide a graphical display of the Knowledge Area Breakdown chart identifying which communication tools belong under which Knowledge area.

Knowledge Area Charts

Figure C.1 shows the communication tools broken down by each Knowledge area. This mapping chart contains every one of the tools in the book, associated to the Project Management Knowledge area. This chart allows you to identify what Knowledge areas the tools are in and what is their associated chapter in the book.

Lifecycle Process Charts

The following section provides a graphical view of the tools broken down by the lifecycle processes. This chart displays what communication tool belong to which lifecycle process. This chart is perfect for printing and attaching to your wall.

Figure C.2 shows the Communication tools broken down by each lifecycle process. This mapping chart contains every one of the tools in the book associated to the project management lifecycle process. This chart enables you to identify what process the tool is under and the chapter of the book in which you can find the tool.

FIGURE C.1

A tool breakdown structure by Knowledge area.

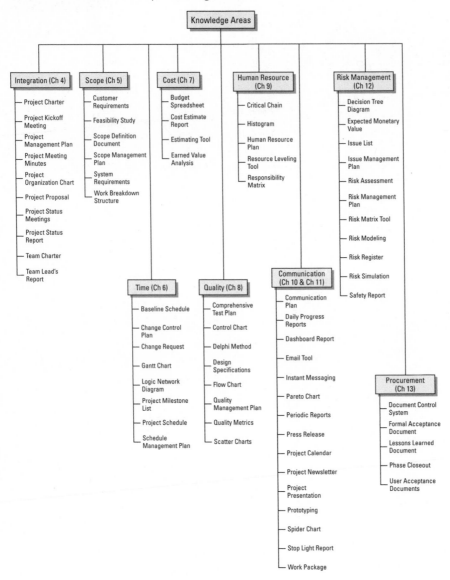

FIGURE C.2

A tool breakdown structure by lifecycle process.

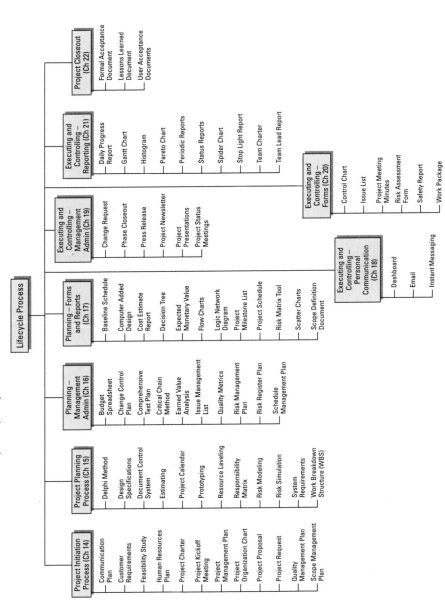

Appendix D

Tools at a Glance

Table D.1 provides a cross reference for every tool in the book. The value of "Tools at a Glance" is that it provides the opportunity for project managers to be able to select the right tools for their projects at a single glance. The breakdown of the tools by knowledge or processes gives the project manager a single reference to draw upon when determine what tools to utilize in what areas of their project. Other benefits of this chart include the size of projects (small, medium, large) to tool mapping where project managers can determine the recommended list of communication tools for the size of project. One of the greatest benefits of this table is it provides project managers with a communication tool checklist.

TABLE D.1

Project Management Communications Tools List

Tool Name	Part 2 (Knowledge Area)	Part 3 (Process)	Knowledge Area	Life Cycle Process (Most Dominant)	Size	Recommended Usage on Projects	Critical Tool on all projects	Industry
Baseline Schedule	6	17	Time	Planning Forms and Reports	Medium	High	Yes	Construction
Budget Spreadsheet	7	16	Cost	Planning Management Admin	Small	High	Yes	Software
Change Control Plan	6	16	Time	Planning Management Admin	Medium	High	Yes	Software
Change Request	6	19	Time	Executing and Controlling Management Admin	Medium	High	Yes	Software
Communication Plan	10	14	Communication	Project initiating	Medium	High	Yes	Software
Comprehensive Test Plan	8	16	Quality	Planning Management Admin	Medium	High	Yes	Software
Control Chart	8	20	Quality	Executing and Controlling Forms	Large	Medium	No	Manufacturing
Cost Estimate Report	7	17	Cost	Planning Forms and Reports	Medium	High	Yes	Construction
Critical Chain	9	16	Human Resources	Planning Management Admin	Large	High	No	Manufacturing

Tool Name	Part 2 (Knowledge Area)	Part 3 (Process)	Knowledge Area	Life Cycle Process (Most Dominant)	Size	Recommended Usage on Projects	Critical Tool on all projects	Industry
Customer Requirements	5	14	Scope	Project initiating	Small	High	Yes	Software
Daily Progress Reports	11	21	Communication	Executing and Controlling Reports	Small	High	Yes	All
Dashboard Report	11	18	Communication	Executing and Controlling Personal Communications	Large	High	No	Software
Decision Tree Diagram	12	17	Risk	Planning Forms and Reports	Large	High	No	Construction
Delphi Method	8	15	Quality	Planning Process	Large	Medium	No	Research
Design Specifications	8	15	Quality	Planning Process	Small	High	Yes	Construction
Document Control System	13	15	Procurement	Planning Process	Medium	High	Yes	Software
Earned Value Analysis	7	16	Cost	Planning Management Admin	Medium	High	Yes	Construction
E-mail Tool	10	18	Communication	Executing and Controlling Personal Communications	Small	High	Yes	All
Estimating Tool	7	15	Cost	Planning Process	Small	High	Yes	Construction
Expected Monetary Value	12	17	Risk	Planning Forms and Reports	Medium	High	Yes	Construction
Feasibility Study	5	14	Scope	Project initiating	Medium	High	Yes	Software

continued

775

TABLE D.1   *(continued)*

Tool Name	Part 2 (Knowledge Area)	Part 3 (Process)	Knowledge Area	Life Cycle Process (Most Dominant)	Size	Recommended Usage on Projects	Critical Tool on all projects	Industry
Flow Chart	8	17	Quality	Planning Forms and Reports	Medium	Low	No	Software
Formal Acceptance Document	13	22	Procurement	Project Closeout	Small	High	Yes	All
Gantt Chart	6	21	Time	Executing and Controlling Reports	Small	High	Yes	All
Histogram	9	21	Human Resources	Executing and Controlling Reports	Medium	Medium	Yes	Construction
Human Resource Plan	9	14	Human Resources	Project initiating	Small	High	Yes	Software
Instant Messaging	10	18	Communication	Executing and Controlling Personal Communications	Small	High	Yes	All
Issue List	12	20	Risk	Executing and Controlling Forms	Medium	High	Yes	All
Issue Management Plan	12	16	Risk	Planning Management Admin	Medium	High	Yes	All
Lessons Learned Document	13	22	Procurement	Project Closeout	Medium	High	Yes	All
Logic Network Diagram	6	17	Time	Planning Forms and Reports	Medium	High	Yes	Construction

Tool Name	Part 2 (Knowledge Area)	Part 3 (Process)	Knowledge Area	Life Cycle Process (Most Dominant)	Size	Recommended Usage on Projects	Critical Tool on all projects	Industry
Pareto Chart	11	21	Communication	Executing and Controlling Reports	Large	High	Yes	Research
Periodic Reports	11	21	Communication	Executing and Controlling Reports	Medium	High	Yes	All Industries will have reports generated on a periodic basis
Phase Closeout	13	19	Procurement	Executing and Controlling Management Admin	Medium	Medium	Yes	Software
Press Release	11	19	Communication	Executing and Controlling Management Admin	Large	Medium	No	Construction
Project Calendar	10	15	Communication	Planning Process	Small	High	Yes	All
Project Charter	4	14	Integration	Project initiating	Medium	High	Yes	All
Project Kickoff Meeting	4	14	Integration	Project initiating	Medium	High	Yes	All
Project Management Plan	4	14	Integration	Project initiating	Medium	High	Yes	Construction
Project Meeting Minutes	4	20	Integration	Executing and Controlling Forms	Small	High	Yes	All
Project Milestone List	6	17	Time	Planning Forms and Reports	Small	High	Yes	Software

continued

TABLE D.1 *(continued)*

Tool Name	Part 2 (Knowledge Area)	Part 3 (Process)	Knowledge Area	Life Cycle Process (Most Dominant)	Size	Recommended Usage on Projects	Critical Tool on all projects	Industry
Project Newsletter	11	19	Communication	Executing and Controlling Management Admin	Medium	High	No	Construction
Project Organization Chart	4	14	Integration	Project initiating	Medium	High	Yes	All
Project Presentation	10	19	Communication	Executing and Controlling Management Admin	Medium	High	Yes	Software
Project Proposal	4	14	Integration	Project initiating	Medium	High	Yes	Construction
Project Schedule	6	17	Time	Planning Forms and Reports	Small	High	Yes	All
Project Status Meetings	4	19	Integration	Executing and Controlling Management Admin	Small	High	Yes	All
Project Status Report	4	21	Integration	Executing and Controlling Reports	Small	High	Yes	All
Prototyping	10	15	Communication	Planning Process	Medium	High	No	Engineering
Quality Management Plan	8	14	Quality	Project initiating	Medium	High	Yes	Construction

Tool Name	Part 2 (Knowledge Area)	Part 3 (Process)	Knowledge Area	Life Cycle Process (Most Dominant)	Size	Recommended Usage on Projects	Critical Tool on all projects	Industry
Quality Metrics	8	16	Quality	Planning Management Admin	Medium	High	Yes	Construction
Resource Leveling Tool	9	15	Human Resources	Planning Process	Medium	High	Yes	Construction
Responsibility Matrix	9	15	Human Resources	Planning Process	Medium	High	Yes	Software
Risk Assessment	12	20	Risk	Executing and Controlling Forms	Medium	High	Yes	Research
Risk Management Plan	12	16	Risk	Planning Management Admin	Medium	High	Yes	Research
Risk Matrix Tool	12	17	Risk	Planning Forms and Reports	Medium	High	Yes	All
Risk Modeling	12	15	Risk	Planning Process	Medium	High	Yes	Construction
Risk Register	12	16	Risk	Planning Management Admin	Medium	High	Yes	All
Risk Simulation	12	15	Risk	Planning Process	Medium	High	Yes	Construction
Safety Report	12	20	Risk	Executing and Controlling Forms	Large	Medium	No	Construction
Scatter Chart	8	17	Quality	Planning Forms and Reports	Large	High	No	Research
Schedule Management Plan	6	16	Time	Planning Management Admin	Medium	High	Yes	All

continued

TABLE D.1 (continued)

Tool Name	Part 2 (Knowledge Area)	Part 3 (Process)	Knowledge Area	Life Cycle Process (Most Dominant)	Size	Recommended Usage on Projects	Critical Tool on all projects	Industry
Scope Definition Document	5	17	Scope	Planning Forms and Reports	Medium	High	Yes	All
Scope Management Plan	5	14	Scope	Project initiating	Medium	High	Yes	All
Spider Chart	11	21	Communication	Executing and Controlling Reports	Medium	High	No	All
Stop Light Report	11	21	Communication	Executing and Controlling Reports	Medium	High	Yes	All
System Requirements	5	15	Scope	Planning Process	Small	High	Yes	Software
Team Charter	4	21	Integration	Executing and Controlling Reports	Small	High	Yes	All
Team Lead's Report	4	21	Integration	Executing and Controlling Reports	Medium	High	Yes	Software
User Acceptance Document	13	22	Procurement	Project Closeout	Small	High	Yes	Software
Work Breakdown Structure	5	15	Scope	Planning Process	Medium	High	Yes	Construction
Work Package	10	20	Communication	Executing and Controlling Forms	Large	High	Yes	Construction

Index

C

G

J

K

L

Q

Wiley Publishing, Inc.
End-User License Agreement

READ THIS. You should carefully read these terms and conditions before opening the software packet(s) included with this book "Book". This is a license agreement "Agreement" between you and Wiley Publishing, Inc. "WPI". By opening the accompanying software packet(s), you acknowledge that you have read and accept the following terms and conditions. If you do not agree and do not want to be bound by such terms and conditions, promptly return the Book and the unopened software packet(s) to the place you obtained them for a full refund.

1. **License Grant.** WPI grants to you (either an individual or entity) a nonexclusive license to use one copy of the enclosed software program(s) (collectively, the "Software," solely for your own personal or business purposes on a single computer (whether a standard computer or a workstation component of a multi-user network). The Software is in use on a computer when it is loaded into temporary memory (RAM) or installed into permanent memory (hard disk, CD-ROM, or other storage device). WPI reserves all rights not expressly granted herein.

2. **Ownership.** WPI is the owner of all right, title, and interest, including copyright, in and to the compilation of the Software recorded on the disk(s) or CD-ROM "Software Media". Copyright to the individual programs recorded on the Software Media is owned by the author or other authorized copyright owner of each program. Ownership of the Software and all proprietary rights relating thereto remain with WPI and its licensers.

3. **Restrictions On Use and Transfer.**

   (a) You may only (i) make one copy of the Software for backup or archival purposes, or (ii) transfer the Software to a single hard disk, provided that you keep the original for backup or archival purposes. You may not (i) rent or lease the Software, (ii) copy or reproduce the Software through a LAN or other network system or through any computer subscriber system or bulletin-board system, or (iii) modify, adapt, or create derivative works based on the Software.

   (b) You may not reverse engineer, decompile, or disassemble the Software. You may transfer the Software and user documentation on a permanent basis, provided that the transferee agrees to accept the terms and conditions of this Agreement and you retain no copies. If the Software is an update or has been updated, any transfer must include the most recent update and all prior versions.

4. **Restrictions on Use of Individual Programs.** You must follow the individual requirements and restrictions detailed for each individual program in the About the CD-ROM appendix of this Book. These limitations are also contained in the individual license agreements recorded on the Software Media. These limitations may include a requirement that after using the program for a specified period of time, the user must pay a registration fee or discontinue use. By opening the Software packet(s), you will be agreeing to abide by the licenses and restrictions for these individual programs that are detailed in the About the CD-ROM appendix and on the Software Media. None of the material on this Software Media or listed in this Book may ever be redistributed, in original or modified form, for commercial purposes.

5. **Limited Warranty.**

(a) WPI warrants that the Software and Software Media are free from defects in materials and workmanship under normal use for a period of sixty (60) days from the date of purchase of this Book. If WPI receives notification within the warranty period of defects in materials or workmanship, WPI will replace the defective Software Media.

(b) WPI AND THE AUTHOR(S) OF THE BOOK DISCLAIM ALL OTHER WARRANTIES, EXPRESS OR IMPLIED, INCLUDING WITHOUT LIMITATION IMPLIED WARRANTIES OF MERCHANTABILITY AND FITNESS FOR A PARTICULAR PURPOSE, WITH RESPECT TO THE SOFTWARE, THE PROGRAMS, THE SOURCE CODE CONTAINED THEREIN, AND/OR THE TECHNIQUES DESCRIBED IN THIS BOOK. WPI DOES NOT WARRANT THAT THE FUNCTIONS CONTAINED IN THE SOFTWARE WILL MEET YOUR REQUIREMENTS OR THAT THE OPERATION OF THE SOFTWARE WILL BE ERROR FREE.

(c) This limited warranty gives you specific legal rights, and you may have other rights that vary from jurisdiction to jurisdiction.

6. **Remedies.**

(a) WPI's entire liability and your exclusive remedy for defects in materials and workmanship shall be limited to replacement of the Software Media, which may be returned to WPI with a copy of your receipt at the following address: Software Media Fulfillment Department, Attn.: *Project Management Communications Bible* Wiley Publishing, Inc., 10475 Crosspoint Blvd., Indianapolis, IN 46256, or call 1-800-762-2974. Please allow four to six weeks for delivery. This Limited Warranty is void if failure of the Software Media has resulted from accident, abuse, or misapplication. Any replacement Software Media will be warranted for the remainder of the original warranty period or thirty (30) days, whichever is longer.

(b) In no event shall WPI or the author be liable for any damages whatsoever (including without limitation damages for loss of business profits, business interruption, loss of business information, or any other pecuniary loss) arising from the use of or inability to use the Book or the Software, even if WPI has been advised of the possibility of such damages.

(c) Because some jurisdictions do not allow the exclusion or limitation of liability for consequential or incidental damages, the above limitation or exclusion may not apply to you.

7. **U.S. Government Restricted Rights.** Use, duplication, or disclosure of the Software for or on behalf of the United States of America, its agencies and/or instrumentalities "U.S. Government" is subject to restrictions as stated in paragraph (c)(1)(ii) of the Rights in Technical Data and Computer Software clause of DFARS 252.227-7013, or subparagraphs (c) (1) and (2) of the Commercial Computer Software - Restricted Rights clause at FAR 52.227-19, and in similar clauses in the NASA FAR supplement, as applicable.

8. **General.** This Agreement constitutes the entire understanding of the parties and revokes and supersedes all prior agreements, oral or written, between them and may not be modified or amended except in a writing signed by both parties hereto that specifically refers to this Agreement. This Agreement shall take precedence over any other documents that may be in conflict herewith. If any one or more provisions contained in this Agreement are held by any court or tribunal to be invalid, illegal, or otherwise unenforceable, each and every other provision shall remain in full force and effect.